리딩이노베이터

실전편

박지성 지음

JH press

리딩이노베이터

실전편

박지성

고려대학교 언어학과 및 영어영문학 졸

현 | 해커스 편입 독해전임
마공스터디 온라인 강사
대치동 용인외대부고 · 휘문고 · 숙명여고 내신
목동 용인외대부고 내신

전 | 강창용편입 독해전임
이패스편입 독해전임
리스공 공무원 강사

저서 | 리딩이노베이터(기본편) 「JH press」
퍼펙트 독해 「JH press」
영어독해 개념이해 「Jonghap Books」
영어독해 문제원리 · 풀이이해 「Jonghap Books」
매그너스 MAGNUS 고등영어 서술형 기본편 6주완성 「오스틴북스」매그너스 MAGNUS 서술형 시리즈 고등영어 서술형 실전편 「오스틴북스」

리딩이노베이터 (실전편)

발 행 일 2025년 7월 16일(개정1판 2쇄)
2024년 3월 8일(개정1판 1쇄)
저 자 박지성
발 행 인 이도경
발 행 처 JH press
주 소 경기도 성남시 분당구 성남대로 331번길 9-14 2층
홈페이지 www.booksellers.co.kr
전자메일 proper002@properenglish.co.kr
대표전화 070-4454-1340
팩 스 031-718-0580

정가 19,800원

ISBN 979-11-984391-8-5 14740

머리말

영문단락을 읽는 방법을 단계적이고 체계적으로 배울 수 있도록 구성된 국내 유일무이한 독해 기본서인 「리딩 이노베이터 기본편」을 처음 선보인 지도 꽤 시간이 지났다. 기존의 책에서 볼 수 없던 책의 독특한 구성과 학습방법으로 인해 초기에 학습자 간 구매 시 "머뭇거림"이 있었지만, 책을 선택해서 직접 학습효과를 본 수험생들 사이에서 입소문이 돌면서 나름 독해 영역에서 입지를 굳히게 되었다. 그런 후 효과를 본 많은 수험생들이 기본편에 이어 중 · 상급 문제풀이집에 대한 갈증을 호소하는 경우가 많아 1년간의 집필 끝에 기본편의 명성을 이어갈 실전편을 마침내 내놓게 되었다.

기본편이 문제풀이 이전 영문단락 읽기에 초점을 두었다면, 실전편은 이름 그대로 문제풀이 방법에 좀 더 치중했다. 편입, 공무원, 텝스, 토플에 등장하는 문제 유형을 모두 반영하고, 각 유형별 접근방법을 상세히 달았다. 시중의 여타 독해책의 맹점이 되는, "문제 – 해석 – 해설 – 어휘"의 강의식 구성에서 벗어나 리딩 이노베이터 기본편과 같은 맥락에서 각 영문지문에 대한 해설을 하나도 빠짐없이 달았고, 무엇보다 문제 유형별 접근방법에 대한 상세한 해설을 첨가했다. 책의 구성을 보면, 각 장은 총 8지문으로 하여 상중하의 지문을 각각 30%, 50%, 20%로 구분, 하나의 개별장은 그 자체로 실전모의고사가 될 수 있도록 구성했으며, 무엇보다 인문과학, 사회과학, 자연과학, 일반상식의 네 분야를 편식하지 않고 다양한 분야를 다뤄 다양한 분야에 대한 적응력을 높일 수 있도록 했다. 총 25회 구성으로 리딩 이노베이터 기본편에 이어 실전편을 꼼꼼하게 학습하다면, 독해파트에 대한 자신감이 더욱 충만될 것이라 자신한다.

박지성

구성과 특징

문제편과 정답 · 해설편 총 두 권으로 구성되어 있다. 25회 분량의 문제편은 8지문을 35분의 제한 시간에 풀 수 있도록 꾸며서 지문의 수에 따라 시간관리를 할 수 있도록 구성했다. 정답 및 해설편의 경우, "정답 – 해설 – 해석" 뿐 아니라 책에 실린 모든 영문지문에 대한 상세한 분석을 달아 혼자서도 충분히 글 전개와 특징을 파악할 수 있도록 했다.

책의 세부 특징은 다음과 같다.

1 상세한 본문분석

본문분석에는 단락분석의 시작인 중심소재와 주제문, 뒷받침 진술, 부연진술, 연결사, 요지문 등의 내용을 상세하게 분석했다. 기본편을 통해 학습한 각 개념들을 실전문제를 통해서 다시 한 번 적용 · 확인할 수 있다.

Passage 1

whereas A, B의 중 글의 무게중심은 A에서 B로 넘어간다. 즉, B에 관한 내용이 본문에 구체적으로 전개됨을 파악하도록 한다.

영문글은 구두점의 활용이 두드러진다. –(dash)의 경우 앞에 전개된 내용을 부연한다(순접부연).

중심소재의 이해
중심소재는 단락분석의 가장 기본이 되는 단위로 포괄적 주제에 해당한다. 중심소재를 찾는

1. Whereas family relationships usually constitute a child's first experience with group life, peer-group interactions soon begin to make their powerful socializing effects felt. 1) From play group to teenage clique, the peer group affords young people many significant learning experiences—① how to achieve status in a circle of friends. Peers are equals in a way parents and their children or teachers and their students are not. A parent or teacher sometimes can force young children to obey rules they neither understand nor like, but peers do not have formal authority to do this; ② thus the true meaning of exchange, cooperation, and equity can be learned more easily in the peer setting. 2. Peer groups increase in importance as the child grows up and reach maximum influence in adolescence, by which time

중심소재: 또래집단 → 청소년 또래집단의 영향

1. 도입부 = 주제문
또래 집단의 중요한 영향 : 사회화 과정을 익힐 수 있는 learning experiences 제공

1) 뒷받침 진술
① 친구들 사이에서 자신의 위치를 성취하는 방법

② 진정한 의미의 상호교류, 협력 그리고 평등을 익힘

2. 정리

2 본문과 분석 간 넘버링

좌측 본문에 해당하는 우측 본문분석에 숫자 또는 영문으로 표시해 글 전체의 흐름과 함께 문장 간 논리적 관계를 쉽게 파악할 수 있도록 했다.

두 문단으로 나눠진 지문이다. 문단별 주제를 설정하고, 궁극적으로 전달하려는 요지를 파악하도록 한다.

구체적 진술을 이끄는 시그널을 확인한다.

1. 1) **The Broken Windows theory** was the brainchild of the criminologists James Wilson and George Kelling. They argued that crime is the inevitable result of disorder. ① If a window is broken and left unrepaired, people walking by will conclude that no one cares and no one is in charge. Soon, more windows will be broken, and the sense of anarchy will spread from the building to the street on which it faces, sending a signal that anything goes here. In a city, relatively minor problems like graffiti, public disorder, and aggressive panhandling are all the equivalent of broken windows

중심소재: 깨진 유리창 이론

1. 첫 번째 문단

1) 주제문
범죄는 무질서의 필연적 결과이다.

① 뒷받침 진술
예시(if)를 통해서 자세히 설명하고 있다

* 첫 번째 문단에선 깨진 창문 이론의 정확한 개념과 어떠한 배경 속에서 범죄가 발생하는지 주목하도록 한다

3 주제문과 요지문

단락 주제문과 요지문은 밑줄을 그어 한 눈에 파악할 수 있도록 하여 주제문과 뒷받침 내용을 바로 구별할 수 있도록 하였다.

두 문단으로 나눠진 지문이다. 문단별 주제를 설정하고, 궁극적으로 전달하려는 요지를 파악하도록 한다.

구체적 진술을 이끄는 시그널을 확인한다.

1. 1) **The Broken Windows theory** was the brainchild of the criminologists James Wilson and George Kelling. They argued that crime is the inevitable result of disorder. ① If a window is broken and left unrepaired, people walking by will conclude that no one cares and no one is in charge. Soon, more windows will be broken, and the sense of anarchy will spread from the building to the street on which it faces, sending a signal that anything goes here. In a city, relatively minor problems like graffiti, public disorder, and aggressive

중심소재: 깨진 유리창 이론

1. 첫 번째 문단

1) 주제문
범죄는 무질서의 필연적 결과이다.

① 뒷받침 진술
예시(if)를 통해서 자세히 설명하고 있다

* 첫 번째 문단에선 깨진 창문 이론의 정확한 개념과 어떠한 배경 속에서 범죄가 발생하는지 주목하도록 한다

4 본문 전개의 도식

책의 날개를 활용하여 기본편에서 다룬 중요 단락구조의 경우 도식화를 통해 학습자의 단락 전개 이해를 도왔다.

통념비판의 패턴을 파악하도록 한다.

통념 A = B
But A ≠ B

뒷받침 진술

2. 1) Conventional economic wisdom, of course, says that the more choices consumers have, the more likely they are to buy, because it is easier for consumers to find the jam that perfectly fits their needs. ① But Iyengar found the opposite to be true. Thirty percent of those who stopped by the six-choice booth ended up buying some jam, while only three percent of those who stopped by the bigger booth bought anything. Ⓐ Why is that? Because buying jam is a snap decision. You say to yourself, instinctively, "I want

선택 사항의 수가 구매 후에 어떤 영향을 미치는가?

2. 두 번째 문단

1) 기존의 관점(통념)

선택의 폭이 넓을수록 구매자의 욕구에 맞는 제품이 있을 가능성이 높기 때문에 판매가 더 잘 이루어질 것이다

①반대의 실험결과

Ⓐ 뒷받침 근거

잼을 사는 행위는 순간의 결정이

5 책의 날개를 활용해 중요내용 강조

본문내용 파악 시 놓치지 말아야 할 중요사항의 경우 책의 날개 부분을 통해 보충설명을 달았으며, 해당 사항을 기본편과 연계하여 학습할 수 있도록 했다.

두 문단으로 나눠진 지문이다. 문단별 주제를 설정하고, 궁극적으로 전달하려는 요지를 파악하도록 한다.

구체적 진술을 이끄는 시그널을 확인한다.

1. 1) **The Broken Windows theory** was the brainchild of the criminologists James Wilson and George Kelling. They argued that crime is the inevitable result of disorder. ① If a window is broken and left unrepaired, people walking by will conclude that no one cares and no one is in charge. Soon, more windows will be broken, and the sense of anarchy will spread from the building to the street on which it faces, sending a signal that anything goes here. In a city, relatively minor problems like graffiti, public disorder, and aggressive panhandling are all the equivalent of broken windows.

중심소재: 깨진 유리창 이론

1. 첫 번째 문단

1) 주제문

범죄는 무질서의 필연적 결과이다.

① 뒷받침 진술

예시(if)를 통해서 자세히 설명하고 있다

* 첫 번째 문단에선 깨진 창문 이론의 정확한 개념과 어떠한 배경 속에서 범죄가 발생하는지 주목하도록 한다.

6 문제풀이 방법

날개를 활용해 문제유형별 접근방법을 상세히 달았다.

New Zealand. They have documented spills of everything from onions to hockey gloves.

정답 1 (D) 2 (B)

해설

1 본문의 주제는 Studying Ocean Currents Through Random Junk이며, 실험을 통해 이를 밝히는 내용임을 글의 도입부에서 파악했다면 보기 (D)가 정답임을 쉽게 접근할 수 있었을 것이다.

2 본문과 일치하지 않는 문제는 문제의 보기 항을 먼저 읽어 본문의 내용을 대략적으로 파악할 수 있도록 한다. 특히, 보기 항에 수치와 관련된 표현이 나올 경우 이를 본문에서 눈여겨봐야 한다. reliable information on 1,600 shoes에서 보기 (B)는 본문과 일치하지 않음을 알 수 있다.

지문해석

오늘날 과학자들은 대양 해류에 대해 점점 더 집중적으로 연구하고 있다. 대개 연구는 위성이나 다른 첨단기술장비를 사용하고 있다. 하지만 해양학자 커티스 에베스마이어(Curtis Ebbesmeyer)는 그 연구를 좀 더 구식으로 하고 있다. 즉, 이리저리 떠다니는 쓰레기의 움직임을 연구하고 있다. 경험이 풍부한과학자인 그는 이방식의 연구를 1990년대 초에 시작했다.

그때 그는 수백 개의 운동선수용 신발이 미국의 북동쪽 해안의 해안가에 쓸려온다는 얘기를 들었다. 굉장히 많은 신발들이 떠밀려오기 때문에 사람들은 그 신발들의 왼짝과 오른짝을 찾아서 팔고 신어보려는 교환 모

내용일치 접근방법

지문을 읽기 전에 문제를 먼저 파악하는 습관을 지니도록 한다. 내용일치·불일치(특히, 불일치) 문제의 경우 지문을 읽기 전 선택지의 내용을 빠르게 파악하는 데 익숙해지면 상당한 효과를 얻을 수 있다. 선택지 중 세 개의 내용은 본문과 일치한다는 것을 알 수 있는데, 일반적으로 본문의 내용을 짧고, 쉬운 표현으로 물어보는 경우가 대다수이므로 선택지의 내용만으로 본문에서 다루는 대략적인 내용을 추론할 수 있다.

책의 활용

본 실전편은 총 25장으로 구분했는데, 각 장은 독해파트로만 보았을 때 하나의 모의고사가 될 수 있도록 구성한 문제집이다. 공부의 왕도가 있지는 않겠지만 아래와 같은 방식을 추천하는 바이다.

1 제한된 시간 안에 풀도록 한다.

수험영어의 특징 중 하나는 제한된 시간 안에 푸는 것이다. 영어실력과 관련 없이 시간관리를 못하면, 실력만큼 점수가 나오지 않게 된다. 제한된 시간 안에 푸는 연습을 해야 문제풀이 시 발생하는 다양한 우발적 상황에 대처하는 방법을 익힐 수 있다. 예를 들어, 어려운 문제에 부딪혔을 때 다른 문제를 먼저 살펴본다든지, 답이 애매할 경우 문제의 선택지를 활용하는 방법 등 나름의 대안을 세울 수 있다.

2 본문분석을 적극 활용한다.

문제풀이 후 정답을 맞힐 때, 바로 해설을 확인하기보다는 본문분석을 먼저 확인하고, 본인이 파악한 내용과 본문분석이 일치하는지 확인한다. 대부분 오답을 고른 경우는 문제 자체의 난이도라기보다는 본문 내용을 정확히 파악하지 못해서 발생하므로 본문분석을 꼼꼼히 살핀 후 틀린 문제를 다시 살펴보도록 한다. 물론, 맞힌 문제도 본문 내용을 바르게 파악하고 풀었는지 확인할 수 있는 좋은 방법이다.

3 답의 근거는 언제나 본문 안에 있다.

오답뿐 아니라 정답을 고른 문제라 하더라도 본인이 찾은 근거와 해설지에서 제시하는 근거가 일치하는지 반드시 확인하도록 한다. 지문을 읽고, "2번이 답일 것 같다"와 같은 근거 없는 "감" 독해는 점수의 기복현상의 결과로 나타난다. 모든 문제의 근거는 본문에 있으므로 이를 찾는 연습을 꾸준히 해야 견고한 성적향상을 이룰 수 있다.

4 유난히 어려웠던 지문은 따로 표시를 해 둔다.

정답률이 낮은 지문은 문제의 난이도라기보다는 본문 내용을 파악하지 못했기 때문이다. 본문내용을 파악하지 못한 데에는 다양한 원인이 있겠으나 1) 어휘를 몰랐거나, 2) 문장의 구조가 까다롭거나 아니면, 3) 내용자체가 이해하기 쉽지 않은 경우가 있다. 특히 어휘와 구조에는 문제가 없었으나 본문 내용 파악이 어려운 경우 지문의 내용을 반복해서 확인하는 동시에 해당 분야의 내용을 우리말 자료로 확인해 두고, 관련 사항도 함께 익혀두어 배경지식을 넓히는 것이 좋다.

5 각 지문은 배경지식을 넓히는 좋은 도구이다.

4번의 배경지식과 관련해 각 장에서 다루는 8개의 지문은 내용 자체가 나름의 배경지식으로 활용될 수 있다. 특히, 까다로웠던 내용을 다룬 지문과 객관적 사실에 해당하는 내용은 앞으로 다루게 될 다른 지문에 직 · 간접적인 배경지식으로 활용될 수 있기에 꼼꼼하게 읽고, 암기해 두는 것도 좋은 방법이다.

목차

BOOK 1 실전문제

목차

BOOK 2 정답 및 해설

리딩이노베이터 | 실전편 |

TEST 01

제한시간 | 35분
정답률 | /21

Passage 1

Whereas family relationships usually constitute a child's first experience with group life, peer-group interactions soon begin to make their powerful socializing effects felt. From play group to teenage clique, the peer group affords young people many significant learning experiences—how to achieve status in a circle of friends. Peers are equals in a way parents and their children or teachers and their students are not. A parent or teacher sometimes can force young children to obey rules they neither understand nor like, but peers do not have formal authority to do this; thus the true meaning of exchange, cooperation, and equity can be learned more easily in the peer setting. Peer groups increase in importance as the child grows up and reach maximum influence in adolescence, by which time they sometimes dictate much of a young person's behavior both in and out of school.

1 According to the passage, which of the following would feel the importance of a peer group the most?

(A) Toddlers
(B) Elementary school students
(C) Kindergarteners
(D) High school students
(E) Adults

2 Which of the following best expresses the main idea of the passage?

(A) Children learn about cooperation in their peer groups.
(B) Peer groups are powerful influences in children's lives.
(C) Parents can force children to do things that a peer group cannot.
(D) Parents have greater influences on children than their teachers do.
(E) Relationships in and out of school provide learning opportunities for children.

Passage 2

There is a whole category of people who are "just" something. To be "just" anything is the worst. It is not to be recognized by society as having much value at all, not now and probably not in the past either. To be "just" anything is to be totally discounted, at least for the present. "Just" a housewife immediately and painfully comes to mind. Sometimes women who have kept a house and reared six children refer to themselves as "just" a housewife. "Just" a bum, "just" a kid, "just" a drunk, old man, student, punk are some others. The "just" category contains present non-earners, people who have no past job history highly valued by society and people whose present jobs are on the low-end of pay and prestige scales. A person can be "just" a cab driver, for example, or "just" a janitor. No one is ever "just" a president, however. We're supposed to be a classless society, but we are not. We don't recognize a titled nobility. We refuse to acknowledge dynastic privilege. But we certainly separate the valued from the valueless, and it has a lot to do with jobs and the importance we attach to them.

1 Which of the following CANNOT be inferred from the passage?

(A) It would be more productive not to limit oneself to just one job.
(B) Non-paying or low-paying careers tend to be less appreciated socially.
(C) We should not discount a person's worth by superficial judgment.
(D) It is worthwhile to manage household affairs and raise children.

2 What is the main idea of the passage?

(A) It is inevitable to judge everybody in terms of the work they do for pay.
(B) Our society has an implicit system of awarding respect based on the jobs we hold.
(C) Placing jobs in a hierarchy is necessary for our work ethic.
(D) We should trivialize jobs that lead to wealth, recognition, and privilege.

3 What is the tone of the passage?

(A) condescending
(B) laudatory
(C) apathetic
(D) critical

Passage 3

Scientists today are studying ocean currents more and more intensely. Most do it using satellites and other high-tech equipment. However, oceanographer Curtis Ebbesmeyer does it in a more old-fashioned way—by studying movements of random junk. A scientist with many years' experience, he started this type of research in the early 1990s when he heard about hundreds of athletic shoes washing up on the shores of the northeast coast of the United States. There were so many shoes that people were holding swap meets to try and match left and right shoes to sell or wear.

Ebbesmeyer started investigating and found out that the shoes—about 60,000 in total—fell into the ocean in a shipping accident. He contacted the shoe company and asked if they wanted the shoes back. Not surprisingly, the company told him that they didn't. Ebbesmeyer realized this could be a great experiment. He learned when and where the shoes went into the water and tracked where they landed, he could learn a lot about __________. The Atlantic Northwest is one of the world's best areas for beachcombing because of converging wind and currents, and as a result, there is a group of serious beachcombers in the area. Ebbesmeyer got help in collecting information about where the shoes landed. In a year he collected reliable information on 1,600 shoes. With this data, he and a colleague were able to test and refine a computer program designed to model ocean currents, and publish the results of their study. Then in 1993, a shipment of colored plastic bathtub toys fell into the North Atlantic Ocean. Ebbesmeyer and his colleagues got even more accurate information from this spill, which resulted in huge amounts of useful new data for their work. As the result of his work, Ebbesmeyer has become known as the scientist to call with questions about any unusual objects found floating in the ocean. He has even started an association of beachcombers and oceanographers, with 500 subscribers from West Africa to New Zealand. They have documented spills of everything from onions to hockey gloves.

1 문맥상 __________에 들어갈 가장 적절한 표현을 고르시오.

(A) the patterns of shoes industry
(B) the patterns of computer program
(C) the patterns of studying junk
(D) the patterns of ocean currents

2 이 글의 내용과 일치하지 않는 것을 고르시오.

(A) Plastic bathtub toys can be a part of a serious scientific study of oceans and ocean currents.
(B) Ebbesmeyer collected reliable information on 60,000 shoes in a year.
(C) The Atlantic Northwest is a good place for beachcombing.
(D) The shoe company didn't want to have the shoes back.

Passage 4

Professor Iyengar of Columbia University conducted an experiment in which she set up a tasting booth with a variety of exotic gourmet jams at an upscale grocery store. Sometimes the booth had six different jams, and sometimes twenty-four different jams on display. She wanted to see whether the number of jam choices made any difference in the number of jams sold. Conventional economic wisdom, of course, says that the more choices consumers have, ① __________, because it is easier for consumers to find the jam that perfectly fits their needs. But Iyengar found the opposite to be true. Thirty percent of those who stopped by the six-choice booth ended up buying some jam, while only three percent of those who stopped by the bigger booth bought anything. Why is that? Because buying jam is a snap decision. You say to yourself, instinctively, "I want that one." And if you are given too many choices, if you are forced to consider much more than your unconscious mind is comfortable with, you get paralyzed. Snap judgments can be made in a snap because they are frugal, and if we want to protect our snap judgments, we have to take steps ② to protect that frugality.

1 Which of the following is the major finding by Professor Iyengar?

(A) Snap judgments require fewer choices to choose from.
(B) Large upscale stores are bound to dominate the market.
(C) Conventional economic wisdom has withstood the test of time.
(D) Consumers are easily pleased with a wide range of selection.
(E) Buyers' unconscious mind weighs each and every option carefully.

2 Which of the following best fits into ①?

(A) the less likely they are to buy
(B) the less likely they are to find their preferences
(C) the less likely they are to find their specific needs
(D) the more likely they are to get confused
(E) the more likely they are to buy

3 Which of the following is an instance of ②?

(A) To restrict the time allowed to make decisions
(B) To reduce the number of available options
(C) To offer a low price on featured products
(D) To overwhelm the decision-making capacity
(E) To discourage buying expensive alternatives

Passage 5

Ethnocentrism is the view that one's own culture is better than all others; it is the way all people feel about themselves as compared to outsiders. There is no one in our society who is not ethnocentric to some degree, no matter how liberal and open-minded he or she might claim to be. People will always find some aspect of another culture distasteful, be it sexual practices, a way of treating friends or relatives, or simply a food that they cannot manage to get down with a smile. This is not something we should be ashamed of, because it is a natural outcome of growing up in any society. However, as anthropologists who study other cultures, it is something we should constantly be aware of, so that when we are tempted to make value judgments about another way of life, we can look at the situation objectively and take our bias into account.

1 According to the passage, the author is ________.

(A) an anthropologist
(B) proud of being ethnocentric
(C) attracted to other cultures than his or her own
(D) opposed to a liberal point of view on other cultures

2 According to the passage, value judgments about other cultures may be balanced when ________.

(A) we become anthropologists
(B) we are critical of our own culture
(C) we do not feel ashamed of being ethnocentric
(D) we take into account our likings for our own culture

Passage 6

History has long made a point of the fact that the magnificent flowering of ancient civilization rested upon the institution of slavery, which released opportunity at the top for the art and literature which became the glory of antiquity. In a way, the mechanization of the present-day world produces the condition of the ancient in that the enormous development of labor-saving devices and of contrivances which amplify the capacities of mankind affords the base for the leisure necessary to widespread cultural pursuits. Mechanization is the present-day slave power, with the difference that in the mechanized society there is no group of the community which does not share in the benefits of its inventions.

1 The main idea of the passage is ________.

(A) slavery in the ancient world
(B) today's community
(C) worthwhile use of leisure
(D) modern slave power

2 Which factor has produced more leisure time?

(A) The abolition of slavery
(B) The glory of antiquity
(C) The development of art and literature
(D) An increase in inventions

3 The flowering of any civilization has always depended on ________.

(A) the institution of slavery
(B) leisure for the workingman
(C) mechanical power
(D) leisure for cultural pursuits

4 The writer's attitude toward mechanization is one of ________.

(A) awe
(B) acceptance
(C) distrust
(D) devotion

Passage 7

How and why did studying the career trajectories of star football players give you a window on better management of business organizations and careers? As research on the National Football League (NFL) reveals, sometimes the specific nature of a job determines whether a great performer at one company can replicate that performance at another. Sports teams are organizations much like many others, subject to the errors that are common elsewhere. But their successes and failures are highly visible and amplified by the fact that they perform in a zero-sum world. In order for one team to win, another team has to lose. As a result, their focus is especially performance-oriented. Teams hire stars on the basis of talent—as do many organizations. Thus, if a star's performance is measured into highly accurate statistical data, they allow researchers to examine whether performance is as (A) <u>portable</u> in a new environment as many in the NFL believe. For business managers, the fact that the star's performance is portable for some positions and not portable for others is necessary to know.

1 밑줄 친 (A)의 문맥상의 의미로 가장 적합한 것을 고르시오.

(A) replicable
(B) measurable
(C) distinguishable
(D) tangible

2 위의 지문의 내용과 가장 일치하는 것을 고르시오.

(A) It is very difficult for star performers to survive in a new organization.
(B) Star performers are at their best in any organizations.
(C) Assigning a proper position is important for star performers' portability.
(D) NFL research finally concludes that star performers should be chosen on the basis of their talent.

Passage 8

The term "globalization" has been snatched away by the powerful to refer to a specific form of international economic integration, one based on investor rights, with the interests of people incidentally neglected. That is why the business press, in its more honest moments, refers to the "free trade agreements" as "free investment agreements" (*Wall Street Journal*). Accordingly, advocates of other forms of globalization are described as "anti-globalization." No sane person is opposed to globalization, that is, international integration. Surely not the left and the workers movements, which were founded on the principle of international solidarity—that is, globalization in a form that attends to the rights of people, not private power systems. There are no serious "theoretical foundations" for any of the versions of globalization, including the investor-rights versions. The international economy is far too poorly understood for there to be systematic "theories" in any serious sense. Certainly the neoliberal programs have no serious theoretical basis, even in the abstract: and their concrete realization is a complex mixture of protectionism and liberalization crafted to meet the interests of the ① _________, not surprisingly.

1 세계 경제 통합으로서의 **"globalization"**에 대한 필자의 입장은?

(A) neutral
(B) ambivalent
(C) supportive
(D) critical

2 위 글에 따르면 **"globalization"**의 정의 문제를 중심으로 형성된 대립하는 두 세력은?

(A) 거대 투자자와 국제 시민노동자 연대
(B) 미국 투자자와 유럽연합 지식인 집단
(C) 선진 자본주의 국가와 후진 농업국
(D) 직업 정치인들과 전문 경제학자들

3 빈칸 ①에 들어갈 집단으로 가장 알맞은 것은?

(A) People
(B) big investors
(C) workers
(D) third world countries

TEST 02

제한시간 | 35분
정답률 | /20

Passage 1

In baseball, pitchers need both psychology and skill to strike out batters. Sometimes pitchers do not need to do anything at all to psych out batters. The pitcher can just stand on the mound and take his time pitching. This messes up the batter's timing. A pitcher might also wait for the batter to step up to home plate, and then step off the pitcher's mound to throw a few balls to first base for practice. One pitcher famous for his fast ball would stand on the pitcher's mound and just stare at the batter.

This gave the batter plenty of time to think about the pitch that was about to be thrown. When the pitcher saw that the batter was starting to feel ill at ease, he let his fast ball fly. It was an excellent tactic for this pitcher.

1 글의 주제로 가장 알맞은 것은?

(A) How pitchers win out psychologically
(B) How pitchers spend their free time
(C) How pitchers develop skills
(D) How pitchers throw fast balls

Passage 2

Typically, people think of genius, whether it manifests in Mozart's composition of symphonies at age five or Einstein's discovery of relativity, as having a quality not just of the supernatural, but also of the eccentric. People see genius as a good abnormality; moreover, they think of genius as a completely unpredictable abnormality. Until recently, psychologists regarded the quirks of genius as too erratic to describe intelligibly; however, Anna Findley's ground-breaking study uncovers predictable patterns in the biographies of geniuses. These patterns, however, even though they occur with regularity, do not completely dispel the common belief that there is a kind of supernatural intervention in the lives of unusually talented men and women. ① ________, Findley shows that all geniuses experience three intensely productive periods in their lives, one of which, mysterious as it may seem, always occurs shortly before their deaths; this is true whether the genius lives to 19 or 90.

1 **Which of the following best fits into ①?**

(A) For example
(B) Despite this
(C) Otherwise
(D) Therefore
(E) Nevertheless

2 **Which of the following would be the best title for the passage?**

(A) Understanding Mozart and Einstein
(B) Predicting the Life of a Genius
(C) Geniuses in Music and Science
(D) Predictable and Unpredictable Aspects of Geniuses
(E) Extreme Hardships that Geniuses Experience

Passage 3

Human beings no longer thrive under the water from which their ancestors emerged, but their relationship with the sea remains close. Over half the world's people live within 100 kilometres (62 miles) of the coast; a tenth are within 10km. On land at least, the sea delights the senses and excites the imagination. The sight and smell of the sea inspire courage and adventure, fear and romance. Though the waves may be rippling or mountainous, the waters angry or calm, the ocean itself is eternal. Its moods pass. Its tides keep to a rhythm. It is unchanging.

Or so it has long seemed. Appearances (가), though. Large parts of the sea may indeed remain unchanged, but in others, especially in the surface and coastal waters where 90% of marine life is to be found, the impact of man's activities is increasingly plain. This should hardly be a surprise. Man has changed the landscape and the atmosphere. It would be odd if the seas, which he has for centuries used for food, for transport, for dumping rubbish and, more recently, for recreation, had not also been affected.

1 **What is the main idea of the passage above?**

(A) The sea has been affected greatly by man's activities.
(B) People like to live in areas close to the sea.
(C) We cannot live without the help of the sea.
(D) There have been various works of literature on the sea.

2 **Which of the following best fills in the blank (가) of the passage above?**

(A) abound
(B) build
(C) deceive
(D) lead

3 **Which technique does the author use to make the point in the first paragraph of the passage above?**

(A) allegory
(B) quotation
(C) definition
(D) enumeration

Passage 4

There are other writing systems similar to the Egyptian one. The most important one still in use is the Chinese script. Such systems are often called logographic, meaning 'word-writing'. Unlike the Egyptian system, the Chinese writing system probably evolved quite independently of other writing systems. It is also considerably younger. The first texts in Chinese date back to around 1200 BC, which means the scripts has now been in use for more than 3,000 years. A logographic system is by its nature more conservative than an alphabetic system. An alphabet conveys sounds, and as the sounds of a spoken language are always in a state of change, the difference between written and spoken language gradually becomes more pronounced. But it is possible to reform the spelling so that the direct connection between the spoken sound and the written symbol is restored. In a script of a more symbolic kind some signs denote meanings without any relation to ⓐ ________. That is, the signs do not convey sounds. For this reason, such a script is more liable to remain unchanged even if the spoken language undergoes considerable change.

1 **Which of the following is NOT stated or implied in the passage?**

(A) The Egyptians develop their writing system earlier than the Chinese.
(B) The Egyptians had an alphabetical writing system.
(C) Sound change causes the distinction between written and spoken language.
(D) Even in a language with a symbolic writing system, its pronunciation can change.
(E) The Egyptian writing system was created under the influence of other scripts.

2 **What is the passage mainly about?**

(A) Characteristics of writing systems
(B) The Egyptians and their writing system
(C) The connection between sounds and signs
(D) Properties of spoken language
(E) The conservation of written language

3 **Which of the following best fits into ⓐ?**

(A) the pronunciation
(B) the vocabulary
(C) the symbol
(D) the grammar

Passage 5

The most important political text of the medieval era was the same one that ended the Christian influence in political theory: Niccolo Machiavelli's The Prince. This book created the conceptual framework in which modern political philosophy operates. Machiavelli wrote the text for the Medici family and included a number of shrewd political actions that one could use to acquire and hold power. The Prince was authored in the midst of the chaos in which a number of factions fought for control of Italy. As such, much of the work centers on balancing the interest of the state with the interest of the public. It also contains advice on dealing with internal and external enemies to the state. Most famously, The Prince is known for its endorsement of cruel or inhumane actions to maintain power. The question addressed in the work provided a conceptual framework that directed the focus of the Enlightenment. Much of this time was spent creating a political body of thought that adhered to the liberal principles of justice and rationality.

1 Which of the following can be inferred about *The Prince*?

(A) It was written to underscore the problems in Italy.
(B) It was intended to advise a certain influential family on how to gain power.
(C) It was regarded by many Italians as unacceptable since it approved cruelty.
(D) It was ignored by most political theorists of the time.

2 Choose the answer which is closest in meaning to "shrewd".

(A) drastic
(B) tenacious
(C) prompt
(D) wily

3 According to the passage, all of the following are true EXCEPT.

(A) Prior to The Prince, churches had an effect on Western political theory.
(B) Machiavelli's book provided the theoretical foundation for modern political philosophy.
(C) Machiavelli's position on how to maintain power was upheld by most Enlightenment thinkers.
(D) During Machiavelli's times, powerful families in Italy feuded with each other.

Passage 6

One of the first principles that you must understand in advertising is that it is limited in both time and space. Television and radio commercials are usually only 10 to 60 seconds long. Print ads are usually no larger than two pages, and usually much smaller. Therefore, an advertisement must do its job quickly. It must get the consumer's attention, identify the product, and deliver the selling message in a small time or space. In order to do this, advertising often breaks the rules of grammar, image, and even society.

The second basic point is that advertisements usually have two parts: copy and illustrations. Copy refers to the words in the advertisement. These words give the sales message. Illustrations are pictures or photographs. Most ads are a combination of copy and illustration. Some advertisements have small illustration and a lot of copy. Some are only an illustration with the name of product. The decision about how much copy and illustration to use depends on how the advertiser wants to present the sales message. Understanding how advertisers make this decision is complex.

1 윗글의 내용과 가장 관계가 없는 문장을 고르시오.

(A) Ads make use of different techniques to accomplish different purposes.
(B) Advertisements contain copy and illustrations.
(C) There are many kinds of advertisements.
(D) The successful ads contain a headline.

2 다음 문장의 빈칸에 가장 적절한 어휘를 고르시오.

> Television advertisements have to give their message in a limited __________.

(A) process
(B) time
(C) information
(D) technique

Passage 7

Cemeteries are not the only "detestable facilities" that have had difficulties in finding locations along with the advent of local autonomous system. Construction of 26 waste management facilities has been suspended throughout the nation. Walls of UNESCO-designated royal palaces in Seoul are wrapped in rubbish. The situations are little better for nuclear waste storages, sewage disposal plants and dams.

Clean, orderly disposal of remnants, either human or material, is the first test of a mature society. Officials should set up a long-term, comprehensive plan on the waste management facilities through the persistent discussion with and persuasion of residents along with convincing incentives. Now is also time for the people to shift from unconditional NIMBY to conditional "YIMBY" (Yes-In-My-Back-Yard) with a broader and pragmatic viewpoint.

1 윗글의 내용과 가장 잘 부합하는 것을 고르시오.

(A) It is time to fully develop the local autonomous system in Korea.
(B) Only the half of 2 waste management facilities have been built.
(C) Some royal palaces in Seoul were surrounded with nuclear waste storages.
(D) The people should open their mind to "detestable facilities"

2 다음 중 **"detestable facilities"**에 속하지 않는 것을 고르시오.

(A) cemeteries
(B) local autonomous system
(C) waste incinerators
(D) sewage disposal plants

Passage 8

Last week, the London Underground was a scene of (A) carnage, not shelter. Three terrorist bombs in the subways (a fourth blew up a bus) killed at least 49 people and wounded 700 more. In one deep tunnel, blocked by the mangled wreckage of a subway car and teeming with rats, rescuers had still not dug out all of the bodies two days after the attack. The message was clear enough to Londoners and the rest of the world: in the age of terror, there are no sanctuaries, no safe places to hide.

The July 7 bombings were the bloodiest day in England since World War II. Still, the toll of "7/7" was nothing compared with the Blitz, which claimed 20,000 civilians between 1940 and '41, as many as 1,500 in one night. "If London can survive the Blitz, it can survive four miserable events like this," said Sir Ian Blair, the London Metropolitan Police commissioner. From the early '70s to the mid-'90s, the British endured more than two decades of terrorist attacks from the Irish Republican Army (though the IRA, in contrast to Al Qaeda, usually called in a warning before setting off a bomb). After last week's attack, British pluck and phlegm were once more the order of the day. A charming child during World War II, Queen Elizabeth II, now dowdy, squat, but unmistakably regal, toured hospitals and declared: "Sadly, we in Britain have been all too familiar with acts of terror, and members of my generation ... know that we have been here before. But those who perpetrate ___________ against innocent people should know that they will not change our way of life." Her message: Hitler tried to terrorize Londoners into submission, too, and, far from conquering Britain, he died a suicide's death in a bunker beneath Berlin.

For Americans, the echoes were more recent and less reassuring, especially when the news first broke. Maybe, many Americans were beginning to hope, the horror of 9/11 had been an (B) <u>aberration</u>, radical Islam's grotesquely lucky shot in the dark, not a harbinger. There have, of course, been many terrorist bombings since 9/11, in places from Bali to Turkey to Kenya to Spain. But Americans feel a _________ with their British cousins, whose common heritage and language made their suffering seem close to home. After the London bombings, repressed fears surfaced, especially for city dwellers who ride subways and buses and wonder if their everyday morning commute will turn deadly.

1 밑줄 친 (A) <u>carnage</u>와 가장 유사한 표현을 찾으시오.

(A) the act of terror
(B) the brutal action of large number of people
(C) the attack of public transportation
(D) the killing of a large number of people

2 이 글의 내용과 일치하는 것은?

(A) Americans feel sympathetic to the July 7 bombings in England.
(B) Hitler conquered Londoners during World War II.
(C) There have been few terrorist attacks since 9/1 in Bali.
(D) Rescuers had dug out all of the bodies two days after the attack.

3 이 글의 논리상 빈칸에 들어갈 가장 적절한 표현끼리 짝지은 것은?

(A) these cruel acts — hostile connection
(B) these protective acts — special brotherhood
(C) these brutal acts — unique kinship
(D) these terrible acts — unique antipathy

4 밑줄 친 (B) **aberration**의 의미를 가장 잘 풀이한 것은?

(A) an incident that is not typical
(B) an incident that is familiar
(C) an incident that is not fortunate
(D) an incident that is fearful

TEST 03

제한시간 | 35분
정답률 | /21

Passage 1

Psychologists find more inaction, conformity, passivity, and reliance on others in the elderly. Yet, desires for mastery and control are likely to remain strong. At the very least, old people are able to continue to make choices and exert control over daily routines. Work of some sort, which imparts a sense of being productive and useful, predicts living to an old age. Research findings suggest that feelings of control actually enhance mental and physical health and promote longevity.

In one series of studies, for instance, psychologists randomly divided nursing home residents from ages 65 to 90 into two groups. Adults in the first group heard a pep talk emphasizing the need to take greater responsibility in caring for themselves and improving the quality of their lives. Members of this high-responsibility group chose a living plant to tend, to symbolize their commitment. The residents in the low-responsibility group were told that the staff would serve them well. Each individual in this group also received a symbolic plant that the nurses would feed and water, just as the nurses planned to take care of them.

What was the result of this experiment? The members of the high-responsibility group thrived. They showed significantly more signs of alertness, active participation, and positive feelings than did those in the low-responsibility group. The differences lasted long. There was an even more remarkable finding: A sense of control appeared ① __________, with more patients in the high-responsibility group surviving than those in the other group by 15 percent eighteen months later.

1 What is the major topic of the passage?

(A) Dramatic changes that occur through aging
(B) Social responsibility of the elderly
(C) Mental health issues of the elderly
(D) Effects of the sense of control in old age
(E) Importance of power relations among the aged

2 Which of the following best fits into ①?

(A) to prolong life
(B) to be negligible
(C) to diminish drastically
(D) to make differences in attitude
(E) to change the sense of responsibility

3 Which of the following is true of the passage?

(A) The sense of control helped people to live longer.
(B) Older people showed a stronger sense of responsibility.
(C) Low-responsibility group subjects tended living plants.
(D) The feeling of control contributed to improved personal relationships.
(E) The low-responsibility group outlived the high-responsibility group.

Passage 2

There was a time—less than a generation—when games weren't just for kids. Before we owned home-entertainment centers, we had game cabinets. But today, with the time drain of television, exhausting commutes and longer working hours, the scatter of extended families and the deepening devotion to home computers and the Internet, it's easy to see how our so-called leisure time has been fractured. Still, there are anachronisms among us—the corporate lawyer who sneaks off to play backgammon at lunch, the longtime pals who arrange joint vacations around bridge tournament. One game master is Ken Tidwell, a California software designer and editor of *The Game Cabinet*, a monthly Web magazine that scouts out games from around the world. He and his wife, Jocelyn, a free-lance writer, host dinner-and-game parties for six to 20 people nearly every week. Often several card or board games rage at once.

1 밑줄 친 부분이 의미하는 것으로 가장 알맞은 것은?

(A) 변호사 등 자유직업인들
(B) 사교모임을 좋아하는 사람들
(C) 게임을 좋아하는 어른들
(D) 도박을 좋아하는 사람들

Passage 3

The apocalyptic scenario begins with an earthquake near Yucca Mountain, a barren ridge that is the burial site for the nation's most lethal nuclear waste. The tremor is minor; but fresh movement in the earth's crust causes ground water to well up suddenly, flooding the repository. Soon, a lethal brew of nuclear poisons seeps into the water that flows underground to nearby Death Valley. Insects, birds and animals drink at the valley's contaminated springs, and slowly the radioactivity spreads into the biosphere. If this scenario becomes a reality, it would be a terrible disaster.

The twin virtues of the Yucca Mountain site are its remoteness and dryness. The only sign of civilization is the dusty trace of a dirt road cutting across a brown, barren valley. The ridge is located on the southwest corner of the Nevada Test Site, where the government explodes nuclear weapons, so access is tightly restricted. Sagebrush* and other desert plants attest to the locale's* remarkable dryness.

Indeed, only six inches of rain fall on the mountain each year, and most of the moisture evaporates, leaving as little as one fiftieth of an inch to soak into the ground. The water table is unusually deep, more than one third of a mile ___(A)___ the surface. According to the Department of Energy, which is charged with building the repository, nuclear waste could be buried far beneath the ground yet still rest safely ___(B)___ the ground water.

*sagebrush (미국 서부 불모지에 많은) 산쑥

1 괄호 (A)와 (B)에 들어갈 낱말의 짝을 고르시오.

(A) away — to
(B) from — near
(C) below — above
(D) upon — beneath

2 윗글의 내용으로 보아 알 수 있는 것을 고르시오.

(A) 유카산은 지진이 빈번한 곳으로 핵폐기물 매립지로는 부적합하다.
(B) 유카산에 매립된 핵폐기물의 유출로 Death Valley가 극도로 황폐되었다.
(C) 지하수반이 깊을수록 핵폐기물을 안전하게 매립하기가 어려워진다.
(D) 유카산을 핵폐기물 매립지로 선정하려는 이유는 외지고 건조하기 때문이다.

Passage 4

Adaptors are nonverbal behaviors designed to satisfy some need. Sometimes the need is physical, as when we scratch to satisfy an itch or when we push our hair out of our eyes. Sometimes the need is psychological, as when we bite our lip when anxious. Sometimes adaptors are directed at increasing comfort, as when we moisten dry lips. When these adaptors occur in private, they occur in their entirety. But in public, adaptors usually occur in <u>abbreviated form</u>. For example, when people are watching us, we might put our fingers to our head and move them around a bit but probably not scratch with the same vigor as when in private. Because publicly emitted adaptors usually occur in such form, it is often difficult for an observer to tell what this partial behavior was intended to accomplish. For example, observing someone's finger on one's head, we cannot be certain for what this behavior was intended.

1 Choose the one closest in meaning to the underlined "abbreviated form".

(A) a full-fledged manner
(B) a reduced way
(C) an exaggerated way
(D) an inexcusable manner

2 Which of the following can be inferred about "adaptors" according to the passage?

(A) They are more effective when combined with speech.
(B) They are intended to bother other people.
(C) They mean different things in different cultures.
(D) They serve a purpose for the person using them.

Passage 5

In every language there seem to be certain "unmentionables"—words of such strong affective connotations that they cannot be used in polite discourse. In English, the first of these to come to mind are, of course, words dealing with excretion and sex. Money is another subject about which communication is in some ways inhibited. When creditors send bills, they practically never mention money, although that is what they are writing about. The fear of death carries over, quite understandably in view of the widespread confusion of symbols with things symbolized, into fear of the words having to do with death. Many people, therefore, instead of saying "died," substitute such expressions as ________. Some of our verbal reticences, especially religious ones, have the authority of the Bible. It appears that there is a feeling that names of the gods are too holy, and the names of evil spirits too terrifying, to be spoken lightly. It could be true that verbal taboos also produce serious problems since they prevent frank discussion of sexual matters. The stronger verbal taboos have, however, a genuine social value. When we are extremely angry and we feel the need of expressing our anger in violence, the uttering of these forbidden words provides us with a relatively harmless verbal substitute for going berserk.

1 According to the passage, creditors seldom talk about money when sending bills because mentioning money ________.

(A) is immoral
(B) is a taboo
(C) is inhabited by law
(D) is not professional
(E) is conventional

2 Which of the following is NOT appropriate for the blank?

(A) "passed away"
(B) "departed"
(C) "cut the corners"
(D) "gone to his reward"
(E) "gone west"

3 According to the passage, verbal taboos ________.

(A) are used only by men
(B) serve as a safety valve in our moments of crisis
(C) may promote friendly communication
(D) are an imaginative way of understanding things
(E) can encourage constructive debates on sex

Passage 6

The collapse of the Communist regime in the German Democratic Republic and the opening of the Berlin Wall in November 1989, were welcomed around the world. But the rapid unification of East and West Germany brought ambivalent reactions, especially from Germany's European neighbors. On the one hand, there were fears of the political and economic dominance of a united Germany in the center of Europe. On the other hand, recollections of the devastating consequences of German national unification movements of the past were rekindled. Voices were heard even within Germany that warned of the emergence of a new sense of nationalism that would slacken ties to Western democracies and promote a new chapter of German assertiveness—one that would seek, for example, to __________ memories of World War II and the Holocaust. Such anxiety was directed in particular toward East Germany because very little was known of their political attitudes.

1 What would be the most appropriate word to fill in the blank?

(A) promote
(B) empower
(C) enhance
(D) share
(E) repress

2 Choose the word that could best replace the underlined rekindled.

(A) remembered
(B) revived
(C) rebutted
(D) revaluated
(E) realized

3 Which title does best describe the above passage?

(A) Cause of the Collapse of East Germany
(B) Relationship between German nationalism and Western democracies
(C) Anxiety and uncertainty of East Germany
(D) German unification and its impact on European countries
(E) Devastating memories of World War II and the Holocaust

Passage 7

Like most people in the Western world, I have grown up in the artificial environment of modern society. It's a place dominated by external timekeepers, calendars, schedules, clocks. Our lives are subdivided into fiscal years, academic years, weekdays, weekends, deadlines. We are taught that there is a time to get up, a time to go to work, a time to eat. We set the clock by a single standard.

Time orders our lives, and inevitably, orders us around. We are so removed from natural rhythms that we rarely confront how 'unnatural' this is.

We didn't always live with this ____a____ timing. In Time Wars, Jeremy Rifkin explains how recently people have been alienated from natural rhythms to those of the schedule, the clock, and now the computer with its nanosecond culture.

The schedule was the invention of the Benedictine monks whose early passion for organizing and filling every minutes of the day grew from St. Benedict's warning that ____b____ His followers reintroduced the roman hour and invented the mechanical clock. Not until the fifteenth century did clocks, those icons of temporal time, begin to rival churches in the city squares. Not until the seventeenth century did clocks have a minute hand. 'Medieval time', writes Rifkin, 'was still sporadic, leisurely, unpredictable and above all tied to experiences rather than abstract numbers'. It was the merchants and factory owners who eventually, and with great difficulty, trained workers—those who had previously lived in accord with seasons—to become as regular as clockwork.

1 Which one best fills blank (a)?

(A) deadly
(B) regular
(C) mechanical
(D) artificial

2 Which one best fills blank (b)?

(A) 'Idleness is the enemy of the soul'.
(B) 'Time and tide wait for no man'.
(C) 'Idle people have the least leisure'.
(D) 'One's time is one's own'.

3 What is meant by 'sporadic'?

(A) occurring at irregular intervals
(B) occurring without any precedent
(C) occurring inaccurately
(D) occurring only once in a while

4 What is meant by 'early' in this context?

(A) youthful
(B) new and original
(C) developed early in life
(D) belonging to an early era

5 Which is true of the above passage?

(A) Merchants and factory owners used mechanical clocks to control the workers.
(B) Modern man's life is controlled by time.
(C) In the old days, workers lived without any sense of time.
(D) We live in a culture in which the computer controls time.

6 We can infer from the above passage that ______________________.

(A) time is the greatest asset in the modern age
(B) the Benedictine monks have done humanity a disservice in inventing the mechanical clock
(C) living by calendars and schedules makes modern man enjoy less leisure
(D) the invention of the mechanical clock is related to the development of trade and industry

Passage 8

The viruses or bacteria that vaccines are made of have been treated so that they do not cause disease. Many vaccines have disease-causing strands of certain bacteria or viruses that have been deactivated or killed. Some use live organisms that resemble strands that do cause a sickness. Others use only parts of germs. Still others are made up of live pathogens that are weakened so they will not cause illnesses. Toxoids are another type of vaccine composed of poisons released by disease-causing organisms. These poisons are chemically treated for use in vaccines, and they provide immunity without causing the disease. Most medical doctors and public health groups agree that required vaccines have greatly reduced disease infection rates. Not only have vaccinations prevented disease in individuals, but the administration of vaccines worldwide has reduced disease epidemics in vulnerable areas where vaccines are inaccessible.

1 According to the passage, vaccines may contain all of the following EXCEPT ________.

(A) active disease-causing viruses
(B) dead bacteria
(C) chemically altered poisons
(D) living organisms

2 Which of the following best paraphrases the underlined sentence?

(A) Vaccinations have prevented disease in some individuals but not in those who live in areas where vaccines are inaccessible.
(B) Individuals in areas of the world which are vulnerable to disease epidemics are less likely to have access to vaccines.
(C) The practice of vaccination has decreased the risk of disease in individuals as well as in populations that do not have access to vaccines.
(D) The administration of vaccines has prevented disease allover the world even though some individuals are more vulnerable than others to certain viruses.

TEST 04

제한시간 | 35분
정답률 | /25

Passage 1

David Melinkof begins his classic account with the statement: "The law is a profession of words." So what words should be chosen when Latin, French, and English each provide a ⓐ copious supply of relevant items? How does one choose between synonyms, or—even more difficult—between two words which seem to be synonymous, but which might just have enough differential meaning to allow a lawyer one day to make an argument based on the difference? The solution, in many cases, was: don't choose, but use both. In Middle English we see the rise of the legal lexical doublets which would become one of the stylistic hallmarks of that profession. Old English goods and Old French chattels resulted in Middle English legalese goods and chattels. The words were often paired to cover distinct nuances, thereby avoiding ambiguity; but sometimes the pairing seems to be no more than a more emphatic expression of a single meaning; and sometimes it seems to be just a stylistic habit, perhaps ⓑ __________ its undoubted rhythmical appeal in oral performance. But whatever the reason, it became a major feature of legal style which continues to the present day.

1 밑줄 친 ⓐ copious와 가장 유사한 의미를 가진 것은?

(A) unimaginable
(B) unsurpassed
(C) extraordinary
(D) abundant

2 빈칸 ⓑ에 들어갈 가장 적절한 표현은?

(A) fostering in
(B) fostered by
(C) is fostered by
(D) is fostering in

3 이 글의 내용에 비추어 볼 때 다음 중 "lexical doublets"에 해당되는 것은?

(A) peace and quiet
(B) shun and maintain
(C) pardon and testament
(D) acknowledge and deny

Passage 2

In cities and large metropolitan areas, the technical experts drill hundreds of feet for new wells; they construct reservoirs to catch and hold rain water; and they build filtration plants for the conversion (a) __________ human use of water in lakes and rivers. However, in rural areas and small settlements remote from pond or stream, the solution is a different one, though the need for water remains the same. Scientists may scoff, and learned people may sneer, but the old notions persist. Very few persons admit to a belief in witches or evil spirits. (b) __________ there are thousands now making use of a water supply that was first located by a 'water witch.' The modern term for a person who can successfully identify a flow of water beneath the earth's surface is 'dowser.' Dowsers ordinarily do not boast about their peculiar talents, but they are frequently considered extremely useful to have around. All they do is secure a forked twig or branch—hazel is preferred but any green wood will serve—and move slowly about the landscape. With the fork held like an inverted Y, lightly pressed against the chest, and with palms up and thumbs turned outward, dowsers walk here and there until the butt of the fork bends downward. Careful dowsers check and recheck their locations, but where twig bends down, they know they have found water. Let city dwellers, technical experts, and the skeptical ridicule. Millions of people now enjoy a good water supply because they were fortunate in finding a person who could 'feel a strong pull' on the stick and say with authority, 'Dig here.'

1 In this selection the best main idea is ______________________.

(A) the water demands of twentieth-century people are so great that the superstitious will even employ a dowser to locate a well

(B) water is a precious liquid; in time of great need it is wise to seek out a dowser

(C) dowsers are thought by many people to have the power to point out a good site for a well

(D) water witches have been practicing their craft for centuries; they are now called dowsers

(E) careful dowsers keep checking their locations until the twig bends down

2 Which word describes best what the author is trying to do?

(A) ridicule
(B) improvise
(C) puzzle
(D) criticize
(E) explain

3 What would be the most appropriate word pair to fill (a)-(b)?

(A) into — Therefore
(B) to — Yet
(C) for — Though
(D) under — But
(E) through — Nevertheless

Passage 3

In her critique, Dorothy Sayers wrote the detective story does not attain the loftiest level of literary achievement. And she suggested that this is because it is "a literature of escape" and not "a literature of expression." I do not know what the loftiest level of literary achievement is; neither did Shakespeare; neither did Miss Sayers. Other things being equal, which they never are, books with a more powerful theme will provoke a more powerful performance. Yet some very dull books have been written about God, and some very fine ones about how to make a living. It is always a matter of who writes the stuff, and what the individual has to write it with. As for literature of expression and literature of escape, this is critics' jargon, a use of abstract words as if they had absolute meanings. Everything written with vitality expresses that vitality; there are no dull subjects, only dull minds. All people who read escape from something else into what lies behind the printed page; the quality of the dream may be argued, but its release has become a functional necessity. All people must escape at times from the deadly rhythm of their private thoughts. It is part of the process of life among thinking beings. I hold no particular brief for the detective story as the ideal escape. I merely say that all reading for pleasure is escape.

1 The author regards the distinction between literature of escape and literature of expression as ________.

(A) an example of literary criticism that means less than it appears
(B) a much more useful concept for beginning writers than for experienced ones
(C) a concept that is less appropriate for critics than for creative writers
(D) an example of the separation of a story's structure from its content

2 The author indicates that the detective story is like other types of literature in that it ________.

(A) is meant to be instructive as well as entertaining
(B) offers an alternative to the reader's own inner world
(C) accurately reflects a writer's deepest personal concerns
(D) permits the reader to understand the motives of fictional characters

Passage 4

It's the height of summer in Mongolia, and the nation is set to celebrate Eriin Gurvan Naadam, an Olympic-like festival where the so-called three manly sports of wrestling, horse racing, and archery take center stage. Naadam is held annually form July 11 to July 13. (가) The timing coincides with the anniversary of the 1921 Mongolian Revolution, in which the nation gained independence from competing Chinese and Russian forces. The festival traces its roots to the 12th century, when the Mongols, led by Genghis Khan, established an empire that at its height stretched across nearly all of Eurasia. Wrestling, horse racing, and archery were necessary skills for success on the battlefield. (나) Making them into sports trained warriors to be better warriors. Naadam traditionally was a time for men who had trained all year to (다) that they have mastered these skills. Often described as the "manly sports," the festival's events were originally limited to men. Today women participate in both the horse racing and archery competitions, and young boys and girls in particular take to the horse racing. The country celebrations attract scattered nomadic herders who gather to take part in friendly competition, to drink a fermented mare's milk, and to feast on a variety of dairy products. Today, the skills are mostly reserved for athletic competition and camaraderie. But the luster and nationalistic pride surrounding Naadam still shines as bright as ever.

1 What can be inferred from the passage about Eriin Gurvan Naadam?

(A) It has been held annually since the days of Genghis Khan.
(B) It was originally aimed at bringing together scattered Mongols all over Eurasia.
(C) Women and children are now allowed to compete in some of the events.
(D) In the past, it was held in the military camps where professional athletes were trained.

2 Which of the following best fills in the blank (다)?

(A) remember
(B) show off
(C) hold fast
(D) assume

3 The underlined clause (가) relates the Naadam festival to ________.

(A) the nationalistic pride
(B) nomadic cultural heritage
(C) the tradition of the "manly sports"
(D) athletic competition and camaraderie

4 The underlined sentence (나) means that ________.

(A) warriors were shaped into athletes
(B) the military enjoyed spectator sports
(C) ancient Mongols loved sport and recreation
(D) sports were used as a course for military training

Passage 5

Superpower though it may be, Microsoft has to tread carefully when its enforcement (A) agents operate on sovereign soil. As a rule, Microsoft's anti-piracy (B) teams provide logistical, investigative and legal support—but are not shoving battering rams through doors or hauling counterfeiters out of their plants. __________, they are at times present during raids and at risk of exposure. When a renowned Bulgarian software pirate was slain gangland style in Sofia in January, a number of Microsoft people who before had been talking openly to (C) us suddenly asked that they (quote) by name. "We are hearing about a lot of death threats against (D) those fighting piracy, particularly in Eastern Europe," says Trainer. "That's why these companies take efforts to conceal the identity of (E) their people in the field."

Microsoft's toughest battleground is in Eastern Europe, where pirates control 70 percent of the market, more than in any other region of the world. From Bucharest to Kiev to Moscow, piracy has roots in the old Soviet policy of keeping pace with Western computer technology by copying it. Now software piracy is just one more black market. Marek Cerniak, a tanklike Polish cop turned private eye who does investigations for Microsoft, says pirates and mobsters are made for each other: "Software pirates have the brains. Organized crime has the muscle."

1 Which is the most appropriate for the blank?

(A) Moreover
(B) Besides
(C) However
(D) Though
(E) Alternatively

2 Which is the most appropriate form for (quote)?

(A) quoted
(B) should quote
(C) didn't quote
(D) are not quoted
(E) not be quoted

3 Which would be the best title of the passage?

(A) Microsoft's War Against Software Piracy
(B) Microsoft As Superpower
(C) The Future of Microsoft
(D) Microsoft in Eastern Europe
(E) Modern Pirates in Moscow

4 Which one is NOT true?

(A) Microsoft must tread carefully when its agents work on foreign soil.

(B) Pirates would be a major menace to the information industry.

(C) Working for Microsoft company can be dangerous.

(D) Microsoft succeeded in developing non-copiable softwares.

(E) More than two-thirds of softwares in Eastern Europe are copied ones.

5 Which one would designate the people different from others?

(A) (A)
(B) (B)
(C) (C)
(D) (D)
(E) (E)

Passage 6

Disneyland is supposed to be "The Happiest Place on Earth," but Liang Ning isn't too happy. The engineer brought his family to Disney's new theme park in Hong Kong from the southern Chinese city of Guangzhou one Saturday in April with high hopes, but by day's end, he was less than spellbound. "I wanted to forget the world and feel like I was in a fairy tale," he says. Instead, he complains, "it's just not big enough and not very different form the amusement parks we have in China." His seven-year-old daughter Yaqin disagrees, calling the park "fantastic," but her father grumbles: "If she wants to come again, I will send her with somebody else."

Hong Kong's Magic Kingdom has so far been a little short on magic. The $1.8 billion theme park, which opened last September, was touted by Disney executives as its biggest and boldest effort to build its brand in China, a potentially vast new market for its toys, DVDs, and movies. The Hong Kong government, which aggressively wooed Disney and is the park's majority owner, hoped the park would help secure the city's reputation as one of Asia's top tourist destinations. However, the conservative approach of Disney and its parter has produced a pint-sized park that so far hasn't matched visitors' lofty expectations. Hong Kong Disneyland has merely 16 attractions compared to 52 at Disneyland Resort Paris. Meanwhile, management glitches involving everything from ticketing to employee relations have further ① __________ the venture's image. In a recent survey conducted by Hong Kong Polytechnic University, 70% of the local residents polled said ② they had a more negative opinion of Disneyland since its opening. ③ "Disney knows the theme-park business, but when it comes to understanding the Chinese guests, it's an entirely new ball game," says John Ap, who is an associate professor at the university's School of Hotel and Tourism Management.

1 According to the passage, who has the biggest stake in Hong Kong Disneyland?

(A) Disney
(B) Disney executives
(C) The Chinese Communist Party
(D) The Hong Kong government

2 Which would be most suitable for the blank ①?

(A) tarnished
(B) distilled
(C) interdicted
(D) improved

3 According to the passage, which of the following statements is true?

(A) Hong Kong Disneyland has far fewer attractions than Disneyland Resort Paris.
(B) Hong Kong's Magic Kingdom opened in the spring advertised as the happiest place on earth.
(C) Disney's new theme park in Hong Kong secures the city's reputation as one of Asia's top tourist destinations.
(D) Hong Kong Disneyland has no management problems with ticketing and employee relations.

4 The underlined pronoun ② they refer to ________.

(A) most of the visitors
(B) most of the local residents
(C) most of the attractions
(D) most of the employees

5 The underlined remark ③ means that ________.

(A) the Chinese guests are unable to understand an entirely new ball game at Disneyland
(B) Chinese guests who visit Disneyland come to understand a new ball game
(C) since Disney knows the theme-park business, it also understands the Chinese guests entirely
(D) Disney's knowledge of the theme-park business does not guarantee it understands its Chinese guests

Passage 7

Bill Smith and Mike Hugh are examples of men who committed three felonies and are now serving life in prison under California's "Three Strikes" law. However, the men's crimes were not violent. Hugh says it is a waste of money to keep people like him locked up for the rest of their lives. Many people agree with him. A new study by the Justice Policy Institute claims that the ten-year-old Three Strikes law has cost California billions of dollars, but it has not reduced crime. The authors of the study believe that sending people to jail is not a good way to reduce crime, and they think that people who commit nonviolent crimes should not suffer from Three Strikes. Some prosecutors agree that the law is unfair and unreasonable, and that it does not deter crime.

The author of the Three Strikes law, Bill Jones, disagrees. According to Jones, Three Strikes has saved California billions of dollars, and crime in the state has gone down by 46 percent. For example, California now has its lowest level of burglaries since 1957. Jones also says there are two million fewer crime victims and 100,000 fewer prisoners than without Three Strikes. He points out that California has not built any new prisons since the law was passed.

1 Which of the following is the best title of the passage?

(A) Criminals and Crime Victims
(B) Violent and Nonviolent Crimes
(C) Advantages of the Three Strikes Law
(D) Controversy Surrounding the Three Strikes Law
(E) Disadvantages of the Three Strikes Law

2 Which of the following did Jones NOT mention as an effect of the Three Strikes law?

(A) California has reformed its prison system.
(B) Crime has gone down by 46 percent.
(C) California has saved billions of dollars.
(D) The number of burglaries has gone down.
(E) There are fewer prison inmates than before.

Passage 8

The average human pulse rate is around seventy beats per minute. This is also the average tempo of most Western music. In fact, it's said that the slow parts of Baroque music induce mental and emotional integration. Concentrating on the rhythm of music affects the rate of breathing, making it more regular, and faster or slower depending on the piece.

There are interesting developments involving music. People are making "bioelectric" music, recording the sounds made by the electric impulses that result from brain activity or muscle movement. The sounds are processed through a computerized gadget for the use of composers, musicians, and even handicapped people who can be taught this means of self-expression. It's possible that by studying the "music" made by cells, microscopic creatures, and plants, we will understand biology much better.

1 글의 제목으로 가장 알맞은 것을 고르시오.

(A) New Developments in Music
(B) Relation of Music to Biology
(C) Use of Computers in Music
(D) Ways to Understand Biology

TEST 05

제한시간 | 35분
정답률 | /27

Passage 1

Cultural imperialism is much more subtle than economic imperialism, which is itself less tangible than political and military imperialism, whose excesses are obvious and easy to denounce. It would be wrong to say that the world domination of English is something deliberately organized and supported by Anglo-Saxon powers, hand in glove with political initiatives or the penetration of the world economy by their transnational firms. The "language war" had very seldom been regarded as a war and has never, anywhere, been declared. The military, diplomatic, political and economic strategies of the major powers can be studied and criticized, but linguistic strategies seem to be ⓐ <u>inconspicuous</u> and tacit, even innocent or nonexistent. Will countries stand ________ domination by a single language?

1 Which of the following best describes the main subject of the passage?

(A) the world economy and transnational firm
(B) the domination of English in the world
(C) the role of English in international relations
(D) Anglo-Saxon powers

2 The main idea of passage is mainly supported by ________.

(A) comparison
(B) examples
(C) cause and effect
(D) an anecdote

3 Which of the following is true to the passage?

(A) The military and diplomatic imperialism of major powers is hard to criticize publicly.
(B) The human civilization has never experienced a linguistic war.
(C) Economic policies are more obvious than linguistic policies.
(D) The growing importance of English is part of a plan by English-speaking nations for global economic domination.

4 Which is the closest in meaning to ⓐ <u>inconspicuous</u>?

(A) unusual
(B) incredulous
(C) indecent
(D) unnoticeable

5 **Which is the most suitable word for blank (가)?**

(A) for
(B) by
(C) up to
(D) up for

Passage 2

In the process of observation, experiment, and logical interpretation, there has grown up the language or rather, the languages, of science that have become in the course of time as essential to it as the material apparatus. Like the apparatus, these languages are not intrinsically strange; they derive from common usage and often come back to it again. A cycle was once kuklos, a wheel, but it lived many centuries as an abstract term for recurring phenomena before it came back to earth as a bicycle. The enormous convenience of making use of quite ordinary words in the forgotten languages of Greece and Rome was to avoid confusion with common meanings. The Greek scientists were under the great disadvantage of not having a (A) roundabout way in plain language—in Greek—for it. They had to express themselves in a roundabout way in plain language—to talk about the subauxiliary gland as "the acorn-like lumps under the jaw." But these practices, though they helped the scientists to discuss more clearly and briefly, had the disadvantage of building up a series of special languages or jargons that effectively, and sometimes deliberately, kept science away from the ordinary man. This barrier, ____(A)____, is by no means necessary. Scientific language is too useful to unlearn, but it can and will infiltrate into common speech once scientific ideas become as familiar adjuncts of everyday life as scientific gadgets.

1 **What does the passage mainly discuss?**

(A) The nature of scientific language
(B) The dissociation of science from ordinary language
(C) The problems with Greek and Latin in terminology
(D) The process of investigative research

2 **The passage supports which of the following statements?**

(A) Some special scientific terms are accepted into ordinary language.
(B) The Greek word "kuklos" fell down from the heaven.
(C) Greek is favored by the Greek scientists.
(D) Ordinary people are willing to learn scientific language.

3 **The word (A) <u>roundabout</u> is closest in meaning to ________.**

(A) forthright
(B) indirect
(C) uncanny
(D) elaborate

4 **Choose one conjunction that correctly completes the sentence.**

(A) besides
(B) however
(C) indeed
(D) therefore

Passage 3

Attitudes are evaluative judgments about objects, people, and thoughts. What is your attitude about religion, soccer, opera, politicians, crossword puzzles, plastic surgery, and the death penalty? As these examples indicate, attitudes can be positive, negative, or neutral; they can also vary greatly in intensity. You may have attitudes of differing intensity about a wide variety of subjects, and those attitudes influence many of your thoughts, behaviors, and interactions. For example, intense political attitudes influence our thoughts about society, our behavior toward others with dissimilar views, and the people whom we call our friends.

Say that you love rollerblading and strap on your "blades" whenever you have a chance. You also enjoy rollerblading because you know that it's excellent exercise and a great way to stay in shape. You have a positive attitude about it. In this description, your love for rollerblading makes up the affective or emotional component of your attitude, your knowledge about the health benefits of rollerblading constitutes the cognitive component, and your action in putting on your blades illustrates the behavioral component.

Although it is easy to see that we all have attitudes, it is more difficult to understand why we have them and what their purpose is. Attitudes serve several distinct functions: ego defense, adjustment, and knowledge.

If a person makes statements that we perceive as threatening, we might say, "He makes comments like that because he's a dumb jock." Attributing threatening statements to the type of individual making them allows us to avoid confronting the possibility that the statements are accurate.

People and behaviors that yield reinforcement are viewed positively; those that yield unpleasant effects are viewed negatively. For example, an individual who is being reinforced on a new job would be likely to say, "I am very impressed with the supervisors on my new job. They are friendly, fair, and understanding people."

The following attitudes may help a person who is trying to understand an apparently unjust situation: "Most football players have skills that others lack. That's why they're paid such incredibly high salaries."

1 윗글의 목적으로 가장 적합한 것을 고르시오.

(A) To describe the components and functions of attitudes
(B) To explain how attitudes are formed in everyday life
(C) To argue how widely attitudes vary from person to person
(D) To illustrate positive and negative attitudes

2 다음 빈칸에 들어갈 가장 적합한 단어를 고르시오.

The part of an attitude that consists of the knowledge we have about something is called ______ component.

(A) affective
(B) emotional
(C) behavioral
(D) cognitive

3 윗글의 내용과 일치하는 것을 고르시오.

(A) Attitudes force us to maximize negative punishments.
(B) Attitudes don't help us maximize positive reinforcements.
(C) Attitudes can't bring order and meaning to our world.
(D) Attitudes protect us from threats to our ego.

Passage 4

Neal Armstrong's famous first words from the moon in 1969 were heard as "That's one small step for man, one giant leap for mankind." But was that what he said? Grammarians have long been annoyed that such a world-famous moment was marred by bad grammar, arguing there should have been an 'a' in front of 'man'. Armstrong has long asserted that he did, in fact, say the 'a', although [A] <u>the acoustic record begged to differ</u>. To set the record straight, Peter Shann Ford, a Sydney-based computer programmer, conducted his own high-tech detective work. By analysing the NASA recording with advanced nerve-based voice analysis software usually used for people who are paralysed, Ford found the missing word. Armstrong did indeed say, "One small step for a man...", but according to Ford, the 'a' lasted a total of only 35 milliseconds. Roger Launius, who chairs the space history division at the Air and Space Museum in Washington, said, "in the overall scheme of world history, it's probably not significant. But it's nice to know that what he thought he said, he actually did say, and that because of the nature of the electronic and communications systems of the time, it [B] ________."

1 **Which one of the following is closest in meaning to the underlined expression [A] the acoustic record begged to differ?**

(A) He asked permission to use the acoustic record in a different way.

(B) What he claimed was different from what the grammarians asserted.

(C) His assertion did not agree with what the acoustic record seemed to indicate.

(D) The acoustic record was not clear enough to identify his words.

(E) The acoustic record was considered to be incorrect by the grammarians.

2 **According to the context, which of the following best fits into [B]?**

(A) just did not get through

(B) turned out to be nothing

(C) was well worth waiting for

(D) did not matter to us anyhow

(E) was decided to accept his assertion

Passage 5

Essentialism presumes 'that particular things have essences which serve to identify them as the particular things that they are'. The most common essentialist view of culture is that 'cultures' are coincidental with countries, regions, and continents, implying that one can 'visit' them while traveling and that they contain 'mutually exclusive types of behavior' so that people 'from' or 'in' French culture are essentially different from those 'from' or 'in' Chinese culture. Common variations on this __________ theme are the association of 'cultures' with religions, political philosophies, ethnicities and languages, where 'Islamic culture', 'black culture', and 'English language culture' take on the same essence of containment.

Much of this essentialism will seem natural and normal to many readers, because it is in many ways the default way of thinking about how we were different from each other. It is, however, problematic because if we think of people's behavior as defined and constrained by the culture in which they live, agency is transferred away from the individual to the culture itself so that we begin to think that 'German culture believes that …', and that 'she belongs to German culture, therefore she …'. There is only a short, easy distance from this essentialist way of thinking to the chauvinistic stereotyping inherent in culturism which allows us to arrive at statements like 'in Middle Eastern culture there is no concept of individualized critical thinking'.

1 **Which is the most suitable to the blank ________?**

(A) geographical

(B) pedagogical

(C) hegemonic

(D) intellectual

2 What message does the author intend to deliver in the passage?

(A) Essentialism has been rooted in many different types of sources over time.

(B) The essential view of culture should be natural and normal to people.

(C) There is a varied range of acceptable interpretations of cultures in the world.

(D) Unconditional acceptance of the essential view of culture is troublesome.

Passage 6

American society has a long-standing tradition of criticizing violence in the media. During the nineteenth century, educators and others warned about the effects of (가) lurid dime novels and newspaper crime stories on the young. In the early twentieth century, motion pictures and radio were both viewed as significant social threats. Today, concerns are expressed about violence in computer games, popular songs, and on the Internet. Throughout the evolving changes in media technology, a fundamental question has remained the same: Do depictions of violence in the media somehow contribute to real-life violence? Since the 1950s, television has been at the center of the debate over media violence. There are several reasons for the focus on television. It is pervasive and thus it is heavily watched. More worse, television shows are frequently violent. In one 1982 study, researchers who analyzed 180 hours of programming counted 1,846 acts of violence. The net result of television's popularity and violent content is that the average American child witnesses eight thousand murders and one hundred thousand other acts of violence by the time he or she finishes elementary school. Many argue that exposure to such quantities of violent depictions damages children and contributes to violence in real life. In particular, critics claim that television violence teaches children that violence is an acceptable solution to problems and fosters a fearful attitude by leading viewers to think that the world is more violent than it really is.

1 The word (가) lurid closest in meaning to ________.

(A) dirty (B) grisly

(C) ludicrous (D) boring

2 Which of the following is the best title of the passage?

(A) History of Media Violence in American Society

(B) Internet Violence Drives Back TV Violence

(C) The Evolving Changes in Media Technology

(D) The Impact of TV Violence on Young Americans

3 Which of the following is true according to the passage?

(A) American society has long been afflicted with acts of violence.
(B) Both radio and newspaper still pose a major threat to the fabric of today's society.
(C) Since the mid-twentieth century, American people have blamed TV as the main source of media source of media violence.
(D) The 1982 study refuted the claim that media violence had been directly responsible for the promotion of aggression.

4 Which of the following is NOT mentioned as the reasons for the focus on TV?

(A) It is widely distributed.
(B) It is very popular.
(C) It is scandalous.
(D) It has violent contents.

Passage 7

The international diamond trade is a peculiar business, routinely described as a bizarre, one-of-a-kind vocation by the very people who earn a living from it. For example, Albert Thomas, deputy manager of the diamond division at the ABNAMBO Bank in Antwerp, says the diamond trade works well, though he calls it "pretty medieval"—a statement supported by the facts.

In today's global market, the $6.8-billion rough-diamond industry is still largely controlled by one company—De Beers Consolidated Mines, which sets the price for uncut, or rough, diamonds and determines supply. Transactions are settled in cash, even when they involve prices of seven figures. Diamond dealers never issue receipts, and deals worth millions of dollars are sealed on a handshake. It's not surprise, then, that the diamond trade is tight-knit family affair so exclusive that entrance is almost impossible unless you're born into the business. "Everything rests on a person's word," says Lerner, whose family has worked with diamonds for five generations. One of a handful of women traders in the business today, she runs her company, Lerner Diamonds, jointly with her husband.

1 Which of the follow is not true of the passage?

(A) Diamond prices are decided on a competitive market.
(B) Diamond trade is a male-dominated business.
(C) Diamond trade is not open to outsiders.
(D) Diamonds are not traded on credit.

Passage 8

Fog is a cloud in contact with or just above the surface of land or sea. It can be a major environmental hazard. Fog on highways can cause chain-reaction accidents involving dozens of cars. Delays and shutdowns at airports can cause economic losses to airlines and inconvenience to thousands of travelers. Fog at sea has always been a danger to navigation. Today, with supertankers carrying vast quantities of oil, fog increases the possibility of catastrophic oil spills.

The most common type of fog, radiation fog, forms at night, when moist air near the ground loses warmth through radiation on a clear night. This type of fog often occurs in valleys, such as California's San Joaquin Valley. Another common type, advection fog, results from the movement of warm, wet air over cold ground. The air loses temperature to the ground and condensation sets in. This type of fog often occurs along the California coast and the shores of the Great Lakes. Advection fog also forms when air associated with a warm ocean current blows across the surface of a cold current. The thick fogs of the Grand Banks off Newfoundland, Canada, are largely of this origin, because here the Labrador Current comes in contact with the warm Gulf Stream.

Two other types of fog are somewhat more unusual. Frontal fog occurs when two fronts of different temperatures meet, and rain from the warm front falls into the colder one, saturating the air. Steam fog appears when cold air picks up moisture by moving over warmer water.

1 The first paragraph focuses on which aspect of fog?

(A) its dangers
(B) its composition
(C) its location
(D) its causes

2 The word catastrophic in the first paragraph is closest in meaning to ________.

(A) accidental
(B) inevitable
(C) unexpected
(D) disastrous

3 According to this passage, fog that occurs along the California coast is generally ________.

(A) radiation fog
(B) advection fog
(C) frontal fog
(D) steam fog

4 It can be inferred from the passage that the Labrador Current is ________.

(A) cold
(B) condensed
(C) clean
(D) warm

5 **The author of this passage organizes the discussion of the different types of fog according to ________.**

(A) their geographic locations
(B) their relative density
(C) the types of problems they cause
(D) their relative frequency

6 **The author of the passage is probably an expert in the field of ___________.**

(A) physics
(B) biology
(C) transportation
(D) meteorology

TEST 05

TEST 06

제한시간 | 35분
정답률 | /22

Passage 1

Plants absorb energy from the sun. This energy flows through a circuit called biota. which may be represented by a ① __________ consisting of layers. The bottom layer is the soil. A plant layer rests on the soil, an insect layer on the plants, and so on up through various animal groups to the apex layer, which consists of the larger carnivores.

The species of a layer are alike not in where they came from, or in what they look like, but rather in what they ② __________. Each successive layer depends on those below it for food and often for other services, and each in turn furnishes food and services to those above. Proceeding upward, each successive layer decreases in numerical abundance. Thus, for every carnivore there are hundreds of his prey, thousands of their prey, millions of insects; uncountable plants.

1 빈칸 ①에 들어갈 가장 알맞은 것은?

(A) ladder
(B) pyramid
(C) sediment
(D) rectangle

2 빈칸 ②에 들어갈 가장 알맞은 것은?

(A) inhabit
(B) serve
(C) supply
(D) eat

Passage 2

Most people feel lonely sometimes, but it usually only lasts between a few minutes and a few hours. For some people, though, loneliness can last for years. Psychologists are studying this complex phenomenon. The most common type of loneliness is temporary. It usually disappears quickly and does not require any special attention. The second kind, situational loneliness, is a natural result of a particular situation—for example, a divorce, the death of a loved one, or moving to a new place. Although this kind of loneliness can cause physical problems, such as headaches and sleeplessness, it usually does not last for more than a year. Situational loneliness is easy to understand and to predict. The third kind of loneliness is the most severe. Unlike the second type, chronic loneliness usually lasts more than two years and has no specific cause. People who experience habitual loneliness have problems socializing and becoming close to others. Many chronically lonely people think there is little or nothing they can do to improve their condition.

1 위 글의 내용과 일치하는 것은?

(A) Chronic loneliness is the most severe.
(B) Situational loneliness usually lasts for two years.
(C) Habitually lonely people experience sleepless nights.
(D) Temporary loneliness does not have a specific cause.

2 다음의 사례는 위 글에 언급된 **loneliness** 중 어떤 유형인가?

> Most researchers agree that the loneliest people are between the ages of 1 and 25. They found that more than 50% of the freshmen were lonely at the beginning of the semester as a result of their new circumstances.

(A) temporary loneliness
(B) situational loneliness
(C) chronic loneliness
(D) habitual loneliness

Passage 3

Bush will lay out his "vision for expanding the space program," which is expected to include long-term moves for manned missions to the moon and an eventual manned mission to Mars, an official said. NASA's target for a moon mission is 2018. The speech will come just a couple of weeks before the anniversary of the breakup of the space shuttle Columbia as it returned to Earth last February 1. All seven astronauts aboard were killed.

The official declined to say where or when Bush will give the speech, but it will likely be after he returns from a summit in Mexico, possibly as early as Wednesday. White House spokesman Scott McClellan, traveling with the president in Florida, confirmed the announcement will take place next week, and said it would be an outgrowth of a review of the space program that began after the shuttle disaster.

Some of the things that had been under consideration were a proposal for a permanent presence on the moon, setting a target for retiring the shuttle fleet, and a plan to phase out the international space station. An administration official said the president is not expected to immediately discuss the potential cost of his new space vision.

The announcement would come more than 31 years after the last moon mission. The last moon flight was December 1972 and some in Congress have argued that it's time to go back. Last month, administration sources told CNN that NASA was urgently debating and refining the proposals. A senior administration official said Vice President Dick Cheney had initial consultations with key members of Congress on the possibility of a revamped and expanded American space program. The Bush administration review also includes choosing a new space vehicle for manned flights.

1 위 기사의 헤드라인으로 가장 알맞은 것은?

(A) Bush to delay the space program
(B) Bush to announce his regret to the NASA project
(C) Bush to help the victims of the Columbia disaster
(D) Bush to seek manned flights to the moon and Mars

2 위 글의 내용과 일치하는 것은?

(A) Bush visited Mexico to discuss the new space program.
(B) The Congress of the United States agreed to expand the space program.
(C) Since the moon flight in 1972 the United States has not been to the moon.
(D) The international space station will get a financial support from the United States.

Passage 4

Flax has been raised for many thousands of years, for many different reasons. Probably the two most important reasons are for the fabric it makes and the oil it produces. The woody stem of the flax plant contains the long, strong fibers that are used to make linen. The seeds are rich in an oil important for its industrial uses. The peoples of ancient Egypt, Assyria, and Mesopotamia raised flax for cloth; Egyptian mummies were wrapped in linen. Since the discovery of its drying ability, the oil from flaxseed, called linseed oil, has been used as a drying agent in paints and varnishes. The best fiber and the best seeds cannot be obtained from the same flax plant. Fiber flax grows tall and has few branches. It needs a short, cool growing season with regular and plentiful rainfall. (A) __________, the plants become woody and the fiber is rough and dry. On the other hand, seed flax grows well in places that are too dry for fiber flax. The plants are lower to the ground and have more branches.

1 Which of the following questions is answered by the passage?

(A) How is flax harvested?
(B) Is flax an edible plant?
(C) Is it possible to produce a new type of flax plant for fabric and oil production?
(D) Can the same flax plant be grown for the best fabric and the best oil?

2 Which is most appropriate for blank (A)?

(A) However
(B) Therefore
(C) Otherwise
(D) Nevertheless

Passage 5

When we look at any scene we tend to concentrate on what interests us and ignore the detail that does not seem relevant. The camera, however, records the entire scene indiscriminately. This is why beginners are often surprised to find unwanted details intruding into their pictures. The single-mindedness of the eye is something the photographer must deliberately impose on the picture by selective focusing so that extraneous detail is excluded, blurred or subordinated to the overall design. To be able to do this, you must learn to see as the camera does. In taking a picture of a group of friends, for instance, it is not enough simply to look at them and make sure they are all in the frame and that nobody's eyes are shut. Having arranged the group in roughly the right position, look through your viewfinder at the whole picture area, ignoring your friends for the moment and examining their ____(A)____. Remember particularly that the three-dimensional scene will be reproduced in only two dimensions on the film and that a post or tree some distance behind the group may therefore appear, ____(B)____, to be joined onto one of your friends like an extra limb. Try to look at other objects in the scene in terms of shapes, patterns, textures, tones or colors to see whether they harmonize with the subject or conflict with it

1 **The best main theme of the passage is "________."**

(A) The similarity between human eye and camera
(B) The limitation of camera
(C) How to tell good stories in films
(D) How to take better pictures
(E) How to choose better cameras

2 **According to the passage, one of the common mistakes made by novice photographers is that they ________.**

(A) tend to ignore small details
(B) hesitate too much before taking pictures
(C) do not know the difference between camera and human eye
(D) shut their eyes when they take pictures
(E) do not choose their subjects carefully

3 **Which of the following is most appropriate in the blank (A)?**

(A) movements
(B) eyes
(C) attitudes
(D) details
(E) surroundings

4 **Which of the following is most appropriate in the blank (B)?**

(A) in the right position
(B) in real life
(C) in the dark
(D) in light
(E) in the picture

Passage 6

At the White House last month, the Southern Baptist Convention's top political officer, Richard Land, told President Bush he was offended by the number of illegal immigrants living with impunity in the United States. "When government does not enforce laws," he told Bush, "it's not doing what God ordained it to do." But Land, whose group counts 16 million followers, favors down-to-earth solutions. "Practically speaking," he says, "the government isn't going to deport 12 million immigrants." So Land told the president he supports Bush's proposed guest-worker program—and that he might even support putting illegal immigrants on a path to citizenship.

Land's take on immigration mirrors an uneasy national ____(A)____. On one hand, Americans seem inclined to preserve their melting-pot heritage, but they also want law and order and harbor post-9/11 fears about national security. The debate is playing out on a variety of stages. Last month, hundreds of thousands marched in the streets in support of immigrants. And last week, the US Senate intensified debate on a host of legislative proposals, ranging from get-tough enforcement measures to guest-worker programs that would put illegals on a path to citizenship. Where it ends up is anybody's guess. "You're in an election year, and this stirs passions on all sides," says Kansas Sen. Sam Brownback. "There's real possibility we won't be able to pull anything together." The issue is so fraught with political and policy differences that even if Congress does pull something off, it is as likely to disappoint all parties involved as it is to satisfy any one of them.

1 According to the passage, Richard Land ________.

(A) asks Mr. Bush to be in support of illegal immigrants
(B) is in favor of Mr. President's proposal on illegal immigrants
(C) doesn't want to have a talk with illegal immigrants
(D) forces the President to expel all the illegal immigrants
(E) advises Mr. Bush to be more practical on illegal immigrants

2 Which one is most appropriate for the blank (A)?

(A) ambivalence
(B) backlash
(C) crisis
(D) orthodox
(E) consensus

3 What would the underlined part "Where it ends up is anybody's guess" mean?

(A) Nobody knows the result.
(B) Anybody can apply for an American citizenship.
(C) They will allow illegal immigrants to stay in the U.S.

(D) There would be a riot in the near future.
(E) Everybody knows what it would be like.

4 Which is NOT true of the above passage?

(A) Mr. Land is demanding that something be done.
(B) Bush's guest-worker program is not pragmatic.
(C) Many Americans want their country to be open to foreigners.
(D) The U.S. government wouldn't try to oust all the illegal immigrants.
(E) It would be impossible to draw a national consensus on the issue.

Passage 7

Although much of the communist system has been jettisoned over the years, all of China's rural land is still owned by the state. Farmers have usually been allowed to lease plots for 30 years at a stretch, after which they can renew the lease. But ownership—and the right to sell—has remained in the hands of village-level leaders and party secretaries. Here in the jurisdiction of Fujin, more than 70 villages have tried to privatize their lands over the past month, according to local farmers. As word of their movement spread on the Internet, they said, farmers in other regions followed suit. The Fujjin farmers focused on 250,000 acres that had been taken over by local officials in the 1990s for sale to private agriculture companies. Only part of the land was in theory redistributed last month, they said, because police moved in and prevented further allocations. But the farmers have since moved beyond the issue of the seized land and asserted the right to own all the collective farmland that they currently work under lease. The (가) nascent movement, although tiny within a peasant population of 700 million, has confronted the Chinese Communist Party with a difficult challenge: If the experience of the past 30 years has shown the wisdom of privatizing state-owned industry and moving toward a market economy, why would it not be wise to privatize the land and bring it into the market economy, as well?

1 The main topic of the passage is ________

(A) a farmer's uprising
(B) the state land policy
(C) the collective farm system
(D) a long-running feud between villages

2 The word (가) nascent is closest in meaning to ________.

(A) emerging
(B) poorly organized
(C) weak
(D) nasty

3 **Which of the following is NOT true according to the passage?**

(A) Much of the communist system has been abandoned in China.
(B) The Fujin farmers have no right to sell their farming plots.
(C) There is a widespread rumor that a great number of farmers will join the movement.
(D) The Chinese Communist Party has successfully pursued a market-driven economy over the years.

Passage 8

Since 1960, worldwide production of meat has quadrupled to more than 280 million tons a year. Even if everyone in the rich nations swore off meat today, consumption would continue to soar. (ⓐ) For this reason, serious environmental planners have recently focused not on eliminating the meat industry but on turning it green. Making beef, pork, or chicken can be an environmentally devastating process. (ⓑ) And among animal proteins, to make a kilogram of beef takes seven times more farmland than is needed to produce a kilo of chicken, and 15 times the area needed for a kilo of pork. Yet scientist, herders, and green groups are convinced they can curb the damage by making adjustments all along the supply chain, changing the way we farm and feed livestock and building a cleaner cow through modern genetics. (ⓒ) When a cow eats, its stomach produces methane as a byproduct. Cows are pretty efficient at eating grass, but the soybeans and corn that most industrial livestock farms feed them make the bovine stomach rumble with excess gas. (ⓓ) To fight this, some farms found they could improve health and boost milk production in the herds, and reduce methane emissions, by eliminating soybean and corn-based feed. Instead, they give their cows old-fashioned alfalfa, which is packed with nutrients and benign fatty acids.

1 **According to the passage, which of the following is true?**

(A) People in the rich nations are trying to stop consuming meat today.
(B) Methane produced by cows is not environmentally harmful.
(C) Cows' stomachs are efficient in digesting soybeans and corn.
(D) To produce a kilo of meat, pork needs less farming area than beef or chicken.

2 **Where does the following sentence fit best in the passage?**

The effort starts with the animals themselves.

(A) ⓐ
(B) ⓑ
(C) ⓒ
(D) ⓓ

TEST 07

제한시간 | 35분
정답률 | /21

Passage 1

What do I love best about the novels of E. L. Doctorow? The answer to that is simple. I love the way he mixes up fact and fiction to create something new and magical. Take Ragtime, for example. In Ragtime he throws together Emma Goldman, the anarchist; Harry Houdini, the "escapologist"; Sigmund Freud, the father of psychoanalysis; Carl Jung, another important psychologist, and Henry Ford, the father of the Model T, turning these historical figures into characters in a novel. Freud and Jung actually went to Coney Island on their visit to America together. That the historians can document. Did they take a ride through the Tunnel of Love, as in the novel? Who knows? But __________. Doctorow employed the facts, showing his creativity to the fullest.

1 **밑줄 친 빈칸에 들어가기에 가장 적합한 것을 고르시오.**

(A) money talks
(B) what a fantastic idea
(C) the historical details do not ring true
(D) the reading public stole the show

2 **What is the author's purpose of mentioning Freud and Jung's ride through the Tunnel of Love?**

(A) To evoke a sense of nostalgia
(B) To commend a happy invention
(C) To document a historic encounter
(D) To take issue with Doctorow's disregard for facts

Passage 2

A young woman whose boyfriend had left her said she could not understand why. "The relationship," she said, "was more important than any substantive issue, so I gave in immediately on everything." A psychiatrist tried to help her understand by saying something along the following lines: "It takes two to have a relationship. Where were you? If you gave in immediately on everything, what were you contributing? If your boyfriend wanted someone to engage in a relationship, someone with interests and views to be taken into account, your giving in, no matter how simple or satisfying that may have seemed to him in the short run, must have made the overall relationship less satisfying."

Giving in does not build a good working relationship. It may avoid arguments, but it also eliminates the opportunity to learn how to talk through problems and to become skillful at reaching solutions. Without such skills, a relationship will be too weak to survive problems that are bound to come along. It is not enough to solve the immediate problem. We have to think ahead to the effect that this transaction will have on the next one, and the ones after that. That is what building a relationship is all about.

1 위 글의 요지로 가장 알맞은 것은?

(A) Demand concessions as a prize for a good relationship.
(B) Consider what effects the present transaction will have.
(C) Don't worry too much about building a good relationship.
(D) Don't try to buy a good relationship by making concessions.

2 [A]와 [B] 단락의 관계로 가장 알맞은 것은?

(A) [A] is an explanation for [B].
(B) [A] is an example to support [B].
(C) [B] is supporting evidence for [A].
(D) [B] is a possible consequence of [A].

Passage 3

In 1604, five years prior to Galileo's development of the telescope, the world beheld a never-before-seen star in the heavens. It was called "nova" for its newness. It flared up near the constellation Sagittarius in October and stayed so prominent through November that Galileo had time to give three public lectures about the newcomer before it faded from bright view. The nova challenged the law of immutability in the heavens, a cherished tenet of the Aristotelian world order. Earthly matter, according to ancient Greek philosophy, contained four base elements—earth, water, air, fire—that underwent constant change, while the heavens as Aristotle described them consisted entirely of a fifth element—the quintessence, or aether—that remained incorruptible. It was thus impossible for a new star to suddenly form. The nova, the Aristotelians argued, must inhabit the sublunar sphere between the Earth and the Moon, __________. But Galileo could see by comparing his nightly observations with those of other stargazers in distant lands that the new star lay far out, beyond the Moon, beyond the planets, among the domain of the old stars.

1 What is the main idea of the passage?

(A) The nova was a great mystery to the early 17th century scientists.
(B) The existence of the fifth element, the quintessence, was denied by Galileo.
(C) The long-held belief in Aristotelian philosophy was challenged by the appearance of a new star.
(D) Galileo's telescope only proved what was already suspected from observations of the naked eye.

2 Which of the following is most appropriate for the blank?

(A) which consisted only of the quintessence
(B) where new stars are regularly formed
(C) which was the seat of other stars
(D) where change was permissible

Passage 4

It has long been known that the air and water encountered by people in their daily lives are filled with all sorts of micro-organisms. ㉮(__________), most of these are benign and even the unsavory ones can usually be washed down the drain without causing any harm. Not always, though. A team of researchers reports that taking showers can pose a danger to some people. They took samples of the biofilm that builds up inside showerheads from 45 sites in nine American cities and analysed the genetic material which it contained. ㉯(__________), in some of the samples they found high concentrations of a microbe which can cause respiratory illnesses. This is found in tap water, but remains harmless unless turned into an aerosol and inhaled—precisely what happens when bug-laden water is forced through a showerhead at high pressure. As the tiny particles are inhaled, they get into the lungs and can start an infection. Is this cause for alarm? Not for healthy people, but those with a compromised immune system or who are at risk of pulmonary diseases such as the elderly may want to take precautions. Cleaning showerheads with bleach will not do since the microbes will simply return with a fresh flow of water. Replacing bug-prone plastic showerheads with metal ones is a good idea.

1 Which of the following best fits into the blanks ㉮ and ㉯?

	㉮	㉯
(A)	Thankfully	Strikingly
(B)	Strikingly	Thankfully
(C)	Happily	Especially
(D)	Especially	Happily

2 According to the passage, which of the following is true?

(A) Elderly people should not take showers too often.
(B) A microbe in tap water causes cardiovascular illnesses.
(C) Healthy people should use metal showerheads instead of plastic ones.
(D) Forcing out microbes from a showerhead at high pressure can make them harmful.

Passage 5

Human memory, formerly believed to be rather inefficient, is really much more sophisticated than that of a computer. Researchers approaching the problem from a variety of points of view have all concluded that there is a great deal more stored in our minds than has been generally supposed. Dr. Wilder Penfield, a Canadian neurosurgeon, proved that by stimulating their brains electrically, he could elicit the total recall of complex events in his subjects' lives. Even dreams and other minor events supposedly forgotten for many years suddenly emerged in detail. The memory trace is the term for whatever forms the internal representation of the specific information about the event stored in the memory. Assumed to have been made by structural changes in the brain, the memory trace is not subject to direct observation, but is, rather, a theoretical construct that is used to speculate about how information presented at a particular time can cause performance at a later time. Most theories include the strength of the memory trace as a variable in the degree of learning, retention, and retrieval possible for a memory. One theory is that the fantastic capacity for storage in the brain is the result of an almost unlimited combination of interconnections between brain cells, stimulated by patterns of activity. Repeated references to the same information support recall. Or, put another way, improved performance is the result of strengthening the chemical (   ) in the memory.

1 Which of the following might be the best title of the passage?

(A) Patterns of Information Processing
(B) Functions of Memory Trace
(C) Human Memory
(D) Memories and Learning

2 Which of the following would fit best in the parenthesis?

(A) bonds
(B) functions
(C) reactions
(D) recognitions

3 Compared with a computer, human memory is ____________.

(A) more durable
(B) more dependable
(C) more complex
(D) more direct

4 What is true about memory trace?

(A) It is an outcome of empirical observation.
(B) Its primary structure remains the same throughout one's life.
(C) It can be strengthened by practice.
(D) It can be fostered only through conscious effort.

Passage 6

In the spring of the year 399 B.C., a famous Greek philosopher was put on trial for having committed two crimes. One was impiety to the gods of the state; the other was the corruption of youth, by teaching them impiety. The penalty for a conviction on these charges was a severe one, possibly death. The prisoner's name was Socrates, and he was seventy years old at that time. There were other reasons, political reasons, for trying Socrates. He had been associated with the old aristocratic regime, now overthrown by the democracy, and he was held in suspicion as a critic of the democracy. Among other things, he became unpopular for his strange doctrine that even politicians ought to know (a) __________ they are doing. Socrates was reputed to be the wisest man of his time. This reputation surprised him, he said, for he considered himself to be an ignorant man; ignorant of the answers to the supreme questions concerning human happiness and human destiny. But he was also sure that no one else knew the answers to these questions, and this furnished him with an explanation of his reputation as a wise man. (b) __________ he was ignorant, he alone knew that he was ignorant, whereas other ignorant men did not know that they were, thinking they had all the answers.

1 Socrates was put on trial for impiety to the gods of the state and for ________.

(A) rude conduct
(B) his writing against democracy
(C) corruption of youth
(D) theft
(E) ignoring some supreme questions

2 Politically Socrates was ________.

(A) for the new democratic regime
(B) a revolutionary
(C) a communist
(D) a monarchist
(E) against the new regime

3 Socrates held that he was ________.

(A) one of the wisest men of the time
(B) one of the most ignorant men of the time
(C) an average thinker
(D) ignorant because he could not answer certain supreme questions
(E) unpopular because his doctrine was opposed by some politicians

4 What would be the most appropriate word pair to fill in (a) and (b)?

(A) how — As
(B) that — If
(C) what — Though
(D) if — Despite
(E) what — Whether

Passage 7

[1] The Renaissance painter Giotto imitated nature so accurately that his teacher swatted at a painted fly on one of Giotto's works. Is this not a superb artistic achievement? If so, the artist's object was mimesis. Beginning during the Renaissance, mimesis was considered the pinnacle of artistic achievement. However, modern art focuses on depicting not only the world of surfaces but also the inner world of abstract thoughts and feelings. Modern art focuses on the way the elements in the work of art interact and what feelings these elements evoke. A quick glance at art produced over the past century reveals that mimesis has been abandoned by the vast majority of artists.

[2] From around 1880 to the outbreak of World War I, a series of sweeping changes in technology and culture created distinctive new modes of thinking about and experiencing time and space. Such radical inventions as the telephone, automobile, airplane, X-Ray machine, cinema, and standard Greenwich time forced people to reconsider perceptions of the world that had been in place for centuries. Distances seemed to shrink. Time grew more particularized and less subject to nature. Artists responded in kind. Intent on representing the shifting sands of reality, painters and novelists abandoned verisimilitude and forged new art forms that explored man's new relationship with his environment.

1 위의 두 지문에서 알게 된 내용으로 가장 적합한 것을 고르시오.

(A) Art before the Renaissance was propelled by its desire for mimetic representation.
(B) Modern technological inventions had little to do with the changes in modern art.
(C) Modern art turned its attention away from producing a mimetic depiction of the world.
(D) Changes in society from around 1880 to 1914 were characterized by speed.

2 Unlike the author of [1], the author of [2] ________.

(A) laments the loss of traditional modes of thought
(B) mentions a revolution in the forms art has taken
(C) fixes the exact moment of a major shift in perspective
(D) points to the cultural factors that led to a shift in artistic style

Passage 8

(A) __________ the smoke from a cigar or pipe contains higher concentration of both tar and nicotine than does cigarette smoke, even a few cigarettes a day poses a greater risk to health than a number of cigars or pipes of tobacco would. This may be because, while it is extremely difficult to smoke cigarettes without inhaling, it is more difficult to inhale cigar or pipe smoke voluntarily. Cigarette smokers tend to inhale actively, deeply and constantly. (B) __________ because the smoke from burning cigar or pipe tobacco is very harsh, it is more difficult to breathe it directly into healthy lungs.

(C) __________, simply switching to a pipe or cigars from cigarettes is likely to increase your risk instead of lessening it. This is because you have probably become accustomed to inhaling. You may find yourself retaining (1) the habit, and you will then be inhaling even more harmful smoke than before.

TEST 07

1 Which of the following sequences fits best in blanks (A), (B), and (C)?

	(A)		(B)		(C)
(A)	But	—	Although	—	However
(B)	But	—	However	—	Although
(C)	Although	—	However	—	But
(D)	Although	—	But	—	However

2 What is the meaning of (1) the habit?

(A) smoking cigars
(B) smoking cigarettes
(C) actively inhaling when smoking
(D) smoking both cigars and cigarettes

3 According to the passage, which of the following is the most harmful?

(A) smoking cigars
(B) smoking cigarettes
(C) exhaling cigar smoke voluntarily
(D) switching from cigarettes to cigars

TEST 08

제한시간 | 35분
정답률 | /20

Passage 1

One creature that faces a significant threat from humans is the frog, whose ecosystem often lies in close proximity to human habitats. One of the <u>unconscious</u> ways we endanger frogs results from our lawn care. Frogs wander into backyards to feed on slugs, snails, and insects. If the area has been treated with pesticides, the frogs will likely be affected by the poisons. Moving logs or piles of stones denies frogs cool dark places to hide and rest. Yet another danger we pose to frogs is caused by the use of cars. Many frogs are killed by motorists unaware that frog paths cross busy roads. But perhaps the most devastating thing a human can do to a frog is to remove it from its environment and take it home as a pet; amphibians are far more likely to perish when brought into a house without the security and familiarity of the wetland to sustain them.

1 What does the underlined word "<u>unconscious</u>" mean?

(A) latent
(B) lifeless
(C) insensible
(D) unintended

2 Why are frogs vulnerable in backyards?

(A) Because they are harmed by the toxins used to eliminate insect life.
(B) Because they are exposed to moving logs that disrupt their feeding.
(C) Because they are endangered by the predators of slugs and snails.
(D) Because they are denied dark places to produce defense mechanism.

Passage 2

What happens to children who are the target of a teacher's anger or sympathy? They often accept the attribution that they think is behind the anger or sympathy: They come to believe that they have made too little effort or have too little ability to succeed. And they perform accordingly. By attributing a student's failure to lack of effort and expressing anger, a teacher can make the student feel guilty. The guilt—the feeling that he or she has let self or teacher down—is a positive motivating force when the student next attempts a task. But by attributing failure to low ability and expressing sympathy, a teacher ordinarily makes a student feel shame. And shame is not a positive motivating force. Instead it can lead a student to withdraw and to feel inferior and helpless. The point of all this is that ① it can backfire. ②It may be a genuine emotion. ③It may express sincere caring about the schoolwork of low-achieving students. But ④it can cause great harm when students think that behind the sympathy is a teacher's belief that they don't have the ability to succeed.

1 Which of the following is commonly referred to by ①, ②, ③, and ④?

(A) Guilt
(B) Failure
(C) Anger
(D) Inferiority
(E) Sympathy

2 Which of the following is NOT stated or implied in the passage?

(A) Guilt produced when a teacher expresses anger is a positive motivator.
(B) When a teacher expresses sympathy, students usually feel shame.
(C) Students may withdraw when they feel shame.
(D) A teacher's anger for poor performance can make students feel guilty.
(E) Students feel frustrated when they are scolded by their teachers.

3 According to the passage, which of the following is the best way for an adult to respond to a child with poor performance?

(A) To be indifferent
(B) To be sympathetic
(C) To express anger
(D) To accept attribution
(E) To pay compliments

Passage 3

[A]

We remember best the things that are most meaningful to us. As you are reading, try to elaborate upon new information with your own examples. Try to integrate what you're studying with what you already know. You will be able to remember new material better if you can link it to something that's already meaningful to you.

[B]

An effective way is to simplify and make information more meaningful. For example, suppose you wanted to remember the colors in the visible spectrum (Red, Orange, Yellow, Green, Blue, Indigo, Violet); you would have to memorize seven "chunks" of information in order.

But if you take the first letter of each color, you can spell the name "Roy G. Biv", and reduce the information to the three "chunks".

[C]

Memory-assisting techniques help us to associate new information with something familiar. For example, to remember a formula or equation, we may use letters of the alphabet to represent certain numbers. Then we can change an abstract formula into a more meaningful word or phrase, so we'll be able to remember it better. Sound-alike associations can be very effective, too, especially while trying to learn a new language. The key is to create your own links, then you won't forget them.

1 [A], [B], [C]의 관계로 가장 알맞은 것은?

(A) [A] explains the cause of [B] and [C], which describe effects.
(B) [B] is an example of [A] and is also an argument for [C].
(C) [B] and [C] give examples of the techniques for [A].
(D) [C] summarizes what has been said in [A] and [B].

2 위 글에서 언급된 방법과 일치하지 않는 것은?

(A) 장소 전치사의 용법을 방의 책상 주변 물건과 관련시켜 기억한다.
(B) 영어 단어의 뜻을 기억하기 위해 단어가 쓰인 문장 전체를 암기한다.
(C) 잘 아는 노래와 관련시켜 한국사의 역사적 사실을 기억한다.
(D) 독해 절차인 Survey, Question, Read, Recite, Review를 SQ3R로 기억한다.

Passage 4

It is clear that the decline of a language must ultimately have political and economic causes: it is not due simply to the bad influence of this or that individual writer. But an effect can become a cause, reinforcing the original cause and producing the same effect in an intensified form, and so on indefinitely. A man may take to drink because he feels himself to be a failure, and then fail all the more completely because he drinks. It is rather the same thing that is happening to the English language. It becomes ugly and inaccurate because our thoughts are foolish but the slovenliness of our language makes it easier for us to have foolish thoughts. The point is that the process is reversible.

1 Which of the following might be the best title of the passage?

(A) Similarity between English and a drunkard
(B) Advantages of learning English
(C) English as a global language
(D) Decline of the English language

2 Which of the following is most likely to be the subsequent part of the essay?

(A) how English can be reshaped
(B) how English was ruined by political leaders
(C) how language changes as society changes
(D) how people get into bad writing habits

3 How does the author describe the relationship between language and its users?

(A) unrelated
(B) complementary
(C) mutually affecting
(D) one-sided

Passage 5

In the 1980s, scientists around the world began to notice something strange: Frogs were disappearing. More recent research has shown that many kinds of amphibians are declining or have become extinct. Scientists are seriously concerned about this question since amphibians are an important source of scientific and medical knowledge. By studying amphibians, scientists have learned about new substances that could be very useful for treating human diseases. Scientists believe that amphibian decline is due to several environmental factors. One of these factors is the destruction of habitat, the natural area where an animal lives. Amphibians are very sensitive to changes in their habitat. If they cannot find the right conditions, they will not lay their eggs. These days, as wild areas are covered with houses, roads, farms, or factories, many kinds of amphibians are no longer laying eggs. There are a number of other factors in amphibian decline. Pollution is one of them. In many industrial areas, air pollution has poisoned the rain, which then falls on ponds and kills the frogs and toads that live there. In farming areas, the heavy use of chemicals on crops has also killed off amphibians. Another factor is that air pollution has led to increased levels of Ultraviolet (UV) light. This endangers amphibians, which seem to be expecially sensitive to UV light. And finally, scientists have discovered a new disease that seems to be killing many species of amphibians in different parts of the world. All these reason for the disappearance of amphibians are also good reasons for more general concern. The destruction of land, the pollution of the air and the water, the changes in our atmosphere, the spread of diseases—these factors affect human beings, too. Amphibians are especially sensitive to environmental change. Perhaps they are like the canary bird that coal miners once used to take down into the mines to detect poisonous gases. When the canary became ill or died, the miners knew that dangerous gases were near and their own lives were in danger.

1 What is the main topic of the passage?

(A) how scientists study amphibians
(B) why amphibians are decreasing in number
(C) how the environment is affecting animals
(D) why amphibians are sensitive to environmental change

2 According to the passage, which is true?

(A) Amphibians are more sensitive to environmental change than most animals.
(B) Amphibians are less sensitive to the levels of UV light than most animals.
(C) Amphibians are more sensitive to detect poisonous gases than most animals.
(D) Amphibians are less sensitive to scientific experiments than most animals.

3 **What do the scientists think of the decline of amphibians?**

(A) The decline of amphibians causes decline in other kinds of animals.
(B) The decline of amphibians is a good sign for human beings.
(C) The decline of amphibians causes environmental change.
(D) The decline of amphibians is a warning signal for human beings.

Passage 6

Trial by jury is a cherished part of the legal system. Yet few people realize that juries are open to the kind of __________ that can actually hinder jurors' ability to arrive at a just decision. For example, in some cases, lawyers create "shadow juries." These juries consist of men and women who possess the same backgrounds, personalities, and habits as the members of a real jury taking part in a trial. By means of the shadow jury, lawyers try to determine the feelings and attitudes of the people they hope to persuade. Then they use that knowledge to try and sway the real jury's verdict. In addition, lawyers consciously employ language they think will influence a jury's verdict. This is particularly obvious in a rape trial. Attorneys for the defense often rely on words that suggest flirtation and romance whereas attorneys for the victim employ the language of force and violence.

1 **Choose the one that best fills in the blank.**

(A) procrastination
(B) manipulation
(C) liberation
(D) discrimination

2 **What is the author's purpose in the passage?**

(A) to claim that rape trials are problematic
(B) to imply that jurors may be influenced by lawyers
(C) to persuade people to refrain from being jurors
(D) to comment that lawyers are deceptive and dishonest

Passage 7

Forty years ago a young, radical journalist helped ignite the War on Poverty with his pioneering book *The Other America*. In its pages, Michael Harrington warned that the recently proclaimed age of affluence was a mirage, that beneath the surface of U.S. prosperity lay tens of millions of people stuck in hopeless poverty that only massive government intervention could help. Today, a new generation of journalists is straining to duplicate Harrington's feat—to convince contemporary America that its economic system doesn't work for millions and that only government can lift them out of poverty. These new journalists face a tougher task than Harrington's though, because all levels of government have spent about $10 trillion on poverty programs since his book appeared, with disappointing, even counterproductive, results. And over the last four decades, millions of poor people, immigrants and native-born alike, have risen from poverty, without recourse to the government programs that Harrington inspired.

1 Which of the following is NOT true according to the passage?

(A) Michael Harrington was a journalist who called for governmental intervention in poverty.
(B) According to *The Other America*, many Americans suffered from poverty.
(C) The contemporary journalists have been influenced by Harrington's claim.
(D) Governmental poverty programs have helped millions of poor people escape from poverty.

2 Which of the following is most likely to follow the passage?

(A) The achievements of Harrington's strong conviction
(B) The re-evaluation of Harrington's argument
(C) Successful examples of the U.S. governmental efforts to help the poor
(D) The positive effects of the U.S. governmental efforts on economy

Passage 8

Each of the two coldest summers in the past 500 years, 1601 and 1816, followed large volcanic upheavals that threw massive amounts of dust into the stratosphere. Over the course of each year, as the slowly spreading dust obscured the Sun, the Earth cooled. As long as an eruption is big enough, the effect works regardless of where on Earth the volcano is located. Tambora, Indonesia, erupted in April 1815, and in Europe, 1816 was known as "the year without a summer." Even the polar ice cap levels of those anomalously cold summers show large quantities of volcanic ash. As recently as 1991, we saw a temporary drop of 1 degree in global temperatures after the explosion of Mount Pinatubo in the Philippines. The evident correlation between volcanic eruptions and global cooling years is easy to understand. On the other hand, we don't know why the period between 1100 and 1250 was warm enough in Europe and America for the Vikings to grow crops in Greenland. __________, 1400 to 1800 was so cool that it is called the "Little Ice Age." Global mean temperatures dropped by a degree or two; the Dutch canals froze over regularly, and the Swedish army invaded Denmark by marching across the iced North Sea. New York harbor occasionally froze, and George Washington experienced a cold winter at Valley Forge—cold but not unusually cold for that era. Were these events due to a shift in winds, a shift in ocean currents, or perhaps even a combination of many factors?

TEST 08

1 Which of the following is true according to the passage?

(A) Earth-induced and water-induced changes in climate are linked to each other.
(B) Some climate anomalies are easy to explain and others are not.
(C) Volcanic eruptions are the most significant causes of global temperature shifts.
(D) Historically, global cooling years were much longer than global warming years.

2 Which of the following best fits in the blank?

(A) Not surprisingly
(B) In any case
(C) Consequently
(D) Conversely

3 Why does the author mention Tambora in the passage?

(A) Because the effect of the eruption of Tambora was far-reaching.
(B) Because the eruption of Tambora caused the explosion of Mount Pinatubo.
(C) Because the summer in 181 was still colder than the summer in 1601.
(D) Because the eruption of Tambora was the largest volcanic upheaval in history.

TEST 09

제한시간 | 35분
정답률 | /20

Passage 1

For the first time in modern history, less than half of the U.S. adult population now reads literature, according to a comprehensive survey released by the National Endowment for the Arts. Reading at Risk, a descriptive survey of national trends in adult (가) reading, presents a detailed but bleak assessment of the decline of reading's role in the nation's culture. The report can be summarized in a single sentence: (나) reading is not only declining rapidly among all groups, but the rate of decline has accelerated, especially among the young. The concerned citizen in search of good news about American (다) culture will study this report in vain. Although the news in the report is dire, I doubt any careful observer of American society will be greatly surprised—except perhaps by the sheer magnitude of decline. Reading at Risk merely documents a huge cultural transformation that most Americans have already noted—our society's massive shift toward electronic media for entertainment and information. Reading a book requires a degree of active attention and engagement. Indeed, reading itself is a progressive skill that depends on years of education and practice. By contrast, most electronic media make fewer demands on their audiences, and indeed often require no more than passive participation. While electronic media offer the considerable advantages of diversity and access, print culture affords irreplaceable forms of focused attention and contemplation that make complex communications and insights possible. To lose such intellectual capability and the many sorts of human continuity, it allows would ________.

1 Which of the following words fits best in blanks (가), (나), and (다)?

(A) literacy
(B) literate
(C) literary
(D) literal

2 Which of the following fits best in blank as a conclusion?

(A) constitute a vast cultural impoverishment
(B) hinder the decline of the reading population
(C) stimulate sales in the book-selling industry
(D) encourage literature lovers to ignore the report

3 **According to the passage, which of the following statements CANNOT be inferred?**

(A) America should not take active and engaged literacy for granted.
(B) Reading is a universal intellectual capability for any human being.
(C) Electronic media have become the major source of entertainment.
(D) Reading at Risk reports serious news about the U.S. reading culture.

Passage 2

It was an exhausting business, but by my mother's accounts it was the most satisfying and rewarding kind of work. As a nurse she was a low person in the professional hierarchy, always running from place to place on orders from the doctors, subject as well to strict discipline from her own administrative superiors on the nursing staff, but none of this came through in her recollections. What she remembered was her usefulness.

Whenever my father talked to me about nurses and their work, he spoke with high regard for them as professionals. Although it was clear in his view that the task of nurses was to do what the doctors told them to, it was also clear that he admired them for being able to do a lot of things he couldn't possibly do, had never been trained to do. On his own rounds later on, when he became an attending physician himself, he consulted the ward nurse for her opinion about problem cases and paid careful attention to her observations and chart notes. In his own days of intern training (perhaps partly under my mother's strong influence, I don't know) he developed a deep and lasting respect for the whole nursing profession.

1 위 글이 주로 다루고 있는 것은?

(A) The position of nurses in the medical profession
(B) The various kinds of work performed by nurses
(C) The division of labor between doctors and nurses
(D) The writer's parents' views of nursing profession

2 위 글의 내용과 일치하는 것은?

(A) The writer has been receiving an intern training to become a physician.
(B) The writer's mother often recalled her difficult experiences in the hospital.
(C) It is certain that the writer's mother lived a fulfilling life as a nurse.
(D) It was due to his wife that the writer's father formed a high regard for nurses.

Passage 3

For hundreds of years, the Sphinx attracted people both as a religious monument and as a work of art. But eventually, the desert sand once again covered the Sphinx, leaving only the head visible. Then, in the 1300s, a religious man named Saim-el-Dahr ordered that the head of the Sphinx be destroyed because it represented a false god. The nose of the Sphinx was broken off, and the face of the statue was damaged. It was not until the 1800s that archeologists began clearing the sand from the statue and began researching the long history of the Sphinx. At last, in the 1920s, all of the sand was finally cleared away and small changes were made to the Great Sphinx in order to fix it up. Special pieces of stone were added to the head of the statue in order to keep the head from falling.

1 글의 내용과 일치하는 것은?

(A) In the 1920s, a new nose was added to the Sphinx.
(B) Head supports were added to the Sphinx in the 1920s.
(C) The Sphinx was made to honor an Egyptian god.
(D) The face of the Sphinx went through complete changes in the 1920s.

Passage 4

The first ethics dealt with the relation between individuals; the Mosaic Decalogue is an example. Later ethics dealt with the relation between the individual and society. The Golden Rule tries to integrate the individual to society; democracy to integrate social organization to the individual.

There is as yet no ethic dealing with man's relation to land and to animals and plants which grow upon it. Land is still property. The land-relation is still strictly economic, entailing privileges but not obligations. The __________ of ethics to this third element in human environment is an evolutionary possibility and ecological necessity.

1 위 글의 제목으로 가장 알맞은 것은?

(A) Evolution of Ethics
(B) Ecological Privileges
(C) Economic Necessity of Ethics
(D) Relation between the Individual and Society

2 빈칸에 들어갈 가장 알맞은 것은?

(A) enclosure
(B) extension
(C) reduction
(D) formation

Passage 5

The discovery of the American continent had nothing to do with intellectual curiosity or even unfathomable human courage. It was almost entirely about one thing: money. And it was a mistake. The Portuguese throughout the sixteenth century ruthlessly and aggressively built a monopoly in the spice trade from the east by dominating the trade routes around the continent of Africa. Spain, on the other hand, began thinking of ways to get around this monopoly by developing a western route to the eastern countries. The problem was that this route was infinitely longer than the trip around Africa, and it lay across such a vast ocean. It was Christopher Columbus who convinced the Spanish Queen to __________ a western expedition to the eastern countries. Europeans also had a good idea as to the circumference of the earth; this circumference, in fact, had been accurately calculated in the second century B.C.

The general view, then, was that a western voyage to India would be a disaster, for the ship would have to travel thousands of miles over open ocean. But Columbus believed that the world was considerably smaller than was imagined in the general view. He was, of course, completely mistaken and had not America gotten in his way, he and his men would have starved or died of dehydration. But fortunately for Columbus, America did get in the way.

1 Choose the word that could best replace the underlined unfathomable.

(A) profound
(B) audacious
(C) curious
(D) noble
(E) mundane

2 According to the passage, which of the following statements is true?

(A) the expedition to the eastern countries was related to territorial expansion.
(B) it was Columbus who calculated the longer circumference of the earth.
(C) Columbus proved that a western voyage to India was shorter than the eastern route.
(D) Spanish Queen wanted to monopolize the spice trade from the west.
(E) the discovery of America saved Columbus' crew members from being starved to death.

3 What would be the most appropriate word to fill in the blank?

(A) forfeit
(B) underwrite
(C) abhor
(D) imagine
(E) inherit

Passage 6

The principle of equality, which makes men independent of each other, gives them a habit and a taste for following in their private actions no other guide than their own will. This complete independence, which they constantly enjoy in regard to their equals and in the intercourse of private life, tends to make them look upon all authority with a jealous eye and speedily suggests to them the notion and the love of political freedom. Men living at such times have a natural bias towards free institutions. Take any one of them at a venture and search if you can his most deep-seated instincts, and you will find that, of all governments, he will soonest conceive and most highly value that government whose head he has himself elected and whose administration he may control. Of all the political effects produced by the equality of conditions, this love of independence is the first to strike the observing and to alarm the timid; nor can it be said that their alarm is wholly misplaced, for anarchy has a more <u>formidable</u> aspect in democratic countries than elsewhere. As the citizens have no direct influence on each other, as soon as the supreme power of the nation fails, which kept them all in their several stations, it would seem that disorder must instantly reach its utmost pitch and that, every man drawing aside in a different direction, the fabric of society must at once crumble away. I am convinced, however, that anarchy is not the principal evil that democratic ages have to fear, but the least.

1 이 글 뒤에 이어질 내용으로 적절한 것은?

(A) the paradoxical aspects of equality
(B) the useless of human independence
(C) the difference between anarchy and democracy
(D) the triumph of human political achievement

2 이 글에 따르면, 민주주의를 가로막는 무정부성을 낳는 근본원인은 무엇인가?

(A) political independence
(B) the principle of equality
(C) governments
(D) private life

3 밑줄 친 단어 **formidable**과 바꿔 쓸 수 있는 말은?

(A) excellent
(B) dubitable
(C) profound
(D) outstanding

Passage 7

Residential racial segregation is an institution that was developed through discriminatory American policies and local acts of racism. Federal and local government housing discriminations, private discrimination, and exclusionary zoning practices have resulted in the continuation of intentional discrimination against minorities, many of whom still remain ① disenfranchised members of society. The devastating effects of residential racial discrimination on the quality of life for minority families and for our culture at large, represent the importance of initiating policies to integrate residential neighborhoods. Without the efforts of integration, the negative effects of decades of ② bigoted housing policies will be exacerbated, therefore ③ perpetuating the existence of segregation and racial division.

1 Which of the following can best replace the underlined ①?

(A) fragmented
(B) dissatisfied
(C) violent
(D) dangerous
(E) deprived

2 Choose the most appropriate pair of the words to replace the underlined ②–③ above.

(A) bipartisan — demolishing
(B) biased — maintaining
(C) neutral — sustaining
(D) impartial — overcoming
(E) capitalistic — subsiding

3 According to the passage, which of the following statements is true?

(A) Bipartisan efforts are needed to deal with residential racial segregation.
(B) Exclusive zoning practices create gap among even the same race.
(C) Residential racial segregation is more serious on local level.
(D) Racial segregation is expected to be solidified unless extra efforts are made.
(E) Residential segregation is a byproduct of legitimate process of industrialization.

Passage 8

In evolutionary biology, an organism is said to behave altruistically when its behaviour benefits other organisms, at a cost to itself. The costs and benefits are measured in terms of reproductive fitness, or expected number of offspring. So by behaving altruistically, an organism reduces the number of offspring it is likely to produce itself, but boosts the number that other organisms are likely to produce. This biological notion of altruism is not identical to the everyday concept. In everyday parlance, an action would only be called "altruistic" if it was done with the conscious intention of helping another. But in the biological sense __________. For the biologist, it is the consequences of an action for reproductive fitness that determine whether the action counts as altruistic, not the intentions, if any, with which the action is performed.

Altruistic behavior is common throughout the animal kingdom, particularly in species with complex social structures. For example, in social insect colonies (e.g., ants and bees), sterile workers devote their whole lives to caring for the queen which is maximally altruistic. From a Darwinian viewpoint, the existence of altruism in nature is at first sight puzzling. Natural selection leads us to expect animals to behave in ways that increase their own chances of survival and reproduction, not those of others. But by behaving altruistically an animal reduces its own fitness, so should be at a selective disadvantage vis-à-vis one which behaves selfishly.

1 What is the main idea of the passage?

(A) The number of offsprings an organism produces is a measure of altruism.
(B) The Darwinian theory of natural selection has been proven wrong by altruism in insects.
(C) For some organisms, altruism is at odds with increasing their chance of survival.
(D) Altruism is a concept usually reserved for humans who have emotions.

2 Which of the following best fills in the blank?

(A) it is completely logical
(B) there is no such requirement
(C) this is a strong tendency
(D) the action is accidental

3 Which of the following CANNOT be inferred from the passage?

(A) Biologists consider altruism to be actions that are an extension of intentions.
(B) For biologists, the notion of altruism involves some degree of self-sacrifice.
(C) Altruistic organisms are more inclined to assist in other's reproduction rather than their own.
(D) The biological view of altruism somewhat contradicts Darwin's theory of natural selection.

TEST 10

제한시간 | 35분
정답률 | /23

Passage 1

The New Year's Day accident was terrible. A rear tire blew out on the Ford SUV ⓐ as it had traveled on Florida's "Alligator Alley" west of Fort Lauderdale, flipping the vehicle and hurling several members of a family onto the highway. A girl perished on the highway; ⓑ her brother would die hours later. Medical personnel who happened to be in the surrounding cars rushed to the rescue of the other victims. A physician helped clear the windpipe of a woman and resuscitate two of the other injured, ⓒ staying long enough to direct the arriving paramedics to those who most needed help. ⓓ Only after he left did anyone realize that the doctor was Bill Frist, [A] incoming majority leader of the U.S. Senate.

[B] Dr. Frist, who doesn't mind his colleagues' addressing him that way instead of as "Senator," keeps a black medical bag in his legislative office and has shown a penchant for coming to the rescue. [C] The Tennessee lawmaker treated victims of a gunman who opened fire in the U.S. Capitol in 1998, and in 2001 came to the aid of Strom Thurmond when [D] the Senator collapsed on the Senate floor. But now, Frist, 50, is beginning a different kind of rescue mission, one that he may not be fully equipped to handle. Congress starts a new session this week, and the patient before Frist is his own party, still reeling from the recent political scandal.

1 Which one of the underlined parts ⓐ–ⓓ is grammatically awkward in the context of the passage?

(A) ⓐ (B) ⓑ
(C) ⓒ (D) ⓓ

2 Which of the following does NOT refer to the same person?

(A) [A] (B) [B]
(C) [C] (D) [D]

Passage 2

From earliest times, and even today among superstitious people, it has been believed that certain persons have the power to injure or even kill other persons or animals or to destroy crops by no more than a <u>malignant</u> glance. Such a person is held to possess the "evil eyes." In ancient Greece, the power of the evil eye was called baskania, in Rome fascinatio. Because no one knew who had the power and the wish to do him or her injury, it was an almost universal custom, in old times, to wear an amulet of some kind which was believed to protect the wearer. Even the cattle were sometimes so adorned. Children were thought to be especially susceptible to the power of the evil eye, and no Roman mother, in classical days, would permit a child of hers to leave the house without a certain amulet called fascinum. Actually, therefore, our word "fascinate," when first brought into English use, meant to cast the evil eye upon one, to put one under the spell of witchcraft. We use the word rarely now in such a literal sense, but employ it rather to mean to hold one's attention irresistibly or to occupy one's thoughts exclusively by pleasing qualities.

1 What would be the most appropriate title for the passage?

(A) The Origin of the Word, Fascinate
(B) The Mysterious Tradition of Wearing Amulet
(C) The Power of Superstition
(D) How to Evade Evil Eye
(E) The Interesting Customs of the World

2 The mode of discourse in the passage is ________.

(A) narration
(B) persuasion
(C) exposition
(D) argumentation
(E) none of the above

3 According to the passage, the power of fascinum is ________.

(A) to cast a dangerous power over people
(B) to protect from evil influences
(C) to possess the power of the evil eye
(D) to hold one's attention
(E) to occupy one's thought irresistibly

4 The underlined <u>malignant</u> cannot be replaced with ________.

(A) malevolent
(B) evil
(C) benign
(D) spiteful
(E) wicked

Passage 3

It has been particularly important to bring to light language that reinforces the dominant culture's views of disability. A useful step in that process has been the construction of the terms *ableist* and *ableism*, which can be used to organize ideas about the centering and domination of the non-disabled experience and point of view. *Ableism* has recently landed in the *Reader's Digest Oxford Wordfinder*, where it is defined as "discrimination in favor of the able-bodied." I would add, extrapolating from the definitions of *racism* and *sexism*, that *ableism* also includes the idea that a person's abilities or characteristics are determined by disability or that people with disabilities as a group are __________ to non-disabled people. Although there is probably greater consensus among the general public on what could be labeled racist or sexist language than there is on what might be considered ableist, that may be because the nature of the oppression of disabled people is not yet as widely understood.

TEST 10

1 장애자의 차별에 대한 서술자의 입장을 가장 잘 표현한 것은?

(A) critical
(B) satirical
(C) flexible
(D) imaginative

2 글의 흐름상 빈칸에 알맞은 것은?

(A) exceptional
(B) inferior
(C) parasitic
(D) extraneous

Passage 4

The Broken Windows theory was the brainchild of the criminologists James Wilson and George Kelling. They argued that crime is the inevitable result of disorder. If a window is broken and left unrepaired, people walking by will conclude that no one cares and no one is in charge. Soon, more windows will be broken, and the sense of anarchy will spread from the building to the street on which it faces, sending a signal that ① __________. In a city, relatively minor problems like graffiti, public disorder, and aggressive panhandling are all the equivalent of broken windows, invitations to more serious crimes.

What does this suggest? It says that the criminal—far from being someone who acts for fundamental, intrinsic reasons and who live in his own world—is actually someone acutely sensitive to his environment, who is alert to all kinds of cues, and who is prompted to commit crimes based on his perception of the world around him. That is an incredibly radical—and in some sense unbelievable—idea. It says that behavior is a function of social context.

1 What is the major theme of the passage?

(A) Most break-ins in the city occur through windows.
(B) An individual's behavior is deeply influenced by the environment.
(C) Minor offenders may become serious criminals in the long run.
(D) Criminals are born to disturb the public peace.
(E) Pedestrians are irresistibly affected by the condition of street-side windows.

2 Which of the following best fits into ①?

(A) anything goes here
(B) the police are around
(C) the windows need fixing
(D) someone is in charge here
(E) it will collapse soon

Passage 5

American culture thrives on contradictions. It (A) individualism yet is (a) rife with the conformity so essential to consumerism. It preaches self-reliance and personal accountability (especially for poor people) while enriching pop psychologists who provide excuses for sins of the middle class. It nurtures feminism and encourages face-lifts. So we shouldn't be entirely surprised by the (B) convergence of reality TV shows with a growing concern about privacy, although the intensity of these opposing trends is particularly dramatic. (b) Democratic and Republican pollsters attest to a "groundswell" of concern about privacy, which politicians rush to address. George W. Bush declares himself a "privacy rights person." Congress considers hundreds of privacy protection bills. (c) Still, people cede their privacy voluntarily every day for the promise for security.

1 Identify the word that best fills in (A).

(A) excavates
(B) exalts
(C) exaggerates
(D) extemporizes

2 Identify the word that best fills in (B).

(A) parallel
(B) paradigmatic
(C) practical
(D) paradoxical

3 Find a word or a phrase that can replace (a).

(A) full of
(B) contending with
(C) delectable
(D) liable to

4 **Find the sentence best expressing the idea inferred in the underlined sentence (b) "Democratic and Republican pollsters attest to a 'groundswell' of concern about privacy, which politicians rush to address."**

(A) Both Democratic and Republican voters agree that politicians should immediately address the issue of privacy.

(B) There is increasing political recognition of invasions of privacy, which is proved by pollsters from both Parties.

(C) The pollsters from both Parties show that they are testing their concerns about privacy, and politicians address the issue in haste.

(D) Privacy has become the groundbreaking issue to both Parties, which presses politicians to address the issue.

5 **Which of the following can be an appropriate example of the underlined statement (c)?**

(A) People stick to a traditional American value, "the right to be let alone," because it guarantees them a sense of self-reliance and personal accountability.

(B) At airport, people are recalcitrant when asked to take off their shoes to be checked by the security guard.

(C) People welcome surveillance cameras in elevators, in parking garages, or at ATMs.

(D) People do not give government the power to wiretap because it guarantees security.

Passage 6

The cultures in Africa vary as much as the terrain. There are over 30 religions on the continent and over one thousand languages spoken. Futhermore, in all parts of Africa, culture is steeped in a dynamic musical tradition. In Northern Africa, Islam influences all parts of life, including the music. The vocals are typically long, fluctuating notes that are as mesmerizing as they are haunting. Singing is usually accompanied by tambourines, drums, bagpipes, and flutes. In other parts of Africa, however, the drum is king. West African music is characterized by throbbing rhythms and call-and-response-style singing. Many music historians attribute the creation of New World music genres such as jazz and rock-and-roll to West African musical influences that were transferred to the Americas through the trans-Atlantic slave trade. Additionally, this is not the only case of African music evolving. In the Democratic Republic of Congo, a style of music called Soukous was created. It is a mixture of traditional Congolese drumming and Afro-Cuban sounds. Soukous has become internationally popular since the 1930s and is performed all over the world.

1 According to the passage, what is true of West African music?

(A) It is heavily influenced by Arabic musical styles.

(B) It is mixed with Afro-Caribbean sounds.

(C) It is based on jazz and rock-and-roll.

(D) It is centered on percussion and rhythmic singing.

2 Choose the answer which is closest in meaning to "mesmerizing".

(A) sobering (B) hypnotizing

(C) tantalizing (D) petrifying

3 Which of the following best paraphrases the underlined sentence?

(A) Music historians contend that without New World genres such as jazz and rock-and-roll, West African music would never be popular.

(B) According to music historians, new music genres in the Americas were inspired by West African music that was transferred during the slave trade.

(C) Music historians have found that jazz and rock-and-roll were created during the trans-Atlantic slave trade.

(D) The West African influences on jazz and rock-and-roll are obvious. and music historians think that they were transferred to Africa through the slave trade.

Passage 7

High-level U.S. officials, interviewed after the close of meetings for the day, said the two sides agreed on many things in principle, such as the need to keep their economies open to other countries. But specific measures and a timetable were less clear, with the United States pushing for rapid change and China seeking to move cautiously. Skepticism toward foreign trade, particularly with China, played a major role in the recent U.S. elections, and proposals for punitive tariffs or other protectionist measures could gain support in Congress next year. "I sense that they have an understanding of the stakes," an official said. "And the stakes are very high. You are talking about a lot of business, a lot of jobs on both sides. We are their No. 1 customer." While most of the day was focused on U.S. requests of Beijing, China also listed some priorities: fewer obstacles to the export of U.S. technology and to Chinese investment in the United States. The complaint about U.S. export controls, in particular, led to some tense exchanges, U.S. delegates said.

1 **Which of the following best describes the author's attitude about the U.S.-China talks on trade?**

(A) optimistic
(B) pessimistic
(C) balanced
(D) cynical
(E) pathetic

2 **Which of the following is NOT stated or implied in the passage?**

(A) China does not want to rapidly open its economy to the U.S.
(B) China wants to import U.S. technology.
(C) There are many obstacles to China's investment in the U.S.
(D) The American Congress is likely to impose heavier taxes on imported items next year.
(E) Americans and Chinese want to have jobs in each other's countries.

Passage 8

Life in ancestral environments was fraught with danger, not just from the obvious predators but also from a variety of microbes, viruses and toxins. Ancestral foods obtained through foraging, scavenging and hunting were quite "natural" and therefore far from healthy. Many plants are full of dangerous toxins and so are dead animals. Also, many animals carry pathogens that adapt easily to life in a human body. The danger is especially high for a "generalist" species like human—that is, one that finds its nutrients in a great variety of sources and adapts to new environments by changing its diet. Being a generalist species requires not only that you have immune defenses like most other species but also that you make specific cognitive adaptations to minimize the danger of contamination and contagion. Rats, too, are generalists; this shows in their extremely cautious approach to novel foods, and in the way they quickly detect the correlation between a new food and various somatic disorders. They detect such connections better than other, non-food-related correlations, which shows that the system that produces such inferences is indeed specialized.

1 **Which of the following made the ancient people more exposed to the danger?**

(A) they didn't cook the food
(B) they heavily relied on dead animals
(C) they had no clothes on
(D) they were surrounded by dangerous animals
(E) they didn't have many weapons to fight with

2 What does it mean to men themselves that they are "generalists"?

(A) They don't have any problems with their new poisoned food.
(B) They are unlikely to survive the next Ice Age.
(C) They can easily cure themselves by taking medicines.
(D) They are likely to face higher risk of food poisoning.
(E) They don't have any preference for their diet.

3 According to the passage, rats can ________.

(A) eat anything without any digestive problems
(B) control his diet whenever they want to
(C) find easily what food is good for their body
(D) go anywhere without being caught by their predators
(E) survive far longer than human beings

TEST 11

제한시간 | 35분
정답률 | /21

Passage 1

If a patient became ill with a fever in the eighteenth century, a surgeon might prescribe leeches. Several of these glossy black worms would be placed on the patient's body, where they would puncture the skin and draw small amounts of blood. If the doctor thought that the patient should be drained of more blood than leeches could drink, he would next turn to bloodletting, which involved cutting a vein and allowing ounces or even whole pints of blood to flow from the body, often until the patient fainted.

During the Civil War, physicians sometimes treated a soldier's open wound by putting maggots, the wormlike larvae of flies, directly onto the patient's damaged flesh. If a patient complained of intestinal problems, the physician might order him to eat dirt.

Do you shudder when you think of such revolting remedies? Are you relieved that advances in medical knowledge have put a stop to these kinds of barbaric treatments? You may be surprised to know that scientists have discovered that many of these old cures actually work; in some cases, they are actually more effective than other, more modern techniques. As a result, a number of disgusting medical remedies are making a comeback in today's hospitals.

Because leeches offer so many benefits, doctors are again beginning to use them for bloodletting. Leeches are proving to be particularly useful after surgeries involving the reattachment of severed body parts. When areas swell with congested blood, leeches are applied to relieve the pressure by sucking up the blood. Leech saliva contains a natural anesthetic, so the bite is pain free. The saliva also contains substances that prevent bacteria from infecting the wound area and cause blood vessels to open wider. Therefore, the worms promote the circulation of blood necessary for healing. Leech saliva also contains a chemical that keeps blood from clotting. Thus the creatures also have been used to unclog blood vessels during heart surgery.

1 According to the passage, which of the following was NOT used as remedies centuries ago?

(A) leeches
(B) bacteria
(C) maggots
(D) dirt

2 Which of the following best states the main idea of the entire passage?

(A) Patients in the past tried anything to be cured of their illness.
(B) Advances in medicine have relieved people from barbaric, disgusting remedies.
(C) Modern scientific research has shown that some old cures are actually effective.
(D) Little progress was made in medicine between the eighteenth and the nineteenth century.

3 Which of the following is true of leeches?

(A) The saliva of leeches is beneficial to humans.
(B) Leeches have been indispensible during heart surgery.
(C) Leeches are particularly helpful to people with damaged flesh.
(D) Using leeches for bloodletting sometimes caused patients to faint.

Passage 2

Noam Chomsky gave the name "Plato's Problem" to the general problem of how we come to know things in conditions of sparse evidence. As Chomsky has shown over the years, this problem arises sharply in the case of language. In linguistics, Plato's Problem is understood to be the problem of explaining how a grammar can be acquired under conditions of poverty of the stimulus.

Plato's Problem refers to the gap between experience and knowledge. To close the gap, we need to either show that learners have more experience than we thought, or that they have some knowledge from another source. Plato took the second approach: learning is but recollection of knowledge we acquired in a previous life. Generative linguists have adopted a version of this solution; that is, to provide the learner with innate knowledge in the form of principles of Universal Grammar (UG). By restricting the set of hypotheses that a learner can formulate, it overcomes, at least to some extent, the poverty of the stimulus, and in this fashion provides a partial solution to Plato's Problem

1 According to the generative linguistics, children learn language through ________.

(A) repeated practice
(B) memorizing grammar rules
(C) inborn grammar structure
(D) various stimuli for language development

2 Which of following is NOT stated in the passage above?

(A) Origin of Plato's Problem
(B) Plato's view of knowledge

(C) Necessity of stimuli in language acquisition
(D) The way of language acquisition

3 What can you infer from the passage above?

(A) Universal Grammar offers stimuli for language development.
(B) Without language, we can have neither knowledge nor experience.
(C) For language acquisition, we necessarily need experience or knowledge.
(D) The concern in the language acquisition is not unique in modern age. It dates back to the ancient Greece.

Passage 3

Grown people know that they do not always know the why of things, and even if they think they know, they do not know where and how they got the proof. Hence the irritation they show when children keep on demanding to know if a thing is so and how the grown folks got the proof of it. It is so troublesome because it is disturbing to the pigeonhole way of life. It is upsetting because until the elders are pushed for an answer, they have never looked to see if it was so, nor how they came by what passes for proof to their acceptances of certain things as true. So, if telling their questioning young to run off and play does not suffice for an answer, a good swat on the child's bottom is held to be proof positive for anything from spelling "Constantinople" to why the sea is salty. It was told to the old folks and that had been enough for them.

1 What is the author's tone in discussing the attitude of grown people?

(A) defiantly resentful
(B) amused and childlike
(C) playfully disapproving
(D) tentative and reasonable

Passage 4

On Feb. 2, 2007. the United Nations scientific panel studying climate change declared that the evidence of a warming trend is ① unequivocal, and that human activity has "very likely" been the driving force in that change over the last 50 years. The last report by the group, the Intergovernmental Panel on Climate Change, in 2001, found that humanity had "likely" played a role.

The addition of that single word "very" did more than reflect mounting scientific evidence that the release of carbon dioxide and other heat-trapping gases from smokestacks, tailpipes and burning forests has played a central role in raising the average surface temperature of the earth by more than I degree Fahrenheit since 1900. It also added new momentum to a debate that now seems centered less over whether humans are warming the planet, but instead over what to do about it. In recent months, business groups have banded together to make ② unprecedented calls for federal regulation of greenhouse gases. The subject had a red-carpeted moment when former Vice President Al Gore's documentary, "An Inconvenient Truth," was awarded an Oscar; and the Supreme Court made its first global warming-related decision, ruling 5 to 4 that the Environmental Protection Agency had not justified its position that it was not authorized to regulate carbon dioxide.

The greenhouse effect has been part of the earth's workings since its earliest days. Gases like carbon dioxide and methane allow sunlight to reach the earth, but prevent some of the resulting heat from radiating back out into space. Without the greenhouse effect, the planet would never have warmed enough to allow life to form. But as ever larger amounts of carbon dioxide have been released along with the development of industrial economies, the atmosphere has grown warmer at an accelerating rate: since 1970, temperatures have gone up at nearly three times the average for the 20th century.

1 Which of the following would be the best title for the above passage?

(A) The Danger of Humanism
(B) The Significance of Carbon Dioxide
(C) A Heated Debate as to the Role of the Supreme Court
(D) Methane and Other Gases
(E) Global Warming-Related Problems

2 The word ① unequivocal is closest in meaning to ________.

(A) certain
(B) unequal
(C) obscure
(D) light
(E) neutral

3 **The word ② <u>unprecedented</u> is closest in meaning to ________.**

(A) out of date
(B) absolutely superb
(C) be destined to
(D) beyond our perception
(E) not known or experienced before

4 **According to the passage, the Supreme Court's decision implies that the Environmental Protection Agency ______________________________.**

(A) supported the policy concerning federal regulation of greenhouse gasses.
(B) played a crucial role in authorizing the use of carbon dioxide.
(C) investigated the principle of the greenhouse effect.
(D) neglected their responsibility to regulate carbon dioxide.
(E) publicized the danger of carbon dioxide through the press.

5 **According to the passage, which of the following is true?**

(A) The main cause of the greenhouse effect is strong sunlight.
(B) The subject of Al Gore's documentary is to inform people of the necessity of the regulation of carbon dioxide.
(C) Gases like carbon dioxide and methane are so absolutely harmful that we have to completely remove them.
(D) Recently, business groups have banded together to invalidate federal regulation of greenhouse gases.
(E) The development of industrial economies has nothing to do with the increase of the average surface temperature of the earth.

TEST 11

Passage 5

Characterization in a play is based almost entirely on action and dialogue. Action can include such subtle devices as a gesture or a change of expression, and dialogue can include a monologue that resembles the expression of thoughts and feelings. In a play, the role of costuming is also important. But the major impression of a character on stage is made by what that character does and what he or she says to others. Compare this with the devices available in fiction. In that more flexible genre you as author can use the character's own thoughts, the thoughts of others, quick glimpses into the past through flashbacks, and direct exposition. Since the devices available to the dramatist are more limited, the tendency is to use them more boldly. Audiences are used to this. Just as the makeup is heavier, the voice louder, characterization is applied more bluntly in a play. It seems natural to use the word 'theatrical' to describe individuals whose personalities are vivid and striking.

1 위 글의 제목으로 가장 적절한 것은?

(A) The History of the Development of the Theatre
(B) The Merits of Fiction Writing
(C) The Nature of Characterization in Drama
(D) The Relationship between the Author and His Audience

2 위 글의 내용과 일치하지 않는 것은?

(A) Fiction provides the author with much more flexibility than does drama.
(B) Monologue is one of the ways in which the playwright deals with characterization.
(C) The novelist often uses flashbacks and direct expositions, devices that are not readily available to the dramatist.
(D) It is often the audience who complains most about the heavy makeup actors must wear on stage.

Passage 6

Among the world's 6,800 tongues, half to 90 percent could become extinct by the end of the century, linguists predict. One reason is because half of all languages are spoken by fewer than 2,500 people each. Languages need at least 100,000 speakers to survive the ages, says UNESCO. War, genocide, fatal natural disasters, the adoption of more dominant languages such as Chinese and Russian, and government bans on languages also contribute to their demise. "In some ways it's similar to what threatens species," said Payal Sampat, a researcher who wrote about ① the issue for the May-June magazine of Worldwatch Institute. He added that Udihe and Arikapu, spoken in Siberia and the Amazon jungle, are also among those that are at risk.

1 Which of the following does the underlined ① refer to?

(A) threatened species
(B) endangered languages
(C) language dominance
(D) language policies for immigrants
(E) diversity in language policies

2 According to the passage, which of the following is true?

(A) Some dead languages have been revived.
(B) The world, linguistically speaking, is becoming more diverse.
(C) Efforts are under way to revive Udihe and Arikapu.
(D) Linguists believe 680 to 3,400 languages could be extinct by 2100.
(E) Governments contribute to the death of some language by banning them.

Passage 7

After failures, backers of Africa aid have changed their tune. Twenty years ago, rock star Bob Geldof raised money with his Live Aid rock concert to help famine victims in Ethiopia. He has since realized that helping Africa is a far more complex business. Much of the money was mismanaged or pocketed by corrupt officials. Geldof's weekend Live 8 concerts to help Africa had a wiser and more realistic aim. They focused on raising awareness and pressuring the leaders of wealthy nations—the Group of Eight (G8). After decades of tossing money at Africa, international organizations are coming to the conclusion, as Geldof has, that more calibrated and sophisticated approaches are needed. Just what those approaches might be are, as yet, unclear. Even so, besides giving generously, three elements seem to be crucial. The G8 would do well to emphasize (가) them, as the World Bank increasingly has: debt cancellation, good governance, and self sufficiency, Africa needs help. It is home to 13% of the world's population and a third of the people in extreme poverty. Incomes are lower than those 30 years ago. Thirteen million have died of AIDS; 26 million are infected. It incubates international disease and terrorism. Realistic help, however, means more than rock concerts and handouts.

1 What can be inferred from the passage?

(A) Bob Geldof will hold a charity concert to get money from the G8 leaders.
(B) Bob Geldof couldn't stand the frustration of not being able to help famine victims.
(C) African aiding mission for decades failed due to a lack of funding and mismanagement.
(D) Backers of Africa aid began to focus accurately planned approaches.

2 What does the pronoun (가) them refer to?

(A) those approaches
(B) three elements
(C) famine victims
(D) international organizations

3 Which of the following is the top priority for the writer in aiding Africa?

(A) realistic help
(B) more volunteers
(C) more money
(D) profit-sharing scheme

Passage 8

Few creatures are held in such awe as lions, tigers, cheetahs and leopards, which we often call the big cats. These agile predators have strong, razor-sharp teeth and claws, muscular bodies and excellent senses. Their beautiful striped and dappled fur camouflages among the trees, allowing them to leap from the shadows to ambush unwary zebras, giraffes and other prey. The first large cats lived 45 million years ago. Many, including the lion, cheetah and leopard still inhabit parts of Africa. Snow leopards dwell in the mountains of Asia. Jaguars are the largest of the big cats in North and South America. They are equally at home swimming in lakes or climbing in trees. Lions are the only big cats that live in groups called "prides," which may be up to thirty in total. The pride roams over an area of $100km^2$ or more, depending on the abundance of prey in that area. The large male lion protects the pride's territory against other prides. The lion also defends the female against other males. Lions, tigers and other big cats are true (A). Lions usually eat large prey such as antelopes and zebras. One giraffe is often enough to feed a whole pride of lions.

1 Which of the following best fits into (A)?

(A) felines
(B) carnivores
(C) canines
(D) herbivores

2 According to the passage, which of the following is NOT true ?

(A) The first big cats are believed to have lived in Africa.
(B) No big cats other than lions are likely to live in groups.
(C) Big cats attract the prey with their striped and dappled fur.
(D) Both snow leopards and jaguars are good at swimming in lakes and climbing in trees.

TEST 12

제한시간 | 35분
정답률 | /22

Passage 1

It's not easy being a mother these days. Most work outside the home in addition to their parenting duties. Because of the high divorce rate, many are rearing their children alone or with only part-time help from fathers. In 2001, an ABC News columnist did some research suggesting that if you paid mothers for all the things they do, they would draw down about $500,000 a year. Moms face a daunting task, whether they have other jobs or not. First, they must make their way through a labyrinth of advice based on vast amounts of research, much of it conflicting. Whatever they do, they're bound to find some study that says they did the wrong thing, didn't do the right thing, or otherwise somehow permanently damaged their offspring. Then there's the whole problem of keeping their children healthy amidst an incessant barrage of messages seducing them to eat more sugar-and fat-loaded snack foods. And of teaching them values in a society that worships materialism. And of helping them find a path through a world filled with diverse beliefs, an overabundance of knowledge and information, and moral ambiguity.

1 What is the general tone of the passage?

(A) ashamed
(B) sympathetic
(C) indignant
(D) threatening

2 Which of the following is the best title for the passage?

(A) Being a Good Mom
(B) Roles of Mom in a Society
(C) Effects of Mom on Child Education
(D) No Job More Challenging Than Being a Mom

Passage 2

The general key to effective listening in interpersonal situations is to listen actively. Perhaps the best preparation for active listening is to act physically and mentally like an alert listener. For many people, this may be the most abused rule of effective listening. Recall, for example, how your body almost automatically reacts to important news: Almost immediately, you assume an upright posture and remain relatively still and quiet. You do this almost reflexively because this is the way you listen most effectively. Even more important than this physical alertness is mental alertness. As a listener, participate in the communication as an equal partner with the speaker, as one who is emotionally and intellectually ready to engage in the sharing of meaning. Active listening is expressive. Let the listener know that you are participating in the communication process. Nonverbally, maintain eye contact, focus your concentration on the speaker rather than on others present, and express your feeling facially. Verbally, ask appropriate questions, signal understanding with "I see" or "yes," and express agreement or disagreement as appropriate. Passive listening is, however, not without merit. Passive listening—listening without talking or directing the speaker in any obvious way—is a powerful means of communicating acceptance. This is the kind of listening that people ask for when they say, "Just listen to me." They are essentially asking you to suspend your judgment and "just listen." Passive listening allows the speaker to develop his or her thoughts and ideas in the presence of another person who accepts but does not evaluate, who supports but does not intrude. By listening passively, you provide a supportive environment. Once that has been established, you may wish to participate in a more active way, verbally and nonverbally.

1 다음 중 적극적인 청취(active listening)와 관계가 없는 것을 고르시오.

(A) The listener must not use nonverbal clues to express his or her feeling.
(B) The listener should try to be an equal partner with the speaker.
(C) The listener should maintain eye contact with the speaker.
(D) The listener had better express disagreement to the speaker when necessary.

2 윗글을 세 단락으로 구분할 때, 셋째 단락은 무엇에 관한 내용인지 다음 중에서 고르시오.

(A) The positive side of passive listening
(B) The negative effects of passive listening in inter-personal situations
(C) The definition and benefits of passive listening
(D) How to develop passive listening in real-life relationships

Passage 3

The correlation observed in English between frequency of usage and etymology is not necessarily true of every language. Some languages—German is ⓐ __________—have traditionally turned to their own resources for enriching the vocabulary with words for more sophisticated notions or new products. For example, Übersetzung is equivalent to our word "translation," but it literally means "setting over." Fernsehen is equivalent to "television," but it literally means "far-seeing." Lautlehre is equivalent to "phonology," but it literally means "sound study." That is, in German, native roots are combined to form new compounds having the same meaning as the classical-based compounds. This method of vocabulary enrichment is familiar also in English: doorbell, horseshoe, lighthouse, shorthand, stronghold are all compounds containing native elements only. However, compared to German, English has been less inventive in producing new words from its own roots; instead, it has added and creatively recycled roots from ⓑ __________.

1 Which of the following fits best in blank ⓐ?

(A) no exception
(B) a case in point
(C) similar to English
(D) an exceptional case

2 Which of the following fits best in blank ⓑ?

(A) English
(B) German
(C) other languages
(D) its own resources

3 According to the passage, which of the following is NOT correct?

(A) Phonology is a classical-based compound.
(B) The word stronghold is formed from English roots.
(C) Fernsehen is a formation from German roots.
(D) English and German form compounds in the same way.

Passage 4

The meaning of "ethics" can seem ambiguous, and the views many people have about ethics are shaky. Many people tend to see ethics as analogous to feelings. However, being ethical is clearly not a matter of merely following one's feelings. A person following his or her feelings may recoil ① ________ doing what is right. In fact, what a person feels frequently deviates from what is ethical. Nor should one identify ethics with religion. Most religions, of course, advocate high ethical standards. Yet if ethics were confined to religion, then ethics would apply only to religious people. However, an atheist or agnostic can maintain high ethical standards, albeit outside the realm of the traditionally religious. ② ________, a deeply religious person might engage in unethical behavior. Religion can set high ethical standards and can provide intense motivations for ethical behavior, yet ethics cannot be confined to religion nor is it the same as religion. Being ethical is also not the same as passively following the law. The law often incorporates ethical standards ③ ________ which most citizens subscribe. But laws, like feelings, can deviate from what is ethical. Our own pre-Civil War slavery laws and the apartheid laws once held in South Africa are grotesquely obvious examples of laws that violate what we view as ethical.

1 Which of the following is NOT consistent with what has been said in the passage?

(A) Being ethical is what your mind dictates you to do.
(B) There have been laws which were downright unethical.
(C) The definition of ethics is often hazy.
(D) Men of religion have perpetrated unscrupulous deeds.

2 Which of the following is most appropriate for blanks ① and ③?

(A) from — on
(B) by — on
(C) from — to
(D) by — to

3 Choose the answer that is most appropriate for blank ②.

(A) In other words
(B) Conversely
(C) Consequently
(D) Otherwise

Passage 5

The monopoly power of a firm refers to the extent of its control over the supply of the product that is produced by the industry of which it is a part. The more firms there are producing and selling a given product the less control any one of the firms can exercise over industry supply. If there are enough firms in an industry so that one firm's output and its control over industry supply are insignificant, we have a market that should tend to be __________. On the other hand, if there is only one firm producing and selling the product, we have a market of pure monopoly. The monopoly power of a firm in an imperfectly competitive market is the larger the firm's output is relative to the output of the industry as a whole. It is less the smaller the firm's output is relative to the output of the entire industry.

1 Choose the one that best fills in the blank.

(A) obsolete
(B) isolated
(C) dormant
(D) competitive

2 Which of the following can be inferred about "monopoly power" according to the passage?

(A) Monopoly power is nonexistent if there is only one producer of a product.
(B) A high level of productivity ensures monopoly power.
(C) Market share can determine the monopoly power of a firm.
(D) Well-known firms have more monopoly power than less known ones.

Passage 6

The Amish have steadfastly subordinated economic value to the values of religion and community. What is too readily overlooked by a secular, exploitive society is that their ways of doing this are not "empty gestures" and are not "backward." In the first place, these ways have kept the communities intact through many varieties of hard times. In the second place, they conserve the land. In the third place, they yield economic benefits. The community, the religious fellowship, has many kinds of value, and among them is economic value. It is the result of the practice of neighborliness, and of the practice of stewardship. What moved me most, what I liked best, in those days we spent with Bill Yoder was the sense of the continuity of the community in his dealings with his children and in their dealings with their children.

1 **The passage implies that ________.**

(A) the Amish value economy over religion and community
(B) the Amish prefer capitalized community to agricultural community
(C) the Amish do not discriminate the value of economy against that of society
(D) the Amish want their community to be continuous in their dealings with their children

2 **Which of the following is NOT suitable to describe the Amish?**

(A) urbanized
(B) conservative
(C) religious
(D) neighborly

Passage 7

The costs associated with a traditional view of masculinity are enormous, and the damage occurs at both personal and societal levels. The belief that a boy should be tough (aggressive, competitive, and daring) can create emotional pain for him. While a few boys experience short-term success for their toughness, there is little security in the long run. Instead, it leads to a series of challenges which few, if any, boys ultimately win. There is no security in being at the top when so many other boys are competing for the same status. Toughness also leads to increased chances of stress, physical injury, and even early death. It is considered manly to take extreme physical risks and voluntarily engage in combative, hostile activities.

The flip side of toughness—nurturance—is not a quality perceived as masculine and ________. Because of this, boys and men experience a greater emotional distance from other people and few opportunities to participate in meaningful interpersonal relationships. Studies consistently show that fathers spend very small amounts of time interacting with their children. In addition, men report that they seldom have intimate relationships with other men. They are afraid of getting too close and don't know how to take down the walls that they have built between themselves.

1 **Choose the one that best fills in the blank.**

(A) accordingly praised
(B) is considered positive
(C) is not criticized
(D) thus not valued

2 **Which of the following can be inferred about "toughness" according to the passage?**

(A) It can atrophy through the socialization process with peers.
(B) It presupposes that boys will avoid risk-taking to survive.
(C) It has a counterpart in nurturance, which emphasizes interpersonal relationships.
(D) It can lead to success in later life for boys who are highly competitive.

3 What is the best title for the passage?

(A) The Feminization of Boys
(B) How Society Shapes Masculinity
(C) The Debate over the Nurturing of Boys
(D) Developing Social Networks Based on Masculinity

Passage 8

The owners of fishing boats do not want to admit it, but there will be virtually no fish in the seas of the world by the middle of the 21st century if current trends of gross overfishing continue, according to a major scientific study. Stocks have collapsed in nearly one-third of sea fisheries, and the rate of decline is accelerating.

Writing in the journal Science, an international team of researchers says fishery decline is closely tied to a broader loss of marine biodiversity. Yet a greater use of protected areas could safeguard existing stocks, giving them time to replenish. "The way we have been using the oceans so far is that we hope and assume there will always be another species to exploit after we've completely gone through the last one," said research leader Boris Worm. "What we're highlighting is there is a finite number of stocks; we have gone through one-third, and we are going to get through the rest, unless restrictions are imposed." One of the other scientists on the project added: "Unless we fundamentally change the way we manage all the ocean species together, as working ecosystems, then this century will be the last century when people can eat wild seafood of any kind." In 2003, 29% of the world's open sea fisheries were in a state of collapse, defined as a decline to less than 10% of their original yield. Bigger vessels, better nets, and new technology for spotting fish are not bringing the world's fleets bigger returns—in fact, the global catch fell by 13% between 1994 and 2003. Fish is already more expensive than beef in many countries; before long it will simply be unavailable to any but millionaires.

TEST 12

1 The passage suggests that fish are being taken from the sea _______.

(A) moderately
(B) ruthlessly
(C) circumspectly
(D) protectively

2 Until now, people have tended to assume that fish supplies are _______.

(A) inexhaustible
(B) ineluctable
(C) inescapable
(D) inextricable

3 **The scientists quoted say that fishing should be restricted in some parts of the sea because ________.**

(A) fish need places where they can rest and play

(B) overfished stocks need to be protected so they can increase again

(C) biodiversity is affected by too many fishing boats working

(D) there are no fish left there

4 **The fact that the global catch fell by 13 between 1994 and 2003 is quoted as a proof that ________.**

(A) fishing techniques have improved greatly

(B) the market for fish is diminishing rapidly

(C) fishing has become much more lucrative

(D) fish stocks have diminished significantly everywhere

5 **The passage includes a clear suggestion that ________.**

(A) the owners of fishing boats are very anxious about the future

(B) there will always be new species of fish that can be caught

(C) not only fish but every kind of marine creature is at risk

(D) millionaires prefer fish to beef

TEST 13

제한시간 | 35분
정답률 | /25

Passage 1

The broadcast and print media regularly provide hype for individuals who have achieved "super" success. These stories are usually about celebrities and superstars from the sports and entertainment world. Society pages and gossip columns serve to keep the social elite informed of each other's doings, allow the rest of us to gawk at their excesses, and help to keep the American dream alive. The print media is also fond of feature stories on corporate empire builders. These stories provide an occasional "insider's" view of the private and corporate life of industrialists by suggesting a rags to riches account of corporate success. These stories tell us that corporate success is a series of smart moves, shrewd acquisitions, timely mergers, and well thought out executive suite shuffles. By painting the upper class in a positive light, innocent of any wrongdoing (labor leaders and union organizations usually get the opposite treatment), the media assures us that wealth and power are ________. One person's capital accumulation is presumed to be good for all. The elite, then, are portrayed as investment wizards, people of special talent and skill, whom even their victims (workers and consumers) can admire.

1 Choose the one closest in meaning to the underlined "to gawk at their excesses."

(A) to marvel at their regard for morals
(B) to gape at their lack of moderation
(C) to pity their longing for luxury
(D) to envy their nonchalant attitude

2 What is the author's purpose in the passage?

(A) to prove that the media is overly devoted to sensational stories
(B) to lament the media's protection of the negligence of the social elite
(C) to criticize the idealization of the social elite by the media
(D) to argue that the social elite need to be more responsible to society

3 Choose the one that best fills in the blank.

(A) ubiquitous
(B) irrelevant
(C) benevolent
(D) multifaceted

Passage 2

Somewhere between 1860 and 1890, the dominant emphasis in American literature was radically changed. But it is obvious that this change was not necessarily a matter of conscious concern to all writers.

In fact, many writers may seem to have been actually unaware of the shifting emphasis. Moreover, it is not possible to trace the steady march of the realistic emphasis from the first feeble notes to its dominant trumpet-note of unquestioned leadership.

The progress of realism is, to change the figure, rather that of a small stream, receiving accessions from its tributaries at unequal points along its course, its progress now and then checked by the sand bars of opposition or the diffusing marshes of error and compromise.

Again it is apparent that any attempts to classify rigidly, as romanticists or realists, the writers of this period are __________, since it is not by virtue of the writer's conscious espousal of the romantic or realistic creed that he does much of his best work, but by virtue of the writer's sincere surrender to the atmosphere of the subject.

1 이 글의 흐름상 빈칸에 들어갈 가장 알맞은 것은?

(A) doomed to failure
(B) welcomed by critics
(C) against our taste
(D) considered reasonable

2 이 글의 내용과 일치하지 <u>않는</u> 것은?

(A) There was a radical change in American literature between 1860 and 1890.
(B) Most writers were conscious of the movement toward realism from the beginning.
(C) Realism could move forward while undergoing resistance and mistakes.
(D) Writers achieved their best works by yielding themselves to the age's mood.

Passage 3

We are sometimes eager to celebrate the influence of our surroundings. In the living room of a house in the Czech Republic, we see an example of how walls, chairs and floors can combine to create an atmosphere in which the best sides of us are offered the opportunity to flourish. We accept with gratitude the power that a single room can possess.

But sensitivity to architecture also has its more problematic aspects. If one room can alter how we feel, if our happiness can hang on the colour of the walls or the shape of a door, what will happen to us in most of the places we are forced to look at and inhabit? What will we experience in a house with prison-like windows, stained carpet tiles and plastic curtains? It is to prevent the possibility of permanent anguish that we can be led to shut our eyes to most of what is around us, for we are never far from damp stains and cracked ceilings, shattered cities and rusting dockyards. We can't remain sensitive indefinitely to environments which __________.

1 Which of the following does the passage mainly discuss?

(A) What makes us less sensitive to architecture
(B) What caused the ugliness of our physical surroundings
(C) How architectural techniques have changed in modern times
(D) What emotions a beautiful room of a Czech house can arouse in us

TEST 13

2 Which of the following best fits in the blank?

(A) cost so many lives, both animal and vegetal
(B) may disappear from our sight any minute now
(C) we don't have the means to alter for the good
(D) have formed our feelings for such a long period

Passage 4

Research on the psychology of happiness has borne out the curmudgeons. Kahneman and Tversky give an everyday example. You open your paycheck and are delighted to find you have been given a five percent raise—until you learn that your co-workers have been given a ten percent raise. According to legend, the diva Maria Callas stipulated that any opera house she sang in had to pay her one dollar more than the next highest paid singer in the company.

People today are safer, healthier, better fed, and longer-lived than at any time in history. Yet we don't spend our lives walking on air, and presumably our ancestors were not chronically glum. It is not reactionary to point out that many of the poor in today's Western nations live in conditions that yesterday's aristocrats could not have dreamed of. People in different classes and countries are often content with their lot until they compare themselves to the more affluent. The amount of violence in a society is more closely related to its ① ________ than to its ② ________. In the second half of the twentieth century, the discontent of the Third World, and later the Second, have been attributed to their glimpses through the mass media of the First.

1 According to the passage, men can be happy only if ________.

(A) they don't have anybody to compare with
(B) they achieve something for which they have worked
(C) they want everything
(D) they have nothing to lose
(E) they fall in love with someone

2 Which one describes the different notion of happiness?

(A) How bitter a thing it is to look into happiness through another man's eye!
(B) Happiness is an agreeable sensation arising from contemplating the misery of others.
(C) It is not enough to succeed. Others must fail.
(D) Anything you're good at contributes to happiness.
(E) When does a hunchback rejoice? When he sees one with a larger hump.

3 Choose one which is most appropriate for the blanks.

	①		②
(A)	poverty	—	dictatorship
(B)	dictatorship	—	atrocity
(C)	inequality	—	poverty
(D)	atrocity	—	politics
(E)	politics	—	inequality

4 **According to the passage, development of mass media would ________.**

(A) destroy the private lives of common people
(B) result in the equal society
(C) make the entertaining businesses prosper
(D) calm down the complaints of the Third World
(E) produce more unhappy people

Passage 5

Sincere comes from two Latin words: sine meaning "without" and cera meaning "wax", but what does the current meaning of sincere have to do with "not having wax"? The current meaning of the word sincere can be attributed ⓐ ________ dishonest merchants over two thousand years ago. In ancient Rome, people used dishware made of clay. As you can imagine, the process of making clay dishes and clay cups was long and difficult, and workers were careful in making the dishware. (가) ________, small cracks would appear in the dishware during this process from time to time. Dishware makers who were not honest would simply apply wax ⓑ ________ an attempt to cover up the flaws in the products. Because this inferior product was almost identical ⓒ ________ a good one, customers rarely identified any problem. Even after a careful inspection of the product, it was virtually impossible to see any problem beforehand. As a result, customers bought the inferior product, took it home, and used it. When the customers washed the dishware with hot water, the wax melted, ⓓ ________ revealed the poor quality of the dishware. (나) ________, customers came to know which dishware merchants sold good products, products that were "sine cera" or sincere. Once customers found a merchant whose products were "without wax," they were able to minimize or perhaps even eliminate the possibility of buying flawed dishware.

1 **Which of the following is most suitable as the title of the above passage?**

(A) Problems Associated with Making Dishware
(B) The Deceptive Art of Ripping Off Customers
(C) The Origin of the Word "Sincere"
(D) How to Avoid Buying Flawed Dishware

2 **Choose the answer in which the most suitable prepositions for the blacks ⓐ, ⓑ and ⓒ are correctly arranged.**

(A) to — in — to
(B) by — in — with
(C) to — on — with
(D) by — on — to

3 **Choose the answer which is most suitable for the black ⓓ.**

(A) it
(B) which
(C) thereby
(D) having

4 **Choose the answer in which the most suitable expressions for the blacks (가) and (나) are correctly arranged.**

(A) Ultimately — Nevertheless
(B) Oddly enough — Unfortunately
(C) Unfortunately — Oddly enough
(D) Nevertheless — Ultimately

Passage 6

The gurus seek bliss amidst mountaintop solitude and serenity in the meditative trance, but I have achieved the oneness with the universe that is known as pure externalization. I have melded my mind with the heavens, communed with the universal consciousness, and experienced the inner calm that externalization brings, and it all started because I bought a car with a G.P.S. Like many men, I quickly established a romantic attachment to my G.P.S. I found comfort in her tranquil and slightly Anglophilic voice. I felt warm and safe following her thin blue line. More than once I experienced her mercy, for each of my transgressions would be greeted by nothing worse than a gentle, "Make a U-turn if possible." After a few weeks, it occurred to me that I could no longer get anywhere without her. Any trip slightly out of the ordinary had me typing the address into her system and then blissfully following her satellite-fed commands. I found that I was quickly shedding all vestiges of a geographic knowledge. It was unnerving at first, but then a relief. Since the dawn of humanity, people have had to worry about how to get from here to there. Precious brainpower has been used storing directions, and memorizing turns. I myself have been trapped at dinner parties at which conversation was devoted exclusively to the topic of commuter routes. My G.P.S. goddess liberated me from this drudgery. She enabled me to externalize geographic information from my own brain to a satellite brain, and you know how it felt? It felt like nirvana.

1 **The narrater's key purpose lies in showing ________.**

(A) why he drove without a G.P.S.
(B) why people use a G.P.S.
(C) why he became fond of his G.P.S.
(D) why people are concerned with geographic information

2 **According to the passage, which of the following best characterizes a G.P.S.?**

(A) solitude and calmness
(B) the outsourced brain
(C) the topic of commuter routes
(D) the trip out of the ordinary

3 **On what ground is the narrator making the point in the passage?**

(A) Based on medical Researches.
(B) Based on professional opinions.
(C) Based on personal experiences.
(D) Based on scientific experiments.

4 **According to the passage, which of the following is TRUE of the narrator?**

(A) The G.P.S. enabled him to forget all traces of geographic knowledge.
(B) He disliked the soft voice of his G.P.S.
(C) In meditation he experienced communion with the universal consciousness.
(D) He liked to memorize directions and turns.

Passage 7

What the blind find difficult are smooth, open spaces. It is just these areas which are assumed by many sighted people to be best for the blind, because there is no danger of tripping. From the blind's point of view, however, a flat, open surface is not negotiable because there are no orientating signals. There is no structure, it is not predictable, because it may end at any moment, and there is no way of telling where you are, once you are on it. The problem for the blind is not falling over, but knowing where he is. For this reason, it is easier to find my way around a campus which is marked out by steps, little hills and valleys, low walls and lots of changes in texture, because I can mark out my route with sections. The structure becomes a sequence when I am moving through it.

1 **According to the passage, the sighted person ________.**

(A) doesn't know much about the blind's situation
(B) thinks much of the blind person's physical condition
(C) believes that the blind can see the light out of darkness
(D) knows a lot about the blind friends
(E) should be taught to live together with the blind

2 **In which situation, would the author get embarrassed most?**

(A) when he is in front of crossroads
(B) when there is a lot of traffic
(C) when he doesn't know where he is
(D) when he doesn't know what to do
(E) when there is no friend to help him

3 **What makes the school campus a nice place for the author to move around?**

(A) its beautiful building
(B) many of kind college students
(C) its considerate atmosphere
(D) the free spirit of college life
(E) its complex structure

Passage 8

Scientific data indicates that the earth has gotten warmer over the past 100 years. Not only have global average temperatures increased, by an average of 0.5 to 1.1 degrees Fahrenheit, but glaciers have retreated, the mean sea level has risen, and other unmistakable signs of warming have been detected. Have these changes been caused, at least in part, by human emissions of greenhouse gases, most notably carbon dioxide? Are even more dramatic changes in store for the future? Ten years ago hundreds of scientists around the world began to work through the Intergovernmental Panel on Climate change to evaluate all the research that has been done on global warming and to reach conclusions about what is known and what remains to be determined. Over time they have become more confident in their projections. Although no one can predict the future with absolute certainty, the scientists believe that the climate has very probably already begun to change because of human activities and they expect a temperature rise of a few degrees in the coming decades. For this reason many climate experts have called for strong international action to reduce human emissions of greenhouse gases. This view has been supported by the world's leading senior scientists, including the majority of living Nobel prize winners in the sciences, who in 1997 called global warming "one of the most serious threats to the planet and to future generations." A temperature changes of a few degrees may not seem like a lot, but it could be enough to alter the range of natural habitats and affect the distribution of the species within them. It would also likely cause changes in precipitation patterns, resulting in more summer dryness in some places but less in others, for example. Rising sea levels caused by melting glaciers and thermally expanding sea water would inundate coastal areas and harm coastal wetlands. Under the best scenarios these changes will occur gradually, but there is a risk of abrupt shifts in climate that could have catastrophic results not only for plants and wildlife but also for the global economy.

1 According to the passage, which of the following does NOT apply to the "more dramatic changes" as underlined above?

(A) the alteration of natural habitats

(B) the reduction of greenhouse gases

(C) the changes in precipitation patterns

(D) the destruction of coastal wetlands

2 Some places may experience more summer dryness because (________).

(A) sea levels are rising and sea water is expanding

(B) there are melting glaciers

(C) some coastal areas are inundated

(D) there is heavy rain in a place where people used to have little rain

3 The Intergovernmental Panel on Climate Change (________).

(A) are confident that the climate changes will occur gradually

(B) are confident that their understanding of global warming is correct

(C) invite living Nobel prize winners to give lectures on climate change

(D) do research on climate change and project its future

TEST 14

제한시간 | 35분
정답률 | /21

Passage 1

There was a time when it was an accomplishment for a PDA to be able to read a written word on a menu, a street sign, or a business card. Today we are living in a world where PDAs are beginning to learn to speak. We're not talking only about simple speech. We are referring to complicated translation engines that will enable the devices to understand not only the content of what is being said, but also the tone and inflection of the speech.

The Phraselator built by Marine Acoustics and sold by VoxTec is one example of such a device. The Phraselator is capable of translating between hundreds of different languages. Five hundred Phraselators are being shipped to troops in Afghanistan. These units have been programmed with special phrases in Urdu that will help the troops. Each of these specially programmed phrases has an associated tone. Phrases such as "Halt!" and "Drop your weapon!" come across sternly and loudly, but a much softer tone is used when asking "Can I help you?"

1 **Choose the best title for the passage.**

(A) PDAs Are Getting Smarter
(B) PDAs Are Getting Popular
(C) PDAs Can Be Good Guides
(D) PDAs Can Be Good Weapons

Passage 2

Suppose you are reading Eliot's the Waste Land, Shakespeare's King Lear, Joyce's Ulysses, or Chekhov's Ward Number Six. What you are reading is a poem, a play, a novel, a short story. We would also say you are reading a work of literature, or of imaginative literature—though in the case of King Lear, some might be inclined to deny that wishing to ______________________________.

Now suppose you are reading the classical Athenian politician Demonsthenes's Philippics, sir Thomas Browne's Um Burial, the Roman Poet Lucretius's On the Nature of Things, or the Sermon on the Mount from the New Testament. What you are reading now is a work oratory, an essay philosophy or __________. Again, we would also say you are reading a work of literature.

Suppose, finally, you are reading Frederick Forsyth's Day of the Jackal, the products of a Victorian poetaster, a story in Just Seventeen, or the Reverend C. T. Awdry's George, the Big Engine. What you are reading now is a novel, poetry (or verse), or stories. We might also say you are reading literature, but we would scarcely say it was serious literature—it is 'popular', or 'light', or 'children's' literature. Or some might say it was not literature at all. It is not good, or important, enough, they might say, to deserve the title of literature.

1 **Choose the best title for the above passage.**

(A) What is Literature?
(B) The Kinds of Literature
(C) Who Utilizes Literature?
(D) The Great Literary Works

2 **Choose the expression that would fit best in (A).**

(A) understand the genres of literature
(B) incorporate all human works into literature
(C) distinguish literature sharply from drama
(D) illustrate the essence of classical literature

3 **According to the passage, which of the following would fit best in (B)?**

(A) scripture
(B) inscription
(C) rhetoric
(D) narrative

Passage 3

Three hundred and fifty years ago, religious freedom was born in North America. Religious tolerance did not begin with the Bill of Rights or with Jefferson's Virginia Statute of Religious Freedom in 1786. With due respect to Roger Williams and his early experiment with "liberty of conscience" in Rhode Island, the United States really owes its enduring strength ① __________ a fragile, scorched document, the Flushing Remonstrance, which was signed by some 30 ordinary citizens on Dec. 27, 1657. It is fitting that this little-known document should be associated with Dutch settlements, because they were the most tolerant in the New World. The Netherlands had enshrined freedom of conscience in 1579, when it clearly established that "no one shall be persecuted or investigated because of his religion." And when the Dutch West India Company set up a trading post at the southern tip of Manhattan in 1625, the purpose was to make money, not to save souls. Because the founding idea was trade, the directors of the firm took pains to ensure that all were ② __________.

1 Who was responsible for the historic but little-known document of religious freedom?

(A) Roger Williams
(B) Dutch preachers
(C) Thomas Jefferson
(D) George Washington

2 What is the most suitable word for ①?

(A) for
(B) by
(C) to
(D) with

3 When was the Flushing Remonstrance signed?

(A) in 1786
(B) in 1657
(C) in 1625
(D) in 1579

4 What is the most suitable word for ②?

(A) greedy
(B) sinful
(C) mercenary
(D) welcome

5 What is the title that best expresses the main idea of the passage?

(A) Religious Freedom in North America
(B) The Founding Idea of Dutch West India Company
(C) The Quakers in the New World
(D) The Puritan Orthodoxy in the New Colony

Passage 4

There is a rich history of mischief and malice in the ① interregnum, particularly during the last transfer of power to take place in the middle of a fiscal firestorm. In 1932 it didn't help that the two men neither liked nor trusted each other: Herbert Hoover called Franklin Roosevelt a "chameleon on plaid," while Roosevelt preferred the image of Hoover as a "fat, timid capon." Since Inauguration Day was not until March 1933, there was an urgent need for action, but Hoover's efforts to reach out to Roosevelt in the name of bipartisan cooperation were dismissed by critics as an attempt to ② __________ the election and obstruct the New Deal. Hoover called Roosevelt a "madman" for digging in his heels on economics and refusing to compromise, which guaranteed that Roosevelt took the oath of office in an atmosphere of crisis.

It would be 20 years before the Democrats had to hand power back, and this didn't go much better. After the 1952 election, Harry Truman wrote in his diary that Eisenhower was being coy about cooperation: "he and his advisers are afraid of some kind of trick. There are no tricks. All I want to do is to make an orderly ③ __________."

1 위 글의 제목으로 가장 알맞은 것은?

(A) Trials of Power Transition
(B) History of Mischief and Malice
(C) Triumph of the American Story
(D) Chameleon on Plaid versus Fat. Timid Capon

2 밑줄 친 ①의 우리말 뜻으로 가장 알맞은 것은?

(A) 내정간섭
(B) 적과의 분쟁
(C) 적과의 동침
(D) 통치공백기간

3 빈칸 ②에 들어갈 가장 알맞은 것은?

(A) justify
(B) accept
(C) validate
(D) annul

4 빈칸 ③에 들어갈 가장 알맞은 것은?

(A) collapse
(B) overturn
(C) turnover
(D) make-up

Passage 5

Given the demand for sensational photographs, everyone regards press photographers as an overbearing lot, as mercenaries in the pay of public curiosity; (A) ever in pursuit, flashgun at the ready, of the unsuspecting victim. Armed to the teeth with the tools of their trade, they elbow their way through the crowd, trampling on the gardens of the famous, jamming their feet into half-closed doors and lying in wait for the widow before the still-opened grave. But are press photographers really cold 'glass-eyewitnesses'? Being up close—that is the curse but also the strength of the photographic medium. A reporter can do his writing from a safe distance behind the lines. A photographer has no choice; he has to be right where the action is. This requires a special temperament. Good photographers seldom fit the corporate mould. They can be a nuisance; most are emotional. Many of them are politically motivated and have (B) a soft spot for the downtrodden since everyday they have to cross the line towards poverty and sickness.

1 **The best title of the passage would be ________.**

(A) How to Take Vivid Photographs
(B) Commercial Use of Photographs
(C) Photography as Blue Collar Work
(D) Difficulties of War Journalists
(E) Dirty Tricks Used by Photographers

2 **The underlined phrase in (A) suggests that photographers ________.**

(A) should be allowed to use a gun in emergency
(B) can be easily victimized
(C) often threaten public safety
(D) carry out the role of the police
(E) invade individual privacy

3 **According to the author of the passage, ________.**

(A) photographers should learn how to behave
(B) objectivity is the curse of the photographic medium
(C) photographers do not like reporters
(D) it is often difficult for photographers to maintain artistic sensitivity
(E) photographers should not be emotional

4 **The underlined phrase in (B) means ________.**

(A) Unwillingness to accept the truth
(B) Sympathy for the underprivileged
(C) Desire for power and authority
(D) Tendency to overlook the poor
(E) A down-to-earth approach

Passage 6

[A]

Today, however, many people say they do not have heroes. It is difficult to find an equivalent of Washington, Kennedy, King, or Gehrig. Political figures in today's world of leaders rarely, if ever, appear larger than life to us. In today's world of prying journalists and a television-age public, it seems difficult for anyone to attain heroic stature. What is worse, we now dredge up information about our past heroes, only to take away their heroism: we now know that John Kennedy ran around with other women; there appear to be evidence that Martin Luther King did, too. And today, more and more of our heroes have been forced to abdicate their hero status as new discoveries of their real lives have been made.

[B]

A hero, it is said, is someone who is "larger than life," whom we can admire for great qualities or abilities that we may never have. Our heroes reflect the values, hopes, and beliefs of a particular time. Heroes have included political and religious leaders, athletes, movie stars, and musicians.

[C]

In the United States, for example, political leaders who led the country to greater freedom and democracy have been heroes to many. George Washington, the nation's first president, John Kennedy, the vibrant young president who inspired hope, and Martin Luther King, the civil rights leader who fought for racial equality, all attained hero status among Americans. Sports were, and still are, the first sources of heroes for many American children. Picture, for example, the 1930s sports stadium: a red-haired, freckled-faced boy sits in the stands, magnetized by the style, grace, and actions of the larger-than-life athlete, Lou Gehrig, the famous baseball player who died of a nerve disease that was later named after him. The young boy was a true believer.

1 위 글을 내용의 흐름에 따라 순서를 정할 때 가장 알맞은 것은?

(A) [A]—[B]—[C]
(B) [B]—[C]—[A]
(C) [C]—[A]—[B]
(D) [C]—[B]—[A]

2 [A]의 내용과 어울리는 말은?

(A) A hero is a man who does what he can.
(B) Self-trust is the essence of heroism.
(C) A hero never dies, but fades away.
(D) Today's hero is a rare species.

Passage 7

The concept of sustainability applies to all aspects of life on Earth and is commonly defined within ecological, social and economic contexts. Due to factors such as overpopulation, lack of education, inadequate financial circumstances and the actions of past generations, sustainability can be difficult to achieve. In an ecological context, sustainability is defined as the ability of an ecosystem to maintain ecological processes, functions, biodiversity and productivity into the future. In a social context, sustainability is expressed as meeting the needs of the present without compromising the ability of future generations to meet their own needs. When applied in an economic context, a business is sustainable if it has adapted its practices for the use of renewable resources and is accountable for the environmental impacts of its activities. To be sustainable, regardless of context, Earth's resources must be used at a rate at which they can be replenished. There is now clear scientific evidence that humanity is living unsustainably, and that an effort is needed to keep human use of natural resources within sustainable limits.

1 **Choose the one closest in meaning to the underlined "<u>compromising the ability.</u>"**

(A) acknowledging the competence
(B) accommodating the fitness
(C) undermining the capacity
(D) rebuking the aptitude

2 **Which of the following <u>CANNOT</u> be inferred about "sustainability" according to the passage?**

(A) It generally refers to maintenance capacity.
(B) It can be attained through orchestrated efforts.
(C) It includes environmental responsibility.
(D) It is an inevitable process of nature.

Passage 8

Drug use in the U.S. is not confined to some narrowly defined, easily excised subculture. Tens of millions of Americans use illegal psychoactives each year, and they come from all walks of life. If we are to undo drugs in America, our policies must reflect the fact that we are the users, the abusers, and the addicts. Although the bulk of all users of psychoactives are casual users, the bulk of all use is by abusers and addicts. And most of the damage done to and by users occurs as a result of addiction and abuse. This is true whether we focus on the adverse health consequences for the users (such as lung cancer for nicotine addicts), adverse health consequences for third parties (such as people killed by drunk drivers), or other adverse effects (such as crimes committed by heroin addicts). Thus, only if we materially alter the behavior of addicts and abusers will our policies yield substantial benefits. Unless and until public policy is shaped to yield a permanent and substantial reduction in use rather than users, few beneficial consequences are likely to result from drug policy.

1 **Which of the following best expresses the main idea of the passage?**

(A) Drug problem should be treated as a crime rather than a medical problem.
(B) Most drug problems result from illegal use, not from casual use.
(C) Restricting casual users is not the best way to prevent addiction.
(D) The drug policy needs to focus on abuse and addiction.

TEST 15

제한시간 | 35분
정답률 | /20

Passage 1

Humans are classed anatomically among the primates, the order of which includes apes, monkeys and lemurs. Among the hundreds of living primate species, only humans are naked. Two kinds of habitat are known to give rise to naked mammals—a ___(A)___ one or a ___(B)___ one. There is a naked Somalian mole rat which never ventures above ground. All other non-human mammals which have lost all or most of their fur are either swimmers like whales and dolphins, or wallowers like hippopotamuses and pigs and tapirs. The rhinoceros and the elephant, though found on land since Africa became drier, bear traces of a more watery past and seize every opportunity of wallowing in mud or water. It has been suggested that humans became hairless "to prevent overheating in the savannah." But no other mammal has ever resorted to this strategy. A covering of hair acts as a defense against the heat of the sun: that is why even the desert-dwelling camel retains its fur. Another version is "to facilitate sweat-cooling." But again many species resort to sweat-cooling quite effectively without needing to lose their hair. One general conclusion seems undeniable from an overall survey of mammalian species: that while a coat of fur provides the best insulation for land mammals the best insulation in water is not fur, but a layer of fat.

1 빈칸 (A)와 (B)에 들어가기에 가장 적절한 것은?

(A) subterranean — wet
(B) icy — humid
(C) tropical — frigid
(D) sandy — grassy

2 위 글의 내용을 추론해 볼 때, 인간은 왜 다른 primate에 비해 몸에 털이 없는가에 대한 가장 적절한 답은?

(A) because they are descended from forest-dwelling apes.
(B) because their earliest ancestors lived in watery places.
(C) because they had to adapt to the hot savannah environment.
(D) because their ancestors had to keep their bodies dry.

Passage 2

We go see a horror movie to re-establish our feelings of essential normality; __________. It urges us to put away our more civilized and adult penchant for analysis and to become children again, seeing things in pure blacks and whites. And we go to have fun. This is where the ground starts to slope away, because this is a very peculiar sort of fun. The fun comes from seeing others menaced—sometimes killed. A critic has suggested that the horror film has become the modern version of the public lynching.

The potential lyncher is in almost all of us, and every now and then, he has to be let loose. Our emotions and our fears form their own body, and we recognize that it demands its own exercise to maintain proper muscle tone. Certain of these emotional muscles are accepted, even exalted, in civilized society. Love, friendship, loyalty, kindness—these are the emotions that we applaud. When we exhibit these emotions, society showers us with positive reinforcement. But anticivilization emotions don't go away, and they demand periodic exercise.

The horror movie has a dirty job to do. It deliberately appeals to all that is worst in us. It is morbidity unchained, our most abject instincts let free, our nastiest fantasies realized. The most aggressive of horror films lifts a trap door in the civilized forebrain and throws a basket of raw meat to the hungry alligators swimming around in that subterranean river beneath. It keeps them from getting out. It keeps them down there and me up here.

1 Choose the one that best fills in the blank.

(A) the horror movie transforms moral standards
(B) the horror movie is innately conventional
(C) the horror movie disavows antisocial desires
(D) the horror movie is traumatic for children

2 Which of the following CANNOT be inferred from the passage?

(A) We tend to use horror movies as an outlet for socially unacceptable emotions.
(B) The simplicity of a horror movie can provide psychic relief to a degree.
(C) A periodic lapse into irrationality enables us to eradicate our fears.
(D) What makes us recoil may at the same time satisfy our unconscious desire.

3 What is the purpose of the passage?

(A) to explain why people crave horror movies
(B) to analyze various types of insanity
(C) to prove everyone is prone to violence
(D) to persuade people to view horror movies

4 **What is the tone of the passage?**

(A) accusatory
(B) analytical
(C inspirational
(D) judgemental

Passage 3

With its booming economy and aspirations to expand its global influence, China may have achieved a victory in American classrooms. Take the private Chinese-American International School in San Francisco, which runs from prekindergarten through eighth grade and offers instruction in all subjects—from math to music half in Mandarin and half in English. The curriculum also includes Chinese history, culture and language studies, and in the 25 years since the school was (A) founded, it has attracted mainly Asian-American children. But in the past few years, it has seen rapid growth in the (B) enrollment of non-Asians. For example, five years ago, the school was 57 percent Asian-American, but this year it is only 49 percent Asian-American, said Sharline Chiang, its spokeswoman, adding that more non-Asian-Americans have been applying in recent years. School officials (C) attribute the changes largely to a (D) growing awareness of China as a global economic force, and to a strong sense among parents that learning Chinese could help their children professionally. As Ms. Chiang said, studying Chinese "is looked at as a long-term benefit." For similar reasons, Chinese language classes are increasingly popular across the country in public schools. Several states—including Kentucky, Minnesota, Washington, Ohio, Kansas and West Virginia—are developing Chinese language related curricula for public schools.

1 **Which of the following uses of the word runs/ran is closest in meaning to the underlined runs in the above passage?**

(A) Bill's father runs an Internet company.
(B) Tonight's repertoire runs from tragedy to comedy.
(C) We ran through the whole symphony four times already.
(D) There's a train that runs from Singapore all the way up to Bangkok.

2 **Among the underlined words (A), (B), (C), and (D), which of the following could be an appropriate substitute?**

(A) discovered
(B) education
(C) contribute
(D) mounting

3 **Which of the following would be the best title for the passage?**

(A) China's Booming Economy

(B) Chinese-American International Schools in the U.S.

(C) Growing Interest in Learning Chinese by Non-Asians

(D) Short-term Benefits of Learning the Chinese Language

Passage 4

A hard line on immigration is getting more popular in politics these days. Politicians throughout Europe have read the writing on the wall and think they've discerned there a populist, anti-immigrant scrawl. Jean-Marie Le Pen's exploitation of the issue helped put him into the second round of France's presidential elections. The new Danish government rode to power astride that issue last fall. So, isn't it only fair to give Europe's politicians a modicum of credit for finally responding to public concern?

Up to a point, yes. When they convene in Seville in August, 2003 for their European Council meeting, European Union leaders will focus on immigration—especially illegal immigration. When it comes to this, Spanish Prime Minister declared, "the masks of hypocrisy have to drop." Yet it seems likely that whatever decisions are made at Seville, more than a few hypocrisies will remain firmly in place. Despite the recognized need for a common E.U. policy on immigration, no number of British warships in the Mediterranean or watchtowers on the Poland-Belarus border are likely to reverse this natural law: __________________. "I don't see any important new developments in migration today," says a top expert on the matter with the OECD. In a political sense, though, much has changed.

1 위 글의 빈칸에 가장 알맞은 것은?

(A) Human beings have always wanted to escape misery

(B) Asylum seekers are provided with shelter and basic necessities

(C) Immigrants have posed a great danger to public safety

(D) The E.U. is a common area of freedom, security and justice

2 위 글의 마지막에 이어질 문장으로 가장 알맞은 것은?

(A) In most E.U. countries, the rate of unemployment among immigrants is hard to measure.

(B) The Mediterranean is glassy calm as the first hint of dawn turns the horizon deep, dark blue.

(C) New arrivals with residence permits must be familiar with the healthcare, education and welfare systems.

(D) When the E.U. leaders gathered in 1999 to launch a policy for immigration, the discussion was suitably noble.

Passage 5

The United States projects its power in varying degrees of rigidity. American military supremacy, or "hard power", is unquestioned. American economic primacy, what might be called "stiff power", perseveres despite erosion in the face of rising economic power in China, India, and the European Union. But "soft power", what Joseph Nye, professor of international relations at the Harvard Kennedy School of Government, describes as the attraction of the international community to the United States based upon its culture, values, and policies, has fallen significantly. The primary cause of this is America's ________, most notably in the Iraq War. The effect has been that other countries are more likely to question America's motives and intentions. While this observation is grim, it also offers an opportunity for decisive action to restore America's moral leadership. The next president can revitalize American soft power through many avenues, two of which seem especially powerful: committing to multilateral diplomacy, and leading by both example and engagement on globally significant issues.

1 According to the passage, the main idea is ________.

(A) need for U.S. soft power in foreign policy
(B) conflict between hard power and soft power
(C) crisis of the U.S. leadership as a super power
(D) priority of keeping faith with the nations in foreign affair

2 Which of the following is the best for the blank?

(A) apathy
(B) hard power
(C) unilateralism
(D) soft policies

3 According to the passage, we can infer that the ideal leadership of a nation is achieved by ________.

(A) the consent of international society
(B) keeping neutral in international conflicts
(C) balance of power in politics and economy
(D) protection of world peace from the evil countries

Passage 6

Why is it so difficult to find a great leader? The answer lies in a very simple truth about leadership. People can only be led where they want to go. The leader follows, though a step ahead. Americans wanted to climb out of the Depression and needed someone to tell them they could do it, and Roosevelt did. The British believed that they could still win the war after the defeats of 1940, and Churchill told them they were right.

A leader rides the waves, moves with the tides, understands the deepest yearnings of his people. He cannot make a nation that wants peace at any price go to war, or stop a nation determined to fight from doing so. His purpose must match the national mood.

1 Which of the following is the best idea of the passage?

(A) Leadership is action, not position.
(B) A leader is merely the sum of us.
(C) Leaders create the state of mind that is society.
(D) Reason and judgment are the qualities of a leader.

Passage 7

Having described the 'structure' of the prison in modern society, Foucault turns finally to the matter of its 'function.' From the moment that the prison came into being, observers recognized that __________ did not reduce crime or rehabilitate criminals. And yet, again and again, even the most enlightened critics in the 1960's called for bigger and better prisons, more effective classification and treatment programs. How then reconcile failure with persistence? How understand the institution's longevity, given so poor a record? Foucault's answer comes quickly: the prison endures because it performs a critical function in capitalist society. By turning criminals into abnormal types of one sort or another, it separates the criminal from the body of the working class. The ultimate purpose of the prison, Foucault declares, is to divide the outlaw from the proletariat, thereby reducing lower-class solidarity and protest. The illegalities of the dominant class survive through the confinement of the illegalities of the lower class.

1 What would be the most appropriate word to fill in the blank?

(A) incarceration
(B) torture
(C) capital punishment
(D) education
(E) euthanasia

2 It can be chiefly inferred from the passage that ________.

(A) the bourgeois manipulated the cohesion of lower-class through the prison system
(B) the modern society has better rehabilitation programs for criminals
(C) the prison system failed to perform a critical function
(D) most outlaws were not considered as belonging to the proletarian class
(E) the prison system justifies the confinement of mental patients away from society

Passage 8

Sibling rivalry can be intense, as anyone who grew up with one or more brothers or sisters knows. But (A) __________ for all concerned, such relationships seldom take a lethal turn. Among a certain bacterial species, however, sibling colonies take competition to a deadly level, researchers report in The Proceedings of the National Academy of Sciences. Related colonies near one another on a bed of low-nutrient agar mutually inhibit growth by secreting an antibacterial compound that in high enough concentrations becomes lethal. Avraham Be'er and Harry Swinney of the University of Texas and colleagues studied colonies of Paenibacillus dendritiformis, which when started as a single droplet grow outward, forming intricate bushlike branches. Using samples from the same bacterial culture (and thus "siblings"), the researchers started two colonies a given distance apart on the agar. After nine hours, the colonies started growing outward. But at 40 hours, the facing fronts of both colonies started to slow down. At 96 hours the facing fronts stopped, leaving a gap between them. The researchers first suspected that the growth slowed down and stopped as the nutrients in the agar were consumed. But several other experiments showed that food was not an issue. Rather, the colonies were secreting a growth-inhibiting compound, one that was killing the bacteria along the facing fronts. An obvious question is why these secretions are deadly between two colonies but not within a single colony on its own. As the researchers put it, why doesn't a single colony (B) __________ its own growth? The researchers devised a simple mathematical model that provides an answer. Basically it comes down to the concentration of the antibacterial compounds. At the growing edge of a colony, the concentration never becomes high enough to be lethal. But with two nearby colonies growing toward each other, the concentration rises to a level to result in mutually assured destruction.

1 밑줄 친 (A)와 (B)에 들어가기에 가장 적합한 것을 고르시오.

(A) consequently — obstruct
(B) significantly — accelerate
(C) curiously — maintain
(D) fortunately — inhibit

2 다음 중 **Paenibacillus dendritiformis**에 대한 설명으로 가장 적합한 것을 고르시오.

(A) Sibling competition is intense but not fatal.

(B) The fatal situation is caused by the want of nutrients.

(C) Growth stops by the secretion of antibacterial compounds within a single colony.

(D) Siblings secrete antibacterial compounds.

TEST 16

제한시간 | 35분
정답률 | /22

Passage 1

Scientists are exploring the seas in search of medicines that may work better than conventional drugs or have fewer side effects. The ocean has already given us osteoporosis drugs derived from salmon, omega-3 fish oils for arthritis and heart disease, and bone replacements from coral. Another marine medicine in the works is a promising new cancer drug derived from bacteria that live inside a moss-like sea creature called Bugula Neritina. Unlike conventional drugs that kill cancer cells, bryostatin-1 makes them revert to normal cells. Researchers at the North Carolina Sea Grant are also developing a peptide antibiotic from mast cells in hybrid striped bass. ㉮ (______) current antibiotics, these antibiotics from mast cells in fish and other animals may even be effective against antibiotic-resistant strains of bacteria.

1 Which is most appropriate for blank ㉮?

(A) Unlike
(B) Due to
(C) Similar to
(D) In addition to

2 Which of the following is the best title for the passage?

(A) Why We Need New Drugs
(B) Different Types of Antibiotics
(C) Fishing the Undersea Pharmacy
(D) Antibiotics with Fewer Side Effects

Passage 2

A Christmas Carol remains one of the rare novels to have infiltrated popular culture, leaving the impress of its characters and language even on those who have never read it. Christmas offered a means for its author, Charles Dickens, to redeem the despair and the terrors of his childhood. After a series of financial embarrassments that left his family insolvent, the 12-year-old Dickens, his schooling interrupted, was sent to work at a shoe blacking factory in a quixotic attempt to remedy his family's plight.

Because Dickens's tribulations were not particular to him but emblematic of the Industrial Revolution, the concerns that inform his fiction were shared by millions of potential readers. Dickens intended to make the sufferings of the most vulnerable of the underclass so pungently real to his readers that they could not continue to ignore their need, not so much for charity as for the means to save themselves: education. At least this was his conscious purpose.

In a sense, replacing the slippery Holy Ghost with anthropomorphized spirits, the infant Christ with a crippled child whose salvation waits on man's—not God's—generosity, Dickens laid claim to a religious festival, handing it over to the gathering forces of secular humanism.

1 Which of the following CANNOT be inferred from the passage?

(A) A Christmas Carol may not have been written had Dickens not faced difficulties in his youth.
(B) Dickens attempted to enlighten the public through religious renderings of a secular society.
(C) The enduring popularity of A Christmas Carol stems from its universally appealing story.
(D) Dickens upheld the ideal that education could be the salvation of the underprivileged.

2 What is the best title for the passage?

(A) Dickens's Humanistic Take on Christmas
(B) A Portrait of the Underclass in Dickens's Novel
(C) How Poverty Shaped the Life of Dickens
(D) Dickens's Christmas Theme of Spiritual Redemption

Passage 3

Clarity is not the prize in writing, nor is it always the principal mark of a good style. There are occasions when obscurity serves a literary yearning, if not a literary purpose, and there are writers whose manner is more overcast than clear. But since writing is communication, clarity can only be a virtue. And although there is no substitute for merit in writing, clarity comes closest to being one.

Even to a writer who is being intentionally obscure or wild of tongue we can say, "Be obscure clearly!"

1 Which of the following is the main idea of the passage?

(A) Be Clear in Writing
(B) Write with a Clear Purpose
(C) Clarity is Not the Prize in Writing
(D) Obscurity Serves a Literary Yearning

Passage 4

Expansion brought problems, not least because of the very different societies of the North and the South. The problem of slavery was first raised over the status of Missouri when it was admitted into the Union in 1821.

The anti-slavery movement gained tremendous support after publication of a book called Uncle Tom's Cabin by Harriet Beecher Stowe. Political divisions over slavery in the Whig and Democratic parties led to the formation of the Republican Party, whose main principle was opposition to the extension of slavery.

When the Republican candidate, Abraham Lincoln, was elected President in 1860, South Carolina announced that its Union with all other states was dissolved and was immediately followed by Mississippi, Florida, Alabama, Georgia, Louisiana and Texas, which together formed a Confederacy with a constitution based on slavery. The Northerners did not want war and Lincoln in his opening speech as President declared that he would not interfere with slavery in the Southern states, but merely affirmed the constitutional right of the Union to determine the status of new states.

Lincoln refused to allow secession to disrupt the Union, however, as civil war became ① __________. Virginia also seceded on the constitutional grounds that every state in the Union enjoyed ② <u>sovereign</u> rights: Nebraska, North Carolina, and Tennessee quickly followed. The twenty-three states of the industrial North, with a population of 22,000,000, were, therefore, opposed by eleven Southern states, almost 4,000,000 of whose 9,000,000 inhabitants were slaves.

1 Which of the following would be the best title for the above passage?

(A) The Imperialism of America
(B) The Formation of Slavery
(C) The Popularity of Uncle Tom's Cabin
(D) The Life of President Lincoln
(E) The American Civil War

2 According to the passage, the first state to secede from the Union was ________.

(A) Missouri
(B) South Carolina
(C) Virginia
(D) Mississippi
(E) Georgia

3 Choose the word that can best fill in the blank ①.

(A) serious
(B) worsened
(C) avoidable
(D) inevitable
(E) significant

4 The word ② sovereign is closest in meaning to ________.

(A) autonomous
(B) powerful
(C) ascending
(D) airy
(E) domestic

5 According to the passage, which of the following is true?

(A) From the very start, the Northerners wanted a war to abolish slavery.
(B) When Abraham Lincoln was elected President, it was Virginia that announced that the Union should be dissolved.
(C) The prime cause of the war is the difference of political stance toward slavery between the North and the South.
(D) The main principle of the Confederacy was opposed to the extension of slavery.
(E) The main theme of *Uncle Tom's Cabin* supported the political principle of the Confederacy.

Passage 5

Can there be a godless morality? Can we assert a superiority for a godless morality over traditional, theistic, and religious morality? Yes, I think that this is possible. Unfortunately, few people even acknowledge the existence of godless moral values, much less their significance. When people talk about moral values, they almost always presume that they have to be talking about religious morality and religious values. The very possibility of godless, irreligious morality is ignored. A popular claim among religious theists is that atheists have no basis for morality—that religion and gods are needed for moral values. Usually they mean their religion and god, but sometimes they seem willing to accept any religion and any god. The truth is that neither religions nor gods are necessary for morality, ethics, or values. They can exist in a godless, secular context just fine, as demonstrated by all the godless atheists who lead moral lives every day.

1 What is the main topic of the passage?

(A) Moral values without gods
(B) Traditional views on morality
(C) Public lives with secular morality
(D) The presumption of religious morality

2 Which of the following best describes the author's view of atheists?

(A) Atheists have no basis for morality because they have no religion.
(B) The atheists who lead moral lives demonstrate the possibility of godless morality.
(C) The significance of secular moral values is ignored by atheists.
(D) Atheists are morally superior to theistic and religious men.

Passage 6

Change has always affected jobs. What is new and scary is that so many jobs are being affected by change. Law is no longer a safe area because there is a new field called jurimetrics that could eliminate the need for many lawyers. Computers would store and organize legal information so that you wouldn't need a lawyer. Instead, people would go to a "law bank" just as we go to a "cash station" for money now. At the "law bank," they would punch in the facts of their case. The computer would analyze all cases like it and then make a decision. The computer could get the facts more cheaply and more easily than a lawyer. It might even decide the case more fairly than a judge.

And what about the changes in the computer science field? Surely, it's one job area a college student can safely bet will exist after graduation. Wrong. The very success of the computer produces less need for computer workers. People are becoming so familiar with computers, they will soon operate them as easily as they drive cars. Psychology is another young field where there are large changes. Research on the brain tells us that many mental illnesses are caused by chemical problems in our brains. If this is true, there won't be the need for the mental health care people we need now.

Although these jobs are disappearing, ____________________. Your job is to develop the ability to cope with change. Find a sense of self that allows you to keep things in balance. Be strong enough to find or create other possibilities. Develop many different skills and interests. Have a good feeling of your own worth and you will be ready for an uncertain future.

1 Choose the phrase that best fills in the blank.

(A) many others are being born
(B) other jobs are becoming unpopular
(C) a few more are in danger
(D) some are becoming extinct

2 Which of the following CANNOT be inferred from the passage?

(A) Specialized computers may take the place of lawyers.
(B) Mental health jobs may disappears in the future.
(C) Jobs in the computer science field are stable.
(D) Advances in computers have helped create the field of jurimetrics.

3 What is the author's purpose in this passage?

(A) To advise job seekers to find high-profile jobs
(B) To alert people to the transitional job market
(C) To explain how to apply for jobs
(D) To describe newly emerging jobs

Passage 7

To those familiar with its principle navigation tools (browsers, e-mail programs etc.), the Internet is not exactly an undiscovered country, but it is certainly a shifting landscape. It is being constantly changed by those who engage it, and by transactions, input, programming languages and devices that further diversify its modes of communication, its routes, and the means through which it is seen and navigated. The impetus for this comes from a spectrum of sources that include both the profit and non-profit sectors of its "community." But undoubtedly its extension is fueled most of all by the corporate sector. Navigation of this terrain requires guidance that not only supplies directional information, but also encourages a critical understanding of informational structures and the systems of micro-power with which they are interwoven. The digital landscape is being shaped not just by the convergence of various new media and information technologies, but also, by a convergence of industry interests from all sectors, especially entertainment and electronics. The "Information Revolution", therefore, is changing the nature of our participation in all spheres of society, and both the way, and the means, by which we perceive these activities. The integration of digital technologies in daily life has especially reconfigured the relationship between the areas of work and leisure, which may share the same tools of information access, only adjusted for the different context.

1 The fundamental topic discussed in this passage is ________.

(A) the mysteries of the Internet
(B) the way different people use the Internet
(C) the future prospects for the Internet
(D) the forces influencing the way the Internet is changing

2 The writer's main contention is that ________.

(A) users of the Internet need to be critically aware of how it is being shaped
(B) ordinary users cannot hope to understand the Internet
(C) the Internet is mainly developing as a means of entertainment
(D) the Internet will greatly increase participation in society

3 The passage maintains that changes in the Internet are mainly caused by ________.

(A) individual users
(B) the demands of consumers
(C) business interests
(D) the needs of entertainment

4 **The final sentence of the passage stresses that ________.**

(A) all work and no play make Jack a dull boy
(B) people now use the same instruments for work and play
(C) the Internet is a great toy
(D) the computer has changed the way people work

5 **The underlined spectrum in the passage could be replaced by the word ________.**

(A) ghost
(B) host
(C) process
(D) variety

Passage 8

Logic is the study of the methods and principles used to distinguish 'correct' from 'incorrect' reasoning. This definition must not be taken to imply that only the student of logic can reason well or correctly. To say so would be as mistaken as to say that to run well requires studying the physics and physiology involved in that activity. Some excellent athletes are quite ignorant of the complex processes that go on inside their bodies when they perform. And, ________, the somewhat elderly professors who know most about such things would perform very poorly were they to risk their dignity on the athletic field. Even given the same basic muscular and nervous apparatus, the person who has such knowledge might not surpass the 'natural athlete.'

1 **What would be the most appropriate word to fill in the blank?**

(A) off the track
(B) beyond description
(C) strange to say
(D) without control
(E) needless to say

2 **Which of the following is implied?**

(A) A person who has studied logic is more certain to reason correctly than one who has not.
(B) The distinction between 'correct' and 'incorrect' reasoning is the central problem with which logic deals.
(C) It is not always the case that excellent athletes know much about physiological processes.
(D) Knowledge on basic muscular and nervous system is indispensible to natural athlete.
(E) The appeal to reason is more effective than emotion in the long run.

TEST 17

제한시간 | 35분
정답률 | /24

Passage 1

When I worked as a part-time bank teller in college, a good-looking young man began making almost daily trips to my window to withdraw or deposit money. I wasn't sure it was because of me until he presented this note with his bank book: "Dear J: I've been SAVING this question in the hope that I might gain some INTEREST. If free Friday, would you care to DEPOSIT yourself beside me at a movie? I've taken into ACCOUNT that you may be previously engaged; if so, I'll WITHDRAW my offer and hope for Saturday. At any RATE, your company would be much enjoyed, and I hope you'll not ASSESS this as too forward. CHECK you later. Sincerely, B." I couldn't resist such a charming and original approach.

1 글의 필자가 청년의 데이트 신청을 받아들인 이유는?

(A) Because he was good-looking.
(B) Because his daily trips to bank moved the author profoundly.
(C) Because he was one of the bank's most valued customers.
(D) Because the words of his note were appropriate and well-chosen.

Passage 2

Although speech is the most advanced form of communication, there are many ways of communicating without using speech. Signals, signs, symbols, and gestures may be found in every known culture. The basic function of a signal is to impinge upon the environment in such a way that it attracts attention, as, for example, the dots and dashes of a telegraph circuit. Coded to refer to speech, the <u>potential</u> for communication is very great. Less adaptable to the codification of words, signs also contain meaning in and of themselves. A stop sign or a barber pole conveys meaning quickly and conveniently. Symbols are more difficult to describe than either signals or signs because of their intricate relationship with the receiver's cultural perceptions. In some cultures, applauding in a theater provides performers with an auditory symbol of approval. Gestures such as waving and handshaking also communicate certain cultural messages.

Although signals, signs, symbols, and gestures are very useful, they do have a major disadvantage. They usually do not allow ideas to be shared without the sender being directly adjacent to the receiver. As a result, means of communication intended to be used for long distances and extended periods are based upon speech. Radio, television, and the telephone are only a few.

1 Which of the following is the best title of the passage?

(A) Communication
(B) Language
(C) Signs and Symbols
(D) Speech

2 What does the author say about speech?

(A) It is the only true form of communication.
(B) It is dependent upon the advances made by inventors.
(C) It is necessary for communication to occur.
(D) It is the most advanced form of communication.

3 According to the passage, what is a signal?

(A) the most difficult form of communication
(B) a form of communication which may be used across long distance
(C) a form of communication that interrupts the environment
(D) the form of communication most related to cultural perceptions

4 The word potential in the first paragraph could best be replaced by ________.

(A) range
(B) advantage
(C) organization
(D) possibility

5 Applauding was cited as an example of ________.

(A) a signal
(B) a sign
(C) a symbol
(D) a gesture

6 Why were the telephone, radio, and TV invented?

(A) People were unable to understand signs, symbols, and signals.
(B) People wanted to communicate across long distance.
(C) People believed that signs, signals, and symbols were obsolete.
(D) People wanted new forms of entertainment.

7 It may be concluded from this passage that ________.

(A) signals, signs, symbols, and gestures are forms of communication
(B) symbols are very easy to define and interpret
(C) only some cultures have signals, signs, and symbols
(D) waving and handshaking are not related to culture

Passage 3

Simply put, positive psychology is the scientific study of human happiness. Positive psychology focuses on what makes people feel good rather than what causes them to feel bad. Until recently, the prevailing focus in the field of psychology has been on mental illness rather than mental wellness. Psychologists asked questions such as why people get depressed, irritable, or anxious. Now some psychologists are examining what makes people happy rather than what makes them sad. Martin Seligman, the illustrious psychologist and professor at the University of Pennsylvania, is the father of positive psychology. Seligman first introduced the world to positive psychology in 1998. The overall goal of positive psychology is to enhance people's experience of love, work, and play. One way to achieve this goal is to teach people how to ① ________ personal qualities such as humor, originality, and generosity into their ② ________ with others to achieve happiness. [I] So what does make us happy? Research suggests that once our basic needs are met, factors such as money, education, high intelligence, sunny weather, or even youth have only a modest effect on happiness. What researchers are discovering is that things such as friends and strong family connections directly affect how happy you are with your life. According to Seligman and other positive psychologists, there are certain personal qualities, or strengths, that directly affect happiness. [II] For example, qualities such as curiosity, optimism, courage, humor, kindness, and generosity are very important in leading a happy life. Seligman encourages people to build on the qualities they already possess. [III] For example, if you are already a generous person by nature, then you should try to practice being generous with friends, coworkers, and even strangers on a daily basis. [IV] Seligman firmly believes that everyone has the ability to be happy. You just have to put some work into it. Seligman should know, because he is actually a self-proclaimed pessimist and has been very open about his own depressive tendencies. He believes optimism is a quality that can be developed. Seligman argues that it does not matter how naturally optimistic or pessimistic you are. People can learn to expand upon their own ability to feel good and develop qualities that lead to happiness. In other words, anyone can lead a happy, if not happier, life.

1 윗글의 제목으로 가장 적절한 것을 고르시오.

(A) The Different Steps of Positive Thinking
(B) Learning about Happiness
(C) How to Overcome Depression
(D) The Negative Side of Positive Psychology

2 빈칸 ①, ②에 들어 갈 가장 적절한 단어를 고르시오.

	①	②
(A)	incorporate	interactions
(B)	include	competition
(C)	divide	dealing
(D)	integrate	struggles

3 윗글에 다음 문장이 들어갈 가장 적절한 곳을 고르시오.

> The more generous you are to others, the more meaning you will have in your life and the happier you will be.

(A) [Ⅰ]
(B) [Ⅱ]
(C) [Ⅲ]
(D) [Ⅳ]

Passage 4

When it comes to leisure activities, Americans aren't quite the funseekers they've been cracked up to be. For one out of five, weekends and vacations are consumed by such drudgeries as housecleaning, yard work, and cooking; only one third of American workers enjoy the luxury of lolling in the sun, going camping, playing sports, or simply relaxing. One thousand employed Americans were recently asked how they occupy themselves on days they are not at work. According to the poll, older people, the affluent, and the well-educated are most apt to spend their spare time doing the things they 'want to do' rather than those they 'have to do'. Overall, high-salaried respondents were more active than those with lower incomes—they reported watching less television and were more likely to engage in social and cultural activities. People who are divorced, widowed, or separated, the survey concluded, are the least likely of any group to take a vacation—and the least likely to attach any importance to it.

1 The passage is most likely to be a part of ________.

(A) an employee handbook
(B) a book review
(C) a newspaper article
(D) a financial report
(E) a product manual

2 According to the passage, which of the following is true about Americans' leisure activities?

(A) Most Americans do what they want in their leisure time.
(B) Fifty percent of Americans spend their vacations in drudgery.
(C) The educated tend to be too busy to take vacations.
(D) People who are separated are likely to take longer vacations.
(E) The high-salaried spend less time watching television than those with low incomes.

Passage 5

The philosophers tell us that art consists essentially, not in performing a moral act, but in making a thing, a work, in making an object with a view not to the human good of the agent, but to the exigencies and the proper good of the object to be made, and by employing ways of realization predetermined by the nature of the object in question. Art thus appears as something foreign in itself to the sphere of the human good, almost as something inhuman, and whose exigencies nevertheless are absolute: for, needless to say, there are not two ways of making an object well, of realizing well the work one has conceived—there is but one way, and it must not be missed.

The philosophers go on to say that this making activity is principally and above all an intellectual activity. Art is a virtue of the intellect, of the practical intellect, and may be termed the virtue proper to working reason. But then, you will say, if art is nothing other than an intellectual virtue of making, whence comes its dignity and its ascendancy among us? Why does this branch of our activity draw to it so much human sap? Why has one always and in all peoples admired the poet as much as the sage? It may be answered first that to create, to produce something intellectually, to make an object rationally constructed, is something very great in the world; for man this alone is already a way of imitating God. And I am speaking here of art in general, such as the ancients understood it—in short, of art as the virtue of the artisan.

1 The philosophers tell us that ________.

(A) an artistic object is something amoral since an object is inhuman
(B) it is needless to say art has something to do with the human good
(C) the making of an object of art is already innate in the object in question
(D) artists must always keep in mind the proper use of the object after the work is done

2 Which of the following is NOT true according to the passage?

(A) An object conceived by the artist has only one way of its realization.
(B) Art as an intellectual activity of making lacks dignity.

(C) Man imitates God by rationally constructing an object.
(D) The ancients understood art as the virtue of the artist.

3 Poets have been admired as much as sages because ________.

(A) poets are creators like God
(B) poets are as religious as sages are
(C) poets are intellectually no less than sages
(D) poets are disciplined under the teachings of sages

Passage 6

Lucas and Speilberg both achieved fame as the brightest young talents in Hollywood ill the late 1970s and early 1980s, Lucas's Star Wars and Speilberg's Close Encounters of the Third Kind, appeared in the same year, 1977, placing both in the race for an Academy Award. The two science fiction films used special effects that had never been seen before. Special computerized cameras were invented and miniature models of spaceships were designed. The effects on screen kept audiences ① breathless. When Lucas and Speilberg worked together on Raiders of the Lost Ark, they once again captured the imagination of the audience and made them feel as if they were a part of the action. This is what made their films so successful.

1 위 글의 내용으로 보아 밑줄 친 ①의 가장 적절한 의미는?

(A) physically exhausted
(B) fascinated and excited
(C) emotionally drained
(D) unable to breathe properly

2 위 글의 내용과 일치하지 않는 것은?

(A) Their movies effectively draw the audience into the action.
(B) Both directors were nominated for an Academy Award in 1977.
(C) Special effects were instrumental to their movies' success.
(D) Lucas and Speilberg collaborated on Star Wars.

Passage 7

Bangladesh's worst ever ferry accident has recently added pressure upon the authorities to improve safety in the shipping sector. According to the official statistics, there have been about 250 ferry accidents in Bangladesh since 1977. These have resulted in more than 2,000 deaths. The latest sinking is typical of many accidents, taking place during the holiday rush at the end of the year. The accident happened in what is believed to be one of the riskiest river channels in the country, an area where accidents occur regularly.

However, the channel remains one of the most important communication links between southern Bangladesh and the capital city, Dhaka. Most of the boats that use this route are constructed in local shipyards, and are often built below international maritime standards. Experts say that the high casualty figures on such vessels are due to a combination of poor manufacturing techniques and the failure of the boat owners to implement adequate safety precautions. The experts point out that although the provision of life jackets or emergency rings is mandatory, the rule has rarely been enforced. Experts also say that many crews and captains lack proper navigation training. They say that the employment of an unskilled workforce in the industry is widespread. Officials at the Shipping Ministry say that they have devised tougher regulations for improving safety standards, but that the problem is one of enforcement rather than of legislation.

1 The passage does NOT clearly say that ________.

(A) Bangladesh has many ferry accidents
(B) Bangladesh ferries are not very well built
(C) Bangladesh ferry crews are inexperienced
(D) Bangladesh people cannot swim well

2 The passage clearly says that life jackets are ________.

(A) usually provided but are no use when accidents happen
(B) sometimes provided but are poorly maintained
(C) required by law to be provided but are usually not available
(D) always available, but in insufficient quantities

3 The passage says that the latest accident was typical of many in that ________.

(A) a lot of people died
(B) it happened in a dangerous place
(C) it could have been prevented
(D) it happened during a holiday rush

4 **The passage explicitly concludes that there will be less accidents if ________.**

(A) better ferries are built
(B) existing safety regulations are applied strictly
(C) stricter laws are enacted
(D) crews are better trained

5 **The best overall title for this text would be ________.**

(A) Tragic loss of life in unique ferry accident
(B) Illegal ferries in multiple accidents
(C) Multiple factors underlie ferry disasters
(D) Tragic ferry accident spurs calls for safer transport

Passage 8

During the evolution of the factory system in the 19th-century, the merchant class became more and more significant in English national life. Cities multiplied in population, labor and life were cheap, and the industrialists developed a philosophy of individualism that would justify their enterprise without involving obligations to society. The Romantic writers were enemies of the idea of social injustice, but they knew little about actual social conditions; they themselves did not come from the ranks of wage earners. But the romantic writers were powerfully affected by the theories developed in France establishing the principles of Liberty, Fraternity and Equality. Before social abuses could be cured, these principles had to be established. The Romantic writers did much to promote them.

1 **19세기 영국에 관한 다음 글의 내용과 일치하지 않는 것은?**

(A) 도시 인구가 증폭되었고, 상인계급이 점점 중요한 역할을 하게 되었다.
(B) 산업자본가들은 사회적 책임을 강조하는 개인주의 철학을 발달시켰다.
(C) 사회정의를 강조했던 낭만주의 작가들은 사회 실상을 잘 알지는 못했다.
(D) 낭만주의 작가들은 프랑스에서 계발된 사상에 많은 영향을 받았다.

TEST 18

제한시간 | 35분
정답률 | /18

Passage 1

Nearly everyone is shy in some ways. If shyness is making you uncomfortable, it may be time for a few lessons in self-confidence. You can build your confidence by following some suggestions from doctors and psychologists. First, make a decision not to hold back in conversations. What you have to say is just as important as what other people say. Second, prepare yourself for being with others in groups. Make a list of the good qualities you have. Then make a list of ideas, experiences, and skills you would like to share with other people. Think about what you would like to say in advance.

Then say it. Finally, if you start feeling self-conscious in a group, take a deep breath and focus your attention on other people. Remember, you are not alone.

No one ever gets over being shy completely, but most people do learn to live with their shyness. Just making the effort to control shyness can have many rewards. But perhaps the best reason to fight shyness is to give other people a chance to know more about you.

1 글을 쓴 목적은?

(A) to account for how shyness originates
(B) to recommend ways of dealing with shyness
(C) to persuade readers that shyness is natural
(D) to prove that shyness can be overcome

Passage 2

Language is not a medium, but a system. This system is not determined by what happens outside of it, in some pre-linguistic space. It is built around an internal arrangement of difference. In a famous [A] __________, language is compared to pieces in a game of chess. You can use anything as chess-pieces (medieval figurines, dolls based on your favorite sit-com, button found in the street), as long as it is clear to the players what defines the system of differences between the various pieces that allows them to move in specific ways. It is not important what you use as king, queen, rook and pawn, as long as everyone knows which is which. In the case of signifiers, it does not matter which particular marks and sounds are used to [B] _________. What makes language work is the difference between one signifier and all others. Language [C] _________ depends not on the perfect way the marks 'cat' define a certain quadruped, but on the complex web of differences which allows us to recognize the minute but [D] _________ distinction between 'cat', 'bat' and so on. Indeed, although this distinction is minute, we are so [E] _________ to language as a system of differences that we consider those who cannot recognize the distinction to be either non-users of our language or suffering from a learning disorder.

1 Which word is the most appropriate in [A]?

(A) analogy
(B) oxymoron
(C) similarity
(D) commonality

2 Which word is the most appropriate in [B]?

(A) defer a particular movement
(B) deny a particular placement
(C) denote a certain object
(D) deter a certain being

3 Which words would be the most appropriate in [C], [D], [E]?

(A) structuration — critiquing — sensible
(B) functionality — contrastive — abstruse
(C) efficiency — crucial — sensitized
(D) capacity — comparative — oblivious

4 What would be the most logical conclusion to the passage above?

(A) Language is a complex body of knowledge which all learners need to eventually learn.
(B) Language is a system of reflection that cannot do without the signified.
(C) Language is not an element arbitrarily linked, but an intricate structure of beliefs defined through the rule of acumen.
(D) Language is not a set of tools haphazardly connected, but a concrete system of conventions built around relationships.

Passage 3

A very large number of people cease when quite young to add anything to a limited stock of judgments. After a certain age, say 25, they consider that their education is finished.

It is perhaps natural that having passed through that painful and boring process, called expressly education, they should suppose it over, and that they are equipped for life to label every event as it occurs and drop it into its given pigeonhole. But one who has a label ready for everything does not bother to observe any more, even such ordinary happenings as he had observed for himself, with attention, before he went to school. He merely acts and reacts.

For people who have stopped noticing, the only possible new or renewed experience, and, therefore, new knowledge, is from a work of art. Because that is the only kind of experience which they are prepared to receive on its own terms, they will come out from their shells and expose themselves to music, to a play, to a book, because it is the accepted method of enjoying ① such things. True, even to plays and books they may bring artistic prejudices which prevent them from seeing that play or comprehending that book. Their artistic sensibilities may be as crusted ②__________ as their minds.

But it is part of an artist's job to break crusts, or let us say rather that artists who work for the public and not merely for themselves are interested in breaking crusts because they want to communicate their intuitions.

1 위 글의 제목으로 알맞은 것은?

(A) The Process of Education
(B) The Origin of Art
(C) Art and the Role of Education
(D) Education and the Role of Art

2 밑줄 친 ①이 가리키는 것은?

(A) some memorable events in one's life
(B) such art forms as music, a play, or a book
(C) anew experience and knowledge
(D) ordinary happenings in one's life

3 빈칸 ②에 알맞은 것은?

(A) over
(B) in
(C) by
(D) under

Passage 4

Lend money to a friend, and you're liable to lose both. But when someone close hits you up for a loan, it can be tough to say no. The first consideration, say financial experts, is whether you can afford it. If you can't afford to give the money away, you can't afford to lend it. Next, get it in writing. For big amounts, a repayment schedule helps to legitimize the loan. "It protects the lender, and can make the recipient more comfortable, so they don't see the loan as charity," says Howard Levine, a chartered accountant. Should you charge interest? It's not mandatory, and may have tax implications. But if your money would be earning 5% on a term deposit, charge the same 5%. Or structure it as a loan but forgo the interest on repayment. And if a pal defaults? For lenders, it's not just the amount that can cause a rift, but the feeling that you're being taken advantage of. Levlne advises ① __________ not to avoid the topic: "Pay back what you can, even if it's just a bit. If you can't pay back, be up-front. Don't just ignore it."

1 Which of the following best describes the author's advice you need when you lend money to a friend?

(A) You should be willing to give the money away just in case.
(B) You should maintain the feeling that you are being abused.
(C) You should not charge any interest to your friends.
(D) You should ask for a repayment schedule from a chartered accountant.
(E) You should be ready to ignore your friend when he or she defaults.

2 Which of the following best fits into ①?

(A) borrowers
(B) accountants
(C) lenders
(D) tax collectors
(E) tellers

Passage 5

The economic world is extremely complicated. There are millions of people and firms, thousands of prices and industries. One possible way of figuring out economic laws in such a setting is by *controlled experiments*. A controlled experiment takes place when everything else __________ the item under investigation is held constant. Thus a scientist trying to determine whether saccharine causes cancer in rats will hold "other things equal" and only vary the amount of saccharine. Same air, same light, same type of rat.

Economists have no such luxury when testing economic laws. They cannot perform the controlled experiments of chemists or biologists because they cannot easily control other important factors. Like astronomers or meteorologists, they generally must be content to observe.

If you are vitally interested in the effects of the 1982 gasoline tax on fuel consumption, you will be vexed by the fact that in the same year when the tax was imposed, the size of cars became smaller. Nevertheless, you must try to isolate the effects of the tax by attempting to figure out what would happen, if "other things were equal." You can perform calculations that correct for the changing car size. Unless you make such corrections, you cannot accurately understand the effects of gasoline taxes.

1 빈칸에 가장 알맞은 것은?

(A) but
(B) besides
(C) with regard to
(D) in favor of

2 위 글이 주로 다루고 있는 것은?

(A) what a controlled experiment is
(B) how economic laws are reached
(C) what effects taxes have on consumption
(D) how science and economics differ

Passage 6

Mainstream scientific organizations worldwide __________ the assessment that most of the observed warming over the last 50 years is likely to have been due to the human-caused increase in greenhouse gas concentrations. However, some critics of the consensus view on global warming have argued that the appearance of overlapping groups of skeptical scientists, commentators and think tanks in seemingly unrelated controversies results from an organized attempt to replace scientific analysis with political ideology. Some claim that the promotion of doubt regarding issues that are politically, but not scientifically, controversial became increasingly prevalent under the Bush Administration and constituted a 'Republican war on science.'

1 **Which title does best describe the passage above?**

(A) Definition of the global warming controversy
(B) Hoax of the global warming
(C) Human responsibilities of the global warming
(D) Political orientation of the global warming controversy
(E) Scientific evidence of the global warming controversy

2 **What would be the most appropriate word to fill in the blank?**

(A) are reluctant to
(B) concur with
(C) become skeptical of
(D) challenge
(E) conciliate

Passage 7

External relationships are just as important as internal ones in predicting team success. A lot of the time that a team spends building trust and a collegial spirit would be better spent scouting for outside sources of new ideas, generating enthusiasm for what the team is doing among upper managers and communicating with everyone the group's work touches, from customers to tech support. __________ about what makes a team work, such as clearly delineated roles and team spirit, tends to correspond to team-member satisfaction, but those variables often don't line up with financial metrics like sales revenue. Companies that thrive in the knowledge-driven global economy are spread out, with loose hierarchies, not rigid centralized structures. They depend on complex, constantly changing streams of information that can't be contained by any one source. And the tasks of groups within these firms link them to people within the company and without. The distributed-yet-interconnected character of contemporary work dictates reaching outward, but years of morale-building retreats and consultants persuade us to keep looking in.

1 **Choose the one that best fills in the blank.**

(A) Conventional wisdom
(B) Financial acumen
(C) Idiosyncratic knowledge
(D) Unsolicited opinion

2 **Which of the following CANNOT be inferred about "team success" according to the passage?**

(A) It must take into consideration the interconnectedness of work.
(B) It depends on a group's communication channels.
(C) It is affected by the sales revenue of the company.
(D) It can be fueled by outside sources and relations with outsiders.

Passage 8

A margin account sounds mysterious to the uninformed. Actually, it is nothing more than a loan the stockbroker makes to you using your securities as collateral to support the loan. Here's how it works: Say you open a margin account by depositing $3,000. (All brokers require a minimum deposit for a margin account, and the Board of Governors of the Federal Reserve System requires an initial margin requirement of 50 percent of the value of securities purchased.) Then, you buy 100 shares of ABC stock at $ (A)__________ a share. Thus, you bought $5,000 worth of stock, ignoring commissions, with only a $3,000 deposit; obviously the other $2,000 came from your broker. Now, what happens if the stock goes up or down in value? No problem, if it goes up. You can sell whenever you like and repay the $2,000 loan plus interest and pocket the difference. If it goes down, keep one simple fact in mind—the loss is all yours. You don't share it with the broker. So if ABC goes down to $30 a share and you then sell, the broker still gets $2,000, plus interest, and you still pocket the difference—$1,000 in this case. You lose $2,000, which is $20 a share times the (B)__________ shares.

1 **How does the author define a margin account?**

(A) what the stockbroker lends to you
(B) what the stockbroker pays to you
(C) what one gets from investment in stocks
(D) what one loses from investment in stocks

2 **밑줄 친 (A)와 (B)에 들어가기에 가장 적합한 것을 고르시오.**

(A) 30 — 50
(B) 50 — 100
(C) 50 — 50
(D) 30 — 100

TEST 19

제한시간 | 35분
정답률 | /18

Passage 1

Communication scholar Kames McCroskey, who has studied communication apprehension for more than twenty year, defines it as "an individual's level of fear or anxiety associated with either real or anticipated communication with another person or persons." As this definition suggests, communication apprehension is not limited to public speaking situations. We may feel worried about almost any kind of communication encounter. If, for example, you are preparing to have a conversation with a romantic partner who, you think, is about to suggest ending the relationship, if your professor has called you into her office to discuss your poor attendance record, or if a police officer has motioned you to pull off the road for a "conversation," you know what communication apprehension is all about.

1 What is the main idea of the passage?

(A) Communication apprehension is hard to define.
(B) Communication apprehension is hard overcome while interaction with others.
(C) Communication apprehension is closely related to the level of anxiety and fear.
(D) Communication apprehension can occur in various kinds of situations.

Passage 2

Thus the critic need not humbly efface himself before the work and submit to its demands; on the contrary, he actively constructs its meaning: he makes the work exist; "there is no Racine en Soi ... Racine exists in the readings of Racine, and apart from the readings there is no Racine." None of these readings is wrong, they all add to the work.

So, a work of literature ultimately consists of everything that has been said about it. As a result, ① no work ever dies; "A work is eternal not because it imposes a single meaning on different men, but because it suggests different meanings to a single man, speaking the same symbolic language in all ages: the work proposes, man disposes."

Barthes's masterpiece, S/Z, remains the exhilarating monument to this total rejection of the critic's passive role. To this one should add Barthes's concomitant insistence on a new emphasis on literature as it really is: a signifying system which characteristically and autonomously employs the specific activities of reading and writing, and which is not simply concerned to deliver a ________ content to the reader.

1 **The paragraph preceding this passage is most likely to argue that ________.**

(A) the critic is given a new role and status
(B) the critic has to be aware of the writer's personal background
(C) the critic should not have any prior knowledge of the work
(D) the critic plays a significant moral role in our society
(E) the critic has to succumb to the demands of the market

2 **According to the passage, no work ever dies in ① because ________.**

(A) the new generation of writers continues to find out new subjects
(B) the meanings of the work always remain unstable
(C) the critic is a passive participant in the work he reads
(D) great works contain a universal truth
(E) writers continuously try to fulfill the reader's demands

3 **Which of the following best fills in the blank?**

(A) predetermined
(B) preoccupied
(C) preliminary
(D) prevailing
(E) preposterous

Passage 3

In everyday life we surround ourselves with an invisible "bubble" that constitutes what we consider our personal space, an area around our body that we reserve for ourselves, intimate acquaintances, and close friends. These personal spaces vary greatly from one culture to another and within cultures when people of different age, race, sex, and social class categories interact. Middle Easterners, for example, have much smaller distance requirements for casual interaction and men often embrace or kiss on the cheek when introduced for the first time—something that makes American men very uncomfortable. ________ living in a very densely-populated country, the Japanese often maintain a larger social space when interacting with strangers. When two Japanese men are introduced, they bow toward one another, an act that requires a distance of about 180cm to prevent bumping heads. In the United States, women are generally far more comfortable touching, hugging, or kissing one another than are men, and women generally will allow other women within their intimate distance, something a man rarely allows from another man, even if they are blood related.

1 **Which of the following best fits in blank?**

(A) Because
(B) Despite
(C) Since
(D) However

2 **According to the passage, which of the following statements is true?**

(A) American men may feel quite uneasy allowing people of the same gender within their "bubble."
(B) It would be offensive to kiss a man on the cheek in Iraq when introduced for he first time.
(C) Japanese culture requires much smaller distance for casual interaction than American culture.
(D) Members within the same cultural groups tend to keep the same amount of personal spaces when interacting with each other.

3 **Which of the following words CANNOT replace the underlined word far?**

(A) way
(B) away
(C) much
(D) considerably

Passage 4

During the past two decades the rise in the real income of manual laborers has been not only great in absolute terms, but also greater in comparison with that of non-manual workers. The effect of this has been to blur the old division between the working and middle classes, many manual workers' families now acquiring habits, tastes, and, to some extent, attitudes which were formerly regarded as "middle class." Due to considerable upward mobility of the working class, social distinctions based on occupation have become ① ________. Whether they exist and what they consist of depend on what part of the country one is looking at, but people today should not assume that a doctor is regarded as several steps on the ladder above a garage keeper, or that the headmaster of the local state school is regarded as a higher being than the skilled worker who now earns not one quarter of his salary, but just as much as he does, if not more.

1 **Which of the following best fits into ①?**

(A) less fuzzy
(B) less clear-cut
(C) more striking
(D) most essential
(E) somewhat prominent

2 Which of the following is stated or implied in the passage?

(A) The things that make up social distinctions are universal.
(B) Occupations are a clear criterion for determining social status across the country.
(C) The rise in manual workers' wages blurred the class distinctions.
(D) All societies have hierarchically structured social distinctions.
(E) Headmasters earn four times as much as some skilled workers.

Passage 5

A thousand years ago, when the earth was reassuringly flat and the universe revolved around it, the ordinary person had no last name, (A) let alone any claim to individualism. The self was subordinated to church and king. Then came the Renaissance explosion of scientific discovery and humanist insight and, as both cause and effect, the rise of individual self-consciousness. All at once, it seemed, humanity had replaced God at the center of earthly life. And perhaps more than any great war or invention or feat of navigation, this upheaval marked the beginning of our modern era. There are now 20 times as many people in the world as there were in the year 1000. Most have last names, and many of us have a personal identity or reasonable expectation of acquiring one. This special (B) issue examines the transformation of identity through different lenses and concludes with reflections on how hard (C) it is, in a time of gathering global conformity, to find one's own way.

1 The best title of this passage is ________.

(A) Identification of humanity
(B) Divinity over individualism
(C) Importance of the Renaissance in the human history
(D) How individual identity was acquired
(E) Relationship between God and humanism

2 What does the underlined (A) means?

(A) to say nothing of any claim to individualism
(B) but for empty claims to individualism
(C) at the same time no claim to individualism
(D) nor any claim at all to individualism
(E) in the end no claim at all to individualism

3 **According to the passage, before the Renaissance ________.**

(A) individualism was respected
(B) people did not have their own personal names
(C) people acquired personal identity
(D) church and king dominated individuals
(E) humanism enhanced individual self-consciousness

4 **밑줄 친 (B) issue의 뜻은?**

(A) 결과
(B) (출판물의) 호
(C) 문제점
(D) 논문
(E) 논쟁

5 **What does the underlined (C) it refer to?**

(A) this special issue
(B) transformation of identity
(C) a personal identity
(D) reasonable expectation of acquiring one
(E) to find one's own way

Passage 6

Surgery that can improve the way a person looks is becoming more and more popular. This kind of surgery is called cosmetic surgery, and both men and women are turning to this treatment as a way of keeping their appearance young as well as keeping competitive in their jobs. Men especially are beginning to turn to face-lifts, liposuction, and implants to help them look younger. As companies downsize and move younger employees into higher position, older employees in their late forties and early fifties feel the need to look and act younger in order to stay competitive. A younger look through cosmetic surgery may give an older employee a few more years on the job. These operations are not without dangers, however.

1 **글의 요지로 가장 알맞은 것은?**

(A) Cosmetic surgery cannot be safe.
(B) There are many kinds of cosmetic surgery.
(C) There are a lot of people who turn to liposuction.
(D) Some people have cosmetic surgery to keep their jobs.

Passage 7

I was in high school when I finally accepted the fact that I was homeless. Until that point I was in complete denial. During those miserable times, my brother and I learned how to become expert liars. We never let our friends in school know where we were living. In some cases we were lucky enough not to be going to the local school, so no one ever walked home with us. If the shelter was near our school or one of our friends caught us coming out of the "bums" building, as the kids in the neighborhood used to call it, then we would tell them our mother worked there and we had to meet her there after school. It is difficult enough to fit in when you are a kid, and worse yet you can never invite anyone home to visit because you don't have a home. Being in those shelters, though, helped me to see that the biggest cause of homeless is not lack of money to pay rent. There were a lot of broken families in these shelters, broken by drugs, alcohol abuse, divorce, AIDS, early pregnancy, lack of education and, most important, lack of information about how to get out of these troubles. Many of the kids I knew at the shelter really wanted to change their circumstances but few of them did—few of them knew how. There weren't many social workers around, and even when they were around and noticed a problem, they rarely followed up. The children in these situations need a listening ear, someone to turn to consistently.

1 In order to hide the fact that they were homeless, the speaker and his brother ________.

(A) didn't come out of the "bums" building
(B) didn't go to meet their mother after school
(C) didn't walk home with anyone
(D) didn't lie about their parents

2 Which is true according to the passage?

(A) Being in homeless shelters can be a helpful experience.
(B) People become homeless mostly because they don't have money to pay rent.
(C) Homeless children do not notice their problem.
(D) People become homeless because there weren't many social workers around.

Passage 8

The school wall is repainted for the fourth time to get rid of graffiti. Creativity is admirable but people should find ways to express themselves that do not inflict extra costs upon society. Why do you spoil the reputation of young people by painting graffiti where it's forbidden? Professional artists do not hang their paintings in the street. Instead they seek funding and gain fame through legal exhibitions.

Buildings, fences and park benches are works of art in themselves. It's really pathetic to spoil this architecture with graffiti. I can't understand why these criminal artists bother as their "artistic works" are just removed from sight over and over again.

1 글의 목적으로 가장 알맞은 것을 고르시오.

(A) To persuade people on the social functions of graffiti
(B) To demonstrate the popularity of graffiti
(C) To present an opinion about graffiti
(D) To explain what graffiti is

TEST 20

제한시간 | 35분
정답률 | /20

Passage 1

Have you ever wondered why the supermarkets you have ever been into are all the same? It is not because the companies that operate them lack imagination. It is because they are all versed in the science of persuading people to buy things. For example, the first thing people come to in most supermarkets is the fresh fruit and vegetables section. For shoppers, this makes no sense. Fruit and vegetables can be easily damaged, so they should be bought at the end, not the beginning, of a shopping trip. But psychology is at work here: selecting good wholesome fresh food is an uplifting way to start shopping, and it makes people feel less guilty about reaching for the stodgy stuff later on. For another example, everyday items like milk are invariably placed towards the back of a store to provide more opportunity to tempt customers. The idea is to boost "dwell time": the length of time people spend in a store.

1 Which of the following is NOT true according to the passage?

(A) Necessities tend to be placed at the rear in stores.
(B) Most stores have the same layout of shopping sections.
(C) Retailers want their customers to stay longer in the store.
(D) Sections in stores are positioned for the best efficiency of customers.

2 Why do retailers place the fresh fruit and vegetables section at the front?

(A) Because fruit and vegetables can be easily spoiled.
(B) Because it can lead customers to stay on a healthy diet.
(C) Because retailers want to save customers time and money.
(D) Because customers can comfort themselves by selecting wholesome food.

Passage 2

(1) Frankenstein has achieved a distinction earned by very few other novels: based on myth, it has itself becomes a myth. The story is of Frankenstein, a scientist who has acquired the ability to light the spark of life in matter. Seeking for perfection and beauty in the creature he makes, and for it to adore him, he creates ⓐ __________ a monster, sewn together from bits of various humans.

(2) Frankenstein's monster is monstrous only in physical appearance. In agony from the wounds that hold it together, the 'monster' inspires loathing in all who see it. Eventually Frankenstein's creation destroys him, his brother, his friend and his bride. Frankenstein pursues it to the Arctic, determined to kill it, but is himself killed as the monster appears to decide that Frankenstein will be his last victim, and he/it will kill himself.

(3) The bare outlines do not do ⓑ __________ to the weight of the story. Frankenstein is an emblem for modern science, the lust for knowledge which creates a power for destruction which it cannot control, and which will eventually destroy the creator and itself. The monster is a symbol of the outsider, subject to fear, loathing and to being an outcast simply through its being different and through ⓒ society's knee-jerk reaction to destroy anything that appears alien.

(4) It is also a version of the myth of the Noble Savage, where something essentially good is corrupted by so-called civilization. There are also hints of the Faust myth, as there are in so many Gothic novels. Frankenstein is seeking to transcend the limitations of humanity, seeking to do what only God is empowered to do, namely give the gift of life. For ⓓ this he must be destroyed, and in true tragic form that destruction will not be limited to him but also affect many innocent people and society in general. To that extent Frankenstein is also a tragedy, in the classical and neo-classical sense of the word.

1 Choose the word that can best fill in the blank ⓐ__________.

(A) likewise
(B) instead
(C) accordingly
(D) extremely
(E) moreover

2 Choose the word that can best fill in the blank ⓑ__________.

(A) justice
(B) mean
(C) positive
(D) property
(E) narrow

3 **What can be inferred about ⓒ society's knee-jerk reaction in paragraph (3)?**

(A) Society is so cruel to the monster because the monster attempts to destroy anything that seems to be alien.

(B) Society never explicitly shows its hostile reaction to the monster.

(C) Human society is caught by a deep-rooted hostility to something totally different and strangers.

(D) Frankenstein is a symbol of the outsider who are persecuted by society's prejudice.

(E) Frankenstein is very adverse to society's reaction to the monster.

4 **In paragraph (4) what does ⓓ this refer to?**

(A) Frankenstein's fear of the monster

(B) Frankenstein's recognition of human limitation

(C) Frankenstein's love of humanity

(D) Frankenstein's attempt to give the gift of life

(E) Frankenstein's glorification of God's power

5 **According to the passage, which of the following is NOT true?**

(A) Myth is an important literary source of Frankenstein.

(B) Frankenstein cannot kill the monster although he pursues it to the Arctic.

(C) Frankenstein is a symbol of modern man who has a thirst for knowledge.

(D) Frankenstein attempts to create the ideal living creature of perfection and beauty.

(E) The monster is very ugly in his/its heart as well as in outward appearance.

Passage 3

William Kidd's story begins in 1696 when he sailed to England from his home in the New York colony. Kidd wanted to captain a Royal Navy warship in the king's army. Unfortunately, the British Board of Trade had other plans for him. Kidd happened to arrive in England during the time that the Board of Trade was coming up with a plan to combat the rampant outbreak of piracy that was just then causing damage to Britain's commercial shipping routes. A "privateer" to do aggressive battle against the pirates on the high sea was wanted by the board. They also wanted their privateer to engage in a little of its own piracy by preying upon French merchantmen. The board more or less roped their reluctant Kidd into doing their dirty work for them by "suggesting" that he might have trouble getting past customs when he returned home to New York. By the time Kidd set sail in his thirty four-gun ship, the Adventure Galley, in February 1696, he had already been pressed into paying the board twenty thousand English pounds bond. In addition, he had contracted that a 10 percent share of any valuables captured be given to the king. Furthermore, Kidd and his crew were to receive their payment out of the loot they confiscated from the pirates and the French.

1 **What did the British Board of Trade want Kidd to do for them?**

(A) To captain a Royal Navy warship in the king's army
(B) To combat the outbreak of piracy in the name of the king
(C) To loot the pirates and French merchantmen on the high sea
(D) To pay twenty thousand English pounds bond in return for his safe return

2 **Which of the following is true according to the passage?**

(A) If Kidd and his crew had failed to get any loot, they would have been paid by the king.
(B) The Board of Trade wanted to conduct piracy but only through a "privateer."
(C) The British Board of Trade accepted Kidd's proposed of service for the king.
(D) In Kidd's time there were lots of French pirates haunting British merchant ships.

Passage 4

The (A) writing of poetry, which has been generally regarded in the West as the most (B) imaginative and loftiest of all literary forms, was in China a common, everyday undertaking of the intellectuals. Chinese poets, unlike some of their Western counterparts who (C) happily built their castles in the air, were on the whole earthbound and (D) mundane. They were disturbed neither by poetic agonies and aesthetic aspirations, nor by the thrills of romantic excursions into the mind and the universe.

(1)__________, they were content with (E) weaving songs out of the materials (F) of daily life and occupation. Almost every educated Chinese was a poet who turned out verses as fast as there was an occasion for them. And in China there were (2)__________ occasions for poetry: court celebrations and religious festivities; weddings and funerals; garden parties, where the beauties of the peonies and chrysanthemums were felicitated; convivial feasts during which, after (G) a generous flow of wine, companies were promoted, merged and dissolved; trips to scenic spots, where even the latent poetic talent would burst into bloom—these and a thousand and one other occasions, on which, no matter how (H) trivial they seemed, poetry was the language that spoke understandingly and pleasurably to the heart.

1 **Which of the following expressions fits best in blank (1)?**

(A) Instead
(B) As a result
(C) Nonetheless
(D) To begin with

2 **Which of the following pairs does NOT make a suitable match?**

(A) (A) writing of poetry — (E) weaving songs
(B) (B) imaginative — (C) happily built their castles in the air
(C) (D) mundane — (F) of daily life and occupation
(D) (G) a generous flow of wine — (H) trivial

3 **Which of the following words fits best in blank (2)?**

(A) rare
(B) numerous
(C) official
(D) traditional

Passage 5

Over the years we have hired many MBAs to work for us. In fact, in my more impressionable days I guess this was one of my own conditioned reflexes: If you have a problem, hire an MBA. As we grew and got to areas in which we had less confidence or expertise, I reasoned that by virtue of their education the MBAs were the best people to run these areas for us.

What I discovered was that a master's in business can sometimes block an ability to master experience. Many of the early MBAs we hired were either naive or victims of their business training. The result was a kind of real-life learning disability—a failure to read people properly or to size up situations.

In fairness to some of our employees, we do have a number of MBAs working for us who have made the adjustment to the real world quite nicely. But to assume, as I once did, that advanced degrees or high IQ scores automatically equal "business smarts" has often proved an expensive error in judgment.

1 위 글의 내용과 가장 어울리는 것은?

(A) Nothing can take the place of experience out in the world.
(B) Learning preserves the errors and wisdom of the past.
(C) Education is a progressive discovery of our own ignorance.
(D) Intelligence enables a man to get along without education.

2 위 글의 내용과 일치하지 않는 것은?

(A) The business abilities of many MBAs disappointed the writer.
(B) The more intelligent a man is, the smarter he runs business.
(C) MBA training can decrease one's ability to cope with realities.
(D) The writer once believed hiring MBAs could solve his problems.

Passage 6

Drug makers are well aware of the power of public relations, and they spend millions of dollars winning and dining the physicians who can make or break their products. Drug makers routinely take physicians to dinner, send them on vacations, or get them tickets to the Super Bowl. Although the physicians who accept these gifts claim that they are not influenced by them, this claim seems hard to believe. In fact, according to Dr. John C. Nelson, an obstetrician who is also a spokesperson for the American Medical Association, studies have shown that a doctor is more likely to prescribe a particular drug if its makers have recently taken the doctor to lunch or dinner. Alarmed by the romance between many doctors and the drug makers, Dr. Robert Goodman, an internist, has set up a website called www.nofreelunch.com. Intended for health care providers, the site makes disturbing reading for patients. For example, in a study run by Harvard Medical School, eighty-five doctors were asked questions about two popularly prescribed drugs. The doctors said that their answers were based on academic research. But the study found that 70 percent of the physicians were repeating information found only in the ads created by the drug makers.

1 Which is true according to the passage?

(A) Doctors prescribe drugs based on academic research.
(B) Drug makers go out on a date with many doctors.
(C) Doctors like to go to the Super Bowl with drug makers.
(D) Doctors are important for the sale of drugs.

2 What does the author mean by the underlined "disturbing reading"?

(A) Doctors prescribe drugs based upon the drug makers' ads.
(B) Doctors are aware of the drug makers' importance.
(C) Harvard Medical School has eighty-five doctors.
(D) Dr. Robert Goodman does not provide a free lunch for health care providers.

Passage 7

It's a warm evening in Baghdad and, not for the first time today, filming of "Love Under Occupation"—Iraq's first soap opera since the second Gulf War—has ground to a halt. Once again the culprit is postwar life. The U.S. Army shut down a radical Islamic newspaper a few hours ago and now thousands of angry Shiite Muslims are demonstrating outside. The crew packs its equipment into a battered car.

Kassem al Malak, the rubber-faced actor who is touted as Iraq's answer to comedian Jim Carrey, looks unfazed. Since filming began in February, gun battles and bomb blasts haven't been confined to the script. When al Malak describes acting as a life-and-death job, he doesn't sound like a drama queen.

Before the toppling of Saddam, the mere notion of making an Iraqi soap opera was impossible. Any drama touching on ordinary lives would have had to mention state-sanctioned torture and secret police—subjects that would earn a writer first-hand experience of both.

The few "real-life" dramas produced had very little action. Now it's the opposite. In the first series alone, al Malak's character, Fawzi Nabil, is arrested on suspicion of being a resistance fighter, gets embroiled in a kidnapping, and loses his devoted mother Zakir in a car-bomb attack.

1 Which of the following does the underlined expression the culprit refer to?

(A) The subject of the soap opera "Love Under Occupation"
(B) The background of the drama "Love Under Occupation"
(C) The primary scene of the drama "Love Under Occupation"
(D) The reason for changing the background of "Love Under Occupation"
(E) The cause of stopping filming "Love Under Occupation"

2 According to the passage, which of the following is NOT true of Kassem al Malak?

(A) He is good at acting with his face.
(B) He gives good answers to Jim Carrey.
(C) He is playing Fawzi Nabil in a drama.
(D) His drama mother dies in a car-bomb attack in the drama.
(E) He is praised as a good actor.

3 According to the passage, which of the following is NOT true?

(A) It was impossible to make an Iraqi soap opera under Saddam's regime.
(B) Many Shiite Muslims are protesting against the U.S. Army shutting down a newspaper.
(C) Iraq's postwar dramas are full of action.
(D) The secret police used to be a popular subject of Iraqi dramas.
(E) In Iraq, gun battles and bomb blasts happen in reality as well as in dramas.

Passage 8

The Romance languages of today came originally from Latin, which was the official language of the Roman Empire. As the Empire spread gradually across a great part of Europe, Latin was introduced everywhere as the official language of government and administration. Spoken Latin was consistent from one area to another in the early days of the Empire. But later, when the Empire began to fall apart, the Roman administrators began to disappear. Gradually, the Latin of each region began to develop in its own way. Separated from each other by great distances and naturally influenced by the speech of the local people, each area slowly developed its own distinctive characteristics to the point where separate languages were formed. The modern Romance languages include the national languages: Italian, French, Spanish, Portuguese and Rumanian.

1 글의 제목으로 가장 알맞은 것을 고르시오.

(A) The formation of European nations
(B) The origin of the Romance languages
(C) The construction of the Roman Empire
(D) The introduction of European languages

TEST 21

제한시간 | 35분
정답률 | /22

Passage 1

In the past few years, there has been ① __________ in a type of television programming called "reality TV." As its name suggests, reality TV is about real people in real situations. Unlike traditional television shows, reality TV shows are completely ② <u>unscripted</u>. They allow viewers to watch how real people react in certain situations. Today, about 69 percent of the world's television watching is devoted to reality TV. In fact, some TV situations are completely dedicated to reality TV shows. Whether you are a fan of reality TV or not, it is definitely good business.

1 Which is the most suitable word for blank ①?

(A) an interface
(B) an elimination
(C) a categorization
(D) an explosion

2 Which is the closest in meaning to ② unscripted?

(A) not written down in advance
(B) contest-based
(C) showing real situations only
(D) based on contract

3 Which of the following is true to the passage?

(A) Reality TV shows are often dangerous.
(B) Reality TV shows cost more than traditional TV shows.
(C) Reality TV shows are becoming popular.
(D) Reality TV shows are rehearsed in reality.

Passage 2

From the ancient Greek historian Thucydides to historical scholars of the Enlightenment and the Romantic periods, historians have maintained in different ways a fundamental distinction between objective knowledge about the past and poetic re-inventions of it. In the last quarter of the 20th century, however, (가) this distinction was challenged by a number of writers and thinkers. (나) Taking their cue from French linguistic theories, these writers have argued that since the human mind understood everything through the medium of language, everything could be regarded, in some sense, as a text. Nothing, indeed, could be shown to exist outside texts. Moreover, (다) the language of which texts were composed bore no demonstrable, direct relation to the concepts of the things to which it referred; it took its meaning from the linguistic context around it. Thus for example *chien* no more suggested in itself a meat-eating, social, four-legged, barking animal than did dog or Hund—the word in question was only understood to have such a reference because it formed part of a larger system of words, a language.

1 The best main theme of the passage is ________.

(A) The conflict between historians and linguistic scholars
(B) History as a literary text
(C) Reinvention of myth through language
(D) How to interpret history objectively
(E) Supremacy of the objective knowledge over its poetic reinterpretations

2 The underlined word in (가) means a distinction between ________.

(A) Ancient Greeks and scholars of the Enlightenment and Romantic periods
(B) knowledge and ignorance
(C) past and present
(D) intellect and emotion
(E) fact and fiction

3 The underlined phrase in (나) means ________.

(A) Opposing French linguistic theories
(B) Following French linguistic theories
(C) Giving rise to French linguistic theories
(D) Replacing French linguistic theories
(E) Preceding French linguistic theories

4 **Which of the following best explains the meaning of the underlined sentence in (다)?**

(A) The relationship between language and things is arbitrary
(B) The meanings of things continue to change
(C) The texts which do not demonstrate clear meanings are difficult to interpret
(D) Texts are getting more important than language
(E) There is no direct relationship between language and text

Passage 3

North Americans do not maintain eye contact during a conversation; however, South Americans do. [I] A person from North America usually meets the other person's eyes for a few seconds, looks away, and then back again, but a South American looks directly into the other person's eyes and considers it impolite not to do so. [II] The South American uses many gestures. The North American, however, uses them only occasionally. [III] The North and South American have more in common regarding the distance each maintains from the person he or she is talking with. Unless a close friendship exists, ①__________ stand(s) about two to three feet from one another. [IV] By studying the differences in body language of a group of North and South Americans, we could probably figure out where each person comes from.

1 위 글에서 빈칸 ①에 들어가기에 가장 적절한 것은?

(A) both the North and the South American
(B) the South American but not the North American
(C) either the North or the South American
(D) the North American but not the South American

2 위 글에서 문맥에 맞게 아래 문장이 들어가기에 가장 적절한 것은?

Another difference is the contrast in using hand movements while speaking.

(A) [I]　　(B) [II]
(C) [III]　　(D) [IV]

Passage 4

Washington, D.C. has traditionally been an unbalanced city when it comes to the life of the mind. It has great national landmarks, from the Smithsonian museums, to the Washington Monument, to the Library of Congress. But day-to-day cultural life can be thin.

Washington has a good claim to be America's intellectual capital. [I] It regularly sucks in a giant share of the country's best brains, It is second only to San Francisco for the proportion of residents twenty-five years and older with a bachelor's degree or higher. [II] But far too much of the city's intellectual life is devoted to the minutiae of the political process. [III]

This is changing. On October 1st, 2007 the Shakespeare Theater Company opened a 775-seat theater in the heart of downtown. [IV] This not only provides a new stage for a theatre company that has hitherto had to make do with the 450-seat Lansburgh Theatre around the comer, but it will also provide a platform for a large number of smaller arts companies. [V]

The danger for Washington is that this intellectual and cultural renaissance will leave some citizens untouched. The capital remains a city deeply divided between well-educated white itinerants and under-educated black locals.

1 Which of the following is NOT stated or implied about Washington, D.C. in the passage?

(A) It is second to none in its residents' level of education.
(B) Some residents still may not enjoy cultural activities.
(C) The facilities for day-to-day culture used to be insufficient.
(D) It has a large number of intellectual people.
(E) It has great historic monuments and museums.

2 Which letter [I], [II], [III], [IV], or [V] can be best replaced by the following sentence?

> Dinner table conversation can all too easily turn to the Presidential election, for example, these days.

(A) [I]
(B) [II]
(C) [III]
(D) [IV]
(E) [V]

3 What is the point that the author is trying to make in the underlined sentence?

(A) The budget problem could now be solved.
(B) The cultural renaissance begins with the opening of the 450-seat theater.
(C) The residents now have more chance to enjoy cultural activities in their daily lives.
(D) A large number of smaller arts companies could penetrate into black neighborhoods. c
(E) There is a change in the atmosphere of the conflict between whites and blacks in Washington, D.C. area.

Passage 5

Have you ever flipped a coin to decide whether or not to do something? People have been flipping coins for more than two thousand years.

Julius Caesar began the practice when he was the dictator in ancient Rome. A picture of Caesar's head was printed on one side of every Roman coin. When Caesar flipped a coin and saw his head, that meant the Roman gods gave a "yes" response to a question. If he didn't see his head, the answer was "no."

Romans began flipping coins to help make important decisions. Coin flips helped people know whom to marry, what house to buy, or who was guilty of a crime. Seeing Caesar's head meant the dictator and the Roman gods __________ with a person's decision.

1 빈칸에 들어갈 가장 알맞은 것은?

(A) deluded
(B) agreed
(C) were angry
(D) were not sure

2 위 글의 제목으로 가장 알맞은 것은?

(A) Roman Gods
(B) Life in Ancient Rome
(C) How Coin Flipping Started
(D) The Story of Julius Caesar

Passage 6

Virtuality tends to skew our experience of the real in several ways. First, it makes ____(A)____ and artificial experiences seem real—let's call it the Disneyland effect. After a brunch on Disneyland's Royal Street, a cappuccino at a restaurant chain called Bonjour Caféat an Anaheim shopping mall may seem real by comparison. After playing a video game in which your opponent is a computer program, the social worlds of Multiple User Dungeon (MUDs) may seem real as well. At least real people play most of the parts and the play space is relatively open. One player compares the roles he was able to play on video games and on MUDs. "Nintendo has a good game where you can play four characters. But even though they are very cool," he says, "they are written up for you." They seem artificial. In contrast, on the MUDs, he says, "There is nothing written up." He says he feels free. MUDs are "for real" because ____(B)____.

Another effect of simulation might be thought of as the (a) artificial crocodile effect. In The Future Does Not Compute: Warnings from the Internet, Stephen L. Talbott quotes educators who say that years of exciting nature programming have ____(C)____ wildlife experiences for children. The animals in the woods are unlikely to perform as dramatically as those captured on the camera. I have a clear memory of a Brownie Scout field trip to the Brooklyn Botanical Gardens where I asked an attendant if she could make the flowers open fast. For a long while, no one understood what I was talking about. Then they figured it out: I was hoping that the attendant could make the flowers behave as they did in the time-lapse photography I had seen in Disney films.

1 Identify the word that best fills in (A).

(A) ordinary
(B) denatured
(C) accustomed
(D) quotidian

2 Find the sentence among the following that best explains the meaning of (a) the artificial crocodile effect.

(A) The fake, like the artificial crocodile, seems more compelling than the real.
(B) Simulation tends to help children get used to wildlife experiences.
(C) Virtuality makes children not afraid of the real as much as the fake.
(D) Like the artificial crocodile, simulation desensitizes children's fear of wildlife.

3 Find the phrase that best fills in (B).

(A) they are not spontaneous
(B) you make them up yourself
(C) they are more realistic than video games
(D) nothing could arise that hadn't already been factored

4 **Find the word(s) that best fills in (C).**

(A) come to an understanding
(B) compromised
(C) brought into disrepute
(D) stroke a balance

5 **Find a phrase that is most appropriate as a title for the passage.**

(A) The Disney Effect
(B) Virtuality and Its Discontents
(C) The Economy of Virtuality
(D) The Loss of the Real

Passage 7

Most households now own two cars, and quite a few own three or four. Sometimes that is necessary—if there are two wage-earners, for example, and both have to commute by car because no other options are available. But if you want the extra car only because it will be a little more convenient, stop and consider two things. First, the mere purchase of a car harms the environment because it encourages the manufacturing of more automobiles. When you picture that new car in your driveway, imagine instead the four tons of carbon and nearly 700 pounds of ordinary pollutants pumped into the atmosphere as a result of its manufacture. Second, not having an extra car will discourage you from making unnecessary car trips and force you to make more effective use of the car you have. This suggestion is a bit like advising a smoker who is trying to quit to keep cigarettes out of the house, or a dieter to buy no sweets. Without that care always at hand, you just might find yourself doubling up with your spouse on trips to the store, hitching rides with friends, perhaps even bicycling or walking.

1 **You may buy an extra car if ________.**

(A) you want to make extra trips to the store
(B) you want to ride with your spouse
(C) your spouse needs it for his or her trip to work
(D) your spouse needs it to carry the four tons of carbon

2 **What benefits are NOT there for not having an extra car?**

(A) you may become healthier
(B) you may have a better relationship with friends
(C) you may spend more time with your spouse
(D) you may encourage car makers to produce more cars

Passage 8

Gift cards are America's most popular present. Retailers like them because they are profitable. But like most goods in the recession, they have become harder to sell, prompting some radical redesigns. Gift cards are profitable because retailers receive money for them up front, and around 10% of them are never redeemed. When people do use them, they often spend more than the amount given, and on products with high margins. But sales of gift cards were down by around 6% last year in America, to about $25 billion, partly because discounts in stores were so steep that customers saw more value in buying merchandise directly. Bankruptcies among retailers also scared people away from gift cards, for fear that stores would not be around to honour them. Some financial-services companies that offer gift cards which can be used in various stores came under fire for charging monthly maintenance fees on unspent balances.

1 According to the passage, which is true?

(A) Big discount in stores made gift cards less popular.
(B) Gift cards will continue to be the most popular present in America.
(C) Retailers do not like gift cards because of high maintenance fees.
(D) Gift cards can be redeemed regardless of the bankruptcies of retailers.

TEST 22

제한시간 | 35분
정답률 | /18

Passage 1

Research studies have shown that high-achieving people are able to envision a detailed, three-dimensional picture of their future in which their goals and aspirations are clearly inscribed. In addition, they are able to construct a mental plan that includes the sequence of steps they will have to take, the amount of time each step will involve, and strategies for overcoming the obstacles they are likely to encounter. Such realistic and compelling concepts of the future enable these people to make sacrifices in the present to achieve their long-term goals. Of course, they may modify these goals as circumstances change and they acquire more information, but ______________________________.

1 밑줄 친 빈칸에 들어갈 내용으로 가장 적절한 것은?

(A) they need to develop an in-depth understanding of themselves
(B) they retain a well-defined flexible plan that charts their life course
(C) they have to make sure that the goals reflect their past and present
(D) they will have difficulty in identifying the most appropriate goals themselves

Passage 2

A writing system is a type of symbolic system used to represent elements or statements expressible in language. Writing systems are distinguished from other possible symbolic communication systems in that one must usually understand something of the associated language to comprehend the text. By contrast, other possible symbolic systems such as information signs, painting, maps, and mathematics often do not require prior knowledge of a spoken language. Every human community possesses language, a feature regarded by many as an innate and defining condition of humankind. However, the development and adoption of writing systems have occurred only sporadically. Once established, writing systems on the whole change more slowly than their spoken counterparts, and often preserve features and expressions which are no longer current in the spoken language. The great benefit of writing systems is their ability to maintain a persistent record of information expressed in a language, which can be retrieved independently of the initial act of formulation. All writing systems require the following things. First, a set of defined base elements or symbols, (①) termed characters or graphemes, and (②)

called a script. Second, a set of rules and conventions understood and shared by a community, which arbitrarily assign meaning to be base elements, their ordering, and relations to one another. Next, a language (generally a spoken language) whose constructions are represented and able to be recalled by the interpretation of these elements and rules. Last, some physical means of distinctly representing the symbols by application to a permanent or semi-permanent medium, so they may be interpreted.

1 In which of the following would you most likely find this passage?

(A) A writing manual
(B) An encyclopedia
(C) An autobiography
(D) A personal diary

2 According to the passage, which of the following statements is true?

(A) All writing systems require prior knowledge of a spoken counterpart.
(B) All human communities possess their own writing systems in different forms.
(C) A writing system is the only symbolic system available to humans.
(D) Information expressed in a written language can be preserved only for a very limited time.

3 Which of the following would fit best in ① and ②?

(A) collectively—cumulatively
(B) individually—discretely
(C) cumulatively—alternatively
(D) individually—collectively

Passage 3

Experiments have shown that relaxing before a learning session positively affects the results. When you take a few minutes to relax deeply, your brain waves slow down. When we experience alpha, or slower, waves, our mind is better able to focus because it's less distracted by muscle tension or irrelevant thoughts. Relaxation also appears to allow the two sides of our brain-the logical, linear left brain and the creative, holistic right brain-to work together. All in all, alpha waves seem to tune up our brains for increased mental performance.

1 글의 주제로 가장 적절한 것을 고르시오.

(A) Brain Waves and Learning
(B) Relaxation and Brain Waves
(C) Brain Waves and Mental Processes
(D) Effects of Relaxing on Mental Performance

Passage 4

Textbooks for primary school students have been accused of containing illustrations that could create a gender bias. Male characters appear about 30 percent ① __________ girls in textbook illustrations and are portrayed as main characters according to a paper coauthored by Prof Kwon Chi-soon of Seoul National University of Education and Kim Kyung-hee, a teacher at Euncheon Elementary School in Seoul.

"Male characters play important roles in many cases while female characters often play passive roles," the research team said in the paper. "Children are ② vulnerable to the biased role models and textbook writers have to remove those sexual stereotypes."

The paper said men are depicted as a president, polttician, judge, doctor, and university professor, while women appear as a teacher, nurse, and bank teller. Male characters play the main roles about 60 percent ③ __________ their counterparts in textbooks, it said.

1 빈칸 ①과 ③에 공통으로 들어갈 표현으로 적당한 것은?

(A) more often than
(B) more rarely than
(C) less rarely than
(D) less often than

2 밑줄 친 ②와 바꾸어 쓸 수 있는 말은?

(A) imperceptive
(B) opposed
(C) susceptible
(D) adamant

Passage 5

Henri Matisse and Marc Chagall were both famous artists. The two men painted in France in the early twentieth century. Their paintings influenced many other artists of their time.

Henri Matisse was born in a small town in France in 1869. He grew up in a wealthy family and showed no early interest in art. Then, while recovering from a surgery in 1890, he began to pass the time by painting. From then on, he considered himself a painter.

In his paintings, Matisse used color in a way that no artist had before. His bold and unusual use of color let the viewer see the world in a new way. When he grew ill and could no longer paint, Matisse did not give up being an artist. He cut out large and colorful paper shapes and arranged them on a canvas. In this way, he was able to create beautiful art until the end of his life.

Marc Chagall was born in a small Russian town in 1887. His family was poor, but young Chagall begged his parents to let him study art. After working for some time as an artist, Chagall decided to go to Paris. He studied and worked there for four years before returning to Russia, where he met and married his wife. Eventually, he moved his family to Paris, where he stayed for most of his remaining years. His later work included murals and stained-glass windows.

Chagall's paintings reminds people of scenes they might see in a dream. Animals and people float in the air. Wonderfully unusual colors add to the dream-like quality. Chagall used ideas from Russian fairy tales and Jewish folk tales in many of his works.

Matisse and Chagall each used art and color to show ideas in new and unusual ways. Today their paintings hang in fine museums all over the world. Along with artists like Monet and Picasso, they are considered pioneers of modern art.

1 What is common between Matisse and Chagall?

(A) Both lived in Russia and moved to Paris.
(B) Both came from wealthy families.
(C) Both painted dream-like scenes all their lives.
(D) Both painted in France in the early twentieth century.

2 What similarities do Chagall's paintings have with those of Matisse?

(A) They include fairy tale scenes.
(B) They present colors in unusual ways.
(C) They are mostly portraits.
(D) They are made of cut-out shapes.

3 What did young Matisse and young Chagall have in common?

(A) Both had large families.
(B) Both grew up in a small town.
(C) Both had an early interest in art.
(D) Both grew up in France.

4 How did Chagall and Matisse differ toward the end of their lives?

(A) Matisse made cut-outs, while Chagall created murals.
(B) Matisse painted fairy tale scenes, while Chagall painted portraits.
(C) Matisse worked in France, while Chagall worked in Russia.
(D) Matisse discovered the effect of black and white, while Chagall used bolder color.

5 **According to the author, what do Matisse and Chagall have in common with Monet and Picasso?**

(A) They all painted until the end of their lives.
(B) They all stopped painting to work on other types of art.
(C) They were all pioneers of modern art.
(D) They all discovered a love for art early in their lives.

Passage 6

As boys, we are taught that masculinity and a concern for style are incompatible. Fashion is the domain of the woman, and too early an immersion in it might put us on the path to becoming sissies. This idea is hammered into us by our fathers and friends throughout childhood and adolescence, typically until we reach our early twenties. Then, an abrupt and complete reversal in philosophy is thrust upon us. Suddenly, "image is everything," "shoes make the man," and "women love a well-dressed man." We set out on a scrambled shopping trips to get ourselves up to date, but, with no acquired style savvy to steer us, we mistakenly let ourselves be guided only by price tags and our favorite colors. The unhappy result? A generation of men that spends too much money on clothes that don't look good on them.

Clearly, this is not a sustainable state of affairs. We need to remedy it. Now we're not about to suggest that men set about raising their sons differently, because we think we're generally doing a good job at that. What we will do, however, is provide males with the information that they need to make it through that troubling transition from not knowing how to dress to knowing how to dress.

1 **The passage is most likely to appear in a book on ________.**

(A) tips for men's style
(B) tips for finding a perfect date
(C) tips for counseling adolescents
(D) tips for becoming a smart shopper

2 **What does the underlined part mean?**

(A) We want to look more masculine.
(B) We become interested in styling ourselves.
(C) We try to save money and impress women.
(D) We begin to realize problems in raising boys.

Passage 7

The new reluctance to punish by killing is part of a historical trend. There was a time when death and torture were spectator sports, when crowds flocked to see prisoners drawn and quartered or beheaded. In some parts of the world, flogging and stoning are still public spectacles. But in the 19th century, supposedly "enlightened" states began looking for more humane ways to serve final justice to kill people without causing too much suffering to either the victims or their executioners. The authorities tried hanging, firing squads, electrocutions, gas chambers, and, more recently, lethal injection. Each method was supposed to be an improvement over the last. ① <u>But the results could be ghastly. Too much depended on the uneven skills of the executioners.</u>

Jurors and prosecutors are steering away from the death penalty because they are both more and less afraid: more apprehensive about killing the innocent and less fearful of crime. As crime rates fell in the 1990s and the first few years of the new century, jurors became more lenient in capital cases. At the same time, prosecutors began to be wary of seeking the death penalty. With legal costs soaring in death cases, states are finding it cheaper to pay for lifetime prison sentences. There may be no such thing as a foolproof system for killing people fairly and painlessly. The smallest glitch can make too much of a difference.

1 위 글의 내용과 가장 거리가 <u>먼</u> 것은?

(A) 배심원들과 검사들은 사형선고를 기피하는 경향이 있다.
(B) 독극물 주입은 가스실 이용보다 비인간적인 처형방식이다.
(C) 군중이 보는 앞에서 태형과 투석형을 시행하는 나라가 있다.
(D) 지난 세기 말 이래로 범죄율이 하락하는 경향이 있다.

2 밑줄 친 ①의 예가 될 수 <u>없는</u> 것은?

(A) lethal injection: Hands shaking, guards sometimes botch inserting the needle, and veins can be hard to find if the inmate was a drug addict.
(B) lethal injection: In Ohio, a prisoner raised his hand to announce, "It's not working."
(C) hanging: Too short a drop and the prisoner slowly strangles: too long a drop and the prisoner can be decapitated.
(D) gas chamber: Today many doctors are willing to play any part in an execution for the law and order of society.

Passage 8

Last week I went to dinner with an eligible doctor. As we were finishing the main course, I struck up conversation with the owner (Marco) in Italian—I speak five languages. My date nearly choked on his linguini and spent the rest of the date mute. I had committed the worst dating faux pas: I had outshone my suitor. Yet it would seem I am not the only woman who is wondering whether it is time to hang up her brain. In America, research shows that successful women are hiding their accomplishments for fear that their academic achievements and financial kudos will scare off potential suitors.

1 Which of the following is true?

(A) My date did not like Italian food.
(B) Marco was smarter than my date.
(C) It turned out that my date was not a doctor.
(D) My date was a kind of man who does not like a smart woman.

2 My mistake was that ________.

(A) I talked too much
(B) I acted in a rude manner
(C) I spoke in Italian
(D) I forgot the fact that my date was a doctor

TEST 23

제한시간 | 35분
정답률 | /19

Passage 1

Many mathematicians play chess, but few excel at it. While creating mathematics and playing chess may require the same kind of thinking, the pace is different. In his work a mathematician can correct his errors upon reflection; in a game he must commit himself quickly and irrevocably, and mathematicians are not exceptionally good at snap decisions. A few mathematicians have exceptional spatial visualization and computational skills. Some have an intuitive feeling for the relationship, for example, between a five-dimensional object and a seven-dimensional space that surround it. And some even have the ability to solve long and complicated problems in their head. As a rule, however, mathematicians cannot do arithmetic as rapidly as accountants.

1 글의 내용으로 보아 수학자들이 체스를 잘하지 못하는 이유로 가장 적절한 것은?

(A) their highly developed intuitive faculty
(B) llieir unwillingness to correct their mistakes
(C) their focus on spacial visualization
(D) their weakness in making prompt decisions

Passage 2

Among the most widespread myths shared by college students is that charm, the social graces, and campus activities will be more important to the first employer after college than any other single fact, such as grades. Another myth suggests that there is a significant connection between the courses we take in college and employment. Facts explode both of these myths. The most concrete information we have relating to college achievement and job performance is the now famous Bell Telephone Study of 1962. Bell examined the careers of 17,000 of its employees. Success with the company was checked against the employees' academic performance, extracurricular activities, as well as which college they attended. Academic excellence closely correlated to success with Bell Telephone. ① Those who had ranked high in their classes were found to be receiving the highest salaries at Bell. It was also found that two thirds of all college graduates are in afield completely different from that for which they thought they were preparing in college.

1 위 글의 제목으로 가장 적절한 것은?

(A) The Myths of High Paying Careers
(B) How to Choose One's Major Wisely
(C) Hiring Practices of the Bell Telephone Company
(D) The Truth behind Employment and College Education

2 다음 중 밑줄 친 ①이 반박하고자 하는 통념은?

(A) Campus club activities are detrimental to one's job search.
(B) College education is essential to procure employment.
(C) Grades are not as important as one's personality.
(D) One's college major determines the nature of one's job.

Passage 3

Historical criticism seeks to understand a literary work by investigating the social, cultural, and intellectual context that produced it—a context that necessarily includes the artist's biography and milieu. Historical critics are less concerned with explaining a work's literary significance for today's readers than with helping us understand the work by re-creating, as nearly as possible, the exact meaning and impact it had on its original audience. A historical reading of a literary work begins by exploring the possible ways in which the meaning of the text has changed over time. Reading ancient literature, no one doubts the value of historical criticism. There have been so many social, cultural, and linguistic changes that some older texts are incomprehensible without scholarly assistance. But historical criticism can even help one better understand modern texts. To return to Weldon's Kee's "For My Daughter" for example, one learns a great deal by considering two rudimentary historical facts—the year in which the poem was first published (1940, when war had broken out in Europe, and America was recovering from the Depression) and the nationality of its author (American)—and then asking how this information has shaped the meaning of the poem. Even this simple historical analysis helps explain at least part of the pessimism of Kee's poem, though a psychological critic would rightly insist that Kee's personality also played a crucial role. Thus, in writing a paper on a poem, you might explore __________.

1 According to the context of the passage, which of the following fits best in the blank?

(A) how the time and place of its creation affect its meaning
(B) what is the only way to explain an author's historical intentions
(C) whether or not linguistic changes in texts are of literary value
(D) why an author decides to have an impact on his or her readers

2 **According to the passage, which of the following statements is true regarding historical criticism?**

(A) Many scholars have expressed serious doubts about its usefulness.
(B) It necessarily includes among other things the understanding of an author's setting.
(C) Older texts have a tendency to become more intelligible with the passage of time.
(D) It is designed to analyze the impact of literature on modern readers.

3 **According to the passage, which of the following statements is the most likely explanation for the pessimism of Kee's poem?**

(A) It was about the daughter he loved the most.
(B) It was issued during World War II.
(C) It was one of his most popular poems.
(D) It was written before the Depression.

Passage 4

Most people are astonished to learn that there are real, stable differences in personality between conservatives and liberals—not just different views or values, but underlying differences in temperament. NYU professor John Jost has demonstrated that conservatives and liberals boast markedly different home and office decor. Liberals are messier than conservatives, their rooms have more clutter and more color, and they tend to have more travel documents, maps of other countries, and flags from around the world. Conservatives are neater, and their rooms are cleaner, better organized, more brightly lit, and more conventional. Liberals have more books, and their books cover a greater variety of topics. And that's just a start. Multiple studies find that liberals are more optimistic. Conservatives are more likely to be religious. Liberals are more likely to like classical music and jazz, conservatives, country music. Liberals are more likely to enjoy abstract art. Conservative men are more likely than liberal men to prefer conventional forms of entertainment like TV and talk radio. Liberal men like romantic comedies more than conservative men. Liberal women are more likely than conservative women to enjoy books, poetry, writing in a diary, acting, and playing musical instruments.

Personality differences between liberals and conservatives are evident in early childhood. In 1969, Berkeley professors Jack and Jeanne Block embarked on a study of childhood personality, asking nursery school teachers to rate children's temperaments. They weren't even thinking about political orientation.

Twenty years later, they decided to compare the subjects' childhood personalities with their political preferences as adults. They found arresting patterns. As kids, liberals had developed close relationships with peers and were rated by their teachers as self-reliant, energetic, impulsive, and resilient. People who were conservative at age 23 had been described by their teachers as easily victimized, easily offended, indecisive, fearful, rigid, inhibited, and vulnerable at age 3.

1 According to the passage, which of the following statements is true?

(A) Conservatives tend to be more untraditional and decisive than liberals.
(B) Liberals tend to be more methodical and inflexible than conservatives.
(C) Conservatives tend to be more pessimistic and well-groomed than liberals.
(D) Liberals tend to be more spiritual and dependent than conservatives.

2 Which of the following statements could be inferred from the last paragraph of this passage?

(A) Insecure kids, because they needed the reassurance of authority, got involved in conservative politics.
(B) Disobedient kids, because they rebelled against their parents, joined liberal political organizations in a search for companionship.
(C) Stable kids, because they felt most comfortable with their peers, tended to avoid involvement in party politics after they grew up.
(D) Independent kids, because they were encouraged by their nursery school teachers, were reluctant to participate in liberal political crusades.

3 John Jost and the Blocks are most likely to be which of the following?

(A) linguists
(B) psychologists
(C) economists
(D) political scientists

Passage 5

Seeds of Peace takes up where governments leave off, attempting to fulfill the hope of peace treaties that are signed but that remain essentially pieces of paper. Seeds of Peace carries out a task that governments are neither equipped for nor very interested in: transforming the hopes for peace into a new reality on the ground among populations that have been taught for decades to distrust and hate one another. The program fosters education, discussion, and emotional growth through both competitive and cooperative activities and emphasizes the importance of developing non-violent mechanisms of resolving conflict. In the three years of its operation, over three hundred male and female teenagers have come from Israel, Palestine, Egypt, Jordan, Morocco, and, for the first time last summer, from Serbia and Bosnia-Herzegovina. Campers are selected in a competitive process; the only prerequisite is that they must have a working knowledge of English. Initially each candidate is recommended by his or her school and then asked to write an essay on the following subject: "Why I want to Make Peace with the Enemy." The final step of the selection process is a personal interview. Candidates are awarded extra points if they demonstrate skill in speaking English. Points are also awarded to children from refugee camps or other underprivileged backgrounds.

1 What is "Seeds of Peace"?

(A) It is a language program that teaches English to teenagers from conflicting countries.

(B) It is a summer camp program that fosters communication among teenagers from conflicting countries.

(C) It is a camp program that carries out a governmental task to transform the hopes for peace into reality.

(D) It is a writing program that helps teenagers from conflicting countries write good essays on world peace.

2 What is the most important qualifications to be admitted to Seeds of Peace?

(A) He or she knows English.

(B) He or she has lived in a refugee camp.

(C) He or she has written on essay on world peace.

(D) He or she has a recommendation from his or her school.

Passage 6

In the United States, there are more women in the work force at higher levels than in any other country in the world—and they still make less than their male counterparts. In Sweden, women's wages are high, but their role in the work force remains relatively traditional. In Germany, maternal leave is generous, but many women drop out of the work force once they have children. In Japan, the gap is not just in wages but also in the basic structure of the way men and women are employed.

In good times and in bad, women's wages have become an increasingly important component of household income and consumer spending. The shift toward service-based economies in the industrialized world has favored women in the work force—one reason they have poured into the labor market over the past three decades.

But what they find ① ________ they get there differs considerably throughout the developed world. That has less to do with gender politics than it does with macroeconomics, and it results in women still being paid less than men in most places and for most jobs. The reasons for this persistent ② ________ are complex, and they vary with geography.

TEST 23

1 Which of the following fits best in blank ①?

(A) because
(B) once
(C) unless
(D) until

2 According to the passage, which of the following statements is NOT correct?

(A) Gender equality in wages has yet to be achieved even in the developed world.
(B) Female earning power is the main cause of generous leaves for child-bearing women.
(C) The gender wage gap is more a matter of economics than of gender politics.
(D) The shift toward service-based economies has benefited job hunting for women.

3 Which of the following fits best in blank ②?

(A) inequity
(B) satisfaction
(C) misunderstanding
(D) harmony

Passage 7

In its battle against the financial crisis, the U.S. government has extended its full faith and credit to an ever-growing swath* of the private sector: first homeowners, then banks, now car companies. Soon, Barack Obama will put the government credit card to work with a massive fiscal boost for the economy. Necessary as these steps are, they raise a worry of their own: Can the United States pay the money back?

The notion seems absurd: Banana republics** default, not the world's biggest, richest economy, right? The United States has unparalleled wealth, a stable legal tradition, responsible macroeconomic policies and a top-notch, triple-A credit rating. U.S. Treasury bonds are routinely called "risk-free," and the United States has the unique privilege of borrowing in the currency that other countries like to hold as foreign exchange reserves.

Yes, default is unlikely. But it is no longer ① __________. Thanks to the advent of credit derivatives—financial contracts that allow investors to speculate on or protect against default—we can now observe how likely global markets think it is that Uncle Sam will ② renege on America's mounting debts. Last week, markets pegged the probabilities of a U.S. default at 6 percent over the next 10 years, compared with just 1 percent a year ago. For technical reasons, this is not a precise reading of investors' views. ③ __________, the trend is real, and it is grounded in some fundamental concerns.

*swath: strip, belt

**Banana republic: a pejorative term for a country with a primitive economy and sometimes a puppet state of a major power

1 위 글의 내용과 일치하지 않는 것은?

(A) 미국은 세계에서 경제규모가 가장 크다.
(B) 미국의 법제도는 안정적이다.
(C) 미국경제의 신용도는 매우 높다.
(D) 미국의 대외 부채 상환율은 증가하는 추세이다.

2 문맥상 빈칸 ①에 들어갈 표현으로 알맞은 것은?

(A) feasible
(B) unthinkable
(C) realistic
(D) constant

3 ② renege와 바꾸어 쓸 수 있는 말을 본문 중에서 고른다면?

(A) default
(B) battle
(C) hold.
(D) speculate

4 글의 흐름상 빈칸 ③에 들어갈 표현으로 알맞은 것은?

(A) Because
(B) Therefore
(C) And
(D) Nonetheless

Passage 8

Yesterday, residents were urged to evacuate about 250 homes, and about 300 guests had to leave a resort hotel as the wind drove the fire downhill into Ventana Canyon. Ventana Canyon is in the foothills of the Santa Catalina Mountains, where the fire has raged since June 18. It has blackened about 85,000 acres. The fire destroyed 415 homes last month in and around the mountaintop vacation hamlet on Mount Lemmon. It skirted fire lines last week and burned a handful of cabins in Willow Canyon. However, a change in weather calmed a wildfire burning about a half-mile from an exclusive desert neighborhood today, greatly reducing the danger to dozens of homes. Relatively high humidity of 30 to 50 percent extinguished flames in some areas above the homes in Ventana Canyon and cooled the fire in others. Still, fire officials said that flare-ups were possible.

TEST 23

1 **Which of the following is CORRECT about the passage?**

(A) Fire burned many cabins in Ventana Canyon.
(B) Rain extinguished fire in a desert neighborhood.
(C) High humidity in the air helped weaken wildfire.
(D) The Ventana Canyon is always closed to the public.

TEST 24

제한시간 | 35분
정답률 | /23

Passage 1

Anorexia nervosa literally means "loss of appetite for nervous reasons." It is characterized by weight loss. However, anorexia nervosa sufferers have not lost their appetite. They have lost weight because they are suppressing their urge to eat. Most anorexia sufferers cannot easily suppress the feeling that they are fat or at risk of becoming fat if they fail to keep their eating in control. Such feelings are usually quite (A) their actual weight. This is referred to as having a distorted body image. There is also a strong cultural component. Anorexia nervosa is more common in Western post-industrialized nations, and, in the United States, whites are more affected than African Americans or Hispanic Americans. While the culture of thinness in which we live is certainly an influential factor in the development of anorexia, it is by no means the sole cause. Anorexia is a response to a complex mix of cultural, social, familial, psychological and biological influences unique to each person. Some possibilities are discussed below. One (B) plausible theory is that people develop anorexia because they seek control over themselves and their lives. Food and weight can be controlled when other aspects of life cannot. Restricting food intake while in the presence of enticing foods (C) feelings of accomplishment. A high Percentage of People struggling with anorexia have a history of abuse, neglect, or other traumatic experiences, and develop anorexia as a coping mechanism. Losing weight provides a concrete way to cope with difficult circumstances because it serves to distract the sufferer from the pain. The following two features seem to be characteristic of many sufferers. First, most have low self-esteem. The second feature is that they find it difficult to deal openly with problematic emotions. This may have something to do with their personality. For instance, they may be obsessional and perfectionist. In general, eating disorders seem to arise in the midst of the difficult business of growing up and developing as a person.

1 Which of the following is the best title for the passage?

(A) Food and Anorexia Nervosa
(B) Emotional Aspects of Anorexia Nervosa
(C) Causes and Symptoms of Anorexia Nervosa
(D) Influence of the Culture of Thinness on Nervosa Anorexia

2 Which of the following best fits into (A) and (C)?

	(A)	(C)
(A)	free from	prohibits
(B)	irrelevant to	controls
(C)	dependent on	provokes
(D)	independent of	evokes

3 Which is closest in meaning to (B)?

(A) feasible
(B) incredible
(C) valuable
(D) comparable

4 According to the passage, which of the following statements is NOT true?

(A) Anorexia nervosa sufferers have doubts about their own worth and competence.
(B) People suffering from anorexia nervosa gain a sense of accomplishment by controlling their eating.
(C) Anorexia nervosa is more common in the developing countries than in advanced technological societies.
(D) Anorexia nervosa helps the sufferers forget about pain-filled experience and survive.

Passage 2

Few people over the age of 10 would list "Happy Birthday" among their favorite songs. But Harvey Alter, now 62, has a special fondness for it. It helped teach him how to talk. One morning in June 2003, Alter, then a self-employed criminologist, was putting a leash on his dog, Sam, in preparation for a walk when suddenly he felt dizzy and disoriented. "My thoughts were intertwined, not making sense," he said in a recent interview. "I knew I was having a stroke." At St. Vincent's Hospital, doctors diagnosed an ischemic stroke, caused by a blockage in blood flow to part of the left half of his brain. As a result, the right side of his body was temporarily paralyzed, the right side of his face drooped and he had trouble coming up with the right words and stringing them into sentences—a condition called aphasia. Within hours of his stroke, Alter met with Loni Burke, a speech therapist. At first he was completely nonverbal; within a few days he could say small words. "Mostly, he said, 'No,'" Burke recalled, "because he was frustrated that he couldn't speak." After two years of painstaking therapy, Alter's paralysis had mostly disappeared and his smile was back to normal. But while he could communicate through small words and the help of a chalkboard, complex verbal communication remained elusive. Using standard speech therapy techniques like reviewing lists of numbers and the days of the week, Burke helped her patient piece together short phrases. But they came slowly and sounded robotic. Then one day, she asked him to sing. "How can I ever sing? I can't talk," Alter recalled thinking. But as soon as Burke began to sing "Happy Birthday," he chimed in. "It sounded good," he said. "Almost like I didn't have anything wrong." The technique, called melodic intonation therapy, was developed in 1973 by Dr. Martin Albert and colleagues at the Boston Veterans Affairs Hospital. The aim was to help patients with damage to Broca's area—the speaking center of the brain, located in its left hemisphere. These patients still had relatively healthy right hemispheres. And while the left hemisphere is largely responsible for speaking, the right hemisphere is used in understanding language, as well as processing melodies and rhythms.

1 Which of the following cannot be inferred from the paragraph?

(A) The damage to Broca's area is related to the paralysis of human body's right part.
(B) The memory loss of linguistic elements is caused by the damage to the left part of human brain.
(C) Melodic intonation therapy is effective on the patients with the body of which the left part is paralyzed by stroke.
(D) The failure in combining phrases into sentences is caused by the damage to Broca's area.

2 Which of the following is CORRECT about the paragraph?

(A) Harvey Alter had damage to the left part of his body.
(B) When Harvey Alter first met his speech therapist, he could speak complex sentences.
(C) Harvey Alter could communicate through full and complex sentences when his paralysis had mostly disappeared.
(D) The function for language faculty in human brain is not totally localized to the left hemisphere of the brain.

Passage 3

Language is our most flexible and most sophisticated medium of expression, but everyone has felt, at one time or another, that it has its limitations. It is accurate enough to convey only the most commonplace distinctions. We have a word, "green" for describing the color of a leaf, and we are able to distinguish between light green, dark green, and a certain number of other shades. But a green leaf that is in the shadow has a very different appearance from one that is in sunlight. Yet our language provides no easy and familiar way of communicating this distinction. (가) __________, we have an extraordinary wealth of words for sounds, such as quaver, rattle, bump, squeak, and splash; but there is no one expression for the phenomenon of a single loud sound followed by gradually diminishing overtones that is heard when a gong or a piano-key is struck. These deficiencies do not reflect the inadequacy of language. They are simply consequences of a fact with which everyone is familiar, the fact that even the most ordinary experience is far more complicated than language can possibly be.

1 빈칸 (가)에 들어갈 가장 알맞은 것은?

(A) Similarly
(B) Strangely
(C) Respectively
(D) Unexpectedly

2 위 글의 제목으로 가장 알맞은 것은?

(A) Limitations of Language
(B) Translation of Language
(C) Various Kinds of Language
(D) Diverse Ways of Expression

3 위 글의 내용과 일치하는 것은?

(A) 경험은 언어보다 복잡하다.
(B) 언어는 부적합한 표현 수단이다.
(C) 문학을 통해서만 섬세한 표현이 가능하다.
(D) 우리는 언어의 유용성을 의식하지 못한다.

Passage 4

Contrary to the image of rolling sand dunes and scorching heat, deserts are much more diverse than most people envision. In addition to the blazing hot temperatures of popular imagination, there are also vast, icy stretches of land known as cold deserts, and though hot deserts and cold deserts are different in some respects, they are similar in ways related to climactic patterns. The climactic differences between hot deserts and cold deserts are obvious from their names. Without cloud cover or water to moderate temperatures, hot deserts can reach up to 120°F during the day. The Sahara:, the largest hot desert in the world, holds the record for the hottest daytime temperature ever recorded at 135°F. ________, the highest average temperature in the wannest month in the Antarctic Desert is 20°F. Although their temperatures are extreme opposites, all desert regions are defined by the same factor, which is their lack of precipitation. The lack of rain in deserts is caused by either of two phenomena: rain shadow or extreme distance from a source of moisture. A rain shadow is created when air masses lose all their moisture as they travel over mountains, leaving no precipitation for the areas on the other side of the mountain. The Antarctic Desert, the largest desert in the world, amazingly receives less than ten millimeters of precipitation per year. Combined with high altitude, precipitation is sparse in Antarctica because weather fronts do not reach inland.

1 According to the passage, what is NOT a reason for the lack of rain or snow in deserts?

(A) Moisture is deposited on one side of a mountain.
(B) Weather fronts do not arrive at certain parts of the continent.
(C) Moist air masses evaporate when they reach desert regions.
(D) The source of the rainwater is very far away.

2 The writer mentions the average temperature in Antarctic in order to ________.

(A) support the claim that hot deserts and cold deserts have nothing in common
(B) recognize the cold temperatures in the desert on the continent of Antarctica
(C) assert that cold deserts have more extreme weather than hot deserts
(D) illustrate the stark differences in temperature between hot and cold deserts

3 Choose the answer which is most appropriate for the blank.

(A) Meanwhile
(B) Therefore
(C) Moreover
(D) Otherwise

Passage 5

A style of singing in Tuva, known as "throat" singing, but, more precisely called overtone singing—the ability to single out and control overtones, phrasing them two or more at a time—finally became known outside of this remote region at the dawn of the 1990s. While everyone has natural harmonics in his or her voice, the Tuvans were able to focus on one of these harmonics, or overtones, create a drone with one overtone and then, vocally, grab a higher pitch, which shapes a melody on top, allowing them to sing duets with themselves. Tuvans divide various overtone styles into three major types, all of which use nature to describe the sounds. Sygyt, for example, is simply an imitation of singing birds or gentle breezes. Xoomei tends to suggest stronger winds, while Kargyraa portends storms. No doubt, people this connected to nature realized that in the birds and rivers and rocks were the spirits. Overtone singing, then, was used __________. There are mountains in the region that make sounds by holding winds before releasing them into the valleys below. Rivers also create sound patterns that vary according to the rocks they hit; supposedly, their sounds contain the origins of overtone singing.

TEST 24

1 Choose the one the best fills in the blank.

(A) shamanically
(B) therapeutically
(C) apocalyptically
(D) prophetically

2 Which of the following CANNOT be inferred from the passage?

(A) In overtone singing, two sounds are simultaneously made like in a duet.
(B) According to the Tuvans, overtone singing stems from the sounds of nature.
(C) The three Tuvans overtone styles have differing degrees of intensity.
(D) The Tuvans have differently shaped vocal cords than other peoples.

Passage 6

The fact is that recent economic numbers have been terrifying, not just in the U.S., but around the world. Manufacturing, in particular, is plunging everywhere. Banks aren't lending; businesses and consumers aren't spending. Let's not mince words: This looks an awful lot like the beginning of a second Great Depression.

We weren't supposed to find ourselves in this situation. For many years most economists believed that preventing another Great Depression would be easy. In 2003, Robert Lucas of the University of Chicago, in his presidential address to the American Economic Association, declared that the "central problem of depression-prevention has been solved, for all practical purposes, and has in fact been solved for many decades." Milton Friedman, in particular, persuaded many economists that the Federal Reserve could have stopped the Depression in its tracks simply by providing banks with more liquidity, which would have prevented a sharp fall in the money supply. Ben Bernanke, the Federal Reserve chairman, famously apologized to Friedman on his institution's behalf: "You're right. We did it. We're very sorry. But thanks to you, we won't do it again."

It turns out, however, that preventing depressions isn't that easy after all. Under Mr. Bernanke's leadership, the Fed has been supplying liquidity like an engine crew trying to put out a five-alarm fire, and the money supply has been rising rapidly. Yet credit remains scarce, and the economy is still in free fall.

Friedman's claim that monetary policy could have prevented the Great Depression was an attempt to refute the analysis' of John Maynard Keynes, who argued that monetary policy is ineffective under depression conditions and that fiscal policy—large-scale deficit spending by the government—is needed to fight mass unemployment. The failure of monetary policy in the current crisis shows that Keynes had it right the first time.

1 According to the passage, many economists in favor of Friedman's theory ________.

(A) developed effective preventive measures for economic depressions
(B) preferred monetary policy to curtail the economic crisis
(C) were successful in predicting causes of the Great Depression
(D) provided a large fiscal spending plan to stop economic depressions

2 The underlined part indicates that the Federal Reserve chairman, Bernanke, ________.

(A) trusts current economic policy and will not change its direction
(B) agrees that spending should not be encouraged for more employment
(C) acknowledges the problems in Friedman's market-oriented economic policy
(D) disagrees with Friedman who believed in lending more money to the poor than to the rich

3 Which one is true about Keynesian economists?

(A) They demand less control of the government for free market.
(B) They believe that government intervention is more effective during the economic crisis.
(C) They want unlimited bank loans and other monetary support to prevent credit default.
(D) They argue against a small government which provides fiscal policy for the unemployed.

Passage 7

Back in my early twenties I tried a diet that was limited to just a few healthy foods. Three weeks into it, I had nearly reached my goal of losing eight pounds. But my progress wasn't as sweet as I had expected. One night I abandoned the diet and gorged on every food I'd been missing. Over the next two weeks, I ate more than ever. No surprise that I quickly regained eight pounds, and put on two more. It sounds like the old diet-binge cycle that we've all heard about so often. My brazen act of indulgence was the direct effect of a boring, restrictive diet. "If you tell someone they cannot have, say, a piece of cheesecake, then that is the first thing they want to have," says Dr. Hubbert. "And then when they eat that piece of cheesecake, they say, 'Oh, now I've blown it, so I might as well blow it every day.'" At Tufts University in Boston, researchers studied 71 healthy men and women aged 20 to 80 years who provided detailed reports of everything they ate for six months. People who routinely ate a variety of nutrient-dense foods such as vegetables, fruits, and whole grains tended to be lean. The researchers found that when people eat a variety of desirable foods, especially vegetables, they eat fewer nutrient-poor, calorie-dense foods such as cookies, candy, and chips. Overall, they consume fewer calories without consciously restricting their intake.

1 Which of the following is the main topic of the passage?

(A) Importance of a restrictive diet
(B) Dangers of calorie-dense foods
(C) Effects of long-term weight training
(D) Advantages of long-term weight control
(E) Importance of eating nutrient-dense foods

2 Which of the following are the researchers most likely to agree with?

(A) Exercise after eating.
(B) Go on a restrictive diet continually.
(C) Eat lots of calorie-dense foods.
(D) Resist the temptation of foods.
(E) Eat a variety of nutrient-rich foods.

3 Which of the following best describes the organization of the passage?

(A) Several different opinions on a theory are presented.
(B) A problem is described, and possible solutions are discussed.
(C) Two solutions for a problem are suggested and both are accepted.
(D) A general idea is introduced, and several specific examples are given.
(E) A recommendation is analyzed and rejected.

Passage 8

Almost every office is looking for additional space. One easy way to get it is to use moveable partitions instead of, or in conjunction with, the solid interior walls of your existing office space. These walls provide several important benefits. First, they let you take maximum advantage of existing space. No more conflicts where one office is just a little too small and another is just a little too big—just move the partition over a foot to adjust the space for everyone. Second, you can change the positions of the partitions as your business needs change. If one project ends and another begins, you can easily change the office space to accomodate project needs. Finally, new materials make these walls both sound-absorbent and lightweight, so they provide the privacy of built-in walls with the advantages of flexible space.

1 What is this article about?

(A) Office redecoration
(B) Moveable partitions
(C) Improving efficiency
(D) Renting new offices

2 Why do partitions create space?

(A) They are cheaper than real walls.
(B) They are narrower than real walls.
(C) You can move them wherever you need them.
(D) They have shelves on them.

3 Why are partitions a good choice for business with different projects?

(A) They can be easily stored.
(B) They make the office look different.
(C) They help you organize information.
(D) You can change the space for different projects.

TEST 25

제한시간 | 35분
정답률 | /23

Passage 1

In Under New Appleby, the author paints a stark yet vivid canvas of a small scottish town, Appleby. Some of the homes in Appleby date back to the 17th century, but now the awesome-powers and tradition-upsetting realities of the 20th century arrive in the form of a nuclear power plant, a proposed fishery, and a Pakistani immigrant family. How the new Appleby, hence the title, deals with these events becomes the subject of a quiet but captivating drama that is sure to move every reader.

1 What is the book Under New Appleby about?

(A) Dangers of nuclear power
(B) Rapid change in village life
(C) 17th century life in Scotland
(D) The effects of immigration on society

2 How does the reviewer regard the book?

(A) As stark
(B) As moving
(C) As awesome
(D) As passionate

Passage 2

Writing plain English is hard work. No one ever learned literature from a textbook. I have never taken a course in writing. I learned to write naturally and on my own. I did not succeed by accident: I succeeded by patient hard work. Verbal dexterity does not make a good book. Too many authors are more concerned with the style of their writing than with the characters they (가) <u>write</u> about. There are too many writers whose styles are often marred by (나) <u>verbosity</u> and self-importance. Few great authors have a brilliant command of language. The indispensable characteristic of a good writer is a style (다) <u>mark</u> by lucidity.

A good writer is wise in his choice of subjects, and exhaustive in his accumulation of materials. A good writer must have an irrepressible confidence in himself and in his ideas.

Good writers know how to excavate significant facts from masses of information. The toughest thing for a writer is (라) <u>maintain</u> the vigor and fertility of his imagination. Most writers fail simply because they lack the indispensable qualification of the genuine writer. They are intensely prejudiced. Their horizon, in spite of their education, is a narrow one.

1 밑줄 친 (나) verbosity와 대체하기에 가장 적절한 어휘는?

(A) tardiness
(B) versatility
(C) wordiness
(D) zealousness

2 윗글로 미루어 알 수 있는 것은?

(A) The author of the above passage made great efforts to succeed in writing.
(B) Great authors make good books by their flowery style.
(C) Good writers should dig out important facts from valueless materials.
(D) A writer can succeed even if he/she holds a biased view.

3 밑줄 친 (가), (다), (라)를 내용과 문법에 맞게 가장 정확히 배열한 것은?

	(가)	(다)	(라)
(A)	are writing	to mark	maintaining
(B)	wrote	marked	to maintain
(C)	wrote	to mark	maintaining
(D)	are writing	marked	to maintain

Passage 3

Every day more than 100 million people hear the sound of background music. They hear it while they are working in offices, shopping in stores, and eating in restaurants. They even hear it while they are sitting in the dentist's chair. Why is background music layed in so many places? The answer is easy. Music is such a powerful force that it can affect people's behavior.

Studies show that background music can affect the sales of business. Ronald Milliman, a marketing professor, measured the effects that fast music, slow music, and no music had on customers in a supermarket. He found that fast music did not affect sales very much when compared with no music.

However, slow music made a big difference. Listening to music played slowly made shoppers move more slowly. When slow music was played, shoppers bought more and sales increased 38 percent.

Milliman also found that restaurant owners can use music to their advantage. In the evening, playing slow music ① __________ the amount of time customers spend in the restaurant. At lunch time, restaurants want people to eat more quickly so that they can serve more customers. Playing lively music at lunchtime encourages customers to eat quickly and leave.

1 **Which is the most suitable word for blank ①?**

(A) truncates
(B) shortens
(C) lengthens
(D) elongates

2 **Who is Ronald Milliman?**

(A) A marketing executive at a supermarket chain.
(B) A psychologist interested in the effect of music on diet.
(C) A regular customer who enjoys music with his meals.
(D) A marketing expert who studied the effect of music.

3 **If you were an owner of a fast food restaurant, what kind of music would you play based on the given information?**

(A) soul music
(B) exciting music
(C) soothing music
(D) irritating music

4 **Which statement best expresses the main idea of the passage?**

(A) Ronald Milliman has discovered the effect of music on human behavior.
(B) When slow music is played, supermarket sales increase.
(C) Background music can help or hurt a store's sales.
(D) Music encourages customers to eat more and spend more.

Passage 4

If our educational system were fashioned after its bookless past we would have the most democratic form of 'college' imaginable. Among the people whom we like to call savages all knowledge inherited by tradition is shared by all. It is taught, to every member of the tribe so that in this respect everybody is equally equipped for life.

Education in the wilderness is not a matter of monetary means. All are entitled to an equal start. There is none of the hurry which, in our society, often hampers the full development of a growing personality. There, a child grows up under the ever-present attention of his/her parents: Therefore the jungle and the savannah know of no 'juvenile delinquency.' No necessity of making a living away from home results in neglect of children, and no father is confronted with his inability to __________ an education for his child.

1 **Which one is most appropriate in the blank?**

(A) share
(B) equip
(C) buy
(D) bind

2 **Which one of the followings is NOT the reason that education in the past is better?**

(A) It costs less.
(B) Parents are always involved in children's learning.
(C) Everybody has equal access to knowledge.
(D) All knowledge inherited by tradition is taught in a hurry.

Passage 5

It might be poisonous emissions wafting from a nearby manufacturing plant. Or it might be the odor surrounding a plant being pushed in Washington that would make it harder for neighbors and local officials in hundreds of communities to know what potentially deadly pollution risks ___(A)___. Twenty years ago, in response to demands from public safety officials and ordinary citizens across the country, Congress passed the Emergency Planning and Community Right-to-Know Act. It came in the wake of the worst industrial accident in history, a chemical spill at a U.S.-owned insecticide plant in India that killed more than 15,000 people, and a serious chemical accident at the same company's plant in West Virginia. The law (B) mandated a publicly accessible annual report, known as the Toxics Release Inventory, on poisonous substances being pumped into the air, water and ground by refineries, chemical plants and others ranging from food processors to makers of kitchen counter tops. By spotlighting where dangerous pollutants come from, it has helped reduce toxic chemical releases by almost 65% over the past two decades.

1 밑줄 친 (A)에 들어갈 가장 적절한 표현은?

(A) they exposed it to
(B) they are being exposed to
(C) they will be exposed
(D) they will expose toxics

2 밑줄 친 (B) mandated와 가장 유사한 뜻을 가진 표현은?

(A) outdated
(B) guided
(C) authorized
(D) protected

3 이 글의 내용과 일치하는 것은?

(A) Local officials always recognize pollution risks.
(B) Ordinary citizens did not support the Emergency Planning Act.

(C) A chemical accident in India killed less than 10,000 people.
(D) Locating the source of pollutants can reduce toxic chemical releases a lot.

Passage 6

Increasing energy use, climate change, and carbon dioxide (CO2) emissions from fossil fuels make switching to low-carbon fuels a high priority. Biofuels are a potential low-carbon energy source, but whether biofuels offer carbon savings depends on ____(A)____. Converting rainforests, peatlands, savannas, or grasslands to produce food-based biofuels in Brazil, Southeast Asia, and the United States (B) <u>creates a 'biofuel carbon debt'</u> by releasing 17 to 420 times more CO2 than the annual greenhouse gas (GHG) reductions these biofuels provide by displacing fossil fuels. In contrast, biofuels made from waste biomass* or from biomass grown on abandoned agricultural lands planted with perennials incur little or no carbon debt and offer immediate and sustained GHG advantages.

*biomass 에너지원으로서의 동식물자원

TEST 25

1 Which of the following is the best for the blank (A)?

(A) how they are produced
(B) when they are produced
(C) what they are produced for
(D) how much they are produced

2 Choose the closest in the meaning to the underlined phrase (B).

(A) emits less carbon than fossil fuel
(B) is likely to diversify the energy sources
(C) generates higher cost than fossil fuel
(D) has low efficiency in curbing emissions

Passage 7

The animals that inhabit the Earth total about one and a quarter million species. Of these, some 80 percent are insects, animals classified in the phylum Arthropoda, the group of joint-legged creatures. [I]

There are only a few __________ insects; some are surface dwellers, others live between tide marks and one midge even lives on the sea bed. But wherever else other animals go, so do the insects—either as free-living forms adapted to an enormous variety of habitats or as parasites living in or on other animals. [II] The insects are a dominant life form from the artic to the equator. Some exist beneath the snow and ice, others in deserts, still others in salt lakes and hot springs.

One of the chief factors in insect success is their ability to fly; apart from the more primitive forms, most species have achieved the freedom of the air, enabling them to colonize new areas and habitats, to escape from predators, to find mates, and to prospect for food much more easily than their nonairborne invertebrate relatives. [III]

Although the insects have scored a great evolutionary success through their powers of flight, their weight/wing ratio is such that theoretically, flight should not be possible. [IV] Actually, however, their wing muscles build up energy and then release it rapidly, the speed of the wing-beat compensating for a theoretical lack of lift.

1 What does the passage mainly discuss?

(A) the evolutionary success of insects
(B) the diverse habitats of insects
(C) the biological importance of insects' flight
(D) a comparison between insects and other creatures

2 Which of the following statements can be inferred from the passage?

(A) The more primitive forms of insects could fly.
(B) Only the insects that could fly survived through their evolution.
(C) The ability to fly is not the only factor of the insects' evolutionary success.
(D) The insects' ability to fly does not increase the success rate of finding mates.

3 The sentence below can be added to the passage. Choose the most appropriate place to insert the sentence from the choices [I] - [IV].

> Numbers alone indicate the success of the class Insecta, but they have also colonized the world more widely than any other group.

(A) [I]
(B) [II]
(C) [III]
(D) [IV]

4 **Which would be most suitable for the blank in the second paragraph?**

(A) coastal
(B) terrestrial
(C) deep-sea
(D) marine

5 **Which of the following is NOT enumerated as the habitat(s) of insects in the passage?**

(A) other animals
(B) high mountains
(C) salt water
(D) water surface

Passage 8

Men and women make different career choices, and we cannot expect an equal distribution of the sexes within every profession. At one extreme, it is foolish to expect equal outcomes for men and women in organizations like the armed forces. Not only are men stronger and more aggressive but the psychology of both sexes has evolved to trust men (and not trust women) in combat, precisely because of this aggression and strength. At the other end of the scale, it is probably an opposite mixture of evolved aptitudes and attitudes that causes the domination by females of professions such as nursing. This is not to say there can be no good female soldiers or male nurses. Patently, there can. But it is not clear evidence of discrimination that they are __________ than their counterparts of the opposite sex. We cannot say where the equilibrium would lie in a world free from discrimination. But we can say with reasonable confidence that this equilibrium will often not be 50/50.

TEST 25

1 **What is the main idea of the passage?**

(A) Men and women are fundamentally different.
(B) We cannot eliminate discrimination due to gender prejudices.
(C) Different career choices do not indicate inferiority or superiority of either sex.
(D) Unequal distribution of men and women in professions is a sign of discrimination.

2 **Which of the following best fits in the blank?**

(A) poorer
(B) richer
(C) rarer
(D) commoner

리딩 이노베이터 **실전편**

READING INNOVATOR

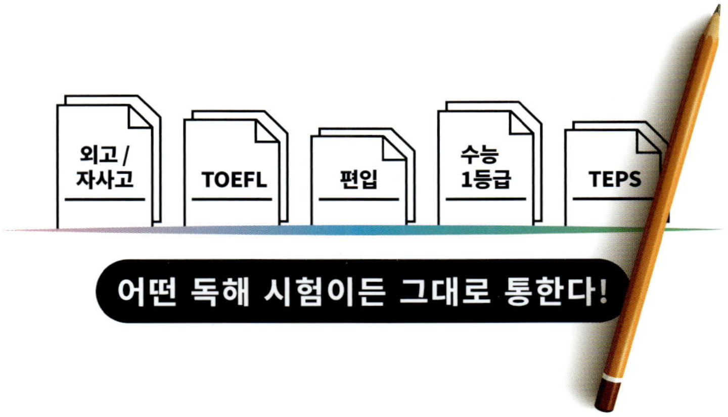

똑같은 지문, 똑같은 시간, 하지만 점수는 다르다 ?

독해의 깊이가 다르기 때문!

영문 독해의 깊이를 더해줄, 최적의 실전 연습 교보재!

JH press

박지성 지음

영어 독해 지문의
종류·유형·전개방식에 따른
영문 독해 패턴 학습

영어 독해 지문의
중심소재와 주제를
한눈에 찾는 연습

킬러 문항도 쉽게 푸는
영어 독해 지문의
통일성과 응집성 훈련

독학 가능한
완벽한 해설
부가 학습 자료 제공

리딩이노베이터

실전편

| 정답 및 해설 |

목차

BOOK 2 정답 및 해설

리딩이노베이터 | 실전편 |

• 정답 및 해설 •

TEST 01

Passage 1

whereas A, B의 중 글의 무게중심은 A에서 B로 넘어간다. 즉, B에 관한 내용이 본문에 구체적으로 전개됨을 파악하도록 한다.

영문글은 구두점의 활용이 두드러진다. -(dash)의 경우 앞에 전개된 내용을 부연한다(순접부연).

중심소재의 이해

중심소재는 단락분석의 가장 기본이 되는 단위로 포괄적 주제에 해당한다. 중심소재를 찾는 방법은 글의 도입부에서 "무엇을 가지고 이야기 하는가"라는 답변을 이끌어내면 쉽게 소재 설정이 가능하다.

1. Whereas family relationships usually constitute a child's first experience with group life, peer-group interactions soon begin to make their powerful socializing effects felt. **1)** From play group to teenage clique, the peer group affords young people many significant learning experiences—① how to achieve status in a circle of friends. Peers are equals in a way parents and their children or teachers and their students are not. A parent or teacher sometimes can force young children to obey rules they neither understand nor like, but peers do not have formal authority to do this; ② thus the true meaning of exchange, cooperation, and equity can be learned more easily in the peer setting. **2.** Peer groups increase in importance as the child grows up and reach maximum influence in adolescence, by which time they sometimes dictate much of a young person's behavior both in and out of school.

중심소재: 또래집단 → 청소년 또래집단의 영향

1. 도입부 = 주제문

또래 집단의 중요한 영향 : 사회화 과정을 익힐 수 있는 learning experiences 제공

1) 뒷받침 진술

① 친구들 사이에서 자신의 위치를 성취하는 방법

② 진정한 의미의 상호교류, 협력 그리고 평등을 익힘

2. 정리

청소년 시기에 또래 집단영향의 중요성 재차강조

정답 1 (D) 2 (B)

해설

1 Peer groups increase in importance as the child grows up and reach maximum influence in adolescence, by which time they sometimes dictate much of a young person's behavior both in and out of school.에서 고등학생이 정답임을 파악할 수 있다.

2 또래 집단의 중요성을 다루는 내용이다. 본문분석을 참조한다.

지문해석

일반적으로 가족관계가 아이들에게 집단생활에 대한 최초의 경험이 되지만, 얼마 안 있어 곧 또래 집단의 상호작용이 사회화에 강력한 영향들을 미치는 것이 느껴지기 시작한다. 놀이 집단에서부터 십대 집단에 이르기까지 또래 집단은 젊은이들에게 친구들 사이에서 어떻게 지위를 얻는가와 같은 중요한 많은 학습 경험들을 제공한다. 또래는 부모와 자식 또는 교사와 학생들의 관계와는 다르게 평등하다. 부모나 교사는 때때로 어린 아이들이 이해하지 못하거나 좋아하지 않는 규칙에 복종하도록 강요할 수 있지만 또래는 이런 것을 할 공식적인 권위가 없다. 그래서 상호교류, 협동, 평등의 진정한 의미는 또래 집단 환경에서 더 쉽게 학습될 수 있다. 또래 집단은 아이들이 성장해감에 따라 점점 더 중요해져서 청소년기에 영향력이 최고에 달한다. 청소년기가 되면 이미 또래 집단이 때때로 학교 안팎에서 젊은이의 많은 행동을 지시한다.

Passage 2

1. There is a whole category of people who are "just" something. To be "just" anything is the worst. It is not to be recognized by society as having much value at all, not now and probably not in the past either. To be "just" anything is to be totally discounted, at least for the present. 1) ① "Just" a housewife immediately and painfully comes to mind. Sometimes women who have kept a house and reared six children refer to themselves as "just" a housewife. "Just" a bum, "just" a kid, "just" a drunk, old man, student, punk are some others.
2) The "just" category contains present non-earners, people who have no past job history highly valued by society and people whose present jobs are on the low-end of pay and prestige scales. ② Ⓐ A person can be "just" a cab driver, for example, or "just" a janitor. Ⓑ No one is ever "just" a president, however. We're supposed to be a classless society, but we are not. 2. We don't recognize a titled nobility. We refuse to acknowledge dynastic privilege. But we certainly separate the valued from the valueless, and it has a lot to do with jobs and the importance we attach to them.

중심소재: 직업군에 따른 가치평가

1. 도입부 = 중심소재 도출

1) "just" 직업군의 특징 1
사회적으로 가치 없는 사람이라 간주됨
① 예시부연
사회에서 부정적으로 인식되는 대표적 대상인 housewife와 함께 다양한 부류의 예 언급

2) "just" 직업군의 특징 2
사회 내에서 수입이 없거나 낮은 임금
② 예시부연(대조)
Ⓐ 운전사, 경비원
Ⓑ 대통령
③ 직업의 내재적 가치를 따지지 않는다.

2. 결론(글의 요지)
우리 사회는 특정 직업군에 중요성을 부여하고, 그에 따른 경제적 가치를 부여하는 시스템을 가지고 있다.

중심소재의 폭이 좁아지면서 구체적 주제로 나아가는 연역적 구조를 파악한다.
just 직업군 → 직업군의 특징 → 특징 1, 2

정답 1 (A) 2 (B) 3 (D)

지문분석
본문의 요지는 Our society has an implicit system of awarding respect based on the jobs we hold.이고, 구체적 진술에서 일반진수로 전개되는 미괄식 구성을 보인다. 영어권 글이 두괄식이 다수를 차지하는 것은 맞지만, 논증과 같이 자신의 주장을 전달하는 글은 미괄식 구성을 취할 수 있다는 점을 기억하도록 한다. 미괄식 구성이 논증에 많이 활용되는 이유 주장의 근거를 본문을 통해서 충분히 제시하면서 독자의 이해를 이끌어 낸 후 이를 바탕으로 결론을 도출할 경우 설득력이 높아지기 때문이다.

해설
1 다양한 일을 하는 것이 더 생산적이라는 말은 본문에 없다.
2 "우리 사회는 가치 있는 직업과 그렇지 않은 직업을 분류하는 체계가 있다(we certainly separate the valued from the valueless, and it has a lot to do with jobs and the importance we attach to them)"가 글의 요지다.
3 문제 2와의 연관해서 우리 사회가 가진 특정 사회적 체계를 비판하는 내용이다.

추론문제는 곧 내용일치라 생각한다.
추론문제의 시작은 본문을 객관적으로 파악하는 내용일치 문제와 같다고 생각한다. 일반적으로 선택지를 만들 때 부분을 전체로 확대 해석하는 일반화 오류나 논리적 비약을 많이 활용한다. 특히 추론 문제에서 이 두 오류를 많이 활용하므로 결국 최대한 주관적 생각을 배제하고, 본문에 나온 내용만을 바탕으로 답을 골라야 한다.

지문해석
"그저" 아무개에 불과한 사람들이라는 범주가 있다. "그저" 아무개가 된다는 것은 최악이다. "그저" 아무개라는 것은 현재에, 그리고 필시 과거에도 가치를 가진 존재로 사회에게 인정받지 못한다는 뜻이기 때문이다. "그저" 아무개에 불과한 존재라는 것은, 적어도 현재로서는, 완전히 무시당하는 것이다. "그저" 주부에 불과한 사람이라는 범주가 얼른 떠올라 마음을 아프게 한다. 때때로 살림을 하고 여섯 아이를 키워낸 여성들은 스스로를 일컬어 "그저" 주부에 불과하다고 말한다. "그저" 하찮은 사람, "그저" 아이에 불과한 존재, "그저"

술주정뱅이, 노인, 학생, "그저" 애송이 등도 이런 하찮게 여겨지는 부류에 속한다. "그저" ~한 사람이라고 분류되는 범주에는 현재 생계비를 벌지 못하는 사람들, 사회가 가치 있다고 여기는 과거 직업 경력을 가지지 못한 사람들 또는 현재 봉급과 명망이 낮은 직장을 가지고 있는 사람들이 포함된다. 예컨대 사람들은 "그저" 택시 운전사이거나, "그저" 수위일 수는 있다. 그러나 누구도 "그저" 대통령일 수는 없다. 우리는 계급 차별이 없는 사회에 살고 있는 듯하지만, 실상은 그렇지 않다. 우리는 작위를 가진 귀족을 인정하지도 않고 왕조의 특권을 인정하지 않지만, 가치 있는 사람과 무가치한 사람들을 분명히 구별하고 있고, 이는 그들의 직업과, 그리고 우리가 그 직업에 부여하는 중요성과, 깊은 관련을 맺고 있다.

Passage 3

However를 기준으로 most와 Curtis가 대조됨을 파악한다.

주제 = Studying Ocean Currents Through Random Junk)

실험의 구체적 내용을 파악하는데, Junk를 통해서 대류의 흐름을 파악하는 내용임을 잊지 않도록 한다.

1. Scientists today are studying ocean currents more and more intensely. **Most** do it using satellites and other high-tech equipment. However, oceanographer Curtis Ebbesmeyer does it ① in a more old-fashioned way—by studying movements of random junk. **1)** ① A scientist with many years' experience, he started this type of research in the early 1990s when he heard about hundreds of athletic shoes washing up on the shores of the northeast coast of the United States. There were so many shoes that people were holding swap meets to try and match left and right shoes to sell or wear.

② Ebbesmeyer started investigating and found out that the shoes—about 60,000 in total—fell into the ocean in a shipping accident. He contacted the shoe company and asked if they wanted the shoes back. Not surprisingly, the company told him that they didn't. Ebbesmeyer realized this could be a great experiment. Ⓐ He learned when and where the shoes went into the water and tracked where they landed, he could learn a lot about __________. The Atlantic Northwest is one of the world's best areas for beachcombing because of converging wind and currents, and as a result, there is a group of serious beachcombers in the area. Ebbesmeyer got help in collecting information about where the shoes landed. In a year he collected reliable information on 1,600 shoes. With this data, he and a colleague were able to test and refine a computer program designed to model ocean currents, and publish the results of their study. Ⓑ Then in 1993, a shipment of colored plastic bathtub toys fell into the North Atlantic Ocean. Ebbesmeyer and his colleagues got even more accurate information from this spill, which resulted in huge amounts of useful new data for their work. As the result of his work, Ebbesmeyer

첫 번째 문장을 통해서 대양해류에 관한 글임을 파악할 수 있다. 중심내용을 바탕으로 구체적 주제를 설정하도록 한다.

중심소재: Ocean currents

1. 도입부 = 주제문

해류연구를 위해 일반인들은 위성과 첨단 장비를 사용하는 반면 Curtis는 오래된 방법(①)을 사용한다고 했으며, 바로 뒤에 그 방법을 소개하고 있다 : studying movements of random junk

1) 뒷받침 진술

① 실험의 배경

② 실험의 구체적 내용 전개

Ⓐ 실험 1
신발을 통한 해류의 흐름 파악

Ⓑ 실험 2
장난감을 통한 해류의 흐름 파악

* 내용일치와 관련해서 본문에 수치가 드러날 경우 구체적으로 어떤 내용과 관련된 사항인지 파악하도록 한다.

has become known as the scientist to call with questions about any unusual objects found floating in the ocean.
He has even started an association of beachcombers and oceanographers, with 500 subscribers from West Africa to New Zealand. They have documented spills of everything from onions to hockey gloves.

정답 1 (D) 2 (B)

해설

1 본문의 주제는 Studying Ocean Currents Through Random Junk이며, 실험을 통해 이를 밝히는 내용임을 글의 도입부에서 파악했다면 보기 (D)가 정답임을 쉽게 접근할 수 있었을 것이다.

2 본문과 일치하지 않는 문제는 문제의 보기 항을 먼저 읽어 본문의 내용을 대략적으로 파악할 수 있도록 한다. 특히, 보기 항에 수치와 관련된 표현이 나올 경우 이를 본문에서 눈여겨봐야 한다. reliable information on 1,600 shoes에서 보기 (B)는 본문과 일치하지 않음을 알 수 있다.

지문해석

오늘날 과학자들은 대양 해류에 대해 점점 더 집중적으로 연구하고 있다. 대개 연구는 위성이나 다른 첨단기술장비를 사용하고 있다. 하지만 해양학자 커티스 에베스마이어(Curtis Ebbesmeyer)는 그 연구를 좀 더 구식으로 하고 있다. 즉, 이리저리 떠다니는 쓰레기의 움직임을 연구하고 있다. 경험이 풍부한과학자인 그는 이방식의 연구를 1990년대 초에 시작했다.
그때 그는 수백 개의 운동선수용 신발이 미국의 북동쪽 해안의 해안가에 쓸려온다는 얘기를 들었다. 굉장히 많은 신발들이 떠밀려오기 때문에 사람들은 그 신발들의 왼짝과 오른짝을 찾아서 팔고 신어보려는 교환 모임도 벌이고 있었다. 에베스마이어는 조사에 착수했고 그 신발들이 전부 6만개쯤 되었는데 선박 사고로 바다에 빠지게 된 사실을 알아냈다. 그는 신발 회사에 연락하여 그들이 그 신발을 다시 회수하고 싶은지 물었다. 당연히 그 회사에서는 그러고 싶지 않다고 말했다. 에베스마이어는 이것이 굉장한 실험이 될 수 있음을 깨달았다. 만약 그 가신 발들이 언제, 그리고 어디에서 바다로 빠졌는지를 알아내고 그 신발이 어느 곳에서 떠밀려 올라왔는지를 알게 된다면 그는 대양 해류의 양상에 대해서 많은 것을 알게 될 것이다. 북서 대서양은 세계에서 많은 물건들이 쓸려 올라오기로 유명한 곳 중 하나인데 그 이유는 바람과 해류가 한데 모이기 때문이다. 결과적으로 이 지역에는 해변에 올라오는 물건을 줍기 위해 오는 사람들이 굉장히 많다. 에베스마이어는 어디쯤에 신발이 떠내려 왔는지에 대한 정보를 수집했다. 1년 동안 그는 천 6백개의 신발에 관한 신빙성 있는 정보를 수집했다. 이 정보로 그와 그의 동료는 대양해류모형을 위해 설계된 컴퓨터 프로그램을 실험하고 개량했으며 연구 결과를 발표했다.
그 후 1993년, 알록달록한 색깔의 플라스틱 목욕탕 장난감의 선적이 북대서양에 가라앉았다. 에베스마이어와 그의 동료들은 이 사고로 인해 좀 더 정확한 정보를 얻을 수 있었는데, 그것이 그들의 연구에 매우 많은 유용한 정보를 제공하였다. 그의 연구 결과로 인해, 에베스마이어는 대양에서 떠다니다가 발견되는 이상한 물체들에 대한 질문에 답하기 위해 소환되는 과학자로 알려지게 되었다. 그는 심지어 해변에서 물건을 줍는 사람과 해양학자들의 협회를 시작했는데 여기에는 서 아프리카에서 뉴질랜드에 이르는 500명의 신청자들이 포함됐다. 그들은 양파에서 하키장갑까지 바다에서 주울 수 있는 모든 것을 문서화 한다.

내용일치 접근방법
지문을 읽기 전에 문제를 먼저 파악하는 습관을 지니도록 한다. 내용일치·불일치(특히, 불일치) 문제의 경우 지문을 읽기 전 선택지의 내용을 빠르게 파악하는 데 익숙해지면 상당한 효과를 얻을 수 있다. 선택지 중 세 개의 내용은 본문과 일치한다는 것을 알 수 있는데다, 일반적으로 본문의 내용을 짧고, 쉬운 표현으로 물어보는 경우가 대다수이므로 선택지의 내용만으로 본문에서 다루는 대략적인 내용을 추론할 수 있다. 선택지에 숫자가 나오는 경우는 본문에 제시된 숫자와 관련된 내용에 집중해서 읽어야 한다.

Passage 4

1. 1) Professor Iyengar of Columbia University conducted an experiment in which she set up a tasting booth with a variety of exotic gourmet jams at an upscale grocery store. Sometimes the booth had six different jams, and sometimes twenty-four different jams on display. ① She wanted to see whether the number of jam choices made any difference in the number of jams sold.

2. 1) Conventional economic wisdom, of course, says that the more choices consumers have, the more likely they are to buy, because it is easier for consumers to find the jam that perfectly fits their needs. ① But Iyengar found the opposite to be true. Thirty percent of those who stopped by the six-choice booth ended up buying some jam, while only three percent of those who stopped by the bigger booth bought anything. Ⓐ Why is that? Because buying jam is a snap decision. You say to yourself, instinctively, "I want that one." And if you are given too many choices, if you are forced to consider much more than your unconscious mind is comfortable with, you get paralyzed. Snap judgments can be made in a snap because they are frugal, and if we want to protect our snap judgments, we have to take steps to protect that frugality.

통념비판의 패턴을 파악하도록 한다.

통념 A = B
But A ≠ B

뒷받침 진술

중심소재: 구매결정에 영향을 미치는 요소

1. 첫 번째 문단

1) 도입부 = 실험

고급 잡화점에 다양한 잼을 선전하는 두 개의 부스 설치: 6개짜리와 24개짜리

① 실험의 목적(주제)
선택 사항의 수가 구매 수에 어떤 영향을 미치는가?

2. 두 번째 문단

1) 기존의 관점(통념)

선택의 폭이 넓을수록 구매자의 욕구에 맞는 제품이 있을 가능성이 높기 때문에 판매가 더 잘 이루어질 것이다

① 반대의 실험결과
Ⓐ 뒷받침 근거
잼을 사는 행위는 순간의 결정이기 때문에 지나치게 선택 사항이 크면 오히려 구매 판단력이 굳어짐

정답 1 (A) 2 (E) 3 (B)

해설

1 잼을 구매하는 행위는 순간적으로 일어난다고 했다. 이를 snap judgement라고 표현하고 있다. 선택 사항이 적을수록 고민하지 않게 되기에 구매로 이어진다고 했으므로 선택지 (A)가 정답이다.

2 because it is easier for consumers to find the jam that perfectly fits their needs에서 밑줄 친 부분의 근거를 바탕으로 빈칸에 넣을 수 있는 가장 적절한 답은 보기 (E)이다. 본문은 조사를 통해 이에 대한 반론을 제기하는 방향으로 전개되고 있다.

3 판단이 frugal 하다는 것은 판단을 내리는 데 요구되는 시간과 노력이 적다는 뜻이므로 그런 frugality를 지킨다는 것은 택할 수 있는 선택가지의 수를 줄이는 것을 의미한다. 따라서 (B)가 적절하다. 소요되는 시간을 줄이는 것이 아니라 허용되는 시간을 제한하는 것은 즉석 결정을 방해할 것이므로 (A)는 부적절하다.

지문해석

콜롬비아 대학(Columbia University)의 아인거(Iyengar) 교수는 다양한 이국적인 미식가를 위한 잼을 가진 시식대를 고급 식료품점에 설치하는 실험을 하였다. 때때로 그 시식대는 6종류의 다양한 잼이 있었고, 때로는 24종류의 다양한 잼을 진열하였다. 그녀는 잼 선택가지의 수가 판매되는 잼의 수에 어떤 차이를 일으키는지 알고 싶어 했다. 물론 경제에 대한 통념은 소비자가 더 많은 선택가지를 가질수록 구입할 가능성이 더 많을 것이라고 말한다. 소비자들이 완벽히 그들의 욕구에 맞는 잼을 더 쉽게 찾을 테니까.
그러나 아인거는 정반대가 사실이라는 것을 알았다. 6종류의 시식대에 멈춘 사람들의 30%가 결국 잼을 산 반면에, 종류가 더 많은 시식대에 머무른 사람 중에는 3%만이 잼을 샀다. 그것은 왜일까? 잼을 사는 것은 즉석 결정이기 때문이다. 당신은 스스로에게 본능적으로 "나는 저것을 원해"라고 말한다. 그런데 너무 많은 선

택가지가 주어지면 즉, 당신의 무의식이 편안하다고 느끼는 것 이상으로 많은 생각을 해야 한다면, 당신의 사고는 마비된다. 즉석 판단은 시간과 노력이 적게 들기 때문에 곧바로 내려질 수 있다. 그래서 우리가 즉석 판단을 지키기를 원한다면 그러한 간소함을 지키기 위한 조치를 취해야 하는 것이다.

Passage 5

1. Ethnocentrism is the view that one's own culture is better than all others; it is the way all people feel about themselves as compared to outsiders. There is no one in our society who is not ethnocentric to some degree, no matter how liberal and open-minded he or she might claim to be. People will always find some aspect of another culture distasteful, be it sexual practices, a way of treating friends or relatives, or simply a food that they cannot manage to get down with a smile. 1) This is not something we should be ashamed of, because it is a natural outcome of growing up in any society. However, as anthropologists who study other cultures, it is something we should constantly be aware of, so that when we are tempted to make value judgments about another way of life, we can look at the situation objectively and take our bias into account.

중심소재: 자민족중심주의

1. 도입부

자민족중심주의의 정의와 특성

1) 요지문

요지를 이끄는 시그널을 확인한다.

정답 1 (A) 2 (D)

세부내용 파악 문제의 경우 문제에서 요구하는 핵심 내용을 최대한 암기하는 연습을 한다. 지문을 읽다가 세부내용에서 묻던 사항이 나왔을 때 바로 답을 구할 수 있는 경우가 대부분이므로 문제를 먼저 읽지 않았을 때 다시 읽어야 하는 시간을 줄일 수 있다.

해설

1 as anthropologists who study other cultures, it is something we should constantly be aware of...에서 인류학자라는 것을 파악할 수 있다.

2 when we are tempted to make value judgments about another way of life, we can look at the situation objectively and take our bias into account.에서 선택지 (D)가 정답임을 파악할 수 있다.

지문해석

자민족중심주의는 자신의 문화가 모든 다른 문화보다 더 좋다고 여기는 관점으로, 모든 사람들이 다른 나라 사람들과 비교하여 스스로에 대해 느끼는 감정이다. 아무리 자신은 관대하거나 편견이 없는 사람이라고 주장 하더라도, 우리사회에서 조금이라도 자민족 중심적이지 않은 사람은 없다. 사람들은 항상 다른 문화에서 불쾌한 면을 찾아낼 것이다. 그것이 성적인 풍습이든, 친구나 친인척을 대하는 방식이든, 혹은 웃는 낯으로 삼킬 수 없는 음식이 되었든 간에 말이다. 이것은 모든 사회에서 발생하는 당연한 결과이기 때문에 우리가 부끄럽게 여겨야 할 것은 아니다. 하지만 다른 문화를 연구하는 인류학자로서 우리는 이 자기 민족중심주의를 항상 인식해야만 한다. 그렇게 함으로써 우리가 다른 생활방식에 대해 가치판단을 내리고 싶어질 때 상황을 객관적으로 보고 우리의 편견까지 고려할 수 있게 된다.

영문단락 전개의 특징

1) 연역적 전개: 포괄적 개념에서 세부개념으로 전개된다. 즉, 일반진술에서 구체적 진술로 이어지는 전개를 염두에 둔다.

2) 진술 또는 견해가 나오면 뒷받침 진술이 따른다.

3) 먼저 언급된 것이 먼저 기술된다(First served, first "described")

Passage 6

1. History has long made a point of the fact that the magnificent flowering of ancient civilization rested upon the institution of slavery, which released opportunity at the top for the art and literature which became the glory of antiquity. 1) In a way, the mechanization of the present-day world produces the condition of the ancient ① in that the enormous development of labor-saving devices and of contrivances which amplify the capacities of mankind affords the base for the leisure necessary to widespread cultural pursuits. 2. Mechanization is the present-day slave power, with the difference that in the mechanized society there is no group of the community which does not share in the benefits of its inventions.

중심소재: 현대판 노예제도인 기계화

1. 도입부

고대문명의 융성은 노예제도에 바탕을 둠

1) 요지

현대판 노예제도 = 기계화

① 뒷받침 근거

기계화로 인해 인간의 노동력이 절약되어 폭넓은 문화추구에 필수적인 여가의 기반이 제공된다.

2. 요지 재진술

기계화는 현대판 노예제도

호흡이 긴 지문과 문제 수의 관계

지문이 길고, 문제가 많은 경우 반드시 문제를 먼저 확인하고 문제에서 요구하는 사항에 맞게 지문을 읽는 연습을 해야 지문과 문제를 여러 번 반복해서 확인하는 시간을 줄일 수가 있다. 물론, 문제 유형(대의파악/내용일치·불일치)에 따라 선택지의 내용까지 읽어야 하는 경우도 있다. 반면, 지문이 짧고, 문제가 많은 경우는 지문을 빠르게 읽고 문제를 푸는 것도 나름의 전략이 된다.

정답 1 (D) 2 (D) 3 (D) 4 (B)

지문분석

이 글은 '기계화'에 초점을 맞추고 있다. 고대 문명이 노예 제도로 융성했듯이 현대인들은 기계화로 폭넓은 문화를 추구하게 되었다는 논지이다. 따라서 글의 주제는 (D)의 "오늘날 노예를 대신하는 힘인 기계화"이다.

해설

1 고대 문명이 노예 제도로 융성했듯이 현대인들은 기계화로 폭넓은 문화를 추구하게 되었다는 것이 요지다. 따라서, "오늘날 노예를 대신하는 힘인 기계화"가 주제다.

2 the enormous development of labor-saving devices and of contrivances which amplify the capacities of mankind에서 (D)가 정답임을 파악할 수 있다.

3 어느 문명이 되었던 여가(the leisure necessary to widespread cultural pursuits)를 바탕으로 문화가 발전했다. (A)는 과거이고, (C)는 현대에만 해당한다.

4 there is no group of the community which does not share in the benefits of its inventions에서 저자는 기계화에 대해 긍정적으로 받아들이는 태도를 보임을 파악할 수 있다.

지문해석

역사는 오랫동안 고대 문명의 화려한 융성은 노예제도에 기초를 두고 있었다는 사실을 강조해 왔는데, 이 노예제도는 귀족들에게 고대의 찬란한 영광이 된 예술과 문학에 대한 기회를 제공했다. 어떤 면에서 인간의 능력을 확대시키는 노동력 절감 기구와 장치의 엄청난 발전이 폭넓은 문화를 추구하는 데 필요한 여가시간의 기반을 제공해 준다는 점에서 현대 사회의 기계화는 고대 시대와 유사한 상황을 조성하고 있다. 기계화는 현대 사회의 노예의 힘이다. 양자의 차이점은 기계화된 현대 사회에서는 발명품(기계 장치)의 혜택을 누리지 못하는 사회 집단이 없다는 것이다.

Passage 7

1. How and why did studying the career trajectories of star football players give you a window on better management of business organizations and careers? 1) ① As research on the National Football League (NFL) reveals, sometimes the specific nature of a job determines whether a great performer at one company can replicate that performance at another. ② Sports teams are organizations much like many others, subject to the errors that are common elsewhere. But their successes and failures are highly visible and amplified by the fact that they perform in a zero-sum world. ③ In order for one team to win, another team has to lose. As a result, their focus is especially performance-oriented. Teams hire stars on the basis of talent—as do many organizations. 2. Thus, if a star's performance is measured into highly accurate statistical data, they allow researchers to examine whether performance is as portable in a new environment as many in the NFL believe. For business managers, the fact that the star's performance is portable for some positions and not portable for others is necessary to know.

중심소재: 스타선수의 경력경로 연구

1. 도입부 = 주제

스타 선수의 경력 경로의 연구의 중요성?

1) 뒷받침 진술

① 선수가 맡게 되는 위치에 따라 선수의 실력이 제대로 발휘될지가 결정된다(스타 선수라 하더라도 어떤 위치에 활동하느냐에 따라 스타성 플레이가 결정되기 때문에 선수의 이전 경력을 보는 것이 왜 중요한지 유추할 수 있다).

② zero-sum법칙(스포츠 경기는 이기거나 지거나 하는 약육강식의 환경)

③ performance-oriented
선수의 실력이 승패에 아주 중요함을 유추할 수 있다.

2. 답변(요지)

첫 번째 문장에서 제시한 의문점에 대한 궁극적인 답변을 제시하고 있다.

글의 도입부에서 제시되는 의문문은 주제에 해당한다.

문단의 위치에 따른 의문문의 의미

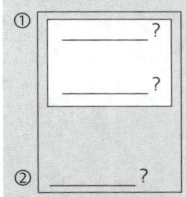

① ________?
________?

② ________?

①과 같이 글의 도입부 또는 중반부에 위치할 경우 주제에 해당하고 답변은 요지이다.
②와 같은 경우는 답변을 요구하지 않는 설의법에 해당하는 제안·권유의 표현으로 요지에 해당한다.

정답 1 (A) 2 (C)

해설

1 portable을 단순히 "휴대의; (다른 곳으로) 이식할 수 있는"의 의미로 파악해서는 답이 나오지 않는다. 독해에서 나오는 어휘문제는 일반적으로 문자적 의미가 아닌 문맥적 의미를 묻는 경우가 많다. 즉, 글의 맥락에 비추어 어떤 의미로 사용되고 있는지 유추해서 답을 골라야 한다. 해당 단어가 들어간 문장을 보면, whether performance is as portable in a new environment인데, '다른 팀으로 이적하면서 가져갈 수 있는'이라는 뜻이므로 '현 팀에서의 성적을 그대로 재현할 수 있는지'를 묻고 있으므로 보기 (A)의 replicable가 가장 근접한 의미로 볼 수 있다.

2 the fact that the star's performance is portable for some positions and not portable for others is necessary to know.를 보면 스타플레이어를 뽑을 때 가장 중요한 것은 어느 위치에서 이전의 역량을 가장 잘 발휘할 수 있을지가 가장 중요하다고 보았으므로 보기 (C)는 본문과 일치한다.

지문해석

어떻게 그리고 왜 스타 축구선수들의 경력 경로를 연구하는 것이 기업체들과 경력의 더 나은 관리를 이해할 수 있는 틀을 제공했는가? 전국프로미식축구연맹(NFL)에 대한 연구가 보여주듯이 때로는 어떤 업무의 구체적인 특성이 한 회사에서 업무를 훌륭히 수행하는 직원이 다른 회사에서도 같은 성과를 낼 수 있는지를 결정한다. 스포츠 팀들은 다른 많은 팀들과 매우 유사한 조직들로서 다른 곳에서 흔히 일어나는 실수의 영향을 받고 있다.
그러나 스포츠 팀의 성공과 실수들은 눈에 잘 띄고 그들이 제로섬(쌍방 득실의 차가 영) 세계에서 벌어진다는 사실 때문에 과장되어 보인다. 한 팀이 이기기 위해서는 다른 팀이 져야 한다. 그 결과 그들의 관심은 특히나 성적 지향적이다. 팀들은 많은 조직들이 그러하듯이 재능을 토대로 스타들을 고용한다.
그래서 한 스타의 성적이 매우 정확하게 통계 자료로 측정되면 그들은 연구가들에게 NFL의 많은 팀들이 믿는 것처럼 경기성적이 새로운 환경에서도 재현될 수 있는지를 조사하도록 한다. 경영자들에게 있어서 스타의 성적이 어떤 포지션에서는 재현 가능하고 다른 포지션에서는 재현될 수 없다는 사실은 알아야 할 필요가 있다.

Passage 8

1. The term “globalization” has been snatched away by the powerful to refer to a specific form of international economic integration, one based on investor rights, with the interests of people incidentally neglected. **1)** ① That is why the business press, in its more honest moments, refers to the “free trade agreements” as “free investment agreements” (*Wall Street Journal*). ② Accordingly, advocates of other forms of globalization are described as “anti-globalization.” No sane person is opposed to globalization, that is, international integration. Surely not the left and the workers movements, which were founded on the principle of international solidarity—that is, globalization in a form that attends to the rights of people, not private power systems. ③ Ⓐ There are no serious “theoretical foundations” for any of the versions of globalization, including the investor-rights versions. Ⓑ The international economy is far too poorly understood for there to be systematic “theories” in any serious sense. **2.** Certainly the neoliberal programs have no serious theoretical basis, even in the abstract: and their concrete realization is a complex mixture of protectionism and liberalization crafted to meet the interests of the big investors, not surprisingly.

중심소재: 세계화

1. 도입부 = 주제문
세계화는 일반 사람들의 이익은 무시된 투자자 권리에 기반을 둔 강자들에게 유리한 국제경제 통합이다.

1) 뒷받침 진술
① 경제지
자유무역협정은 자유투자협정
② 다른 형태의 세계화는 반-세계화로 낙인
③ 문제점
Ⓐ 국제화에 대한 이론적 기반의 부재
Ⓑ 국제 경제에 대한 체계적 이론 성립을 위한 이해부족

2. 주제문 재진술
세계화란 거대 투자자들의 이익만을 충족시키는 보호무역주의와 자유주의의 혼합체로 드러날 뿐이다.

문제를 먼저 읽을 때 얻을 수 있는 효과를 잘 보여주는 예다. 문제 1, 2를 통해서 지문은 “세계화”라는 중심소재를 다루는 글임을 쉽게 파악할 수 있는 동시에 2번 문제를 통해 세계화 정의에 대한 상반된 두 견해를 가진 집단이 본문에 언급될 것을 파악할 수 있다.

정답 1 (D) 2 (A) 3 (B)

해설

1 글쓴이는 세계통합으로서의 세계화에 대해서는 긍정적이지만(No sane person is opposed to globalization, that is, international integration) 세계경제통합으로서의 세계화에 대해서는 비판적이다

2 본문에 드러난 세계화의 두 가지 정의는 거대 투자자들의 권익에 근거한 세계경제통합으로서의 세계화와 국제연대 원칙에 근거한 노동자 운동이 주장하는 각국 국민들의 권익 관심을 갖는 세계통합으로서의 세계화이다. 그러므로 대립된 두 세력은 거대 투자자와 국제 시민노동자 연대임을 파악할 수 있다.

3 빈칸이 들어간 문장은 다음과 같다. their concrete realization is a complex mixture of protectionism and liberalization crafted to meet the interests of the ① __________. 우선 their이 가리키는 대상 the neoliberal programs이다. 본문은 첫 번째 문장에서도 잘 나왔듯이 경제 통합으로서의 세계화는 일반인의 득은 무시되고, 투자자들의 권리만을 옹호한다. 신자유의란 자유주의와 보호무역을 통해 거대 투자자(특히 대기업)의 권익을 위한 제도임을 비판하는 내용이다. 빈칸에 들어갈 내용은 선택지 (B)의 big investors가 가장 적절하다.

지문해석

“세계화”라는 용어는 강자들이 가로채 특정한 형태의 국제경제 통합을 일컫는데 사용되어 왔는데, 투자자의 권익에 근거해 국민들의 이익을 자연스레 무시하는 것이다. 그것이 바로 경제지가 가장 정직한 순간에 “자유

무역협정"을 "자유투자협정"이라고 부르는 이유이다(월스트리트 저널). 따라서 다른 형태의 세계화를 옹호하는 사람들이 "반 세계화" 세력으로 묘사되기도 한다. 제정신인 사람이라면 세계화, 즉 세계 통합에 반대하지 않는다.

좌파와 노동자 운동 측도 반대하지 않는 것이 분명한데, 이들은 국제 연대의 원칙 즉 사적인 권력시스템이 아닌 국민들의 권익에 관심을 쏟는 형태의 세계화에 근거를 두고 있다. 투자자 권익을 포함한 그 어떤 세계화에 대한 해석에도 진정한 "이론적 토대"는 없다. 국제 경제는 너무나 형편없이 이해되고 있어 그 어떤 진정한 의미에서도 체계적인 "이론"이 있을 수 없다. 신자유주의 프로그램들은 심지어 개략적으로라도 진지한 이론적 근거를 가지고 있지 않음이 분명하다.

그 구체적인 구현 형태가 대형 투자자들의 이익을 충족시키기 위해 복잡하게 만들어진 보호무역주의와 자유주의의 혼합이라는 것은 그다지 놀라운 일이 아니다.

TEST 02

특정 대상은 앞 선 일반 진술에 대한 구체적 진술을 이끄는 시그널이다. 구체적 진술의 종류는 다음과 같다.
1) for example, for instance, let's say
2) when, if
3) consider, imagine, picture
4) 구체적 대상 언급
5) 시간의 부사(recently, for the last X years 등등)

Passage 1

1. In baseball, pitchers need both psychology and skill to strike out batters. 1) ① Sometimes pitchers do not need to do anything at all to psych out batters. The pitcher can just stand on the mound and take his time pitching. This messes up the batter's timing. ② A pitcher might also wait for the batter to step up to home plate, and then step off the pitcher's mound to throw a few balls to first base for practice. Ⓐ One pitcher famous for his fast ball would stand on the pitcher's mound and just stare at the batter. This gave the batter plenty of time to think about the pitch that was about to be thrown. When the pitcher saw that the batter was starting to feel ill at ease, he let his fast ball fly. It was an excellent tactic for this pitcher.

중심소재: 타자를 압도하는 방법

1. 도입부 = 주제문
야구에서 투수는 타자를 이기기 위해 심리전과 기술을 함께 사용한다.

1) 뒷받침 진술
심리적으로 타자를 압도하는지 구체적 방법을 언급하고 있다.
①방법 1
②방법 2
Ⓐ 부연 예시

정답 **1** (A)

해설
투수가 심리전을 통해서 상대(타자)를 이기는 방법에 대해 언급되어있다. 주제: How pitchers win out psychologically

지문해석
야구에서, 투수가 타자를 삼진으로 아웃시키려면 심리전과 기술 모두가 필요하다. 때때로 투수는 타자와의 심리전에서 이기기 위해서 아무것도 할 필요가 없을 때도 있다. 투수는 그저 마운드에 서서 뜸을 들이며 천천히 공을 던진다. 이것이 타자의 타이밍을 흩뜨려버린다. 투수는 또한 타자가 홈 플레이트에 들어서길 기다렸다가, 마운드에서 발을 빼고 1루 베이스로 몇 개의 공을 던지기도 한다. 강속구로 유명한 어떤 투수는 투수 마운드에 서서 타자를 노려보기만 하곤 했다. 이것은 타자에게 던져질 투구에 대해 생각할 충분한 시간을 주었다. 타자가 불안감을 느끼기 시작했다는 낌새가 보일 때, 그 투수는 그의 빠른 공을 던졌다. 그것은 이 투수의 훌륭한 전략이었다.

Passage 2

통념의 패턴을 파악하도록 한다.

1. Typically, people think of genius, whether it manifests in Mozart's composition of symphonies at age five or Einstein's discovery of relativity, as having a quality not just of the supernatural, but also of the eccentric. 1) People see genius as a good abnormality; moreover, they think of genius as a completely unpredictable abnormality. ① Until recently, psychologists regarded the quirks of genius as too

중심소재: 천재의 속성

1. 도입부 = 천재
초자연적일 뿐 아니라 괴짜

1) 불예측성
천재들의 불예측성은 일정한 패턴이 없어 설명하기 어렵다.

erratic to describe intelligibly; **however**, Anna Findley's ground-breaking study uncovers predictable patterns in the biographies of geniuses. Ⓐ ⓐ These patterns, however, even though they occur with regularity, do not completely dispel the common belief that there is a kind of supernatural intervention in the lives of unusually talented men and women. ⓑ For example, Findley shows that all geniuses experience three intensely productive periods in their lives, one of which, mysterious as it may seem, always occurs shortly before their deaths; this is true whether the genius lives to 19 or 90.

① 논리적 반전 = 주제문
However를 기점으로 과거와 달리 천재들에도 예측 가능한 패턴이 있다.
Ⓐ 뒷받침 진술
ⓐ 특성
초자연적 요소가 결합된 예측 가능한 패턴이 있다.
ⓑ 예시(For example)

통념의 글 전개와 But의 기능

people say A = B
But A ≠ B A = C
뒷받침 진술

But의 두 기능
① 역접(본문)
② 순접강조추가

A = B
But A = B + A = C
뒷받침 진술

TEST 02

정답 1 (A) 2 (D)

해설

1 앞의 내용에 대한 예시를 제시하는 내용이 빈칸 이후에 전개되고 있다.

2 However 이후 실험을 통해 "천재들의 예측 가능성과 불가능성"을 을 다루는 글이다.

지문해석

천재성이 5살 때 모차르트의 교향곡 작곡에서 나타나건 아인슈타인의 상대성 발견에서 나타나건 대체로 사람들은 천재는 초인의 특징뿐 아니라 기인의 특징도 가지고 있는 것으로 여긴다. 사람들은 천재를 좋은 비정상으로 여긴다. 게다가 사람들은 천재를 전혀 예측 불가능한 비정상으로 여긴다. 최근까지 심리학자들은 천재들의 기발함을 너무 엉뚱해서 명료하게 설명할 수 없는 것으로 간주했다. 그러나 아나 핀들리(Anna Findley)의 혁신적인 연구가 천재들의 전기에서 예측 가능한 패턴들을 밝혀낸다. 그러나 이러한 패턴들은 일정하게 발생함에도 불구하고 특별히 재능 있는 사람들의 삶에는 일종의 초자연적인 개입이 있다는 일반적인 믿음을 완전히 없애지는 못한다. 예를 들면 핀들리는 모든 천재들은 그들의 삶에서 3번의 매우 생산적인 기간을 경험한다는 것을 보여준다. 신비하게 여겨지겠지만 그 중의 한 시기는 그들이 죽기 직전에 항상 발생한다. 천재가 19세까지 살건 90세까지 살건 이것은 사실이다.

Passage 3

1. Human beings no longer thrive under the water from which their ancestors emerged, but their relationship with the sea remains close. ① Over half the world's people live within 100 kilometres (62 miles) of the coast; a tenth are within 10km. 1) ① On land at least, the sea delights the senses and excites the imagination. The sight and smell of the sea inspire courage and adventure, fear and romance. Though the waves may be rippling or mountainous, the waters angry or calm, the ocean itself is eternal. Its moods pass. Its tides keep to a rhythm. It is unchanging.
② Or so it has long seemed. Appearances deceive, though. Large parts of the sea may indeed remain unchanged, but

바다(중심소재)와 관련된 다양한 주제를 다루고 있으므로 화제가 바뀔 때마다 내용을 정리하도록 한다.
중심소재: 바다와의 관계

1. 도입부
인간은 바다와 밀접한 관계를 유지
① 뒷받침 부연
세계인구의 절반이 바다와 근접해 위치하고 있으므로 언급
1) 구체적 진술
① 육지에서 바라본 바다의 모습
전반적으로 바다의 긍정적 이미지와 함께 영속적 속성을 드러내고 있다.

역접의 'but'을 확인하고, 글쓴이가 강조하려는 부분은 바로 뒤에 이어지는 진술이다

글의 논리적 반전을 이끄는 시그널 though를 확인한다.

가정법은 가정의 현상을 설정하면서 실제 현상을 강조한다.

in others, especially in the surface and coastal waters where 90% of marine life is to be found, the impact of man's activities is increasingly plain. This should hardly be a surprise. Man has changed the landscape and the atmosphere. It would be odd if the seas, which he has for centuries used for food, for transport, for dumping rubbish and, more recently, for recreation, had not also been affected.

② 실제 현상(요지)
though를 기점으로 앞서 변치 않은 바다의 속성과 달리 but이후 실제는 인간의 활용으로 인해 부정적 영향을 받았다는 내용으로 전개되고 있다.

정답 1 (A) 2 (C) 3 (D)

해설

1 첫째 단락에서 바다의 모습을 둘째 단락에서는 그 영원할 것처럼 보이는 바다가 육상과 대기처럼 인간의 활동에 영향을 받아 변화했다는 것을 이야기하고 있으므로 이 글의 주제는 (A)가 적절하다.

2 글의 전후 관계에서 겉으로 보기에 영원한 것처럼 보이 지만 실제로는 인간에 의해 변화했다는 것을 언급하므로 '겉모습은 거짓말을 한다.'의 의미가 적절하다.

3 첫째 단락에서 주장을 밝히고자 사용한 기법은 바다의 모습을 구체적으로 하나하나 기술한 열거이다.

지문해석

인간은 자신의 조상이 출현했던 물 아래에서 더 이상 번성하지 못하지만 바다와 그들의 관계는 밀접하다. 전 세계 사람들의 반 이상이 해안으로부터 100킬로미터 이내에서 살고 있으며 10분의 1은 10킬로미터 이내에 있다. 적어도 육상에서 보면 바다는 감각들을 기쁘게 하며 상상력을 자극한다. 바다의 광경과 냄새는 용기와 모험 두려움과 낭만을 자극한다. 비록 파도가 잔물결이 일거나 산과같이 거대할 수도 있고 바다가 분노 하거나 고요할 수도 있지만 바다 자체는 영원하다. 바다의 변덕은 지나간다. 바다의 조수는 규칙적 반복을 지킨다. 바다는 변하지 않는다.

아니 그렇게 오랫동안 바다는 보여 왔다. 그러나 겉모습은 믿을 수 없다. 바다의 많은 지역들이 실제로 변화하지 않았을지 모르지만 다른 지역들에서 특히 해양 생명체의 90%가 발견될 수 있는 해수면과 해안에서 인간 활동이 미치는 영향은 점점 명백해지고 있다. 이는 놀라운 일이 아닐 것이다. 인간은 주변의 풍경과 대기도 바꾸어 놓고 있다. 만약 인간이 수 세기 동안 식량 운송 쓰레기 투기 그리고 보다 최근에는 휴양을 위해 이용해왔던 바다도 또한 인간의 활동에 영향을 받지 않았다면 이상할 것이다.

글의 도입부에서 중심소재의 폭이 좁아지고 있다: other writing systems → the Chinese script

Passage 4

1. There are other writing systems similar to the Egyptian one. The most important one still in use is the Chinese script. Such systems are often called logographic, meaning 'word-writing'. 1) Unlike the Egyptian system, the Chinese writing system probably evolved quite independently of other writing systems. It is also considerably younger. The first texts in Chinese date back to around 1200 BC, which means the scripts has now been in use for more than 3,000 years. ① A logographic system is by its nature more conservative than an alphabetic system. Ⓐ An alphabet conveys sounds, and as the sounds of a spoken language

영문단락 전개의 특징: 연역적 전개

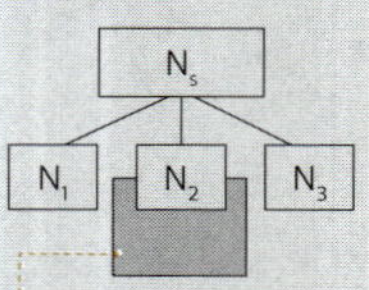

N_2로 중심소재가 좁아지며 구체적 주제가 드러난다

중심소재: 중국문자

1. 도입부 = 중심소재 파악
로고그래픽에 속하는 중국문자
1) 중국문자에 관한 간략한 배경

① 주제문
알파벳보다 보수적이다.
Ⓐ 뒷받침 진술
소리의 변화에 영향에 받지 않는 로고그래픽의 보수적 특징을 알파벳과의 대조를 통해서 상술하고 있다.

are always in a state of change, the difference between written and spoken language gradually becomes more pronounced. But it is possible to reform the spelling so that the direct connection between the spoken sound and the written symbol is restored. In a script of a more symbolic kind some signs denote meanings without any relation to the pronunciation. That is, the signs do not convey sounds. For this reason, such a script is more liable to remain unchanged even if the spoken language undergoes considerable change.

정답 **1** (B) **2** (A) **3** (A)

지문분석

문자의 특성을 다루는 글로 특히 대조의 글 전개방식을 활용하여 특히 logographic이라 불리는 중국의 문자의 특성을 다루고 있다.

해설

1 이집트 문자와 비슷한 체계로 중국의 문자를 언급하면서, 중국문자의 특징을 알파벳과 대조하고 있다. 고로 이집트 문자가 알파벳 문자를 포함하고 있다는 선택지 (B)는 틀린 진술이다. It is also considerably younger.와 이후 진술로 선택지 (A)는 옳은 진술이다. An alphabet conveys sounds, and as the sounds of a spoken language are always in a state of change, the difference between written and spoken language gradually becomes more pronounced.부분에서 선택지 (C)의 내용을 확인할 수 있다. 선택지 (D)의 경우 본문 마지막 부분에서 상징적 문자에서도 발음은 변할 수 있다고 언급되어 있다. Unlike the Egyptian system, the Chinese writing system probably evolved quite independently of other writing systems.에서 이집트의 문자는 다른 문자에 영향을 받았다는 것을 유추할 수 있다. 고로 선택지 (E)도 옳은 진술이다.

2 문자의 특성을 다루는 글로 특히 대조의 글 전개방식을 활용하여 특히 logographic이라 불리는 중국의 문자의 특성을 다루고 있다.

3 바로 뒤에 이어지는 재진술 that is를 활용한다. the signs do not conveys sounds.'부분에서 알 수 있듯이 빈칸에는 sounds에 해당하는 선택지 (A)가 가장 적절하다.

지문해석

이집트 문자와 유사한 다른 문자들이 있다. 지금도 여전히 사용되는 가장 중요한 문자는 중국 문자이다. 이러한 문자 체계는 종종 '로고그래픽'이라 불리는 것으로 '단어-쓰기'라는 의미이다. 이집트 문자와 달리, 중국의 문자는 아마도 다른 문자와는 전혀 독립적으로 발달한 듯하다. 또한 아주 최근의 것이다. 중국의 첫 번째 텍스트는 약 기원전 1200년으로 거슬러 올라가는데, 이 글이 현재 3000년 이상 사용이 되어 왔다는 의미이다. '로고그래픽' 문자는 알파벳 체제보다 그 특성상 더 보수적이다. 알파벳은 소리를 전달하고, 구어의 소리는 항상 변화를 겪고 있기에, 문어와 구어 사이의 구별이 점차적으로 더 뚜렷해진다. 그러나 말의 소리와 문자의 상징 사이의 직접적 관계가 다시 생겨나도록 철자를 바꾸는 것이 가능하다. 좀 더 상징적인 종류의 글에서 특정 기호는 발음과 전혀 관련성이 없이 의미를 나타낸다. 다시 말해, 이 기호는 소리를 전달하지 않는다. 이러한 이유에서 이러한 글은 비록 구어가 상당한 변화를 겪지만 변화하지 않고 좀 더 지속된다.

글 전개방식의 종류(문제에서 물어볼 수 있는 유형이므로 해당 영어표현도 암기하도록 한다)

1) 나열
(listing, enumeration)
2) 비교·대조
(comparison·contrast)
중심소재가 두 개이며, 대조의 글이 특히 시험에 잘 나온다. 1대 다수의 법칙을 활용한 통념의 글도 대조의 글의 한 유형이다.
3) 인과
(cause and effect)
현상의 글에서 자주 활용되는 글 전개방식이다.
4) 시간
(chronologic order)·
공간(spacial order)·
단계(procedure)

Passage 5

1. The most important political text of the medieval era was the same one that ended the Christian influence in political theory: Niccolo Machiavelli's *The Prince*. 1) ① This book created the conceptual framework in which modern political philosophy operates. Ⓐ Machiavelli wrote the text for the Medici family and included a number of shrewd political actions that one could use to acquire and hold power. Ⓑ *The Prince* was authored in the midst of the chaos in which a number of factions fought for control of Italy. Ⓒ As such, much of the work centers on balancing the interest of the state with the interest of the public. ② It also contains advice on dealing with internal and external enemies to the state. Most famously, *The Prince* is known for its endorsement of cruel or inhumane actions to maintain power. 2. The question addressed in the work provided a conceptual framework that directed the focus of the Enlightenment. Much of this time was spent creating a political body of thought that adhered to the liberal principles of justice and rationality.

중심소재: 마키아벨리의 군주론

1. 도입부 = 중심소재 도출
마키아벨리의 군주론에 관한 글이다.

1) 구체적 진술

①특징 1
현대 정치정학의 이론적 틀 제공
Ⓐ 저작의 목적
메디치 가문이 권력을 얻고 유지하는데 사용할 수 있는 수많은 정치적 계략을 포함.
Ⓑ 역사적 배경
다양한 당파가 이탈리아의 통치권을 차지하기 위한 싸움을 벌이던 혼란 속에서 집필됨
Ⓒ 내용
국가의 이해관계를 국민의 이해관계와 균형을 이루는데 집중

②특징 2
내외에 존재하는 국가의 적을 다루는 방법이 포함되어 있는데, 아주 잔인하고 비인간적인 방법을 추구한 것으로 악명이 높음

2. 역사적 의의(영향)
군주론의 잔인성에 대한 회의적 태도는 정의와 합리성의 자유주의 원칙고수라는 계몽주의가 추구할 방향의 틀 제공

정답 **1** (B) **2** (D) **3** (C)

지문분석

마키아벨리의 '군주론'에 관한 전반적인 내용을 개괄적으로 다루고 있다. 소개되는 각각의 내용을 정확히 파악하도록 한다.

해설

1 셋째 문장에서 마키아벨리가 군주론을 저술한 목적은 메디치 가문이 지속적으로 권력을 장악하고 유지하는데 도움을 주려는 것이었다고 언급하고 있다.

2 "교활하다"는 의미로 (D) wily가 정답이다.

3 권력을 유지하기 위해 수단과 방법을 가리지 않았던 마키아벨리의 입장과는 달리 자유주의적 계몽주의 사상가들은 정의와 합리성에 의거하는 정치사상체를 모색하게 된다. 따라서 계몽주의 사상가들과 마키아벨리의 입장은 서로 상치되고 있으므로 "계몽주의 사상가들이 마키아벨리의 입장을 지지했다"는 (C)는 사실과 거리가 멀다.

지문해석

중세 시대의 가장 중요한 정치 서적은 정치 이론에 있어 기독교적 영향력을 종식시켰던 것과 동일한 서적인 니콜로 마키아벨리의 '군주론'이었다. 이 책은 현대 정치철학이 운용되고 있는 이론적인 틀을 창시했다. 마키아벨리는 메디치 가문을 위해서 이 책을 저술했으며, 책에는 권력을 획득하고 유지하기 위해 이용할 수 있는 수많은 정치적 계략이 담겨 있다. 군주론은 이탈리아의 통치권을 차지하기 위해 수많은 파벌들이 싸우고 있던 혼란스런 시대에 저술되었다. 그러한 것으로서 이 책의 내용 중 많은 부분은 국가의 이해관계를 대중의 이해관계와 균형을 이루게 하는 것에 집중되어 있다. 그것은 또한 국가의 대내외적인 적들을 다루는 데 대한 충고를 담고 있다. 가장 유명한 것은, 군주론이 권력을 유지하기 위해서는 잔인하거나 비인간적인 조치를 취

해도 무방하다고 인정한 것으로 잘 알려져 있다. 이 작품에서 다룬 문제는 계몽주의 시대가 중점적으로 추구할 방향을 정한 이론적인 틀을 제공했다. 계몽주의 시대에는 정의와 합리성의 자유주의적 원칙을 고수하는 정치사상체제를 창출하는 데 많은 시간을 보냈다.

Passage 6

1. One of the first principles that you must understand in advertising is that 1) ① it is limited in both time and space. Ⓐ Television and radio commercials are usually only 10 to 60 seconds long. Ⓑ Print ads are usually no larger than two pages, and usually much smaller. Therefore, an advertisement must do its job quickly. ⓐ It must get the consumer's attention, identify the product, and deliver the selling message in a small time or space. In order to do this, advertising often breaks the rules of grammar, image, and even society.

② The second basic point is that advertisements usually have two parts: copy and illustrations. Ⓐ Copy refers to the words in the advertisement. These words give the sales message. Ⓑ Illustrations are pictures or photographs. Most ads are a combination of copy and illustration. ⓐ Some advertisements have small illustration and a lot of copy. Some are only an illustration with the name of product. The decision about how much copy and illustration to use depends on how the advertiser wants to present the sales message. Understanding how advertisers make this decision is complex.

중심소재: 광고

1. 도입부 = 주제설정

One of the principles에서 알 수 있듯이 "광고의 원칙"을 다루는 글임

1) 뒷받침 진술

①광고의 원칙 1
시간과 공간의 제약
Ⓐ 시간: 10~60초
Ⓑ 공간: 2 페이지 내
ⓐ 제약된 시간과 공간으로 인해 문법, 이미지 그리고 사회의 규칙을 깸

②광고의 원칙 2
카피와 삽화로 구성됨
Ⓐ 카피의 개념과 기능
Ⓑ 삽화의 개념
ⓐ 부연진술
카피와 삽화를 활용한 광고

첫 번째 문장을 통해 중심소재인 광고(포괄적 주제)에 관한 글임을 파악할 수 있다. 중심내용을 바탕으로 포괄적 주제의 폭을 좁혀 구체적 주제를 설정하도록 한다.

영문단락 전개:
먼저 언급된 것 먼저 기술된다.

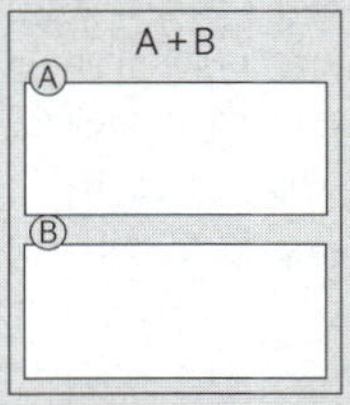

정답 **1** (D) **2** (B)

해설

1 본문 후반부에서 다양한 방법을 통해 광고를 전달함을 통해 보기 (A)는 옳다는 것을 알 수 있다. 선택지 (B)의 경우도 광고의 두 번째 원칙에 잘 드러나 있다. 선택지 (3) 또한 본문 마지막을 통해서 알 수 있는데, 본문에서 성공적인 광고가 반드시 헤드라인을 포함해야 한다는 내용은 없다. 참고로, 선택지 (A)와 (D)는 서로 의미가 상충한다는 의미에서 둘 중 하나가 답임을 어느 정도 파악할 수도 있다.

2 it is limited in both time and space.에서 선택지 (B)가 정답임을 알 수 있다.

지문해석

광고기법에 있어 이해해야 할 가장 중요한 원리 중 하나는 광고가 시간과 공간 면에서 제한성이 있다는 것이다. 텔레비전이나 라디오의 상업 광고는 길이가 대개 10내지 60초에 불과하다. 인쇄물 광고는 대개 두 페이지를 넘지 않거나 대개 이보다도 훨씬 분량이 적다. 따라서 광고는 신속히 제 할 일을 해내야 한다. 소비자의 주의를 끌고, 제품의 용도를 밝히고, 판매 목적을 담은 메시지를 전하는 일을 짧은 시간이나 작은 공간 안에 해내야 하는 것이다. 이렇게 하기 위해 광고는 종종 문법, 영상, 심지어는 사회의 규칙까지도 어기는 경우가 있다. 두 번째 기본적인 점은 대개 광고는 광고 문안과 삽화라는 두 부분으로 구성되어 있다는 것이다. 광

고 문안은 광고 속의 글을 가리키는데 이 글이 판매 메시지를 전달한다. 삽화는 그림이나 사진이다. 대부분의 광고는 광고 문안과 삽화가 공동으로 결합된 것이다. 적은 삽화와 많은 광고 문안으로 된 광고도 있고 제품의 이름과 함께 삽화만 덜렁 있는 광고도 있다. 광고 문안과 삽화 사용의 분량을 정하는 결정은 광고주의 판매 메시지 전달 선호도에 달려 있다. 광고주가 어떻게 이런 결정을 내리는가를 이해하는 것은 복잡한 일이다.

응집성

응집성이란 문장 또는 문단 간의 논리적 연결을 말한다. 일반적으로 문장 또는 문단 간의 응집성을 드러내는 시그널은 다음과 같다.

1) 연결사
2) 대명사(지시대명사, 지시형용사, 부정대명사의 순서)
3) a N → the N → it/that
4) 순차적 행위를 나타내는 동사
5) 글 전개와 유형

본문의 경우 유형의 측면에서 "현상 → 문제점 지적 → 대안"의 패턴으로 이어지는 유형이다.

Passage 7

1. Cemeteries are not the only "detestable facilities" that have had difficulties in finding locations along with the advent of local autonomous system. **1)** Construction of 26 waste management facilities has been suspended throughout the nation. Walls of UNESCO-designated royal palaces in Seoul are wrapped in rubbish. The situations are little better for nuclear waste storages, sewage disposal plants and dams.

2. Clean, orderly disposal of remnants, either human or material, is the first test of a mature society. **1)** ① Officials should set up a long-term, comprehensive plan on the waste management facilities through the persistent discussion with and persuasion of residents along with convincing incentives. Now is also time for the people to shift from unconditional NIMBY to conditional "YIMBY" (Yes-In-My-Back-Yard) with a broader and pragmatic viewpoint.

중심소재: 혐오시설

1. 첫 번째 문단

1) 도입부 = 현상(문제점)

지방지치제의 도입으로 혐오시설을 설치할 장소를 찾기 어려움

① 구체적 진술

26개 폐기물 처리시설 건설이 중단된 상태

Ⓐ 핵폐기물저장소와 하수처리공장 또한 동일한 상황

2. 두 번째 문단

1) 대안

① 정부 차원

주민과의 충분한 대화와 설득 + 인센티브 제공

② 지방시민차원

unconditional NIMBY → conditional "YIMBY"라는 실용적 관점의 필요

정답 1 (D) 2 (B)

해설

1 Now is also time for the people to shift from unconditional NIMBY to conditional "YIMBY" (Yes-In-My-Back-Yard) with a broader and pragmatic viewpoint. 부분에서 선택지 (D)의 내용을 파악할 수 있다.

2 (B)는 혐오시설 기피현상의 원인에 해당하는 것이지 혐오시설 자체가 아니다.

지문해석

공동묘지가 지방자치 제도의 도래와 더불어 장소 선정에 어려움을 겪어 온 유일한 "혐오 시설"인 것은 아니다. 전국적으로 26개 폐기물 관리 시설의 –그 중 반은 퇴적장이고 나머지 반은 소각장인데– 건설이 일시 중지 상태에 처해 있다. 서울에 있는 유네스코 지정 왕궁들의 담벼락들은 쓰레기로 둘러싸여 있다. 폐기물 저장소, 하수 처리장, 댐 등의 경우도 상황은 더 나을 것이 없다.

인간이 남긴 찌꺼기이든 물질찌꺼기이든, 찌꺼기를 깨끗하고 말끔하게 처리하는 것이 성숙된 사회의 첫째가는 시금석이다. 관청에서는 납득할 만한 보상제도와 아울러 주민들과의 지속적인 토론과 설득을 통해 폐기물 관리 시설에 대한 장기적이고 포괄적인 계획을 수립해야 한다. 이제 또한 전 국민이 보다 넓고 실용적인 시각을 가지고, 무조건적인 '님비'에서 조건적인 "임비(Yes-In-My-Back-Yard)"로 옮겨 가야할 때인 것이다.

Passage 8

1. 1) Last week, the London Underground was a scene of carnage, not shelter. ① Three terrorist bombs in the subways (a fourth blew up a bus) killed at least 49 people and wounded 700 more. In one deep tunnel, blocked by the mangled wreckage of a subway car and teeming with rats, rescuers had still not dug out all of the bodies two days after the attack. The message was clear enough to Londoners and the rest of the world: in the age of terror, there are no sanctuaries, no safe places to hide.

2. 1) ① The July 7 bombings were the bloodiest day in England since World War II. Still, the toll of "7/7" was nothing compared with the Blitz, which claimed 20,000 civilians between 1940 and '41, as many as 1,500 in one night. "If London can survive the Blitz, it can survive four miserable events like this," said Sir Ian Blair, the London Metropolitan Police commissioner. ② From the early '70s to the mid-'90s, the British endured more than two decades of terrorist attacks from the Irish Republican Army (though the IRA, in contrast to Al Qaeda, usually called in a warning before setting off a bomb).

3. After last week's attack, British pluck and phlegm were once more the order of the day. A charming child during World War II, Queen Elizabeth II, now dowdy, squat, but unmistakably regal, toured hospitals and declared: "Sadly, we in Britain have been all too familiar with acts of terror, and members of my generation ... know that we have been here before. But those who perpetrate these brutal acts against innocent people should know that they will not change our way of life." Her message: Hitler tried to terrorize Londoners into submission, too, and, far from conquering Britain, he died a suicide's death in a bunker beneath Berlin.

4. 1) For Americans, the echoes were more recent and less reassuring, especially when the news first broke. Maybe, many Americans were beginning to hope, the horror of 9/11 had been an aberration, radical Islam's grotesquely lucky shot in the dark, not a harbinger. There have, of course, been many terrorist bombings since 9/11, in places from Bali to Turkey to Kenya to Spain. But Americans feel a unique kinship with their British cousins, whose common

중심소재: 테러사건

1. 첫 번째 문단

1) 도입부 = 현상(사건)

엄청난 인명 피해가 발생한 런던 테러

① 구체적 진술

2. 두 번째 문단

과거 이보다 더 처참한 사건을 견딘 런던 사람들을 언급하면서 현재의 어려움도 이겨 낼 수 있다는 메시지를 전달하고 있다.

1) 구체적 진술

① 7/7 폭격

② 70년대 두 차례의 테러

3. 세 번째 문단

다시 현재의 사건으로 돌아와 희생자를 살피는 여왕의 모습을 그리면서 과거에도 그랬듯이 현재의 테러도 우리는 변하지 않을 것이라는 확고한 신념을 드러내고 있다. 히틀러를 언급하면서 영국이 현 상황을 잘 이겨내고 궁극적으로 승리하게 됨을 다시 강조하고 있다.

4. 네 번째 문단

1) 미국인들의 반응

9/11이후 세계 곳곳에 테러가 있었지만, 같은 역사와 언어적 유산을 공유하는 영국에 이러한 불미스러운 사건의 여파로 두려움에 쌓인 미국인들을 언급하고 있다.

뉴스체의 기사이다. 육하원칙에 따라 글을 파악하되, 사건(현상)을 중심으로 파악한다.

글의 통일성(중요)

통일성이란 하나의 단락은 하나의 주제만을 다룬다는 내용이다. 여러 단락으로 구성된 글은 각 단락의 소주제를 설정하고, 각 소주제의 공통분모를 바탕으로 "하나의 주제"를 다시 설정하여 통일성을 이룬다. 평소 각 단락별 소주제를 설정하는 연습을 꾸준히 하면, 글의 논리성을 묻는 순서배열, 문단 나누기와 같은 고난도 문제에 대비가 가능하다.

heritage and language made their suffering seem close to home. After the London bombings, repressed fears surfaced, especially for city dwellers who ride subways and buses and wonder if their everyday morning commute will turn deadly.

정답 **1**(D) **2**(A) **3**(C) **4**(A)

해설

1 carnage는 "대량학살"이란 뜻이다. 밑줄 친 단어의 뜻을 모른다 하더라도 바로 뒤에 이어지는 상황(Three terrorist bombs in the subways killed at least 4 people and wounded 700 more)을 통해 답을 유추할 수 있는 문제다.

어휘와 문장해석 능력의 중요성
영어시험의 꽃은 일반적으로 독해라는 측면에서 글 읽는 능력의 중요성이 강조되는 것은 맞지만, 결국 글을 파악하는 가장 기본은 어휘와 문장단위 해석이다. 본 지문의 문제에서 알 수 있듯이 어휘실력은 곧 문제풀이와 직결된다는 것을 알 수 있다. 단순히 본문에 나온 어휘만을 암기하는 수준에 그치지 말고, 사전을 통해 동의어와 숙어 등을 함께 확인하는 능동적 학습이 필요하다. 영어실력을 결정짓는 궁극적 요소는 어휘임을 잊지 말아야 한다.

2 But Americans feel a unique kinship with their British cousins, whose common heritage and language made their suffering seem close to home.에서 알 수 있듯이 미국인들은 문화적 유산과 언어를 공유하는 영국인들의 최근 참사에 동정심을 느낀다고 언급하고 있다. close to home을 해석할 수 있는지를 묻는 문제로 평소 관용어구 표현을 주의를 기울여야 한다.

3 첫 번째 빈칸이 들어간 문장에서 those는 무고한 사람들(innocent people)에게 피해를 입히는 대상이 됨으로 선택지 (A), (B), (D)가 적절함을 알 수 있다. 두 번째 빈칸의 경우 빈칸을 한정하는 with their British cousins을 통해서 unique kinship을 쉽게 파악할 수 있다.

4 aberration은 "일탈, 비정상"이란 뜻이므로 선택지 (A)가 가장 적절한 의미를 전달하고 있다.

지문해석

지난주 런던 지하철은 대피소가 아니라 대학살의 현장이었다. 세 건의 폭탄 테러로(네 번째는 버스를 폭파시킴) 최소한 49명이 사망했고 700명 이상이 부상당했다. 망가진 지하철 잔해와 쥐들로 가득 찬 깊은 터널에서 구조대원들은 공격 발생 후 이틀이 지나서까지도 시신을 모두 수습하지 못했다. 런던 사람들과 세계 여러 다른 나라들에게 전해진 교훈은 분명하고도 남았다. 테러의 시대에는 피난처도, 숨기에 안전한 장소도 없다.

7월 7일의 폭격은 제2차 세계대전 이후 영국에서 가장 유혈이 낭자한 날이었다. 그러나 이른바 "7/7" 사건의 사상자 수도 런던 대공습*(the Blitz)에 비하면 아무 것도 아니었는데, 당시엔 1940년–41년 사이에 2만 명의 목숨을 앗아갔고 하룻밤에 1,500명이 사망하기도 했다. "런던이 런던 대공습을 잘 이겨낼 수 있으면 이 같은 네 건의 비참한 사건 역시 극복할 수 있다."고 런던 경찰국장 이안 블레어(Ian Blair) 경은 말했다. 70년대 초부터 90년대 중반까지 영국인들은 아일랜드 공화국군(IRA)의 20년 이상 계속된 테러 공격을 참아 왔다(아일랜드 공화국군은 알 카에다와는 대조적으로 폭탄을 터트리기 전에 전화로 경고를 했다). 지난 주 공격 이후 영국인들의 용기와 침착함은 다시 한 번 유행이 되었다. 제2차 세계대전 당시 매력적인 소녀였던 엘리자베스 2세 여왕은 이제는 촌스럽고 구부정하지만 분명 위엄 있는 모습으로 병원들을 돌아다니며 "슬프게도 영국에 있는 우리 모두 테러 행위들에 너무나 익숙해져 왔고 우리 세대 구성원들은 ... 우리가 이전에도 이곳에 있어왔다는 것을 알고 있다. 그러나 무고한 사람들을 상대로 이러한 잔인한 행위를 저지른 사람들은 자신들이 우리의 생활양식을 바꿀 수 없다는 점을 알아야만 한다."고 단언했다. 그녀가 전달하고자 하는 메시지는 분명하다. 히틀러 역시 런던 사람들을 위협해 굴복시키려 했으나 영국을 정복하기는커녕 베를린 지하 벙커에서 자살했다는 것이다.

미국인들에게는 그 반향이 더욱 새롭고 안심을 앗아가는 것이었는데, 특히 그 소식이 처음 알려졌을 때 그러했다. 어쩌면 많은 미국인들은 9/11의 공포가 어떠한 조짐이 아니라 일탈, 이슬람 급진주의자들의 기괴한 요행이길 바라기 시작했다. 물론 9/11 이후 발리에서부터 터키, 케냐, 스페인에 이르는 여러 지역에서 테러범들의 폭격이 많았다. 그러나 미국인들은 그들의 영국 사촌들에게 특유의 연대감을 느꼈고 영국인들의 공통된 유산과 언어는 그들의 고통을 절실히 보이게 했다. 런던 폭탄 테러 사건 이후 억눌렸던 공포가 표출되었는데, 특히 지하철과 버스를 탑승하는 그들의 매일 아침 출근길이 치명적으로 변할 것을 걱정하는 도시인들 사이에서 그러했다.

*런던 대공습(the Blitz): 1940년 독일군에 의한 폭격 작전

TEST 03

Passage 1

1. Psychologists find more inaction, conformity, passivity, and reliance on others in the elderly. Yet, desires for mastery and control are likely to remain strong. 1) At the very least, old people are able to continue to make choices and exert control over daily routines. Work of some sort, which imparts a sense of being productive and useful, predicts living to an old age. ① Research findings suggest that feelings of control actually enhance mental and physical health and promote longevity.
Ⓐ In one series of studies, for instance, psychologists randomly divided nursing home residents from ages 65 to 90 into two groups. Adults in the first group heard a pep talk emphasizing the need to take greater responsibility in caring for themselves and improving the quality of their lives. Members of this high-responsibility group chose a living plant to tend, to symbolize their commitment. The residents in the low-responsibility group were told that the staff would serve them well. Each individual in this group also received a symbolic plant that the nurses would feed and water, just as the nurses planned to take care of them.
2. What was the result of this experiment? The members of the high-responsibility group thrived. They showed significantly more signs of alertness, active participation, and positive feelings than did those in the low-responsibility group. The differences lasted long. There was an even more remarkable finding: A sense of control appeared to prolong life, with more patients in the high-responsibility group surviving than those in the other group by 15 percent eighteen months later.

중심소재: 노인들의 지배와 통제 욕망

1. 도입부
일반적 통념과 달리 노인들은 지배와 통제하려는 욕망은 여전히 남아 있음

1) 효과(요지)
일에 대한 지배와 통제는 생산적이고, 여전히 유용하다는 감정을 심어 주어 수명연장의 효과가 있다.

① 뒷받침 부연(요지)
연구를 통해 수명연장의 효과를 증명
Ⓐ 실험의 구체적 내용

2. 실험의 결과(요지)
일에 대한 지배와 통제력은 수명 연장에 도움을 준다.

실험·조사·연구
실험·조사·연구의 글에서 실험의 목적은 주제가 되고, 결과가 곧 요지가 됨을 기억한다. 요지를 이끄는 시그널은 다음과 같다.
1) find out, discover
2) show, reveal, indicate, suggest
3) result, discovery

위와 같은 표현 다음에 나오는 내용은 곧 글의 요지가 된다.

정답 1 (D) 2 (A) 3 (A)

지문분석
글 전반에 요지가 드러나는 글로 "삶에 대한 통제 의식은 수명을 연장하는 효과가 있다."는 내용이다.

해설
1 본문은 삶에 대한 통제 의식은 수명을 연장하는 효과가 있다는 내용이 요지다.
2 with more patients in the high-responsibility group surviving than those in the other group by 1 percent eighteen months later에서 답의 직접적인 힌트를 발견할 수 있다.

3 내용일치의 경우 선택지 중 하나만 본문과 일치한다는 점에서 일반적으로 글의 요지가 답인 경우가 많다. 본 문제도 글의 요지를 고르는 내용일치 문제다.

지문해석

심리학자들은 노인들에게서 더 많은 게으름, 순종, 수동성, 다른 사람들에 대한 의존을 발견한다. 그러나 지배와 관리에 대한 욕망은 강하게 남아있는 것 같다. 적어도 노인들은 계속해서 선택을 하고 일상생활에 대한 관리를 할 수 있다. 생산적이고 유용하다는 느낌을 주는 어떤 종류의 일은 장수를 예측한다. 연구결과는 생활을 제대로 관리하고 있다는 느낌은 정신 건강과 육체 건강을 고취시키고 장수를 촉진한다고 암시한다.

예를 들면 일련의 연구들에서 심리학자들은 65세에서 90세에 이르는 요양원 거주자들을 무작위로 두 집단으로 나누었다. 첫 번째 집단의 노인들은 자기 자신들을 돌보고 그들의 삶의 질을 향상시키는 데 있어서 더 큰 책임감의 필요성을 강조하는 격려의 말을 들었다. 이러한 책임감이 높은 집단의 사람들은 그들의 책임을 상징하는 것으로 그들이 돌볼 식물을 골랐다. 책임감이 낮은 집단에 속한 거주자들은 직원들이 그들을 잘 보살필 것이라는 말을 들었다. 이 집단의 사람들 또한 간호사들이 그들을 돌보는 것처럼 간호사들이 기르고 물을 줄 상징적인 식물을 받았다.

이 실험의 결과는 무엇이었는가? 책임감이 높은 집단의 사람들은 성장했다. 그들은 책임감이 낮은 집단에 있는 사람들보다 상당히 더 많은 조심성, 능동적인 참여, 그리고 긍정적인 감정의 표시를 보여주었다. 그 차이들은 오래 지속되었다. 훨씬 더 주목할 만한 발견이 있었다. 책임감이 높은 집단의 환자들이 다른 집단의 환자들보다 18개월 후 15%만큼 더 많이 생존해 있었기 때문에 관리 의식이 수명을 연장시키는 것 같았다.

Passage 2

but을 기준으로 과거와 현재가 대조된다. 시간의 대조는 내용의 대조임을 기억한다.

과거
⊕
현재
⊖

1\. 1) There was a time—less than a generation—when games weren't just for kids. ① Before we owned home-entertainment centers, we had game cabinets. But ② today, with the time drain of television, exhausting commutes and longer working hours, the scatter of extended families and the deepening devotion to home computers and the Internet, it's easy to see how our so-called leisure time has been fractured. Ⓐ Still, there are anachronisms among us—ⓐ the corporate lawyer who sneaks off to play backgammon at lunch, the longtime pals who arrange joint vacations around bridge tournament. One game master is Ken Tidwell, a California software designer and editor of The Game Cabinet, a monthly Web magazine that scouts out games from around the world. He and his wife, Jocelyn, a free-lance writer, host dinner-and-game parties for six to 20 people nearly every week. Often several card or board games rage at once.

중심소재: 게임

1. 도입부 = 현상

1) 이후 과거와 현재를 대조되는 현상을 제시하고 있다.

① 과거

집에서 게임을 즐김

② 현재

TV, 통근, 장시간의 근무 등으로 대가족이 무너지고 컴퓨터와 인터넷으로 인해 여가시간(오락시간)이 줄어들었다.

Ⓐ 주제문

이런 상황에서도 여전히 게임을 즐기는 사람(anachronism)이 있다고 소개하고 있다.

ⓐ 뒷받침 사례

정답 1 (C)

해설

첫 문단에서 "오늘날에는 여러 가지 일로 여가 시간에 게임을 하기 어렵지만 옛날에는 어른들도 게임을 즐겼다"고 했으므로 시대에 뒤진 사람들(anachronism)이란 옛날처럼 게임을 즐기는 어른들을 의미한다.

지문해석

게임이 아이들만을 위한 것이 아니었던 시기—한 세대도 채 안 된—가 있었다. 우리가 가정 놀이 센터를 소유하기 전에 우리는 게임용 방을 가지고 있었다. 그러나 오늘날에는, 텔레비전에 시간을 빼앗기고, 힘든 출퇴근과 더 오랜 근무에 시간을 보내고, 확대 가족들이 흩어져 살게 되고, 개인용 컴퓨터와 인터넷에 점점 더 깊이 몰입하는 것 등으로 인해, 소위 여가 시간이 어떻게 균열되어 왔는가는 쉽게 알 수 있다. 그러나 우리들 중에는 시대에 뒤떨어진 사람들이 있다. 점심시간에 배개먼(서양 주사위놀이)을 하기 위해 몰래 나오는 회사 변호사, 브리지게임 시합장에서 같이 휴가를 보내기로 하는 오래된 친구들. 한 게임의 대가는 캘리포니아의 소프트웨어 디자이너이며 전 세계의 게임을 찾아다니는 월간 잡지인 게임 캐비닛의 편집자인 켄 티드웰이다. 그와 프리랜서 작가인 그의 아내 조셀린은 거의 매주 6 내지 20명의 사람들에게 게임과 만찬을 곁들인 파티를 연다. 흔히 파티장은 몇몇 카드게임이나 보드게임으로 즉시 달아오른다.

Passage 3

1. 1) The apocalyptic scenario begins with an earthquake near Yucca Mountain, a barren ridge that is the burial site for the nation's most lethal nuclear waste. The tremor is minor; but fresh movement in the earth's crust causes ground water to well up suddenly, flooding the repository. Soon, a lethal brew of nuclear poisons seeps into the water that flows underground to nearby Death Valley. Insects, birds and animals drink at the valley's contaminated springs, and slowly the radioactivity spreads into the biosphere. If this scenario becomes a reality, it would be a terrible disaster.

2) The twin virtues of the Yucca Mountain site are its remoteness and dryness. The only sign of civilization is the dusty trace of a dirt road cutting across a brown, barren valley. ① The ridge is located on the southwest corner of the Nevada Test Site, where the government explodes nuclear weapons, so access is tightly restricted. ② Sagebrush and other desert plants attest to the locale's remarkable dryness.

③ Indeed, only six inches of rain fall on the mountain each year, and most of the moisture evaporates, leaving as little as one fiftieth of an inch to soak into the ground. The water table is unusually deep, more than one third of a mile below the surface. Ⓐ According to the Department of Energy, which is charged with building the repository, nuclear waste could be buried far beneath the ground yet still rest safely above the ground water.

중심소재: 핵폐기물처리장인 유카산

1. 도입부

핵폐기물 처리장인 유카산에 관한 글임을 파악하도록 한다.

1) 유카산을 중심으로 세계종말 시나리오를 전개하고 있다.

지진 → 지하수 상승 → 핵폐기물 처리장 범람 → 유독한 핵폐기물이 근처 Death Valley로 이동 → 근처 동물이 오염됨 → 점차적으로 생태계에 번짐 → 엄청난 재앙

2) 뒷받침 근거

유카산을 핵폐기물 처리장으로 선정한 두 가지 장점(지역적 조건과 건조한 환경)

①지역적 조건에 대한 부연

②건조한 환경에 대한 부연

순접추가부연을 확인한다.

③추가적 장점

비가 거의 내리지 않고, 건조한 기후로 습기는 모두 증발 + 지하수면이 아주 깊이 매장되어 있음

Ⓐ 핵폐기물은 지하수면보다 훨씬 더 아래 매장되어 있고, 그 위에 매장되어도 안전함

정답 1 (C) 2 (D)

지문분석

첫 번째 문단에서 지구종말의 시나리오를 가정하고 있지만, 두 번째와 세 번째 문단을 통해 유카산이 핵폐기물 지역으로

안전하다는 내용을 전달하고 있다.

해설

1 바로 앞 내용을 보면, "지하수면은 매우 깊은 곳에 있다"고 했으므로 첫 번째 빈칸에는 거리가 멀리 떨어져 있거나 또는 아래를 나타내는 전치사가 필요하다는 점과 바로 앞 문장에 "핵폐기물은 지하 훨씬 밑에 묻힐 수도 있으나"라고 하였으므로 below임을 알 수 있다. 두 번째 빈칸은 "물이 갑자기 분출하게 하여 폐기물 저장소를 물에 잠기게 한다"는 내용으로 미루어 핵폐기물은 지하수위에 있다는 것을 알 수 있다.

2 본문의 The twin virtues of the Yucca Mountain site are its remoteness and dryness와 이후 전개되는 부연진술을 통해서 선택지 (D)는 옳음을 파악할 수 있다.

선택지가 한글인 경우 먼저 읽고 지문을 읽는다.

지문해석

세계 종말의 시나리오는 유카(Yucca)산 근처에서 발생한 지진과 함께 시작하는데, 이 황폐한 봉우리는 그 나라에서 가장 치명적인 핵폐기물을 매립한 지역이다. (지진의) 진동은 미미하지만, 지각의 새로운 움직임은 지면 가까이 있던 물을 갑자기 분출하게 하여 그 폐기물 저장소를 물에 잠기게 된다. 곧 죽음의 계곡(Death Valley) 근처를 향해 흐르던 지하수에 치명적인 핵 유해 물질을 지닌 액체가 스며들게 된다. 벌레, 새, 그리고 동물들은 계곡의 오염된 샘에서 물을 마시고, 곧 이어 방사능은 생물권 전체로 퍼지게 된다. 만약 이 시나리오가 현실이 된다면, 그것은 끔찍한 재앙이 될 것이다. 유카산 지역의 두 가지 장점은 도시와 멀리 떨어져 있다는 점과 건조하다는 점이다. 문명화를 보여주는 유일한 표시는 갈색의 메마른 계곡을 가로지르는 진흙길의 먼지 가득한 흔적뿐이다. 그 봉우리는 네바다 주의 핵실험 장소인 남서쪽의 구석진 곳에 위치해 있는데, 이곳은 정부가 핵무기를 폭파시키기 때문에 접근이 엄격히 제한되어 있다. 산쑥과 다른 사막 식물들은 그 지역이 현저히 건조하다는 것을 증명한다. 게다가, 그 산에는 비가 연간 6인치밖에 안되는데, 대부분의 수분은 증발되고, 50분의 1인치의 수분만이 지하로 스며들게 된다. 지표면 아래로 3분의 1마일 이상이나 되는 곳에 지하수면은 위치해 있다. 매립지 건설을 담당하는 동력자원부에 따르면, 핵폐기물은 지하 훨씬 밑에 묻힐 수도 있으나, 지하수위에서도 안전하게 놓여있다고 한다.

어댑터의 의도(목적), 특징을 다루는 글이다. 다양한 내용을 다루기에 특정한 내용을 바탕으로 주제를 설정하지 말아야 한다.

주제와 내용일치·불일치 선택지 (오류) 만드는 원리

1) Paraphrasing(문장의 구조를 변경하거나 동의어 및 영영활용)
2) 부분 → 전체로 확대 해석(일반화오류)
3) 논리적 비약(예: 그는 자전거를 잘 탄다. 고로, 자가용도 잘 운전할 것이다)
4) 선택지에 숫자가 언급되면, 본문에 언급된 해당 숫자에 주의한다.
5) 대조되는 두 대상이 언급되는 지문의 경우 두 대상의 특징을 교차하는 경우가 많다.

Passage 4

1. Adaptors are nonverbal behaviors designed to satisfy some need. 1) Sometimes the need is ① physical, as when we scratch to satisfy an itch or when we push our hair out of our eyes. Sometimes the need is ② psychological, as when we bite our lip when anxious. Sometimes adaptors are directed at increasing comfort, as when we moisten dry lips. 2) When these adaptors occur in private, they occur in their entirety. But in public, adaptors usually occur in abbreviated form. ① For example, when people are watching us, we might put our fingers to our head and move them around a bit but probably not scratch with the same vigor as when in private. Because publicly emitted adaptors usually occur in such form, it is often difficult for an observer to tell what this partial behavior was intended to accomplish. For example, observing someone's finger on one's head, we cannot be certain for what this behavior was intended.

중심소재: 어댑터

1. 도입부 = 중심소재 도출

어댑터의 목적: 특정 욕구를 충족시키는 비언어적 행동

1) 어댑터의 특징 1

두 가지 종류의 욕구

① 신체적 욕구만족

② 심리적 욕구만족

2) 어댑터의 특징 2

사적 영역과 공공 영역에서 어댑터의 특징

① 부연예시

정답 1 (B) 2 (D)

해설

1 축약된 형태라는 뜻이며, 선택지 (A)와 (C)는 정반대의 의미이다.

2 Adaptors are nonverbal behaviors designed to satisfy some need.에서 알 수 있듯이 어댑터는 특정 목적을 수행하기 위해서 사용된다.

지문해석

어댑터는 특정 욕구를 충족시키기 위한 비언어적 행동이다. 때로 이 욕구는 우리가 가려운 곳을 긁을 때나 우리가 눈에 거슬리는 머리카락을 밀어내는 것과 같은 물리적일 수도 있으며, 다른 경우 심리적인 것으로 우리가 긴장할 때 입술을 깨무는 것과 같은 경우다. 또한 우리가 마른 입술을 적시는 것과 같이 더욱 편안함을 느끼도록 만든다. 이러한 어댑터가 사적인 차원에서 발생할 경우, 이것들은 온전하게(온전한 형태로) 드러난다. 그러나 공공장소에선 어댑터는 일반적으로 축약된 형태로 발생한다. 예를 들어, 사람들이 우리를 바라볼 때, 우리는 손가락을 머리에 대고, 약간 움직이지만 이것은 아마도 우리가 혼자 있을 때와 같은 힘으로 긁는 것은 아니다.

공개적으로 발생하는 어댑터들은 보통 이러한 형태를 띠고 있기 때문에, 우리는 이러한 부분적 행동이 무엇을 의도한 것인지 관찰해내기 어려울 때가 많다. 예를 들어, 어떤 사람이 자신의 머리 위에 손가락을 올려놓았을 경우, 우리는 이것이 어떤 행위를 의도한 것인지 확실하게 말할 수 없다.

Passage 5

1. In every language there seem to be certain "unmentionables" —words of such strong affective connotations that they cannot be used in polite discourse. 1) In English, the first of these to come to mind are, of course, ① words dealing with excretion and sex. ② Money is another subject about which communication is in some ways inhibited. Ⓐ When creditors send bills, they practically never mention money, although that is what they are writing about. ③ The fear of death carries over, quite understandably in view of the widespread confusion of symbols with things symbolized, into fear of the words having to do with death. Many people, therefore, instead of saying "died," substitute such expressions as passed away. ④ Some of our verbal reticences, especially religious ones, have the authority of the Bible. It appears that there is a feeling that names of the gods are too holy, and the names of evil spirits too terrifying, to be spoken lightly.

중심소재: verbal taboo

1. 도입부 = 주제문

1) 뒷받침 진술

금언의 구체적 예

① 배설과 성과 관련된 표현

② 돈과 관련된 내용

Ⓐ 부연진술

③ 죽음과 관련된 표현

④ 종교와 관련된 표현

구체적 진술을 이끄는 시그널로 이를 통해 앞 문장과 같은 맥락에서 좀 더 세부적인 사항을 다룰 것을 예상할 수 있다.

정답 1 (B) 2 (C) 3 (B)

해설

1 채권자가 언급된 곳을 보면, when으로 시작하는 구체적 진술의 시그널을 파악할 수 있다. 바로 앞 문장의 내용에 대한 상술에 해당함으로 앞 문장의 내용을 바탕으로 답의 힌트를 얻을 수 있다. Money is another subject about which communication is in some ways inhibited.를 통해 선택지 B가 정답임을 파악할 수 있다.

2 죽음과 관련된 표현이 아닌 것을 고르는 문제다. cut the corners는 "불필요한 부분을 잘라내다", "지름길로 가다"의 의미다.

3 공손한 상황에서 사용하지 말아야 할 불쾌, 불편, 지나치게 경건한 표현을 언급하지 않으므로 그 상황에 발생할 부정적인 결과를 예방하는 효과를 얻을 수 있으므로 선택지 B가 본문과 가장 일맥상통한다.

지문해석

모든 언어에는 '언급할 수 없는 특정한 말' – 점잖은 대화에서 사용할 수 없을 정도의 아주 강한 정서를 내포하는 단어가 있는 듯하다. 영어에서 바로 생각나는 첫 번째 단어는 물론 배설과 성의 내용을 다루는 단어이다. 돈 역시, 그에 관한 언급이 다소 꺼려지는 또 다른 주제이다. 채권자가 청구서를 보낼 때, 이들은 실질적으로 돈을 절대 언급하지 않는다. 돈이 그 청구서를 보내는 바로 그 이유임에도 불구하고 말이다. 죽음에 대한 공포는 죽음과 관련된 단어에 대한 공포로 전이된다. 그리고 이는 상징화된 물건이 지니는 상징의 혼돈이 널리 퍼져있다는 것을 볼 때 꽤 이해할 만한 것이다. 그러므로 많은 이들은 '죽었다'라는 말 대신 '돌아가셨다'라는 표현으로 대체한다. 우리가 꺼려하는 말 중에서 특정 단어, 특히 종교적인 것은 성경의 권위를 지니는 것이다. 하나님을 지칭하는 이름은 너무나 거룩하며, 악령을 드러내는 말은 가볍게 말하기에는 너무 두렵다는 감정이 존재하는 것처럼 보인다. 금언(금지된 말) 또한, 이것들이 성적인 문제를 솔직하게 나누지 못하게 하기에, 심각한 문제를 일으킬 수 있다는 것도 사실일 수 있다. 그러나 강력하게 금지된 말들은 진정한 사회적 가치를 지니고 있다. 우리가 아주 극도로 화가 나고 우리의 분노를 폭력으로 표현할 필요가 있다고 생각될 때, 이렇게 금지된 말을 하는 것이 우리가 난폭해지지 않고, 우리에게 상대적으로 해롭지 않은 언어적 대체물이 되기 때문이다.

Passage 6

연역적 전개

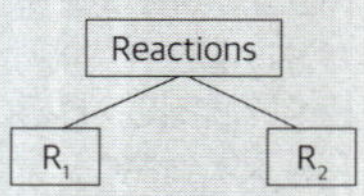

1. The collapse of the Communist regime in the German Democratic Republic and the opening of the Berlin Wall in November 1989, were welcomed around the world. 1) But the rapid unification of East and West Germany brought ambivalent reactions, especially from Germany's European neighbors. ① Ⓐ On the one hand, there were fears of the political and economic dominance of a united Germany in the center of Europe. Ⓑ On the other hand, recollections of the devastating consequences of German national unification movements of the past were rekindled. ⓐ Voices were heard even within Germany that warned of the emergence of a new sense of nationalism that would slacken ties to Western democracies and promote a new chapter of German assertiveness - one that would seek, for example, to repress memories of World War II and the Holocaust. Such anxiety was directed in particular toward East Germany because very little was known of their political attitudes.

중심소재: 독일통일의 반응

1. 도입부 = 중심소재 도출

독일의 통일

1) 주제문

동독과 서독의 갑작스러운 통일은 독일의 주변국의 상반된 반응을 일으켰다.

① 뒷받침 진술

Ⓐ 반응 1

통일된 독일은 유럽의 정치/경제의 중심이 될 것이라는 두려움

Ⓑ 반응 2

과거 통일 독일의 끔찍했던 기억이 재현

ⓐ 예시부연(for example)

정답 1 (E) 2 (B) 3 (D)

해설

1 빈칸 앞에 전개된 내용을 보면, 통일된 독일의 민족주의가 가져올 수 있는 위험을 언급하면서 독일의 독단주의 예를 들고 있으므로 "억누르려 한다(repress)"가 적절하다.

2 rekindle은 "어떤 기억 등을 다시 되살리다"라는 뜻이므로 revived가 적절하다.

3 본문은 독일 통일에 대한 유럽 주변 국가들의 상반된(ambivalent) 반응에 대해 기술하고 있다. 한편에서는 통일된 동독의 정치적, 경제적 패권에 대한 두려움에 대해 말하고, 다른 한편에서는 독일 민족주의 부활에 대한 우려를 표명하고 있다는 내용이므로 이에 대한 제목으로는 D의 "독일 통일과 유럽 국가들에 독일 통일이 미친 영향(German unification and its impact on European countries)"이 가장 잘 어울린다.

지문해석

1989년 11월, 독일민주공화국(동독)의 공산주의 체제 붕괴와 베를린 장벽의 개방은 전 세계적으로 환영받았다. 하지만, 동독과 서독의 급격한 통일은 상반된 반응을, 특히 독일의 유럽 이웃국가들로부터 불러 일으켰다. 한편으로는 통일된 독일이 가질 유럽 중앙에서의 정치적, 경제적 패권에 대한 두려움이 있었다. 다른 한편으로는 과거 독일 민족의 통일운동이 가져왔던 끔찍했던 결과에 대한 기억들이 되어 살아났다. 심지어 독일 내에서도 새로운 민족주의의 출현을 경고하는 목소리가 나왔다. 이런 민족주의의 출현은 서구 민주주의 국가들과의 유대 관계를 느슨하게 할 수 있고, 독단적인 독일(이런 독단주의는 제2차 세계대전과 유대인 대학살 등의 기억들을 억누르고자 할 것이다)의 새 장을 열어줄 수 있는 것이다. 이런 불안감은 주로 동독인들에게 향했는데, 이는 그들의 정치적 성향에 대해 알려진 바가 거의 없었기 때문이었다.

Passage 7

1. 1] Like most people in the Western world, I have grown up in the artificial environment of modern society. It's a place dominated by external timekeepers, calendars, schedules, clocks. Our lives are subdivided into fiscal years, academic years, weekdays, weekends, deadlines. We are taught that there is a time to get up, a time to go to work, a time to eat. We set the clock by a single standard. Time orders our lives, and inevitably, orders us around. ① We are so removed from natural rhythms that we rarely confront how 'unnatural' this is. Ⓐ We didn't always live with this artificial timing. In Time wars, Jeremy Rifkin explains how recently people have been alienated from natural rhythms to those of the schedule, the clock, and now the computer with its nanosecond culture.

2. The schedule was the invention of the Benedictine monks whose early passion for organizing and filling every minute of the day grew from St. Benedict's warning that **1]** 'Idleness is the enemy of the soul.' His followers reintroduced the roman hour and invented the mechanical clock. ① Not until the fifteenth century did clocks, those icons of temporal time, begin to rival churches in the city squares. Not until the seventeenth century did clocks have a minute hand. ② 'Medieval time,' writes Rifkin,'was still sporadic, leisurely, unpredictable and above all tied to experiences rather than abstract numbers.' ③ It was the merchants and factory owners who eventually, and with great differently, trained workers—those who had previously lived in accord with seasons—to become as regular as clockwork.

중심소재: 시간에 따른 인위적 환경의 틀

1. 첫 번째 문단

1) 도입부 = 현상(문제점 지적)
현대인들은 시간이라는 인위적인 틀에 맞추어 살아간다.

① 부정적 결과
인간은 자연의 리듬(시간)에 너무 소외되어 자신이 얼마나 부자연스러운 삶을 사는지 인식하지 못하는 지경에 이르렀다.

Ⓐ 부연
인간이 자연의 리듬에서 멀어진 것은 최근의 사건이라는 내용을 유명한 책을 통해 전달

* 첫 번째 문단은 "자연의 리듬에서 소외된 인간은 인위적인 시간에 따라 살고 있다."라는 문제점을 지적하는 내용이다.

2. 두 번째 문단
인위적인 시간에 따라 살아가는 현대인의 삶의 기원을 밝히고 있다.

1) 배경
중세 수도사들은 게으름이 영혼의 적이라 생각해 시간에 맞추어 생활하기 위해 스케줄을 만들어 냄

① 시간이 지나면서 세속적 성격의 시계가 서서히 발달함

② 중세의 특징
sporadic, leisurely, unpredictable and tied to experiences

③ 현대의 특징
상인과 공장주가 현대의 노동자들을 인위적 시간에 맞추어 살도록 조작

주제·요지·제목의 구별과 주의사항

• 주제: 글을 통해 말하고자 하는 내용 즉, "무엇에 관한 글"인지를 파악하는 것
• 요지: 주제를 통해 궁극적으로 전달하고자 하는 내용
• 제목: 독자의 주의를 환기시키는 주제 또는 요지를 반영한 직·간접적인 표현. 주제를 곧 제목으로 설정할 수 있으나 그럴 경우 독자의 관심을 유발하기가 쉽지 않다. 예를 들어, 소시지 제품의 제목을 "소지지" 즉, 내용물을 주제로 설정할 경우보다 "천하장사"와 같은 표현을 쓰면 좀 더 독자의 관심을 유발할 수 있으며, 그러면서도 주제인 소시지를 먹으면 "건강하고, 강해진다"는 요지까지 잘 반영할 수 있게 되어 구매를 유도할 수 있게 된다. 제목은 글의 요지를 반영할 수 있다는 점에서 주제보다 한 단계 난이도가 높은 문제유형이라 볼 수 있다.

기원의 글

기원의 글의 경우 일반적으로 현재→과거→현재, 현재→과거, 과거→현재의 패턴으로 흐른다. 공통점은 본문은 과거의 시제가 쓰임을 확인한다.

정답 **1** (D) **2** (A) **3** (A) **4** (B) **5** (B) **6** (D)

지문분석

문단을 나눈 후 각 문단의 주제 및 요지를 정리한 후 전체 주제와 요지를 적는다. 두 문단의 내용을 정리하면, "현대인은 인위적인 시간에 따라 부자연스러운 삶을 살며, 이런 부자연스러운 시간에 따라 살도록 조작된 근원은 바로 상인과 공장주에 의한 것이다"라는 점을 밝히고 있다.

해설

1 바로 앞 문단에서 언급되고 있는 시간의 특징을 드러내는 표현들의 공통점을 파악한다.

2 수도사들이 스케줄을 짜고, "하루를 매 분 단위로 준비하고 직무 수행"하는 이유가 무엇이었을지 생각해 본다.

3 sporadic은 "불규칙적으로 산발적인"이란 뜻이다.

4 수도사가 되어 "처음 가지는 새로운" 열정이란 의미이므로 선택지 (B)가 가장 적절하다.

5 선택지 (B)의 내용은 첫 번째 문단에서 확인할 수 있다.

6 It was the merchants and factory owners who eventually, and with great difficulty, trained workers—those who had previously lived in accord with seasons—to become as regular as clockwork.에서 선택지 (D)의 관계를 파악할 수 있다.

지문해석

서구 세계의 대부분의 사람들처럼 나는 현대 사회의 인위적인 환경 속에서 자라왔다. 그 곳은 외부 시간 기록원, 달력, 일정, 시계에 의해 지배되는 곳이다. 우리의 삶은 회계 연도, 학년, 평일, 주말, 마감일로 세분화된다. 우리는 일어날 시간, 출근할 시간, 식사 시간이 있다고 배운다. 우리는 단일 표준에 따라 시계를 맞춘다.

시간은 우리의 삶을 규제하고 불가피하게도 우리에게 이런저런 일을 시킨다. 우리는 자연의 리듬으로부터 너무나 동떨어져 있어서 이런 삶이 얼마나 '부자연스러운지' 좀처럼 깨닫지 못한다. 우리가 항상 이렇게 인위적인 시간에 맞춰 살아온 것은 아니었다. 「시간과의 전쟁」이라는 저서에서 제레미 리프킨(Jeremy Rifkin)은 근래 들어 사람들이 어떻게 자연스러운 리듬으로부터 멀어져 일정과 시계의 리듬에, 그리고 이제는 10억분의 1단위 문화를 가진 컴퓨터에 이르게 되었는지를 설명한다.

일정은 베네딕트회 수사들이 만들었던 것으로, 하루를 매 분 단위로 준비하고 직무 수행하려는 그들의 초기 열정은 '태만은 영혼의 적'이라는 성 베네딕트(St. Benedict)의 경고에서 비롯되었다. 그의 추종자들은 로마식 시간을 재도입하였고 기계로 작동되는 시계를 발명했다. 15세기가 되어서야 속세 시간의 우상인 시계가 도시 광장에서 교회에 필적하기 시작했다. 17세기에 들어서는 시계에 분침이 생겼다. 리프킨은 '중세의 시간은 여전히 산발적이었고, 느긋했으며, 예측할 수 없었고, 무엇보다도 추상적인 숫자들보다는 경험에 얽혀있었다.'고 저술했다. 마침내 엄청난 어려움을 극복하고 과거에 계절과 조화를 이루며 살았던 노동자들이 태엽장치처럼 규칙적이 되도록 훈련시킨 이들은 상인들과 공장주들이었다.

Passage 8

1. 1) The viruses or bacteria that vaccines are made of have been treated so that they do not cause disease. ① Ⓐ Many vaccines have disease-causing strands of certain bacteria or viruses that have been deactivated or killed. Ⓑ Some use live organisms that resemble strands that do cause a sickness. Ⓒ Others use only parts of germs. Ⓓ Still others are made up of live pathogens that are weakened so they will not cause illnesses. ⓐ Toxoids are another type of vaccine composed of poisons released by disease-causing organisms. These poisons are chemically treated for use in vaccines, and they provide immunity without causing the disease.

2. 1) Most medical doctors and public health groups agree that required vaccines have greatly reduced disease infection rates. Not only have vaccinations prevented disease in individuals, but the administration of vaccines worldwide has reduced disease epidemics in vulnerable areas where vaccines are inaccessible.

중심소재: 백신용 박테리아

1. 첫 번째 문단

1) 도입부 = 중심소재 도출

백신용 박테리아는 병을 일으키지 않도록 처리됨

① 백신으로 활용되는 종류

Ⓐ 질병을 유발하는 죽은 박테리아

Ⓑ 특정 질병을 유발하는 종을 닮은 유기체 활용

Ⓒ 세균의 일부활용

Ⓓ 질병을 유발하지 않는 약화된 병원균

ⓐ 예시부연: 톡소이도

질병을 일으키는 유기체가 유발시키는 독소로 구성된 백신으로 화학적으로 처리되고, 면역성 제공

2. 두 번째 문단

1) 백신의 효과

전 세계적으로 질병 감염률을 크게 줄이는 동시에 개인의 질병 예방

연역적 구조 확인

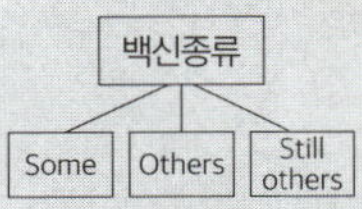

세부내용 파악 중 불일치하는 것을 고르는 문제다.

선택지 중 하나만 틀린 대상이므로 문제를 통해 본문에 언급될 대상을 먼저 확인하고 지문을 읽도록 한다.

정답 **1** (A) **2** (C)

해설

1 질병을 발병케 하는 활성 바이러스는 백신의 성분으로 사용할 수가 없다.

2 백신 접종을 통해 개인의 질병 예방은 물론 백신을 구할 수 없는 취약한 여러 지역에 사는 사람들을 전염병에 걸리지 않게 했다는 의미로 선택지 (C)가 정답이다.

지문해석

백신의 원료인 바이러스나 박테리아는 병을 일으키지 않도록 처리된 것이다. 많은 백신에는 어떤 박테리아나 바이러스의 질병유발 요소들을 무기력하게 하거나 죽여 놓은 것이 들어있다. 일부 백신에서는 질병유발 요소와 흡사한 살아 있는 유기체가 사용되고, 다른 일부 백신에서는 세균의 일부분들만이 사용된다. 그리고 또 다른 일부 백신은 질병을 일으키지 않도록 약화시킨 살아있는 병원체로 구성되어 있다. 변성독소는 병을 일으키는 유기체에서 방출되는 독성물질로 구성된 또 다른 유형의 백신이다. 이런 독성물질을 백신으로 사용하기 위해서는 화학적으로 처리를 한다. 그러면 독성물질은 병을 일으키지 않고 면역기능을 부여한다. 대부분의 의사들과 공중보건 단체들은 필요한 백신이 질병 감염들을 현격하게 감소시켰다는 데 동의한다. 백신 접종은 개개인이 질병에 걸리지 않게 해주었을 뿐 아니라 전 세계적인 백신 접종은 백신을 구할 수 없는 취약한 여러 지역에서 전염병을 감소시켰다.

TEST 04

Passage 1

글의 도입부에서 제시되는 의문문은 주제에 해당하고, 이에 대한 답변은 요지다. 글의 말미에 제시되는 의문문은 답변을 요하지 않는 수사의 문문(설의법)에 해당하는 것으로 요지를 이끈다.

1. David Melinkof begins his classic account with the statement: "The law is a profession of words." **1)** So what words should be chosen when Latin, French, and English each provide a copious supply of relevant items? How does one choose between synonyms, or—even more difficult—between two words which seem to be synonymous, but which might just have enough differential meaning to allow a lawyer one day to make an argument based on the difference? ① The solution, in many cases, was: don't choose, but use both. In Middle English we see the rise of the legal lexical doublets which would become one of the stylistic hallmarks of that profession. Ⓐ Old English goods and Old French chattels resulted in Middle English legalese goods and chattels. ⓐ The words were often paired to cover distinct nuances, thereby avoiding ambiguity; but sometimes the pairing seems to be no more than a more emphatic expression of a single meaning; and ⓑ sometimes it seems to be just a stylistic habit, perhaps fostered by its undoubted rhythmical appeal in oral performance. **2.** But whatever the reason, it became a major feature of legal style which continues to the present day.

중심소재:
법률 용어 → lexical doublets

1. 도입부 = 중심소재 도출
법률 용어에 관한 글이다.

1) 의문문(주제)
동의어 또는 유사표현이지만 사실 의미상의 차이점으로 법정 사건의 결과에 영향을 미칠 단어를 어떻게 선택할 수 있는가? ← 주제: Legal Doublets

① 답변(요지)
두 단어를 함께 사용(legal lexical doublets).

Ⓐ 뒷받침 예시
Goods and Chattels

ⓐ 독특한 뉘앙스를 통해 애매성을 피함

ⓑ 말의 리드미컬한 효과

2. 정리
doublet은 법률 문체의 주된 특징

정답 1 (D) 2 (B) 3 (A)

해설

1 copious는 "매우 풍부한"이란 의미다.

2 타동사인 foster의 목적어인 a stylistic habit가 앞으로 도치되고, 분사구문의 형태를 취하는 선택지 (B)가 올바른 표현이다.

3 Lexical doublets의 정의는 다음과 같다. synonyms between two words which seem to be synonymous, but which might just have enough differential meaning to allow a lawyer one day to make an argument based on the difference이다. 즉, 동의어처럼 보이지만, 두 단어의 차이점을 기반으로 주장을 펼칠 수 있다는 짝이 되어야 함으로 peace an quiet가 가장 적절하다. 선택지 (B)는 "피하고, 유지하다"는 의미고, (C)는 "용서와 신앙고백", (D)는 "인정과 부인"이므로 lexical doublets의 정의에 부합되지 않은 짝이다.

지문해석

데이비드 멜린코프(David Melinkof)는 다음과 같은 진술로 본인 최고의 말을 시작한다. "법이란 말의 직업이다." 그럼 관련 사항이 라틴어, 프랑스어, 영어에 각각 상당한 분량이 있다고 할 때, 어떤 단어를 선정해야 하는 걸까? 동의어 또는 – 더욱 까다롭게 – 동의어로 보이지만 둘의 차이점을 바탕으로 변호사가 충분히 다른 의미를 가질 수 있는 두 단어 중 어떤 것을 골라야 할까?
많은 경우 해결책은 (어느 하나를) 선택하지 않고, 둘 다 사용하는 것이다. 중세 영어에서 우리는 이 분야 문체의 주된 특징 중 하나인 법률 이중어(lexical doublet)의 발생을 볼 수 있다. 고대 영국의 물건들과 고대 프랑스의 가재도구가 중세 영어의 난해한 법률 가재도구가 되었다. 말은 종종 독특한 뉘앙스를 없애기 위해 짝을 이루어 애매함을 피했다. 그러나 때로 이런 짝은 개별적 한 단어의 의미를 더욱 강조하는 표현에 지나지 않는 것처럼 보이기도 하고, 때로는 단지 문체의 습관처럼 보이기도 하는데, 이는 아마도 말을 할 때 억양의 확실한 매력에 의해서 만들어지는 듯하다. 그러나 어떤 이유에서든 이것은 오늘날까지 지속되는 주된 법 문체의 특징이다.

Passage 2

1. In cities and large metropolitan areas, the technical experts drill hundreds of feet for new wells; they construct reservoirs to catch and hold rain water; and they build filtration plants for the conversion to human use of water in lakes and rivers. **However**, in rural areas and small settlements remote from pond or stream, the solution is a different one, though the need for water remains the same. 1) Scientists may scoff, and learned people may sneer, but the old notions persist. Very few persons admit to a belief in witches or evil spirits. **Yet** there are thousands now making use of a water supply that was first located by a 'water witch.' ① The modern term for a person who can successfully identify a flow of water beneath the earth's surface is 'dowser.' Dowsers ordinarily do not boast about their peculiar talents, but they are frequently considered extremely useful to have around. ② All they do is secure a forked twig or branch—hazel is preferred but any green wood will serve—and move slowly about the landscape. With the fork held like an inverted Y, lightly pressed against the chest, and with palms up and thumbs turned outward, dowsers walk here and there until the butt of the fork bends downward. Careful dowsers check and recheck their locations, but where twig bends down, they know they have found water. Let city dwellers, technical experts, and the skeptical ridicule. Ⓐ Millions of people now enjoy a good water supply because they were fortunate in finding a person who could 'feel a strong pull' on the stick and say with authority, 'Dig here.'

중심소재: 물을 얻는 방법(수맥탐지)

1. 도입부
대시와 지방의 물 얻는 방법의 차이점을 기술하고 있다.

1) 현상
수맥탐지를 통한 물 공급이 유행하고 있다.
① 수맥 탐지자의 간략한 정의

② 수맥을 찾는 구체적 방법이 소개되고 있다.

Ⓐ 많은 이들이 수맥을 찾는 사람에 의해 원하는 물을 즐기고 있다.

However를 기준으로 도시와 시골의 차이점을 다루는데, 물을 얻는 방법의 차이점을 언급하고 있다. 일반적으로 중립적인 입장에서 두 대상의 차이점을 기술하는 글이 아니라면 However 이후의 내용이 글의 중심이 된다.

도입부의 내용을 통해 본문은 적어도 "물 찾는 방법"과 관련된 내용임을 파악할 수 있다. 이후 전개되는 내용을 바탕으로 중심소재의 폭을 좁히도록 한다.

현상의 시그널을 이끄는 현재진행을 파악한다.

현상의 시그널
1) 현재완료(have + p.p), 현재 진행형(be + V-ing)
2) 시간의 부사 (recently, today, for the last X years)

현상의 글의 제목설정
현상의 글의 경우 현상 자체를 제목으로 설정하거나 문제점으로 드러나는 현상의 대안을 반영한 표현을 제목으로 설정하는 경우가 대부분이다.

정답 **1** (C) **2** (E) **3** (B)

해설
1 물 수급이 쉽지 않은 지방에서 물을 구하는 "현상"에 관한 글이다. 대도시의 경우 물을 찾거나 이용하는 데 전문 기

술자들이 과학적인 방법을 사용하는 반면, 아직도 오래전 과거부터 사용되어온 나뭇가지 등을 이용해 수맥을 찾는 이들(예전에는 이들을 water witch라고 불렀고, 요즘에는 dowser라고 지칭한다고 나온다)이 존재한다고 밝히고 있다. 본문의 요지는 현상을 가장 잘 반영하는 선택지는 수맥탐지사(dowser)의 능력을 믿는 이들이 많다고 밝힌 (C)가 가장 적절하다.

2 수맥탐지사는 어떤 이들인지, 유래와 이들이 수맥을 찾는 방법 등을 객관적 입장에서 설명하는 글로 보는 것이 적절하다.

3 (a)의 빈칸이 들어간 문장은 다음과 같다. they build filtration plants for the conversion (a)________ human use of water in lakes and rivers. for the conversion의 for는 "~용"이란 의미로 "전환을 위한 필터공장을 세운다"는 내용에서 활용된 것이고, 이러한 공장을 짓는 이유는 바로 강과 호수의 물을 식수로 전환하기 위함이다. 이때 "~로의 전환"에 해당하는 표현은 conversion to라 한다. to는 전치사이다. (b)의 경우, 과거와 현재가 대조되면서 과학자들이 웃고 넘길 그런 물 수급방법이 최근 활용되고 있다는 내용이므로 역접의 Yet이 적절하다. 그러므로 정답은 (B)이다.

지문해석

도시와 대도시 지역에서는 전문 기술자들이 새로운 우물을 위해 수백 피트를 드릴로 판다. 또한 그들은 빗물을 받아 보관할 저수지를 짓기도 하고, 호수와 강의 물을 사람들이 사용할 수 있도록 여과할 수 있는 설비를 짓는다. 그러나 비록 물에 대한 필요가 같더라도, 연못이나 지류로부터 멀리 떨어진 시골 지역과 작은 취락지에서는 그에 대한 해결 방법이 다르다. 과학자들은 비웃고 식자는 조롱할지도 모르지만 오래전 생각이 지금도 이어지고 있다. 마녀나 악령의 존재를 믿는다고 인정할 사람은 거의 없다. 하지만, 수맥을 찾는 사람(water witch)에 의해 최초로 위치가 파악된 상수원을 현재 수천 명의 사람들이 사용하고 있다. 지표 아래의 물줄기를 성공적으로 찾아낼 수 있는 사람을 현대 용어로 수맥탐지사(dowser)라고 부른다. 수맥 탐지사는 보통 그들의 특별한 재능을 뽐내진 않지만, 사람들은 그들이 곁에 있으면, 매우 유용하다고 여긴다. 그들이 하는 일이란 두 갈래로 나뉜 나뭇가지(개암나무가 주로 선호되지만 일반 나무도 가능하다)를 찾아 수맥이 있을 만한 곳을 천천히 움직이는 것이 전부다. 역전된 Y형태로 나뭇가지를 쥐는데, 이를 가볍게 가슴에 대고 손바닥은 위로, 엄지는 바깥쪽으로 향하여 들고 나뭇가지의 밑동인 길쭉한 부분이 아래쪽을 향할 때까지 여기저기를 걷는다. 신중한 수맥탐지사들은 발견 장소를 반복해서 점검하지만, 결국에는 나뭇가지가 아래를 향하는 곳에 다다르면 자신들이 물을 찾았다는 것을 확신하게 된다. 도시에 사는 이들과 전문 기술자들, 회의적인 사람들이 비웃도록 내버려 두자, 수백만의 사람들이 지금 좋은 급수를 즐기고 있는 이유는 바로 그들에게 막대에 강력한 당김을 느끼고 '여기를 파라'라고 권위 있게 말할 수 있는 사람을 운 좋게 찾을 수 있었기 때문이다.

Passage 3

본문은 특정 대상에 대한 두 견해가 제시되고, 처음에 제시되는 견해와 상반되는 견해가 곧 글쓴이의 주장으로 이어지는 형태이다.

1. **1)** In her critique, Dorothy Sayers wrote the detective story does not attain the loftiest level of literary achievement. And she suggested that this is ① because it is "a literature of escape" and not "a literature of expression." **2)** I do not know what the loftiest level of literary achievement is; neither did Shakespeare; neither did Miss Sayers. ① Other things being equal, which they never are, books with a more powerful theme will provoke a more powerful performance.
Yet some very dull books have been written about God, and some very fine ones about how to make a living. It is always

중심소재: 탐정소설

1. 도입부
탐정소설에 대한 특정 인물의 견해가 드러난다.

1) Dorothy Sayers의 견해
탐정소설은 높은 경지의 문학적 성취를 달성하지 못한다.

①근거
탐정소설은 표현의 문학이 아니라 도피는 문학이기 때문이다.

a matter of who writes the stuff, and what the individual has to write it with. As for literature of expression and literature of escape, this is critics' jargon, a use of abstract words as if they had absolute meanings. ② Everything written with vitality expresses that vitality; there are no dull subjects, only dull minds. 2. All people who read escape from something else into what lies behind the printed page; the quality of the dream may be argued, but its release has become a functional necessity. All people must escape at times from the deadly rhythm of their private thoughts. It is part of the process of life among thinking beings. I hold no particular brief for the detective story as the ideal escape. I merely say that all reading for pleasure is escape.

2) 글쓴이의 견해

① 강력한 주제를 다루는 책은 큰 즐거움을 줄 수 있다.

② 생명력(앞에서 언급한 powerful과 같은 개념)이 넘치는 글은 그 생명력을 표현한다.

2. 요지

글을 읽는 사람은 근본적으로 인쇄된 면 뒤에 숨겨진 곳으로 도피하는 것이며, 모든 사람은 개인의 케케묵은 사고에서 때로 탈출해야 하며, 즐거움을 위한 독서는 근본적으로 '도피'이다.

글쓴이의 견해를 직접적으로 드러내는 표현을 놓치지 않도록 한다: must, I merely say that...

TEST 04

정답 1 (A) 2 (B)

해설

1 도피의 문학과 표현의 문학은 문학 비평에서 사용하는 전문용어로서 그 용어 자체에 절대적인 뜻이 있는 것은 아니다(As for literature of expression and literature of escape, this is critics' jargon, a use of abstract words as if they had absolute meanings).

2 탐정소설은 다른 문학들처럼 삶의 따분한 과정에서 돌파구가 되므로 독자의 고유한 내면세계에 대안을 제시해 줄 수 있다.

지문해석

도로시 세이어(Dorothy Sayers)는 그녀의 비평에서, 탐정소설이 문학적 성취의 높은 경지에는 오를 수 없다고 하였다. 왜냐하면 그녀는 탐정소설이 '표현의 문학'이 아니라 '도피의 문학'이기 때문이라고 주장했다. 나는 문학적 성취의 가장 고상한 경지가 무엇인지 모른다. 셰익스피어도 몰랐고 도로시 세이어도 몰랐다. 절대 그럴 수는 없겠지만 다른 모든 조건이 똑같다면 좀 더 강렬한 주제를 지닌 책들이 좀 더 엄청난 흥행을 가져왔을 것이다. 일부 지루한 책들은 신에 대해 쓰였고 일부 매우 좋은 책들은 돈을 버는 방법에 대해 쓰였다. 중요한 것은 누가 그 내용을 썼는가 하는 것과 그가 그 내용을 어떻게 썼느냐 하는 것이다. 표현의 문학이니 도피의 문학이니 하는 것은 비평 용어일 뿐이고 마치 그 용어에 절대적인 뜻이 있는 것처럼 보이려고 추상적인 어휘를 쓰는 것뿐이다. 생동감 있게 쓴 모든 것은 생동감이 표현된다. 모든 주제는 지루하지 않고 단지 그 정신이 지루할 뿐이다. 책을 읽는 모든 사람들은 어떤 무언가로부터 인쇄된 종이 뒤에 숨겨진 것으로 도피해 간다. 이 대목에서 꿈의 속성이 논의될 수도 있지만, 그 꿈의 표출은 기능적 필요가 되어 왔다. 모든 사람들은 때때로 개인적인 생각의 따분한 리듬으로부터 반드시 도피해야만 한다. 이것은 생각하는 존재로서 살아가는 과정의 일부이다. 나는 탐정 소설이 이상적인 도피구라는 특별한 신념을 갖고 있는 것은 아니다. 단지 즐거움을 위한 모든 독서가 돌파구라는 것을 말하고 싶을 뿐이다.

Passage 4

1. It's the height of summer in Mongolia, and the nation is set to celebrate Eriin Gurvan Naadam, an Olympic-like festival where the so-called three manly sports of wrestling, horse racing, and archery take center stage. 1) ① Naadam is held annually form July 11 to July 13. The timing coincides with the anniversary of the 1921 Mongolian Revolution, in which the nation gained independence from competing Chinese and Russian forces. ② The festival traces its roots to the 12th century, when the Mongols, led by Genghis Khan, established an empire that at its height stretched across nearly all of Eurasia. Wrestling, horse racing, and archery were necessary skills for success on the battlefield. Making them into sports trained warriors to be better warriors. Naadam traditionally was a time for men who had trained all year to show off that they have mastered these skills. ③ Often described as the "manly sports," the festival's events were originally limited to men. Today women participate in both the horse racing and archery competitions, and young boys and girls in particular take to the horse racing. The country celebrations attract scattered nomadic herders who gather to take part in friendly competition, to drink a fermented mare's milk, and to feast on a variety of dairy products. ④ Today, the skills are mostly reserved for athletic competition and camaraderie. But the luster and nationalistic pride surrounding Naadam still shines as bright as ever.

시간의 대조는 내용의 대조

중심소재: 몽골의 스포츠 축제

1. 도입부 = 중심소재 도출
올림픽과 유사한 몽골의 스포츠 축제인 Eriin Grvan Naadam

1) 구체적 진술
① 출제가 열리는 시점은 1921년 몽골혁명과 일치

② 축제의 기원

③ 축제의 특징
manly sports에서 알 수 있듯이 원래 남자에게만 한정되었지만, 오늘날은 다양한 계층이 여러 게임에 출전

④ 현대의미
역사적으로 대제국 건설의 기반이 바로 이런 기술임에 대한 국가적 자부심은 여전히 대단

정답 **1** (C) **2** (B) **3** (A) **4** (D)

해설

1 글의 중반 이후에 오늘날 여성 뿐 아니라 젊은 소년, 소녀들도 참여할 수 있다고 했으므로 선택지 (C)는 옳다.
2 앞뒤 내용상 배운 기술을 "뽐내다"인 선택지 (B)가 가장 적절하다.
3 마지막 문장과의 연계해서 몽고혁명의 기념일과 관련짓는 의미는 "국가적 자부심"이 가장 적절하다.
4 빈칸 바로 앞 문장의 내용을 보면 "레슬링, 말 경주 그리고 활쏘기는 전장의 승리를 위한 필수적 요소"라고 했으므로 선택지 (D)가 정답임을 파악할 수 있다.

지문해석

그때는 몽골에서의 여름의 절정이고, 그 나라는 소위 3개의 남자다운 스포츠인 레슬링, 경마, 그리고 궁술이 중심무대를 차지하는 올림픽과 같은 축제인 Eriin Grvan Naadam을 축하하기 위해 관심이 향해 있다. Naadam은 매년 7월 11일부터 7월 13일 개최된다. (가) 그때는 1921년 몽골혁명의 기념일과 우연히 일치된다. 이것은 그 나라가 중국과 러시아 세력과 싸워 독립을 얻게 된 혁명이다. 그 축제는 12세기로 그 기원을 거슬러 올라가는데 그때 징기스칸이 이끈 몽골족은 그 힘이 거의 유라시아 전체를 가로질러 뻗어 있는 제국을 설립했다. 레슬링, 경마, 그리고 궁술은 전쟁터에서 성공을 위한 필요한 기술들이었다. (나) 그것들을 스포츠로 만든 것은 전사들을 더 좋은 전사들로 훈련시켰다. Naadam은 전통적으로 일 년 내내 훈련 받았던 남

자들이 그들이 이러한 기술들을 정복했다는 것을 (다) (과시하기) 위한 시간이었다. 종종 "남자다운 스포츠"로 묘사되었던 그 축제의 행사들은 원래는 남자들에게 국한되어 있었다. 오늘날 여자들은 경마와 궁술 시합 둘 다 참가하고 젊은 소년, 소녀들은 특별히 경마에 몰두한다. 국가의 축전들은 친밀한 경쟁에 참여하고 발효된 암말의 우유를 마시고 여러 가지 낙농 제품들로 잔치를 벌이기 위해 모인 흩어진 유목민들의 목자들에게 매력을 준다. 오늘날, 그 기술들은 대개 운동 경연과 우정을 위해 보존해 둔다. 그러나 열망하는 사람과 Naadam을 둘러싸고 있는 민족주의적인 자부심은 여전히 여태까지 만큼 밝게 빛나고 있다.

Passage 5

1. 1) Superpower though it may be, Microsoft has to tread carefully when its enforcement agents operate on sovereign soil. ① As a rule, Microsoft's anti-piracy teams provide logistical, investigative and legal support—but are not shoving battering rams through doors or hauling counterfeiters out of their plants. However, they are at times present during raids and at risk of exposure. Ⓐ When a renowned Bulgarian software pirate was slain gangland style in Sofia in January, a number of Microsoft people who before had been talking openly to us suddenly asked that they not be quoted by name. "We are hearing about a lot of death threats against those fighting piracy, particularly in Eastern Europe," says Trainer. "That's why these companies take efforts to conceal the identity of their people in the field."

2. 1) Microsoft's toughest battleground is in Eastern Europe, where pirates control 70 percent of the market, more than in any other region of the world. ① From Bucharest to Kiev to Moscow, piracy has roots in the old Soviet policy of keeping pace with Western computer technology by copying it. Now software piracy is just one more black market. **2.** Marek Cerniak, a tanklike Polish cop turned private eye who does investigations for Microsoft, says pirates and mobsters are made for each other: "Software pirates have the brains. Organized crime has the muscle."

중심소재: 마이크로소프트(M)사의 불법복제 단속

1. 첫 번째 문단

1) 도입부 = 주제문

M사는 해외에서 불법단속을 할 때 조심해야 한다.

① M사의 대처와 문제점

불법복제 팀을 통해 간접적인 지원을 제공하지만, 때로 강압적인 방법을 취하고, 이는 단속반의 제한적 범위를 넘은 월권행위임

Ⓐ 부연

불법복제 단원 중 한명이 살해되고, 불법복제단체로부터 협박으로 인해 마이크로소프트사 익명 요구

2. 두 번째 문단

1) 현상(문제점)

동유럽 내 불법복제의 심각성

① 배경

불법복제가 성행하게 된 배경

2. 요지문

폴란드의 한 경찰의 말을 인용하면서 M사에 첫 번째 문장에서 밝힌 주의를 재차 강조

정답 1 (C) 2 (E) 3 (A) 4 (D) 5 (C)

해설

1 As a rule, Microsoft's anti-piracy teams ... are not shoving battering rams through doors or hauling counterfeiters out of their plants. __________, they are at times present during raids and at risk of exposure.의 내용 중 빈칸을 중심으로 밑줄 친 부분이 서로 대조되고 있다.

2 역접을 드러내는 "suddenly"와 문맥적 정황을 활용하여 접근한다. 우선, quote의 형태를 긍정문에 맞출 것인지 부정문에 맞출 것인지 판단해야 한다. 주어가 마이크로소프트사의 직원이므로 자신의 이름이 드러나지 않기를 원할 것이다. suddenly를 기준으로 이전과 이후가 대조되어야 한다는 점을 활용해도 이를 파악할 수 있다. 또

구체적 진술을 이끄는 시그널을 확인한다.

역접을 드러내는 부사에 주목!

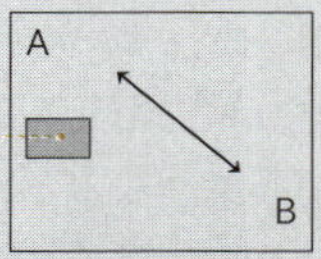

Usually, Normally, Suddenly를 중심으로 A와 B는 서로 대조의 내용을 가진다.

한 ask that S (should) V의 구문을 함께 파악할 수 있어야 한다. 그러므로 답은 선택지 (E)의 (should) not be quoted의 형태가 된다.

3 본문은 "마이크로소프트사의 소프트웨어 불법복제 단속"에 관한 글이다.

4 선택지 (D)와 같이 마이크로소프트사가 복제 방지된 소프트웨어 개발에 성공했다는 내용은 본문에 언급되어 있지 않다.

5 (C)는 media(reporters), 나머지 선택지 항은 모두 마이크로소프트사의 anti-piracy team을 지칭한다.

지문해석

비록 마이크로소프트(Microsoft) 사(社)가 막강한 힘을 가지고 있을지는 모르지만 그 집행 담당자들이 (미국 외) 주권국에서 활동할 때는 신중을 기해야 한다. 대체로 마이크로소프트의 불법복제 단속팀들은 물류 및 연구, 법률 지원을 제공하지만 문 사이로 성벽을 부수는 망치를 밀어 넣거나 공장에서 나오는 복제범들을 체포하진 않는다. 하지만 그들은 가끔씩 불시 단속 현장에 나타나 신분 노출의 위험을 무릅쓴다. 악명 높은 불가리아의 소프트웨어 복제범이 지난 1월 소피아(Sofia)에서 조직폭력배들의 방식으로 살해됐을 때 이전까지는 우리에게 스스럼없이 이야기하던 마이크로소프트사 직원 여러 명이 갑작스레 실명으로 거론되지 않게 해달라고 요청해왔다. "우리는 그들 복제 단속팀에 대한 수많은 살해 위협에 대해 전해 듣고 있습니다. 특히 동유럽에서요."라고 트레이너(Trainer)씨는 말한다. "그것이 이런 기업들이 해당 업계에서 그들 직원들의 신분을 숨기려고 노력하는 이유입니다."

마이크로소프트사의 가장 치열한 전쟁터는 동유럽인데, 거기서 불법복제는 시장의 70%를 통제하고 있고 이는 전 세계 그 어떤 곳보다도 높은 비율이다. 부카레스트(Bucharest)에서부터 키예프(Kiev), 모스크바(Moscow)에 이르기까지 저작권 침해는 복제를 통해 서구 컴퓨터 기술을 따라잡으려는 구소련 정책에 뿌리를 두고 있다. 이제 소프트웨어 불법 복제는 또 하나의 암시장에 불과하다. 건장한 폴란드 경찰 출신으로 사립 탐정이 되 마이크로소프트사의 수사를 담당하고 있는 마렉 세미악(Marek Cemiak)씨는 불법 복제단들과 조직 폭력배들이 천생 연분이라고 말한다. "소프트웨어 불법 복제단들은 두뇌가 있고, 조직 폭력배들은 힘이 있습니다."

Passage 6

1. 1) Disneyland is supposed to be "The Happiest Place on Earth," but Liang Ning isn't too happy. The engineer brought his family to Disney's new theme park in Hong Kong from the southern Chinese city of Guangzhou one Saturday in April with high hopes, but by day's end, he was less than spellbound. "I wanted to forget the world and feel like I was in a fairy tale," he says. ① Instead, he complains, "it's just not big enough and not very different form the amusement parks we have in China." His seven-year-old daughter Yaqin disagrees, calling the park "fantastic," but her father grumbles: "If she wants to come again, I will send her with somebody else."

2. 1) Hong Kong's Magic Kingdom has so far been a little short on magic. The $1.8 billion theme park, which opened last September, was touted by Disney executives as its biggest and boldest effort to build its brand in China, a potentially vast new market for its toys, DVDs, and movies. The Hong

중심소재: 중국에 들어선 홍콩 디즈니랜드

1. 첫 번째 문단

1) 구체적 진술

Liang Ning이란 특정 인물의 경험을 통해서 불만족스러운 디즈니랜드 언급

① 작은 규모와 색다른 것 없는 평범함

2. 두 번째 문단

1) 문제점 지적

Kong government, which aggressively wooed Disney and is the park's majority owner, hoped the park would help secure the city's reputation as one of Asia's top tourist destinations. Ⓐ However, the conservative approach of Disney and its parter has produced a pint-sized park that so far hasn't matched visitors' lofty expectations. ⓐ Hong Kong Disneyland has merely 16 attractions compared to 52 at Disneyland Resort Paris. ⓑ Meanwhile, management glitches involving everything from ticketing to employee relations have further tarnished the venture's image. ⓒ In a recent survey conducted by Hong Kong Polytechnic University, 70% of the local residents polled said they had a more negative opinion of Disneyland since its opening. "Disney knows the theme-park business, but when it comes to understanding the Chinese guests, it's an entirely new ball game," says John Ap, who is an associate professor at the university's School of Hotel and Tourism Management.

① 아직까지는 홍콩의 디즈니랜드는 기대에 미치지 못함을 드러냄
Ⓐ 처음 들어섰을 때의 자신감과 기대감 언급 이후 however 이후 구체적 문제점 지적
ⓐ 적은 놀이기구 수
ⓑ 기계적 결함
ⓒ 중국고객에 대한 이해 부족

정답 **1** (D) **2** (A) **3** (A) **4** (B) **5** (D)

해설

1 "The Hong Kong government, which aggressively wooed Disney and is the park's majority owner, hoped the park would help secure the city's reputation as one of Asia's top tourist destinations."에서 알 수 있듯이 홍콩정부가 대소유주이며, 아시아 최대 관광지로서의 홍콩의 명성에 도움 될 것으로 기대한다고 했으므로, 홍콩 디즈니랜드에 가장 큰 이해관계가 걸려있는 측은 홍콩 정부이다.

2 주부와 서술부의 인과관계를 파악하면 쉽게 접근이 가능하다.

management glitches → have further tarnished the venture's image 경영 결함 벤처사업의 이미지 손상

3 Hong Kong Disneyland has merely 16 attractions compared to 52 at Disneyland Resort Paris. 에서 선택지 (A)는 옳은 진술임을 파악할 수 있다. (B)의 경우 봄이 아니라 가을인 9월에 개장했다. (C) 또한 "the conservative approach of Disney and its parter has produced a pint-sized park that so far hasn't matched visitors' lofty expectations."로 보아 틀린 문장이다. 선택지 (D)의 경우 2번 문제를 참고한다.

4 주절의 주어인 "조사에 응한 지역주민의 70%"를 가리키므로 선택지 (B)의 "대부분의 지역주민"이라 할 수 있다.

5 디즈니 관계자는 테마파크 사업에는 익숙하나, 중국 고객에 대한 이해는 부족함을 언급하고 있다.

지문해석

디즈니랜드는 "지구상에서 가장 행복한 장소"여야 하지만 리앙닝(Liang Ning)은 그다지 행복하지 않다. 기술자인 그는 큰 기대를 안고 4월의 어느 토요일 중국 남쪽도시인 광저우에서 그의 가족을 데리고 홍콩에 있는 디즈니의 새로운 테마파크로 왔지만, 날이 저물도록 전혀 넋을 잃지 않았다. "저는 세상일을 잊어버리고 동화 속에 있는 것처럼 느끼기를 원했어요"라고 그는 말한다. 대신에 그는 "그다지 크지도 않고 중국에 있는 놀이공원과 크게 다르지 않다"고 불평한다. 그의 일곱 살 난 딸인 야퀸(Yaqin)은 이에 동의하지 않으며 그 공원이 "환상적"이라고 말하지만, 그녀의 아버지는 "만약 제 딸이 다시 오고 싶어 하면 저는 다른 사람과 같이 가도록 할 겁니다"라고 투덜거린다. 홍콩의 마법 왕국은 지금까지 마법이 조금 부족했다. 지난 9월에 개장한 18억 달러짜리 테마 공원은 회사의 브랜드를 중국에 심기 위한 가장 크고 대담한 작업이었다고 디즈니사 임

원들에 의해 홍보되었는데, 중국은 장난감, DVD, 영화의 잠재적인 거대 신흥 시장이다. 적극적으로 디즈니사를 설득했던 그 공원의 대주주인 홍콩 정부는 그 공원이 아시아 최고 여행지로서 그 도시의 명성을 견고히 하는 데 도움이 되기를 희망했다. 하지만 디즈니사와 동업자의 보수적인 접근 방식이 현재까지는 방문객들의 높은 기대치에 부응하지 못하는 소규모의 공원을 만들었다. 홍콩 디즈니랜드는 52개의 놀이기구가 있는 파리 디즈니 리조트에 비해 겨우 16개의 놀이기구를 가지고 있다. 한편, 매표에서 고용관계까지 모든 것이 관련된 경영상의 결함은 이 모험적인 사업의 이미지를 더욱 손상시켜왔다. 홍콩 폴리테크 대학이 실시한 최근 조사에서 설문에 응한 지역 주민의 70%가 공원 개장 이후 디즈니랜드에 대해 더욱 부정적인 견해를 갖게 되었다고 응답했다. 그 대학의 호텔관광 경영학교 조교수인 존 앱(John Ap)은 "디즈니사가 테마공원 사업에 대해서는 잘 알지만, 중국 고객들을 이해하는 문제에 있어서는 상황이 완전 뒤바뀌었다."고 말한다.

Passage 7

1. Bill Smith and Mike Hugh are examples of men who committed three felonies and are now serving life in prison under California's "Three Strikes" law. However, the men's crimes were not violent. **1)**① Hugh says it is a waste of money to keep people like him locked up for the rest of their lives. Many people agree with him. ⓐ A new study by the Justice Policy Institute claims that the ten-year-old Three Strikes law has cost California billions of dollars, but it has not reduced crime. The authors of the study believe that sending people to jail is not a good way to reduce crime, and they think that people who commit nonviolent crimes should not suffer from Three Strikes. Some prosecutors agree that the law is unfair and unreasonable, and that it does not deter crime.

② The author of the Three Strikes law, Bill Jones, disagrees. Ⓐ According to Jones, Three Strikes has saved California billions of dollars, and crime in the state has gone down by 46 percent. ⓐ For example, California now has its lowest level of burglaries since 1957. Jones also says there are two million fewer crime victims and 100,000 fewer prisoners than without Three Strikes. He points out that California has not built any new prisons since the law was passed.

중심소재: Three Strikes Law

1. 도입부 = 중심소재 도출
구체적 사례를 통해서 Three Strikes Law를 소개하고 있다.

1) 구체적 진술
①반대 입장
Ⓐ 뒷받침 근거
돈 낭비
ⓐ 부연(조사)
비용만 많이 들 뿐 실리적으로 범죄율을 낮추지 못하고, 비폭력적 범죄를 저지른 사람의 경우 현행 법에 의해 처벌받지 말아야 한다.

②찬성 입장
Ⓐ 근거
비용 절감과 실제 범죄율을 낮추었다.
ⓐ 예시부연

정답 **1** (D) **2** (A)

해설

1 본문분석을 참조한다.

2 He points out that California has not built any new prisons since the law was passed.의 내용에서 감옥의 신설도 없으면, 감옥제도의 개혁도 언급되어 있지 않다.

지문해석

빌 스미스(Bill Smith)와 마이크 휴(Mike Hugh)는 3번의 중죄를 저지르고 지금 캘리포니아의 'Three Strikes' 법 아래서 종신형을 복역 중인 사람들의 예이다. 그러나 그들의 범죄는 폭력적이지는 않았다. 휴는 자신과 같은 사람들을 남은 인생동안 가두어놓는 것은 돈 낭비라고 말한다. 많은 사람들이 그의 의견에 동의한다. 사법 정책 연구소(the Justice Policy Institute)에 의한 한 새로운 연구는 10년이 된 Three Strikes 법은 캘리포니아 주로 하여금 수십억 달러의 비용을 쓰게 했지만 범죄를 줄이지는 못했다고 주장한다. 연구의 집필자들은 사람들을 감옥에 보내는 것은 범죄를 줄이는 좋은 방법은 아니라고 믿으며 비폭력적인 범죄를 저지르는 사람들은 Three Strikes 법의 적용을 받지 말아야 한다고 생각한다. 몇몇 검사들 또한 그 법은 불공정하고 불합리하며 범죄를 막지 못한다는 데 동의한다.

Three Strikes 법의 창시자인 빌 존스(Bill Jones)는 동의하지 않는다. 존스에 따르면 Three strikes는 캘리포니아 주로 하여금 수십억 달러를 절약하게 해왔고 캘리포니아 주의 범죄는 46%만큼 감소했다. 예를 들면 캘리포니아 주는 현재 1957년 이래로 가장 낮은 강도범죄 수치를 나타내고 있다. 또한 Three Strikes가 없을 때보다 2백만 명의 범죄피해자와 십만 명의 죄수가 줄었다고 존스는 말한다. 캘리포니아 주는 그 법이 통과된 이후로 어떠한 새로운 감옥도 건설하지 않았다고 그는 지적하고 있다.

Passage 8

1. **1)** The average human pulse rate is around seventy beats per minute. This is also the average tempo of most Western music. ① Ⓐ In fact, it's said that the slow parts of Baroque music induce mental and emotional integration. Ⓑ Concentrating on the rhythm of music affects the rate of breathing, making it more regular, and faster or slower depending on the piece.

2. There are interesting developments involving music. People are making "bioelectric" music, recording the sounds made by the electric impulses that result from brain activity or muscle movement. **1)** Ⓐ The sounds are processed through a computerized gadget for the use of composers, musicians, and even handicapped people who can be taught this means of self-expression. Ⓑ It's possible that by studying the "music" made by cells, microscopic creatures, and plants, we will understand biology much better.

중심소재: 인간의 신체와 음악

1. 첫 번째 문단

1) 도입부

인간의 평균박동 수와 서양 음악의 템포가 거의 비슷 = 인간의 신체와 음악

① 관계

Ⓐ 바로크 음악은 정신과 감정의 통합을 이끌어 낸다.

Ⓑ 음악의 리듬에 따라 호흡율에 영향을 미친다.

2. 두 번째 문단

1) 주제문

인간 뇌 또는 근육의 움직을 통해 발생하는 전기적 파장을 이용해 "biolectric" 음악을 만듦

① 구체적 진술

Ⓐ 방법

Ⓑ 의의

첫 번째 문단은 "음악과 신체"의 관계를 다루고 있다.

정답 1 (B)

해설

첫 번째 문단의 주된 내용은 "인간의 신체와 음악의 관계"이고, 두 번째 문단은 "신체를 활용한 음악과 관련된 흥미로운 개발, 즉 신체를 활용한 음악"이 됨으로 주제로 가장 적절한 것은 (B)에 해당한다.

지문해석

보통 사람의 맥박 속도는 1분에 약 70회이다. 이것은 대부분 서구 음악의 평균 박자이기도 하다. 실제로, 바로크 음악의 느린 부분은 정신과 감정의 통합을 이끌어낸다고들 한다. 음악의 리듬에 집중하는 것은 호흡의 속도에도 영향을 미쳐서, 호흡을 더욱 규칙적이게 하고, 곡에 따라 호흡은 더 빨라지거나 느려진다.

음악과 관련된 흥미 있는 개발이 있다. 사람들은 뇌의 활동이나 근육 움직임에 의해 생겨나는 전기적인 파장에 의해서 만들어진 소리를 녹음하여 '생물 조직의 전기 에너지' 음악을 만든다. 그 소리는 컴퓨터 장비를 통해 가공되어 작곡가들, 음악가들이 사용할 수 있고, 심지어 장애인들은 이를 배워 자기표현의 수단으로 이용할 수 있다. 세포, 미세 생물, 식물의 '음악'을 연구하여 생물을 훨씬 더 잘 이해하는 것이 가능하게 되었다.

TEST 05

Passage 1

문화제국주의 중 한 형태인 영어의 세계지배로 중심소재의 폭이 좁아짐을 파악한다.

1. Cultural imperialism is much more subtle than economic imperialism, which is itself less tangible than political and military imperialism, whose excesses are obvious and easy to denounce. 1) It would be wrong to say that the world domination of English is something deliberately organized and supported by Anglo-Saxon powers, hand in glove with political initiatives or the penetration of the world economy by their transnational firms. The "language war" had very seldom been regarded as a war and has never, anywhere, been declared. ① The military, diplomatic, political and economic strategies of the major powers can be studied and criticized, but linguistic strategies seem to be inconspicuous and tacit, even innocent or nonexistent. Will countries stand up to domination by a single language?

중심소재: 문화제국주의 → 영어

1. 도입부 = 중심소재 도출
문화제국주의의 특징: much more subtle to denounce

1) 현상
영어의 세계지배는 언어전쟁으로 간주되지 않음을 지적하고 있다.
① 이유
눈에 띄지 않고, 암묵적임 (inconspicuous and tacit)

대조의 글 전개방식을 파악하도록 한다.

글 전개방식과 유형의 관계
1) 대조 - 통념
통념은 1대 다수의 법칙으로 대조의 글 전개를 활용한다. 다수를 설정하고, 적절한 뒷받침을 통한 반박은 필자의 주장을 더욱 두드러지게 하는 효과가 있기에 통념의 글에서 주로 활용된다.
2) 인과 - 현상
글의 도입부에서 "결과적" 현상이 기술되고, 현상의 원인이 따르는 인과의 전개 방식이 활용된다.

정답 1 (B) 2 (A) 3 (C) 4 (D) 5 (D)

해설

1 글의 도입부에서 정치 · 군사 제국주의와 다른 문화제국주의를 언급한 후 그중에서도 영어의 세계 지배로 그 주제의 폭을 좁히고 있다.

2 기존의 제국주의와 비교하면서 문화제국주의 중 문화 제국주의의 특징을 언급하고 있다.

3 Cultural imperialism is much more subtle than economic imperialism, which is itself less tangible than political and military imperialism, whose excesses are obvious and easy to denounce를 보면, 문화제국주의는 경제 제국주의보다 훨씬 더 미묘하며, 정치·군사 제국주의보다는 덜 분명하다고 했다. 즉, 경제 정책은 문화정책보다 훨씬 더 분명하게 인식할 수 있다. 본문과 일치하는 선택지는 (C)이다.

4 inconspicuous and tacit에서 A and B는 A=B이므로 inconspicuous의 의미를 모른다고 할 때 tacit과 가장 근접한 단어를 고르는 문제로 보아도 된다.

5 linguistic strategies seem to be ⓐinconspicuous and tacit, even innocent or nonexistent. Will countries stand up to domination by a single language?에서 언어 전략은 눈에 띄지 않고, 암묵적이며 심지어 해롭지 않게 보인다고 했으므로 이런 문화적 지배에 "저항할 수 있을지"라고 묻는 것이 문맥에 가장 적절하다.
글의 도입부에서 정치 · 군사 제국주의와 다른 문화제국주의를 언급한 후 그중에서도 영어의 세계 지배로 그 주제의 폭을 좁히고 있다.

지문해석

문화제국주의는 경제 제국주의보다 훨씬 더 미묘한데, 이는 문화 제국주의가 지나침이 뻔히 보이고 맹렬한 비난을 하기 쉬운 정치나 군사 제국주의보다 훨씬 덜 분명하기 때문이다. 영어가 전 세계를 지배하고 있는 것은, 정치 조직들과 손을 잡은 앵글로색슨 족들의 힘으로 인하여 고의적으로 조작되었거나 지원받았기 때문이라고 말하는 것, 혹은 그들의 범국가적 회사들로 인하여 세계 경제에 영어가 깊이 뿌리박혀 있다고 말하는 것은 잘못된 일일 것이다. "언어 전쟁"은 좀처럼 전쟁으로 생각되지 않으며, 이제껏 그 어디에서도 선포된 적이 없다. 주된 강대국의 군사, 외교, 정치, 경제적 전략은 연구된 후 비판될 수 있지만, 언어전략은 두

드러지지 않고 암묵적이며, 심지어 해롭지 않거나 존재하지 않는 것 같이 보이기도 한다. 한 언어가 독점적 위치를 차지하고 있는 현실에 대해, 다른 나라들은 저항하고 일어설 것인가?

Passage 2

1. In the process of observation, experiment, and logical interpretation, there has grown up the language or rather, the languages, of science that have become in the course of time as essential to it as the material apparatus. 1) ① Like the apparatus, these languages are not intrinsically strange; they derive from common usage and often come back to it again. Ⓐ A cycle was once kuklos, a wheel, but it lived many centuries as an abstract term for recurring phenomena before it came back to earth as a bicycle. ② The enormous convenience of making use of quite ordinary words in the forgotten languages of Greece and Rome was to avoid confusion with common meanings. The Greek scientists were under the great disadvantage of not having a roundabout way in plain language—in Greek—for it. They had to express themselves in a roundabout way in plain language—to talk about the subauxiliary gland as "the acorn-like lumps under the jaw." Ⓐ But these practices, though they helped the scientists to discuss more clearly and briefly, had the disadvantage of building up a series of special languages or jargons that effectively, and sometimes deliberately, kept science away from the ordinary man. Ⓑ This barrier, however, is by no means necessary. Scientific language is too useful to unlearn, but it can and will infiltrate into common speech once scientific ideas become as familiar adjuncts of everyday life as scientific gadgets.

중심소재: 과학언어

1. 도입부
관찰, 실험 그리고 논리적 해석의 과정에서 과학의 중요한 도구로써의 과학언어

1) 구체적 진술

① 과학언어의 특징 1
일상적 용어에서 가져와 과학용어로 활용하고 다시 일상의 용어로 활용된다
Ⓐ 예시부여(*kuklos*)

② 과학언어의 특성 2
일상용어와 혼동을 피하기 위해 그리스와 로마와 같은 사라진 언어를 사용
Ⓐ 단점부연
일반인들이 다가가기 힘든 언어의 사용으로 과학과 일상의 괴리가 수 있는 단점은 있다.
Ⓑ 논리적 반전(however)
과학의 언어는 너무나 유용하고 일단 익숙해지면, 다시 일상의 언어로 자리를 잡는다.

정답 1 (A) 2 (A) 3 (B) 4 (B)

해설

1 글의 도입부에서 중심소재인 "과학언어"을 파악할 수 있었다면 쉽게 선택지를 파악할 수 있다. 과학언어의 특징을 두 가지 측면에서 다루면서 그 유용성까지 부연하는 글이다.

2 once scientific ideas become as familiar adjuncts of everyday life as scientific gadgets에서 선택지 (A)의 내용을 파악할 수 있다.

3 roundabout는 "우회적인, 돌려서 말하는"의 뜻이다.

4 빈칸을 중심으로 과학언어의 단점과 장점이 언급되고 있으므로 역접의 선택지 (B)가 가장 적절하다.

지문해석

관찰, 실험 그리고 논리적 해석의 과정에서 언어, 더 정확히 말하자면 시간이 흐르면서 실질적인 (과학적) 도구들처럼 과학에 필수적인 것이 된 과학 언어가 등장했다. 이러한 언어는 도구들처럼 본질적으로 낯선 것은 아니다. 왜냐하면 그 언어들은 일상적인 용법에서 유래되어 종종 다시 제자리로 돌아오기 때문이다. 사이클

중심소재
중심소재는 대의파악 문제뿐 아니라 모든 유형의 문제풀이의 시작이다. 글의 도입부에서 언급되는 대상 또는 내용이 반복될 경우 중심소재가 될 가능성이 높다는 점을 기억한다.

중심소재와 주제와의 관계
주제는 글의 도입부에서 설정한 포괄적 주제인 중심소재의 폭을 본문의 내용을 바탕으로 폭을 좁힌 것임을 잊지 않도록 한다.

응집성 연습
연결사 문제 풀이의 정확성을 높이는 방법 중 하나는 문제의 선택지를 보기 전에 빈칸에 들어갈 내용이 순접인지 역접인지와 아래와 같은 세부 사항 중 어느 것인지를 먼저 파악하는 것이다.
순접: 예시(for example), 나열(first, second), 첨어(in addition, furthermore), 인과, 재진술(that is to say), 요약·정리(therefore, so)

(cycle)이란 말은 한때 바퀴를 뜻하는 kuklos란 말에서 유래된 것이지만, 자전거라는 의미로 일상생활에 쓰이기 전까지는 반복되는 현상에 대한 추상적 언어로서 수세기 동안 쓰여 왔다. 이제는 사용되지 않는 그리스와 로마어의 아주 평범한 말들을 사용하는 큰 이점은 일반적인 의미와의 혼동을 피할 수 있다는 점이다. 그리스 과학자들은 과학 용어를 쉬운 그리스어로 다르게 표현하기 힘들었다. 예를 들면 엽액하 분비선(葉腋下分泌腺)을 쉬운 말로 표현하려면 '턱 아래 있는 도토리 같은 덩어리'로 다른 방식으로 설명해야 했다. 비록 이런 관행들은 과학자들이 더 정확하고 간결하게 의사소통하는 데 유용하긴 하지만 사실상, 때로는 의도적으로 과학을 평범한 사람들로부터 멀어지게 하는 특수용어나 (과학적) 전문용어를 늘린다는 점에서는 좋지 않다. 그러나 이것이 반드시 장벽이 되는 것은 아니다. 과학적 언어는 너무나 유용해서 배운 것을 쉽게 잊어버릴 수가 없다. 일단 과학적 개념이 과학적 장치들만큼 일상생활의 친숙한 부속물이 되기만 하면 그것(과학적 언어)은 일상적인 언어 속에 스며들 수 있고 스며들게 될 것이다.

Passage 3

1. Attitudes are evaluative judgments about objects, people, and thoughts. What is your attitude about religion, soccer, opera, politicians, crossword puzzles, plastic surgery, and the death penalty? 1) As these examples indicate, attitudes can be positive, negative, or neutral; they can also vary greatly in intensity. You may have attitudes of differing intensity about a wide variety of subjects, and those attitudes influence many of your thoughts, behaviors, and interactions. Ⓐ For example, intense political attitudes influence our thoughts about society, our behavior toward others with dissimilar views, and the people whom we call our friends. Say that you love rollerblading and strap on your "blades" whenever you have a chance. You also enjoy rollerblading because you know that it's excellent exercise and a great way to stay in shape. You have a positive attitude about it. 2) In this description, your love for rollerblading makes up the affective or emotional component of your attitude, your knowledge about the health benefits of rollerblading constitutes the cognitive component, and your action in putting on your blades illustrates the behavioral component. Although it is easy to see that we all have attitudes, it is more difficult to understand why we have them and what their purpose is. 3) Attitudes serve several distinct functions: ego defense, adjustment, and knowledge. Ⓐ If a person makes statements that we perceive as threatening, we might say, "He makes comments like that because he's a dumb jock." Attributing threatening statements to the type of individual making them allows us to avoid confronting the possibility

도입부에서 정의되는 대상은 중심소재가 됨을 기억한다.

구체적 진술을 이끄는 시그널을 확인한다.

중심소재: 태도

1. 도입부 = 중심소재 도출
태도의 정의

1) 태도의 종류와 정도
태도에는 긍정, 부정, 중립의 종류가 있고, 정도에 차이가 있다.
Ⓐ 예시

2) 태도의 요소(component)
① affective or emotional component
② cognitive component
③ behavioral component

3) 태도의 기능
① ego defense
② adjustment
③ knowledge
Ⓐ 각 기능 부연

that the statements are accurate. People and behaviors that yield reinforcement are viewed positively; those that yield unpleasant effects are viewed negatively. For example, an individual who is being reinforced on a new job would be likely to say, "I am very impressed with the supervisors on my new job. They are friendly, fair, and understanding people." The following attitudes may help a person who is trying to understand an apparently unjust situation: "Most football players have skills that others lack. That's why they're paid such incredibly high salaries."

정답 **1** (A) **2** (D) **3** (D)

해설

1 본문분석을 참조한다.

2 두 번째 단락에서 your knowledge about the health benefits of rollerblading constitutes the cognitive component를 보면, 태도 중 지식의 구성은 인지적 요소라고 했으므로 선택지 (D)가 정답이다.

3 세 번째 문단의 마지막 부분인 Attitudes serve several distinct functions: ego defense, adjustment, and knowledge.를 통해 선택지 (D)가 본문의 내용과 일치함을 파악할 수 있다.

지문해석

태도라는 것은 사물이나 사람, 생각에 대한 평가적 판단이다. 종교, 축구, 오페라, 정치인, 낱말 맞추기 게임, 성형수술, 사형제도 등에 대한 당신의 태도는 어떠한가? 이런 예들이 보여주듯, 태도는 긍정적, 혹은 부정적 이거나 중립적일 수 있고 이런 태도들의 강도 또한 다양할 수 있다. 당신은 아주 다양한 주제에 대하여 서로 다른 강도의 태도를 가질 수 있고, 그 태도들은 당신의 생각 ,행동, 대화에 많은 영향을 준다. 예를 들면, 정치에 대해 강한 태도를 가지고 있다면, 이는 사회에 대한 우리의 생각, 다른 의견을 가지고 있는 사람들에 대한 우리의 행동, 그리고 우리가 친구라고 부르는 사람들에 영향을 준다. 당신이 롤러블레이드를 타는 것을 좋아해서 기회가 있을 때마다 블레이드를 탄다고 해보자. 당신은 또한 롤러블레이드가 훌륭한 운동이고 몸을 건강하게 유지하는 좋은 방법임을 알기 때문에 롤러블레이드 타는 것을 즐기기도 한다. 당신은 롤러블레이드에 대해서 긍정적인 태도를 가지고 있다. 이 상황에서, 당신이 롤러블레이드를 매우 좋아한다는 사실은 당신의 태도에 있어 정서적인, 혹은 감정적인 요소를 구성하고 있으며, 롤러블레이드를 타는 것이 건강에 이롭다는 것을 알고 있다는 사실은 인지적 요소를 구성하며, 당신이 실제로 롤러블레이드를 신는 행동은 행동적 요소를 보여준다. 우리 모두 태도를 가지고 있다는 것은 알기 쉽지만, 왜 우리가 그런 태도를 가지고 있고, 그 태도들의 목적이 무엇인지를 이해하는 것은 더 어렵다. 태도는 자아 방어, 적응, 그리고 지식과 같은 몇 가지 명백한 기능을 한다. 만약 어떤 사람이 위협한 발언으로 여겨지는 말을 하면 "그는 무식이 철철 넘치니까 그런 말을 하는 거야"라고 말할 수도 있다. 위험한 말을 하는 것을, 그런 말을 하는 사람의 유형탓으로 돌려 버리면, 그런 말이 옳을 가능성에 맞서 대처할 필요가 없게 된다. 사람은 자신의 주장을 더욱 강화시켜주는 사람이나 행동은 긍정적으로 보고, 불쾌한 결과를 가져다주는 사람과 행동은 부정적으로 본다. 예를 들면 새로운 직장에서 이러한 강화 효과를 얻고 있는 사람은 "나는 새 직장 관리자들에게서 매우 감명 받고 있어요. 그들은 친절하고 공평하며 사려 깊은 분들이에요"라고 말하기 쉬울 것이다. 다음과 같은 태도는 일견 불공평해 보이는 상황을 이해하기 위해서 노력하는 사람에게 도움이 될 수도 있다. "대부분의 축구 선수들은 다른 사람들에게 부족한 기술을 가지고 있다. 그 때문에 그들이 그렇게 높은 연봉을 받는 것이다."

Passage 4

1. Neal Armstrong's famous first words from the moon in 1969 were heard as "That's one small step for man, one giant leap for mankind." But was that what he said? Grammarians have long been annoyed that such a world-famous moment was marred by bad grammar, arguing there should have been an 'a' in front of 'man'. 1) Armstrong has long asserted that he did, in fact, say the 'a', although the acoustic record begged to differ.

① To set the record straight, Peter Shann Ford, a Sydney-based computer programmer, conducted his own high-tech detective work. By analysing the NASA recording with advanced nerve-based voice analysis software usually used for people who are paralysed, Ford found the missing word. Armstrong did indeed say, "One small step for a man...", but according to Ford, the 'a' lasted a total of only 35 milliseconds. 2. Roger Launius, who chairs the space history division at the Air and Space Museum in Washington, said, "in the overall scheme of world history, it's probably not significant. But it's nice to know that what he thought he said, he actually did say, and that because of the nature of the electronic and communications systems of the time, it just did not get through."

요지를 이끄는 시그널을 확인한다.

중심소재: 암스트롱이 달에서 남긴 말

1. 도입부 = 중심소재 도출
암스트롱이 달에서 한 역사적인 첫 말에 문법적 오류: a를 발음하지 않아 문법적으로 오점을 남겼다.

1) 암스트롱의 주장
본인은 a를 했다고 하나 기록이 이를 증명해 주지 못한다.

① 뒷받침 근거(실험)
최첨단 장비를 통해 그가 a를 발음했음을 확인

2. 결론
역사적으로 중대한 사건에서 암스트롱이 문법적 오류를 남기지 않았다는 점을 언급하고 있다.

정답 1 (D) 2 (A)

해설

1 beg to differ라는 표현은 "~에 찬성하지 않는다, 반대하다"의 의미이다. 그러므로 음성기록은 암스트롱의 주장인 'a' 발음을 했다는 내용과 반대의 의미를 전달해야 함으로 선택지 (D)가 정답이다.

2 빈칸의 주어인 it이 지칭하는 것은 암스트롱이 말한 a이다. 당시 장비의 한계로 인해 그 소리가 들리지 않았다는 내용이 되어야 자연스러운 문맥을 형성함으로 선택지 (A)가 정답이다.

지문해석

1969년 달에서 닐 암스트롱이 말한 유명한 첫 마디는 "이는 (한) 사람에게 있어서는 작은 한걸음이지만, 인류에 있어서는 거대한 진보이다."처럼 들렸다. 그러나 그가 말한 것이 정말 이것이었나? 문법학자들은 오래동안 세계적으로 이렇게 중요한 순간에 문법적 실수로 인해 오점이 생겼다고 오랫동안 불편함을 드러냈다. 그들은 '인간' 앞에 '한'이 있어야 했다고 말한다. 암스트롱은 오랫동안 그가 실제로 '한'을 말했다고 주장했지만, 녹취는 이를 뒷받침하지 못했다.

이 기록을 바로 잡기 위해서 시드니에 기반을 둔 컴퓨터 프로그래머인 Peter Shann Ford는 자신의 최첨단 탐지 작업을 실행했다. 원래 마비된 사람들에게 사용되던, 신경기반으로 목소리를 분석하는 고도 소프트웨어를 사용하여 Ford는 NASA의 기록을 분석했고, 들리지 않던 단어를 발견했다. 암스트롱은 확실히 "한 인간을 위한 작은 한걸음"이라고 말했지만, Ford에 따르면 '한'이란 단어는 단지 35 밀리세컨드만 지속되었다고 한다.

워싱턴의 항공우주 박물관에서 우주역사 부서의 의장으로 있는 Roger Launius는 "전 세계 역사에서 이것은 아마도 그리 중요하지 않을 것이다. 그러나 그가 말했다고 생각한 것이 실질적으로 말해졌다는 것, 그리고 그 당시의 전자 및 통신 시스템의 특성으로 인해, 이것이 들리지 않았다는 것을 알게 되어 기쁘다."라고 말했다.

Passage 5

1. 1) Essentialism presumes 'that particular things have essences which serve to identify them as the particular things that they are'. ① The most common essentialist view of culture is that 'cultures' are coincidental with countries, regions, and continents, implying that one can 'visit' them while traveling and that they contain 'mutually exclusive types of behavior' so that people 'from' or 'in' French culture are essentially different from those 'from' or 'in' Chinese culture. Ⓐ Common variations on this geographical theme are the association of 'cultures' with religions, political philosophies, ethnicities and languages, where 'Islamic culture', 'black culture', and 'English language culture' take on the same essence of containment.

2. 1) Much of this essentialism will seem natural and normal to many readers, because it is in many ways the default way of thinking about how we were different from each other. ① It is, however, problematic because if we think of people's behavior as defined and constrained by the culture in which they live, agency is transferred away from the individual to the culture itself so that we begin to think that 'German culture believes that ...', and that 'she belongs to German culture, therefore she ...'. Ⓐ There is only a short, easy distance from this essentialist way of thinking to the chauvinistic stereotyping inherent in culturism which allows us to arrive at statements like 'in Middle Eastern culture there is no concept of individualized critical thinking'.

중심소재: 문화 → 문화에 대한 본질주의자들의 견해

1. 첫 번째 문단

1) 도입부

특정 사물은 다른 것과 구별되는 그 사물만의 특정한 본질이 있다.

① 문화에 대한 견해

문화는 나라, 지역 그리고 대륙과 일치하며, 어느 나라 출신인지에 따라 상호배타적인 행동양식을 취하게 되어 문화 간 차별이 생긴다.

Ⓐ 지리적 차이로 인해 그 지역의 특정 문화는 종교, 정치 철학, 민족성 그리고 언어와 연계됨

2. 두 번째 문단

1) 일반통념

일반인들은 본질주의를 당연한 것으로 간주한다.

① 문제점 지적(요지)

만약 사람들의 행위를 문화에 따라 제약된 것으로 본다면, 행위주체성(agency)이 인간에서 문화로 전위되는 현상이 발생하게 된다.

Ⓐ 본질주의는 맹목적 애국주의라는 고정관념으로 쉽게 발달할 수 있다.

문화와 지리의 관계를 바탕으로 전개한 견해

통념비판의 글임을 드러내는 시그널을 확인하고, however 이후 이어지는 내용은 글쓴이가 궁극적으로 전달하고자 하는

글의 유형
① 통념(대다수)
② 현황(인과)
③ 실험·모의·연구
④ 시간의 대조

TEST 05

정답 1 A) 2 D)

해설

1 두 번째 문장의 cultures' are coincidental with countries, regions, and continents를 통해 "지리적"이란 표현이 빈칸에 적절함을 파악할 수 있다.

2 문화에 대한 본질주의적 관점의 문제점을 지적하는 내용이다.

지문해석

본질주의는 특정한 (개별적인) 것들이 본질들을 갖고 있다고 가정하는데 그 본질들을 현재 존재하는 특정한 것들로 확인하는 데 기여한다고 본다. 문화에 대한 가장 일반적인 본질주의 견해는 '문화들'은 나라와 지역, 그리고 대륙과 동시에 발생한다는 것인데 이러한 견해는 어떤 사람이 여행하면서 문화들을 '방문'할 수 있고 문화들은 '상호 배타적인 행동 양식들'을 내포하고 있어서 프랑스 문화'로부터' 또는 프랑스 문화 '내의' 사람들은 중국 문화'로부터' 또는 중국 문화 '내의' 사람들과는 본질적으로 다르다는 의미를 내포하고 있다. 이러한 지리적 주제와 마찬가지인 또 다른 일반적 변인들은 '문화들'을 종교, 정치철학, 인종, 언어들과 연관 지은

것들인데, '이슬람 문화', '흑인 문화' 그리고 '영어권 문화'는 모두 똑같이 본질을 포함하고 있다. 이러한 본질주의의 많은 부분은 많은 독자들에게 자연스럽고 정상적으로 여겨지게 되는데, 그 이유는 우리가 어떻게 서로 달랐는가에 대해 생각할 때 특별한 경우가 아니면 많은 면에서 바로 그렇게 (본질주의적으로) 생각하기 때문이다. 그러나 만약 우리가 사람들의 행동이 그들이 살고 있는 문화에 의해 정의되고 제환되는 것으로 생각한다면 행위주체성은 개인으로부터 문화 그 자체로 옮겨지고 그 결과 우리는 '독일 문화는 무엇이 어떻다고 믿는다'라거나 '그녀는 독인 문화에 속해 있어서 어떠어떠하다'라는 생각을 갖게 되기 때문에 본질주의는 문제가 있다. 이러한 본질주의적 사고방식으로부터 문화주의에 내재해 있는 쇼비니즘(맹목적 애국주의)적 고정관념으로 발전하는 것은 너무나 쉬운 순식간의 일이고, 그렇게 되면 우리는 "중동 문화에는 개인화된 비판적 사고라는 개념이 존재하지 않는다"는 말까지도 내뱉게 된다.

Passage 6

시간의 글 전개 확인

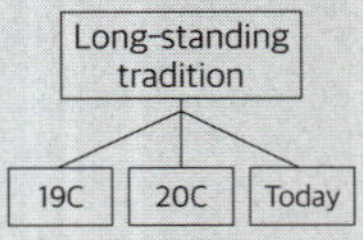

1. 1) American society has a long-standing tradition of criticizing violence in the media. ① Ⓐ During the nineteenth century, educators and others warned about the effects of lurid dime novels and newspaper crime stories on the young. Ⓑ In the early twentieth century, motion pictures and radio were both viewed as significant social threats. Ⓒ Today, concerns are expressed about violence in computer games, popular songs, and on the Internet.

2. 1) Throughout the evolving changes in media technology, a fundamental question has remained the same: Do depictions of violence in the media somehow contribute to real-life violence? ① Since the 1950s, television has been at the center of the debate over media violence. Ⓐ There are several reasons for the focus on television. ⓐ It is pervasive and thus it is heavily watched. ⓑ More worse, television shows are frequently violent. In one 1982 study, researchers who analyzed 180 hours of programming counted 1,846 acts of violence. The net result of television's popularity and violent content is that the average American child witnesses eight thousand murders and one hundred thousand other acts of violence by the time he or she finishes elementary school. ⓒ Many argue that exposure to such quantities of violent depictions damages children and contributes to violence in real life. In particular, critics claim that television violence teaches children that violence is an acceptable solution to problems and fosters a fearful attitude by leading viewers to think that the world is more violent than it really is.

중심소재: 미디어의 폭력

1. 첫 번째 문단

1) 도입부 = 중심소재 도출

미디어로 표현되는 폭력 비판은 미국 사회에서 과거에서 현재까지 이어지는(long-standing) 전통

① 뒷받침 진술

Ⓐ 19세기

교육가를 중심으로 젊은이들에게 부정적인 영향을 미치는 무시무시한 싸구려 소설과 신문의 범죄이야기 비판

Ⓑ 20세기 초

영화와 라디오: 심각한 사회에 위협을 미치는 요소로 비판

Ⓒ Today

컴퓨터 게임, 대중음악, 인터넷의 폭력성

2. 두 번째 문단

1) 의문문(주제)

미디어를 통해 표현되는 폭력성이 현실 폭력으로 드러나는가?

① 답변(요지)

TV는 실제폭력 논의의 중심

Ⓐ 뒷받침 근거

ⓐ 보편화되어서 많이 봄

ⓑ 폭력적 장면이 자주 등장

- 부연

ⓒ 폭력적 장면은 아이들에게 나쁜 영향을 미치고 실제 생활의 폭력으로 이어짐

- 부연

정답 **1**(B) **2**(D) **3**(C) **4**(C)

해설

1 lurid는 "무시무시한"의 뜻으로 가장 근접한 의미의 단어는 grisly다.

2 젊은이에게 미치는 TV의 부정적인 영향을 다루는 글이다. 본문 분석을 참조한다.

3 Since the 1950s, television has been at the center of the debate over media violence.에서 선택지 (C)는 본문과 일치함을 알 수 있다.

4 It is pervasive and thus it is heavily watched. More worse, television shows are frequently violent.를 통해 선택지 (C)는 언급되어 있지 않다.

지문해석

미국 사회는 대중매체 속 폭력을 비판하는 오래된 전통을 가지고 있다. 19세기 내내 교육가들과 다른 사람들은 무시무시한 싸구려 소설과 신문의 범죄 이야기가 젊은이들에게 미치는 영향들에 대해 경고했다. 20세기 초에는 영화와 라디오 둘 다 중대한 사회적 위협들로 간주되었다. 오늘날 컴퓨터 게임과 대중음악, 인터넷에 표현된 폭력에 대한 우려가 나타나고 있다. 대중매체 기술의 진화하는 변화 속에서 근본적인 의문 하나가 여전히 변치 않고 남아 있다. 대중매체 속 폭력 묘사들이 어떻게든지 실생활 속 폭력에 기여하는가? 1950년대 이래 텔레비전은 대중매체 폭력에 대한 논쟁의 중심에 있어 왔다. 텔레비전에 초점을 맞추는 이유는 몇 가지 있다. 그것은 널리 보급되어 있고 따라서 많이 시청된다. 더욱 심각한 것은 텔레비전 쇼들이 빈번히 폭력적이라는 점이다. 1982년 한 연구에서 180시간 분의 프로그램을 분석했던 연구진들은 1,846건의 폭력 행위를 집계했다. 텔레비전의 인기와 폭력적인 콘텐츠의 최종 결과는 평균적인 미국 어린이가 초등학교를 마칠 때까지 8천 건의 살인과 10만 건의 기타 폭력 행위들을 시청한다는 것이다. 그런 양의 폭력적인 묘사에 노출되는 것은 어린이들에게 해를 끼치고 실생활의 폭력에 기여한다고 많은 이들이 주장한다. 특히 텔레비전 속 폭력은 폭력이 문제들을 푸는 적합한 해결책이라고 아이들을 가르치고 세상이 실제보다 더욱 폭력적이라고 생각하도록 시청자들을 유도함으로써 두려움이 가득 찬 태도를 갖게 한다고 비평가들은 주장한다.

Passage 7

1. The international diamond trade is a peculiar business, routinely described as a bizarre, one-of-a-kind vocation by the very people who earn a living from it. For example, Albert Thomas, deputy manager of the diamond division at the ABNAMBO Bank in Antwerp, says the diamond trade works well, though he calls it "pretty medieval"— a statement supported by the facts.

1) ① In today's global market, the $6.8-billion rough-diamond industry is still largely controlled by one company—De Beers Consolidated Mines, which sets the price for uncut, or rough, diamonds and determines supply. ② Transactions are settled in cash, even when they involve prices of seven figures. Diamond dealers never issue receipts, and deals worth millions of dollars are sealed on a handshake. ③ It's not surprise, then, that the diamond trade is tight-knit family affair so exclusive that entrance is almost impossible unless you're born into the business. "Everything rests on a person's word," says Lerner, whose family has worked with diamonds for five generations. ④ One of a handful of women traders in the business today, she runs her company, Lerner Diamonds, jointly with her husband.

중심소재: 국제 다이아몬드 무역

1. 도입부 = 주제문

국제 다이아몬드 무역은 중세적 성격의 아주 독특한 특징을 가진다.

1) 뒷받침 진술

①특징 1
독점

②특징 2
현금거래, 영수증 X, 계약서 X

③특징 3
가족 중심의 세습적이고, 배타적

④특징 4
남성중심

나열은 연역적 전개의 대표적 사례

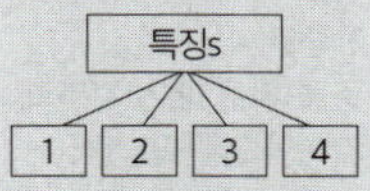

정답 1 (A)

해설

마지막 문장에서 a handful of women traders라고 했으므로 다이아몬드 무역이 남성 중심의 사업이라고 볼 수 있고, 그 무역이 대부분 세습적 성격을 지닌 긴밀하게 짜여진 가업이라고 했으므로 외부 사람들에게는 개방되지 않았다는 것을 알 수 있다. 또한 Transactions are settled in cash, even when they involve prices of seven figures.부분을 통해 다이아몬드는 오로지 현금으로만 거래되고 신용대부로는 거래되지 않음을 알 수 있다. 독점무역이라는 점에서 선택지 (A)만 본문과 일치하지 않음을 알 수 있다.

지문해석

국제 다이아몬드 무역은 그것으로 생계를 꾸리는 사람들조차 특이하고 독특한 직업이라고 흔히들 말하는 유별난 사업이다. 예를 들어 앤트워프에 있는 ABN 암로(ABN AMRO) 은행 다이아몬드 부서의 부 지배인인 앨버트 토머스는 다이아몬드 무역이 잘되고 있지만 "상당히 중세적인" 사업이라고 부르는데, 이는 사실에 근거한 주장이다.
오늘날 세계시장에서 68억 달러 규모의 다이아몬드 원석 산업은 아직까지 드 비어즈 통합 광산(De Beers Consolidated Mines)이라는 한 개의 회사에 의해 지배되고 있는데, 이 회사는 세공되지 않고 거친 다이아몬드의 가격과 공급량을 결정한다. 거래는 수백만 달러가 오고가지만 현금으로만 결제된다. 다이아몬드 거래 상인들은 결코 영수증을 발급하지 않고, 수백만 달러 가치의 거래들이 악수로 마무리된다. 다이아몬드 무역은 너무도 배타적이고 긴밀한 가업이어서 그 가업을 잇는 집안에서 태어나지 않았으면 진입 자체가 거의 불가능하다 해도 놀랄 일이 아니다.
"모든 것은 한 사람의 지시에 달려 있다"고 Lerner는 말하는데, 그의 가족은 5대째 다이아몬드 사업을 하고 있다. 오늘날 몇 안 되는 여성 다이아몬드 무역업자 중 한 사람인 그녀는 자신의 회사인 레너 다이아몬드사를 남편과 공동으로 운영하고 있다.

Passage 8

여러 단락으로 글이 구성될 경우 각 단락별 주제를 설정하도록 한다.

글의 도입부에서 정의되는 대상은 중심소재가 된다.

단락구성의 두 원리
1) 통일성
글을 읽을 때는 지문의 길이와 관련 없이 주제는 하나라는 점을 잊지 말아야 본문 끝까지 일관성 있는 글 읽기가 가능하다. 그러므로 주제 파악의 첫 시작인 중심소재 설정의 중요성을 다시 인식하고, 글의 도입부에서 중심소재 설정에 주목한다.
2) 응집성
문장 또는 문단 간의 논리적 고리인 응집성은 고난도 문제인 문장배열, 문장삽입, 빈칸문제에 자주 활용된다. 평소 문장과 문단 간의 논리적 관계를 꾸준히 연습하여 이러한 문제에 대비해야 한다.

1. Fog is a cloud in contact with or just above the surface of land or sea. 1) It can be a major environmental hazard. ① Fog on highways can cause chain-reaction accidents involving dozens of cars. ② Delays and shutdowns at airports can cause economic losses to airlines and inconvenience to thousands of travelers. ③ Fog at sea has always been a danger to navigation. ④ Today, with supertankers carrying vast quantities of oil, fog increases the possibility of catastrophic oil spills.

2. 1) ① The most common type of fog, radiation fog, forms at night, when moist air near the ground loses warmth through radiation on a clear night. This type of fog often occurs in valleys, such as California's San Joaquin Valley. ② Another common type, advection fog, results from the movement of warm, wet air over cold ground. The air loses temperature to the ground and condensation sets in. This type of fog often occurs along the California coast and the shores of the Great Lakes. Advection fog also forms when air associated with a warm ocean current blows across the surface of a cold current. The thick fogs of the Grand Banks off Newfoundland, Canada, are largely of this origin,

중심소재: 안개

1. 첫 번째 문단
1) 도입부 = 중심소재 도출
안개의 정의
① 단락 주제문
안개는 주된 환경적 문제를 야기한다.
Ⓐ 뒷받침 예시
①, ②, ③, ④

2. 두 번째 문단
1) 안개의 두 종류(①, ②)
흔히 발생하는 안개의 두 가지 종류, 형성과정, 원인에 관한 내용을 자세히 다루고 있다.

because here the Labrador Current comes in contact with the warm Gulf Stream.
3. Two other types of fog are somewhat more unusual. ③ Frontal fog occurs when two fronts of different temperatures meet, and rain from the warm front falls into the colder one, saturating the air. ④ Steam fog appears when cold air picks up moisture by moving over warmer water.

3. 세 번째 문단
추가적 안개의 종류(③, ④)

정답 **1** (A) **2** (D) **3** (B) **4** (A) **5** (A) **6** (D)

해설

1 첫 번째 단락은 안개로 인해 교통사고나 석유누출 사고 등의 위험성이 커지고 있다고 이야기하고 있으므로 선택지 (A)가 정답이다.

2 catastrophic는 "대변동[큰 재앙]의, 파멸적인"의 뜻으로 disastrous의 의미가 가장 근접하다.

3 캘리포니아 해변에 형성되는 안개는 보통 수평류 안개이다.

4 윗글에 의하면 복사 안개는 공기가 따뜻한 해류와 만나 찬 바다를 지날 때 형성되는데, 따뜻한 멕시코 만류와 래브라도 해류가 만나 복사 안개가 형성된다고 했으므로 래브라도 해류는 차다.

5 작가는 각각의 다른 종류의 안개들을 발생하는 지역에 따라 분류하여 설명하고 있다.

6 안개에 대해 해박한 지식을 가진 것으로 보아 저자는 기상학 전문가일 것이다.

지문해석

안개는 땅이나 바다의 표면 바로 위에 접하고 있는 구름이다. 그것은 환경적으로 크게 위험할 수 있다. 고속도로의 안개는 수십 개의 차를 동반하는 연쇄 사고를 일으키게 하기도 한다. 공항의 (운항)지연과 일시 폐쇄는 항공사측에 경제적 손실을 주고 여행객들을 불편하게 할 수 있다. 바다의 안개는 항해에 항상 위험한 존재였다. 오늘날, 초대형 유조선이 광대한 양의 석유를 나를 때, 안개는 석유 누출로 인한 비극적인 해중 오염의 가능성을 높이기도 한다.
가장 일반적인 형태의 안개인 복사 안개는 청명한 밤에 방열(放熱)로 온기를 잃은 축축한 공기가 지면 가까이에 있을 때 형성된다. 이 형태의 안개는 캘리포니아의 San Joaquin Valley 같은 계곡에서 종종 발생한다. 또 다른 평범한 형태의 안개인 복사 안개는 습한 공기가 차가운 대지를 지날 때 온기의 움직임 때문에 발생한다. 대기는 지면에 온도를 빼앗기고 응결이 일어날 때 온도를 빼앗긴다. 이런 형태의 안개는 종종 캘리포니아 연안이나 미국의 5대호 기슭에서 생긴다. 복사 안개는 공기가 따뜻한 해류와 만나 찬 해류의 표면을 지나 바람에 날릴 때 형성된다. 뉴펀들랜드, 캐나다의 Grand Bank의 두꺼운 안개는 대개 이러한 경로로 생긴 것인데, 왜냐하면 래브라도 해류가 따뜻한 멕시코 만류와 접하게 되기 때문이다.
두 가지 다른 형태의 안개는 약간 더 특이하다. 전선(前線) 안개는 다른 온도의 두 전선이 만나는 때와 비가 따뜻한 전선에서 차가운 전선으로 내릴 때 발생한다. 뭉개 안개는 찬 공기가 따뜻한 물 위를 지나면서 습기를 머금을 때 생긴다.

TEST 06

Passage 1

1. 1) Plants absorb energy from the sun. ① This energy flows through a circuit called **biota**, which may be represented by a pyramid consisting of layers. Ⓐ The bottom layer is the soil. A plant layer rests on the soil, an insect layer on the plants, and so on up through various animal groups to the apex layer, which consists of the larger carnivores.

2. The species of a layer are alike not in where they came from, or in what they look like, but rather in what they eat. Each successive layer depends on those below it for food and often for other services, and each in turn furnishes food and services to those above. Proceeding upward, each successive layer decreases in numerical abundance. Thus, for every carnivore there are hundreds of his prey, thousands of their prey, millions of insects; uncountable plants.

중심소재: Biota

1. 첫 번째 문단

1) 도입부 = 중심소재 도출

biota 정의

①단락 주제문

Ⓐ각 층에 대한 설명
식물 층(가장 밑바닥의 토양) → 곤충 층(식물 위) → 다양한 동물 층 → 육식 동물이 거하는 가장 위 층(Apex layer)

2. 두 번째 문단

각 층의 특징과 상호관계를 밝히고 있다.

정답 1 (B) 2 (D)

지문분석

하나의 단락은 하나의 주제만 다루는 통일성의 원칙을 반드시 지켜야 한다. 단락이 두 개로 나뉘면, 각 단락의 소주제를 설정하고 두 문단의 공통 또는 전체 주제를 설정하도록 한다.

해설

1 먹이 피라미드의 각 층과 상호관계에 관한 설명의 글이다.

2 먹이 사슬에 관한 내용이 두 번째 문단에 서술되고 있고 빈칸 다음 문장에도 먹을 것을 위해 아래층에 의존한다는 내용이 있으므로 (D)가 적합하다.

지문해석

식물들은 태양으로부터 에너지를 흡수한다. 이 에너지는 생물상(相)이라는 경로를 통해 흘러가는데 이 경로는 여러 층으로 구성된 피라미드에 의해 나타낼 수 있다. 바닥층은 토양이다. 식물 층이 그 위에 위치하고 곤충이 그 위층인 식으로 해서 다양한 동물 집단들을 거쳐 더 큰 육식동물로 구성된 맨 위층에까지 이른다.
한 층의 종은 그들의 출생지나 혹은 생김새에 있어서 유사한 것이 아니라 그들이 먹는 것에 있어서 다소 유사하다. 각각의 연속적인 층이 먹이와 그 외 다른 서비스를 위해 그 아래층들에 의존하며, 각각의 층은 또한 그 위층에 먹이와 서비스를 제공한다. 위쪽으로 가면서 연속적인 각층은 수적인 풍부함이 감소하게 된다. 따라서 모든 육식동물 한 마리에게 수백 마리의 먹이가 있고 그 먹이의 먹이들은 수천 마리가 있고 수백 만 마리의 곤충이 있고, 셀 수 없는 식물이 있는 것이다.

Passage 2

1. Most people feel lonely sometimes, **but** it usually only lasts between a few minutes and a few hours. For some people, though, loneliness can last for years. Psychologists are studying this complex phenomenon. 1) ① The most common type of loneliness is temporary. Ⓐ It usually disappears quickly and does not require any special attention. ② The second kind, situational loneliness, is a natural result of a particular situation—for example, a divorce, the death of a loved one, or moving to a new place. Ⓑ Although this kind of loneliness can cause physical problems, such as headaches and sleeplessness, it usually does not last for more than a year. Situational loneliness is easy to understand and to predict. ③ The third kind of loneliness is the most severe. Unlike the second type, chronic loneliness usually lasts more than two years and has no specific cause. Ⓒ People who experience habitual loneliness have problems socializing and becoming close to others. Many chronically lonely people think there is little or nothing they can do to improve their condition.

중심소재: 외로움

1. 도입부 = 중심소재 도출

but이후 외로움이 사람에 따라 다양한 형태로 드러난다고 말한 후 심리학자의 연구를 통해 다양한 종류의 외로움을 밝히는 글로 전개되고 있다. 주제 : Kinds of Loneliness (나열의 글 전개방식)

1) 뒷받침 진술

①Temporary loneliness
Ⓐ부연진술

②Situational loneliness
Ⓑ부연진술

③Chronic Loneliness
Ⓒ부연진술

첫 번째 문장은 글 전체의 방향성을 제시해 주는 나침반과 같은 역할을 한다. 주제문이 드러날 경우 글의 주제 및 중심내용을 이끌어 낼 수 있다. 적어도 주제를 드러내는 중심소재는 글의 도입부에서 설정할 수 있어야 한다.

나열의 글 전개를 드러내는 시그널로 top-to-bottom 형태의 대표적 유형으로 중요도에 따른 나열이다.

TEST 06

정답 **1** (A) **2** (B)

지문분석

다양한 종류의 외로움을 소개하는 글이다. 글의 종류는 설명이며, 나열의 전개방식을 취하고 있다. 이런 종류의 글은 내용파악을 물어보는 내용일치 또는 구체적 세부사항 문제가 나올 가능성이 높기에 각 종류별 특징을 정확히 파악해야 한다.

해설

1 일시적인 외로움이나 상황적인 외로움과 달리 만성적인 외로움은 매우 심각하다고 하였다.

2 여기에서 언급된 사례는 다음과 같다. "대부분의 조사자들은 가장 외로운 사람들이 18세에서 25세 사이의 사람들이라는 데에 동의했다. 그들은 50%이상의 신입생들이 학기 초에 새로운 환경으로 인해 외로워한다는 것을 발견했다." 이것은 외로움의 두 번째 유형인 상황적인 외로움이다.

지문해석

대부분의 사람들이 때로는 외로움을 느끼지만 일반적으로 이것은 몇 분에서 몇 시간 동안만 지속된다. 하지만, 어떤 사람들에게는 외로움이 수년간 지속될 수 있다. 심리학자들은 이 복잡한 현상을 연구하고 있다. 외로움의 가장 흔한 유형은 일시적 외로움이다. 이것은 대개 금방 사라지고 특별한 주의를 요하지 않는다. 두 번째 유형인 상황적인 외로움은 특별한 상황, 예를 들어, 이혼, 사랑하는 이의 죽음, 새로운 장소로의 이동과 같은 상황에 의한 자연스런 결과이다. 이러한 종류의 외로움이 두통, 불면증과 같은 건강상의 문제를 일으킬 수도 있지만, 그것은 대개 일년 이상 지속되지 않는다. 상황적인 외로움은 이해하고 예측하기 쉽다. 세 번째 유형의 외로움이 가장 심각하다. 두 번째 유형과 달리 만성적 외로움은 2년 이상 지속되는 것이 일반적이며 특별한 원인도 없다. 습관적으로 외로움을 느끼는 사람들은 사회화하거나 다른 이들과 가까워지는 데 문제가 있다. 만성적으로 외로움을 타는 많은 사람들은 그들의 상황을 개선하기 위해 자기가 할 수 있는 일이 거의 없거나 혹은 전혀 없다고 생각한다.

Passage 3

1. Bush will lay out his "vision for expanding the space program," which is expected to include long-term moves for manned missions to the moon and an eventual manned mission to Mars, an official said. NASA's target for a moon mission is 2018. 1) ① The speech will come just a couple of weeks before the anniversary of the breakup of the space shuttle Columbia as it returned to Earth last February 1. All seven astronauts aboard were killed.

② The official declined to say where or when Bush will give the speech, but it will likely be after he returns from a summit in Mexico, possibly as early as Wednesday. White House spokesman Scott McClellan, traveling with the president in Florida, confirmed the announcement will take place next week, and said it would be an outgrowth of a review of the space program that began after the shuttle disaster.

Ⓐ Some of the things that had been under consideration were a proposal for a permanent presence on the moon, setting a target for retiring the shuttle fleet, and a plan to phase out the international space station. An administration official said the president is not expected to immediately discuss the potential cost of his new space vision.

2. The announcement would come more than 31 years after the last moon mission. The last moon flight was December 1972 and some in Congress have argued that it's time to go back. Last month, administration sources told CNN that NASA was urgently debating and refining the proposals. A senior administration official said Vice President Dick Cheney had initial consultations with key members of Congress on the possibility of a revamped and expanded American space program. The Bush administration review also includes choosing a new space vehicle for manned flights.

중심소재: 부시의 우주탐사 프로그램

1. 도입부

우주탐사에 관한 부시 대통령의 계획: 달, 나아가 화성에 유인 우주선을 보내는 장기적인 계획

1) 구체적 진술

①시기

부시의 연설은 우주 프로그램으로 발생한 참사의 기념하는 날 이주 전에 할 예정

②공식입장

관계자는 부시가 언제 어디서 연설할지에 대한 정보를 묵인하지만, 아마도 멕시코 정상회담 이후 할 것으로 예정이며 연설의 주된 내용은 우주 프로그램에 대한 재검토

Ⓐ 재검토 내용부연

영구적 기지 달에 건설, 낡은 우주선 복귀 시기, 국제 우주정거장 단계적 설계. 하지만 새로운 우주 계획의 비용에 대한 논의는 없을 것

2. 배경

우주탐사 프로그램 재고의 배경

정답 1 (D) 2 (C)

해설

1 글 전반에 걸쳐 우주왕복선 콜롬비아호의 공중폭발 참사 후 부시 행정부가 유인우주탐사를 재개할 계획이라는 내용을 다루고 있다.

2 마지막 달 탐험은 1972년 12월에 있었다(The last moon flight was December 1972)고 언급되어 있다. 따라서 (C)가 본문의 내용과 일치한다.

지문해석

조지 W. 부시 미국 대통령은 '우주개발 프로그램 확대에 대한 비전'을 제시할 것이며 이 우주 프로그램에는

달에 인간을 착륙시키고 궁극적으로는 화성에 유인우주선을 보낸다는 장기적인 계획이 포함될 것이라고 미 정부관계자가 밝혔다. 미 항공우주국(NASA)은 달 착륙 목표연도를 2018년으로 잡고 있다. 이 같은 내용을 담은 연설은 지난 2월 1일 지구로 귀환하던 중 폭발한 우주왕복선 콜롬비아호의 폭발 참사 1주기 2, 3주 전에 행해질 것이다. 우주비행사 7명은 전원 사망했다. 이 정부관계자는 부시가 연설할 장소와 시간을 밝히기를 거부했으나 부시 대통령이 멕시코 정상회담을 마치고 귀국한 후 이르면 수요일에 발표가 있을 것으로 예상된다. 스콧 매클렌런(Scott McClellan) 백악관 대변인은 부시대통령과 플로리다(Florida) 주 순회 중 다음 주에 발표가 있을 것임을 확인하고 이번 발표는 콜롬비아호 폭발 참사 이후 시작된 우주개발 프로그램을 재검토한 결과보고가 될 것이라고 전했다. 고려 중에 있는 몇 가지 계획에 따르면 달에 영구기지를 건설하고, 낡은 우주왕복선 편대를 퇴역시키고, 국제우주정거장(ISS)에서 단계적으로 철수한다는 계획이다. 한 행정부 관리는 부시 대통령이 새 우주개발비전의 잠재 비용에 대해 즉각적인 논의를 할 것으로 보이지는 않는다고 밝혔다. 이번 우주개발계획은 달 탐사 임무가 끝난 지 31년 만에 발표되는 것이다. 마지막 달 탐사는 지난 1972년 12월 이후 중단되었다. 일부 미국 국회의원들은 이제 달 탐사를 재개해야 한다고 주장했다. 지난달 미 행정부 소식통은 나사(NASA)가 이 안건을 긴급 토의 및 검토 중이라고 CNN에 말했다. 미 행정부의 고위 관계자는 딕 체니(Dick Cheney) 부통령이 미 우주개발 프로그램의 개선 및 확장 가능성에 대해 국회 주요 인사들과 첫 회의를 가졌다고 밝혔다. 부시 행정부의 차세대 우주개발계획 재검토 작업에는 유인 우주비행을 실현할 새 우주탐사선 선정 과정도 포함되어 있다.

Passage 4

1. 1) Flax has been raised for many thousands of years, for many different reasons. ① Probably the two most important reasons are for the fabric it makes and the oil it produces. Ⓐ The woody stem of the flax plant contains the long, strong fibers that are used to make linen. Ⓑ The seeds are rich in an oil important for its industrial uses. ⓐ The peoples of ancient Egypt, Assyria, and Mesopotamia raised flax for cloth; Egyptian mummies were wrapped in linen. Since the discovery of its drying ability, the oil from flaxseed, called linseed oil, has been used as a drying agent in paints and varnishes.

2. 1) The best fiber and the best seeds cannot be obtained from the same flax plant. ① Fiber flax grows tall and has few branches. Ⓐ It needs a short, cool growing season with regular and plentiful rainfall. Otherwise, the plants become woody and the fiber is rough and dry. Ⓑ On the other hand, seed flax grows well in places that are too dry for fiber flax. The plants are lower to the ground and have more branches.

중심소재: 아마

1. 첫 번째 문단

1) 도입부 = 단락 주제문
아마는 다양한 이유에서 기른다.

① 뒷받침 진술
fabric과 oil을 얻기 위해 아마 재배
Ⓐ 아마의 딱딱한 나무줄기에서 아마포를 만드는데 사용하는 fabric 생산
Ⓑ 아마 씨앗에 산업용 oil이 풍부하게 포함되어 있다.
ⓐ 고대 사회부터 옷을 만들기 위해 아마를 기름 + 씨앗에서 추출한 oil을 그림 또는 광택에 포함된 건조제로 활용

2. 두 번째 문단

1) 단락 주제문
fiber와 oil은 동일한 아마에서 구할 수 없다.

① 뒷받침 진술
Ⓐ fiber를 얻을 수 있는 키가 크고 가지가 없는 아마의 경우 비가 많이 오는 서늘한 하지만 짧은 시즌을 필요로 한다.
Ⓑ 반면, oil을 얻을 수 있는 아마(seed flax)의 경우 건조한 기후에서 자란다.

본문에 구체적으로 다뤄질 중심내용이다.

대조의 글 전개를 확인한다.

정답 1(D) 2(C)

해설

1 본문 후반부에 The best fiber and the best seeds cannot be obtained from the same flax plant(동일한 아마풀에서 최고급 섬유와 최고급 씨를 같이 얻을 수는 없다)라고 분명히 명시되어 있으며 이는 (D)의 질문에 대한 답으로 볼 수 있다. (A), (B), (C)는 본문에 언급되지 않은 사항이다.

2 빈칸 앞의 문장에서는 섬유용 아마풀은 "짧고 서늘한 재배기간(a short, cool growing season)"과 "정기적으로 많은 양의 강우(regular and plentiful rainfall)"가 필요하다고 했고, 빈칸 뒤의 문장은 "아마풀이 나무처럼 딱딱해지면서 섬유가 거칠고 건조해진다(the plants become woody and the fiber is rough and dry)"라는 내용이므로 앞에서 언급된 조건이 "만족되지 않으며", "그렇지 않으면"과 같은 맥락의 연결사가 되어야 하므로 선택지 Otherwise가 적절하다.

지문해석

아마는 수천 년 동안 다양한 이유로 재배되었다. 아마 가장 중요한 두 가지 이유는 아마로 만드는 섬유와 아마로 만드는 기름 때문일 것이다. 아마풀의 나무같이 딱딱한 줄기는 린네르천을 만드는데 사용되는 길고 뻣뻣한 섬유를 함유하고 있다. 아마씨엔 공업적 용도로 중요하게 여겨지는 기름이 풍부하다. 고대 이집트, 아시리아, 메소포타미아 인들은 아마를 옷감으로 길렀고, 이집트의 미라는 린네르천으로 감싸여 있다. 건조능력이 발견된 이래, 아마인유로 불리는 아마씨 기름은 물감이나 광택제에 포함되는 건조제로 사용되어 왔다. 동일한 아마풀에서 최고급 섬유와 최고급 씨를 같이 얻을 수는 없다. 섬유용 아마는 높이 자라고 가지가 얼마 없다. 섬유용 아마는 짧으면서 서늘한 재배기간에 정기적으로 풍부한 양의 강우가 필요하다. 그렇지 않으면, 아마풀이 나무처럼 딱딱해지면서 섬유가 거칠고 건조해진다. 반면에 씨용 아마는 섬유용 아마가 자라기에 너무 건조한 곳에서 잘 자란다. 이 아마풀은 섬유용 아마풀보다 땅으로 낮게 자라고 가지가 더 많다.

Passage 5

요지를 이끄는 시그널
1. not A but B = B, not A
2. not only[just/merely] A but also[rather] B
3. not so much A as B = B rather than A (B가 중요)
4. 역접의 연결사 뒤
5. 양보구문에서 뒤의 주절의 내용
6. Because S + V, S + V에서 결과에 해당하는 주절의 내용
7. To + V, S V에서 주절의 내용
8. must/have to/should 가 들어간 문장
8. 최상급 표현이 들어간 문장
9. The 비교급 ~, the 비교급~ 구문
10. So, Thus, Therefore, 등의 결론을 유도하는 연결사 다음에 나오는 내용
11. In short, In brief, In Summary, To sum up, To put it simply, Put simply 등의 요약을 유도하는 연결사 다음에 나오는 내용

1. When we look at any scene we tend to concentrate on what interests us and ignore the detail that does not seem relevant. The camera, however, records the entire scene indiscriminately. 1) This is why beginners are often surprised to find unwanted details intruding into their pictures. ① The single-mindedness of the eye is something the photographer must deliberately impose on the picture by selective focusing so that extraneous detail is excluded, blurred or subordinated to the overall design. Ⓐ To be able to do this, you must learn to see as the camera does. In taking a picture of a group of friends, for instance, it is not enough simply to look at them and make sure they are all in the frame and that nobody's eyes are shut. Having arranged the group in roughly the right position, look through your viewfinder at the whole picture area, ignoring your friends for the moment and examining their surroundings. Remember particularly that the three-dimensional scene will be reproduced in only two dimensions on the film and that a post or tree some distance behind the group may thereforeappear, in the picture, to be joined onto one of your friendslike an extra limb. Try to look at other objects in

중심소재: 인간과 카메라

1. 도입부 = 중심소재 도출
However를 중심으로 인간과 카메라의 차이점 언급: 인간은 관심이 있는 것에만 집중하는 반면, 카메라는 전체의 장면을 구별 없이 모두 담아냄

1) 문제점
무분별하게 모든 장면을 담아내는 카메라의 특징으로 인해 초보자들이 어려움을 겪는다.
① 대안(요지)
초보 사진작가들은 선택적인 장면에만 초점을 맞출 수 있도록 해야한다.
Ⓐ 구체적 방법상술
카메라와 같이 보는 방법을 예시와 함께 본문 끝까지 상술하고 있다.

the scene interms of shapes, patterns, textures, tones or colors to see whether they harmonize with the subject or conflict with it.

정답 1 D) 2 C) 3 E) 4 E)

해설

1 글의 도입부에서 언급된 문제점을 해결하는 방법에 관한 글이다. To be able to do this, you must learn to see as the camera does 부분을 통해 (D)가 글의 주제임을 파악할 수 있다.

2 인간은 특정 장면을 바라볼 때 관심이 있는 것만 집중하는 반면, 카레마를 전 장면을 무분별하게 받아들이기에 이에 대한 차이점을 인식해야 하는데, 초보는 이런 점을 인식하지 못한다. 글의 도입부 세 문장을 주목한다.

3 In taking a picture of a group of friends, for instance, it is not enough simply to look at them and make sure they are all in the frame and that nobody's eyes are shut. Having arranged the group in roughly the right position, look through your viewfinder at the whole picture area, ignoring your friends for the moment and examining their ___(A)___.
분사구문은 앞의 문장에 대한 부연이므로 빈칸의 힌트는 앞에 전개된 내용에서 찾을 수 있다. 친구들의 단체 사진을 찍을 때 단지 사람에게만 초점을 맞추지 말고, 사진 전체를 보라고 했으므로 잠시 친구를 무시하고 전체 배경을 보라는 내용이 되어야 함으로 surroundings가 빈칸에 적절하다.

4 3차원의 장면이 사진이라는 2차원에 담겨지는 내용이므로 in the picture가 정답이다.

지문해석

어떤 장면을 바라볼 때, 우리는 흥미로운 것에만 집중하고 사소해 보이는 세부사항은 무시하는 경향이 있다. 그렇지만, 카메라는 이러한 구별 없이 전체 장면을 기록한다. 이것이 바로 초보자들이 그들의 사진 속에 들어있는 불필요한 세부사항들을 발견하고는 종종 놀라는 이유이다. 포토그래퍼는 사진에서 가장 중요하게 찍혀야 할 부분에만 선택적으로 초점을 맞추고 그 외의 세부 장면은 빼거나 흐릿하게 하거나 전체 구도에 부속시킴으로써 인간의 눈의, 관심 있는 것만 집중적으로 보는 특성(single-mindedness)을 사진 속에 반드시 구현한다. 이렇게 하기 위해서는 카메라처럼 보는 법을 배워야 한다. 예를 들어 친구들을 촬영할 때, 단순히 친구들을 바라보고, 모두가 테두리 안으로 들어오도록 하고, 눈 감은 사람이 아무도 없도록 확인하는 것만으로는 불충분하다. 올바른 위치에 친구들을 배치하고, 뷰파인더를 통해 전체 사진의 범위를 확인하고, 일단은 친구들을 무시하고 주변 환경부터 자세히 보라. 특히 3차원의 장면이 필름 속에서는 단지 2차원으로 재연되고, 사람들 뒤로 멀리 떨어져 있는 장대나 나무가 사진 속에서는 친구들 중 한 명에게 마치 또 다른 팔다리처럼 붙어있는 것처럼 보일 수도 있다는 사실을 명심하라. 현장의 다른 사물들을 모양, 패턴, 질감, 색조, 색의 관점에서 바라보고 그것들이 피사체와 조화를 이루는지 충돌을 빚고 있는지 확인해야 한다.

12. 주장, 제안, 충고 등을 나타내는 명령형 문장
13. 글의 말미에 등장하는 수사의문문
14. For example/For instance 등과 같은 예시 앞 문장
15. necessary/im portant/imperative/require 등의 표현이 있는 문장
16. 글의 도입부의 의문문은 글의 주제며, 답변은 요지다.
17. 논증의 글에서 I think/believe/feel~ 등의 필자의 견해가 있는 문장
18. 비유는 요지의 간접적 전달이며, 비유되는 대상을 통해 전달하는 말이 곧 요지다.
19. Storytelling(이야기체) 글이 아닌 논설문이나 설명문에서 " "(인용부호(Quotation Mark)가 있으면 대부분 핵심내용이다.

Passage 6

1. 1) At the White House last month, the Southern Baptist Convention's top political officer, Richard Land, told President Bush he was offended by the number of illegal immigrants living with impunity in the United States. ① Ⓐ "When government does not enforce laws," he told Bush, "it's not doing what God ordained it to do." Ⓑ But Land, whose group counts 16 million followers, favors down-to-earth solutions. "Practically speaking," he says, "the government isn't going to deport 12 million immigrants."

중심소재: 불법이민자

1. 첫 번째 문단

1) 도입부 = 현상(문제점)

Richard Land를 통해 불법이민자들에 대한 문제점 언급

①대안

Ⓐ 원칙적 접근
정부차원의 법적 처리

So Land told the president he supports Bush's proposed guest-worker program—and that he might even support putting illegal immigrants on a path to citizenship. 2. 1) Land's take on immigration mirrors an uneasy national ____(A)____. ① Ⓐ On one hand, Americans seem inclined to preserve their melting-pot heritage, but they also want law and order and harbor post-9/11 fears about national security. Ⓑ The debate is playing out on a variety of stages. Last month, hundreds of thousands marched in the streets in support of immigrants. And last week, the US Senate intensified debate on a host of legislative proposals, ranging from get-tough enforcement measures to guest-worker programs that would put illegals on a path to citizenship. Ⓒ Where it ends up is anybody's guess. "You're in an election year, and this stirs passions on all sides," says Kansas Sen. Sam Brownback. "There's real possibility we won't be able to pull anything together." The issue is so fraught with political and policy differences that even if Congress does pull something off, it is as likely to disappoint all parties involved as it is to satisfy any one of them.

Ⓑ Richard Land의 현실적 접근
현실적으로 이들을 추방할 수 없으며, 이들이 오히려 법 안에 들어올 수 있도록 하는 부시의 정책을 지지

2. 두 번째 문단

1) 단락주제

불법이민문제에 대한 논란

① 뒷받침 진술

Ⓐ 다문화 전통 유지와 함께 9/11사태로 인한 보안 강화

Ⓑ 반응
이미자를 지지하는 거두행진과 국회 내 이를 지지하는 정책과 불법 이민에 대한 강경책의 충돌

Ⓒ 불법 이민자에 대한 문제가 쉽게 되지 않을 것임을 본문 끝까지 언급

주제 : A Controversial Issue of Illegal immigrants

정답 1(B) 2(A) 3(A) 4(B)

해설

1 So Land told the president he supports Bush's proposed guest-worker program—and that he might even support putting illegal immigrants on a path to citizenship.에서 알 수 있듯이 Land는 불법 이민자에 대한 Bush의 정책에 찬성하는 것을 파악할 수 있다.

2 바로 이어지는 내용인 On one hand, Americans seem inclined to preserve their melting-pot heritage, but they also want law and order and harbor post-9/11 fears about national security.로 보아 Land의 입장은 미국인들의 양면적 성격을 드러냄을 파악할 수 있다.

3 anyone's guess란 누구도 짐작만 할 뿐 확실히 모르는 상황을 가리킬 때 쓰는 표현이다. [예문] When he comes is anybody's guess.(그가 언제 오는지 정확히 알지는 못한다.)

4 'Practically speaking,' he says, 'the government isn't going to deport 12 million immigrant에서 부시의 정책은 실용적임을 파악할 수 있다.

지문해석

지난달 백악관에서 미국 남침례회연맹의 최고 행정관인 리처드 랜드(Richard Land)는 부시 대통령에게 미국에서 처벌받지 않고 거주하고 있는 불법이민자들의 숫자에 화가 난다고 말했다. 그는 부시 대통령에게 "정부가 법을 집행하지 않는다면 그것은 신께서 정부에게 명한 일을 하지 않는 것"이라고 말했다. 그러나 1,600만 명의 신도들이 있는 교단에 속한 랜드는 현실적인 해결책을 지지한다. 그는 "현실적으로 정부가 1,200만 명에 이르는 이민자들을 추방하지는 않을 것"라고 말한다. 그래서 랜드는 대통령에게 자신은 대통령이 제안한 이주 노동자 프로그램을 지지하고, 심지어 불법이민자들이 시민권을 취득할 수 있도록 길을 열어주는 것에도 지지를 표할 수 있다고 밝혔다.

이민에 대한 랜드의 태도는 불안한 국민적 모순을 반영하고 있다. 한편으로 미국인들은 그들의 용광로 유산을 보호하는 쪽으로 마음이 기운 것처럼 보이지만, 동시에 법과 질서를 원하고 국가 안보에 대한 9/11 사태

이후의 불안감을 계속해서 품고 있다. 그 논쟁은 다양한 측면으로 진행되고 있다. 지난달 수십만 명의 사람들이 이민자를 지지하는 거리 시위를 벌였다. 또한 지난주 미국 상원은 강경한 강제조치부터 불법이민자들에게 시민권 취득의 길을 허용하는 이주 노동자 프로그램에 이르기까지 다양한 다수의 입법 제안들에 대한 논쟁에 불을 지폈다. 그 논쟁이 어디에서 끝날지는 어느 누구도 예측하기 어렵다. "올해엔 선거가 있고 이 논쟁은 사방에서 격한 감정을 자극한다. 우리가 어떤 식으로도 협력할 수 없을 가능성이 실재한다."고 캔자스주 상원의원인 샘 브라운백(Sam Brownback)은 말한다. 그 문제에는 정치적, 정책적 차이가 너무나 많아 설사 의회가 어떤 성과를 달성한다고 해도 관여한 정당 중 어느 측을 만족시키는 것만큼이나 모든 정당을 실망시킬 가능성이 크다.

Passage 7

1. Although much of the communist system has been jettisoned over the years, all of China's rural land is still owned by the state. **1)** Farmers have usually been allowed to lease plots for 30 years at a stretch, after which they can renew the lease. But ownership—and the right to sell—has remained in the hands of village-level leaders and party secretaries. ① Here in the jurisdiction of Fujin, more than 70 villages have tried to privatize their lands over the past month, according to local farmers. As word of their movement spread on the Internet, they said, farmers in other regions followed suit. Ⓐ ⓐ The Fujjin farmers focused on 250,000 acres that had been taken over by local officials in the 1990s for sale to private agriculture companies. Only part of the land was in theory redistributed last month, they said, because police moved in and prevented further allocations. ⓑ But the farmers have since moved beyond the issue of the seized land and asserted the right to own all the collective farmland that they currently work under lease. The nascent movement, although tiny within a peasant population of 700 million, has confronted the Chinese Communist Party with a difficult challenge: **2.** If the experience of the past 30 years has shown the wisdom of privatizing state-owned industry and moving toward a market economy, why would it not be wise to privatize the land and bring it into the market economy, as well?

중심소재: 국영토지제도

1. 도입부 = 중심소재 도출
중국의 모든 토지는 국가 소유

1) 개괄적 설명
농부는 최장 30년간 소규모 밭을 임대하고, 이후 갱신하는 형식을 취하며, 소유권은 주로 촌락과 당 지도자에 있음

① 현상
Fujin지역에서 확산된 농지의 사유화 시도

Ⓐ 전개

ⓐ 1990년대 지역 관료에게 넘어간 땅에 대한 소유권(부분적 소유권)을 주장했지만, 일부만 재분배되고, 경찰의 개입으로 더 이상의 분배는 저지됨

ⓑ 경찰의 개입으로 소유권에 대한 분쟁이 정부쪽의 강압적 승리로 끝났지만, 농민들은 정부에 넘어간 땅 문제를 넘어 현지 차용으로 일구는 집단 경작지에 대한 소유권을 주장하면서 중국공산당과 충돌

2. 요지문
국가주도 산업의 민영화를 통해 이룬 지혜로운 조치와 마찬가지로 토지소유권도 자유 시장경제에 맡기자!

연상의 시그널을 확인한다.

글의 말미에 제시되는 의문문은 제안, 권유로 요지에 해당한다.

정답 **1** (B) **2** (A) **3** (D)

해설

1 국영토지제도에 관한 글이다. 본문분석을 참조한다.

2 nascent는 "초기의, 발생기의"란 뜻으로 emerging이 가장 비슷한 의미를 전달한다.

3 글 전체의 내용이 농부들의 토지 국영화 반대이다. 마지막 문장인 If the experience of the past **30** years has shown the wisdom of privatizing state-owned industry and moving toward a market economy, why would it not be wise to privatize the land and bring it into the market economy, as well?의 밑줄 친 부분에서 알 수 있듯이 중국 공산당이 국가 소유의 산업을 민영화 하는 지혜를 보인 것과 같이 토지의 사유화와 시장경제로의 움직임을 주장하고 있다. 그러므로 선택지 (D)와 같이 정부가 성공적으로 시장경제를 추구했다는 말은 옳지 못하다.

지문해석

비록 공산주의 체제 대부분이 수년에 걸쳐 폐기되어 왔지만 여전히 중국의 전체 시골 토지는 국가 소유다. 농부들은 보통 30년 동안 연속해서 소규모 밭을 임대하도록 허가되어 왔고 그 후에 임대 계약을 연장할 수 있었다. 그러나 소유권(과 판매권)은 촌락 단위의 지도자들과 당 서기들의 수중에 남아 있었다. 지역 농부들에 따르면 이곳 푸진(Fujin) 관할 구역에서 70개 이상의 마을이 지난 달 토지를 사유화하려고 시도했다. 그들이 전하길 그들의 움직임이 인터넷에 소문나자 다른 지역의 농부들도 동참했다고 한다. 푸진 지역 농부들은 1990년대 민간 농업기업들에 팔려고 지역 관료들에 의해 인수된 25만 에이커에 주의를 기울였다. 영토의 일부만이 원칙적으로 지난 달 재분배되었는데 그들에 따르면 경찰이 개입해 추가적인 배분을 막았기 때문이다. 그러나 그때 이후로 농부들은 수탈당한 토지 문제를 뛰어넘어 운동을 벌였고 그들이 임대 계약 하에 현재 작업하고 있는 집단 농장 전체를 소유할 권리를 주장하고 나섰다. 이 초기 운동은 비록 7억 명의 농부들 가운데 극히 일부 사이에서 일어났지만 어려운 도전 과제를 들고 중국 공산당에 대항하고 있다. 지난 30년의 경험을 통해 국가 소유의 산업을 민영화하고 시장경제를 향해 나아간 것이 현명했음을 보여주었다면 영토를 사유화해 이를 시장경제로 들이는 것 또한 현명하지 않을까?

Passage 8

1. Since 1960, worldwide production of meat has quadrupled to more than 280 million tons a year. Even if everyone in the rich nations swore off meat today, consumption would continue to soar. 1) For this reason, serious environmental planners have recently focused not on eliminating the meat industry but on turning it green.① Making beef, pork, or chicken can be an environmentally devastating process. And among animal proteins, to make a kilogram of beef takes seven times more farmland than is needed to produce a kilo of chicken, and 15 times the area needed for a kilo of pork. ② **Yet** scientists, herders, and green groups are convinced they can curb the damage by Ⓐ making adjustments all along the supply chain, changing the way we farm and feed livestock and building a cleaner cow through modern genetics. ⓐ The effort starts with the animals themselves. When a cow eats, its stomach produces methane as a byproduct. Cows are pretty efficient at eating grass, but the soybeans and corn thatmost industrial livestock farms feed them make the bovine stomach rumble with excess gas. To fight this, some farms found they could improve health and boost milk production in the herds, and reduce methane emissions, by eliminatingsoybean and corn-based feed. Instead, they give

중심소재: 고기소비의 급증

1. 도입부 = 현상

세계적으로 고기 생산량 급증 부유한 나라에서 모든 이가 고기를 끊겠다고 맹세했으면서도 여전히 소비량 급증

1) 환경입안자의 대안

고기 산업을 없애려는 시도보단 고기 산업을 환경친화적으로(green) 변화시키려는 시도

①이유

글의 도입부에서 제시된 바와 같이 고기소비를 줄인다는 것은 비현실적이며, 동물 단백질의 경우 소고기 1kg을 만드는 데 같은 양의 돼지고기를 생산하는 것보다 7배의 더 많은 목초지가 필요

②구체적 방법

Ⓐ를 통해서 현재의 피해를 최소화 할 수 있다.

ⓐ부연

soybeans and corn를 alfalfa로 대체

their cows old-fashioned alfalfa, which is packed with nutrients and benign fatty acids.

정답 **1** (D) **2** (C)

해설

1 to make a kilogram of beef takes seven times more farmland than is needed to produce a kilo of chicken, and 15 times the area needed for a kilo of pork에서 알 수 있듯이 소고기 1kg를 만들기 위해선 돼지고기 1kg에 필요한 양의 15배나 많은 농지가 필요하다고 했으므로 선택지 (D)는 본문과 일치한다.

2 육류 생산의 전면적 중단은 현실성이 떨어진다는 점을 지적하면서, 친환경 생산과정의 도입을 주장하는 글이다. 제시된 문장의 the effort는 글쓴이가 궁극적으로 전달하려는 대안이 언급되는 시작점이므로 선택지 (C)가 적절하다. 만약 (D)에 넣을 경우 제시문의 내용이 to fight this에서 밑줄 친 부분이 되어야 함으로 문장 간 응집성이 결여된다. 문장삽입의 경우 1) 연결사 2) 대명사 3) a N → the N → it/that 4) 순차적 행위를 나타낸 동사 및 동적 명사 5) 글 전개/유형 등을 활용한다.

지문해석

1960부터 전 세계 육류 생산이 4배인 연간 2억 8천만 톤으로 증가했다. 부유한 국가의 모든 사람이 오늘 고기를 그만 먹겠다고 맹세하더라도 (육류) 소비는 계속 증가할 것이다. 이 때문에 생각 있는 환경계획 입안자들은 최근에 육류산업을 없애는 것이 아니라 육류산업을 친환경화 하는 것에 집중하기 시작했다. 소고기, 돼지고기, 또는 닭고기를 만드는 것은 환경적으로 재앙을 불러오는 과정이 될 수 있다. 그리고 동물성 단백질 중에서도 1kg의 소고기를 만들기 위해서는 닭고기 1kg을 만들기 위해 필요한 것보다 7배나 많은 농지가 필요하고, 돼지고기 1kg을 만들기 위해 필요한 것보다 15배나 많은 농지가 필요하다. 하지만 과학자, 농장주, 환경단체 등은 우리가 가축을 사육하고 먹이는 방식을 바꾸고 현재의 유전학을 통해 소를 더 깨끗하게 만들어서 육류 공급망 전체에 조정을 가하는 방식으로 이 같은 피해를 억제할 수 있다고 확신한다. 이러한 노력은 가축들에서부터 시작된다. 소가 먹이를 먹을 때 소의 위는 메탄을 부산물로 생산한다. 소는 풀을 섭취하는데 있어선 꽤 효율적이지만, 대부분 산업형태의 가축농장에서 소에게 먹이는 콩이나 옥수수는 소의 위가 과도한 가스로 울렁이게 만든다. 이에 대처하기 위해, 콩 및 옥수수로 된 먹이를 없앰으로서 무리 중의 건강을 향상시키고 우유 생산을 증진시키며 매탄가스 발생을 줄일 수 있음을 몇몇 농장에서는 발견했다. 그 대신에, 농장에서는 옛날 방식으로 소에게 영양소와 무해한 지방산이 가득한 알팔파를 먹이로 준다.

TEST 07

Passage 1

1. What do I love best about the novels of E. L. Doctorow? The answer to that is simple. 1) I love the way he mixes up fact and fiction to create something new and magical. ① Take Ragtime, for example. In Ragtime he throws together Emma Goldman, the anarchist; Harry Houdini, the "escapologist"; Sigmund Freud, the father of psychoanalysis; Carl Jung, another important psychologist, and Henry Ford, the father of the Model T, turning these historical figures into characters in a novel. Ⓐ Freud and Jung actually went to Coney Island on their visit to America together. That the historians can document. Ⓑ Did they take a ride through the Tunnel of Love, as in the novel? Who knows? But what a fantastic idea. 2. Doctorow employed the facts, showing his creativity to the fullest.

중심소재: E.L Doctorow의 소설

1. 도입부 = 주제

E.L Doctorow의 소설을 좋아하는 이유

1) 답변(요지)

사실과 허구를 섞어 새로운 것을 만들어내는 창조력

① 뒷받침 진술(예시)

Ⓐ fact에 해당하는 내용

Ⓑ fiction에 해당하는 내용

즉, fact를 fiction에 접목

2. 요지 재진술

정답 **1** (B) **2** (B)

해설

1 "Who knows?"란 앞에서 언급한 내용이 사실인지 허구인지 분명치 않다는 말이지만, 역접을 이끄는 접속사가 이어지면서 결과적으로 Did they take a ride through the Tunnel of Love에서 밑줄 친 표현을 통해 소설의 허구적 요소를 반영함으로서 창조적 표현임을 드러내고 있다.

2 프로이드와 융이 사랑의 터널을 차를 타고 통과했다는 것은 사실인지, 허구인지 알 수 없다. 이는 E. L. Doctorow의 창의력이 뛰어남을 보여주려고 언급한 것이다.

지문해석

닥터로(E. L. Doctorow)의 소설들에서 내가 가장 좋아하는 점은 무엇인가? 답하기는 매우 쉽다. 나는 사실과 허구를 혼합해서 새롭고 매혹적인 무엇인가를 창조하는 그의 기법을 좋아한다. '랙타임(Ragtime)'을 예로 들어보자. 랙타임에서 그는 무정부주의자 에마 골드만, 동아줄을 빠져나가는 곡예사 해리 후디니, 정신분석의 창시자 지그문트 프로이트, 또 다른 저명한 심리학자 칼융, 그리고 포드자동차 T모델의 창시자 헨리 포드까지 역사적 인물들을 긁어모아, 한 소설 속의 등장인물들로 전환한다. 실제로 프로이트와 융은 미국 방문길에 코니아일랜드에 함께 갔다. 그 점은 역사가들이 문서로 증명할 수 있다. (그런데) 그들이 실제 소설 속에서처럼 차를 타고 사랑의 터널을 통과해갔나? 누가 알겠는가? 그러나 얼마나 멋진 생각인가? 닥터로는 사실들을 이용해서 자기의 창조성을 최고로 보여주었다.

Passage 2

1\. 1) A young woman whose boyfriend had left her said she could not understand why. "The relationship," she said, "was more important than any substantive issue, so I gave in immediately on everything." A psychiatrist tried to help her understand by saying something along the following lines: "It takes two to have a relationship. Where were you? If you gave in immediately on everything, what were you contributing? If your boyfriend wanted someone to engage in a relationship, someone with interests and views to be taken into account, ① your giving in, no matter how simple or satisfying that may have seemed to him in the short run, must have made the overall relationship less satisfying."

2\. 1) Giving in does not build a good working relationship. ① It may avoid arguments, but it also eliminates the opportunity to learn how to talk through problems and to become skillful at reaching solutions. Without such skills, a relationship will be too weak to survive problems that are bound to come along. It is not enough to solve the immediate problem. 2) We have to think ahead to the effect that this transaction will have on the next one, and the ones after that. That is what building a relationship is all about·.

1\. 첫 번째 문단(구체적 진술)

1) 구체적 사례

남자친구를 잃은 한 여자의 이야기

① 요지

상담심리사를 통해 궁극적으로 전달하려는 내용이 드러나 있다: 양보하는 것이 전반적 관계를 오히려 덜 만족스럽게 만들었음에 틀림이 없다(무조건 양보하는 것이 좋은 것이 아님을 의미한다).

2\. 두 번째 문단(일반진술)

1) 주제문

용서하는 것이 좋은 관계를 형성하지 못한다.

① 뒷받침 진술

2) 요지문

구체적 진술의 시그널을 확인한다.

요지를 이끄는 시그널을 확인하도록 한다.

TEST 07

정답 1 (D) 2 (B)

해설

1 "건강한 관계를 쌓으려면 양보하는 것만으로는 부족하다"는 것을 글의 요지로 볼 수 있다.

2 남자친구를 잃은 한 젊은 영성에 대한 하나의 사례가 나오고 그 뒤에 일반적인 내용의 글이 나온다. 따라서 (B)가 적절하다.

지문해석

남자친구가 떠나버린 한 젊은 여성은 왜 그가 자기를 떠났는지 이해할 수 없다고 말했다. 그녀가 말했다. "그 관계는 어떤 것보다도 더 중요했어요. 그래서 나는 모든 것에서 즉시 양보했지요." 정신과 의사는 그녀가 이해하는 데 도움을 주려고 애쓰면서 다음과 같은 이야기를 했다. "관계를 맺는 데에는 두 사람이 필요해요. 당신은 어디에 있었습니까? 당신이 모든 것을 즉시 양보했다면 당신은 관계에 어떤 기여를 했습니까? 당신의 남자친구가 관계에 참여할 수 있는 어떤 사람, 즉 그가 고려해야 할 관심사와 관점을 지니고 있는 이와 관계를 맺기 원했다면, 당신의 양보가 단기적으로 그에게 얼마나 편하거나 만족스러웠든지 간에 그 양보는 전반적으로 덜 만족스러운 관계를 만들 수밖에 없었을 것입니다."

양보로 훌륭히 작용하는 관계를 형성할 수 없다. 양보로 논쟁을 피할 수 있지만 동시에 문제를 통해 서로 대화하는 법을 배우고, 해결책을 찾는 데 숙련될 기회도 잃게 된다. 그러한 기술들 없이는, 관계가 너무 약해서 필연적으로 등장할 수밖에 없는 문제들을 해결하지도 못하고 깨어져 버리게 된다. 당장의 문제들을 해결하는 것만으로는 충분치 않다. 우리는 이런 식의 처리가 다음번에 그리고 그 다음번에 미치게 될 영향에 대해 미리 생각해야 한다. 이것이 관계를 형성하는 것에서 가장 중요한 것이다.

단순 도입부와 중심소재의 관계

첫 번째 문장 또는 글의 도입부에 주제문이 제시되는 경우 글의 중심 소재와 함께 주제가 드러나기 때문에 글 전체의 내용적 방향성을 잡을 수 있다. 하지만, 단순 도입부일 경우 주제문이 중반 또는 말미에 나올 수 있기에 글이 전개되는 내용에 따라 주제를 설정해야 한다. 하지만, 이런 경우라도 글의 도입부에서 포괄적인 주제인 중심소재는 설정할 수 있다는 점은 기억하고, 중심소재 파악을 게을리 해선 안 된다.

Passage 3

1. In 1604, five years prior to Galileo's development of the telescope, the world beheld a never-before-seen star in the heavens. It was called "nova" for its newness. It flared up near the constellation Sagittarius in October and stayed so prominent through November that Galileo had time to give three public lectures about the newcomer before it faded from bright view. 1) The nova challenged the law of immutability in the heavens, a cherished tenet of the Aristotelian world order. 2) ① Earthly matter, according to ancient Greek philosophy, contained four base elements—earth, water, air, fire—that underwent constant change, while the heavens as Aristotle described them consisted entirely of a fifth element—the quintessence, or aether—that remained incorruptible. It was thus impossible for a new star to suddenly form. ② The nova, the Aristotelians argued, must inhabit the sublunar sphere between the Earth and the Moon, where change was permissible. But Galileo could see by comparing his nightly observations with those of other stargazers in distant lands that the new star lay far out, beyond the Moon, beyond the planets, among the domain of the old stars.

중심소재: Nova(초신성)

1. 도입부 = 중심소재 도출

'Nova'라 불리는 초신성의 목격을 그리면서, 이에 대한 갈릴레오의 강의가 언급되고 있다.

1) 주제문: 초신성의 의의

아리스토텔레스가 주장한 천체 불변의 법칙에 도전(요지)

2) 뒷받침 근거

① 아리스토텔레스의 이론 1

지구의 물질은 흙, 물, 공기, 불로 구성되고 이것은 변화할 수 있지만, 천체는 제 5원소인 에테르로 구성되어 있기에 변하지 않음. 고로 우주에 변화(초신성)가 생긴다는 것은 가정할 수 없다.

② 아리스토텔레스의 이론 2

변화는 지구와 달 사이에만 존재해야 하는데, 신성은 달, 행성을 넘어 목격됨

정답 1 (C) 2 (D)

해설

1 하늘은 제 5원소로 이루어져 있으며 절대 불변한다는 아리스토텔레스의 가설이 새로운 별, 신성의 출현으로 도전받고 있다는 것이 이 글의 요지이다.

2 아리스토텔레스의 이론에 따르면 하늘은 불변하는 것인데, 이 새로운 별의 출현을 이론에 모순되지 않게 설명할 수 있으려면 신성이 변화가 허용되는 곳이 있다는 선택지 (D)가 가장 적절하다.

지문해석

갈릴레오가 망원경을 개발하기 5년 전인 1604년, 세계는 전에는 한 번도 본적이 없었던 하늘에 떠 있는 별을 주시하고 있었다. 그 별의 새로움 때문에 사람들은 그 별을 신성이라 불렀다. 그 별은 10월의 궁수자리 근처에서 빛나고 11월까지 그 자리에서 뚜렷하게 머물러서 갈릴레오는 그 밝게 빛나는 별이 지기 전에 신성에 대해 세 번의 대중 강연을 할 시간을 가졌다. 그 신성은 하늘의 불변성 법칙이라는 아리스토텔레스적 세계 질서의 소중한 교리에 도전을 한 셈이었다. 고대 그리스 철학에 의하면 지구상의 물질은 흙, 물, 바람, 불이라는 네 가지 기본 원소를 포함하며 그 원소들은 끊임없이 변화한다. 한편 아리스토텔레스는 하늘이 오로지 다섯 번째 원소, 즉 불후의 제 5원소 또는 에테르로만 이루어져 있다고 묘사하였다. 그래서 새로운 별이 갑자기 나타나는 것은 불가능한 것이다. 아리스토텔레스주의자들은 이 신성이 지구와 달 중간에 변화가 허용되는 달 궤도 영향 하에 있다고 주장하였다. 하지만 갈릴레오는 멀리 떨어진 지역에 살고 있는 다른 천문학자와 그의 관찰을 비교하여 새로운 별이 달 넘어, 행성들을 넘어, 오래된 별들의 영역 가운데에 멀리 존재한다는 것을 알 수 있었다.

Passage 4

1. It has long been known that the air and water encountered by people in their daily lives are filled with all sorts of micro-organisms. Thankfully, most of these are benign and even the unsavory ones can usually be washed down the drain without causing any harm. 1) Not always, though. A team of researchers reports that taking showers can pose a danger to some people. ① Ⓐ They took samples of the biofilm that builds up inside showerheads from 45 sites in nine American cities and analysed the genetic material which it contained. Strikingly, in some of the samples they found high concentrations of a microbe which can cause respiratory illnesses. Ⓑ This is found in tap water, but remains harmless unless turned into an aerosol and inhaled-precisely what happens when bug-laden water is forced through a showerhead at high pressure. As the tiny particles are inhaled, they get into the lungs and can start an infection. 2. Is this cause for alarm? Not for healthy people, but those with a compromised immune system or who are at risk of pulmonary diseases such as the elderly may want to take precautions. Cleaning showerheads with bleach will not do since the microbes will simply return with a fresh flow of water. Replacing bug-prone plastic showerheads with metal ones is a better idea.

중심소재: 샤워 중 위험 요소

1. 도입부 = 통념

일상에서 접하는 공기와 물은 다양한 미생물로 가득하지만 일반적으로 해가 없다.

1) 주제문

샤워를 할 때 앞에 언급한 공기와 물은 특정 사람에게 위험할 수 있다(연구결과)

① 뒷받침 진술(연구)

Ⓐ 샤워

샤워 모자 속 균막 샘플을 수집한 결과 호흡기 질환을 일으킬 가능성 있음

Ⓑ 수돗물

구체적으로 어떤 과정을 통해 병이 발생하는지 설명하고 있다.

2. 주의 및 제안(요지)

이러 현상이 모든 이에게 일어나는 것은 아니며, 면역이 손상된 또는 폐질환의 위험이 있는 나이든 사람은 주의해야 한다고 강조하고 있다(not A but B구문)

③ 금속 재질로 된 샤워헤드를 제안하고 있다.

통념으로 시작하는 글임을 파악한다.

통념을 뒤집는 시그널을 확인하고, 이후 주제문이 뒤따른다.

TEST 07

정답 1 (A) 2 (D)

해설

1 Not always, though.를 기점으로 대조적인 내용이 전개되고 있다. 선택지 (A)와 (B)가 답이 될 수 있다. 빈칸 이후의 내용으로 보아 선택지 (A)가 가장 적절하다.
(A) benign and even the unsavory ones can usually be washed down the drain without causing any harm → Thankfully
(B) in some of the samples they found high concentrations of a microbe which can cause respiratory illnesses → Strikingly

2 선택지 (D)의 내용은 This is found in tap water, but remains harmless unless turned into an aerosol and inhaled-precisely what happens when bug-laden water is forced through a showerhead at high pressure.에 명시되어 있다.

지문해석

오랫동안 사람들이 일상생활에서 마주하는 공기와 물이 모든 종류의 미생물로 가득차 있다는 것은 오래전부터 알려져 있었다. 다행히도 대부분의 미생물은 해가 없고, 심지어 좋지 못한 것들도 보통은 어떤 해도 끼치지 않고 하수구로 쓸려 내려가 버린다. 그러나 항상 그런 것은 아니다. 일군의 연구자들은 샤워를 하는 것이 어떤 사람들에게는 위험을 가져다준다는 연구를 발표했다. 이들은 샤워꼭지 안에서 형성되는 세균군락의 샘플을 9곳의 미국 도시의 45개 장소에서 추출한 다음 그 세균군락에 포함된 유전물질을 분석했다. 충격적인

사실은, 샘플 중 몇 가지에서 호흡기 질환을 일으킬 수 있는 높은 농도의 미생물을 발견했다. 이 미생물들은 수돗물에서 발견이 되는데, 분말입자 형태로 변해 흡입되기 전까지는 무해하다. 문제는 세균이 들어찬 물이 고압 상태에서 샤워꼭지를 통해 뿜어 나오게 됐을 때 정확히 벌어지는 상황이 이것이다(즉, 미세분말 형태로 뿜어져 나와서 사람이 흡입하게 됨). 미세분말은 흡입되면 폐로 들어가서 감염을 유발한다. 이것이 우려할 상황인가? 건강한 사람의 경우는 그렇지 않다. 하지만 제 기능을 발휘하지 못하는 면역 체계를 가진 사람이나 노인처럼 폐질환에 걸릴 위험이 높은 사람은 주의를 기울어야 한다. 표백제로 샤워꼭지를 청소하는 것은 도움이 되지 않으며 이유는 미생물들이 물이 새로 흘러들면 다시 돌아올 것이기 때문이다. 세균이 끼기 쉬운 플라스틱 샤워꼭지를 금속으로 바꾸는 것이 좋은 해결방안이다.

Passage 5

첫 번째 문장을 보면 일반통념비판의 글과 비슷한 유형으로 전개된다. formerly believed와 역접을 이끄는 really를 확인한다.

1. Human memory, formerly believed to be rather inefficient, is really much more sophisticated than that of a computer. 1) ① Researchers approaching the problem from a variety of points of view have all concluded that there is a great deal more stored in our minds than has been generally supposed. ② Dr. Wilder Penfield, a Canadian neurosurgeon, proved that by stimulating their brains electrically, he could elicit the total recall of complex events in his subjects' lives. Even dreams and other minor events supposedly forgotten for many years suddenly emerged in detail. ③ The memory trace is the term for whatever forms the internal representation of the specific information about the event stored in the memory. Ⓐ Assumed to have been made by structural changes in the brain, the memory trace is not subject to direct observation, but is, rather, a theoretical construct that is used to speculate about how information presented at a particular time can cause performance at a later time. Most theories include the strength of the memory trace as a variable in the degree of learning, retention, and retrieval possible for a memory. Ⓑ One theory is that the fantastic capacity for storage in the brain is the result of an almost unlimited combination of interconnections between brain cells, stimulated by patterns of activity. Repeated references to the same information support recall. Or, put another way, improved performance is the result of strengthening the chemical bonds in the memory.

중심소재: 인간의 기억

1. 도입부 = 주제문

인간은 기억은 컴퓨터보다 더 섬세하다.

1) 뒷받침 진술

①근거1

우리 마음속에는 훨씬 더 많은 정보가 저장되어 있다.

②근거2

실험을 통해 기억 회상의 놀라운 능력을 확인

③인간기억의 특징

Ⓐ memory trace의 개념

구조적 변화를 겪는 기억흔적은 직접적 관찰이 아니라 이론적 구조이며, 기억흔적은 학습, 보존, 회상의 능력 강화가 가능

Ⓑ 회상이론을 통해 기억의 저장 능력: 패턴을 띄는 외부행위에 자극을 받은 뇌세포의 끊임없는 상호작용의 조합의 결과

정답 1 (C) 2 (A) 3 (C) 4 (C)

지문분석

본문의 제목을 설정할 때 부분적인 내용에 얽매이지 말고, 전체를 포괄하는 동시에 구체적 내용으로 설정한다.

해설

1 일반 통념과는 달리 인간의 기억력이 컴퓨터보다 우수하다는 내용을 다양한 근거를 통해 제시하는 글이다. 선택지 (C)가 제목으로 가장 적절하다.

2 the fantastic capacity for storage in the brain is the result of an almost unlimited combination of interconnections between brain cells, stimulated by patterns of activity.에서 뇌의 놀라운 저장능력은 바로 세포 간의 끊임없는 상호연계성임을 알 수 있다. 이를 가장 잘 드러내는 선택지는 bonds이다.

3 human memory much more sophisticated than that of a computer에서 선택지 (C)가 정답임을 알 수 있다.

4 Repeated references to the same information support recall을 보면, 기억추적 이 글의 끝부분에 "똑같은 정보에 반복된 관련사항들이 회상을 지탱해 준다"고 했으므로 기억추적은 연습에 의해서 강화될 수 있다는 선택지 (C)가 정답이다.

지문해석

이전에는 다소 비효율적인 것으로 믿어졌던 인간의 기억력은 실제로 컴퓨터의 메모리보다 훨씬 더 복잡하다. 다양한 관점에서 그 문제를 연구하고 있는 사람들은 모두 다음과 같은 결론을 내렸다. 일반적으로 생각되었던 것보다 훨씬 많은 것들이 우리의 마음에 저장된다는 것이다. 캐나다의 신경외과 의사인 와일더 펜필드(Wilder Penfield) 박사는 전기를 통해 뇌를 자극시킴으로써 그의 피실험자들의 생활 속에서 나타나는 복잡한 사건들의 전체적인 기억을 이끌어 낼 수 있음을 증명했다. 심지어 수년 동안 잊혔던 것으로 여겨졌던 꿈들과 다른 사소한 사건들도 갑자기 상세하게 기억되었다. 기억추적이란, 기억 속에 저장되어 있는 어떤 사건에 대한 구체적 정보가 내적으로 표현되는 모든 형태를 나타내는 용어이다. 기억 추적은 뇌 속에서 구조적 변화를 겪으며 생성되었다고 여겨지기 때문에, 이는 직접적인 관찰에 의해 영향받지 않으며, 오히려 특정 시기에 정보가 제시되는 방식이 나중에 실행될지를 추론하는 이론적 구조물이라 할 수 있다. 대부분의 이론들은 기억 추적의 강도를, 무언가를 배우고, 이를 계속 기억하며, 기억 속에서 끄집어낼 수 있는 과정 속의 하나의 변수로 생각한다. 한 이론은 우리 뇌 속의 엄청난 저장 능력은, 활동 유형들로 인해 자극을 받은 뇌세포 간의 상호 작용이 거의 무제한적으로 이루어진 결과라고 말한다. 동일한 정보에 반복적으로 수반되는 사항들이 기억을 돕는다. 혹은 다른 말로 설명하자면, 기억력의 강화는 기억 속의 화학적 결합이 강화되어 나타나는 것이다.

대의파악 문제 접근방법

대의파악 문제 중 특히 주제와 제목의 경우 짧은 구를 빠르게 파악하고 본문의 내용을 추론할 수 있다. 예를 들어, (A)의 경우, 중심소재는 정보이고, 중심내용은 정보처리의 다양한 패턴에 관한 내용임을 알 수 있다. 이는 글의 도입부에 정보가 제시되고, 본문에 나열의 전개방식을 바탕으로 다양한 패턴을 다룰 것을 추론할 수 있다는 말이다. 문제의 선택지를 먼저 읽을 경우 글의 중반 이전에 대부분의 답을 구할 수 있다. 또 다른 활용으로 글을 다 읽은 다음에 무슨 말인지 모를 경우 각각의 선택지가 답일 경우 본인이 읽었던 내용에 관한 내용인지를 자문하면 읽었던 내용이 좀 더 명확하게 다가와 답을 이끌어 낼 수 있게 된다.

Passage 6

1. 1) In the spring of the year 399 B.C., a famous Greek philosopher was put on trial for having committed two crimes. ① Ⓐ One was impiety to the gods of the state; the other was the corruption of youth, by teaching them impiety. The penalty for a conviction on these charges was a severe one, possibly death. The prisoner's name was Socrates, and he was seventy years old at that time. Ⓑ There were other reasons, political reasons, for trying Socrates. He had been associated with the old aristocratic regime, now overthrown by the democracy, and he was held in suspicion as a critic of the democracy.

2. 1) Among other things, he became unpopular for ① his strange doctrine that even politicians ought to know what they are doing. ② Socrates was reputed to be the wisest

중심소재: 소크라테스의 재판과 그의 철학

1. 첫 번째 문단

1) 도입부
두 가지 죄목으로 재판을 받게 된 그리스의 철학자
① 구체적 진술
Ⓐ 첫 번째 죄목
국가의 신을 섬기지 않음
Ⓑ 두 번째 죄목
민주주의를 비판한 인물(귀족주의)

2. 두 번째 문단

1) 현인으로서의 소크라테스와 그의 철학
① 철학자조차 자신이 하는 것을 알아야 한다(너 자신을 알라)

man of his time. This reputation surprised him, he said, for he considered himself to be an ignorant man; ignorant of the answers to the supreme questions concerning human happiness and human destiny. But he was also sure that no one else knew the answers to these questions, and this furnished him with an explanation of his reputation as a wise man. Though he was ignorant, he alone knew that he was ignorant, whereas other ignorant men did not know that they were, thinking they had all the answers.

① 철학자조차 자신이 하는 것을 알아야 한다(너 자신을 알라)
② 소크라테스가 진정 현인인 이유를 본문 끝까지 언급하고 있다.

정답 **1**(C) **2**(E) **3**(D) **4**(C)

해설

1 소크라테스의 두 죄명은 신에 대한 불경죄와 민주주의 비판이다

2 과거 귀족주의와 연관성이 있으면서 현 민주주의에 대해 비평한 것으로 보아 현 정부에 대한 비판적 입장을 취했다고 보아야 한다.
두 번째 문단 중간 이후에 소크라테스는 "인간의 행복과 인간의 운명이라는 궁극적 질문들에 대한 답을 알지 못한다"라고 하면서 스스로를 무지하다고 보고 있다.

4 먼저 (가)에 들어갈 단어는, doing의 목적어이면서 동시에 본동사 know의 목적어에 해당하는 명사구를 이끌 수 있는 단어가 들어가야 한다. 따라서 선행사를 포함하는 관계대명사인 what이 적절하다. (나)는 접속사가 올 자리로 빈칸이 들어있는 문장의 내용을 보면, 소크라테스는 무지했으나, 오직 그만이 이런 사실을 알았다고 말하고 있으므로 양보의 의미를 담는 Though가 적절하다.

지문해석

기원전 399년 봄, 한 유명한 그리스 철학자가 2개의 죄명으로 재판에 회부되었다. 하나는 국가의 신들에 대한 불경죄였고, 다른 하나는 젊은이들에게도 불경을 가르쳐서 그들을 타락시켰다는 죄명이었다. 이러한 고발에 대해 유죄 판결이 날 경우 사형까지 가능한 중대한 범죄였다. 그 죄수의 이름은 소크라테스였고, 그는 당시 70세였다. 소크라테스를 심판하려는 데에는 다른 이유, 즉 정치적 이유도 있었다. 그는 민주 정권에 의해 전복된 이전 귀족정과 관계가 있었고, 현재의 민주 정권에 대한 비판자라는 의심을 받고 있었다. 다른 모든 비판 중에서도, 심지어 정치가들도 그들이 무엇을 하고 있는지는 알아야 한다는 그의 이상한 교리 때문에 대중들로부터 인기가 없었다. 소크라테스는 그의 시대에 가장 현명한 사람이라고 평판이 나 있었다. 그는 스스로를 무지한 사람으로 여겼으며, 인간의 행복과 인간의 운명이라는 궁극적 질문들에 대한 답을 알지 못한다고 생각했기 때문에, 사람들의 이런 평판에 그는 놀랐다고 주장했다. 그러나 그는 또한 다른 어느 누구도 이런 문제들에 대한 해답을 모를 것이라고 확신했고, 이것은 현인이라는 그의 명성에 대한 설명을 부여해 주는 것이었다. 그는 무지했지만 그 혼자서 자신이 무지하다는 사실을 알았던 반면, 다른 무지한 사람들은 그들이 모든 해답을 알고 있다고 생각하면서 자신들이 무지하다는 사실을 깨닫지 못했다.

Passage 7

[1] 1) ① The Renaissance painter Giotto imitated nature so accurately that his teacher swatted at a painted fly on one of Giotto's works. Is this not a superb artistic achievement? If so, the artist's object was mimesis. Beginning during the Renaissance, mimesis was considered the pinnacle of artistic achievement. ② However, modern art focuses on depicting not only the world of surfaces but also Ⓐ the inner world of abstract thoughts and feelings. Ⓑ Modern art focuses on the way the elements in the work of art interact and what feelings these elements evoke. A quick glance at art produced over the past century reveals that mimesis has been abandoned by the vast majority of artists.

[2] 1) From around 1880 to the outbreak of World War I, a series of sweeping changes in technology and culture created distinctive new modes of thinking about and experiencing time and space. ① Ⓐ Such radical inventions as the telephone, automobile, airplane, X-Ray machine, cinema, and standard Greenwich time forced people to reconsider perceptions of the world that had been in place for centuries. Distances seemed to shrink. Time grew more particularized and less subject to nature. Ⓑ Artists responded in kind. Intent on representing the shifting sands of reality, painters and novelists abandoned verisimilitude and forged new art forms that explored man's new relationship with his environment.

1. 첫 번째 단락

1) 도입부

① 르네상스 예술의 특징: 자연의 모방

② 현대 예술의 특징

Ⓐ 추상적 생각과 감정의 내적 세계 강조

Ⓑ 예술 작품의 내적 요소가 어떻게 상호작용하고, 이러한 요소가 어떻게 예술을 감상하는 사람의 감정을 일으키는지에 초점

2. 두 번째 단락

1) 현상

기술과 문화의 큰 변화가 일어난 1880년대와 1차 세계대전 사이의 배경을 바탕으로 시간과 공간에 대한 새로운 양식의 사고와 경험이 출현

① 영향

Ⓐ 기술변화의 영향

세상을 바로 보는 관점의 변화

Ⓑ 예술에 미친 영향

자연과 인간의 새로운 관계를 연구하는 예술의 형태 발달

시간의 대조를 파악한다.

대조의 글 전개를 확인한다.

먼저 기술된 것이 먼저 상술됨.

T+C

Ⓣ

Ⓒ

정답 1 (C) 2 (D)

해설

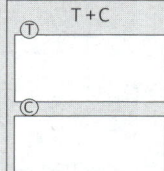

1 [1]과 [2]의 내용은 르네상스 시대의 모방이 현대예술가들에 의해 단념되었다는 내용이므로 "현대예술은 세계를 모방하는 것을 만드는 데서 관심을 돌렸다"는 (C)가 적절하다.

2 [1]의 저자와는 달리 [2]의 저자는 문화와 기술의 맹렬한 변화들이 시간과 공간에 대한 인식들을 재고하게 한 여러 요소들을 나열하므로 "예술방식에서 변화를 초래했던 문화적 요소들을 지적한다"는 (D)가 적절하다.

지문해석

[1] 르네상스 화가 조토는 자연을 너무 정확히 모방해서 그의 스승은 조토의 작품들 중 한 작품 위에 그려진 파리를 찰싹 때렸다. 이것이 탁월한 예술적 성취가 아닌가? 그렇다면 예술가의 목표는 모방이었다. 르네상스 기간에 시작한 모방은 예술성취의 정점으로 간주되었다. 그러나 현대예술은 표면세계뿐만 아니라 추상적인 생각과 감정의 내면세계도 묘사하는 데 집중한다. 현대예술은 예술작품 속의 요소들이 상호작용하는 방법과 이러한 요소들이 불러내는 모든 감정들에 집중한다. 지난 세기 동안에 생산된 예술은 얼핏 보기만 해도 모방이 대다수의 예술가들에 의해 단념되었음을 보여준다.

[2] 대략 1880년경부터 1차 세계대전이 발발할 때까지 기술과 문화에서 연속적인 대대적인 변화들은 시간과 공간에 대해 생각하고 시간과 공간을 경험하는 특이한 새로운 방식들을 창출했다. 전화 자동차 비행기 X선 기기, 영화, 그리고 그리니치 표준시간 같은 그런 급진적인 발명들은 사람들로 하여금 수 세기 동안 적절했던 세상에 대한 인식

들을 재고하도록 강요했다. 거리가 줄어드는 것처럼 보였다. 시간은 더 특수하게 되었고 자연에 덜 종속되었다. 예술가들도 같은 식으로 반응했다. 현실의 흐르는 모래(변화)를 표현하는 데 열중하여 화가들과 소설가들은 박진성(현실과의 유사성)을 버리고 사람과 환경의 새로운 관계를 탐구하는 새로운 예술 형태들을 만들어냈다.

Passage 8

1. Although the smoke from a cigar or pipe contains higher concentration of both tar and nicotine than does cigarette smoke, 1) even a few cigarettes a day poses a greater risk to health than a number of cigars or pipes of tobacco would. ① Ⓐ This may be because, while it is extremely difficult to smoke cigarettes without inhaling, it is more difficult to inhale cigar or pipe smoke voluntarily. Cigarette smokers tend to inhale actively, deeply and constantly. Ⓑ But because the smoke from burning cigar or pipe tobacco is very harsh, it is more difficult to breathe it directly into healthy lungs.

2. 1) However, simply switching to a pipe or cigars from cigarettes is likely to increase your risk instead of lessening it. ① This is because you have probably become accustomed to inhaling. You may find yourself retaining the habit, and you will then be inhaling even more harmful smoke than before.

중심소재: 담배 → 담배의 위험성

1. 첫 번째 문단

1) 도입부 = 단락 주제문

담배가 시가나 파이프 담배보다 훨씬 건강에 안 좋다.

① 뒷받침 진술

Ⓐ 담배를 깊이 지속적으로 흡인하기가 훨씬 쉬움

Ⓑ 시가와 파이프 담배는 훨씬 독하기 때문에 폐 깊숙이 흡입하기 쉽지 않음

2. 두 번째 문단

1) 단락 주제문

시가나 파이프 담배가 그냥 담배보다 덜 해롭지만, 그렇다고 담배를 끊고 시가나 파이프 담배를 대신 피우지 말아야 한다.

① 뒷받침 근거

정답 1 (D) 2 (C) 3 (D)

해설

1 서로 상반되는 내용의 두 절을 연결한다는 점은 같아도 but이 이끄는 절은 반드시 뒤에 와야 하고 although가 이끄는 절은 앞, 뒤 모두 올 수 있어 although가 문두에 올 수 있다. 따라서 첫 번째 빈칸은 although이다. 둘째 빈칸 다음은 두 개의 절이 because에 의해 연결되어 있고 셋째 빈칸 다음은 접속사 없이 하나의 단문으로 되어 있다. 이런 경우는 빈칸 앞의 문장을 마치 하나의 절로 생각하여 빈칸에는 접속사 but과 부사 however가 모두 쓰일 수 있는데, 다만 but 다음은 콤마가 없고 however 다음은 콤마가 있다. 따라서 둘째 빈칸은 but이고 셋째 빈칸은 however이다.

2 담배를 피우면서 연기를 깊이 들이 마시는 습관을 말한다.

3 두 번째 단락 첫 번째 문장에서 알 수 있듯이 궐련에서 여송연으로 그냥 바꾸는 것은 궐련을 피울 때의 위험을 더욱 증가시키므로 가장 위험하다.

지문해석

비록 궐련 담배 연기보다 여송연이나 파이프 담배 연기가 더 높은 농도의 타르와 니코틴을 가지고 있다 할지라도, 궐련 담배는 하루 몇 개만으로도 많은 여송연이나 파이프 담배보다 건강에 더 큰 위험이 된다. 이것은 궐련을 연기를 들이마시지 않고 피우는 것이 매우 어렵긴 하지만, 여송연이나 파이프 담배 연기를 의도적으로 들이마시는 것은 더 어렵기 때문일지도 모른다. 궐련 담배흡연자들은 능동적으로, 깊이 그리고 끊임없이 담배 연기를 들이 마시는 경향이 있다. 그러나 타고 있는 여송연이나 파이프 담배 연기는 매우 독하기 때문에 그것을 직접 건강한 폐로 들이마시는 것은 더 어렵다.

하지만, 궐련 담배에서 파이프나 여송연 담배로 그냥 바꾸는 것은 위험성을 줄이는 대신 위험성을 증가시킬 것 같다. 이것은 당신이 아마도 담배 연기를 깊이 들이 마시는 것에 익숙해졌기 때문일 것이다. 당신은 그 습관을 계속 갖고 있을지도 모른다. 그러면 해로운 담배연기를 전보다 훨씬 더 많이 들이 마시게 될 것이다.

TEST 08

Passage 1

1. 1) One creature that faces a significant threat from humans is the frog, whose ecosystem often lies. One of the unconscious ways we endanger frogs results from our lawn care. ① Ⓐ Frogs wander into backyards to feed on slugs, snails, and insects. If the area has been treated with pesticides, the frogs will likely be affected by the poisons. Moving logs or piles of stones denies frogs cool dark places to hide and rest. Ⓑ Yet another danger we pose to frogs is caused by the use of cars. Many frogs are killed by motorists unaware that frog paths cross busy roads. Ⓒ But perhaps the most devastating thing a human can do to a frog is to remove it from its environment and take it home as a pet; amphibians are far more likely to perish when brought into a house without the security and familiarity of the wetland to sustain them.

중심소재: 개구리

1. 도입부 = 현상(중심소재 도출)
인간의 위협으로 위협에 처한 개구리

1) 주제문(현상의 원인)
인간과의 근접성으로 인해 개구리가 위험해 처하게 되었다.

① 뒷받침 진술
- Ⓐ 잔디밭 살충제의 사용
- Ⓑ 자동차
- Ⓒ 애완동물

개구리를 자신의 터전에서 분리한 후 애완동물로 취급한 것이 가장 큰 위험요소라 지적함

Yet과 But은 역접의 기능이 아닌 추가적 정보의 기능

정답 **1** (A) **2** (D)

해설

1 문맥 속 동의어를 고르는 문제이다. 본문에서 unconscious는 "의도하지 않은; 예기치 않은"으로 사용되고 있다. 즉, "다른 해로운 곤충을 죽이기 위해 사용된 살충제가 개구리에 간접적인 피해를 미친다"는 이후 진술로 그 의미를 찾아내야 한다. 선택지 (D)가 가장 적절하다.

2 구체적 사실 확인문제이다. 문제의 내용을 정확히 파악한 후 본문 어디에 언급이 되어 있지는 찾으면 된다. 다음 본문에서 답을 구할 수 있다. Frogs wander into backyards to feed on slugs, snails, and insects. If the area has been treated with pesticides, the frogs will likely be affected by the poisons.

지문해석

인간으로부터 심각한 위협에 처한 생물 중 하나는 종종 인간 거주지에 밀접한 곳에 생태계가 위치해 있는 개구리이다. 우리가 깨닫지 못하는 상태에서 개구리를 위험에 빠뜨리는 방법 중 하나는 우리의 잔디관리에 기인한다. 개구리는 민달팽이, 달팽이, 벌레 등을 먹기 위해 이리저리 돌아다니다 뒤뜰로 흘러 들어온다. 만약 그 뒤뜰이 살충제로 처리가 되어 있으면 개구리는 살충제의 독에 영향 받을 가능성이 높다. 통나무나 돌무더기를 옮기는 행위는 개구리가 숨어서 쉴 수 있는 서늘하고 어두운 장소를 빼앗는 행위이다. 게다가 우리가 개구리에 가하는 또 다른 위험은 자동차를 타는 것으로 인해 발생한다. 많은 개구리는 개구리가 다니는 길이 혼잡한 도로와 교차되는지 모르고 있는 운전자에 의해 죽임을 당한다. 하지만 아마 인간이 개구리에게 행하는 가장 파괴적인 행위는 개구리가 사는 환경에서 개구리를 빼낸 다음에 애완용으로 집으로 데려가는 일일 것이다. 양서류가 살 수 있게 유지시켜 주는 습지대의 안전함과 친숙함이 없는 인간의 집으로 들어오게 되면 양서류는 죽을 가능성이 훨씬 높아진다.

Passage 2

질문은 곧 글에서 다루려는 주제이고, 이에 대한 답변은 글의 요지가 된다.

1. What happens to children who are the target of a teacher's anger or sympathy? 1) They often accept the attribution that they think is behind the anger or sympathy: They come to believe that they have made too little effort or have too little ability to succeed. And they perform accordingly. ① Ⓐ By attributing a student's failure to lack of effort and expressing anger, a teacher can make the student feel guilty. That guilt—the feeling that he or she has let self or teacher down—is a positive motivating force when the student next attempts a task. Ⓑ But by attributing failure to low ability and expressing sympathy, a teacher ordinarily makes a student feel shame. And shame is not a positive motivating force. Instead it can lead a student to withdraw and to feel inferior and helpless. The point of all this is that it can backfire. It may be a genuine emotion. It may express sincere caring about the schoolwork of low-achieving students. But it can cause great harm when students think that behind the sympathy is a teacher's belief that they don't have the ability to succeed.

대조의 글 전개를 확인한다.

중심소재: 선생이 아이에게 화를 낼 때와 동정심을 보일 때 발생하는 현상

1. 도입부 = 주제 도출
선생이 아이에게 화를 낼 때와 동정심을 보일 때 발생하는 현상

1) 요지문
화를 냈을 때는 노력을 하지 않았기 때문임을 믿게 되고, 동정심을 보일 때 성공할 능력이 없다고 느끼게 된다.

① 뒷받침 진술
Ⓐ 화를 내는 상황

Ⓑ 동정을 보였을 때 상황

정답 1 (E) 2 (E) 3 (C)

해설

1 부정적인 영향을 미치는 요소는 sympathy이므로 선택지 (E)가 정답이다.

2 본문에서 anger는 긍정적 요소로 작용하고 있다. 학생이 수치심을 느끼는 원인은 shame이라고 했으므로 선택지 (D)는 틀린 표현이다.

3 선생의 동정은 부정적 결과를 낳고, 화를 내는 것은 학생 스스로 노력을 하지 않는 결과로 빚어진 것이라 죄책감을 갖고, 다음에 열심히 할 동기를 얻게 되는 것이므로 선택지 (C)가 적절한 답이 된다.

지문해석

선생님의 분노나 동정의 대상인 아이들에게 무슨 일이 일어날까? 그들은 그 분노나 동정 뒤에 있다고 생각되는 속성을 종종 받아들인다. 그들은 그들이 너무 노력을 안 하거나 성공할 능력을 가지고 있지 않다고 믿게 된다. 그리고 그들은 그것에 따라서 행동한다. 학생의 실패를 노력 부족의 탓으로 돌리고 분노를 표현함으로써 선생님은 학생들이 잘못했다고 느끼게 만들 수 있다. 그러한 죄의식 즉, 자신이나 선생님을 실망시켰다는 느낌은 그 학생이 다음 일을 시도할 때 긍정적인 동기부여 요인이 된다. 그러나 실패를 능력 부족의 탓으로 돌리고 동정을 표현하면 선생님은 보통 학생으로 하여금 수치심을 느끼게 한다. 그리고 수치심은 긍정적인 동기부여 요인이 아니다. 대신에 수치심은 학생을 움츠리게 하여 열등하고 무기력하게 느끼게 한다. 이 모든 것의 요점은 동정이 역효과를 일으킬 수도 있다는 것이다. 동정이 진짜 감정일 수도 있다. 동정은 성취도가 낮은 학생의 학업에 대한 진실한 관심을 표현할 수도 있다. 그러나 학생에게 성공할 능력이 없다는 선생님의 믿음이 동정 뒤에 있다고 학생들이 생각할 때는 동정이 큰 피해를 일으킬 수 있다.

Passage 3

[A] 1. We remember best the things that are most meaningful to us. 1) As you are reading, try to elaborate upon new information with your own examples. Try to integrate what you're studying with what you already know. You will be able to remember new material better if you can link it to something that's already meaningful to you.
[B] 2. An effective way is to simplify and make information more meaningful. 1) For example, suppose you wanted to remember the colors in the visible spectrum (Red, Orange, Yellow, Green, Blue, Indigo, Violet); you would have to memorize seven "chunks" of information in order. But if you take the first letter of each color, you can spell the name "Roy G. Biv", and reduce the information to the three "chunks".
[C] 3. Memory-assisting techniques help us to associate new information with something familiar. 1) For example, to remember a formula or equation, we may use letters of the alphabet to represent certain numbers. Then we can change an abstract formula into a more meaningful word or phrase, so we'll be able to remember it better. Sound-alike associations can be very effective, too, especially while trying to learn a new language. The key is to create your own links, then you won't forget them.

중심소재: 암기

[A]
1. 도입부 = 단락 주제문
본인에게 의미 있는 것이 가장 잘 외워진다.
1) 뒷받침 진술
자신에게 의미 있고, 이미 알고 있는 지식과 연관 지을 때 새로운 내용을 잘 기억할 수 있게 된다.

구체적 진술의 시그널을 확인한다.

[B]
2. 도입부 = 주제문
정보를 단순화 시키고, 의미 있게 만들라.
1) 뒷받침 예시

[C]
3. 도입부 = 주제문
익숙한 정보를 새로운 정보와 연관 지어라.
1) 뒷받침 예시

TEST 08

정답 1 (C) 2 (B)

해설
1 [B]와 [C]는 [A]의 기억을 돕는 방법을 보여 주는 예이다.
2 (A)와 (C)는 친근한 어떤 것(책상 주변 물건, 잘 아는 노래)과 새로운 정보를 관련시키는 방법이고 (D)는 정보를 단순화시켜 기억하는 방법이다.

지문해석
[A] 우리는 우리에게 가장 의미 있는 것들을 가장 잘 기억한다. 책을 읽을 때, 당신 자신의 예들을 가지고, 새로운 정보를 이해하도록 노력해라. 지금 공부하고 있는 것을 이미 알고 있는 것과 통합시키도록 노력해라. 만일 당신이 새로운 것을 이미 당신에게 의미 있는 어떤 것과 연결시킬 수 있다면 그 새로운 것을 더 잘 기억할 수 있을 것이다.
[B] 효과적인 방법은 정보를 단순화시키고 더 의미 있게 만드는 것이다. 예를 들어, 당신이 가시광선 스펙트럼(빨강, 주황, 노랑, 초록, 파랑, 남색, 보라) 색깔을 기억하고자 한다고 가정해보자. 그러면 당신은 정보의 7가지 '덩어리'를 순서대로 기억해야만 할 것이다. 그러나 만일 당신이 각 색깔의 첫 글자를 딴다면, Roy G. Biv라는 이름을 쓸 수 있을 것이다. 그리고 세 가지 '덩어리'로 정보를 축소시킬 수 있을 것이다.
[C] 기억을 돕는 기법은 새로운 정보를 낯익은 어떤 것과 연관시키도록 도움을 준다. 예를 들어, 어떤 공식이나 방정식을 기억하기 위해, 우리는 어떤 숫자를 나타내는 알파벳 글자들을 사용할 수도 있다. 그리고 나서 우리는 추상적인 공식을 더 의미 있는 단어나 구로 바꿀 수 있다. 그래서 우리는 그것을 더 잘 기억할 수 있게 될 것이다. 특히 새로운 언어를 배우려고 할 때 비슷한 소리 연상법도 역시 매우 효과적이다. 비결은 당신 자신의 연결고리를 창조하는 것인데, 그리고 나면 당신은 그것을 잊지 않게 될 것이다.

Passage 4

1. It is clear that the decline of a language must ultimately have political and economic causes: it is not due simply to the bad influence of this or that individual writer. But **1)** an effect can become a cause, reinforcing the original cause and producing the same effect in an intensified form, and so on indefinitely. ① A man may take to drink because he feels himself to be a failure, and then fail all the more completely because he drinks. **2.** It is rather the same thing that is happening to the English language. It becomes ugly and inaccurate because our thoughts are foolish but the slovenliness of our language makes it easier for us to have foolish thoughts. The point is that the process is reversible.

중심소재: 언어 → 언어의 쇠퇴

1. 도입부 = 주제
언어(영어)의 쇠퇴의 원인

1) 구체적 진술
결과가 원인이 되고, 원래의 원인이 강화되며 반복된다.

① 술주정뱅이 비유부연

2. 요지
어리석은 생각으로 인해 언어가 부정확해지고, 이로 인한 언어의 부정이 다시 어리석은 생각을 이끈다.

정답 1 (D) 2 (A) 3 (C)

해설

1 영어라는 언어의 쇠퇴원인(Decline of the English Language)을 논하고 있는 글이다.

2 마지막에 영어가 타락하는 과정을 바꿀 수 있다(reversible)고 하였으니 영어를 다시 재형성하는 방법이 나와야 적합하다. 1번 문제와 함께 생각해야 할 문제이다. 따라서 정답은 (A)이다.

3 A man may take to drink because he feels himself to be a failure, and then fail all the more completely because he drinks. It is rather the same thing that is happening to the English language.의 비유를 통해서 답을 이끌어 낼 수 있다. 술은 사람에게 영향을 미치고, 다시 사람이 술에 영향을 미치는 순환적 사고를 발견할 수 있다. 이는 곧 영어라는 언어에도 일어나고 있다고 했으므로 영어 사용자와 영어는 "상호 영향을 미치는 관계"로 파악하는 것이 옳다.

지문해석

한 언어의 쇠퇴에는 궁극적으로 정치적, 경제적 원인이 있음이 분명하다. 언어가 쇠퇴하는 것은 단지 이런 저런 개별 작가들의 나쁜 영향 때문만은 아니다. 그러나 결과가 원인이 되어서 원래의 원인을 강화하고 똑같은 결과를 더 심각한 형태로 만들 수 있으며 이런 식으로 무한정 계속될 수 있다. 사람은 자신이 실패자라고 느껴서 술을 마시겠지만 술을 마시기 때문에 더 확실하게 실패한다. 영어에 벌어지는 일도 바로 이와 같은 일이다. 영어는 우리의 생각이 아둔하기 때문에 추해지고 부정확해지지만, 우리 언어(영어)의 단정치 못함 때문에 우리는 바보 같은 생각을 더 쉽게 하게 된다. 요점은 이 과정을 돌이킬 수 있다는 것이다.

Passage 5

구체적 진술의 시그널을 확인한다.

1. 1) In the 1980s, scientists around the world began to notice something strange: Frogs were disappearing. ① Ⓐ More recent research has shown that many kinds of amphibians are declining or have become extinct. Ⓑ Scientists are seriously concerned about this question since amphibians are an important source of scientific and medical knowledge. ⓐ By studying amphibians, scientists

중심소재: 개구리 개체수 감소

1. 첫 번째 문단

1) 도입부 = 현상
1980년대 전 세계적으로 개구리가 사라짐

① 구체적 진술
Ⓐ 많은 종류의 양서류가 줄어들거나 멸종 위기

have learned about new substances that could be very useful for treating human diseases.

2. 1) Scientists believe that amphibian decline is ① due to several environmental factors. Ⓐ One of these factors is the destruction of habitat, the natural area where an animal lives. Amphibians are very sensitive to changes in their habitat. If they cannot find the right conditions, they will not lay their eggs. These days, as wild areas are covered with houses, roads, farms, or factories, many kinds of amphibians are no longer laying eggs. There are a number of other factors in amphibian decline. Ⓑ Pollution is one of them. ⓐ In many industrial areas, air pollution has poisoned the rain, which then falls on ponds and kills the frogs and toads that live there. ⓑ In farming areas, the heavy use of chemicals on crops has also killed off amphibians. ⓒ Another factor is that air pollution has led to increased levels of Ultraviolet (UV) light. This endangers amphibians, which seem to be expecially sensitive to UV light. ⓓ And finally, scientists have discovered a new disease that seems to be killing many species of amphibians in different parts of the world.

3. 1) All these reasons for the disappearance of amphibians are also good reasons for more general concern. The destruction of land, the pollution of the air and the water, the changes in our atmosphere, the spread of diseases—these factors affect human beings, too. Amphibians are especially sensitive to environmental change. ① Perhaps they are like the canary bird that coal miners once used to take down into the mines to detect poisonous gases. When the canary became ill or died, the miners knew that dangerous gases were near and their own lives were in danger.

Ⓑ 양서류가 줄어드는 것에 대한 우려 및 이런 현상에 대한 대안 필요성과 중요성 지적
ⓐ 이유
양서류는 과학과 의학 지식에 중요한 원천이기 때문

2. 두 번째 문단

1) 현상의 원인

① 환경적 요인
Ⓐ 주거지 파괴
양서류는 특히 주거지 변화에 민감하고, 적절한 장소가 없을 경우 알을 낳지 않음(족종번식의 부적절성)
Ⓑ 오염
ⓐ 공업지대로 인한 공기 오염 → 산성비 → 개구리에 영향
ⓑ 농업지역의 심각한 살충제(화학약품) 사용
ⓒ 공기 오염으로 인한 UV증가 - UV에 민감한 양서류
ⓓ 양서류에서 치명적인 새로운 질병

3. 세 번째 문단

1) 양서류에게 미치는 이런 유해한 요소들은 인간에게도 동일하게 적용된다.

① 카나리아와 광부의 이야기를 비유로 양서류의 위기는 곧 인류의 위험이 될 수 있다고 말하면서 이에 대한 적극적 대안의 필요성을 강조하고 있다.

두번째 문단 본문에 기술될 중심내용이다. 나열의 글전개를 예측할 수 있다.

one, other, another은 나열의 시그널

TEST 08

정답 **1** (B) **2** (A) **3** (D)

해설

1 현상은 곧 주제 또는 제목으로 반영된다. 첫 번째, 두 번째 문장에 제시된 바와 같이 "왜 양서류들의 숫자가 감소하고 있는가?"가 주제임을 파악할 수 있다.

2 마지막 단락 셋째 문장에 "양서류들은 환경 변화에 특히 민감하다"라고 나와 있다.

3 마지막 두 문장에서, 양서류가 옛날 광부들의 카나리아 새와 같다고 하고 카나리아 새가 아프거나 죽으면 광부들이 위험을 알았다고 했으므로, 양서류의 감소도 인간에게 경고 신호가 되는 것이다.

지문해석

1980년대 전 세계 과학자들은 어딘가 이상한 것을 인지하기 시작했다. 그것은 바로 개구리들이 사라지고 있다는 것이었다. 보다 최근의 조사에서 많은 종류의 양서류들의 수가 감소하고 있거나 멸종된 것으로 나타났

다. 과학자들은 양서류들이 과학과 의학 지식의 중요한 원천이기 때문에 이 문제에 심각한 우려를 나타내고 있다. 양서류들의 연구를 통해 과학자들은 인간의 질병들을 치료하는 데 매우 유용할 수 있는 신물질들에 대해 알게 되었다. 과학자들은 양서류의 감소가 몇 가지 환경적 요인들 때문이라고 믿고 있다. 이러한 요인들 중 하나는 어떤 동물이 살아가는 자연 지역인 서식지의 파괴이다. 양서류들은 서식지의 변화에 매우 민감하다. 만약 그들이 알맞은 환경 조건을 찾지 못한다면 그들은 알을 낳지 않을 것이다. 요즘 야생 지역들이 주택, 도로, 농장, 또는 공장들로 뒤덮여버림에 따라 많은 종류의 양서류들이 더 이상 알을 낳지 않는다.

양서류의 감소에는 다른 많은 요인들이 있다. 오염은 그 요인들 중 하나다. 많은 산업 지역들에서 대기 오염이 비를 오염시켰고, 그 비가 연못에 내려 그것에 사는 개구리들과 두꺼비들을 죽게 만든다. 농지들에서는 농작물에 대한 과다한 화학약품의 사용 또한 양서류들을 죽게 했다. 또 다른 요인은 대기 오염이 자외선 양의 증가를 낳았다는 것이다. 이것은 자외선에 특히 민감해 보이는 양서류들을 위험에 빠뜨리고 있다. 그리고 마지막으로, 과학자들은 전 세계 각지에 있는 많은 종류의 양서류들을 죽이는 것처럼 보이는 새로운 병을 발견했다.

양서류들의 소실에 대한 이 모든 이유들은 또한 좀 더 일반적인 관심을 불러일으킬 충반한 이유들이 되고 있다. 땅의 파괴, 대기와 수질의 오염, 대기의 변화, 질병의 만연과 같은 이러한 요인들은 인간에게도 영향을 준다. 양서류들은 환경 변화에 특히 민감하다. 아마 그들은 한때 석탄 광부들이 유독 가스를 감지하기 위해 (탄광) 아래로 데리고 들어갔던 카나리아 새와 같을지 모른다. 카나리아 새가 아프거나 죽게 되면 광부들은 가까이에 유독가스가 있고 그들의 목숨도 위태롭다는 것을 알았다.

Passage 6

1. Trial by jury is a cherished part of the legal system. Yet few people realize that juries are open to the kind of manipulation that can actually hinder jurors' ability to arrive at a just decision. 1) For example, in some cases, lawyers create Ⓐ "shadow juries." These juries consist of men and women who possess the same backgrounds, personalities, and habits as the members of a real jury taking part in a trial. By means of the shadow jury, lawyers try to determine the feelings and attitudes of the people they hope to persuade. Then they use that knowledge to try and sway the real jury's verdict. Ⓑ In addition, lawyers consciously employ language they think will influence a jury's verdict. This is particularly obvious in a rape trial. Attorneys for the defense often rely on words that suggest flirtation and romance whereas attorneys for the victim employ the language of force and violence.

통념비판의 패턴을 파악하도록 한다.

연결 시의 순서
①For example→ in addition
②For example→ anther example→ in addition
위 ①, ②와 같이 연결사만으로도 순서가 정해짐을 파악하도록 한다.

중심소재: 배심원재판

1. 도입부 = 중심소재 도출
배심원제도

1) 주제문
배심원의 판단력을 흐리게 하는 조작이 있을 수 있다.

① 뒷받침 진술
변호사들의 조작의 구체적
Ⓐ 예시 1
shadow juries

Ⓑ 예시 2
의도적으로 특정 언어를 도입해 배심원의 판단에 영향을 미침

정답 **1 (B) 2 (B)**

해설

1 빈칸에 들어갈 표현에 영향을 미치는 요소는 바로 이어지는 관계대명사절과 이후 전개되는 예시(For example)이다. 빈칸의 의미를 한정하는 "that"에 걸리는 절의 내용이 곧 답에 들어갈 표현을 결정한다.

that can actually hinder jurors' ability to arrive at a just decision

배심원의 바른 결단력에 방해를 미치는 요소이므로 빈칸에 들어갈 표현은 부정적 어감이 되어야 한다. 또한, for example의 내용을 보면 변호사들이 조작을 통해 배심원의 판단에 영향을 미치고 있다는 점으로 보아 선택지 (B)가 가장 적절하다.

2 주제문의 위치를 파악했다면 별 어려움 없이 답을 구할 수 있다. 주제문의 위치는 다음과 같은 시그널을 통해서도 파악할 수 있다. however 뒤 for example 앞에 해당한다.

지문해석

배심 재판은 사법제도에서 중요하게 지켜져 온 부분이다. 그러나 공정한 결정에 이를 수 있는 배심원들의 능력을 실제로 방해할 수 있는 교묘한 조작에 배심원들이 노출되어 있다는 사실을 아는 이는 거의 없다. 예를 들어 일부 재판에서 변호사들은 "그림자 배심원들"을 만든다. 이 배심원들은 재판에 참여하는 실제 배심원단의 구성원들과 똑같은 출신 배경, 성격, 습관을 가진 남녀들로 구성된다. 그림자 배심원을 이용하여 변호사들은 그들이 설득하길 원하는 사람들의 감정과 사고방식을 알아보려고 한다. 그런 다음 그들은 거기서 얻은 지식을 이용해 진짜 배심원단의 평결을 흔들기 위해 노력한다. 게다가 변호사들은 배심원단의 평결에 영향을 줄 것이라 생각되는 언어를 의식적으로 사용한다. 이는 특히 강간에 대한 재판에서 두드러진다. 피고 측 변호인들은 흔히 남녀의 시시덕거림이나 연애를 암시하는 단어들에 의존하는 반면 원고 측 변호인들은 강압과 폭력에 관한 언어를 차용한다.

Passage 7

1. Forty years ago a young, radical journalist helped ignite the War on Poverty with his pioneering book *The Other America*. In its pages, Michael Harrington warned that the recently proclaimed age of affluence was a mirage, that beneath the surface of U.S. prosperity lay tens of millions of people stuck in hopeless poverty that only massive government intervention could help.

1) Today, a new generation of journalists is straining to duplicate Harrington's feat—to convince contemporary America that its economic system doesn't work for millions and ① that only government can lift them out of poverty. Ⓐ These new journalists face a tougher task than Harrington's though, because Ⓐ all levels of government have spent about $10 trillion on poverty programs since his book appeared, with disappointing, even counterproductive, results. Ⓑ And over the last four decades, millions of poor people, immigrants and native-born alike, have risen from poverty, without recourse to the government programs that Harrington inspired.

중심소재: 빈곤퇴치

1. 도입부 = 중심소재파악

40년 전 Michael Harrington은 빈곤문제와 함께 정부의 개입의 필요성 언급

1) 현상

빈곤 퇴치와 관련 현 경제제도는 효과가 없음

① 대안(신세대 기자들의 주장)

정부역할 강화를 강조

Ⓐ 난관

Ⓐ 지금껏 빈곤 퇴치를 위한 정부의 엄청난 노력 - 효과 없음

Ⓑ 정부의 지원 없이 빈곤을 이기고 성공한 사람들의 예

정답 1 (D) 2 (B)

TEST 08

해설

1 끝에서 두 번째 문장에서 all levels of government have spent about $10 trillion on poverty programs since his book appeared, with disappointing, even counter-productive, results고 한 것으로 보아 선택지 (D)와 같이 "정부의 빈곤 퇴치 프로그램으로 수백만 명의 빈곤층이 가난으로부터 벗어났다"는 진술은 본문에 부합하지 않는다.

2 새로운 기자들의 주장은 해링턴과 같이 정부개입(government intervention)을 통한 빈곤퇴치이다. 하지만, 해링턴의 접근방법과 달리 정부의 도움 없이 빈곤을 이기고 성공한 사람들의 예가 글 마지막 부분에 제시되는 점으로 보아 해밀턴에 주장에 대한 "재평가"가 이루어진다는 선택지 (B)가 가장 적절하다.

지문해석

40년 전 젊고 급진적인 기자 한 명이 그의 선구적인 저서 〈또 다른 미국(The Other America)〉을 통해 가난과의 전쟁에 불을 붙였다. 그 책에서 마이클 해링턴(Michael Harrington)은 최근에 선포된 풍요의 시대가 신기루에 불과하고 미국의 번영 이면에는 수천만 명의 사람들이 오직 정부의 개입만이 도울 수 있는 희망 없는 빈곤에 빠져있다고 경고했다.

오늘날 신세대 기자들은 해링턴의 위업을 재현하기 위해 노력 중인데, 동시대 미국인들에게 그들의 경제 체제가 수백만 명의 사람들에게 작동하지 않고 있고 정부만이 그들을 가난으로부터 구해낼 수 있다는 것을 설득시키는 일이다. 하지만 이 신참 기자들은 해링턴보다 더욱 어려운 과제를 직면하고 있는데, 각계각층의 정부 체제가 해링턴의 책이 출판된 이후 10조 달러 이상을 빈곤 대책들에 투입했지만 실망스럽고 심지어는 역효과를 낳는 결과만을 초래했기 때문이다. 그리고 지난 40년 간 가난한 사람들, 이민자들, 미국 토박이들을 막론하고 수백만 명이 해링턴이 권장한 정부 프로그램에 의존하지 않고도 가난으로부터 탈출했다.

Passage 8

1. 1) ① Each of the two coldest summers in the past 500 years, 1601 and 1816, followed large volcanic upheavals that threw massive amounts of dust into the stratosphere. Over the course of each year, as the slowly spreading dust obscured the Sun, the Earth cooled. As long as an eruption is big enough, the effect works regardless of where on Earth the volcano is located. Tambora, Indonesia, erupted in April 1815, and in Europe, 1816 was known as "the year without a summer." Even the polar ice cap levels of those anomalously cold summers show large quantities of volcanic ash. As recently as 1991, we saw a temporary drop of 1 degree in global temperatures after the explosion of Mount Pinatubo in the Philippines. The evident correlation between volcanic eruptions and global cooling years is easy to understand.

대조의 글 전개를 파악한다.

2. 1) ① On the other hand, we don't know why the period between 1100 and 1250 was warm enough in Europe and America for the Vikings to grow crops in Greenland. Conversely, 1400 to 1800 was so cool that it is called the "Little Ice Age." Global mean temperatures dropped by a degree or two; the Dutch canals froze over regularly, and

중심소재: 지구이상기온의 원인

1. 첫 번째 문단

1) 지구이상기온의 원인이 명확한 사례

① 시간의 글 전개방식에 따라 역사적 사례를 제시하면서 "거대한 화산활동으로 인한 지구의 온도 하락"의 관계를 밝히고 있다.

2. 두 번째 문단

1) 지구이상기온의 원인이 불명료한 경우

① 앞 문단에서 언급된 내용과 달리 "이상기온에 대한 원인을 파악할 수 없다"는 내용을 역사적 사례로 들면서 언급하고 있다.

the Swedish army invaded Denmark by marching across the iced North Sea. New York harbor occasionally froze, and George Washington experienced a cold winter at Valley Forge—cold but not unusually cold for that era. Were these events due to a shift in winds, a shift in ocean currents, or perhaps even a combination of many factors?

정답 **1** (B) **2** (D) **3** (A)

해설

1 이 글은 이유를 알 수 있는 기상 이변과 이유를 알 수 없는 기상 이변으로 문단을 나누어 기술하고 있다

2 빈칸 앞에는 이상 온난화가, 빈칸 뒤에는 이상 한파의 예가 나오므로 '거꾸로, 반대로'라는 부사 conversely가 들어가서 문장의 의미를 역접으로 이어주는 것이 적절하다.

3 인도네시아에서 폭발한 탐보라 화산의 영향으로 다음 해 유럽에 이상 한파가 불어 닥쳤다는 예를 든 것은 화산이 어디서 폭발하든 그 영향이 멀리까지 미칠 수 있음을 보여주기 위해서이다.

지문해석

지난 500년 사이에 1601년과 1816년 두 차례 대규모 화산분출로 인해 엄청난 양의 먼지가 성층권으로 유입되어 가장 추운 여름이 찾아왔다. 그 두 해에는 각각 연중 내내 천천히 퍼져나간 먼지가 태양을 가렸고, 지구는 식었다. 분출이 충분히 크기만 하다면, 지구의 어디에 화산이 위치하고 있든 상관없이 그 영향은 힘을 발휘한다. 인도네시아의 탐보라 화산은 1815년 4월에 분출했고, 유럽에서는 그 다음 해인 1816년이 '여름이 없는 해'가 되었다. 그렇게 이례적으로 추운 여름철에는 극지방의 만년설에서조차 다량의 화산재들이 발견된다. 최근 1991년에는 필리핀의 피나투보 화산이 폭발한 이후, 우리는 지구 온도가 일시적으로 1도 떨어지는 것을 목격했다.

화산 분출과 지구 냉각 사이의 명백한 상관관계는 이해하기 어렵지 않다. 반면에, 유럽과 미국에서 1100년과 1250년 사이의 기간은 바이킹족들이 그린랜드(Greenland)에서 곡식을 기를 수 있을 정도로 매우 더웠는데 그 이유는 알 수 없다. 그와 반대로, 1400년에서 1800년까지는 너무나 추워서 '소빙기(Little Ice Age)'라고 불리어진다. 당시 지구의 평균 기온은 1 내지 2도 떨어졌고, 네덜란드의 운하들은 자주 얼어버렸고, 스웨덴 군대는 얼음이 언 북해(North Sea)를 건너 행진해서 덴마크를 침공했다. 뉴욕 항이 어는 경우도 때로 있었고, 춥긴 해도 그 시대에는 특히 춥지는 않은 곳이었던 밸리포지(Valley Forge)에서 조지 워싱턴이 추운 겨울을 겪기도 했다. 이러한 일들은 바람의 변화 때문이었는가, 해류의 변화 때문이었는가, 아니면 아마도 많은 요인들의 결합으로 인한 것이었는가?

TEST 09

Passage 1

객관성을 확보할 수 있는 조사를 통해 현상의 문제점을 지적하고 있다.

1. For the first time in modern history, less than half of the U.S. adult population now reads literature, according to a comprehensive survey released by the National Endowment for the Arts. 1) Reading at Risk, a descriptive survey of national trends in adult literary reading, presents a detailed but bleak assessment of the decline of reading's role in the nation's culture. ① The report can be summarized in a single sentence: literary reading is not only declining rapidly among all groups, but the rate of decline has accelerated, especially among the young. The concerned citizen in search of good news about American literary culture will study this report in vain. Although the news in the report is dire, I doubt any careful observer of American society will be greatly surprised—except perhaps by the sheer magnitude of decline. 2) ① Reading at Risk merely documents a huge cultural transformation that most Americans have already noted—our society's massive shift toward electronic media for entertainment and information.

3) Reading a book requires a degree of active attention and engagement. Indeed, reading itself is a progressive skill that depends on years of education and practice. By contrast, most electronic media make fewer demands on their audiences, and indeed often require no more than passive participation. While electronic media offer the considerable advantages of diversity and access, print culture affords irreplaceable forms of focused attention and contemplation that make complex communications and insights possible. To lose such intellectual capability and the many sorts of human continuity it allows would constitute a vast cultural impoverishment.

중심소재: 문학읽기

1. 도입부 = 현상
미국 성인인구의 절반도 되지 않는 인구만이 문학을 읽는다.

1) 상황의 심각성
Reading at Risk의 조사를 통해 독서가 줄어들고 있는 암울한 현상 제시

① 부연(보고서 요약)
모든 층의 인구가 독서행위가 떨어질 뿐 아니라 젊은 사람들 내 독서가 급격히 줄어들고 있음

2) 현상의 이유
① 대부분의 미국인들이 이미 연예와 정보를 얻기 위한 수단으로 전자미디어에 의존하고 있다.

3) 현상의 의의
전자미디어와 달리 독서는 집중력을 요구하기 때문. 이러한 능력의 상실은 엄청난 문화적 빈곤에 해당한다.

정답 **1**(C) **2**(A) **3**(B)

지문분석

미국인들의 문학읽기의 실태(현상)를 다루는 글로 첫 번째 문단에서 다룬 독서 감소의 원인으로 전자미디어를 들면서 "인쇄문화의 감소를 비판적"으로 바라보고 있다.

해설

1 미국인들의 문학읽기의 실태(현상)를 다루는 글이다. "문학의"라는 뜻의 표현은 선택지 (C)이다.

2 글의 문맥에 맞게 인과의 논리를 완성한다. 문학을 읽지 않는 것은 곧 "지적 능력과 과거부터 내려오는 인간의 문화의 연속성"을 상실하는 것이라고 했으므로 선택지 (A)가 빈칸의 내용으로 가장 적절하다.

3 불일치 문제 또는 유추할 수 없는 문제의 경우 선택지를 먼저 읽고 접근하는 것이 문제풀이의 시간을 줄이는 방법 중 하나이다. Reading a book requires a degree of active attention and engagement.부분에서 알 수 있듯이 독서란 모든 인간이 갖출 수 있는 보편적인 지적 능력이 아니다. 일정한 노력의 결과를 통해서 학습의 산물임을 유추할 수 있다. 선택지 (B)는 틀린 진술이다.

불일치 문제의 경우 문제의 선택지를 먼저 읽을 경우 다음과 같은 내용을 파악할 수 있는지 주목한다.
1) 중심소재
2) 본문에 구체적으로 전개되는 중심내용
3) 주제설정
4) 모순되는 두 선택지 (둘 중 하나가 답일 가능성 높음)

지문해석

현대 역사상 처음으로, 미국 성인 인구의 절반 이하만이 현재 문학을 읽고 있다는 사실이, 국립예술기부단체(the National Endowment for the Arts)가 발표한 종합적 연구에서 드러났다. 나라별로 성인들이 문학을 얼마나 읽고 있는가에 대한 실태조사인 Reading at Risk는 전 국가의 문화에 있어 독서의 역할이 줄어들고 있다는 것에 대한 자세하면서도 암울한 평가를 제시하고 있다.

이 보고서는 한 문장으로 요약이 될 수 있다. 문학 독서가 모든 층에서 급격하게 하락하고 있을 뿐 아니라 하락률이 특히 젊은이 사이에서 가속화되고 있다는 것이다. 미국 독서문화에 대한 좋은 소식을 찾아 고민하는 시민이라면 이 보고서를 연구하는 것은 헛된 일이 될 것이다.

비록 보고서의 내용이 암울하긴 하지만, 나는 미국 사회에 대해서 주의 깊게 관찰한 사람이라면 아무도 놀라지 않을 것이라 생각한다. 감소의 규모를 제외한다면 말이다. 이번 조사는 단지 대부분의 미국인들이 인식하고 있는 거대한 문화적 변화를 문서로 옮겨놓은 것뿐이다. 그 변화란 우리 사회가 오락과 정보에 있어 전자미디어 쪽으로 광범위하게 옮겨갔다는 것이다. 책을 읽는 것은 어느 정도의 능동적인 집중력과 참여도를 필요로 한다. 실제로, 독서 그 자체는 수년간의 교육과 실행에 따라 달라지는 점진적인 기술이다. 이와 대조적으로, 대부분의 전자미디어는 이를 사용하는 사람들에게 요구하는 것이 더 적으며, 수동적인 참여 이상의 것을 요구하지 않는 경우가 많다. 전자미디어가 다양성과 접근성 측면에서 많은 이점을 제공하는 반면, 인쇄문화(독서)는 다른 것을 줄 수 없는 형태의 또렷한 집중력과 복잡한 의사소통과 통찰력을 얻을 수 있는 깊은 사고력을 제공할 수 있다. 이러한 지적 능력과 독서가 줄 수 있는 다양한 인간의 연속성을 얻지 못하는 것은 엄청난 문화적 빈곤화를 가져온다.

TEST 09

Passage 2

1. 1) ① It was an exhausting business, but by my mother's accounts it was the most satisfying and rewarding kind of work. As a nurse she was a low person in the professional hierarchy, always running from place to place on orders from the doctors, subject as well to strict discipline from her own administrative superiors on the nursing staff, but none of this came through in her recollections. What she remembered was her usefulness.

2) ② Whenever my father talked to me about nurses and their work, he spoke with high regard for them as professionals. Although it was clear in his view that the task of nurses was to do what the doctors told them to, it was also clear that he admired them for being able to do a lot of things he couldn't possibly do, had never been trained to do. On his own rounds later on, when he became an attending physician himself, he consulted the ward nurse

중심소재: 간호사 직업

1. 도입부 = 중심소재 도출

1) 뒷받침 진술 1
간호사 직업에 대한 관점
① 어머니의 관점
밑줄 친 두 문장에 간호사에 대한 어머니의 견해가 잘 반영되고 있다.

2) 뒷받침 진술 2
② 아버지의 관점
의사로서 아버지가 가진 간호사에 대한 존경의 견해가 잘 드러나 있다.

두 문단으로 나눠진 지문이다. 첫 번째 문단에선 간호사에 대한 어머니의 관점이 드러나고, 두 번째 문단은 아버지의 관점에서 기술되고 있다.

for her opinion about problem cases and paid careful attention to her observations and chart notes. In his own days of intern training (perhaps partly under my mother's strong influence, I don't know) he developed a deep and lasting respect for the whole nursing profession.

정답 **1 (D) 2 (C)**

해설

1 본문은 아버지와 어머니를 통해서 간접적으로 '간호사'에 대한 견해를 드러내는 글이다.

2 어머니가 예전에 간호사였던 자신에 대해 회상하는 부분은 그녀의 유용함이었다. 선택지 (D)의 경우 아버지가 간호사에 대해서 깊은 존경심을 갖게 된 것은 일부 어머니의 영향도 있겠지만 전적인 것은 아니다. 일반적으로 극단적 표현을 담는 선택지는 본문에 언급되지 않는 경우 오답일 가능성이 높다. 선택지 오답 유형에는 1) 극단적 표현 2) 부분을 전체로 확대하는 일반화 오류 3) 논리적 비약 4) 대조되는 두 대상의 특징 혼동 5) 수치, 날짜 6) 행동의 주체와 객체 혼동 등등이 있다.

지문해석

매우 힘든 일이긴 하지만 우리 어머니의 말로는 그처럼 만족스러우면서도 보람된 일이 없다고 했다. 간호사로서 어머니는 직책상 아래 사람이었고 언제나 의사의 지시에 따라 이리저리 뛰어다녀야 했으며 간호 스태프의 상사가 지시하는 엄격한 규율도 지켜야 했다. 하지만 이 중 어느 것도 그녀의 추억을 바꾸어 놓을 수는 없었다. 그녀가 기억하는 것은 자신의 유용함이었다. 나의 아버지는 나에게 간호사나 그들의 일에 대해서 말하실 때마다 그들을 전문적인 사람으로 높이 평가하셨다. 분명 아버지의 생각에 간호사의 일이란 의사가 지시한 것을 행하는 일임에도 불구하고 아버지가 간호사들에 대해 감탄하셨던 부분은 자신이 한번도 훈련받은 적이 없었기 때문에 할 수 없었던 많은 일들을 간호사들은 할 수 있었기 때문이다. 나중에 아버지가 주치의로 근무하며, 회진을 할 때, 그는 병동 간호사에게 어떤 문제에 대한 의견을 묻고선 그 간호사의 관찰과 그녀의 기록에 주의를 기울였다. 아버지가 인턴으로 근무하는 동안에 (아마 내가 모르는 우리 어머니의 강한 영향력도 한몫 했겠지만) 아버지는 전체 간호사들에 대한 깊고 지속적인 존경심을 키웠다.

Passage 3

1. For hundreds of years, the Sphinx attracted people both as a religious monument and as a work of art. But eventually, the desert sand once again covered the Sphinx, leaving only the head visible. Then, in the 1300s, a religious man named Saim-el-Dahr ordered that the head of the Sphinx be destroyed because it represented a false god. The nose of the Sphinx was broken off, and the face of the statue was damaged. It was not until the 1800s that archeologists began clearing the sand from the statue and began researching the long history of the Sphinx. At last, in the 1920s, all of the sand was finally cleared away and small changes were made to the Great Sphinx in order to fix it up. Special pieces of stone were added to the head of the statue in order to keep the head from falling.

중심소재: the Great Sphinx

1. the Great Sphinx의 복원을 시간의 순서(시간의 시그널 확인)에 따라 기술하고 있다. 이런 종류의 글을 읽을 땐, 언제 어떤 일이 일어났는지를 시간과 대비하여 잘 파악해 두어야 내용일치 문제를 풀 때, 시간을 절약할 수 있다.

정답 1 (B)

해설

1920년대에 스핑크스의 머리가 떨어지지 않도록 지탱하기 위해 작은 조각들을 붙였다는 내용이 본문 마지막에 드러난다.

지문해석

수백 년 동안, 스핑크스는 종교적 기념물과 예술 작품으로서 사람들을 매혹해왔다. 그러나 결국에, 머리만 보이도록 남겨준 채, 사막 모래는 다시 스핑크스를 덮었다. 그러다가 1300년대에 사임-엘-다흐르라는 한 신앙심이 깊은 사람이 스핑크스가 거짓 신을 나타낸다는 이유로 스핑크스 머리를 파괴하라고 명령했다. 스핑크스의 코는 떨어져 버렸고, 그 상(像)의 얼굴은 손상되었다. 1800년대가 되어서야 비로소 고고학자들이 그 상(像)으로부터 모래를 제거하고 스핑크스의 오랜 역사를 조사하기 시작했다. 마침내 1920년대에 모든 모래가 제거되었고 그것을 고치기 위해 위대한 스핑크스에 조그만 변화가 일어났다. 특이한 돌조각이 머리가 떨어지지 않도록 보호하기 위해 그 상의 머리에 붙여졌다.

Passage 4

1. 1) The first ethics dealt with the relation between individuals; ① the Mosaic Decalogue is an example. **2)** Later ethics dealt with the relation between the individual and society. ② The Golden Rule tries to integrate the individual to society; democracy to integrate social organization to the individual.

2. 1) There is as yet no ethic dealing with man's relation to land and to animals and plants which grow upon it. Land is still property. ① The land-relation is still strictly economic, entailing privileges but not obligations. **2)** The extension of ethics to this third element in human environment is an evolutionary possibility and ecological necessity.

중심소재: 자연친화적 윤리

1. 첫 번째 문단

1) 최초 윤리의 특징

개인 간의 관계에 초점

① 예시부연 - 모세 십계명

2) 후기 윤리의 특징

개인과 사회관계에 초점

② 예시부연 - 황금률

2. 두 번째 문단

1) 새로운 윤리의 필요성

인간과 자연의 관계를 다루는 윤리는 없다

① 문제점 지적

인간과 땅의 관계는 여전히 인간이 자연에 행사할 의무가 아닌 착취할 특권으로 인식하는 경제적 관점

2) 글쓴이의 주장

자연친화적 관점의 윤리로 진화와 필요성

정답 1 (A) 2 (B)

해설

1 최초의 윤리에서 최근의 윤리까지 윤리가 다루는 범위를 설명하고 있으므로 선택지 (A)의 "윤리의 진화"가 제목으로 적절하다.

2 윤리의 범위가 개인에서 사회로 그리고 세 번째 요소인 토지와 동식물(생태계)로 넓어지는 것이므로 확장을 뜻하는 extension이 정답이다.

지문해석

최초의 윤리는 개인 간의 관계를 다루었다. 모세의 십계명이 한 예이다. 나중에 윤리는 개인과 사회의 관계를 다루었다. 황금률(행동규범)은 개인을 사회에 융합시키려 하고, 민주주의는 사회 조직을 개인에 융합시키려 한다. 그러나 아직은 인간과 토지의 관계, 인간과 토지 위에서 자라는 동식물의 관계를 다루는 윤리는 없

다. 토지는 아직도 재산이다. 토지 관계는 아직 엄격하게 경제적이고 권리를 수반하지 의무를 수반하지는 않는다. 윤리가 인간 환경에서의 이 세 번째 요소로까지 확장되는 것은 진화적으로 가능하고 생태계를 위해 필요하다.

Passage 5

먼저 언급된 것 먼저 기술된다.

1. The discovery of the American continent had nothing to do with intellectual curiosity or even unfathomable human courage. 1) It was almost entirely about one thing: money. And it was a mistake. ① Ⓐ The Portuguese throughout the sixteenth century ruthlessly and aggressively built a monopoly in the spice trade from the east by dominating the trade routes around the continent of Africa. Ⓑ Spain, on the other hand, began thinking of ways to get around this monopoly by developing a western route to the eastern countries. ⓐ The problem was that this route was infinitely longer than the trip around Africa, and it lay across such a vast ocean. ⓑ It was Christopher Columbus who convinced the Spanish Queen to underwrite a western expedition to the eastern countries. Europeans also had a good idea as to the circumference of the earth; this circumference, in fact, had been accurately calculated in the second century B.C.

② Ⓐ The general view, then, was that a western voyage to India would be a disaster, for the ship would have to travel thousands of miles over open ocean. Ⓑ But Columbus believed that the world was considerably smaller than was imagined in the general view. He was, of course, completely mistaken and had not America gotten in his way, he and his men would have starved or died of dehydration. But fortunately for Columbus, America did get in the way.

중심소재: 미국의 발견

1. 도입부 = 중심소재 도출
미국의 발견은 지적 호기심 또는 인간의 용기와는 전혀 관련이 없다.

1) 주제문
미국발견의 배경 = 돈과 실수

① 뒷받침 진술 1(돈)
Ⓐ 포르투갈
아프리카 대륙 무역로를 주도함으로 향신로 무역 독점
Ⓑ 스페인
동양으로 이르는 서쪽 길을 뚫어 포르투갈의 독점을 우회하려는 계획을 세움
ⓐ 문제점
거리가 너무 멀고, 그 사이에 대양이 놓여 있다.
ⓑ 콜롬버스의 설득
콜럼버스는 동양국가로 향하는 여행경비를 받을 수 있도록 스페인 여왕을 설득(당시 이런 설득을 할 수 있었던 것은 유럽 사람들은 지구원주에 대한 개념을 잘 알고 있었기 때문)

② 뒷받침 진술 2(실수)
Ⓐ 일반적 관점
인도로의 항해는 배로 항해가 불가능한 거리이기 때문에 재앙이 될 것이다.
Ⓑ 콜럼버스의 관점
콜럼버스는 세상이 일반적 관점보다 더 작다고 착각

정답 **1** (A) **2** (E) **3** (B)

해설

1 unfathomable은 "측정하기 어려운, 심오한"의 뜻이므로 정답은 (A)이다.

2 (A)의 경우, 동방 국가로의 원정은 영토 확장이 아닌 경제적 측면과 관련이 있다. 지구의 원주에 대한 개념은 이미 유럽사람이 잘 파악하고 있었다는 내용이 언급되어 있으므로 선택지 (B)는 옳지 않으며, (C)의 경우는 Columbus가 증명한 것이 아니라 그렇게 개인적으로 믿었다고 했으므로 틀린 진술이다. had not America gotten in his way, he and his men would have starved or died of dehydration. But fortunately for Columbus, America did get in the way.부분을 통해 선택지 (E)는 옳은 진술임을 파악할 수 있다.

3 Columbus는 스페인 여왕을 설득해 서방 원정을 지원해 달라고 설득하는 내용이므로 선택지 (B)가 정답이다.

지문해석

아메리카 대륙의 발견은 지적 호기심이나 심오한 인간의 용기와는 아무 관련이 없었다. 이는 거의 전적으로 한 가지와 관련이 있었는데, 이는 바로 돈이었다. 그리고 이는 실수에 의한 것이었다. 16세기를 통틀어 포르투칼 인들은 동방으로부터의 향료무역에서 아프리카 대륙을 돌아가는 무역로를 지배함으로써 거침없고 공격적으로 독점을 이뤘다. 반면에 스페인은 동방 국가까지의 서쪽항로를 개발함으로써 이 독점을 회피하는 방법을 생각해내기 시작했다. 문제는 이 항로는 아프리카 대륙을 둘러가는 여정보다 훨씬 길고 광대한 대양을 가로질러 놓여 있다는 것이었다. 스페인 여왕에게 동방국가로 가는 서쪽 원정 비용을 지원해 줄 것을 설득한 것은 Christopher Columbus였다. 유럽인들은 지구 둘레 길이에 대해 상당한 지식이 있었다. 이 원주는 사실상 기원전 2세기에 정확하게 계산되어진 바 있다. 그 당시의 일반적인 시각으로는 배가 공해 위로 수천 마일을 항해해야 했으므로 인도를 향한 서쪽으로의 항해는 재앙이 될 것이라는 것이었다. 그러나 Columbus는 세상이 일반인들이 생각하는 것보다 훨씬 작을 것이라고 믿었다. 물론 이는 그가 완벽하게 잘못 판단한 것이었으며, 아메리카 대륙이 그를 막아서지 않았더라면, 그와 그의 부하들은 굶거나 탈수로 목숨을 잃었을 것이다. 그러나 Columbus에게는 운이 좋게도 아메리카 대륙이 그들의 길목에 있었다.

Passage 6

1. The principle of equality, which makes men independent of each other, gives them a habit and a taste for following in their private actions no other guide than their own will. This complete independence, which they constantly enjoy in regard to their equals and in the intercourse of private life, tends to make them look upon all authority with a jealous eye and speedily suggests to them the notion and the love of political freedom. Men living at such times have a natural bias towards free institutions. 1) Take any one of them at a venture and search if you can his most deepseated instincts, and you will find that, of all governments, he will soonest conceive and most highly value that government whose head he has himself elected and whose administration he may control. Of all the political effects produced by the equality of conditions, this love of independence is the first to strike the observing and to alarm the timid; nor can it be said that their alarm is wholly misplaced, for anarchy has a more formidable aspect in democratic countries than elsewhere. As the citizens have no direct influence on each other, as soon as the supreme power of the nation fails, which kept them all in their several stations, it would seem that disorder must instantly reach its utmost pitch and that, every man drawing aside in a different direction, the fabric of society must at once crumble away. 2. I am convinced, however, that anarchy is not the principal evil that democratic ages have to fear, but the least.

중심소재: 평등의 원칙과 무정부주의

1. 도입부 = 주제문

온전한 독립을 강조하는 평등의 원칙은 정치적 자유를 추구하게 만들고, 결국 어디에도 구속받지 않은 자유로운 제도를 갈망(무정부주의)

1) 뒷받침 진술

앞서 언급한 평등의 원칙이 결국 무정부주의로 이르러 결국 사회조직이 붕괴하게 된다는 내용을 단계적으로 상술하고 있다.

2. 글쓴이의 견해

무정부주의는 민주의주의가 두려워야 할 대상이 아님

구체적 진술의 시그널을 확인한다.
Take = take on example of

TEST 09

정답 1 (A) 2 (B) 3 (D)

해설

1 민주주의의 기반이 되는 평등의 원칙으로 인해 발생하는 모순은 바로 "무정부주의"라고 말하고 있다. 그러나 본문 마지막 부분에서 however를 기준으로 이런 평등에 의한 무정부주의가 민주주의 시대가 두려워할 대상이 아니라고 하고 있으므로 이후에는 앞에서 언급한 내용과 대조되는 역설적 측면이 제시되는 것이 글의 논리적 전개로 바람직하다.

2 본문 분석을 참조한다.

3 formidable은 "가공할, 대단한, 뛰어난"의 뜻으로 선택지 (D)의 outstanding이 가장 유사한 의미를 전달한다.

지문해석

평등의 원칙은 인간을 서로에게서 독립적으로 만드는 것으로, 인간이 사적인 행동에 있어서 오직 자신의 의지 외에는 어떤 지침도 따르지 않도록 하는 습관과 취향을 갖게 한다. 이 완전한 독립은 그들이 자신과 동등한 사람들과의 관계 속에서 또한 사생활의 교제 속에서 끊임없이 즐기는 것으로, 그들로 하여금 모든 권위를 질투어린 눈으로 보게끔 하는 경향이 있고 곧장 정치적 자유라는 관념과 욕망을 갖게 한다. 그러한 시대를 살아가는 사람들은 자연스럽게 자유로운 단체들에 치우치게 된다. 그들 중의 한 사람을 무작위로 골라서 가장 깊숙이 자리 잡은 본능을 자세히 살펴보면 당신은 그가 모든 정부들 중에서도 직접 지도부를 선출하고 행정부를 통제할 수 있는 정부를 가장 먼저 떠올리고 가장 가치 있게 생각한다는 사실을 알게 될 것이다. 제조건의 평등(the equality of conditions)이 만들어낸 모든 정치적 효과들 중에 이 독립에 대한 욕망은 가장 먼저 빈틈없는 사람들을 놀라게 하고 용기 없는 이들을 불안하게 하는 것이다. 그들의 불안이 전적으로 부적절하다고 말할 수 없는데, 무정부 상태는 그 어떤 곳보다도 민주주의 국가에서 어마어마한 양상을 나타내기 때문이다. 시민들은 서로에게 어떠한 직접적인 영향도 미치지 않기 때문에 그들 모두가 몇 개의 지위를 유지할 수 있도록 하는 국가의 절대 권력이 무너지자마자 무질서는 즉각적으로 최고조에 이를 것이 틀림없고 모든 사람들이 각기 다른 방향으로 비켜서 있는 동안 사회 구조는 즉시 무너져 내릴 것이다. 하지만 내가 확신하건대 무정부 상태는 민주주의 시대가 두려워해야 할 주된 악이 아니라 가장 두려워하지 않아도 될 것이다.

Passage 7

1. Residential racial segregation is an institution that was developed through discriminatory American policies and local acts of racism. 1) Federal and local government housing discriminations, private discrimination, and exclusionary zoning practices have resulted in the continuation of intentional discrimination against minorities, many of whom still remain disenfranchised members of society. 2. The devastating effects of residential racial discrimination on the quality of life for minority families and for our culture at large, represent the importance of initiating policies to integrate residential neighborhoods. ① Without the efforts of integration, the negative effects of decades of bigoted housing policies will be exacerbated, therefore perpetuating the existence of segregation and racial division.

중심소재: 주거 인종차별

1. 도입부 = 중심소재 도출

주거 인종차별은 차별적 미국 정책과 지역 인종차별 행위를 바탕으로 발달한 제도

1) 결과적 현상

정부와 지역정부의 차별적 주택 정책, 배타적 지역설정 등은 소수민족에 대한 의도적 차별을 영속하려는 결과를 가져왔기에 여전히 많은 이들이 사회에서 소외된 구성원으로 남아있음

2. 대안(요지)

지역주민 통합을 위한 정책의 중요성

① 뒷받침 근거

이러한 통합의 노력이 없다면, 한쪽으로 치우친 주택정책이 악화되고, 차별이 영속될 것이다.

정답 1(E) 2(B) 3(D)

해설

1 disenfranchise는 "(선거권)을 빼앗다 (법인 등의) 특권을 박탈하다"라는 뜻으로 deprived가 밑줄 친 부분과 가장 유사한 뜻을 가지고 있다.

2 bigoted는 "편향된(biased)", perpetuating는 "영속하는, 지속되는(maintaining)"을 각각 의미한다.

3 Without the efforts of integration, the negative effects of decades of bigoted housing policies will be exacerbated, therefore perpetuating the existence of segregation and racial division.에서 초당파적 노력이 아니라 "통합의 노력"이 필요함을 알 수 있으며, exclusionary zoning practices have resulted in the continuation of intentional discrimination against minorities에서 the same race가 아니라 "소수민족"이 옳다. Without the efforts of integration, the negative effects of decades of bigoted housing policies will be exacerbated, therefore perpetuating the existence of segregation and racial division.를 통해 "통합의 노력"이 없다면, 인종차별은 지속된다는 점을 파악할 수 있다.

지문해석

주거에 관한 인종차별은 차별적인 미국의 정책과 인종차별에 관한 지역 법안을 통해 발전되어 온 제도이다. 연방정부와 지방정부의 주거지 차별, 개인적 차별, 배타적 지역제 시행은 소수 민족들에 대한 의도적인 차별이 계속되는 결과를 낳았는데, 소수 민족들 중 많은 이들은 아직까지 선거권을 박탈당한 사회구성원으로 남아있다. 주거에 관한 인종차별이 소수 민족 가족들과 일반적인 우리 문화에 미치는 파괴적인 영향력은 인근 거주 지역들을 통합하는 정책 제안의 중요성을 나타낸다. 통합을 위한 노력이 없으면 수십 년간 계속된 편협한 주거 정책의 부정적인 영향이 더욱 악화될 것이고 인종차별과 인종분리가 영구적으로 존재하게 될 것이다.

Passage 8

1. 1) In evolutionary biology, an organism is said to behave altruistically when its behaviour benefits other organisms, at a cost to itself. 1) The costs and benefits are measured in terms of reproductive fitness, or expected number of offspring. So by behaving altruistically, an organism reduces the number of offspring it is likely to produce itself, but boosts the number that other organisms are likely to produce. 2) This biological notion of altruism is not identical to the everyday concept. Ⓐ In everyday parlance, an action would only be called "altruistic" if it was done with the conscious intention of helping another. But in the biological sense there is no such requirement. For the biologist, it is the consequences of an action for reproductive fitness that determine whether the action counts as altruistic, not the intentions, if any, with which the action is performed.

2. 1) Altruistic behavior is common throughout the animal kingdom, particularly in species with complex social structures. ① For example, in social insect colonies (e.g., ants and bees), sterile workers devote their whole lives to caring for the queen which is maximally altruistic. 2) From

중심소재: 이타적 행위

1. 첫 번째 문단

1) 도입부 = 현상

진화생물학에서 이타적 행위는 자신을 희생하고 다른 유기체에게 득을 주는 행위

1) 현상의 이유와 의미

이타적 행위로 인해 자신이 나을 수 있는 자손은 줄지만, 다른 유기체의 자손의 수는 높여준다.

2) 생물학적 개념의 이타주의는 일상적 개념과 상이

Ⓐ 일상의 의미에서 이타주의란 '의도적 행위'인 반면 생물학적 이타주의는 종족 번식을 위한 이타주의로 간주되는 적절성의 결과

2. 두 번째 문단

1) 이타주의 발생 배경

이타적 행위는 특히나 복잡한 사회 구조를 가진 종에서 발생한다.

① 뒷받침 예시

현상의 글의 중요 유형

유형 1. 부정적 현상

현상 | 문제점 지적 | 원인 | 대안

유형 2. 특정 예외적 현상

현상 | 원인 | 회의

유형 3. Trend

현상 | 사례 | 전망

TEST 09

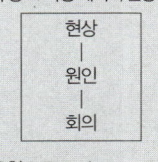

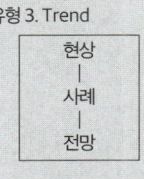

a Darwinian viewpoint, the existence of altruism in nature is at first sight puzzling. Natural selection leads us to expect animals to behave in ways that increase their own chances of survival and reproduction, not those of others. But by behaving altruistically an animal reduces its own fitness, so should be at a selective disadvantage vis-à-vis one which behaves selfishly.

2) 다윈주의 관점에서의 의미
다윈의 관점에서 자연계 내 이타적 행위의 존재는 얼핏 보기에 이상해 보이지만, 사실 자신의 적응능력을 낮추므로 다른 동물의 생존능력을 높이는 기여를 하기에 "자연도태"의 개념과 어긋나지 않는다.

정답 1 (C) 2 (B) 3 (A)

지문분석

본문의 주제는 "개체 자체의 생존과는 상충되는 생물의 이타주의"이다.

해설

1 첫 문장에서 "유기체는 비록 자신을 희생하더라도 자신의 행동이 다른 유기체에 이로울 때는 이타적으로 행동한다"고 했고, 마지막 부분에서는 이러한 행태가 진화론 일반의 관점에서 보면 당혹스럽다고 했으므로 개체 자체의 생존과는 상충되는 생물의 이타주의에 대한 내용이 이 글의 주제이다. 따라서 선택지 (C)가 글의 요지로 가장 적절하다.

2 빈칸 바로 앞의 내용을 보면, 일상적인 어법에서는 "다른 사람을 돕는 의식적인 의도"가 어떤 행동이 이타적이기 위한 요건으로 기술되는 반면, 다음 문장을 통해 생물학에서는 이타적 행동을 결정하는 것은 "의도(intentions)가 아니라고 했으므로 "그런 요건은 없다"고 한 (B)가 적절하다.

3 첫 문단 끝에 "의도가 없다(not the intentions)"고 했으므로 선택지 (A)는 적절하지 않다.

지문해석

진화 생물학에 따르면 유기체(생물)는 비록 자신을 희생하더라도 자신의 행동이 다른 유기체에 이로울 때는 이타적으로 행동한다고 한다. 희생과 이로움은 생식능력 즉 예상되는 자손의 수를 통해 측정된다. 그래서 이타적으로 행동함으로써 유기체는 자신이 낳을 수 있는 자손의 수는 줄이지만 다른 유기체들이 낳을 수 있는 수를 늘린다. 생물학에서 쓰이는 이러한 이타주의 개념은 일상적인 개념과는 다르다. 일상적인 어법에서는, 남을 돕는다는 의식적인 의도를 갖고 행한 행동이라면 '이타적'이라 부를 수 있다. 그러나 생물학적 이타성의 개념에 그런 요건은 없다. 생물학자들이 보기에, 어떤 행동이 이타적인가 아닌가를 결정하는 것은 그 행동의 의도가 아니라 그 행동이 낳는 생식능력 면에서의 결과이다.

이타적 행위는 동물계 전체에 나타나며 특히 복잡한 사회 조직을 갖춘 종에서 흔하다. 예를 들어 (개미와 꿀벌처럼) 군집사회를 이루는 곤충 집단에서는, 새끼를 못 낳는 일개미(일벌)들은 여왕개미(여왕벌)를 돌보는 데 평생 헌신하는데, 이것은 더할 나위 없이 이타적인 행동이다. 다윈주의의 관점에서 보면 자연계에 나타나는 이타주의는 언뜻 보기에 아주 당혹스럽다. 자연 선택에 의하면 동물은 당연히 다른 동물이 아니라 그들 자신의 생존 기회와 번식을 늘리는 방법으로 행동할 것이라고 예상하게 된다. 그러나 이타적인 행동을 함으로써 동물은 자신의 적응능력을 감소시키고 그래서 이기적으로 행동하는 다른 동물에 비해 선택적으로 불리한 조건에 놓이게 된다.

TEST 10

Passage 1

1. 1) The New Year's Day accident was terrible. 1) A rear tire blew out on the Ford SUV as if it had traveled on Florida's "Alligator Alley" west of Fort Lauderdale, flipping the vehicle and hurling several members of a family onto the highway. A girl perished on the highway; her brother would die hours later. Medical personnel who happened to be in the surrounding cars rushed to the rescue of the other victims. ① A physician helped clear the windpipe of a woman and resuscitate two of the other injured, staying long enough to direct the arriving paramedics to those who most needed help. ② Only after he left did anyone realize that the doctor was Bill Frist, incoming majority leader of the U.S. Senate. 2. 1) Dr. Frist, who doesn't mind his colleagues' addressing him that way instead of as "Senator," keeps a black medical bag in his legislative office and ① has shown a penchant for coming to the rescue. Ⓐ The Tennessee lawmaker treated victims of a gunman who opened fire in the U.S. Capitol in 1998, and in 2001 came to the aid of Strom Thurmond when the Senator collapsed on the Senate floor. 2. 1) But now, Frist, 50, is beginning a different kind of rescue mission, one that he may not be fully equipped to handle. ① Congress starts a new session this week, and the patient before Frist is his own party, still reeling from the recent political scandal.

중심소재: Bill Frist

1. 첫 번째 문단

1) 도입부 = 끔찍한 사건

구체적 진술

자동차 사고로 다친 사람을 도와주는 한 의사(①)를 소개하고 있다. 첫 번째 마지막 문장(②)을 통해 상원 소속의 새로 부인한 다수당 지도자인 Bill Frist(글에서 궁극적으로 다루려는 대상)임을 소개하고 있다.

* 첫 번째 문단: 어려움을 지나치지 못한 의사 Bill Frist

2. 두 번째 문단

1) 구체적 진술

문단이 바뀌면서 Bill First의 성품과 함께 그의 간략한 업적이 드러난다.

① 성품

상원의원으로서 의사로 불리는 점을 마다하지 않으며, 언제나 남을 도우려는 성향을 지님

Ⓐ 부연예시

남을 도왔던 구체적 예시

2. 요지

1) 새로운 구조미션

지금까지 의사로서 사람의 목숨을 구하는 역할을 했다면, 이제 새로운 미션을 시작함 ← 미션에 대한 구체적 진술이 이어질 것을 예상할 수 있다.

① 구체적 진술

최근 정치적 스캔들로 휘청거리는 새로 국회를 "고쳐야"하는 지도자의 모습

두 문단으로 구성된 지문이다. 각 문단별 요지를 먼저 파악하고 두 문단의 공통 또는 포괄하는 주제(제목)를 설정하도록 한다.

앞서 언급한 내용을 바탕으로 글을 통해 궁극적으로 전달하려는 내용이 제시된다.

TEST 10

정답 1 (A) 2 (D)

지문분석

본문은 과거에 남을 헌신적으로 돕는 의사에서 현재는 국회를 이끌 새로운 지도자로 직면한 Bill Frist에 관한 글이다.

해설

1 문맥 상 as 이하의 내용은 실제 상황이 아닌 가정의 내용이므로 혼합가정법을 써야 한다. as를 가정법 as if로 고치도록 한다.

2 (D)의 상원의원은 Dr. Frist가 돕는 쓰러진 Strom Thurmond에 해당한다.

지문해석

정월 초하루에 있었던 사고는 끔찍했다. 마치 포트 로더데일 서쪽 플로리다의 '엘리게이터 앨리'를 달린 것처

럼 포드 레저용 차량의 뒤쪽 타이어가 폭발하며 자동차는 뒤집어지고 식구들 몇몇은 고속도로 위로 날아갔다. 한 소녀는 고속도로 위에서 죽었고 남동생은 몇 시간 뒤에 죽었다. 우연히 주변 차에 타고 있던 의료 요원들이 다른 희생자들을 구하러 달려갔다. 한 의사가 여자의 숨통이 트이도록 돕고 다른 부상자 중 둘을 인공호흡 했고 의료진이 도착할 때까지 가장 도움이 필요한 희생자들이 살아 있도록 곁에 있었다. 그가 떠난 후 조금 후에 사람들은 그 의사가 미국 상원의 차기 다수당 원내 총무인 빌 프리스트(Bill Frist)라는 것을 알았다. 프리스트 의사는 동료들이 그를 상원이라고 부르는 대신에 의사라고 부르는 것을 개의치 않는데, 입법부 사무실에 검은 의료 가방을 갖고 있으며 구조하러 가는 것을 아주 즐긴다. 이 테네시 주 법률제정자는 1998년에 미국 국회 의사당 내에서 총을 쏘았던 총잡이의 희생자를 치료하였다. 2001년에는 의사당 바닥에 쓰러진 상원의원 스트롬 써몬드(Strom Thurmond)를 구조했다. 하지만 지금 프리스트는 50세로 다른 구조 임무를 시작하고 있다. 그는 그 구조 임무를 처리할 장비를 완전히 갖추지도 못했을 것이다. 의회는 이 주에 새로운 회기를 시작할 것이고, 프리스트 앞에 놓은 환자는 다름 아닌 그가 속한 당인데, 이 환자는 최근 정치적인 스캔들로 여전히 비틀거리고 있다.

Passage 2

"악마의 눈"이란 소재를 통해서 궁극적으로 fascinate란 단어의 기원을 따지는 글이다.

1. From earliest times, and even today among superstitious people, it has been believed that certain persons have the power to injure or even kill other persons or animals or to destroy crops by no more than a malignant glance. Such a person is held to possess the "evil eyes." 1) ① In ancient Greece, the power of the evil eye was called baskania, in Rome fascinatio. Because no one knew who had the power and the wish to do him or her injury, it was an almost universal custom, in old times, to wear an amulet of some kind which was believed to protect the wearer. Even the cattle were sometimes so adorned. Children were thought to be especially susceptible to the power of the evil eye, and no Roman mother, in classical days, would permit a child of hers to leave the house without a certain amulet called fascinum. 2. Actually, therefore, our word "fascinate," when first brought into English use, meant to cast the evil eye upon one, to put one under the spell of witchcraft. We use the word rarely now in such a literal sense, but employ it rather to mean to hold one's attention irresistibly or to occupy one's thoughts exclusively by pleasing qualities.

요지를 이끄는 시그널을 확인한다.

중심소재: evil eyes

1. 도입부 = 중심소재 도출
"악마의 눈"이란 미신을 언급하고 있다.

1) 구체적 진술
고대 그리스로 거슬러 올라가 "악마의 눈"의 기원을 살피고 있다.
① "악마의 눈"으로 인해 모든 이가 부적을 차게 됨. 특히 아이들은 반드시 집을 나설 때 fascinum이란 부적을 가지고 나감

2. 결론(요지)
영어에서 fascinate는 처음에 이와 같은 부정적인 의미로 사용되다, 현대에는 긍정적 의미로 "다른 이의 마음을 앗아가다"는 의미의 변화를 기술하고 있다.

정답 **1**(A) **2**(C) **3**(B) **4**(C)

해설

1 fascinate란 현대 표현의 기원을 살피는 글이다. 일반적으로 기원을 따지는 글은 현대에서 과거 또는 과거에서 현재의 시간의 글 전개방식이 주로 활용되는 점을 기억하도록 한다.

2 기원을 설명하는 글이다. narration 서사, persuasion 논증, exposition 설명 description 묘사

3 amulet은 부적이란 뜻이다. 사악한 힘으로부터 아이를 보호하는 의미에서 부적을 차지 않은 아이는 밖에 내보내지 않는다는 내용을 파악할 수 있다. Children were thought to be especially susceptible to the power

of the evil eye, and no Roman mother, in classical days, would permit a child of hers to leave the house without a certain amulet called fascinum.의 밑줄 친 표현을 확인한다.

4 malignant(악의 있는)와 benign(친절한, 자애적인)은 서로 반의어 관계이다.

지문해석

태곳적부터 오늘날까지, 미신을 믿는 사람들은, 다른 사람이나 동물을 해하거나 죽일 수 있으며, 혹은 단지 악의에 찬 눈빛만으로 곡식을 망가뜨릴 수 있는 능력을 가지고 있는 사람이 있다고 믿고 있다. 이러한 사람은 '악마의 눈'을 가지고 있다고 여겨진다. 악마의 눈의 힘은 고대 그리스에서 baskania, 로마에선 fascinatio으로 불렀다. 어느 누구도 누가 힘을 가지고 있는지, 혹은 누구를 다치게 하고 싶어 하는지 몰랐기에, 고대에는 부적을 가지고 다니는 풍습이 거의 보편적이었다. 부적은 이를 지니는 사람을 보호해준다고 여겨졌기 때문이다. 때로는 소들까지 부적으로 장식되었다. 아이들은 악마의 눈의 영향력에 특별히 취약하다고 여겨졌기에, 고대 시대에는 fascinum이라는 부적을 지니지 않고 아이를 밖에 내보내는 엄마는 아무도 없었다. 따라서 영어로 처음 옮겨졌을 때, 우리가 "fascinate" 이라 사용하는 단어는 실제로 다른 사람에게 악마의 눈을 던져 마녀의 마법에 걸리게 하는 것을 의미했다. 우리는 이 단어를 현재 이런 문자 그대로의 의미로 거의 사용하지 않고, 저항할 수 없을 정도로 다른 사람의 관심을 이끌어 내거나 매력적인 특징으로 다른 이의 생각을 사로잡는 의미로 이것을 사용한다.

Passage 3

1. It has been particularly important to bring to light language that reinforces the dominant culture's views of disability. 1) ① A useful step in that process has been the construction of the terms *ableist* and *ableism,* which can be used to organize ideas about the centering and domination of the non-disabled experience and point of view. Ⓐ *Ableism* has recently landed in the *Reader's Digest Oxford Wordfinder,* where it is defined as "discrimination in favor of the able-bodied." Ⓑ I would add, extrapolating from the definitions of *racism* and *sexism,* that *ableism* also includes the idea that a person's abilities or characteristics are determined by disability or that people with disabilities as a group are inferior to non-disabled people. ② Although there is probably greater consensus among the general public on what could be labeled racist or sexist language than there is on what might be considered ableist, that may be because the nature of the oppression of disabled people is not yet as widely understood.

중심소재: ableist and ableism

1. 도입부 = 중심소재 도출

장애에 대한 주류문화의 관점을 강화시키는 언어

1) 구체적 진술

① *ableist*와 *ableism*

정상인의 관점의 중심과 지배를 강화하는 용어

Ⓐ Ableism의 의미 1

정상적 신체능력을 선호하는 차별

Ⓑ Ableism의 의미 2

*ableism*은 인종적 편견 또는 성차별의 같은 맥락에서 한 사람의 능력 또는 특성이 장애에 의해서 정의되거나 이들은 정상인보다 열등한 사람이라는 것을 조장

② ableism에 대한 인식부족의 문제점 지적

글쓴이의 견해를 드러내는 표현을 확인한다.

정답 **1** (A) **2** (B)

지문분석

본문은 장애에 대한 주류문화의 왜곡된 관점을 강화시키는 언어인 ableism을 비판적으로 바라보고 있다.

해설

1 장애인차별을 인종차별과 성차별의 연장선상에서 보고 있다는 점에서 장애인차별에 대해 판적인 입장임을 알 수

있다.

2 흑인은 백인보다 열등하다는 인종차별과 여성은 남성보다 열등하다는 성차별과 마찬가지로 장애인차별주의에서 장애인은 정상인보다 열등하다고 인식될 것을 유추할 수 있다.

지문해석

특별히 중요한 것은 장애에 대한 지배적 문화의 관점을 강화하는 언어를 드러내는 것이다. 그 과정에서 유용한 시작은 장애차별이라는 용어를 만들어가는 것이다. 이 용어들은 중심적이고 지배적인 비장애적 경험과 시각에 대한 생각들의 조직화에 사용될 수 있다. 장애차별이라는 용어는 최근 리더스 다이제스트 옥스퍼드 단어찾기에 수록되었다. 그곳에서 그 용어는 '장애 없는 육신에 대한 선호로 인한 차별'이라고 정의된다. 나는 인종차별과 성차별의 정의를 참고해서 장애차별은 사람의 능력이나 성격이 장애에 의해 결정되거나 또는 장애를 가진 사람들이 그렇지 않은 사람들보다 열등하다는 생각이라고 덧붙일 것이다. 일반 대중 사이에는 무엇이 장애차별적인 말인지에 대해서보다 인종차별적이거나 성차별적인 말인지에 대해서 더 많은 공감대가 있을 것이다. 그것은 장애인에 대한 억압에 대해 아직 널리 이해되지 못하고 있어서일 것이다.

Passage 4

두 문단으로 나눠진 지문이다. 문단별 주제를 설정하고, 궁극적으로 전달하려는 요지를 파악하도록 한다.

구체적 진술을 이끄는 시그널을 확인한다.

글에서 궁극적으로 밝히려는 사항을 제시하는 문단이다. 첫 번째 문단에서 제시한 깨진 창문 이론을 통해서 말하려는 바는 무엇인가?

1\. 1) **The Broken Windows theory** was the brainchild of the criminologists James Wilson and George Kelling. They argued that crime is the inevitable result of disorder. ① If a window is broken and left unrepaired, people walking by will conclude that no one cares and no one is in charge. Soon, more windows will be broken, and the sense of anarchy will spread from the building to the street on which it faces, sending a signal that anything goes here. In a city, relatively minor problems like graffiti, public disorder, and aggressive panhandling are all the equivalent of broken windows, invitations to more serious crimes.

2\. 1) What does this suggest? It says that ① Ⓐ the criminal — far from being someone who acts for fundamental, intrinsic reasons and who live in his own world — is actually someone acutely sensitive to his environment, who is alert to all kinds of cues, and who is prompted to commit crimes based on his perception of the world around him. That is an incredibly radical — and in some sense unbelievable — idea. It says that Ⓑ behavior is a function of social context.

중심소재: 깨진 유리창 이론

1\. 첫 번째 문단

1) 주제문
범죄는 무질서의 필연적 결과이다.

① 뒷받침 진술
예시(if)를 통해서 자세히 설명하고 있다

* 첫 번째 문단에선 깨진 창문 이론의 정확한 개념과 어떠한 배경 속에서 범죄가 발생하는지 주목하도록 한다.

2\. 두 번째 문단

1) 의문문 = 주제

① 답변(요지)
범죄(행위)는 환경의 산물이다 (Ⓐ+Ⓑ)

정답 1 (B) 2 (A)

해설

1 깨친 창문 이론을 통해서 사람의 행동은 환경에 영향을 받는다는 내용을 전달하고 있으므로 선택지 (B)가 정답이다.

2 무질서에 대한 의심이 심어지면 범죄로 이어진다. "어떤 짓을 해도 된다"는 논리는 내가 범죄를 저질러도 현재의 무질서한 상황이 방치되는 것처럼 나도 괜찮을 것이란 논리가 반영된 것이므로 선택지 (A)가 적절하다.

지문해석

'깨진 창문' 이론은 범죄학자인 제임스 윌슨(James Wilson)과 조지 켈링(George Kelling)의 창작물이었다. 그들은 범죄는 혼란의 불가피한 결과라고 말했다. 창문이 깨져서 수리되지 않은 채로 방치되면 지나가는 사람들은 어느 누구도 관심을 가지고 있지 않고 책임자가 없다고 결론을 내릴 것이다. 곧 더 많은 창문이 깨질 것이고 무질서 의식이 건물로부터 그 건물이 면해 있는 거리로까지 퍼져서 여기서는 무슨 짓이든 해도 된다는 신호를 보내게 될 것이다. 도시에서는 낙서, 공공질서 위반, 공격적인 구걸과 같은 비교적 사소한 문제들이 모두 깨진 창문에 해당하는 것으로, 더 심각한 범죄를 초래한다.

이것이 무엇을 암시하는가? 그것은 범죄자란 근본적이고 본질적인 이유에 따라 행동하고 자신의 세계 안에서 사는 사람이 아니라, 실제로는 자신의 환경에 매우 민감하고 모든 종류의 신호들에 주의하고 주변 세계의 인지에 근거해 범죄를 저지르게 되는 사람이라는 것을 말한다. 그것은 대단히 급진적이고 어떤 의미에서는 믿을 수 없는 생각이다. 그것은 행동은 사회적 상황의 상관관계라고 말하고 있다.

Passage 5

1. American culture thrives on contradictions. 1) It exalts individualism yet is rife with the conformity so essential to consumerism. It preaches self-reliance and personal accountability (especially for poor people) while enriching pop psychologists who provide excuses for sins of the middle class. It nurtures feminism and encourages face-lifts. So we shouldn't be entirely surprised by the paradoxical convergence of reality TV shows with a growing concern about privacy, although the intensity of these opposing trends is particularly dramatic. Democratic and Republican pollsters attest to a "groundswell" of concern about privacy, which politicians rush to address. George W. Bush declares himself a "privacy rights person." Congress considers hundreds of privacy protection bills. Still, people cede their privacy voluntarily every day for the promise for security.

중심소재: 미국문화

1. 도입부 = 주제문

미국문화는 모순에 바탕을 두고 성장했다.

1) 뒷받침 문장

미국 문화의 모순적 성장에 대한 구체적 진술이 이어지는데, 본문에서 대조를 드러내는 yet, while, paradoxical, although, still의 표현을 확인할 수 있다.

본문에 구체적으로 전개될 중심내용으로 대조의 글 전개를 예측할 수 있다.

중심소재의 반복을 확보한다.

TEST 10

정답 **1** (B) **2** (D) **3** (A) **4** (D) 5. (C)

해설

1 역접의 Yet을 활용한다. "미국문화가 개인주의를 찬양하지만 소비자 중심주의에 있어서 대단히 필수적인 순응, 즉, 복종으로 가득 차 있다."는 내용으로 yet 앞의 내용과 뒤의 내용이 반대가 되려면 앞의 내용은 긍정적 내용의 exalt가 와야 한다.

2 we shouldn't be entirely surprised by the (B) convergence of reality TV shows with a growing concern about privacy, although the intensity of these opposing trends is particularly dramatic.를 보면 밑줄 친 두 부분이 서로 역설적인 관계를 나타낸다.

3 rife는 "유행하고 있는, 만연한, 풍부한, 가득 찬"이란 뜻이다.

4 "민주당과 공화당의 여론 조사원들은 사생활에 대한 걱정의 "(여론의) 들끓음"을 입증하고 있으며, 정치가들인 앞다투어 이에 대한 발언을 하고자 한다."의 내용을 가장 잘 드러내는 선택지는 (D)이다.

5 "사람들은 안전을 위해 자신의 사생활을 양보한다"는 내용이므로 선택지 (C)가 이러한 예로 가장 적절하다.

지문해석

미국 문화는 모순 속에서 번창한다. 미국문화는 개인주의를 찬양하지만 소비 지상주의에 필수적 요소인 순응으로 가득 차 있다. 미국 문화는 (특히 가난한 사람들에게 있어서) 자립정신과 개인적 책임을 역설한다. 반면 인기 있는 심리학자들은 중산층의 죄에 대한 변명을 만들어주며 번성하고 있다. 미국문화는 페미니즘을 조장하면서 동시에 주름을 펴주는 얼굴성형 수술을 권장한다. 따라서 우리는 사생활에 대한 우려가 점점 커져가는 리얼리티 티비쇼들로 집중되는 모순적 현상에 대해 완전히 놀랄 것도 없다. 이러한 반대적 경향들의 강도가 특별히 극적이라 해도 말이다. 민주당과 공화당의 여론 조사원들은 사생활에 대한 걱정의 "(여론의) 들끓음"을 입증하고 있으며, 정치가들인 앞 다투어 이에 대한 발언을 하고자 한다. 조지 부시 대통령은 자신을 "사생활 보호권"의 대통령이라 역설한다. 국회는 수백 가지의 사생활 보호 법안을 심사하고 있다. 그러나 국회는 수백 가지의 사생활 보호 법안을 고려하고 있다. 그럼에도 불구하고, 사람들은 매일매일 안전에 대한 약속을 위해 자신의 사생활을 마지못해 양도하고 있다.

Passage 6

다양한 아프리카 문화에서 음악으로 중심소재의 폭이 좁아짐을 파악하도록 한다.

1. The cultures in Africa vary as much as the terrain. There are over 30 religions on the continent and over one thousand languages spoken. 1) Futhermore, in all parts of Africa, culture is steeped in a dynamic musical tradition. ① Ⓐ In Northern Africa, Islam influences all parts of life, including the music. The vocals are typically long, fluctuating notes that are as mesmerizing as they are haunting. Singing is usually accompanied by tambourines, drums, bagpipes, and flutes. Ⓑ In other parts of Africa, however, the drum is king. West African music is characterized by throbbing rhythms and call-and-response-style singing. ② Many music historians attribute the creation of New World music genres such as jazz and rock-and-roll to West African musical influences that were transferred to the Americas through the trans-Atlantic slave trade. ③ Additionally, this is not the only case of African music evolving. Ⓐ In the Democratic Republic of Congo, a style of music called Soukous was created. It is a mixture of traditional Congolese drumming and Afro-Cuban sounds. Soukous has become internationally popular since the 1930s and is performed all over the world.

중심소재: 아프리카의 역동적인 음악

1. 도입부
다양한 아프리카 문화 언급

1) 구체적 진술
아프리카의 역동적인 음악

① 지역적 특징
Ⓐ 북아프리카의 특징
Ⓑ 서아프리카의 특징

② 영향
노예무역으로 인해 신대륙의 음악(재즈와 록큰롤)에 영향을 미침

③ 추가적 특징
새로운 음악의 창조
Ⓐ 예시

정답 1 (D) 2 (B) 3 (B)

해설

1 본문에서 서아프리카의 음악의 특징으로는 가슴을 박동케 하는 리듬과 서로 호응하며 부르는 노래가 특징이라고 언급하고 있다.

2 구어체에서 hypnotizying을 "매혹적, 매혹시키는"이라는 의미로 쓴다.

3 Many music historians attribute the creation of New World music genres .... to the Americas through the trans-Atlantic slave trade.를 통해 신대륙 미국에서 발전했던 재즈와 록큰롤 같은 음악장르는 노

예무역을 통해 미주대륙으로 전파된 서아프리카 음악에서 영향을 받고 발전한 것임을 파악할 수 있으므로 선택지 (B)가 정답이다. attribute의 문장 내 정확한 용례를 적용한 제이다. [attribute A(결과) to B(원인)]의 구조로 "A의 결과는 B로 기인한다"로 해석한다.

지문해석

아프리카의 문화는 지형만큼이나 다양하다. 아프리카 대륙에서는 사람들이 믿는 종교가 30가지 이상이 있고 그들이 말하는 언어는 100가지가 넘는다. 게다가 아프리카 어디에서나 문화에는 역동적인 음악전통이 배어 있다. 북아프리카에서는 이슬람 종교가 음악을 포함해서 삶의 전반에 영향을 미치고 있다. 그 노래 소리는 일반적으로 길고도 고조변화가 심한 곡조여서 잊혀지지 않을 정도로 매혹적이다. 노래는 대개 탬버린, 북, 백파이프, 그리고 피리 반주에 맞추어 부르곤 한다. 그러나 아프리카 다른 지역에서는 북이야말로 으뜸이다. 서아프리카의 음악은 가슴을 박동케 하는 리듬과 그리고 서로 호응하며 부르는 노래가 특징을 이루고 있다. 수많은 음악 역사가들은 신대륙의 재즈나 록큰롤과 같은 음악장르의 탄생은 대서양을 가로지른 노예무역을 통해 미주대륙으로 전파된 서아프리카음악의 영향력 때문이라고 생각한다. 하나 덧붙이자면, 이것만이 아프리카 음악이 발전한 유일한 사례는 아니다. 콩고 민주공화국에서는 수쿠스(Soukous)라는 음악형식이 탄생되었다. 수쿠스는 전통적인 콩고의 북소리와 아프로큐반 사운드가 혼합된 형태이다. 수쿠스는 1930년대 이후 국제적으로 유행하기 시작했고 지금은 전 세계에서 연주되고 있다.

Passage 7

1. High-level U.S. officials, interviewed after the close of meetings for the day, said the two sides agreed on many things in principle, such as the need to keep their economies open to other countries. 1) But specific measures and a timetable were less clear, with the United States pushing for rapid change and China seeking to move cautiously. ① Ⓐ Skepticism toward foreign trade, particularly with China, played a major role in the recent U.S. elections, and proposals for punitive tariffs or other protectionist measures could gain support in Congress next year. "I sense that they have an understanding of the stakes," an official said. "And the stakes are very high. You are talking about a lot of business, a lot of jobs on both sides. We are their No. 1 customer." Ⓑ While most of the day was focused on U.S. requests of Beijing, China also listed some priorities: fewer obstacles to the export of U.S. technology and to Chinese investment in the United States. The complaint about U.S. export controls, in particular, led to some tense exchanges, U.S. delegates said.

중심소재: 경제 개방에 대한 미국과 중국의 입장

1. 도입부
미국과 중국 모두 경제 개방의 필요성 동의

1) 구체적 진술(논리적 반전)
접근방법(미국은 빠른 변화를 밀어붙이는 반면, 중국은 조심스런 움직임)의 상이점으로 인해 구체적 조치의 내용과 시기에 대해 불분명

① 각국의 구체적 입장
Ⓐ 미국
외국 무역(특히 중국과)에 대한 회의주의가 최근의 미국선거에 큰 영향력을 미쳤으며, 보복세 또는 보호무역주의 조치가 내년에 지지를 얻을 것
Ⓑ 중국
미국 기술 수출에 대한 제약과 미국에 대한 중국의 투자 제약을 제거 + 미국 수출 통제에 대한 불만

정답 1 (C) 2 (E)

해설

1 미국과 중국의 입장을 중립적 입장에서 기술하고 있다는 점에서 균형 잡힌 관점의 글이다.

2 And the stakes are very high. You are talking about a lot of business, a lot of jobs on both sides. 에서 언급되고 있는 직업은 각국의 고용상황을 반영한 표현이지, 해외고용 창출과 관련된 표현으로 보아서는 안 된다. 본문의 내용을 바탕으로 답을 고를 때, 지나친 비약은 오답을 유도하는 함정이므로 좀 더 객관적 입장에서 본

문을 분석하고 답에 접근하도록 노력한다.

지문해석

미국의 고위 관료들은 그 날의 회담을 마친 후 한 인터뷰에서 양 진영이 자국 경제를 타국에 개방해야 할 필요성과 같은 많은 사항들에 있어서 원칙적으로 합의했다고 밝혔다. 그러나 구체적인 정책들과 일정표는 다소 불분명한데, 미국은 즉각적인 변화를 요구한 반면 중국은 신중하게 진척해가는 것을 추구하고 있다. 해외무역, 특히 중국과의 무역에 대한 회의론은 최근의 미국 선거에 있어서 중요한 역할을 했고, 보복 관세나 다른 보호무역정책들에 대한 제안이 내년도 의회에서 지지를 얻을 수 있다. 한 관료는 "나는 그들이 이해관계들을 이해하고 있음을 알고 있다. 중대한 이해관계가 걸려 있다. 양 쪽 모두 많은 일감과 많은 일자리에 대해 이야기하고 있다. 우리는 그들에게 제1의 고객이다."라고 말했다. 그 날의 대부분이 중국 정부에 대한 미국의 요구에 중점을 두었지만 중국 또한 몇 가지 우선 사항들을 열거했다. 즉, 미국 기술의 수출에 대한 제약 및 미국 내 중국 투자에 대한 제약의 축소이다. 특히나 미국의 수출 규제에 대한 항의가 날카로운 언쟁으로 이어졌다고 미국 측 대표들은 말했다.

Passage 8

1. Life in ancestral environments was fraught with danger, not just from the obvious predators but also from a variety of microbes, viruses and toxins. 1) Ancestral foods obtained through foraging, scavenging and hunting were quite "natural" and therefore far from healthy. ① Many plants are full of dangerous toxins and so are dead animals. Also, many animals carry pathogens that adapt easily to life in a human body. Ⓐ The danger is especially high for a "generalist" species like human—that is, one that finds its nutrients in a great variety of sources and adapts to new environments by changing its diet. 2. Being a generalist species requires not only that you have immune defenses like most other species but also that you make specific cognitive adaptations to minimize the danger of contamination and contagion. 1) Rats, too, are generalists; this shows in their extremely cautious approach to novel foods, and in the way they quickly detect the correlation between a new food and various somatic disorders. They detect such connections better than other, non-food-related correlations, which shows that the system that produces such inferences is indeed specialized.

중심소재: 고대환경의 적응

1. 도입부 = 고대의 환경

포식자뿐 아니라 다양한 세균, 바이러스 독소들로 가득해 고대조상은 채집, 수집, 사냥을 통해 식량을 구했기 때문에 몸에 건강한 식량과는 거리가 멀다.

1) 뒷받침 사례

자연에서 얻은 위험한 음식의 예를 구체적으로 언급하고 있다.

① 잡식성이 인간에게 더욱 위험

2. 주제문

잡식성의 경우 이러한 환경에서 살아남기 위해 면역 체계뿐 아니라 오염과 전염을 낮출 수 있는 인지 적응력을 갖춰야 한다.

1) 뒷받침 사례

인지 적응력이 뛰어난 잡시성의 또 다른 예인 쥐를 언급하고 있다.

정답 1 (A) 2 (D) 3 (C)

해설

1 글의 초반부에 "조상들의 음식은 자연 상태 그대로의 것이어서 건강에 좋지 못하다"라고 언급된 것으로 보아 (A)에서 "음식을 요리하지(익히지) 않았던 것이 조상들을 위험에 노출시킨 원인"으로 작용했다고 볼 수 있다.

2 본문의 중간에서 "그 위험은 인간 같은 잡식성의 경우 특히 높은데, 잡식성은 굉장히 다양한 원천에서 영양분을 찾

고 먹는 음식을 바꿈으로써 새로운 환경에 적응하는 그런 종이다"라는 언급으로 보아 (D)의 "식중독의 더 높은 위험에 직면하게 될 것 같다"가 적절하다.

3 마지막 부분에서 "쥐들이 새로운 음식과 다양한 신체 질병들 사이에 상호 관련성을 빨리 간파한다."는 언급으로 보아 (C)가 적절하다.

지문해석

조상들이 살았던 환경에서는 생활 속에 위험이 가득했는데, 명백한 약탈자들로부터의 위험뿐 아니라 다양한 미생물, 바이러스 그리고 독소로부터의 위험도 있었다. 조상들이 채집과 수집 그리고 사냥을 통해 얻은 음식들은 아주 '자연 상태 그대로의 것'이어서 결코 건강에 좋지 못했다. 많은 식물들은 위험한 독소들로 가득하고 죽은 동물들 또한 그렇다. 또한 많은 동물들은 인체 안에서 삶에 쉽게 적응하는 병원균들을 지니고 있다. 그 위험은 인간 같은 '잡식성 동물' 종(種)의 경우 특히 높은데, 잡식성이란 굉장히 다양한 원천에서 영양분을 찾고, 먹는 음식을 바꿈으로써 새로운 환경에 적응하는 그런 종을 말한다. 잡식성이 되려면 대부분의 다른 종처럼 면역 방어기제를 갖고 있어야 할 뿐 아니라 오염과 감염의 위험을 최소화하기 위해 특정한 인식을 적응시킬 줄 알아야 한다. 쥐들도 또한 잡식성인데, 이 점은 새로운 음식에 대한 그들의 대단히 조심스러운 접근과 새로운 음식과 다양한 신체 질병들 사이의 상호관련성을 빨리 간파하는 방식에서 드러난다. 쥐들은 그런 관련성을 음식 이외의 것이 관련된 상호관련성보다 더 잘 간파한다. 이것은 그러한 추론을 낳는 인식체계가 정말 특화되어 있다는 것을 보여주는 것이다.

TEST 11

Passage 1

시간의 글 전개를 파악하도록 한다.

1. 1) If a patient became ill with a fever in the eighteenth century, a surgeon might prescribe leeches. ① Several of these glossy black worms would be placed on the patient's body, where they would puncture the skin and draw small amounts of blood. If the doctor thought that the patient should be drained of more blood than leeches could drink, he would next turn to bloodletting, which involved cutting a vein and allowing ounces or even whole pints of blood to flow from the body, often until the patient fainted.

2. 1) **During the Civil War**, physicians sometimes treated a soldier's open wound by putting maggots, the wormlike larvae of flies, directly onto the patient's damaged flesh. ① If a patient complained of intestinal problems, the physician might order him to eat dirt.

3. 1) Do you shudder when you think of such revolting remedies? Are you relieved that advances in medical knowledge have put a stop to these kinds of barbaric treatments? ① You may be surprised to know that scientists have discovered that many of these old cures actually work; in some cases, they are actually more effective than other, more modern techniques. ② As a result, a number of disgusting medical remedies are making a comeback in today's hospitals.

4. 1) Because leeches offer so many benefits, doctors are again beginning to use them for bloodletting. Leeches are proving to be particularly useful after surgeries involving the reattachment of severed body parts. When areas swell with congested blood, leeches are applied to relieve the pressure by sucking up the blood. ① Ⓐ Leech saliva contains a natural anesthetic, so the bite is pain free. Ⓑ The saliva also contains substances that prevent bacteria from infecting the wound area and cause blood vessels to open wider. Therefore, the worms promote the circulation of blood necessary for healing. Ⓒ Leech saliva also contains a chemical that keeps blood from clotting. Thus the creatures also have been used to unclog blood vessels during heart surgery.

중심소재: 거머리 치료법

1. 첫 번째 문단

1) 도입부

18세기에 거머리를 활용하여 환자를 치료

① 구체적 진술

치료 방법을 자세히 상술하고 있다.

2. 두 번째 문단

1) 남북전쟁 당시 구더기를 활용하여 상처를 치료함

① 치료방법 상술

3. 세 번째 문단

1) 현대인의 관점에서 지금까지 언급한 치료방법이 이상할 수 있지만 현대 과학은 이러한 치료법이 실제 효과가 있음을 발견했다는 내용이 기술되고 있다(①).

② 현상(요지)

많은 병원들이 실제 활용

4. 네 번째 문단

1) 단락주제문(②의 뒷받침 내용)

거머리의 봉합수술에 아주 유용함

① 뒷받침 근거

거머리 침의 특성

Ⓐ 천연마취제

Ⓑ 박테리아 예방 물질 함유
치료에 필요한 혈액순환을 활발하게 만든다.

Ⓒ 피의 응고를 막는 물질 함유
심장 수술 동안 혈관이 막히지 않도록 하는 데 활용된다.

정답 1 (B) 2 (C) 3 (A)

해설

1 거머리, 구더기, 흙은 과거에 의사들이 병을 치료하기 위해 쓰인 방법으로 언급되었지만 "박테리아"는 상처 부위를 감염시키는 요인으로 설명하고 있으며 치료법(remedies)으로 언급하지는 않고 있다.

2 이 글에서는 과거 특정 치료방식을 소개하는 글이다. 비록 이런 치료 방식이 야만적으로 보일지라도 과학연구에서 효과가 있는 것으로 드러나, 현대에 들어서 다시 사용되고 있다는 현상을 설명하는 글이다.

3 거머리의 침은 수술 후에 사용되는데, 통증이 없으며 박테리아를 막아주는 화학성분을 가지고 있다는 것은 인간에게 beneficial하다고 볼 수 있다.

지문해석

18세기에는 환자가 열병을 앓게 되면 외과의사는 아마도 거머리를 처방했을 것이다. 이 광택이 나는 검은 색 벌레 몇 마리가 환자의 몸 위에 놓여서, 피부를 찌르고 적은 양의 피를 흡수했다. 만약에 의사가 거머리가 흡수할 수 있는 것보다 더 많은 피를 환자가 배출해야 한다고 생각하면 의사는 그 다음으로 방혈이라는 방법을 사용하는데, 이는 혈관을 잘라서 몇 온스의 피나 심지어는 몇 파인트의 피가 몸에서 흘러나오도록 하는 것이었으며, 종종 환자가 의식을 잃을 때까지 유지한다.

남북전쟁 동안에 의사들은 때때로 벌레처럼 생긴 파리의 유충인 구더기를 직접 환자의 부상을 당한 살 위에 올려놓아 병사들의 벌어진 상처를 치료했다. 만약에 환자가 내장의 문제가 있다고 호소하면 의사들은 흙을 먹으라고 지시했을 것이다.

이와 같은 혐오스러운 치료를 생각할 때 소름이 끼치는가? 의학 지식의 진보가 이런 야만적인 치료를 멈추게 했다는 것에 안도되어 지는가? 당신은 과학자들이 이런 많은 오래된 치료법(논란이 되었던)이 실제로 효과가 있다는 것을 발견했다는 사실을 알게 되면 놀랄지도 모른다. 몇몇 경우에는 실제로 다른 현대적인 기술보다 더 효과가 있다. 그 결과, 많은 혐오스러운 의학 치료법이 오늘날 병원에서 다시 시행되고 있다. 거머리는 굉장히 많은 이득이 있으므로, 의사들은 다시 방혈을 위해 거머리를 쓰기 시작하고 있다. 거머리는 절단된 몸 부위를 다시 붙이는 수술 후에 특히 유용한 것으로 드러나고 있다. 부위가 응혈된 피로 부풀어 오르면 거머리는 피를 빨아드림으로써 압력을 완화시키는 데 사용된다. 거머리의 침에는 자연적인 마취 성분이 들어있어서 물리는 데 있어 고통이 수반되지 않는다. 그 침은 또한 박테리아가 상처부위를 감염시키는 것을 막고 혈관을 더 넓어지게 해주는 물질을 포함하고 있다. 따라서 그 벌레들은 치료에 있어 필수적인 피의 순환을 증진시킨다. 거머리 침은 또한 혈액이 응고하는 것을 막아주는 화학 성분을 포함하고 있다. 따라서 이 생물은 심장수술을 하는 동안 혈관이 막히지 않게 하는 데 사용되어 왔다.

Passage 2

Noam Chomsky가 제시한 "Plato's Problem"에 관한 글로 아이들이 언어를 어떻게 습득하게 되는지를 다루는 내용이다.

1. 1) Noam Chomsky gave the name "Plato's Problem" to the general problem of how we come to know things in conditions of sparse evidence. As Chomsky has shown over the years, this problem arises sharply in the case of language. ① In linguistics, Plato's Problem is understood to be the problem of explaining how a grammar can be acquired under conditions of poverty of the stimulus.

2. 1) Plato's Problem refers to the gap between experience and knowledge. ① To close the gap, we need to either show that Ⓐ learners have more experience than we thought, or that Ⓑ they have some knowledge from another source.

중심소재: Plato's Problems in Linguistics

1. 첫 번째 문단

1) 도입부 = 소재도출

부족한 정보의 상황에서 세상을 이해하게 되는 Plato's Problems가 언어학에서 이러한 문제점이 대두됨

① 언어학적 의미

언어적 자극의 부재 상황에서 문법을 습득하게 됨

2. 두 번째 문단

앞에서 언급한 언어학적 의미를 두 번째 문단에서 더욱 깊이 다루고 있다.

TEST 11

본문의 내용을 통해 촘스키는 생성언어학자임을 파악할 수 있다.

2) Plato took the second approach: learning is but recollection of knowledge we acquired in a previous life. ① Generative linguists have adopted a version of this solution; that is, to provide the learner with innate knowledge in the form of principles of Universal Grammar (UG). By restricting the set of hypotheses that a learner can formulate, it overcomes, at least to some extent, the poverty of the stimulus, and in this fashion provides a partial solution to Plato's Problem

1) Plato's Problems의 간략한 정의
경험과 지식의 차로 경험할 수 있는 언어적 정보가 적음에도 아이들은 언어를 배운다는 뜻
① 언어학적 의미
Ⓐ 아이들은 우리가 생각하는 것보다 더 많은 언어 경험을 한다.
Ⓑ 경험이 아닌 다른 원천에서 지식을 습득
2) 플라톤의 경우 두 번째
이전의 삶에서 얻은 지식을 회상
① 생성언어학자
아이들은 UG라는 형태로 언어를 배울 수 있는 내재적 지식을 가지고 태어난다는 플라톤의 접근법을 받아들임

정답 1 (C) 2 (C) 3 (C)

해설

1 본문 마지막 부분에서 생성언어학자들은 학습자들이 보편문법이라는 원칙을 가지고 태어난다고 보았으므로 선택지 (C)가 정답이다. "Generative linguists have adopted a version of this solution; that is, to provide the learner with innate knowledge in the form of principles of Universal Grammar (UG)."부분을 참고한다.

2 본문에서 언급하고 있는 플라톤의 문제는 언어학습이 외부의 자극(언어적 입력)이 반드시 필요하다는 내용이 아니라 언어를 배울 수 있는 능력을 내재하고 있다는 내용이므로 선택지 (C)는 옳지 않다.

3 To close the gap, we need to either show that learners have more experience than we thought, or that they have some knowledge from another source.로 보아 언어학습은 경험 또는 지식 경험 외 지식 즉, 내재적 언어적 지식이 필요하다는 내용이므로 선택지 (C)가 옳다. (A)의 경우, 보편문법은 외부 자극이 아니라 내적 지식과 관련되므로 옳지 않다. 본문에서 지식과 경험을 위해선 언어가 필수라는 내용은 없다. 선택지 (B)도 옳지 않으며, 글의 도입부에서 최근 대두된 언어적 문제는 플라톤 문제와 연관성이 있으므로 선택지 (D)도 옳지 않다.

지문해석

Noam Chomsky는 정보가 거의 없는 상황에서 지식을 얻는 (come to know things) 방법이 지니는 일반적 문제들을 Plato's Problem이라 불렀다. Chomsky가 수십 년에 걸쳐 입증한 바대로 이 문제는 특히 언어학에서 두드러진다. 언어학에서 Plato's Problem은 인간이 자극(정보입력)이 없는 상황에서도 문법체계를 획득하는 방식을 설명하는 문제이다.

즉, Plato's Problem은 경험과 지식 사이의 간극을 의미한다. 그 간극을 좁히기 위해서는 학습자가 생각보다 많은 경험을 지녔다는 것을 보여주거나 다른 경로를 통해 지식을 이미 갖췄음을 보여주어야 한다. Plato는 두 번째 접근법을 택했다: 학습이란 전생에 배운 지식을 회상하는 것에 불과하다. 발생언어학자들은 이러한 플라톤식 해결책을 채택했다; 즉, 학습자에게 일반문법(Universal Grammar) 원리라는 선험적 지식을 부여한 것이다. 학습자가 만들어낼 수 있는 가설의 수를 제한함으로써 일반문법은 자극(정보)의 부족을 극복하게 해주고 Plato's Problem을 해결한다.

Passage 3

1. Grown people know that they do not always know the why of things, and even if they think they know, they do not know where and how they got the proof. 1) ① Hence the irritation they show when children keep on demanding to know if a thing is so and how the grown folks got the proof of it. It is so troublesome Ⓐ because it is disturbing to the pigeonhole way of life. ② It is upsetting Ⓐ because until the elders are pushed for an answer, they have never looked to see if it was so, nor how they came by what passes for proof to their acceptances of certain things as true. 2. So, if Ⓐ telling their questioning young to run off and play does not suffice for an answer, Ⓑ a good swat on the child's bottom is held to be proof positive for anything from spelling "Constantinople" to why the sea is salty. It was told to the old folks and that had been enough for them.

중심소재: 호기심

1. 도입부

호기심 많은 아이들의 질문에 대한 어른들의 성향을 제시하고 있다.

1) 구체적 진술

①짜증을 낸다.

Ⓐ부연근거

irritation한 이유가 언급되고 있다.

②마음이 괴롭다.

Ⓐ부연근거

2. 어른들의 대안

Ⓐ telling the young to run off and play

Ⓑ a good swat on the child's bottom.

정답 1 (C)

지문분석

글 전반에 걸쳐 호기심 많은 아이에 대한 어른들의 반응에 대한 충분한 근거를 제시하면서도, 유희적 요소를 섞어가면서 비판적으로 바라보고 있다.

해설

저자는 아이들의 숱한 질문들에 당황하고 귀찮아하는 어른들의 태도를 이해하면서도 그다지 바람직한 행동이라고 생각하지는 않는다. 마지막에서 두 번째 문장은 playful한 분위기를 잘 보여주고 있다.

지문해석

성인들은 그들이 어떤 일들의 원인을 항상 알 수는 없다는 사실을 알고 있으며, 그들이 안다고 생각할 때조차도 그들이 어디서 어떻게 근거를 얻는지 모른다. 그래서 성인들은 어린이들이 왜 어떤 것이 그러한지, 어른들이 거기에 대해서 어떻게 근거를 댈 건지 계속 물으면 짜증을 내기도 한다. 그것은 정리해놓은 삶의 방식을 혼란시키기 때문에 그렇게 골치 아픈 것이다. 그것이 이렇게 귀찮은 이유는 어른들이 대답하도록 압력을 받기 전까지는 그게 그랬었는지 여부나 어떻게 그것을 사실로 수용하게 하는 증거들이 그러한 증거가 됐는지 알려고 시도하지 않았었기 때문이다. 그래서 캐묻기 좋아하는 아이들에게 나가서 놀라고 말하는 것이 충분한 대답이 되지 않는다면, 아이들에게 콘스탄티노플의 스펠링부터 왜 바닷물이 짠지에 대한 자신 있는 증거 대신 아이의 볼기짝을 실컷 두들겨 주는 것이 효과적이다. 이것이 어른들이 들어온 것이고, 그들에게는 충분했었다.

Passage 4

1. 1) On Feb, **2.** 2007, the United Nations scientific panel studying climate change declared that the evidence of a warming trend is unequivocal, and that human activity has "very likely" been the driving force in that change over the last 50 years. ① The last report by the group, the Intergovernmental Panel on Climate Change, in 2001, found that humanity had "likely" played a role.

2. 1) The addition of that single word "very" did more than reflect mounting scientific evidence that ① the release of carbon dioxide and other heat-trapping gases from smokestacks, tailpipes and burning forests has played a central role in raising the average surface temperature of the earth by more than I degree Fahrenheit since 1900.

3. 1) It also added new momentum to a debate that now seems centered less over whether humans are warming the planet, but instead over what to do about it. ① In recent months, Ⓐ business groups have banded together to make unprecedented calls for federal regulation of greenhouse gases. Ⓑ The subject had a red-carpeted moment when former Vice President Al Gore's documentary, "An Inconvenient Truth," was awarded an Oscar; and the Supreme Court made its first global warming-related decision, ruling 5 to 4 that the Environmental Protection Agency had not justified its position that it was not authorized to regulate carbon dioxide.

4. 1) The greenhouse effect has been part of the earth's workings since its earliest days. Gases like carbon dioxide and methane allow sunlight to reach the earth, but prevent some of the resulting heat from radiating back out into space. Without the greenhouse effect, the planet would never have warmed enough to allow life to form. But as ever larger amounts of carbon dioxide have been released along with the development of industrial economies, the atmosphere has grown warmer at an accelerating rate: since 1970, temperatures have gone up at nearly three times the average for the 20th century.

중심소재: 온난화 현상

1. 첫 번째 문단

1) 도입부 현상

온난화는 분명한 추세이며, 그 원인은 "인간의 인위적 활동"일 가능성이 농후

① 뒷받침 근거

2001년의 보고서(likely)

2. 두 번째 문단

1) 현상의 원인

① 인간의 인위적 활동이 온도 변화의 주된 원인

3. 세 번째 문단

1) 새로운 쟁점

이제는 온난화의 주범을 밝히는 논의가 아닌 구체적 대안이 논의의 쟁점이 되고 있음

① 뒷받침 근거(Ⓐ, Ⓑ)

엘 고어의 다큐를 소개하면서 온실가스에 대한 정부의 규제 강화가 옳음을 정당화하고 있다.

4. 네 번째 문단

1) 현상의 배경

온실효과가 생명에 필요한 자연의 기능이지만, 인간의 인위적 활동(산업경제 발달)으로 지나치게 많은 양이 방출되면서 지국의 온도가 급격하게 증가하게 됨

정답 **1** (E) **2** (A) **3** (E) **4** (D) **5** (B)

해설

1 이 글은 지구온난화에 대한 보고와 반응을 설명하고 있으므로 제목으로 선택지 (E)가 적절하다.

2 equivocal(모호한)은 obscure와 unequivocal(명백한)은 certain의 의미와 각각 근접하다.

3 unprecedented는 "전례 없는, 유례없는"의 뜻이다.
4 환경청이 자신들은 이산화탄소를 규제할 권한이 없다는 입장을 밝힌 것은 이산화탄소 규제의 책임을 소홀히 한 것이며 그런 입장은 정당하지 않다는 법원의 결정이 여기에 일침을 가한 것이다.
5 (B) 앨 고어의 다큐멘터리 영화의 수상으로 온실가스 규제 문제가 세간의 주목을 받았다는 것은 이 영화의 주제가 온실 가스 규제의 필요성을 널리 알리는 것임을 말해준다.

지문해석

2007년 2월 2일 기후 변화를 연구하는 유엔 과학 위원단은 온난화 추세의 증거는 명백하며 인류의 활동이 지난 50년간 기후변화에 주도적 역할을 했을 '가능성이 아주 농후'하다고 선언했다. 2001년 정부 간 기후변화 위원단의 최종 보고서는 인간이 어느 정도 역할을 했을 가능성을 밝혔다.
'아주'라는 한 단어를 덧붙인 것은 공장, 굴뚝, 자동차배기관, 그리고 산불에서 발생하는 이산화탄소와 기타 열을 가두는 기체들의 방출이 1900년 이후 지구의 평균 표면온도를 화씨 1도 이상 끌어올리는 데 핵심적인 역할을 했다는 점증하는 과학적 증거를 반영한 것 이상의 일이었다. 이는 또한 인간이 지구를 덥히고 있는지 아닌지가 아니라 이 문제에 대해 무엇을 해야 하는지에 더 큰 비중을 둔 논쟁을 촉발시키는 새로운 계기를 제공하였다. 최근 몇 달 새 기업들은 한 목소리로 온실가스에 대한 연방정부의 규제를 요청하는 유례를 찾기 어려운 요구를 하였다. 이 주제는 전 부통령 앨 고어의 다큐멘터리 영화인 불편한 진실(An Inconvenient Truth)이 오스카상을 수상하고 미 연방대법원이 미 환경청은 이산화탄소를 규제할 권한이 없다는 입장을 정당화하지 못했다고 하는 지구온난화 관련 최초의 결정을 5대 4로 내리자 세간의 주목을 받게 되었다.
온실효과는 지구의 초창기 이후로 지구 작용의 일부였다. 이산화탄소 메탄가스 같은 기체들은 햇빛이 지구에 도달하도록 허용하지만 그 결과 발생한 열의 일부가 방사되어 우주공간으로 돌아가지 못하게 막아버린다. 온실효과가 없었다면 지구는 결코 생명체가 형성되는 데 충분할 만큼 데워지지 못했을 것이다. 그러나 산업 경제가 발달하면서 이산화탄소의 배출량이 늘어남에 따라 대기는 점점 더 빠른 속도로 따뜻해져 왔다. 1970년 이래 기온은 20세기 평균 상승률의 거의 3배로 상승했다.

Passage 5

1. Characterization in a play is based almost entirely on action and dialogue. 1) Action can include such subtle devices as a gesture or a change of expression, and dialogue can include a monologue that resembles the expression of thoughts and feelings. In a play, the role of costuming is also important. **But** the major impression of a character on stage is made by what that character does and what he or she says to others. ① Compare this with the devices available in fiction. In that more flexible genre you as author can use the character's own thoughts, the thoughts of others, quick glimpses into the past through flashbacks, and direct exposition. Since the devices available to the dramatist are more limited, the tendency is to use them more boldly. Audiences are used to this. Ⓐ Just as the makeup is heavier, the voice louder, characterization is applied more bluntly in a play. It seems natural to use the word 'theatrical' to describe individuals whose personalities are vivid and striking.

중심소재: 연극의 성격묘사

1. 도입부 = 주제문
성격묘사는 주로 행동과 대화에 기초한다.

1) 뒷받침 진술
행동과 대화의 종류 언급 후 but(강조용법) 행동과 대화가 무대 위 인물 인상의 주된 요소임을 다시 강조하고 있다.

① 이유
소설과 달리 연극에선 성격 묘사의 장치가 제한되기에 더욱 강하게 행동, 대화를 사용하는 경향이 있다.

Ⓐ 부연
화장과 목소리 등이 과장되어 표현됨.

본문은 크게 두 문단으로 나눠진다. 각 문단의 공통된 중심내용을 파악하여 주제를 설정하도록 한다. 첫 번째 문장에서 중심소재와 함께 주제문 여부를 확인한다.

TEST 11

아주 간단한 구조의 글이다. 현상 - 문제점(심각성) - 원인으로 이어지는 전형적인 시사지문의 패턴을 따르고 있다.

정답 1 (C) 2 (D)

해설

1 본문은 "연극의 성격묘사"를 다루는 글이다. 본문분석을 참조한다.

2 내용불일치 문제의 경우 선택지 중 세 개는 본문과 일치하기 때문에 경우에 따라선(특히 긴 글의 경우) 글의 중심 소재, 중심내용을 파악할 수 있는 동시에 주제까지 파악할 수 있다. 문제를 먼저 보고 지문을 보는 것이 유리한 경우이다. in that more flexible genre~에서 선택지 (A)가 옳다는 것을 알 수 있고, (B)의 경우 dialogue can include a monologue that resembles the expression of thoughts and feelings.에서 인물묘사에 독백이 사용됨을 알 수 있다. Since the devices available to the dramatist are more limited, the tendency is to use them more boldly.에서 선택지 (C)도 확인할 수 있다. Audiences are used to this. Just as the makeup is heavier, the voice louder, characterization is applied more bluntly in a play.에 비추어 볼 때 선택지 (D)는 틀린 표현이다.

지문해석

연극에서 인물의 성격묘사는 거의 몸짓과 대화로 이루어진다. 몸짓에는 동작이나 표정 변화와 같은 섬세한 장치가 포함될 수 있고 대화에는 생각이나 감정의 표현과 유사한 독백이 포함될 수 있다. 연극에서 의상의 역할 또한 중요하다. 그러나 무대에서 등장인물의 주된 인상은 그 인물이 무엇을 하는가와 그/그녀가 다른 사람에게 무슨 말을 하는가에 의해 주어진다. 이를 소설에서 쓰일 수 있는 장치들과 한 번 비교해 보자. 더 융통성 있는 장르인 소설에서, 작가인 당신은 등장인물 자신의 생각, 다른 사람의 생각, 플래시백을 하여 과거 사건을 빠르게 들여다보기, 직접 설명하기 등의 장치를 사용할 수 있다. 극작가가 사용할 수 있는 장치가 더 제한적이기 때문에 그들은 이러한 장치들을 더 과감히 사용하려는 경향이 있다. 관객은 이런 경향에 익숙하다. 분장이 더 짙고 목소리가 더 커짐에 따라 연극에서 인물의 성격묘사는 더 직설적이고 솔직하게 행해진다. 성격이 뚜렷하고 두드러지는 사람들에게 연극적이라는 표현을 쓰는 것은 당연해 보인다.

Passage 6

1. Among the world's 6,800 tongues, half to 90 percent could become extinct by the end of the century, linguists predict. 1) ① One reason is because half of all languages are spoken by fewer than 2,500 people each. Languages need at least 100,000 speakers to survive the ages, says UNESCO. ② War, genocide, fatal natural disasters, the adoption of more dominant languages such as Chinese and Russian, and government bans on languages also contribute to their demise. "In some ways it's similar to what threatens species," said Payal Sampat, a researcher who wrote about the issue for the May-June magazine of Worldwatch Institute. He added that Udihe and Arikapu, spoken in Siberia and the Amazon jungle, are also among those that are at risk.

중심소재: 언어

1. 도입부 = 현상의 전망

90%의 반의 언어가 곧 살아질 것이다.

1) 뒷받침 근거

①이유 1

②이유 2

정답 1 (B) 2 (E)

해설

1 밑줄 친 the issue는 endangered languages(멸종 위기에 처한 언어들)를 가리킨다.

2 네 번째 문장에서 정부의 금지정책이 소수 언어들의 소멸을 야기한다(War, genocide, fatal natural disasters, the adoption of more dominant languages such as Chinese and Russian, and government bans on languages also contribute to their demise.)고 언급되어 있다.

지문해석

전 세계 6,800개 언어들 중에서, 50에서 90퍼센트의 언어들은 금세기 말까지 사어(死語)가 될 것이라고 언어학자들은 예측한다. 한 가지 이유는 모든 언어들 중에서 절반에 달하는 언어들이 2500명도 안 되는 사람들에 의해서만 사용되기 때문이다. 언어가 오랫동안 살아남기 위해서는 적어도 10만 명 이상의 사람들이 그 언어를 사용해야 한다고 유네스코(Unesco)는 전한다. 전쟁, 집단 학살, 치명적 자연재해, 중국어나 러시아어와 같은 보다 우세한 언어들의 사용, 그리고 군소 언어들에 대한 중앙 정부의 금지방침 등이 그 언어들을 사라지게 한다. "어떤 점에서 그것은 종의 멸종 위협과 유사하다"라고 세계 감시 협회(Worldwatch Institute)의 5-6월호 잡지에 그 주제에 대한 글을 기고한 한 연구자인 페이얼 삼파트(Payal Sampat)는 말했다. 시베리아 지역에서 사용되는 우디히어(Udihe)와 아마존 정글에서 사용되는 아리카푸어(Arikapu) 또한 위험에 처한 언어들에 속한다고 그는 덧붙였다.

Passage 7

1. After failures, backers of Africa aid have changed their tune. **1)** Twenty years ago, rock star Bob Geldof raised money with his Live Aid rock concert to help famine victims in Ethiopia. He has since realized that helping Africa is a far more complex business. ① Much of the money was mismanaged or pocketed by corrupt officials.
2) Geldof's weekend Live 8 concerts to help Africa had a wiser and more realistic aim. ① They focused on raising awareness and pressuring the leaders of wealthy nations — the Group of Eight (G8). ② After decades of tossing money at Africa, international organizations are coming to the conclusion, as Geldof has, that more calibrated and sophisticated approaches are needed. Just what those approaches might be are, as yet, unclear. Ⓐ Even so, besides giving generously, three elements seem to be crucial. The G8 would do well to emphasize them, as the World Bank increasingly has: debt cancellation, good governance, and self sufficiency, Africa needs help.
2. It is home to 13% of the world's population and a third of the people in extreme poverty. Incomes are lower than those 30 years ago. Thirteen million have died of AIDS; 26 million are infected. It incubates international disease and terrorism. Realistic help, however, means more than rock concerts and handouts.

중심소재: 아프리카 원조

1. 도입부
아프리카 원조의 방향 선회

1) 기존의 방법
락 콘서트를 통해서 이디오피아의 기근피해자 원조

① 문제점
부패한 관료로 인해 기금이 잘못 운영되거나 이들의 손에 들어감

2) 방향전환
좀 더 현실적인 목적과 방안

① 원조에 대한 G8 지도자들의 인식증가와 압력

② 국제단체
좀 더 정교한 접근 필요
- Ⓐ 원조와 함께 고려해야 할 중요한 요소
- ⓐ 빚 청산
- ⓑ 바른 정부운영
- ⓒ 자급자족

2. 요약정리
아프리카의 심각한 상황을 기술하면서 세계 원조의 필요성과 함께 음악을 통한 기금마련과 원조만으로 부족함을 강조하고 있다.

정답 1 (D) 2 (B) 3 (A)

TEST 11

해설

1 글의 도입부에서 기존의 아프리카 원조가 실패하면서 그 방향을 바꾸었다고 하고 있다. Much of the money was mismanaged or pocketed by corrupt officials.에서 알 수 있듯이 기존의 아프리카 원조가 제대로 이루어지지 않은 것을 파악하고, a wiser and more realistic aim한 방향으로 선회했다고 했으므로 선택지 (D)는 옳은 진술이다.

2 The G8 would do well to emphasize them, (as the World Bank increasingly has): debt cancellation, good governance, and self sufficiency에서 순접부연 중 나열을 이끄는 콜론을 활용하여 them은 밑줄 친 세 가지 사항을 지칭함을 알 수 있으므로, 정답은 three elements가 됨을 알 수 있다.

3 Thirteen million have died of AIDS; 26 million are infected. It incubates international disease and terrorism. Realistic help, however, means more than rock concerts and handouts.에서 알 수 있듯이 아프리카의 심각한 상황에 실질적인 도움이 되는지가 관건이다.

지문해석

몇 번의 실패 끝에 아프리카 원조의 후원자들은 그들의 방식을 바꿨다. 20년 전 록 스타인 밥 겔도프(Bob Geldof)는 에티오피아의 기근 희생자들을 돕기 위한 라이브 에이드(Live Aid) 록 공연으로 기금을 모금했다. 이후 그는 아프리카를 돕는 것이 훨씬 더 복잡한 일이라는 것을 깨닫게 되었다. 대부분의 돈이 부패한 공무원들에 의해 잘못 운용되거나 착복되었던 것이다. 겔도프의 아프리카를 돕기 위한 주말 라이브 8(Live 8) 공연은 좀 더 현명하고 현실적인 목표를 갖게 되었다. 그들은 인식을 제고하고 부유한 국가들(이른바 G8)에 압력을 가하는 일에 중점을 두었다. 수십 년 동안 아프리카를 금전적으로 도운 후 국제기구들은 겔도프가 그랬던 것처럼 결론에 이르렀는데 더욱 정확히 조정된 정교한 접근들이 필요하다는 것이었다. 그 접근이 무엇인지는 현재로서 분명하지 않다. 그럼에도 후하게 베푸는 것 외에 3가지 요소가 중요하다고 보인다. 세계은행이 점차 그런 것처럼 G8 국가들도 이 3가지를 강조하는 것이 당연할 텐데 그것은 부채 탕감, 훌륭한 통치, 자급자족이다. 아프리카는 도움이 필요하다. 그곳은 전 세계 인구의 13 퍼센트가 살아가는 곳이고 그들 중 3분의 1이 지독한 가난에 처해있다. 소득은 30년 전보다 낮다. 1300만 명이 에이즈로 사망했고 2600만 명이 감염된 상태다. 그곳은 국제적인 질병과 테러를 배양하고 있다. 그러나 실질적인 도움은 록 공연과 지원금 이상을 의미한다.

Passage 8

1. Few creatures are held in such awe as lions, tigers, cheetahs and leopards, which we often call the big cats. 1) ① Ⓐ These agile predators have strong, razor-sharp teeth and claws, muscular bodies and excellent senses. Their beautiful striped and dappled fur camouflages among the trees, allowing them to leap from the shadows to ambush unwary zebras, giraffes and other prey. Ⓑ The first large cats lived 45 million years ago. Many, including the lion, cheetah and leopard still inhabit parts of Africa. Snow leopards dwell in the mountains of Asia. Jaguars are the largest of the big cats in North and South America. They are equally at home swimming in lakes or climbing in trees.
2. 1) Lions are the only big cats that ① live in groups called

중심소재: 큰 고양이과와 사자

1. 첫 번째 문단

1) 도입부

큰 고양이과에 속하는 동물을 언급하고 있다.

① 구체적 진술

Ⓐ 내외적 특성

Ⓑ 종에 따라 다양한 지역에 분포

"prides," which may be up to thirty in total. ② The pride roams over an area of 100km^2 or more, depending on the abundance of prey in that area. ③ The large male lion protects the pride's territory against other prides. The lion also defends the female against other males. ④ Lions, tigers and other big cats are true carnivores. Ⓐ Lions usually eat large prey such as antelopes and zebras. One giraffe is often enough to feed a whole pride of lions.

2. 두 번째 문단
큰고양이과 중 특히 사자의 특징을 다루고 있다.

1) 구체적 진술
① 유일하게 prides라 불리는 집단 생활
② 먹이의 풍부함을 따라 광범위한 지역을 돌아다님
③ 우두머리 수컷 사자는 다른 집단에 저항해 영토를 지키고 다른 수컷이 자신의 암컷을 넘보지 못하게 함
④ 엄청난 육식동물
Ⓐ 부연

정답 1 (B) 2 (C)

해설

1 뒤에 이어지는 내용을 보면, "영양이나 얼룩말과 같은 먹이를 먹는다"고 했으므로 육식성 동물임을 파악할 수 있다.

2 큰 고양이과 동물들은 줄무늬와 얼룩 털로 그들의 먹이를 끈다고 한 것은 그 글 앞에 위장하기 위한 것이라는 내용과 맞지 않다.

지문해석

사자, 호랑이, 치타, 그리고 표범과 같이 경외심을 갖게 되는 동물은 거의 없는데 이것을 우리는 종종 큰 고양이과라고 부른다. 이런 민첩한 육식동물들은 강하고, 면도날처럼 날카로운 이빨, 발톱, 근육질의 몸 그리고 뛰어난 감각들을 갖고 있다. 그들의 아름다운 줄무늬와 얼룩진 털은 나무들 사이에서 위장해주고, 그들이 의식하지 못하는 얼룩말, 기린과 다른 먹이를 잠복해서 어둠으로부터 뛰어 오르는 것을 허락하게 해 준다. 최초의 큰 고양이과 동물들은 4천 5백만년 전에 살았다. 사자를 포함해서 많은 치타와 표범은 여전히 아프리카의 여러 지역에 살고 있다. 눈표범은 아시아의 산악지역에 살고 있다. 재규어는 북미와 남미의 큰 고양이과들 중에서 가장 크다. 그것들은 편하게 호수에서 헤엄치고 나무를 오르는 것에서 똑같다. 사자는 "사자떼"라고 불리워지는 무리를 지어 사는 유일한 큰 고양이과 동물인데 이것은 전체적으로 30마리까지 될 수 있다. 사자떼는 100km^2 혹은 그 이상의 지역에 걸쳐 돌아다니는데 이것은 그 지역에 있는 먹이의 풍부함에 달려있다. 큰 수사자는 다른 사자떼에 대항해서 자기 사자떼의 영역을 보호해 준다. 사자는 또한 다른 수컷들에 대해 암컷들을 지켜준다. 사자, 호랑이, 그리고 다른 큰 고양이과 동물들은 진짜 육식성이다. 사자들은 보통 영양이나 얼룩말과 같은 큰 먹이를 먹는다. 한 마리의 얼룩말은 종종 전체 사자떼를 먹일 수 있을 만큼 충분하다.

TEST 12

Passage 1

1. It's not easy being a mother these days. 1) ① Most work outside the home in addition to their parenting duties. Because of the high divorce rate, many are rearing their children alone or with only part-time help from fathers, Ⓐ In 2001, an ABC News columnist did some research suggesting that if you paid mothers for all the things they do, they would draw down about $500,000 a year. ② Moms face a daunting task, whether they have other jobs or not. Ⓐ First, they must make their way through a labyrinth of advice based on vast amounts of research, much of it conflicting. Ⓑ Whatever they do, they're bound to find some study that says they did the wrong thing, didn't do the right thing, or otherwise somehow permanently damaged their offspring. Ⓒ Then there's the whole problem of keeping their children healthy amidst an incessant barrage of messages seducing them to eat more sugar-and fat-loaded snack foods. Ⓓ And of teaching them values in a society that worships materialism. Ⓔ And of helping them find a path through a world filled with diverse beliefs, an overabundance of knowledge and information, and moral ambiguity.

중심소재: A job as a mother

1. 도입부 = 주제문
어머니가 된다는 것은 쉽지 않다고 말하고 있다(현상).

1) 뒷받침 근거

① 일을 하는 동시에 이혼으로 인해 홀로 아이와 일을 병행
 Ⓐ 뒷받침 부연
 구체적 연구를 통해 어머니가 하는 일이 얼마나 많고 힘든지 강조하고 있다.

② 추가적 이유
 Ⓐ 상충하는 지나치게 많은 조언의 홍수
 Ⓑ 부모의 잘못한 점만을 강조하는 연구 보고서
 Ⓒ 설탕과 지방이 가득한 스낵으로 인해 아이의 건강한 식습관 유지가 쉽지 않음
 Ⓓ 물질주의를 숭배하는 사회적 가치 속에서 아이에게 바른 길을 제시하는 어려움
 Ⓔ 지나치게 다양한 신념, 지식의 홍수 그리고 흔들리는 도덕성 속에서 아이를 지도해야 하는 어려움

정답 1 (B) 2 (D)

지문분석

첫 번째 문장에서 알 수 있듯이, '힘겨운 어머니란 직업'을 다루고 있다. 이후 이러한 현상(결과)에 대한 이유를 본문 끝까지 다양한 측면에서 제시하고 있다.

해설

1 전체적으로 "힘겨운 어머니"에 대해 "동정심"을 느낄 수 있다. 선택지 (B)가 가장 적절하다.

2 "힘겨운 어머니라는 직업"의 주제를 가장 잘 전달하는 선택지는 (D)이다.

지문해석

요즘 엄마로 사는 것은 쉬운 일이 아니다. 대부분의 어머니는 아이를 돌보는 임무에 더해 집 밖에서 일을 한다. 이혼율이 높아서, 많은 어머니들은 아이를 홀로 키우거나 아이의 아버지로부터 일부 시간만 도움을 받을 뿐이다. 2001년 ABC뉴스의 한 칼럼니스트가 만약 어머니들이 하는 모든 일에 비용을 지불한다면 어머니는 1년에 50만 달러를 급료로 받게 될 것이라는 내용의 연구를 했다. 어머니들은 다른 직업이 있든 없든 간에 엄청난 업무에 맞닥뜨리게 된다. 먼저, 어머니들은 미로와 같이 복잡한 조언들의 홍수를 헤쳐 나가야 한다. 이러한 조언들은 상당한 양의 연구에 그 기반을 두고 있지만 대부분이 서로 상충하는 조언들이다. (따라서) 어머니들은 무엇을 하든지, 자신이 잘못하고 있다거나, 올바른 일을 하지 않고 있다거나, 혹은 자녀에게

영구적인 장애를 주고 있다고 말하는 연구와 마주할 수밖에 없다. 그리고 아이들에게 더욱 설탕과 지방으로 가득한 간식거리를 먹으라고 유혹하면서 끊임없이 빗발치며 날아드는 (광고) 메시지 속에서 아이들의 건강을 유지해야 하는 문제도 있다. 또한 물질주의를 숭배하는 사회에서 아이들에게 가치 있는 것을 가르쳐야 하는 문제도 있다. 게다가 다양한 믿음과, 과도한 지식과 정보, 도덕적으로 확실치 않은 것들로 가득한 세상을 헤쳐 나가는 길을 찾도록 아이를 인도해야 하는 문제도 있다.

Passage 2

1. 1) The general key to effective listening in interpersonal situations is to listen actively. Perhaps the best preparation for active listening is to act physically and mentally like an alert listener. For many people, this may be the most abused rule of effective listening. ① Recall, for example, how your body almost automatically reacts to important news: Almost immediately, you assume an upright posture and remain relatively still and quiet. You do this almost reflexively because this is the way you listen most effectively. Even more important than this physical alertness is mental alertness.

2. 2) ① As a listener, participate in the communication as an equal partner with the speaker, as one who is emotionally and intellectually ready to engage in the sharing of meaning. ② Active listening is expressive. Let the listener know that you are participating in the communication process. ③ Nonverbally, maintain eye contact, focus your concentration on the speaker rather than on others present, and express your feeling facially. Verbally, ask appropriate questions, signal understanding with "I see" or "yes," and express agreement or disagreement as appropriate. Passive listening is, however, not without merit.

3. 3) ① Passive listening—listening without talking or directing the speaker in any obvious way—is a powerful means of communicating acceptance. This is the kind of listening that people ask for when they say, "Just listen to me." They are essentially asking you to suspend your judgment and "just listen." ② Passive listening allows the speaker to develop his or her thoughts and ideas in the presence of another person who accepts but does not evaluate, who supports but does not intrude. By listening passively, you provide a supportive environment. Once that has been established, you may wish to participate in a more active way, verbally and nonverbally.

중심소재: 청취 요건

1. 첫 번째 단락

1) 효과적인 청취 요건 1

적극적 청취를 위해 육체적·정신적으로 행동

① 예시부연

2. 두 번째 단락

2) 효과적인 청취 요건 2

① 정서적이고 지적으로 대화에 참여하는 사람과 같이 화자와 동등한 파트너의 입장에서 대화에 참여

② 표현의 풍부함

③ 언어적 요소와 비언어적 요소의 활용

3. 세 번째 단락

3) 수동적 청취의 효과

① 수동적 청취의 정의

② 수동적 청취의 효과

정답 1 (A) 2 (C)

해설

1 두 번째 단락에서 적극적인 청취에 대해 자세히 설명하고 있다. 적극적인 청취에는 언어적(verbal), 비언어적(non-verbal) 수단이 모두 동원된다. 본문분석을 참조한다.

2 셋째 단락에서는 수동적인 청취가 무엇인지 정의하고 얻을 수 있는 효과는 무엇인지 설명하고 있다. 본문분석을 참조한다.

지문해석

대인관계와 관련 있는 상황에서 효과적인 경청 일반적 관건은 적극적으로 듣는 것이다. 아마도 적극적으로 청취를 하기 위한 최상의 준비는 육체적 · 정신적으로 방심하지 않는 경청자처럼 행동하는 것이다. 많은 사람들은 효과적 청취에 있어 이 규칙을 제대로 지키지 못한다. 예를 들면, 중요한 뉴스를 들었을 때 당신의 몸이 거의 자동적으로 반응하는 모습을 상기해 보아라. 거의 즉시 당신은 직립자세를 취하며 비교적 움직이지 않고 조용히 있을 것이다. 당신은 이것을 거의 반사적으로 행하는데 왜냐하면 이것이 바로 당신이 가장 효과적으로 듣는 방법이기 때문이다.

이렇게 신체적으로 면밀한 자세를 취하는 것보다 더 중요한 것은 정신적인 면밀함을 갖추는 것이다. 청취자로서, 당신은 정서적으로, 그리고 지적으로 의미를 함께 나눌 준비가 되어 있는 말하는 사람과 동등한 파트너로서 대화에 참여해야 한다. 적극적인 청취는 표현하는 것이다. 청취자에게 당신이 의사교환 과정에 참여하고 있다는 것을 알려라. 비언어적으로는(신체적으로는), 눈을 계속 맞추고, 참석한 다른 사람이 아니라 바로 화자에게 주의를 집중하며, 당신의 감정을 얼굴로 표현하라. 언어적으로는(말로는) 적절한 질문을 하고, "알겠어요" 나 "예" 라는 말로 상대방의 말을 이해했음을 알리며, 동의나 반대를 적절하게 표현해라.

그러나 수동적인 청취에도 좋은 점은 있다. 말도 하지 않고 그 어떤 명백한 방법으로도 화자의 주의를 끌지 않고 청취하는 수동적인 청취는 수락의 의미를 전달하는 강력한 수단이다. 이것은 사람들이 "그냥 내 말 좀 들어봐." 라고 말할 때 바라는 청취이다. 그들은 본질적으로 당신에게 판단을 보류하고 그냥 듣기만을 요청하고 있다. 수동적인 청취는 화자로 하여금, 수락만 하고 평가하지 않으며 지지만 하고 참견하지 않는 그런 다른 사람 앞에서 자신의 생각과 아이디어를 전개하도록 해준다. 수동적 청취는 당신을 지지하는 환경을 만들어준다. 이러한 환경이 일단 만들어지고 나면, 당신은 언어적으로나 비언어적으로나 더욱 적극적으로 대화에 참여하길 희망할 수도 있다.

Passage 3

1. The correlation observed in English between frequency of usage and etymology is not necessarily true of every language. 1) ① Some languages—German is a case in point—have traditionally turned to their own resources for enriching the vocabulary with words for more sophisticated notions or new products. Ⓐ For example, Übersetzung is equivalent to our word "translation," but it literally means "setting over." Fernsehen is equivalent to "television," but it literally means "far-seeing." Lautlehre is equivalent to "phonology," but it literally means "sound study." That is, in German, native roots are combined to form new compounds having the same meaning as the classical-based compounds. ② This method of vocabulary enrichment is

독일어와의 대조를 통해서 영어의 특징을 부각시키고 있음을 파악한다.

중심소재: 영어의 특징

1. 도입부 = 주제도출
영어에서 용례의 빈도와 어원의 관계

1) 구체적 진술
① 독일어의 경우
자신의 어근을 활용하여 새로운 언어를 만들어냄
Ⓐ 구체적 예시

② 영어의 경우
새로운 단어를 만들어낸 이러한 방법이 영어에도 존재하지만 다른 언어의 어근을 추가하면서 창조적 재사용(요지)

familiar also in English: doorbell, horseshoe, lighthouse, shorthand, stronghold are all compounds containing native elements only. However, compared to German, English has been less inventive in producing new words from its own roots; instead, it has added and creatively recycled roots from other languages.

정답 1 B) 2 C) 3 D)

해설

1 첫 번째 문장에서 언급하고 있는 영어 표현의 용례와 어원 사이의 관계가 다른 언어에 동일하게 적용되지 않는다고 하면서 그 예로 독일어를 제시하는 것이므로 선택지 (B)가 빈칸에 가장 적절하다.

2 역접을 이끄는 instead를 활용한다. 독일어 같이 자신의 뿌리에서 새로운 언어를 만들어내지 못하는 것이 영어라고 했으므로 다른 언어에서 새로운 언어를 만들어 낸다는 선택지 (C)가 빈칸에 가장 적절한 표현이다.

3 Lautlehre is equivalent to "phonology," but it literally means "sound study." That is, in German, native roots are combined to form new compounds having the same meaning as the classical-based compounds.에서 선택지 (A)는 옳다는 것을 알 수 있다. This method of vocabulary enrichment is familiar also in English: doorbell, horseshoe, lighthouse, shorthand, stronghold are all compounds containing native elements only.에서 알 수 있듯이 stronghold는 영어의 뿌리에서 형성된 단어임을 알 수 있다. Ferneshen는 Some languages have traditionally turned to their own resources for enriching the vocabulary with words for more sophisticated notions or new products의 내용에 대한 예시이므로 독일어의 뿌리에서 형성된 표현이라는 선택지 (C)도 옳다. 선택지 (D)는 첫 번째 문장과 마지막 문장과 반대되는 내용이다.

지문해석

영어에서 볼 수 있는, 빈번한 용례와 어원 사이의 상호관계는 모든 언어에서 반드시 적용되는 것은 아니다. 어떤 언어의 경우 — 독일어가 바로 현재의 논의를 잘 보여주고 있는데 — 예부터, 더욱 세련된 개념 또는 새로운 상품을 나타낼 때, 원래 있던 단어들을 사용하여 그 언어를 풍부하게 만든다. 예를 들어, Übersetzung는 우리말의 '번역'에 해당하지만, 문자 그대로의 의미는 '~위에 놓다'를 의미한다. Fernehen의 경우 'TV'이지만 이것의 문자 그대로의 의미는 '멀리 보는 것'이다. Lautlehre는 '음성학'이지만 이것은 문자적으로 '소리 연구'를 의미한다.

다시 말해 독일어에서는 원래의 어근이 결합하여, 기존의 합성어와 같은 의미를 지니는 새로운 합성어를 형성하는 것이다. 어휘를 확장하는 이런 방법은 영어에서도 흔히 찾아볼 수 있다. 현관 벨, 말발굽, 등대, 속기, 요새는 모두 기본 요소만을 포함한 합성어이다. 그러나 독일어와 비교했을 때, 영어는 자신의 뿌리에서 새로운 단어를 만들어내는 데 재능이 덜하다. 대신, 영어는 다른 언어의 어근을 더하여 창조적으로 재사용했다.

Passage 4

1. The meaning of "ethics" can seem ambiguous, and the views many people have about ethics are shaky. 1) Many people tend to see ethics as analogous to feelings. ① However, being ethical is clearly not a matter of merely following one's feelings. Ⓐ A person following his or her feelings may recoil from doing what is right. ⓐ In fact, what a person feels frequently deviates from what is ethical.
2) Nor should one identify ethics with religion. Most religions, of course, advocate high ethical standards. ① Yet if ethics were confined to religion, then ethics would apply only to religious people. However, an atheist or agnostic can maintain high ethical standards, albeit outside the realm of the traditionally religious. Conversely, a deeply religious person might engage in unethical behavior. Religion can set high ethical standards and can provide intense motivations for ethical behavior, yet ethics cannot be confined to religion nor is it the same as religion.
3) Being ethical is also not the same as passively following the law. ① The law often incorporates ethical standards to which most citizens subscribe. But laws, like feelings, can deviate from what is ethical. Ⓐ Our own pre-Civil War slavery laws and the apartheid laws once held in South Africa are grotesquely obvious examples of laws that violate what we view as ethical.

중심소재: 윤리

1. 도입부 = 중심소재 도출
모호한 윤리의 의미

1) 윤리의 특징 1
통념: 일반인들은 윤리를 감정과 비슷한 것으로 간주

① 통념비판
윤리적이란 말은 단순히 자신의 감정을 따르는 문제가 아니다.

Ⓐ 뒷받침 근거
자신의 감정을 따르다보면 오히려 옳은 일을 꺼리게 되는 경우도 생긴다.

ⓐ 부연강조(in fact)
자신의 감정을 따르는 것은 오히려 윤리적인 것에서 탈선되는 경우가 많다.

2) 윤리의 특징 2
윤리는 종교와 같지도 않다.

① 뒷받침 근거
만약 윤리가 종교적인 것이라면 윤리는 종교인에게만 해당되는 것이어야 하지만 무신론자나 불가지론자도 윤리를 잘 따르며, 오히려 종교적인 사람이 윤리적이지 않은 경우도 있다.

3) 윤리의 특징 3
윤리적이라는 것은 법을 수동적으로 따르는 것도 아니다.

① 뒷받침 근거
법도 윤리적인 것에서 벗어날 수 있다.

Ⓐ 부연 예시
시민전쟁 이전 노예제도

정답 1 (A) 2 (C) 3 (B)

해설

1 본문에서 '사람이 느끼는 대로 행동하는 것은 종종 윤리적이지 못한 것'이라고 언급되어 있기 때문에 정답은 (A)이다.

2 빈칸 ①은 "주춤거리다"의 의미에서 recoil from이고 빈칸 ③은 "동의하다"의 의미에서 subscribe to이다.

3 앞 문장은 비종교적인 사람이 윤리적일 수 있다고 했고 빈칸 다음에서는 종교적인 사람이 비윤리적일 수 있다고 했는데, 이것은 앞 문장과는 반대되는 경우를 말한 것이다. 따라서 빈칸에는 "거꾸로, 반대로"라는 뜻의 (B)가 적절하다.

지문해석

"윤리"의 의미는 모호한 것처럼 보일 수 있으며 윤리에 대한 사람들의 견해도 확실하지 않다. 많은 사람들이 윤리를 감정과 유사한 것이라고 생각한다. 그러나 윤리적이라는 것은 단순히 자신의 여러 가지 감정을 따라가는 문제는 분명 아니다. 자신의 감정을 따르는 사람들은 올바른 일을 하는 데 있어 머뭇거릴 수가 있다. 사실 사람이 느끼는 바는 종종 윤리적인 것에서 벗어나기도 한다. 또한 사람들은 윤리를 종교와 동일시해서도 안 된다. 물론 대부분의 종교에서는 높은 윤리 기준을 옹호하고 있다. 그러나 윤리를 종교에만 국한시켜 버린다면 윤리는 오로지 종교인들에게만 적용될 것이다. 하지만 무신론자나 불가지론자들도 비록 전통적으로 종교적인 영역 밖에 있긴 하지만 높은 윤리기준을 견지할 수 있다. 반대로 신앙심이 깊은 사람이 비윤리적인 행동을 할 수도 있다. 종교가 높은 윤리 기준을 설정하고 윤리적인 행동에 대한 강렬한 동기를 부여할 수 있지만, 윤리는 종교에만 국한시킬 수는 없는 것이며 또한 종교와 같을 수도 없는 것이다. 윤리적이라는 것은 또한 소극적으로 법을 준수하는 것과 동일한 것이 아니다. 법은 종종 대부분의 시민들이 동의하는 윤리 기준들을 통합하고 있다. 그러나 법도 감정처럼 윤리적인 것에서 벗어날 수 있다. 남북전쟁 이전의 미국의 노예제도 법과 남아프리카공화국에서 제정되었던 인종차별정책 법은 윤리적이라고 생각되는 것에 위배되는, 법의 괴상하리만치 명백한 예들이다.

Passage 5

1. The monopoly power of a firm refers to the extent of its control over the supply of the product that is produced by the industry of which it is a part. 1) ① The more firms there are producing and selling a given product the less control any one of the firms can exercise over industry supply. If there are enough firms in an industry so that one firm's output and its control over industry supply are insignificant, we have a market that should tend to be competitive. ② On the other hand, if there is only one firm producing and selling the product, we have a market of pure monopoly. The monopoly power of a firm in an imperfectly competitive market is greater the larger the firm's output is relative to the output of the industry as a whole. It is less the smaller the firm's output is relative to the output of the entire industry.

중심소재: 기업의 시장지배력

1. 도입부 = 정의
기업의 시장지배력: 시장 내 생산되는 제품 공급에 대한 기업의 지배력

1) 구체적 진술

① 시장지배력이↓ 경우
특정 상품을 생산하는 회사가 많으면 많을수록 그 상품에 대한 한 회사의 시장공급이 낮고, 경쟁이 심한 시장을 형성함

② 시장지배력이↑ 경우
동일 상품을 하나의 회사가 생산하여 판매할 경우 순수 독점 시장을 형성하고, 산업 전체의 생산량에 비해 특정 회사의 생산량이 크면 클수록 시장지배력이 큼

글의 도입부에서 정의되는 대상은 중심소재다.

대조의 글 전개를 확인한다.

TEST 12

정답 1 (D) 2 (C)

해설

1 특정 분야에서 다수의 회사가 존재하고, 각 회사는 그 분야의 시장 내 형성된 제품 전체공급(량)에 미치는 지배력이 적다면 독점이 없는 경쟁적인 시장이 형성될 것이다.

2 마지막 두 문장에서 알 수 있듯이 특정 회사의 제품 생산량이 그 제품이 속한 산업의 생산량과 비슷하면 그 회사의 시장 지배력이 크다고 했으므로, 시장점유율이 곧 독점을 결정짓는 요인임을 유추할 수 있다.

지문해석

한 기업의 독점력이란 그 기업이 속한 산업에 의해 생산되는 제품의 공급에 대해 그 기업이 지배하는 정도를 가리킨다. 특정 제품을 생산하고 판매하는 회사들이 많으면 많을수록 그중 어느 한 회사가 산업 전체의 공급에 대해 행사할 수 있는 지배력은 줄어든다. 어떤 산업 분야에 많은 회사들이 있어서 한 회사의 생산량과 산업 전체의 공급에 대한 그 회사의 지배력이 대단치 않다면 우리는 경쟁적 경향의 시장을 갖게 된다. 반면에 그 제품을 생산하고 판매하는 회사가 단 하나뿐이라면 우리는 순수 독점시장을 갖게 된다. 불완전 경쟁시장에서는 어떤 회사의 생산량이 전체 업계의 생산량 대비 상대적으로 크면 클수록 그 회사의 독점력은 더욱 커진다. 회사의 생산량이 전체 업계의 생산량에 비해 작으면 작을수록 그 회사의 독점력은 더 작아진다.

Passage 6

1. The Amish have steadfastly subordinated economic value to the values of religion and community. 1) What is too readily overlooked by a secular, exploitive society is that their ways of doing this are not "empty gestures" and are not "backward." ① In the first place, these ways have kept the communities intact through many varieties of hard times. ② In the second place, they conserve the land. ③ In the third place, they yield economic benefits. Ⓐ The community, the religious fellowship, has many kinds of value, and among them is economic value. It is the result of the practice of neighborliness, and of the practice of stewardship. ④ What moved me most, what I liked best, in those days we spent with Bill Yoder was the sense of the continuity of the community in his dealings with his children and in their dealings with their children.

중심소재: 아미시파 교도들의 특징

1. 도입부 = 주제문
경제적 가치보다 종교와 공동체를 더 중시함

1) 뒷받침 진술
① 고난에 잘 대처해 왔음
② 토지보존
③ 경제적 이익 추구
Ⓐ 부연
④ 공동체와의 연계성의 관점에서 자녀양육

정답 1 (C) 2 (A)

지문분석

나열의 글 전개방식을 확인한다.

해설

1 아미시파 교인들이 비록 종교와 공동체보다는 경제적 가치를 경시하긴 하지만, "많은 가치 중 경제적 가치도 있다"는 언급으로 보아 선택지 (C)는 본문과 일치한다.

2 아미시파 교인들은 공동체를 온전하게 유지하는 사람들이므로, 보수적인 사람으로 볼 수 있고, 좋은 이웃이 되고자 실천한다는 말에서 neighborly도 옳다. 땅을 보존하는 종교단체라는 점에서 선택지 (A)는 옳지 않다.

지문해석

아미시파 교인들은 변함없이 경제적 가치를 종교와 공동체보다 경시했다. 세속적이고 착취적인 사회에 의해 너무 선뜻 간과된 것은 아미시파 교인들이 경시하는 방식은 단지 "말뿐인"것도 아니었고 (공동체를) "퇴보시킨"것도 아니었다는 점이다. 첫째로 이들의 방식은 자신들의 공동체를 다양한 고난 속에서도 온전하게 유지해 왔다. 둘째로 이들은 땅을 보존했다. 셋째로 이들은 경제적 이득을 거두었다. 종교적 단체인 아미시파 공동체는 많은 가치를 갖고 있으며 그중에는 경제적 가치도 있다. 이는 좋은 이웃이 되고자 실천한 결과였으며 책무를 실천한 결과였다. 우리가 Bill Yoder와 함께 보낸 그 기간 동안 나를 가장 감동시키고 내가 가장 좋아했던 것은 그가 자신의 아이들을 다룰 때와 공동체의 사람들이 자신들의 아이들을 다룰 때 보여준 공동체 내의 연속성이었다.

Passage 7

1. The costs associated with a traditional view of masculinity are enormous, and the damage occurs at both personal and societal levels. 1) ① The belief that a boy should be tough (aggressive, competitive, and daring) can create emotional pain for him. While a few boys experience short-term success for their toughness, there is little security in the long run. Instead, it leads to a series of challenges which few, if any, boys ultimately win. Ⓐ There is no security in being at the top when so many other boys are competing for the same status. Ⓑ Toughness also leads to increased chances of stress, physical injury, and even early death. It is considered manly to take extreme physical risks and voluntarily engage in combative, hostile activities.
② The flip side of toughness—nurturance—is not a quality perceived as masculine and thus not valued. Because of this, boys and men experience a greater emotional distance from other people and few opportunities to participate in meaningful interpersonal relationships. Ⓐ Studies consistently show that fathers spend very small amounts of time interacting with their children. In addition, men report that they seldom have intimate relationships with other men. They are afraid of getting too close and don't know how to take down the walls that they have built between themselves.

중심소재: 남성다움에 대한 전통적 관점

1. 도입부 = 주제문
전통적 관점과 관련된 남성다움의 '희생'은 개인과 사회적 차원에서 발생한다.

1) 뒷받침 진술
①개인적 차원
남자는 강해야 한다는 신념은 아이에게 emotional pain을 안겨준다
Ⓐ no security in being at the top
Ⓑ stress, physical injury, and even early death

②사회적 차원
아이들은 다른 사람과 정서적 거리감을 가지게 되어 의미 있는 사람과의 사회적 관계를 유지하지 못한다.
Ⓐ 뒷받침 진술(연구)

먼저 언급된 것 먼저 기술

Both A and B
Ⓐ
Ⓑ

TEST 12

정답 1 (D) 2 (C) 3 (C)

해설

1 A and B는 A=B임을 활용한다. 앞에서 강인함의 또 다른 측면은 바로 남성다움이라 여겨지는 특징이 아니라고 했으므로 바로 뒤에 이어지는 내용도 부정적인 어감의 표현이 들어가야 한다. 선택지 (D)가 정답이다. 선택지만을 볼 때 (A), (B), (C) 모두 긍정적 어감이라는 것도 확인하도록 한다.

2 The flip side of toughness—nurturance—is not a quality perceived as masculine and thus not valued. Because of this, boys and men experience a greater emotional distance from other people and few opportunities to participate in meaningful interpersonal relationships.를 보면, toughness가 nurturance의 반대이며, 사람과의 감성적 교감이 없어 의미 있는 대인관계 형성을 어렵게 만든다고 하고 있으므로 선택지 (C)는 옳은 진술임을 알 수 있다.

3 남자 아이들을 남성답게 양육하는 논의를 개인적 차원과 사회적 차원에서 다루는 글이다.

지문해석

남자다움에 대한 전통적인 관점 때문에 치러야 하는 대가는 엄청나고 그 피해는 개인과 사회적 차원에서 나타난다. 남자 아이는 강인해야 한다는 (또한 적극적이고, 경쟁심이 강하며, 대담해야 한다는) 믿음은 아이에게 정서적인 고통을 초래할 수 있다. 몇몇 아이들은 그들의 강인함 덕분에 단기적인 성공을 맛볼 수 있지만, 장기적인 안도감은 거의 없다. 이는 오히려 일련의 도전 과제들로 이어지는데, 극히 일부의 남자 아이들만이 이를 결국 이겨낸다. 다른 많은 남자 아이들이 동등한 위치를 놓고 경쟁을 벌일 때 선두에 있다고 안심하지

못한다. 또한 강인함은 스트레스, 신체 부상, 심지어 요절의 가능성을 높일 수도 있다. 극심한 신체적 위험을 무릅쓰고 전투적이고 적대적인 활동에 자발적으로 참여하는 것은 남자답다고 여겨진다.
강인함의 반대편에 있는 양육은 남자답다고 인식되는 자질이 아니고 그래서 가치 있게 여겨지지 않는다. 이 때문에 남자 아이들과 성인 남성들은 다른 사람들로부터 더 큰 정서적 거리감을 경험하고, 의미 있는 대인 관계에 참여할 기회를 거의 갖지 못한다. 연구들은 아버지들이 자녀들과 소통하는 데 매우 적은 시간을 쓴다는 점을 일관되게 보여준다. 게다가 남성들은 다른 남성들과 좀처럼 친밀한 관계를 갖지 않는다고 보고한다. 그들은 지나치게 가까워지기를 두려워하고 그들 사이에 쌓아놓은 장벽을 허무는 방법을 알지 못한다.

Passage 8

1. 1) The owners of fishing boats do not want to admit it, but there will be virtually no fish in the seas of the world by the middle of the 21st century if current trends of gross overfishing continue, according to a major scientific study. ① Stocks have collapsed in nearly one-third of sea fisheries, and the rate of decline is accelerating.
2. 1) Writing in the journal Science, an international team of researchers says fishery decline is closely tied to a broader loss of marine biodiversity. ① Yet a greater use of protected areas could safeguard existing stocks, giving them time to replenish. Ⓐ "The way we have been using the oceans so far is that we hope and assume there will always be another species to exploit after we've completely gone through the last one," said research leader Boris Worm. "What we're highlighting is there is a finite number of stocks; we have gone through one-third, and we are going to get through the rest, unless restrictions are imposed." ⓐ One of the other scientists on the project added: "Unless we fundamentally change the way we manage all the ocean species together, as working ecosystems, then this century will be the last century when people can eat wild seafood of any kind."
3. 1) ① In 2003, 29% of the world's open sea fisheries were in a state of collapse, defined as a decline to less than 10% of their original yield. Ⓐ Bigger vessels, better nets, and new technology for spotting fish are not bringing the world's fleets bigger returns—in fact, the global catch fell by 13% between 1994 and 2003. Fish is already more expensive than beef in many countries; before long it will simply be unavailable to any but millionaires.

중심소재: 어업실태

1. 첫 번째 문단

1) 도입부 = 현상
과도한 현 어업행태를 계속할 경우 21세기 중반에 바다에 남아 있을 고기가 전혀 없게 된다.
① 현상의 심각성
바다 어획량의 1/3이 줄었고, 점점 이 속도가 가속화되고 있다.

2. 두 번째 문단

1) 현상의 원인
어장 감소는 바다 생물의 다양성이 줄어드는 것과 관련이 있다.
① 대안
보호구역을 더 확대하고 제도적 장치를 통한 규제
Ⓐ 현상의 근본적 원인
바다는 끊임없이 착취할 수 있는 대상으로 인식
ⓐ 현상의 심각성을 강조하면 시급한 대처의 필요성을 뒷받침하고 있다.

3. 세 번째 문단

1) 현상과 원인과 결과
① 현상
2003년 어획량이 10% 이하
Ⓐ 기술발전으로 인한 무차별적 어업활동은 결국 어획량의 궁극적 감소로 이어진다는 내용

정답 1 (B) 2 (A) 3 (B) 4 (D) 5 (C)

해설

1 The owners of fishing boats do not want to admit it, but there will be virtually no fish in the seas

of the world by the middle of the 21st century if current trends of gross overfishing continue의 밑줄 친 표현을 보면 "과도한 현 어업행위가 지속된다면, 21세기 중반에는 바다에 고기가 전혀 없을 것이다"라고 했으므로 "무차별적으로"란 ruthlessly가 빈칸에 가장 적절하다.

2 we hope an assume there will be always be another species to exploit after we've completely gone through the last one의 밑줄 친 표현에서 사람들은 물고기가 "무한대로 있다"라고 가정함으로 선택지 (A)의 inexhaustible가 적절하다.

3 Yet a greater use of protected areas could safeguard existing stocks, giving them time to replenish의 밑줄 친 내용으로 보아, "기존의 어류가 다시 번성할 수 있도록" 하기 위해 보호해야 함을 파악할 수 있다.

4 Bigger vessels, better nets, and new technology for spotting fish are not bringing the world's fleets bigger returns—in fact, the global catch fell by 13% between 1994 and 2003에서 알 수 있듯이, 더 나은 고기 잡는 기술의 발달은 "전 세계 어류의 급격한 감소"로 이어졌다는 현상의 객관적 뒷받침 자료임을 파악할 수 있다.

5 본문의 then this century will be the last century when people can eat wild seafood of any kind에서 알 수 있듯이 "모든 해양생물이 위기에 처해 있다"는 것을 파악할 수 있다.

지문해석

고깃배 주인들은 인정하지 않으려 하겠지만, 주요 과학적 연구에 의하면, 만약 엄청난 남획이 현재 추세대로 간다면 21세기 중반에 가서는 사실상 전 세계 바다에 남아 있는 물고기는 한 마리도 없을 것이다. 어장의 거의 3분의 1에서 어류는 급격히 감소했고 감소 속도는 가속화되고 있다. 한 국제 연구팀은 사이언스지에서 어장 감소는 보다 광범위한 해양생물 다양성의 손실과 밀접하게 연결되어 있다고 주장한다. 그러나 보호구역의 보다 많은 이용은 보충할 수 있는 시간을 제공하기 때문에 현존하는 어류를 지킬 수가 있다. 연구 책임자인 보리스 웜은 "지금까지 우리가 바다를 사용해 온 방식은 마지막 남은 어종까지 깡그리 잡아들인 후에도 또 다른 종이 있을 것이라고 희망하고 가정하는 것이다"라고 말한다. "우리가 강조하는 것은 어족 자원은 한정되어 있다는 것이다. 우리는 3분의 1을 고갈시켰고 만약 이에 대한 제한이 없다면 그 나머지는 고갈될 것이다." 연구의 과학자들 중 다른 이는 다음과 같이 덧붙였다. "현재 작동하고 있는 생태계처럼, 만약 우리가 모든 해양 어종 전체를 관리하는 방법을 근본적으로 바꾸지 않으면 이번 세기는 사람들이 어떤 종류가 됐건 천연 해산물을 먹을 수 있는 마지막 세기가 될 것이다." 2003년에 세계 대양 어장의 29%가 원래 공급량의 10% 미만으로 정의되면서 급감상태에 빠졌다. 더 큰 배, 더 좋은 그물, 어류를 잡는 신기술은 전 세계 선단에 더 많은 수확을 가져다주지 못하고 있다. 사실 1994년에서 2003년 사이에 전 세계 어획량은 13% 감소했다. 많은 나라에서 생선은 이미 쇠고기보다 비싸다. 머지않아 생선은 백만장자들 외에는 먹지도 못하게 될 것이다.

TEST 13

첫 번째 문장은 전체 지문 내용의 방향성을 제시한다는 점에서 아주 중요하다. 우선 중심소재를 설정하고, 중심소재를 중심으로 어떤 내용을 전개하는지 파악하도록 한다.

Passage 1

1. The broadcast and print media regularly provide hype for individuals who have achieved "super" success. 1) ① These stories are usually about celebrities and superstars from the sports and entertainment world. Ⓐ Society pages and gossip columns serve to keep the social elite informed of each other's doings, allow the rest of us to gawk at their excesses, and help to keep the American dream alive. ② The print media is also fond of feature stories on corporate empire builders. Ⓑ These stories provide an occasional "insider's" view of the private and corporate life of industrialists by suggesting a rags to riches account of corporate success. These stories tell us that corporate success is a series of smart moves, shrewd acquisitions, timely mergers, and well thought out executive suite shuffles. 2. By painting the upper class in a positive light, innocent of any wrongdoing (labor leaders and union organizations usually get the opposite treatment), the media assures us that wealth and power are benevolent. One person's capital accumulation is presumed to be good for all. The elite, then, are portrayed as investment wizards, people of special talent and skill, whom even their victims (workers and consumers) can admire.

중심소재: 미디어

1. 도입부 = 주제문

미디어(중심소재)는 성공한 사람들을 과대 선전하는 경향이 있다.

1) 뒷받침 진술

①유명인과 스포츠 스타를 다룸

Ⓐ부연

사회 엘리트 계층의 정보를 다루면서 일반인들을 이들의 과소비 형태를 바라보게 하면서 아메리카 드림을 계속 유지하게 하도록 작용

②거대 기업 창시자에 초점

Ⓑ부연

벼락부자가 된 사업 성공이야기와 이들이 성공하게 된 원인을 함께 언급

2. 주제문 재진술

상류계층의 사람들을 긍정적으로 묘사하고 이들의 물질적 성공을 선으로 포장하고 있는 미디어를 비판하고 있다.

정답 1 (B) 2 (C) 3 (C)

지문분석

본문은 엘리트층을 과대 포장하여 선전하는 미디어의 행태를 비판하는 '현상 비판'의 유형이다.

해설

1 gawk at their excesses는 "그들의 과소비 행태를 멍하니 바라보다"의 뜻이므로 "절제의 부족함(lack of moderation)을 멍하니 바라본다"는 의미로 볼 수 있다.

2 사회 상류 사람들을 이상적인 모습으로 묘사하는 미디어를 비판하고 있다. 본문분석을 참조한다.

3 상류층 기업가 집단을 호의적으로 취급하는 중심소재가 media이므로 빈칸에 들어갈 표현은 이런 상류층 기업가가 가진 부와 권력에 "호의적"일 것을 예상할 수 있다.

지문해석

방송과 인쇄 매체들은 "엄청난" 성공을 거둔 사람들에 대한 과장된 기사를 자주 내보낸다. 이런 기사들은 대개 스포츠와 연예계 출신의 유명인사와 슈퍼스타들에 관한 것이다. 사회면이나 가십난은 사회의 엘리트들에게 서로 간의 일을 계속해서 알리는 역할을 하고, 나머지 사람들에게는 엘리트들의 무절제함을 멍하니 넋을 잃고 바라보게 하면서 아메리칸 드림이 살아 있도록 돕는다. 또한 인쇄 매체들은 거대 기업을 일구어낸 사람

들에 관한 특집 기사를 좋아한다. 이런 기사들은 무일푼에서 부자가 된 기업의 성공에 대해 기사를 실으면서 기업 경영자들의 사생활과 회사생활에 대한 "내부자"의 견해를 이따금씩 제공하기도 한다. 이런 기사들은 기업의 성공이란 일련의 현명한 움직임, 재빠른 인수, 시기적절한 합병, 그리고 용의주도한 임원진의 옷을 바꿔 입는 것이라고 우리에게 말해준다. 상류 계층을 긍정적인 시선으로 어떠한 부정행위에 대해서도 모르는 듯 묘사함으로써 (노조 지도자들이나 노조 단체들은 보통 정반대의 대우를 받음) 대중매체는 부와 권력이 자비로운 것이라고 우리에게 확언한다. 한 사람의 자본 축적은 모두에게 이로운 것으로 간주된다. 그러고는 엘리트 계층의 사람들은 투자의 귀재, 특별한 재능과 기술을 가진 존재로 그려지는데, 심지어 그들에게 피해를 당한 사람들(노동자와 소비자들)조차 그들을 존경할 수 있다.

Passage 2

1. Somewhere between 1860 and 1890, the dominant emphasis in American literature was radically changed. 1) But ① it is obvious that this change was not necessarily a matter of conscious concern to all writers. In fact, many writers may seem to have been actually unaware of the shifting emphasis. Ⓐ Moreover, it is not possible to trace the steady march of the realistic emphasis from the first feeble notes to its dominant trumpet-note of unquestioned leadership.

ⓐ The progress of realism is, to change the figure, rather that of a small stream, receiving accessions from its tributaries at unequal points along its course, its progress now and then checked by the sand bars of opposition or the diffusing marshes of error and compromise.

2. Again it is apparent that any attempts to classify rigidly, as romanticists or realists, the writers of this period are doomed to failure, since it is not by virtue of the writer's conscious espousal of the romantic or realistic creed that he does much of his best work, but by virtue of the writer's sincere surrender to the atmosphere of the subject.

중심소재: 1860년대와 1890년대 사이 미국문학의 변화 →변화에 대한 반응

1. 도입부 = 현상

1860년대와 1890년대 사이 미국 문학 중심에 큰 변화가 생겼다.

1) 예외적 반응

① 첫 번째 문장에서 언급된 "radical"한 변화와 달리 많은 작가들은 이런 변화를 인식하지 못함

Ⓐ 배경
사실주의로의 변천이 아주 미미하면서 천천히 발생하기 때문

ⓐ 비유부연
하천의 비유를 통해 작가들이 이 시기에 발생한 문학적 흐름의 변화를 빠르게 인식하지 못했던 이유를 부연하고 있다.

2. 결론

이 시기에는 구체적 주제의 분위기에 전적으로 따르는 분위기로 인해 낭만주의와 사실주의 작가로 구별하는 것은 실패하기 마련이다.

역접의 대조를 파악한다.

But의 세 가지 기능

① 역접

A = B
But
A ≠ B

② 순접강조추가

A = B
But A = A
A = C

③ 소재의 폭↓

N_s
But N

N_s→N

TEST 13

정답 1 (A) 2 (B)

해설

1 낭만주의에서 사실주의로의 문학사조 변천이 급격하게 일어나지 않고 not necessarily a matter of conscious concern to all writers라고 했으므로 낭만주의와 사실주의를 엄격하게 구별하려는 시도는 성공하지 못할 것을 알 수 있다. 선택지 (A)가 정답이다.

2 this change was not necessarily a matter of conscious concern to all writers.를 보면, "이러한 변화가 반드시 필연적으로 모든 작가에서 의식적 관심의 문제는 아니었다"고 했으므로 선택지 (B)는 본문의 내용과 정반대임을 알 수 있다.

지문해석

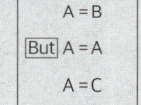

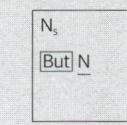

미국 문학에 있어서 지배적인 강조점은 1860년대에서 1890년도 사이, 근본적으로 변했다. 그러나 분명한 것은, 이러한 변화가 모든 작가들과 연관이 있는 의식차이의 문제일 필요는 없었다는 것이다. 사실, 많은 작가

들은 실제로 이러한 주안점의 변화를 인식하지 못한 것처럼 보일 수 있다. 더구나 사실주의의 비중이 처음에는 미미하다가 확실히 당당한 주도적 위치로 점차 이동해 간 것을 알아채기란 불가능하다. 비유적으로 보자면, 사실주의의 발전 과정은, 작은 냇가의 형성과정과도 같다. 길을 따라 내려오면서 각기 다른 장소에서 지류들이 유입되고, 이따금씩 반대편의 모래언덕이나 여기저기 퍼져있는 오류와 타협의 늪지에 의해 저지되며 하천으로 발전해가는 것이다. 다시 말하지만, 이 시기의 작가들을 낭만주의자, 혹은 사실주의자 등으로 엄격히 분류하려는 시도는 모두 실패할 것이 명백하다. 왜냐하면 최고의 작품을 이루는 것은 작가가 의식적으로 낭만주의, 혹은 사실주의 신조를 지지해서가 아니라, 작가가 해당 주제의 분위기를 전적으로 따랐기 때문이다.

Passage 3

1. 1) We are sometimes eager to celebrate the influence of our surroundings. ① In the living room of a house in the Czech Republic, we see an example of how walls, chairs and floors can combine to create an atmosphere in which the best sides of us are offered the opportunity to flourish. We accept with gratitude the power that a single room can possess.

2. 1) But sensitivity to architecture also has its more problematic aspects. ① If one room can alter how we feel, if our happiness can hang on the colour of the walls or the shape of a door, what will happen to us in most of the places we are forced to look at and inhabit? What will we experience in a house with prison-like windows, stained carpet tiles and plastic curtains? **2)** It is to prevent the possibility of permanent anguish that we can be led to shut our eyes to most of what is around us, for we are never far from damp stains and cracked ceilings, shattered cities and rusting dockyards. We can't remain sensitive indefinitely to environments which we don't have the means to alter for the good.

It ~ that강조용법을 활용하여 글쓴이의 주장이 드러난다.

중심소재: 주변 환경(건축물)에 반응

1. 첫 번째 단락

1) 도입부

주변 환경에 영향을 받는다.

① 예시부연

2. 두 번째 단락

1) 주제문

민감하게 건축물에 반응하는 것은 부정적 영향을 미친다.

① 뒷받침 진술

외부 건축물에 민감하게 반응하게 되었을 때 발생하는 부정적 결과

2) 요지문

더 나은 환경으로 바꿀 수 없을 경우 우리의 눈을 감아 외부 건축물에 의해서 발생하는 지속적인 고뇌의 가능성을 회피해야 한다.

정답 **1** (A) **2** (C)

해설

1 외부 건축물에 민감하게 반응하게 되었을 때 발생하는 부정적 측면을 다룬 후 이에 대한 대안을 제시하는 글이다. 요지를 중심으로 설정한 선택지 (A)가 주제로 가장 적절하다.

2 environments를 수식하는 적절한 표현인데, can't remain sensitive indefinitely to로 보아 environments는 부정적 건축물을 나타낸다고 볼 수 있다. 또한 we are never far from damp stains and cracked ceilings, shattered cities and rusting dockyards에서 부정적인 외부의 건축물에서 자유로울 수 없다고 했으므로 빈칸에 들어갈 내용은 "바꿀 수 있는 수단이 없는"이 가장 적절하다.

지문해석

우리는 때때로 주변 환경의 영향을 찬양하는 데 매우 열심이다. 예를 들어, 체코 공화국의 주택 거실에서 우리는 벽과, 의자와, 바닥이 서로 어우러져 우리가 지닌 최고의 모습들이 잘 자라날 기회를 주는 분위기를 만들어내는 모습을 보게 된다. 우리는 하나의 방이 지닐 수 있는 힘을 감사하며 받아들인다.

그러나 건축에 대해 민감하게 반응하는 것은 더욱 문제가 될 수 있는 측면들도 있다. 만약 하나의 방이 우리의 감정을 바꿀 수 있다면, 또 우리의 행복이 벽의 색깔이나 문의 모양에 좌우된다면, 우리가 바라보고 살아갈 수밖에 없는 대부분의 장소에서는 우리에게 어떤 일이 일어나겠는가? 감옥처럼 보이는 창문과 얼룩진 카펫 타일과 플라스틱 커튼이 있는 집에서는 무엇을 경험하겠는가? 우리가 우리를 둘러싼 대부분의 것에 눈을 감게 되는 것은 바로 영원한 고통을 막기 위해서이다. 왜냐하면 우리는 축축한 얼룩, 금이 간 천장, 부서진 도시, 그리고 녹슨 조선소와 결코 멀리 있지 않기 때문이다. 우리는 좋은 것으로 바꿀 수단을 갖추지 못한 환경에 언제까지나 민감하게 반응할 수는 없다.

Passage 4

1. Research on the psychology of happiness has borne out the curmudgeons. 1) ① Kahneman and Tversky give an everyday example. You open your paycheck and are delighted to find you have been given a five percent raise—until you learn that your co-workers have been given a ten percent raise. ② According to legend, the diva Maria Callas stipulated that any opera house she sang in had to pay her one dollar more than the next highest paid singer in the company. 2. 1) People today are safer, healthier, better fed, and longer-lived than at any time in history. Yet we don't spend our lives walking on air, and presumably our ancestors were not chronically glum. It is not reactionary to point out that many of the poor in today's Western nations live in conditions that yesterday's aristocrats could not have dreamed of. ① People in different classes and countries are often content with their lot until they compare themselves to the more affluent. The amount of violence in a society is more closely related to its inequality than to its poverty. In the second half of the twentieth century, the discontent of the Third World, and later the Second, have been attributed to their glimpses through the mass media of the First.

중심소재: 행복

1. 첫 번째 문단

1) 도입부 = 단락 주제문

행복은 심술궂은 구두쇠를 지지한다.

1) 뒷받침 예시(①, ②)

행복이란 상대적인 것으로 다른 이보다 더 많이 받을 때 행복을 느낌

2. 두 번째 문단

1) 도입부 = 단락주제 도출

현대 사람들이 과거 사람들보다 더 건강하고, 안전하고 잘 먹지만 그렇다고 현대가 과거보다 더 행복하다고 말할 수 없다.

1) 이유(요지문)

비교로 인한 상대적 불행

① 폭력과의 관계부연

특정 사회에 폭력이 증가하는 것은 수입이 적어서가 아니라 상대적 수입의 불평등을 느끼기 때문이다.

첫 번째 문단의 주된 글 전개방식은 예시이고, 두 번째 문단은 대조임을 파악한다.

정답 1 (A) 2 (D) 3 (C) 4 (E)

해설

1 People in different classes and countries are often content with their lot until they compare themselves to the more affluent를 보면, "자신보다 부유한 사람과 비교하지 않을 때 자신의 인생에 만족함을 느낀다"의 뜻이므로 선택지 (A)가 적절하다.

2 (D)를 제외한 모든 선택지는 다른 사람과의 비교를 통한 행복을 언급하고 있다.

3 People in different classes and countries are often content with their lot until they compare themselves to the more affluent에서 나보다 잘 사는 사람과 비교할 때 나는 불만을 느끼게 됨을 알 수 있고, In the second half of the twentieth century, the discontent of the Third World, and later the Second, have been attributed to their glimpses through the mass media of the First.에서 미디어를

통한 비교로 인해 제 3세계가 불만족함을 알 수 있다. 즉, 빈곤 자체로 인해서 사람들이 불만을 느끼는 것이 아니라 남과의 비교에 따른 불평등에 의해서 불만을 느끼게 됨을 추론할 수 있다.

4 제 2, 3세계의 불만은 미디어를 통해 제 1세계의 삶과 비교하기에 일어난다고 본문 마지막에 드러나므로 선택지 (E)가 정답이다.

지문해석

행복의 심리에 대한 연구가 심술궂은 구두쇠를 옹호해주었다. 카네만(Kahneman)과 트베르스키(Tversky)는 일상적인 예를 보여준다. 당신은 급여수표를 보고 급여가 5퍼센트 인상된 것을 알고는 기뻐하지만 동료들은 10퍼센트 인상을 받았다는 것을 알고 나면 그 기쁨이 멈추게 된다. 한 일화에 따르면, 여가수 마리아 칼라스(Maria Callas)는 자신이 노래하는 어떤 오페라 극장이건, 자기 다음으로 가장 많이 돈을 받는 가수보다 1달러 더 많이 자신에게 돈을 지불해야 한다고 오페라단과의 계약에 명기했다고 한다.

사람들은 오늘날 그 어떤 시기보다도 더 안전하며, 더 건강하고, 더 잘 먹으며, 더 오래 살고 있다. 그러나 우리는 우리의 삶을 기뻐 날뛰면서 보내고 있지도 않고, 우리의 선조들도 아마, 만성적으로 우울해하지 않았을 것이다. 오늘날 서구 국가들에 있는 많은 가난한 사람들이 과거의 귀족들조차 꿈꾸지 못했던 상태에서 살고 있다는 사실을 지적한다고 해서 반발을 일으킬 일은 아니다. 다양한 계층과 국가의 사람들은 자신을 더 부유한 사람들과 비교하기 전까지 그들의 운명에 만족해하는 경우가 많다. 한 사회에서 폭력의 양은 그 사회의 가난보다는 그 사회의 불평등과 더 밀접하게 관련되어 있다. 20세기 후반에 일어난 제 3세계의 불만과 후에 제 2세계의 불만은 모두 제 1세계의 생활상을 대중매체를 통해 알게 되었기 때문이다.

Passage 5

기원의 글은 시간적으로 현재에서 과거로 거슬러 올라가거나 과거에서 현재로 기술되며, 본문의 시제는 과거이다. 밑줄 친 표현을 확인하도록 한다.

1. Sincere comes from two Latin words: sine meaning "without" and cera meaning "wax", but what does the current meaning of sincere have to do with "not having wax"? The current meaning of the word sincere can be attributed to dishonest merchants over two thousand years ago. 1) In ancient Rome, people used dishware made of clay. As you can imagine, the process of making clay dishes and clay cups was long and difficult, and workers were careful in making the dishware. Nevertheless, small cracks would appear in the dishware during this process from time to time. Dishware makers who were not honest would simply apply wax in an attempt to cover up the flaws in the products. Because this inferior product was almost identical to a good one, customers rarely identified any problem. Even after a careful inspection of the product, it was virtually impossible to see any problem beforehand. As a result, customers bought the inferior product, took it home, and used it. When the customers washed the dishware with hot water, the wax melted, which revealed the poor quality of the dishware. Ultimately, customers came to know which dishware merchants sold good products, products that were "sine cera" or sincere. Once customers found a merchant whose products were "without wax," they were

중심소재: sincere

1. 도입부 = 주제도출

sincere이란 단어의 기원에 관한 글임을 come from과 be attributed to와 같은 표현에서 쉽게 파악할 수 있다.

1) 구체적 진술

로마시대로 거슬러 올라가 어떻게 sincere라는 단어가 not having wax와 어떤 의미에서 관련이 되어 "정직한"의 의미가 되었는지 살펴보고 있다.

able to minimize or perhaps even eliminate the possibility of buying flawed dishware.

정답 **1** (C) **2** (A) **3** (B) **4** (D)

지문분석

글의 도입부에서 특정 단어의 기원을 다루는 글임을 알 수 있다. originate와 같은 기원을 드러내는 표현인 come from을 첫 번째 문장에서 볼 수 있으며, 이후 sine과 cera라는 표현이 어떻게 sincere라는 표현이 되었는지 기술하는 설명문이다.

해설

1 글의 도입부에서 특정 단어의 기원을 다루는 글임을 알 수 있다. originate와 같은 기원을 드러내는 표현인 come from을 첫 번째 문장에서 볼 수 있으며, 이후 sine과 cera라는 표현이 어떻게 sincere라는 표현이 되었는지 설명하고 있다.

2 A is attributed to B는 "A의 원인은 B이다"는 뜻이고, in an attempt to는 "~하려는 시도"라는 의미의 전치사구이다. A is identical to B는 "A와 B는 동일하다"의 의미다.

3 접속사와 주어역할을 함께 하면서 코마를 받을 수 있는 계속적 용법의 which가 정답이다.

4 (가)의 경우 앞뒤 문장이 서로 논리적 반전을 이루고 있으므로 양보의 nevertheless가 가장 적절하며, (나)의 경우 앞에서 전개된 내용이 판단의 근거가 됨으로 결과를 이끄는 표현을 넣어야 한다.

지문해석

성실함(Sincere)이란 단어는 두 개의 라틴 단어에서 유래했다. sine는 'without'을 의미하고 cera는 'wax'를 의미하지만, 현재 성실하다는 의미가 '왁스가 없다'는 뜻과 어떤 관련이 있는가? 성실함이란 단어의 현 의미는 이천 년 전의 부정한 상인에서 생겼다. 고대 로마에서 사람들은 흙으로 빚은 그릇을 사용했다. 흙으로 빚은 그릇과 컵을 만드는 과정은 시간이 오래 걸리고 까다로우며, 짐작할 수 있듯, 작업자들은 그릇을 만드는 데 아주 주의해야 했다. 그럼에도 불구하고, 때로 이런 과정에서 작은 금이 그릇에 생기곤 했다. 그릇 제작자들 중 정직하지 못했던 사람들은 제품의 하자를 가리기 위한 시도로 그냥 그 위에 왁스를 덧바르곤 했다. 이러한 불량제품은 정상제품과 거의 동일하기 때문에 손님들은 좀처럼 미리 문제를 인식하지 못했다. 제품을 아주 자세히 검토한 후에도 문제를 미리 발견하기란 사실상 거의 불가능했다. 따라서 고객은 불량 제품을 구입한 뒤, 집에 가져가 사용했다. 그리고 고객이 뜨거운 물로 그릇을 씻을 때, 왁스가 녹아 불량임을 드러났다. 결국 고객은 어느 그릇 상인이 좋은 상품 즉, 왁스가 없는 진정한 상품을 파는지 알게 된다. 일단 고객이 '왁스가 없는' 제품을 파는 상인을 찾게 되면, 이들은 불량품을 살 가능성이 최소화되거나 그럴 가능성이 아예 없어졌다.

Passage 6

1. 1) The gurus seek bliss amidst mountaintop solitude and serenity in the meditative trance, but I have achieved the oneness with the universe that is known as pure externalization. I have melded my mind with the heavens, communed with the universal consciousness, and experienced the inner calm that externalization brings, and ① it all started because I bought a car with a G.P.S. Like many men, I quickly established a romantic attachment to my G.P.S. Ⓐ I found comfort in ⓐ her tranquil and slightly Anglophilic

중심소재: G.P.S

1. 첫 번째 단락

1) 도입부 = 중심소재 파악

G.P.S 구입으로 인해 힌두교 지도자와 같은 열반의 경지에 오름

①단락주제

G.P.S에 대한 애착

Ⓐ 뒷받침 근거(이유)

ⓐ 목소리

글 전반에 걸쳐 개인의 경험담을 통해 G.P.S를 좋아하게 된 근거를 제시하고 있다.

TEST 13

voice. ⓑ I felt warm and safe following her thin blue line. ⓒ More than once I experienced her mercy, for each of my transgressions would be greeted by nothing worse than a gentle, “Make a U-turn if possible.”

2. 1) After a few weeks, it occurred to me that I could no longer get anywhere without her. Any trip slightly out of the ordinary had me typing the address into her system and then blissfully following her satellite-fed commands. I found that I was quickly shedding all vestiges of a geographic knowledge. ① It was unnerving at first, but then a relief. Ⓐ Since the dawn of humanity, people have had to worry about how to get from here to there. Precious brainpower has been used storing directions, and memorizing turns. I myself have been trapped at dinner parties at which conversation was devoted exclusively to the topic of commuter routes. ② My G.P.S. goddess liberated me from this drudgery. She enabled me to externalize geographic information from my own brain to a satellite brain, and you know how it felt? It felt like nirvana.

ⓑ 파란 예상 경로 선을 따라가면서 "따뜻함과 안전함"을 느낌
ⓒ 교통 위반 시에도 친절하게 무엇을 해야 할지 알려줌

2. 두 번째 단락

1) 구체적 진술(문제점 발생)
G.P.S가 없으면 어디도 갈 수 없는 상황

①단락 주제문 ①+②단락 요지
But 이후 안도의 한숨
Ⓐ 뒷받침 근거(이유)
장소 이동에 대한 인류의 고민거리를 해결한 G.P.S를 열반에 오른 경지와 비유하면 뒷받침 근거를 제시하고 있다.

정답 **1** (C) **2** (B) **3** (C) **4** (A)

지문분석
본문은 G.P.S로 인해 얻게 된 마음의 상태를 마치 힌두교 지도자가 열반의 경지에 이른 것과 비유하며, 재치(wit)가 넘치는 글이다.

해설

1 I quickly established a romantic attachment to my G.P.S. 진술 이후 G.P.S를 좋아하게 된 이유를 기술하고 있다. 선택지 (C)가 글의 목적으로 가장 적절하다.

2 Any trip slightly out of the ordinary had me typing the address into her system and then blissfully following her satellite-fed commands.에서 글쓴이 I가 가야할 길을 알려주는 기능을 하고 있다는 점에서 선택지 (B)가 가장 적절하다.

3 일인칭 시점(first person)의 글로 "개인의 경험담"을 바탕으로 쓴 글이다.

4 I found that I was quickly shedding all vestiges of a geographic knowledge.부분을 통해 선택지 (A)는 옳음을 알 수 있다.

지문해석
힌두교 지도자들은 산 정상의 고독 속에서 행복을 구하고 명상 상태에서 평정을 찾지만 나는 완전한 객관화로 알려진 우주와의 일체를 달성해왔다. 나는 내 정신을 하늘과 연결시키고, 보편적인 의식과 교제하며, 객관화가 가져다주는 내적 평온을 경험해 왔다. 그리고 이 모든 것들은 GPS가 장착된 자동차를 사면서 시작되었다. 많은 남성들처럼 나는 재빨리 내 GPS에 낭만적인 애착을 가졌다. 나는 고요하고 약간의 영국 악센트가 섞인 목소리에서 위안을 찾았다. 나는 그녀의 가늘고 파란 선을 따라가면서 따뜻함과 안전함을 느꼈다. 내가 자비를 경험한 것은 한 번 이상인데, 교통 법규를 위반할 때마다 "가능하면 유턴하세요."라는 친절한 말 외에는 별다른 이야기를 들은 일이 없다. 몇 주가 지난 후 내가 GPS 없이는 어디도 갈 수 없다는 것을 알게 되었다. 일상에서 조금만 벗어나는 이동을 할 때도 나는 주소를 시스템에 입력하고 난 후 행복에 넘친 채 기계의 위성 제공 지시를 따랐다. 나는 스스로 온갖 지리적 지식의 흔적을 버리고 있는 모습을 발견했다. 처

음에는 불안했지만 이후엔 안도감이 들었다. 인류의 기원 이래 사람들은 여기서 저기로 어떻게 가는지에 대해 걱정해야만 했다. 귀중한 지능이 방향 정보를 저장하고 회전을 기억하는 데 사용되어 왔다. 대화가 전적으로 출근 경로에 관한 것인 저녁 파티에 내 자신이 갇혀있기도 했다. 내 GPS 여신은 이런 고역으로부터 나를 해방시켰다. 그녀는 지리 정보를 내 두뇌에서 꺼내 위성 두뇌에 외부화할 수 있었는데 이게 어떤 기분인지 당신은 아는가? 마치 해탈의 경지에 이른 것 같았다.

Passage 7

1. What the blind find difficult are smooth, open spaces, It is just these areas which are assumed by many sighted people to be best for the blind, because there is no danger of tripping. 1) From the blind's point of view, however, a flat, open surface is not negotiable because there are no orientating signals. ① There is no structure, it is not predictable, because it may end at any moment, and there is no way of telling where you are, once you are on it. The problem for the blind is not falling over, but knowing where he is. 2. For this reason, it is easier to find my way around a campus which is marked out by steps, little hills and valleys, low walls and lots of changes in texture, because I can mark out my route with sections. The structure becomes a sequence when I am moving through it.

중심소재: Open spaces (for the blind)

통념의 시그널을 확인한다.

1. 도입부 = 주제문
일반인과 달리 장애인에게 평평하고, 트인 공간이 더 위험하다.

1) 뒷받침 진술
일반인과 달리 트인 공간은 방향을 안내하는 시그널이 없기에 더 불편하다.
① 장애인에게 문제가 되는 근본적인 것은 바로 자신이 어디에 있는지의 "방향감각"

2. 요지문
이러한 이유에서 장애물이 많은 캠퍼스가 더 길을 찾기 쉽다고 말하고 있다.

정답 **1** (A) **2** (C) **3** (E)

해설

1 It is just these areas which are assumed by many sighted people to be best for the blind, because there is no danger of tripping.의 문장은 Many sighted people assume that these areas are best for the blind. 정도로 바꾸어 표현할 수 있다. 즉, 글쓴이(I) 한 명과 대조되는 다수를 설정할 경우 다수의 생각은 글쓴이가 반대하는 입장이 될 가능성이 있다는 점을 고려하고 글을 읽으면 쉽게 접근이 가능하다. 뒤에 이어지는 내용을 보면, "눈이 보이는" 사람들이 생각하는 것과 smooth하고 open된 공각은 시각장애인에게는 방향을 드러내는 지형지물이 없기에 더욱 위험한데, 이러한 것을 일반인들은 잘 모른다는 내용이다. 고로, 선택지 (A)가 옳은 진술이다.

2 우선 글쓴이가 누구인지 파악하는 것이 중요한다. it is easier to find my way around a campus which is marked out by steps, little hills and valleys, low walls and lots of changes in texture, because I can mark out my route with sections의 밑줄 친 부분을 통해 글쓴이는 장애인임을 파악할 수 있다. 장애인으로 글쓴이가 당황할 수 있는 경우는 바로 The problem for the blind is not falling over, but knowing where he is.에서 알 수 있듯이 "넘어지는 것이 아니라, 자신이 어디 있는지를 모르는 경우"이다.

3 a campus which is marked out by steps, little hills and valleys, low walls and lots of changes in texture에서 선택지 (E)가 정답임을 파악할 수 있다.

지문해석

시각장애인들이 어렵다고 생각하는 것은 평탄하고 탁 트인 장소들이다. 그곳은 시력이 있는 많은 사람들에 의해 시각장애인들에게 매우 좋다고 생각되는 장소인데, 왜냐하면 발을 헛디딜 위험이 없기 때문이다. 그러나 시각장애인들의 관점에서 보면 평탄하고 탁 트인 지면은 위치를 알려주는 신호들이 없기 때문에 통행할 수 없다.
아무런 구조물이 없고, 그런 지면은 예측할 수도 없는데, 왜냐하면 그곳은 어느 순간에든 끝날 수 있으며 일단 그곳에 있으면 어디에 있는지 알 방법이 없기 때문이다. 시각장애인들에게 있어서 문제는 넘어지는 것이 아니라 자신이 어디에 있는지 아는 것이다. 이런 이유 때문에 계단, 작은 언덕과 계곡, 낮은 담벼락 그리고 구조상 변화들이 많은 캠퍼스 주변은 길을 찾기가 보다 수월한데 내가 다니는 길을 여러 구역 별로 구획할 수 있기 때문이다. 그 구조는 내가 그곳을 지나가는 순서이다.

Passage 8

1. 1) Scientific data indicates that the earth has gotten warmer over the past 100 years. ① Not only have global average temperatures increased, by an average of 0.5 to 1.1 degrees Fahrenheit, but glaciers have retreated, the mean sea level has risen, and other unmistakable signs of warming have been detected. Ⓐ Have these changes been caused, at least in part, by human emissions of greenhouse gases, most notably carbon dioxide? Are even more dramatic changes in store for the future? ⓐ Ten years ago hundreds of scientists around the world began to work through the Intergovernmental Panel on Climate change to evaluate all the research that has been done on global warming and to reach conclusions about what is known and what remains to be determined. Over time they have become more confident in their projections. Although no one can predict the future with absolute certainty, the scientists believe that the climate has very probably already begun to change because of human activities and they expect a temperature rise of a few degrees in the coming decades.

2. 1) For this reason many climate experts have called for strong international action to reduce human emissions of greenhouse gases. This view has been supported by the world's leading senior scientists, including the majority of living Nobel prize winners in the sciences, who in 1997 called global warming "one of the most serious threats to the planet and to future generations." ① A temperature changes of a few degrees may not seem like a lot, but Ⓐ it could be enough to alter the range of natural habitats and affect the distribution of the species within them. Ⓑ It would also likely cause changes in precipitation patterns, resulting in more summer dryness in some places but less in others, for example. Ⓒ Rising sea levels caused by melting glaciers

중심소재: 지구의 온도상승

1. 첫 번째 문단

1) 도입부 = 현상
지구가 지난 100년 동안 기온이 올랐다.

① 구체적 진술
온도뿐 아니라 빙하도 줄어들고, 평균 해수면 증가 그리고 온난화의 신호 감지
Ⓐ 현상의 원인과 전망
ⓐ 인간의 인위적 활동이 원인이며, 앞으로 기후가 상승할 것이다.

2. 두 번째 문단

1) 대안(요지)
권위 있는 과학자들을 언급하면서 온실가스를 줄여야 한다는 주장하고 있다.

① 뒷받침 근거(이유)
Ⓐ 동물 서식지와 종의 분배에 영향
Ⓑ 지역에 따른 강수량의 패턴 변화
Ⓒ 해수면 상승으로 해안가의 범람과 해안 습지 파괴
Ⓓ 경제적 재앙

and thermally expanding sea water would inundate coastal areas and harm coastal wetlands. Ⓓ Under the best scenarios these changes will occur gradually, but there is a risk of abrupt shifts in climate that could have catastrophic results not only for plants and wildlife but also for the global economy.

정답 1 (B) 2 (D) 3 (D)

해설

1 급격한 온도 변화에 따른 변화를 언급하는 내용이므로 서식지, 강수의 패턴, 해안가의 습지 등의 변화는 해당 변화의 결과로 일어날 가능성 있는 현상이다. 온실가스 삭감은 급격한 변화로 인한 결과라기보단 현상의 대안으로 제시되는 내용이 되어야 한다.

2 It would also likely cause changes in precipitation patterns, resulting in more summer dryness in some places but less in others.에서 여름 건조현상의 심화는 강수량 변화와 관련성이 있음을 파악할 수 있다.

3 Over time they have become more confident in their projections.부분을 통해서 선택지 (B)로 갈 수 있겠으니 이어지는 내용을 보면, 누구도 미래에 대한 예측이 옳은지는 확신할 수 없다고 했으므로 답이 될 수 없다. Ten years ago hundreds of scientists around the world began to work through the Intergovernmental Panel on Climate change to evaluate all the research that has been done on global warming and to reach conclusions about what is known and what remains to be determined.에서 패널은 온난화에 관해 연구하고 예측하는 단체임을 파악할 수 있다.

지문해석

과학적 데이터에 따르면 지구는 지난 100년간 더욱 따뜻해지고 있다. 지구의 평균 기온이 화씨로 평균 0.5도에서 1.1도 올라갔을 뿐 아니라 빙하가 쑥 들어가고, 평균 해면이 상승하고, 그 외의 분명한 온난화의 신호들도 감지되었다. 과연 이 같은 변화는, 최소한 일부가, 이산화탄소를 가장 두드러진 예로 들 수 있는 온실가스가 인간에 의해 배출되었기 때문인가? 미래에는 더욱 극적인 변화가 우리에게 닥칠 준비를 하고 있을까? 10년 전 전 세계의 수백 명의 과학자들은 기후변화에 관한 정부간 패널(Intergovernmental Panel on Climate Change)을 통해 기후변화에 관련해 이루어진 모든 연구를 평가했고 현재 알려진 사항과 앞으로 결정이 필요한 사항에 대해 합의를 했다. 시간이 지나면서 그 과학자들은 자신들이 예상한 것에 더욱 확신을 가졌다. 비록 아무도 미래를 절대적으로 확실히 예측할 수는 없지만, 과학자들은 인간의 활동 때문에 기후가 이미 변화하기 시작했을 가능성이 매우 높다고 생각했으며 앞으로 다가오는 수십 년 안에는 기온이 상승할 것으로 예측했다. 이 때문에 많은 기후 전문가들은 인간의 온실가스 배출을 줄이기 위해 힘 있는 국제적 행동을 요청해 왔다. 이 같은 시각은 세계의 저명한 원로 과학자들로부터 지지를 얻어왔으며, 그중에는 현재 생존한 과학 분야 노벨상 수상자들 대다수도 포함된다. 이들은 1997년에 지구 온난화를 "지구와 미래세대에 있어 가장 심각한 위협 중 하나"로 일컬었다. 몇 도의 기온의 변화는 큰 것으로 보이지는 않을 것이나, 그 약간의 기온 변화는 자연 서식지의 범위를 변화시키고 그곳에 살고 있는 종의 분포에 영향을 미치기에 충분하다. 또한 기온의 변화는 강수 패턴의 변화를 야기하는데 예를 들자면 몇몇 지역에서는 여름 건조가 심해지게 하지만, 다른 곳에서는 덜해지게 한다. 빙하가 녹고 열로 인해 해수가 증가한 결과로 상승하는 해수면은 해안 지역을 침수시키고 해안 습지에 해를 끼친다. 이 같은 변화가 점진적으로 일어나는 것이 최상의 시나리오지만, 기후에 급격한 변화가 일어나 식물과 야생동물뿐 아니라 세계 경제에도 재앙과 같은 결과를 낳을 위험성도 존재한다.

TEST 14

Passage 1

1. There was a time when it was an accomplishment for a PDA to be able to read a written word on a menu, a street sign, or a business card. 1) Today we are living in a world where PDAs are beginning to learn to speak. We're not talking only about simple speech. We are referring to complicated translation engines that will enable the devices to understand not only the content of what is being said, but also the tone and inflection of the speech.
① The Phraselator built by Marine Acoustics and sold by VoxTec is one example of such a device. Ⓐ The Phraselator is capable of translating between hundreds of different languages. Five hundred Phraselators are being shipped to troops in Afghanistan. These units have been programmed with special phrases in Urdu that will help the troops. Each of these specially programmed phrases has an associated tone. Phrases such as "Halt!" and "Drop your weapon!" come across sternly and loudly, but a much softer tone is used when asking "Can I help you?"

중심소재: PDA

1. 도입부 = 중심소재 도출
과거와 현재를 대조하며 최근의 PDA의 특징을 언급하고 있다.

1) 주제문
PDA가 단순한 언어사용이 아닌 복잡한 번역이 가능하게 되었다.

① 뒷받침 사례
프레이즈레이터
Ⓐ 특징부연

정답 1 (A)

해설
제목을 설정할 때는 주제를 통해서 궁극적으로 전달하고자 하는 요지를 반영하여 설정할 수 있다. 본문은 최근 PDA(중심소재)는 글을 읽을 뿐만 아니라 말하기도 하며 여러 언어를 번역하기도 하므로 PDA가 더 똑똑해진다는 것이 반영된 제목이 가장 적절하다.

지문해석
PDA(개인 휴대용 단말기)가 메뉴나 길거리 표지판, 업무용 명함에 쓰인 글씨를 읽을 수 있는 것이 대단한 일이던 시절이 있었다. 오늘날 우리는 PDA가 말을 배우기 시작하는 세상에 살고 있다. 간단한 말에 국한해서 이야기하는 것이 아니다. 그 기계장치가 말의 내용뿐만 아니라 그 말의 어조와 억양까지도 이해할 수 있는 정교한 번역기에 대해 말하는 것이다.
마린 어쿠스틱스(Marine Acoustics)사에 의해 제작되고 복스텍(VoxTec)이 판매하는 프레이즈레이터(Phraselator)는 그런 장치의 한 예이다. 프레이즈레이터는 서로 다른 수백 가지의 언어를 번역할 수 있다. 오백 개의 프레이즈레이터가 아프가니스탄 주둔군으로 배송되고 있다. 이 기계들은 그곳 군대를 돕기 위한 우르두어 특수 구문들이 프로그램화 되어 있다. 특별히 프로그램화된 구문 각각은 관련된 어조를 가지고 있다. "꼼짝 마!"나 "무기를 내려놔!"와 같은 구문들은 단호하고 큰 소리로 나오지만 "도와 드릴까요?"라고 물을 때는 훨씬 더 부드러운 어조가 사용된다.

Passage 2

1\. 1) Suppose you are reading Eliot's the Waste Land, Shakespeare's King Lear, Joyce's Ulysses, or Chekhov's Ward Number Six. What you are reading is a poem, a play, a novel, a short story. 1) We would also say you are reading a work of literature, or of imaginative literature - though in the case of King Lear, some might be inclined to deny that wishing to distinguish literature sharply from drama.

2) Now suppose you are reading the classical Athenian politician Demonsthenes's Philippics, sir Thomas Browne's Um Burial, the Roman Poet Lucretius's On the Nature of Things, or the Sermon on the Mount from the New Testament. What you are reading now is a work oratory, an essay philosophy or scripture. Again, we would also say you are reading a work of literature.

3) Suppose, finally, you are reading Frederick Forsyth's Day of the Jackal, the products of a Victorian poetaster*, a story in Just Seventeen, or the Reverend C. T. Awdry's George, the Big Engine. What you are reading now is a novel, poetry (or verse), or stories. We might also say you are reading literature, but we would scarcely say it was serious literature - it is 'popular', or 'light', or 'children's' literature. Or some might say it was not literature at all. It is not good, or important, enough, they might say, to deserve the title of literature.

중심소재: 문학작품 → 문학작품의 종류

1\. 도입부 = 구체적 진술

1) 구체적 진술 1
다양한 종류의 문학작품

2) 구체적 진술 2
또 다른 종류의 문학작품

3) 구체적 진술 3
진지하지 않은 문학작품의 종류

세 문단으로 구성된 글로 모두 suppose로 시작하여 구체적 진술이 나온다. 각 문단을 통해 궁극적으로 전달하려는 일반진술을 이끌어 내도록 한다.

정답 **1**(B) **2**(C) **3**(A)

지문분석

본문은 문학작품의 종류를 전달하는 것으로 글의 특징이라면 문학작품과 그렇지 않은 작품을 대조적으로 제시함으로 구체적으로 어떤 것이 문학작품으로 분류되는지 설명하고 있다.

* 일반적으로 A의 특징을 설명할 때 효과적인 방법은 A와 상반되는 또는 다른 특징을 지닌 B라는 대상을 언급하면서 A의 특징을 강조하면 설명할 수 있다. 이런 경우 A와 B의 특징을 중립적으로 전달하는 것이 아니라 한 쪽의 특징을 부각시키고 다른 한 쪽의 특징을 대조구로 설정한다는 점을 기억하자. 주제는 당연히 'A의 특징'이 된다.

해설

1 문학작품이 될 수 있는 것과 그렇지 못한 것을 구별하면서 궁극적으로 "문학작품의 종류"를 다루는 글이다.

2 Shakespeare's King Lear는 a play라고 했으므로 문학과 drama를 구별하는 의도에서 King Lear는 문학이라는 점을 부인한다는 내용이다.

3 A, B and C는 A=B=C이므로 "a work oratory, an essay philosophy or ______."에서 빈칸은 책의 장르에 관한 내용이 나와야 한다. "the Sermon on the Mount from the New Testament"에 해당하는 성서가 가장 적절하다.

지문해석

당신이 엘리엇의 '황무지'를, 세익스피어의 '리어왕'을, 조이스의 '율리시즈'를, 아니면 체홉의 '제 6병동'을 읽는다고 가정해보자. 당신은 시, 희곡, 소설, 혹은 단편 소설을 읽는 것이다. 또한 문학작품을, 혹은 상상의

TEST 14

작품을 읽고 있다고 말할 수도 있다. 뭐, 리어왕의 경우에는 드라마와 문학작품은 엄밀히 말해 다르다며 이를 부인하는 사람이 있을지도 모르겠지만 말이다. 이제 당신이 아테네 정치가인 데모스테네스의 고전 '필립포스 탄핵'이나 토마스 브라운의 '납골 항아리'나, 로마시인 루크레티우스의 '사물의 본질에 대하여'나, 신약성경에 나오는 '산상수훈'을 읽고 있다고 가정해보자. 당신은 연설문, 수필, 철학서 또는 성서를 읽는 것이다. 다시, 이번에도 우리는 당신이 문학 작품을 읽고 있다고 말할 수 있다. 마지막으로, 당신이 프레더릭 포사이스의 '자칼의 날'이나 빅토리아 시대의 삼류 시인들의 작품들이나 잡지 '저스트 세븐틴'에 실린 이야기나, C. T. 오드리 목사의 'George, the Big Engine'을 읽는다고 해보자. 당신은 소설, 시, 혹은 이야기를 읽고 있다고 할 수 있다. 당신은 문학 작품을 읽고 있다고 말할 수도 있겠지만, 진중한 문학이라고 말할 수는 없을 것이다. 왜냐하면 이것들은 '대중적'이고 '가벼우며,' '아동 문학'이기 때문이다. 혹자는 아예 문학이라고 할 수 조차 없다고 말할지 모른다. 그들은 이것들이 문학이라는 타이틀을 가지기에는 충분히 훌륭하거나 중요도를 가지지 못한다고 말한다.

Passage 3

1. Three hundred and fifty years ago, religious freedom was born in North America. 1) Religious tolerance did not begin with the Bill of Rights or with Jefferson's Virginia Statute of Religious Freedom in 1786. With due respect to Roger Williams and his early experiment with "liberty of conscience" in Rhode Island, the United States really owes its enduring strength to a fragile, scorched document, the Flushing Remonstrance, which was signed by some 30 ordinary citizens on Dec. 27, 1657. ① It is fitting that this little-known document should be associated with Dutch settlements, because they were the most tolerant in the New World. The Netherlands had enshrined freedom of conscience in 1579, when it clearly established that "no one shall be persecuted or investigated because of his religion." And when the Dutch West India Company set up a trading post at the southern tip of Manhattan in 1625, Ⓐ the purpose was to make money, not to save souls. Because the founding idea was trade, the directors of the firm took pains to ensure that all were welcome.

중심소재: 종교의 자유

1. 도입부 = 중심소재 도출

종교적 자유의 기원에 관한 글

1) 주제문

종교의 자유의 기원은 권리장전 또는 제퍼슨의 종교자유 선문법이 아니라 플러싱 진정서이다.

① 뒷받침 진술

진정서는 네덜란드 정착민과 관련된 것으로 이들은 신세계에서 가장 관용이 넘치던 사람이었음

Ⓐ 관용의 배경

경제적 이유

정답 1 (B) 2 (C) 3 (B) 4 (D) 5 (A)

지문분석

본문은 미국의 초기 종교적 자유의 탄생이 일반인들이 알고 있는 지식과 달리 "플러싱 진정서"라고 언급한 후, 이 진정서의 성격은 "종교라기보단 경제적 이유"가 강했다고 말하고 있다. 북아메리카에서 종교적 자유의 기원을 기술한 글이다. 주제: Religious Freedom in North America

해설

1 It is fitting that this little-known document should be associated with Dutch settlements 부분에서 Dutch settlements임을 알 수 있는데 종교의 자유와 관련된 문서임을 감안할 때 (B)의 Dutch preachers가 가장 적절하다.

2 owe something to a person은 "~ 에게 빚지다, 은혜 입다"의 뜻이다.

3 두 번째 문장 마지막 부분인 the Flushing Remonstrance, which was signed by some 30 ordinary citizens on Dec. 27, 1657에서 "1657년 12월 27일 30명의 일반 시민들이 서명했다"고 나온다.

4 the purpose was to make money, not to save souls. Because the founding idea was trade의 밑줄 친 표현에서 알 수 있듯이 "종교적 목적이 아니라 돈을 벌어들이기 위한 수단"이었으므로 모든 사람을 환영한다는 welcome이 가장 적절하다.

5 북아메리카에서 종교적 자유의 기원을 기술한 글이다.

지문해석

350년 전에 북아메리카에서 종교의 자유가 탄생했다. 종교에 대한 관용은 권리 장전이나 1786년 제퍼슨이 만든 버지니아 주 종교자유 선문법과 더불어 시작된 것이 아니다. 로저 윌리엄스와 그가 초창기에 로드아일랜드 주에서 행한 '양심의 자유'에 관한 실험에 마땅한 경의를 표하는 미국이 그러한 인내력을 갖게 된 것은 사실은 플러싱 진정서라는 힘없고 그을린 한 문서 덕택이라고 볼 수 있는데, 이 문서는 1657년 12월 27일 약 30명의 일반 시민들이 서명한 것이다. 사람들이 거의 알지 못하는 이 문서는 네덜란드 정착지와 관련되어 있다고 보는 것이 적절하다. 왜냐하면 그들은 신대륙에서 가장 관대하였기 때문이다. 네덜란드는 1579년에 양심의 자유를 공식 문서화 했었는데, 그때에 그 나라는 "어느 누구도 종교적 이유로 박해받거나 조사받지 않는다."라는 점을 명확히 확립시켰다. 그리고 네덜란드 서인도 회사가 1625년 맨허튼 남단에 무역 기지를 개설했을 때, 그 목적은 돈을 벌기 위한 것이었지, 영혼을 구하고자 한 것이 아니었다. 설립 취지가 무역이었기 때문에, 그 회사의 중역들은 모든 사람을 환영한다는 것을 보장하기 위해 애를 썼던 것이다.

Passage 4

1. There is a rich history of mischief and malice in the interregnum, particularly during the last transfer of power to take place in the middle of a fiscal firestorm. 1) ① In 1932 it didn't help that the two men neither liked nor trusted each other: Herbert Hoover called Franklin Roosevelt a "chameleon on plaid," while Roosevelt preferred the image of Hoover as a "fat, timid capon." Since Inauguration Day was not until March 1933, there was an urgent need for action, but Hoover's efforts to reach out to Roosevelt in the name of bipartisan cooperation were dismissed by critics as an attempt to annul the election and obstruct the New Deal. Hoover called Roosevelt a "madman" for digging in his heels on economics and refusing to compromise, which guaranteed that Roosevelt took the oath of office in an atmosphere of crisis.

② It would be 20 years before the Democrats had to hand power back, and this didn't go much better. After the 1952 election, Harry Truman wrote in his diary that Eisenhower was being coy about cooperation: "he and his advisers are afraid of some kind of trick. There are no tricks. All I want to do is to make an orderly turnover."

중심소재: 권력이동 시 발생하는 현상

1. 도입부 = 주제문
재정위기의 시기에 권력 이동 중 발생하는 비행과 악행

구체적 진술을 이끄는 시그널을 파악한다.

1) 뒷받침 진술
① 사례 1
후버와 루즈벨트

② 사례 2
트루먼과 아이젠하워

TEST 14

정답 **1** (A) **2** (D) **3** (D) **4** (C)

해설

1 권력 이전시기에 발생하는 어려움을 다루는 지문이므로 (A)가 적합하다.

2 interregnum은 "권력 공백 기간, 통치 공백 기간" 등의 의미다.

3 후임으로 당선된 루즈벨트의 뉴딜정책을 방해하다는 말이 순접의 and 다음에 있으므로 같은 맥락에서 앞에서도 그가 당선된 선거를 "무효화하다"라고 하는 것이 적절하다.

4 권력 이양의 어려움에 대한 예를 제시하고 있으므로 "이전"을 뜻하는 turnover가 맞다. overturn은 "전복, 타도"의 뜻임에 주의한다.

지문해석

통치 공백 기간에는, 특히 국가재정의 대혼란 속에 행해지는 최종 권력 이전 시기에는, 역사적으로 비행과 악행이 저질러진 예가 많다. 1932년의 경우에는 두 사람이 서로 좋아하지도 믿지도 않았다는 것은 도움이 되지 않았다. 허버트 후버(Herbert Hoover)는 프랭클린 루즈벨트(Franklin Roosevelt)를 '격자무늬 위의 카멜레온'이라고 불렀고, 루즈벨트는 후버의 '뚱뚱하고 소심한 겁쟁이'로서의 이미지를 즐겼다. 취임식이 1933년 3월까지도 열리지 않았고 조치를 취해야 할 시급한 필요가 있었지만, 양당 협조라는 이름하에 루즈벨트에게 손을 내밀고자 한 후버의 노력은 선거를 무효화하고 뉴딜정책을 방해하는 것으로 비판자들에 의해 무시되었다. 후버는 경제에 관한 자신의 입장을 고집하고 타협하기를 거부하는 것 때문에 루즈벨트를 '미치광이'라고 불렀는데. 이것이 루즈벨트를 위기의 분위기에서 취임하게 만들었다.

그로부터 20년이 지난 후 민주당원들이 권력을 다시 건네주게 되었는데, 이때도 그다지 나아지지 않았다. 1952년 선거 후에 헤리 트루먼(Harry Truman)이 그의 일기장에 아이젠하워(Eisenhower)가 협조에 대해 주저한다고 썼다. "아이크(Ike)와 그의 보좌관들은 속임수를 두려워한다. 속임수란 없다. 내가 원하는 것은 질서 정연한 권력 이양일 뿐이다."

Passage 5

통념으로 시작하는 글임을 파악한다.

논리적 반전을 통해 앞서 언급된 기자에 대한 부정적 견해를 뒤집고 있다.

1. Given the demand for sensational photographs, everyone regards press photographers as an overbearing lot, as mercenaries in the pay of public curiosity; ever in pursuit, flashgun at the ready, of the unsuspecting victim. Armed to the teeth with the tools of their trade, they elbow their way through the crowd, trampling on the gardens of the famous, jamming their feet into half-closed doors and lying in wait for the widow before the still-opened grave. 1) But are press photographers really cold 'glass-eyewitnesses'? Being up close—that is the curse but also the strength of the photographic medium. ① A reporter can do his writing from a safe distance behind the lines. A photographer has no choice; he has to be right where the action is. This requires a special temperament. Good photographers seldom fit the corporate mould. They can be a nuisance; most are emotional. Many of them are politically motivated and have a soft spot for the downtrodden since everyday they have to cross the line towards poverty and sickness.

중심소재: 언론 사진기자

1. 도입부 = 통념

대중의 호기심을 바탕으로 돈을 버는 용병으로 묘사되는 언론 사진사

1) 의문문(주제)

언론 사진사들은 정말 냉정한 '목격자인가?

① 답변(요지)

대조되는 기자와 달리 사진사들은 현장에서 빈곤과 질병의 최전선을 오가는 약자에게 마음 약한 사람들이다.

정답 1 (C) 2 (E) 3 (B) 4 (B)

해설

1 통념비판의 글이다. But 이후 현장에서 떨어져 집안에서 안락하게 글만 쓰면 되는 기자와 달리 글쓴이는 사진기자는 "빈곤과 질병의 경계를 넘나드는 현장에서 위험한 일을 감수해야 한다"는 내용을 다음의 밑줄 친 표현에서 파악할 수 있다. A reporter can do his writing from a safe distance behind the lines. A photographer has no choice; he has to be right where the action is + everyday they have to cross the line towards poverty and sickness.

2 밑줄 친 표현은 "항시 카메라 플래시를 터뜨릴 준비가 된 상태로 순진한 희생자를 쫓는"이므로 개인의 사생활을 침입하는 모습을 묘사하는 것임을 알 수 있다(press photographers as an overbearing lot, as mercenaries in the pay of public curiosity).

3 객관적 보도를 위해 사진 기자들은 현장에 있어야 한다고 했다(he has to be right where the action is). 이것이 저주이면서도 동시에 강점이라고 했으므로(Being up close – that is the curse but also the strength of the photographic medium.) 선택지 (B)는 옳은 진술이다.

4 "짓밟힌 사람들에 약한 마음을 가진" 사람으로 묘사되고 있으므로 선택지 (B)가 가장 적절한 풀이라고 볼 수 있다.

지문해석

선정적인 사진에 대한 수요를 고려할 때 모든 이들이 언론 사진 기자들을 거만한 패거리이자 대중의 호기심을 위해 고용된 돈벌레로 여긴다. 즉, 항시 카메라 플래시를 터뜨릴 준비가 된 상태로 순진한 희생자를 쫓는 사람으로 여기는 것이다. 그들은 자신들의 직업에 필요한 장비들로 완전 무장한 채 팔꿈치로 인파들 사이를 헤집고 다니고 유명인들의 정원을 밟아 뭉개며 반쯤 열린 문 사이로 발을 들이밀고 아직 열려 있는 무덤 앞에서 미망인을 기다리며 엎드려 있다. 그러나 언론 사진 기자들이 정말로 냉정한 '(사진)렌즈를 낀 목격자'인가? 가까이에 있는 것, 그것이야말로 사진 매체의 저주이자 강점이다. 기자는 후방의 안전거리에서 그의 글을 쓸 수 있다. 그러나 사진 기자는 선택의 여지없이 사건이 있는 바로 그곳에 있어야만 한다. 이는 특별한 기질을 요구한다. 훌륭한 사진 기자들은 좀처럼 회사 체질이 아니다. 그들은 귀찮은 존재일 수 있고 대부분은 감정적이다. 그들 중 많은 이들이 정치적으로 적극적이고 억압받는 이들에 대해 호의적인데 그들이 매일 가난과 질병을 향해 나아가기 때문이다.

TEST 14

Passage 6

[B]

1. A hero, it is said, is someone who is "larger than life," whom we can admire for great qualities or abilities that we may never have. Our heroes reflect the values, hopes, and beliefs of a particular time. Heroes have included political and religious leaders, athletes, movie stars, and musicians.

[B] 첫 번째 문단
1. 영웅의 정의
특징, 역할, 종류

[C]

1. 1) In the United States, for example, ① political leaders who led the country to greater freedom and democracy have been heroes to many. George Washington, the nation's first president, John Kennedy, the vibrant young president who inspired hope, and Martin Luther King, the civil rights leader who fought for racial equality, all attained hero status among Americans. ② Sports were, and still are, the first sources of heroes for many American children.

[C] 두 번째 문단
1. for example에서 알 수 있듯이 과거의 정치와 스포츠의 영웅을 구체적 예와 함께 다루고 있다.
1) 구체적 진술
① 정치 영웅의 예
② 스포츠 영웅의 예

Picture, for example, the 1930s sports stadium: a red-haired, freckled-faced boy sits in the stands, magnetized by the style, grace, and actions of the larger-than-life athlete, Lou Gehrig, the famous baseball player who died of a nerve disease that was later named after him. The young boy was a true believer.

[A]

1. 1) Today, however, many people say they do not have heroes. It is difficult to find an equivalent of Washington, Kennedy, King, or Gehrig. Political figures in today's world of leaders rarely, if ever, appear larger than life to us. ① In today's world of prying journalists and a television-age public, it seems difficult for anyone to attain heroic stature. What is worse, we now dredge up information about our past heroes, only to take away their heroism: we now know that John Kennedy ran around with other women; there appear to be evidence that Martin Luther King did, too. And today, more and more of our heroes have been forced to abdicate their hero status as new discoveries of their real lives have been made.

[A] 세 번째 문단

1. However를 중심으로 앞 문단의 과거와 대조를 이루는 오늘날의 이야기를 다루고 있다.

1) 현실(현상)

영웅 부재의 현실

①원인

남의 사생활을 캐기 좋아하는 저널리스트와 TV시대로 인해 영웅의 과거가 드러나면서 영웅으로서의 지위를 유지하기가 힘들게 되었다.

정답 **1** (B) **2** (D)

해설

however와 for example을 통해 문장의 흐름을 알 수 있다. [B]에서는 영웅에 대한 전반적인 이야기를 하고 있고 [C]에서는 영웅의 구체적 예에 대해, [A]에서는 과거와 다르게 오늘날에는 영웅이 거의 존재하지 않는다는 이야기를 하고 있다. 영웅 부재 현상을 다루는 내용이다.

지문해석

[B] 영웅은 "현실과 동떨어진" 사람, 우리가 결코 가질 수 없는 위대한 자질과 능력을 가지고 있어서 우리가 존경할 수 있는 사람이라고들 한다. 우리의 영웅들은 특정한 시대의 가치와 희망, 신념을 반영한다. 영웅에는 정치 및 종교 지도자와 운동선수, 영화배우, 음악가들이 포함되어 왔다.

[C] 예를 들어 미국에서는 미국을 더 큰 자유와 민주주의로 이끌었던 정치 지도자들이 많은 이들에게 영웅이 되어왔다. 미국의 초대 대통령인 조지 워싱턴(George Washington), 희망을 불어 넣어준 정력적이고 젊은 대통령 존 에프 케네디(John F. Kennedy), 인종 평등을 위해 싸웠던 민권 지도자 마틴 루터 킹(Martin Luther King)은 모두 미국인들 사이에서 영웅적 지위를 얻었다. 스포츠는 과거에도 현재에도 많은 미국 어린이들에게 가장 중요한 영웅의 원천이다. 예를 들어 1930년대 운동 경기장을 상상해 보아라. 빨간 머리, 주근깨 얼굴의 소년이 관람석에 앉아, 이후 그의 이름을 따서 이름 붙여진 신경계 질환으로 사망한 유명 야구 선수인 루 게릭(Lou Gehrig)이라는 영웅적인 운동선수의 스타일과 우아함과 행동에 매료되어 있다. 그 어린 소년은 진정한 신봉자였다.

[A] 그러나 오늘날 많은 사람들은 영웅을 가지고 있지 않다고 말한다. 워싱턴이나 케네디, 마틴 루터 킹, 루 게릭에 필적할 만한 사람을 찾는 것은 어려운 일이다. 오늘날 지도자인 세계의 정치인들은, 만약 있긴 한다면, 좀처럼 우리에게 영웅적으로 보이지 않는다. 오늘날 엿보기 좋아하는 언론인들과 텔레비전 시대의 대중들이 살아가는 세상에서 어떤 사람이 영웅적인 위상을 얻는다는 것은 힘들어 보인다. 설상가상으로 우리는 우리의 과거 영웅들에 대한 정보를 들추어내다가 결국엔 그들에게서 영웅적 지

위를 빼앗기도 한다. 이제 우리는 존 에프 케네디가 다른 여성들과 깊은 관계를 맺었음을 알게 되었다. 마틴 루터 킹 역시 그랬다는 증거가 있는 듯이 보인다. 그래서 오늘날 점점 더 많은 우리의 영웅들이 그들의 실생활에 대한 새로운 사실들이 발견되면서 영웅의 지위를 포기하지 않을 수 없게 되었다.

Passage 7

1. 1) The concept of sustainability applies to all aspects of life on Earth and is commonly defined within ecological, social and economic contexts. Due to factors such as overpopulation, lack of education, inadequate financial circumstances and the actions of past generations, sustainability can be difficult to achieve. ① Ⓐ **In an ecological context**, sustainability is defined as the ability of an ecosystem to maintain ecological processes, functions, biodiversity and productivity into the future. Ⓑ **In a social context**, sustainability is expressed as meeting the needs of the present without compromising the ability of future generations to meet their own needs. Ⓒ When applied **in an economic context**, a business is sustainable if it has adapted its practices for the use of renewable resources and is accountable for the environmental impacts of its activities.

2. 1) To be sustainable, regardless of context, Earth's resources must be used at a rate at which they can be replenished. There is now clear scientific evidence that humanity is living unsustainably, and that an effort is needed to keep human use of natural resources within sustainable limits.

먼저 언급된 것 먼저 기술

E+S+E

Ⓔ

Ⓢ

Ⓔ

중심소재: sustainability

1. 첫 번째 문단

1) 도입부 = 중심소재 도출

지속가능성의 정의를 세 분야로 나누어 살펴보고 있다.

① 구체적 진술

Ⓐ Ecological Context
생태학적 상황에서 바라본 지속가능성의 정의

Ⓑ Social Context
사회적 상황에서 바라본 지속가능성의 정의

Ⓒ Economic Context
사회적 상황에서 바라본 지속가능성의 정의

2. 두 번째 문단

1) 지속가능성의 조건과 필요성

TEST 14

정답 1 (C) 2 (D)

해설

1 compromise는 "손상시키다"는 뜻으로 선택지 (C)가 의미상 가장 근접하다.

2 본문 마지막에 문장인 an effort is needed to keep human use of natural resources within sustainable limits.를 통해 지속발전 가능한 제한 내에서 천연자원을 사용해야 함을 강조하고 있으므로 지속가능성의 개념은 "불가피한 과정"이 아니라 인위적 노력이 뒷받침되어야 함을 파악할 수 있으므로 선택지 (D)는 적절치 못하다.

지문해석

지속가능성(sustainability)이라는 개념은 지구 생명체의 모든 양상에 적용되며 흔히 생태학적, 사회적, 경제적 상황 내에서 정의된다. 이를테면 인구과잉, 교육 부족, 불충분한 재정 상황, 과거 세대의 행위 등의 요인 때문에 지속 가능성은 달성하기 어려울 수 있다. 생태학적인 상황에서 지속 가능성은 생태 과정, 기능, 생물의 다양성 그리고 생산성을 미래로까지 유지할 수 있는 생태계의 능력이라 정의할 수 있다. 사회적 상황에서 지속 가능성은 미래 세대의 욕구 충족 능력을 손상시키지 않고 현재의 욕구를 충족시키는 것이라 표현된다. 경제적 상황에서 적용되는 지속가능성이란, 한 기업이 지속되려면 재생 가능한 자원을 이용하기 위해 기업 관행을 바꾸고 기업의 활동이 환경에 미치는 영향에 대해 책임을 져야 한다는 뜻이다. 어떤 상황에서든 지속

가능하려면 자원은 다시 보충될 수 있는 속도로 이용되어야 한다. 인류는 현재 지속 불가능한 방식으로 살아가고 있으며 인류가 천연자원을 지속가능한 한계 내에서만 이용하도록 하기 위해 노력해야 할 필요가 있다는 분명한 과학적 증거가 있다.

Passage 8

1. Drug use in the U.S. is not confined to some narrowly defined, easily excised subculture. Tens of millions of Americans use illegal psychoactives each year, and they come from all walks of life. **1)** If we are to undo drugs in America, our policies must reflect the fact that we are the users, the abusers, and the addicts. ① Although the bulk of all users of psychoactives are casual users, the bulk of all use is by abusers and addicts. And most of the damage done to and by users occurs as a result of addiction and abuse. This is true whether we focus on the adverse health consequences for the users (such as lung cancer for nicotine addicts), adverse health consequences for third parties (such as people killed by drunk drivers), or other adverse effects (such as crimes committed by heroin addicts). **2.** Thus, ③ only if we materially alter the behavior of addicts and abusers will our policies yield substantial benefits. Unless and until public policy is shaped to yield a permanent and substantial reduction in use rather than users, few beneficial consequences are likely to result from drug policy.

요지를 이끄는 시그널을 확인한다.

중심소재: 정신활성제

1. 도입부 = 현상(문제점 지적)
마약사용 범위에 대한 정의를 내리면서 미국 사회 내 만연해 있는 정신활성제의 불법 사용을 지적하고 있다.

1) 대안(요지)
미국 사회에서 불법마약사용을 없애기 위해선 우선, 우리 스스로 마약을 남용하고 중독된 점을 반영해야 한다.

① 문제점
일반사용자가 아닌 중독과 남용으로 이어지는 마약중독자에 의한 정신활성제 소비가 문제

2. 대안(요지)
중독자와 남용자의 실질적 행동을 변화시킬 정책과 마약의 영구적 사용량 감축을 위한 정책적 차원에서 제약이 필요함

정답 1 (D)

해설
마약 사용자들이 입는 피해와 그들이 입히는 피해는 대부분은 중독과 남용의 결과이며 중독자와 남용자의 행동을 변화시켜야 효과가 있다고 하였으므로 선택지 (D) "마약정책은 남용과 중독에 초점을 맞출 필요가 있다"가 적절하다.

지문해석
미국에서 약물 사용은 제한적으로 정의되고 쉽게 잘라낼 수 있는 어떤 하위문화에 한정된 것이 아니다. 수천만 명의 미국인들이 불법 정신활성제들을 매년 사용하는데 그들은 사회 각계각층의 사람들이다. 우리가 약물 없는 미국을 만들고자 한다면 우리의 정책들은 우리가 사용자, 남용자, 중독자라는 사실을 반영해야 한다. 정신활성제 사용자의 대부분은 이따금 사용하는 사람들이지만 전체 사용량의 대부분이 남용자들과 중독자들에 의한 것이다. 그리고 사용자들에게 가해진 피해와 사용자들이 가한 피해의 대부분이 중독과 남용의 결과로 발생한다. 이것은 우리가 사용자들에게 미치는 (니코틴 중독자들의 폐암과 같은) 건강상의 부정적인 결과들에 초점을 맞추든, 제 3자들에게 미치는 (음주 운전자들에 의해 사망한 사람들과 같은) 건강상의 부정적인 결과들에 초점을 맞추든, 아니면 (헤로인 중독자들에 의해 저질러진 범죄들과 같은) 다른 악영향들에 초점을 맞추든 사실이다. 따라서 우리가 중독자들과 남용자들의 행동을 실질적으로 바꾸어 놓는 경우에 한해 우리의 정책들은 상당한 이득들을 이끌어낼 것이다. 사용자 수보다는 사용량의 영구적이고 상당한 감소를 이끌어내도록 공공정책이 만들어지기 전까지 약물 정책에서 얻을 수 있는 유익한 결과들은 거의 없을 것 같다.

TEST 15

Passage 1

1. 1) Humans are classed anatomically among the primates, the order of which includes apes, monkeys and lemurs. Among the hundreds of living primate species, only humans are naked. ① Two kinds of habitat are known to give rise to naked mammals - a subterranean one or a wet one. Ⓐ There is a naked Somalian mole rat which never ventures above ground. All other non-human mammals which have lost all or most of their fur are either swimmers like whales and dolphins, or wallowers like hippopotamuses and pigs and tapirs. ⓐ The rhinoceros and the elephant, though found on land since Africa became drier, bear traces of a more watery past and seize every opportunity of wallowing in mud or water. 2. 1) It has been suggested that ① humans became hairless "to prevent overheating in the savannah." But no other mammal has ever resorted to this strategy. Ⓐ A covering of hair acts as a defense against the heat of the sun: that is why even the desert-dwelling camel retains its fur. ② Another version is "to facilitate sweat-cooling." But again many species resort to sweat-cooling quite effectively without needing to lose their hair. 2) One general conclusion seems undeniable from an overall survey of mammalian species: that while a coat of fur provides the best insulation for land mammals the best insulation in water is not fur, but a layer of fat.

중심소재: 인간의 특징 → 털이 없음

1. 첫 번째 문단

1) 도입부 = 인간의 예외적 특징
영장류 중 유일하게 털이 없다.
① 원인
땅 속 또는 물과 같은 두 종류의 서식지의 영향
Ⓐ 뒷받침 진술
Somalian mole rat만 땅 속에서 생활하고, 나머지는 모두 털이 없는 바다생물이거나 물에서 뒹구는 하마와 같은 종류
ⓐ wallower에 대한 세부부연

2. 두 번째 문단

1) 인간이 털이 없게 된 배경
① 가설 1
대초원의 지나친 열을 막기 위한 도구일 수 있지만, 다른 어떤 포유류도 이러한 방법을 쓰지 않기에 설득력이 떨어짐
Ⓐ 예시부연
② 가설 2
땀을 효율적으로 식히기 위함이지만, 여전히 털이 있으면서도 효율적으로 땀을 식히는 포유류가 많음
2) 일반적 결론(요지)
바다에선 털보단 지방층이 단열재로 가장 적합함 ← 인간의 서식지가 바다에 기원을 두고 있음을 추론할 수 있는 부분

첫 번째 문단에선 주로 일반적인 동물이 털이 없게 된 배경을 서식지 측면에서 바라보고 있다. 특정 대상의 예외적 특징이 언급되면 이에 대한 원인 파악의 내용으로 전개되는 경우가 많음을 기억한다.

정답 1 (A) 2 (B)

해설

1 빈칸에는 털이 없는 포유류가 사는 두 종류의 서식지의 속성에 해당하는 단어가 들어가야 한다. 빈칸이 있는 문장 이후에, "땅 위로 나오지 않는" 두더지와 아울러 "헤엄치거나 진창을 뒹구는" 고래, 하마, 돼지 등이 언급되고 있으므로, ①에는 "지하의"라는 뜻을 가진 subterranean이, ②에는 "물기가 있는, 젖은"의 뜻을 가진 wet이 들어가는 것이 가장 적절하다. 나머지 선택지들은 본문에서 언급한 속성과 거리가 멀다.

2 마지막 문단을 통해 추론해 보면, 인간의 몸에 털이 거의 없는 이유는 인류의 조상이 털을 필요로 하는 육지보다는 지방층의 역할이 더욱 중요한 수중에서 살았기 때문임을 알 수 있다.

지문해석

인간은 해부학적으로 볼 때, 유인원, 원숭이, 여우 원숭이 등이 속해 있는 영장류계에 속한다. 현존하는 수백 종의 영장류 가운데 인간만이 털이 없다. 지하 혹은 물이 있는 곳, 이 두 종류의 서식지에서 털이 없는 포유류가 생겨나는 것으로 알려져 있다. 땅 위로 결코 나오지 않는 벌거숭이 소말리아 두더지가 있다. 인간을 제

외하고 털이 거의 없거나 완전히 없는 포유류는 고래나 돌고래 같이 헤엄치는 동물들 혹은 하마나 돼지, 맥(貘)과 같이 뒹굴면서 다니는 동물들이다. 아프리카 대륙이 점차 건조지대가 된 이래로, 육지에서 발견할 수 있는 코뿔소와 코끼리는 과거에는 물속에서 지냈음을 짐작케 하는 여러 흔적들을 몸에 지니고 있으며, 기회만 되면 진흙이나 물속에서 뒹구는 걸 자주 볼 수 있다. 인간이 '열대 지방의 초원에서 몸이 지나치게 뜨거워지는 것을 막기 위해' 털이 없어졌다는 견해도 있어 왔다. 그러나 이런 방법에 의지한 다른 포유동물은 전혀 없었다. 털로 덮여 있는 것은 태양열에 대한 보호막 역할을 하기 때문이다. 사막에 사는 낙타조차도 털을 가지고 있는 것이 바로 그런 이유에서다. '땀을 흘려 몸의 체온을 낮추는 것을 용이하게 하기 위한 것'이라는 주장도 있다. 그러나 역시 여러 종들이 털을 잃지 않고도 꽤 효과적으로 땀을 흘리는 것을 통해 체온조절을 하고 있다. 그렇기 때문에 설득력이 부족하다. 포유동물의 종합적인 조사로부터 얻은 한 가지 부인할 수 없는 일반적인 결론이 있다. 그것은 동물의 외피가 육지 동물을 위한 최고의 단열재 역할을 하는 반면, 수중에서의 최고의 단열재는 털이 아니라 지방층이라는 사실이다.

Passage 2

1. 1) We go see a horror movie ① to re-establish our feelings of essential normality; the horror movie is innately conventional. It urges us to put away our more civilized and adult penchant for analysis and to become children again, seeing things in pure blacks and whites. And we go ② to have fun. This is where the ground starts to slope away, because this is a very peculiar sort of fun. Ⓐ The fun comes from seeing others menaced—sometimes killed. A critic has suggested that the horror film has become the modern version of the public lynching.

2. 1) The potential lyncher is in almost all of us, and every now and then, he has to be let loose. Our emotions and our fears form their own body, and we recognize that it demands its own exercise to maintain proper muscle tone. Certain of these emotional muscles are accepted, even exalted, in civilized society. Love, friendship, loyalty, kindness—these are the emotions that we applaud. When we exhibit these emotions, society showers us with positive reinforcement. ① But anticivilization emotions don't go away, and they demand periodic exercise.

3. The horror movie has a dirty job to do. It deliberately appeals to all that is worst in us. It is morbidity unchained, our most abject instincts let free, our nastiest fantasies realized. The most aggressive of horror films lifts a trap door in the civilized forebrain and throws a basket of raw meat to the hungry alligators swimming around in that subterranean river beneath. It keeps them from getting out. It keeps them down there and me up here.

중심소재: 공포영화

1. 첫 번째 문단

1) 도입부 = 단락주제

공포 영화를 보러가는 이유

1) 구체적 진술

①기능 1
인간의 근본적 상태를 재회복하기 위한 기능

②기능 2
독특한 종류의 기쁨을 누리기 위함
Ⓐ 괴롭힘을 당하는 사람, 심지어는 죽는 것을 보고 즐거워함

2. 두 번째 문단

1) 기능 3의 뒷받침 근거

인간은 사람에게 고통을 가하고자 하는 본능이 존재하지만 사회적으로 받아들여지지 않는 행위로 간주됨

① 하지만 이러한 반문명적 감정이 사라지지 않고, 표출을 요구함

3. 기능 3

반사회적 감정의 표출을 공포영화가 대신해 주면서, 인간의 내면에 표출되기 원하는 반사회적 감정을 억제해 준다.

정답 **1** (B) **2** (C) **3** (A) **4** (B)

해설

1 It urges us to put away our more civilized and adult penchant for analysis and to become children again을 보면, 공포영화란 문화적으로 습득된 측면과 어른이 되어 가지게 되는 분석적 성향을 버리고 다시 단순하고, 어린 인간의 본성으로 돌아간다고 했으므로 선택지 (B)가 빈칸에 가장 적절하다.

2 anticivilization emotions don't go away, and they demand periodic exercise.의 밑줄 친 표현을 보면, 반문명적 감정은 가시지 않는다고 했다. 영화를 통해 이러한 감정을 주기적으로 표출함으로 무의식적 욕망을 만족시킨다고 했으므로 선택지 (C)는 본문과 일치하지 않는다.

3 공포영화를 보는 이유와 그것의 역할을 다룬 내용이므로 선택지 (A)가 적절하다. 본문분석을 참조한다.

4 공포영화의 심리적 기제를 설명한 깊이로 미루어 보아 분석적인(analytical) 어조의 글이다.

지문해석

공포영화를 보러 가는 것은 정상상태 그 자체에 대한 우리의 감정을 회복하기 위함이다. 공포영화란 본래 정해진 공식이 있기 마련이다. 공포영화는 분석을 위한 보다 세련되고 어른스러운 성향을 버리고 다시 어린아이가 되어 순전한 흑백의 관점에서 바라보도록 몰아친다. 그리고 우리는 재미있으려고 공포영화를 보러 간다. 그런데 바로 여기에서 공포영화의 존재 기반은 무너지기 시작한다. 공포영화의 재미는 매우 기묘한 종류의 재미이기 때문이다. 그 재미는 다른 사람들이 위협받거나 때로는 죽는 것을 보는 데에서 온다. 어떤 비평가는 공포영화가 현대판 공개 린치 행위가 되었다고 말한다.

잠재적인 린치 가해자로서의 특성은 거의 누구에게나 내재되어 있으며 때때로 이를 속박에서 풀어주어야 한다. 우리의 감정과 두려움이 그의 형체를 만들어냈고 우리는 그것이 적절한 근육활동을 유지하기 위해 운동을 필요로 함을 깨닫는다. 문명사회는 이러한 감정의 근육 중 특정한 것들은 수용하며 심지어 고양하기도 한다. 사랑, 우정, 충심, 친절 등은 우리가 찬양하는 감정들이다. 우리가 이런 감정들을 드러내면 사회는 우리에게 긍정적 보상을 퍼붓는다. 그러나 반문명적 감정들은 사라지지 않으며, 이러한 감정들은 주기적으로 운동을 필요로 한다.

공포영화는 꼭 해야만 하는 궂은일을 해준다. 공포영화는 우리 내부에 존재하는 최악의 것들에 주도면밀하게 호소한다. 공포영화는 우리의 병적 상태를 속박에서 풀어주고 가장 비열한 본능을 자유롭게 하며 가장 역겨운 환상을 실현시킨다. 공포영화 중에서도 가장 공격적인 영화들은 문명화된 전뇌(前腦)에 나있는 뚜껑문을 들어올리고, 그 아래 지하의 강을 이리저리 헤엄치고 있는 배고픈 악어와 같은 최악의 감정들에게 날고기 한 바가지를 던져주는 역할을 한다. 공포영화는 악한 인간의 감정들이 나오지 못하게 가두는 역할을 하는 것이다. 공포영화는 악한 감정들은 저 아래에 가두어 두고 문명화된 나를 이 위에 있게 해준다.

Passage 3

1. With its booming economy and aspirations to expand its global influence, China may have achieved a victory in American classrooms. 1) Take the private Chinese-American International School in San Francisco, which runs from prekindergarten through eighth grade and offers instruction in all subjects—from math to music half in Mandarin and half in English. The curriculum also includes Chinese history, culture and language studies, and in the 25 years since the school was founded, it has attracted mainly Asian-American children. ① But in the past few years, it has seen rapid growth in the enrollment of non-Asians. Ⓐ For example,

중심소재: 미국교육 내 중국의 영향력↑

1. 도입부

중국이 미국의 교육에서 승리를 거두었다.

1) 구체적 진술

① 현상

과거와 달리 비아시아계 미국인들이 중국계 미국인 국제 학교에 입학하고 있다.

Ⓐ 수치 부연 예시

구체적 진술을 이끄는 시그널을 확인한다.

과거와 대조를 통해서 현재를 강조하는 시간의 대조를 확인한다.

five years ago, the school was 57 percent Asian-American, but this year it is only 49 percent Asian-American, said Sharline Chiang, its spokeswoman, adding that more non-Asian-Americans have been applying in recent years. ② Ⓐ School officials attribute the changes largely to a growing awareness of China as a global economic force, Ⓑ and to a strong sense among parents that learning Chinese could help their children professionally. ⓐ As Ms. Chiang said, studying Chinese "is looked at as a long-term benefit." For similar reasons, Chinese language classes are increasingly popular across the country in public schools. Several states—including Kentucky, Minnesota, Washington, Ohio, Kansas and West Virginia—are developing Chinese language related curricula for public schools.

②현상의 원인
Ⓐ 세계 경제의 핵심 축으로 중국에 대한 인식 증가
Ⓑ 중국어 학습이 세계화의 전문성↑ → 같은 맥락에서 중국어교육 증가 → 장기적 관점에서 경제력↑

ⓐ 여파
다양한 주에서 중국어 관련 수업을 개설

정답 1 (B) 2 (D) 3 (C)

해설

1 본문의 run은 "(범위가) ~에 이르다, 미치다, 걸치다"의 의미인데 (A)는 "경영하다, 운영하다"이고, (C)는 "예행연습을 하다"이며, (D)는 "운행하다, 달리다"의 의미이다.

2 (A)의 found는 "건립하다"이고, (B)의 enrollment는 "입학"이란 뜻이다. (C)의 attribute A to B는 "A는 B로 인한 것이다"의 뜻이다. contribute는 "공헌하다"의 뜻이다. 선택지 (D)의 growing은 "늘어나는, 증가하는"의 mounting과 대체할 수 있다.

3 현상의 글은 일반적으로 "현상" 자체를 제목으로 설정하는 경우가 많다. "비(非)아시아계의 중국계 미국 국제학교에 등록이 늘어가고 있다"와 "이런 변화를 주로 세계 경제국으로 중국을 점차 인식시키고 있는 것과 중국어를 배우는 것이 아이들을 전문적으로 도울 수 있다는 부모들의 강한 의식으로 그 원인을 돌리고 있다"는 것을 통해 제목으로 적절한 것은 선택지 (C)의 "중국어 학습에 비(非) 아시아인의 증대되는 관심"이 적절하다.

지문해석

급속한 성장을 이루고 있는 경제와 세계적 영향력을 확대하려는 열망을 가진 중국은 일종의 성과를 냈는지도 모르겠다. 미국의 학교 내에서 말이다. 샌프란시스코에 있는 한 사립 중국계 미국 국제 학교를 예로 들어보자. 이 학교는 유치원 이전 과정부터 8학년에 이르는 과정을 운영하고 있으며, 수학에서 음악에 이르는 전 과목을 반은 만다린 어로, 반은 영어로 가르친다. 커리큘럼 역시 중국사와 중국 문화, 중국어를 포함하고 있으며, 학교가 창립된 이후 지금까지 25년 동안 주로 아시아계 미국 아이들을 유치했다. 그러나 최근 몇 년간, 비 아시아계 학생들의 입학이 급격하게 증가했다. 예를 들어, 오년 전, 아시아계 미국 학생들의 비율은 57퍼센트에 달했지만 올해는 49퍼센트에 지나지 않는다고, 학교의 대변인 샬린 치앙(Sharline Chiang)은 전했다. 그녀는 또한, 비 아시아계 학생들의 지원이 최근 몇 년간 더욱 증가하고 있다고 덧붙였다. 학교 관계자들은 중국을 세계 경제 대국으로 인식하는 경향이 커진 것과, 중국어를 배우면 아이들이 직업적으로 혜택을 입을 것이라고 굳게 믿는 부모들이 이러한 변화를 만들어낸 주된 이유라 보고 있다. Ms. Chiang이 말했듯, 중국어를 공부하는 것은 "장기적으로 도움이 되는 것처럼 보인다." 또한 이와 유사한 이유로 중국어 수업은 전국의 공립학교에서 날로 인기를 더해가고 있다. 켄터키, 미네소타, 워싱턴, 오하이오, 켄사스, 웨스트버지니아를 포함한 몇몇 주들은 공립학교를 위한 중국어 관련 교과과정들을 개발하고 있다.

Passage 4

1. A hard line on immigration is getting more popular in politics these days. Politicians throughout Europe have read the writing on the wall and think they've discerned there a populist, anti-immigrant scrawl. 1) ① Jean-Marie Le Pen's exploitation of the issue helped put him into the second round of France's presidential elections. ② The new Danish government rode to power astride that issue last fall. 2) So, isn't it only fair to give Europe's politicians a modicum of credit for finally responding to public concern?

① Up to a point, yes. When they convene in Seville in August, 2003 for their European Council meeting, European Union leaders will focus on immigration—especially illegal immigration. When it comes to this, Spanish Prime Minister declared, "the masks of hypocrisy have to drop." Yet it seems likely that whatever decisions are made at Seville, more than a few hypocrisies will remain firmly in place. Despite the recognized need for a common E.U. policy on immigration, no number of British warships in the Mediterranean or watchtowers on the Poland-Belarus border are likely to reverse this natural law: Ⓐ Human beings have always wanted to escape misery. "I don't see any important new developments in migration today," says a top expert on the matter with the OECD. In a political sense, though, much has changed.

중심소재: 이민정책

1. 도입부 = 현상

이민자에 대한 유럽의 강경책으로 유럽전역에 반이민정서 확산

1) 배경

① 프랑스의 경우

반이민정서를 활용하여 대선을 노리는 정치인

② 덴마크의 경우

반이민정서를 이용하여 새로운 정부 설립

2) 의문문(주제)

국민정서를 반영한 유럽 정치인의 공로 인정?

① 답변(요지)

스페인 총리를 통해 현 이민정책의 모순적 측면을 EU회의에서 모두 청산해야 함을 언급하지만, Yet을 중심으로 불법 이민이 없어지지 않을 것이라는 사실을 언급하고 있다.

Ⓐ 근거

인간은 언제나 비극적인 상황을 회피하기를 원하기 때문(본문의 문맥상 이민을 통해서)

up to a point, yes에서 알 수 있듯이 궁극적으로 글쓴이는 앞의 의문점에 반대하는 견해를 제시할 것을 예측할 수 있다.

TEST 15

정답 1 (A) 2 (D)

해설

1 지중해에 떠 있는 수없는 전함이나 국경선의 감시탑도 "이 자연의 법칙" 즉, 이민현상을 막을 수 없다는 내용으로 가장 적절한 것은 "비참한 현실을 떠나 더 나은 삶을 찾기를 원한다"는 선택지 (A)이다.

2 "정치적인 관점에서 볼 때 많이 달라졌다."는 긍정적 의미를 내포하는 마지막 문장 다음에 올 내용으로 가장 적절한 것은 (D)이다.

지문해석

요즘 들어 이민에 대한 강경노선이 정치에서 점점 더 많은 지지를 얻고 있다. 전 유럽의 정치인들이 대자보를 읽었고, 거기에서 대중의 인기에 영합하는 이민 반대 의사를 발견했다. 장 마리 르펜(Jean-Marie Le Pen)은 이 관심사를 이용해 프랑스 대통령 선거 2차 투표까지 갈 수 있었다. 덴마크의 새로운 정부는 지난 가을 이 문제를 이용해 정권을 잡았다. 그러니 대중의 관심에 마침내 반응한 것에 대해 유럽 정치인들에게 조금이라도 점수를 주는 것이 정당한 것 아닌가?

어느 정도까지는 그렇다. 그들이 2003년 8월 유럽 이사회 회담을 위해 세비야(Seville)에 모일 때 유럽 연합 지도자들은 이민, 특히 불법 이민을 중점적으로 다룰 것이다. 이에 관해 스페인 총리는 "위선의 가면을 벗어야 한다"고 선언했다. 그러나 세비야에서 어떤 결정이 내려지든 적지 않은 위선적 행위들이 변함없이 지속될 것으로 보인다. 이민에 대한 유럽 연합의 공동 정책이 필요하다는 공감대가 형성되어 있음에도 지중해 연안의 영국 군함이나 폴란드-벨로루시 경계에 있는 망루 중 어느 하나도 인간은 언제나 불행에서 벗어나길 원

했다는 자연 법칙을 뒤엎을 것 같지 않다. "나는 오늘 이민에 관한 어떠한 새로운 진전도 보지 못했다"라고 이 사항과 관련된 OECD의 최고 전문가는 말한다. 그러나 정치적 관점에서 볼 때는 많은 것이 변했다. 1999년에 유럽 연합 지도자들이 이민 정책을 시행하기 위해 모였을 때 당시의 논의는 상당히 고차원적이었다.

Passage 5

국제 사회에서 미국의 power에 관한 글이다. 글의 도입부에서 3가지 종류의 power를 언급하는데, 궁극적으로 But 이후의 soft power에 관한 글로 그 주제의 폭이 좁혀지고 있다.

글의 논리적 전환을 이끄는 역접은 글의 무게중심을 But 이후로 전환한다.

1. The United States projects its power in varying degrees of rigidity. American military supremacy, or "hard power", is unquestioned. American economic primacy, what might be called "stiff power", perseveres despite erosion in the face of rising economic power in China, India, and the European Union. 1) But "soft power", what Joseph Nye, professor of international relations at the Harvard Kennedy School of Government, describes as the attraction of the international community to the United States based upon its culture, values, and policies, has fallen significantly. ① The primary cause of this is America's unilateralism, most notably in the Iraq War. The effect has been that other countries are more likely to question America's motives and intentions. 2. While this observation is grim, it also offers an opportunity for decisive action to restore America's moral leadership. The next president can revitalize American soft power through many avenues, two of which seem especially powerful: committing to multilateral diplomacy, and leading by both example and engagement on globally significant issues.

중심소재: American's Power

1. 도입부
미국이 국제사회에 행사하는 군사력(hard power)과 경제력(stiff power)은 여전히 건재함

1) 현상(문제점)
외교력인 Soft power는 그 영향력이 많이 줄어들었다.

① 원인
이라크 전에 있어 미국의 일방주의로 인해 다른 나라들이 미국의 동기와 의도를 의심하게 됨

2. 대안(요지)
세계 중요문제에 모범이 되면서 적극적으로 개입함으로 미국의 외교력을 회복할 수 있다.

정답 1 (A) 2 (C) 3 (A)

해설

1 주로 미국의 외교력인 soft power에 관한 글임을 글의 전반부에서 파악했다면 쉽게 답을 구할 수 있다. 본문 분석을 참조하도록 한다.

2 soft power를 회복하는 두 가지 방법 중 하나로 multilateral diplomacy가 제시되었다. other countries are more likely to question America's motives and intentions의 밑줄 친 부분을 볼 때 soft power의 약화 원인으로 "일방주의(unilateralism)"를 보는 것이 논리적이다.

3 The effect has been that other countries are more likely to question America's motives and intentions.와 committing to multilateral diplomacy, and leading by both example and engagement on globally significant issues.의 두 내용을 통해 이상적 지도력은 "국제 사회의 동의"를 바탕으로 이뤄짐을 파악할 수 있다.

지문해석

미국의 파워는 다양한 강도로 표현된다. 미국의 군사적 패권 또는 "hard power"는 확고하다. 중국, 인도, 유럽연합 등 경제 강국들의 부상에 불구하고 "stiff power"라고도 불릴 수 있는 미국의 경제적 우위 역시 지속되고 있다. 그러나 Harvard Kennedy School of Government의 Joseph Nye교수에 따르면 미국의 문화, 가치, 정치에 기반을 두고 국제사회를 흡인할 수 있는 능력인 "soft power"는 상당히 약화되었다. 이러한 현상

의 주요 원인은 특히 이라크 전쟁에서 가장 크게 부각된 미국의 일방주의이다. 그 결과 다른 국가들은 미국의 (이라크 전쟁에 대한) 동기와 의도에 대해 의심할 가능성이 커진다. 이러한 상황이 암울해 보이긴 하지만 한편 미국의 도덕적 리더십을 회복하기 위한 단호한 조치를 취할 기회를 제공하기도 한다. 차기 대통령은 여러 수단을 강구해 미국의 soft power를 회복시킬 수 있다. 그 수단들 중 특히 강력한 것은 다자간 외교에 힘쓰는 것과 전 세계적으로 중요한 사안에 대해 참여와 모범을 보임으로써 지도력을 발휘하는 것이다.

Passage 6

1. Why is it so difficult to find a great leader? ① The answer lies in a very simple truth about leadership. 1) People can only be led where they want to go. The leader follows, though a step ahead. ① Americans wanted to climb out of the Depression and needed someone to tell them they could do it, and Roosevelt did. The British believed that they could still win the war after the defeats of 1940, and Churchill told them they were right.

2. A leader rides the waves, moves with the tides, understands the deepest yearnings of his people. He cannot make a nation that wants peace at any price go to war, or stop a nation determined to fight from doing so. His purpose must match the national mood.

중심소재: 지도자의 부재

1. 도입부 = 주제
위대한 지도자를 찾기 힘든 이유

1) 주제문(요지문)
사람들은 자신이 원하는 방향으로 이끌리길 원하기 때문에, 지도자는 앞서가면서도, 사람들을 따라야 한다(국민의 견해를 따르는 지도자).
① 뒷받침 사례

2. 요지 재진술
국민의 마음을 대변하는 지도자

정답 1 (B)

해설
진정한 지도자란 국민이 원하는 바를 성취할 수 있도록 이끄는 사람이다. 이러한 내용을 가장 잘 드러내는 것은 선택지 (B)이다.

지문해석
위대한 지도자를 찾는 것이 왜 그렇게 어려운 일인가? 그 대답은 리더십에 관한 매우 단순한 사실에 있다. 사람들은 오직 그들이 가고 싶어 하는 곳으로 인도된다. 지도자는 한 발 앞서서 따라가는 것뿐이다. 미국인들은 대공황에서 빠져나오고 싶었고 그들에게 할 수 있다고 말해주는 누군가를 필요로 했는데 루즈벨트(Roosevelt)가 그걸 해주었다. 영국인들은 1940년 전쟁에서 패배한 후에도 여전히 전쟁에서 이길 수 있다고 믿었고, 처칠(Churchill)은 그들이 옳다고 말해주었다. 지도자는 최고의 지위를 누리기도 하고 시류를 따르기도 하면서 그의 국민들 가슴 속 깊이 있는 열망을 이해한다. 그는 어떤 대가를 치르더라도 평화를 원하는 국민을 전쟁터로 내몰 수 없고, 그러려고 싸우기로 결심한 국민을 멈출 수도 없다. 그의 목표는 국민의 분위기에 맞춰야만 한다.

첫 번째 문장에서 글의 방향성을 설정할 수 있다. 어느 지문을 막론하고 첫 번째 문장의 이해도가 곧 글 전체의 이해도와 직결된다는 점을 잊지 말아야한다.

Passage 7

1. Having described the 'structure' of the prison in modern society, Foucault turns finally to the matter of its 'function.' 1) From the moment that the prison came into being, observers recognized that incarceration did not reduce crime or rehabilitate criminals. And yet, again and again, even the most enlightened critics in the 1960's called for bigger and better prisons, more effective classification and treatment programs. ① How then reconcile failure with persistence? How understand the institution's longevity, given so poor a record? Ⓐ Foucault's answer comes quickly: the prison endures because it performs a critical function in capitalist society. ⓐ By turning criminals into abnormal types of one sort or another, it separates the criminal from the body of the working class. The ultimate purpose of the prison, Foucault declares, is to divide the outlaw from the proletariat, thereby reducing lower-class solidarity and protest. The illegalities of the dominant class survive through the confinement of the illegalities of the lower class.

중심소재: 감옥

1. 도입부 = 중심소재 도출
감옥의 기능

1) 예외적 현상
범죄를 줄이거나 범죄자를 회복시키지 못했음에도 불구하고, 1960년대에 더 크고 더 나은 감옥이 요구되었다.

① 의문점(주제)
감옥의 기능 상실과 지속을 어떻게 해결했는가?

Ⓐ 답변(요지)
자본주의 사회에서 중요한 역할을 하기 때문이다

ⓐ 뒷받침 진술
감옥의 기능 상술

정답 **1 (A) 2 (A)**

해설

1 From the moment that the prison came into being, observers recognized that ________ did not reduce crime or rehabilitate criminals. And yet, again and again, even the most enlightened critics in the 1960's called for bigger and better prisons에서 빈칸을 중심으로 전개되는 내용은 "감옥이 생긴 후 ____가 범죄를 줄이거나 범죄자를 교화시키지 못했다. 하지만 1960년대 비평가는 여전히 더 큰 감옥을 요구했다"라는 내용이므로 빈칸에 들어갈 표현은 "감옥에 가두는 것"에 해당하는 선택지 (A)가 가장 적절하다.

2 글의 중심내용인 "감옥의 기능"을 중심으로 본문과 일치하는 내용을 선택해야 한다. By turning criminals into abnormal types of one sort or another, it separates the criminal from the body of the working class. The ultimate purpose of the prison, Foucault declares, is to divide the outlaw from the proletariat, thereby reducing lower-class solidarity and protest.에서 밑줄 친 내용을 보면 "죄수를 비정상적인 사람으로 바꿈으로 노동계급 집단으로부터 분류한다. 감옥의 궁극적 목적(기능)은 노동계급으로부터 '범죄자'를 분리해 노동자 계층의 유대와 저항을 줄인다."고 말하고 있다. 이는 사회로부터 감옥을 옹호하는 사람들이 보기에 "정신이상자"를 분리하는 것을 정당화시키는 도구로 활용함을 유추할 수 있다. 부르주아는 노동자들이 서로 유대감을 형성하는 것을 반대함으로 선택지 (A)는 옳지 않다.

지문해석

현대 사회에서의 감옥의 구조를 자세히 기술한 후 푸코(Foucault)는 마침내 그 '기능'의 문제로 시선을 돌렸다. 감옥이 존재하기 시작한 순간부터 관찰자들은 투옥이 범죄를 줄이거나 범죄자들을 교화시키지 않는다는 사실을 깨달았다. 그러나 1960년대의 가장 계몽된 비평가들조차 더 크고 좋은 감옥, 더욱 효율적인 분류와 치료 프로그램을 계속해서 요구했다. 그렇다면 (감옥이 제구실을 못한) 실패와 (그럼에도 불구하고 감옥이 오늘날까지 계속되는) 지속성을 어떻게 조절해야 할까? 성과가 너무도 안 좋았던 기관이 이토록 장수하는 것을 어떻게 이해해야 할까? 푸코는 재빨리 대답한다. 감옥이 자본주의 사회에서 중요한 기능을 수행하기 때문에 존속한다는 것이다. 범죄자들을 이런 저런 종류의 비정상적인 유형으로 변경시켜 노동계급 집단으로부터 분리시킨다. 푸코는 감옥의 궁극적 목적이 상습적 범죄자를 노동자 계급으로부터 분리해내서 하층계급의 결속과 저항을 줄이는 것이라고 단언한다. 지배계급의 불법행위는 하층계급의 불법행위를 제한하면서 지금까지 살아남은 것이다.

Passage 8

1. 1) Sibling rivalry can be intense, as anyone who grew up with one or more brothers or sisters knows. But fortunately for all concerned, such relationships seldom take a lethal turn. Among a certain bacterial species, however, sibling colonies take competition to a deadly level, researchers report in The Proceedings of the National Academy of Sciences. ① Related colonies near one another on a bed of low-nutrient agar mutually inhibit growth by secreting an antibacterial compound that in high enough concentrations becomes lethal.

2. 1) Avraham Be'er and Harry Swinney of the University of Texas and colleagues studied colonies of Paenibacillus dendritiformis, which when started as a single droplet grow outward, forming intricate bushlike branches. Using samples from the same bacterial culture (and thus "siblings"), the researchers started two colonies a given distance apart on the agar. After nine hours, the colonies started growing outward. But at 40 hours, the facing fronts of both colonies started to slow down. At 96 hours the facing fronts stopped, leaving a gap between them. The researchers first suspected that the growth slowed down and stopped as the nutrients in the agar were consumed. But several other experiments showed that food was not an issue. ① Rather, the colonies were secreting a growth-inhibiting compound, one that was killing the bacteria along the facing fronts.

3. 1) An obvious question is why these secretions are deadly between two colonies but not within a single colony on its own. As the researchers put it, why doesn't a single colony inhibit its own growth? The researchers devised a simple mathematical model that provides an answer. ① Basically it comes down to the concentration of the antibacterial compounds. Ⓐ At the growing edge of a colony, the concentration never becomes high enough to be lethal. But with two nearby colonies growing toward each other, the concentration rises to a level to result in mutually assured destruction.

중심소재: sibling colonies

1. 첫 번째 문단

1) 도입부 = 현상

일반적으로 형제·자매간의 경쟁과 달리 형제·자매 군락의 경쟁은 치명적인 수준까지 이른다.

① 구체적 진술

낮은 영양분의 배양판을 중심으로 양쪽의 군락은 서로 치명적 수준의 항박테리아를 분배

2. 두 번째 문단

1) 실험의 구체적 내용

① 실험 결과

한쪽 군락이 다른 군락의 박테리아를 죽임

3. 세 번째 문단

1) 의문점(문단 주제)

성장방해 합성물의 분비는 자체 군락의 성장을 왜 저해하지 않는 것인가?

① 답변(단락요지)

항박테리아 혼합물의 농도

Ⓐ 부연

라이벌 군락이 서로 마주보고 있을 경우 분비물의 농도가 높아져 치명적이게 된다.

TEST 15

정답 1 (D) 2 (D)

해설

1 (A)는 경쟁이 격렬할 수 있다고 했는데 그 관계들이 치명적이 아니므로 다행이라는 fortunately가 적절하며, (B)는 앞 내용에서 두 군락 사이에서는 서로 성장을 방해하나 한 군락이 자신의 성장은 방해하지 않으므로 inhibit가 적절하다.

2 Paenibacillus dendritiformis는 형제 사이의 경쟁에 대한 실험을 하기 위해 배양한 군락으로 경쟁이 치명적이므로 (A)는 부적합하고 영양소가 문제가 아니라고 했으므로 (B)도 부적절하며 (C)는 두 군락 사이에서 성장이 멈추므로 부적절하며 형제군락들은 항박테리아 합성물을 분비해서 성장을 저해하므로 (D)가 타당하다.

지문해석

여러 형제나 자매와 함께 성장한 사람이면 누구나 알고 있듯이 형제나 자매 사이의 경쟁은 격렬할 수 있다. 그러나 관련된 모든 사람에게 다행하게도 그런 관계들이 좀처럼 치명적인 관계로 변하지는 않는다. 그러나 어떤 박테리아 종들 중에서는 형제군락이 치명적인 수준으로까지 경쟁을 한다고 '국립과학학회 회보'에서 조사자들은 보고한다. 낮은 영양분의 한천배양판에서 서로 가까이 있는 관련된 군락들은 농도가 충분히 높으면 치명적이게 되는 항박테리아 합성물을 분비함으로써 상호 간에 성장을 방해한다.

텍사스 대학의 아브라함 베어르와 핸리 스위니와 동료들은 Paenibacillus dendritiformis의 군락들을 연구했는데 그것들은 한 방울로 시작할 때는 밖으로 성장해서 복잡한 덤불 숲 같은 가지들을 형성한다. 같은 박테리아 배양균(그래서 형제들)으로부터 추출한 박테리아 샘플을 사용하여 그 조사자들은 두 개의 군락을 한천 배양판 위에서 서로 일정한 거리를 두고 시작하게 했다. 9시간 후에 그 군락들은 밖으로 성장하기 시작했다. 그러나 40시간이 경과하자 양 군락의 대면하는 앞쪽 부분들은 성장이 둔화되기 시작했다. 96시간 경과 시에는 대면하는 앞쪽 부분들이 성장을 멈추었고 그들 사이에는 간격이 생겨났다. 조사자들은 한천 배양기의 영양분들이 소비되었기 때문에 성장이 둔화되고 멈추었다고 처음에는 생각했다. 그러나 여러 다른 실험들은 양분이 문제가 아니었음을 보여주었다. 오히려 군락들은 대면하는 앞쪽 부분들에 있는 박테리아를 죽이고 있는 성장 방해 합성물을 분비하고 있었다.

분명한 의문점은 왜 이러한 분비물들이 두 군락 사이에 서는 치명적이지만 한 군락 안에서 그자체로는 치명적이지 않는가 하는 것이다. 조사자들의 표현을 빌리자면 왜 한 군락은 자기 자신의 성장을 방해하지 않는가? 조사자들은 답을 제공하는 간단한 수학적 모델을 고안했다. 기본적으로 그것은 항박테리아 합성물들의 농도로 귀착된다. 한 군락의 성장하는 가장자리에서는 그 농도가 결코 치명적일만큼 충분히 높아지지 않는다. 그러나 인접한 두 군락들이 서로를 향해 성장할 때는 그 농도가 상호간에 분명한 파괴를 초래할 수준으로까지 상승한다.

TEST 16

Passage 1

1. Scientists are exploring the seas in search of medicines that may work better than conventional drugs or have fewer side effects. 1) ① The ocean has already given us osteoporosis drugs derived from salmon, omega-3 fish oils for arthritis and heart disease, and bone replacements from coral. ② Another marine medicine in the works is a promising new cancer drug derived from bacteria that live inside a moss-like sea creature called Bugula Neritina. Ⓐ Unlike conventional drugs that kill cancer cells bryostatin-l makes them revert to normal cells. Researchers at the North ③ Carolina Sea Grant are also developing a peptide antibiotic from mast cells in hybrid striped bass. Ⓑ Unlike current antibiotics, these antibiotics from mast cells in fish and other animals may even be effective against antibiotic-resistant strains of bacteria.

중심소재: Drugs from the sea

1. 도입부 = 주제문
과학자들이 새로운 약을 개발하기 위해 바다를 탐험하고 있다.
(주제: Finding New Drugs from the sea)

1) 뒷받침 진술
① 이미 입증된 약
- osteoporosis drugs
- omega-3 fish oils
- bone replacements
② 진행 중인 항암 의약품
Bugula Neritina
Ⓐ 장점부연
③ 또 다른 제품
peptide antibiotic
Ⓑ 장점 부연

정답 1 (A) 2 (C)

해설

1 기존의 약(current antibiotics)에 비해 뛰어난 "물고기에서 만든 항생제"를 설명하고 있다. 앞에서 이미 사용된 대조를 통해 new drugs from the sea를 강조하므로 선택지 (A)가 정답이다.

2 제목을 고르는 문제이다. 주제인 new drugs from the sea를 가장 잘 반영한 것은 선택지 (C)이다.

지문해석

과학자들은 기존의 약보다 효능이 좋거나 부작용이 적은 약을 찾아 바다를 탐사하고 있다. 대양은 이미 우리에게 연어로부터 추출된 골다공증약, 관절염과 심장병에 쓰이는 오메가-3 어유(魚油), 그리고 산호에서 추출한 골대체제 등을 제공해 주었다. 현재 개발 중인 해양성분으로 만든 의약품 중에는 Bugula Neritina라는 이름의 나방 모양의 해상 식물의 신체에 사는 박테리아에서 추출한 장래성 있는 항암 의약품이 있다. 암세포를 죽이는 기존의 약과 달리, bryostatin-1은 암세포가 정상세포로 되돌아가도록 만든다. North Carolina Sea Grant의 연구진들은 또한 hybrid striped bass의 비만세포에서 펩티드 항생제를 개발 중에 있다. 현재의 항생제와는 달리 물고기 및 다른 동물의 비만세포에서 추출한 신 항생제는 항생제에 내성을 가진 박테리아 변종에 한층 효과적일 것이다.

찰스 디킨슨의 작품인 크리스마스 캐럴에 관한 글임을 알 수 있다. 작품과 관련하여 어떤 이야기를 하려는지 파악하도록 한다.

이후 문단과 관련하여 중요한 사항은 바로 개인이 교육을 통해서 스스로의 곤경을 이겨낼 수 있다는 인본주의적 관점이 드러난다는 점이다.

Passage 2

1. A Christmas Carol remains one of the rare novels to have infiltrated popular culture, leaving the impress of its characters and language even on those who have never read it. 1) Christmas offered a means for its author, Charles Dickens, to redeem the despair and the terrors of his childhood. ① After a series of financial embarrassments that left his family insolvent, the 12-year-old Dickens, his schooling interrupted, was sent to work at a shoe blacking factory in a quixotic attempt to remedy his family's plight. ② Because Dickens's tribulations were not particular to him but emblematic of the Industrial Revolution, the concerns that inform his fiction were shared by millions of potential readers. Ⓐ Dickens intended to make the sufferings of the most vulnerable of the underclass so pungently real to his readers that they could not continue to ignore their need, not so much for charity as for the means to save themselves: education. At least this was his conscious purpose.

2. In a sense, replacing the slippery Holy Ghost with anthropomorphized spirits, the infant Christ with a crippled child whose salvation waits on man's—not God's—generosity, Dickens laid claim to a religious festival, handing it over to the gathering forces of secular humanism.

중심소재: 찰스디킨스의 크리스마스 캐럴

1. 도입부
크리스마스 캐럴은 대중문화에 침투하여 대중의 마음에 작품의 등장인물과 언어라는 측면에서 깊은 인상을 남긴다.

1) 구체적 진술

① 크리스마스 소재의 선정 배경
개인적 차원의 구원: 자신의 어린 시절의 절망과 공포를 회복하는 도구

② 대중적 차원의 구원으로 확대
디킨슨의 어린 시절의 고난이 단지 개인적인 사항이 아닌 그 당시의 보편적 상황임을 언급하면서 소설 속에 다룬 관심사의 대중성을 언급하고 있다.

Ⓐ 해결책
곤궁한 대중에 대한 해결책은 단순한 자선이 아닌 교육의 제공이다.

2. 궁극적 의미(요지)
현재의 곤궁의 극복은 신의 개입을 통한 수동적 접근이 아닌 '인간에 의한 인간의 구제'인 세속적 인본주의

정답 **1** (B) **2** (A)

해설

1 본문 마지막 문장(Dickens laid claim to a religious festival, handing it over to the gathering forces of secular humanism)에서도 알 수 있듯이 디킨슨은 종교적 축제를 세속적 인본주의에 넘기려는 시도를 한다. 그러므로 선택지 (B)와 같이 세속적 사회를 종교적으로 묘사(religious renderings of a secular society)한다는 표현은 옳지 못하다.

2 디킨슨을 크리스마스 캐럴을 통해 인류의 구원은 인간의 손에 달려 있다는 세속적 인문주의 관점을 드러내고 있다. 선택지 (A)가 가장 적절한 제목이다.

지문해석

크리스마스 캐럴은 대중문화에 침투하여, 그 소설을 읽지 않은 사람들에게조차 등장인물과 언어에 대해 깊은 인상을 남긴, 흔치 않은 소설이다. 크리스마스는 그 작가인 찰스 디킨스로 하여금 자신의 어린 시절의 절망과 공포를 상쇄시킬 수 있는 도구를 제시했다. 가정을 파산시킨 잇따른 금전적 곤란을 겪은 후, 12살의 디킨스는 학업을 마치지 못하고 구두닦이 공장으로 보내진다. 이는 가정의 궁핍함을 구제하고자 했던 터무니없는 시도였다.
디킨스가 겪은 시련들은 특별히 그에게만 있었던 것이 아니라 산업 혁명기의 전형적 표상이었기 때문에, 그의 소설을 특징짓는 여러 주요 사건들은 수백만의 잠재적 독자들도 함께 느낄 수 있었다. 디킨스의 의도는 최하층의 가장 취약한 사람들의 고통을 아주 현실적으로 그려내어 그의 독자들이 스스로를 구제할 수 있는 수단으로 동정이 아닌, 그들에게 진정으로 필요한 것, 즉 교육을 지속적으로 무시하지 못하도록 하는 것이었다. 적어도 그의 고의적인 목적은 그랬다.

어떤 면에서 손에 잡히지 않는 성령을 인격화된 영혼들로, 아기 예수를 – 신이 아닌 – 인간의 관용을 기다리는 절름발이 아이로 바꾸어 놓음으로써, 디킨스는 더욱 힘을 얻어가는 세속적 인본주의에 넘겨주며 종교의 향연(크리스마스)에 대한 권리를 주장한 것이다.

Passage 3

1. Clarity is not the prize in writing, nor is it always the principal mark of a good style. There are occasions when obscurity serves a literary yearning, if not a literary purpose, and there are writers whose manner is more overcast than clear. 1) <u>But since writing is communication, clarity can only be a virtue.</u> ① And although there is no substitute for merit in writing, clarity comes closest to being one. Even to a writer who is being intentionally obscure or wild of tongue we can say, 2. "Be obscure clearly!"

중심소재: 글의 명료함

1. 도입부 = 중심소재 도출

애매함을 통해 문학적 목적을 달성하는 측면에서 명료함이 글쓰기에서 가장 중요한 요소는 아니다.

1) 주제문

논리적 반전을 통해 명료함의 중요성을 강조하고 있다.

① 뒷받침 진술

2. 요지 재진술

정답 1 (A)

해설

명료한 글을 쓰는 방법에 대해 이야기하고 있다.

지문해석

명료함은 글쓰기에 있어 가장 중요한 것은 아니다. 그리고 그것이 항상 좋은 문체를 나타내 주는 중요한 특징인 것도 아니다. 모호함이 문학적인 목적은 아니라고 하더라도, 문학적인 열정에 부응할 때가 있고, 작풍이 명료하기보다는 모호한 작가가 있다. 그러나 글쓰기는 의사전달이기 때문에 명료함은 미덕일 수밖에 없다. 그리고 비록 글쓰기 기술에 대한 대체물이 없긴 하지만, 명료함은 장점과 가장 가깝다. 의도적으로 모호하거나 거친 말을 하는 작가에게조차도 우리는 "명료하게 모호해져라"라고 말할 수 있다.

Passage 4

1. Expansion brought problems, not least because of the very different societies of the North and the South. The problem of slavery was first raised over the status of Missouri when it was admitted into the Union in 1821.

1) ① The anti-slavery movement gained tremendous support after publication of a book called Uncle Tom's Cabin by Harriet Beecher Stowe. ② Political divisions over slavery in the Whig and Democratic parties led to the formation of the Republican Party, whose main principle was opposition to the extension of slavery.

③ When the Republican candidate, Abraham Lincoln, was elected President in 1860, South Carolina announced that its Union with all other states was dissolved and was

중심소재: 남북전쟁과 노예제도

1. 도입부 = 문제점 지적

노예제도의 문제점 언급

1) 구체적 진술

① Uncle Tom's Cabin으로 반노예제도 운동의 가속도가 붙음

② 공화당의 형성과 노예제도 확장 반대

③ 공화당 후보 링컨이 대통령으로 뽑히면서 남부의 여러 주가 Union에서 탈퇴하고, 노예제를 기반으로 한 남부연방을 형성

immediately followed by Mississippi, Florida, Alabama, Georgia, Louisiana and Texas, which together formed a Confederacy with a constitution based on slavery. The Northerners did not want war and Lincoln in his opening speech as President declared that he would not interfere with slavery in the Southern states, but merely affirmed the constitutional right of the Union to determine the status of new states.

④ Lincoln refused to allow secession to disrupt the Union, however, as civil war became inevitable. Virginia also seceded on the constitutional grounds that every state in the Union enjoyed sovereign rights: Nebraska, North Carolina, and Tennessee quickly followed. The twenty-three states of the industrial North, with a population of 22,000,000, were, therefore, opposed by eleven Southern states, almost 4,000,000 of whose 9,000,000 inhabitants were slaves.

④남북전쟁 발발
남부 11주의 연방탈퇴를 링컨이 승인하지 않아 남북전쟁이 시작됨

정답 **1**(E) **2**(B) **3**(D) **4**(A) **5**(C)

해설

1 본문은 노예제도가 남북전쟁의 원인이었음을 밝힌 글이므로 "남북전쟁"이나 "남북전쟁의 발단" 등이 제목으로 적절하다. 다소 포괄적 소재를 바탕으로 제목을 설정해야 하는 문제로 전반적으로 남북전재의 발단을 언급하면서 노예제도를 언급하고 있기에, 선택지 (B)와 같이 "노예제도의 형성"이라고는 볼 수 없다.

2 셋째 단락에서 링컨이 당선되자 South Carolina가 연합의 해체를 먼저 발표했고 다른 주들이 뒤따랐다.

3 탈퇴를 허용하지 않으면 탈퇴하려는 주들과의 충돌은 불가피해질 것이다.

4 "sovereign(자주적인)"은 "autonomous(자치의, 독립한)"와 가장 가까운 의미이다.

5 노예제도에 대한 정치적 입장 차는 정당 간에도 있었고, 남부와 북부 사이에도 있었는데 이로 인해 일부 주가 연방을 탈퇴하려 하자 링컨은 탈퇴를 허용하지 않고, 이로 인해 남북전쟁이 불가피해졌다고 했다.

지문해석

영토 확장은 특히 북부와 남부의 매우 다른 사회들로 인해 여러 문제를 불러왔다. 노예제도 문제는 미주리 주가 1821년 미합중국에 가입되었을 때 미주리 주의 위상을 둘러싸고 처음으로 제기되었다.
노예제 반대 운동은 해리엇 비처 스토우가 '엉클톰스캐빈'이라는 책을 출판한 후 큰 지지를 얻었다. 휘그당과 민주당 내의 노예제도에 대한 정치적 분열로 인해 공화당이 만들어졌으며 공화당의 주된 원칙은 노예제의 확대에 반대하는 것이었다.
공화당 대통령 후보인 에이브러햄 링컨이 1880년 대통령에 선출되자 사우스캐롤라이나 주는 다른 모든 주들과의 연합이 해체되었다고 발표했고 곧바로 미시시피, 플로리다, 앨라배마, 조지아, 루이지애나, 그리고 텍사스 주가 그 뒤를 이었으며 이 주들은 노예제도를 근간으로 한 헌법을 채택하여 남부 연방을 함께 만들었다. 북부 여러 주의 사람들은 전쟁을 원치 않았으며 링컨은 대통령 취임 연설에서 남부 주들의 노예제도를 간섭하지 않을 것이라고 선언하였고 단지 미합중국이 신생주의 위상을 결정하는 헌법상의 권한을 가지고 있음을 천명하였다. 그러나 링컨이 미합중국을 깨뜨리는 연방 탈퇴를 허용하지 않자 남북전쟁이 피할 수 없게 되었고, 버지니아 주 또한 미합중국의 모든 주는 자치권을 행사한다는 헌법을 근거로 연방을 탈퇴하자 네브래스카 노스캐롤라이나 테네시 주도 재빠르게 뒤를 이었다. 따라서 22,000,000명의 인구를 가진 공업중심의 북부 23개 주는 거주인구 9백만 명 중 거의 4백만 명이 노예인 11개의 남부 주와 대립하게 되었다.

Passage 5

1. Can there be a godless morality? Can we assert a superiority for a godless morality over traditional, theistic, and religious morality? 1) Yes, I think that this is possible. ① Unfortunately, few people even acknowledge the existence of godless moral values, much less their significance. When people talk about moral values, they almost always presume that they have to be talking about religious morality and religious values. The very possibility of godless, irreligious morality is ignored. A popular claim among religious theists is that atheists have no basis for morality—that religion and gods are needed for moral values. Usually they mean their religion and god, but sometimes they seem willing to accept any religion and any god. Ⓐ The truth is that neither religions nor gods are necessary for morality, ethics, or values. They can exist in a godless, secular context just fine, as demonstrated by all the godless atheists who lead moral lives every day.

중심소재: 신 없는 도덕성→그 가능성

1. 도입부=주제도출

신 없는 도덕성, 이것이 전통적인 종교적 도덕성보다 우월할 수 있을까?

1) 답변(요지)

가능하다고 말하고 있다.

① 뒷받침 진술

religious theists의 주장을 반대하면서 Ⓐ에서 글쓴이의 주장의 근거가 드러난다.

의문점 제기 : 주제, 제목
답변 : 글의 요지(주제, 제목 도출)

정답 1 (A) 2 (B)

해설

1 본문은 "신이 없는 도덕적 가치"의 가능함을 주장하고 있는 글이다.

2 본문 마지막 부분에서 도덕적 삶을 살고 있는 무신론자들을 통해 신이 없는 도덕의 가능성을 실제로 보여주고 있다.

지문해석

신의 존재를 부인하는 도덕이 있을 수 있을까? 신이 없는 도덕이 전통적이고, 유신론적이며, 종교적인 도덕보다 더 우월하다고 주장할 수 있을까? 그렇다, 내 생각에 그것은 가능한 일이다. 불행히도, 신을 배제한 도덕적 가치들의 중요성은 말할 것도 없고 그런 가치가 존재한다는 사실조차 받아들이고 있는 사람들은 거의 없다. 사람들은 도덕적 가치에 대해서 이야기할 때는 거의 항상 종교적 도덕과 종교적 가치들에 대해서 말해야 한다고 가정한다. 신이 없는, 비종교적인 도덕의 가능성 자체를 무시하는 것이다. 유신론자들의 일반적 주장은 무신론자들은 도덕이 성립할 수 있는 기반이 없다는 것이다. 즉, 도덕적 가치가 존재하기 위해서는 종교와 신이 있어야 한다는 것이다. 보통 그것들은 그들 자신의 종교와 신을 의미하지만, 때로는 어떠한 종교나 신이라도 기꺼이 받아들이는 것처럼 보이기도 한다. 실은 도덕, 윤리, 또는 가치를 위해서는 종교도 신도 필요하지 않다. 매일 윤리적인 삶을 살아가고 있는 모든 무신론자들에 의해 입증되고 있듯이 도덕과 윤리와 가치는 신이 없는, 세속적인 환경에서도 얼마든지 제대로 존재할 수 있다.

Passage 6

소재의 폭이 좁혀짐을 파악하도록 한다: so many jobs → law

1. 1) Change has always affected jobs. What is new and scary is that so many jobs are being affected by change. Law is no longer a safe area because there is a new field called jurimetrics that could eliminate the need for many lawyers. ① Computers would store and organize legal information so that you wouldn't need a lawyer. Ⓐ Instead, people would go to a "law bank" just as we go to a "cash station" for money now. At the "law bank," they would punch in the facts of their case. The computer would analyze all cases like it and then make a decision. The computer could get the facts more cheaply and more easily than a lawyer. It might even decide the case more fairly than a judge.

2. 1) And what about the changes in the computer science field? Surely, it's one job area a college student can safely bet will exist after graduation. Wrong. ① The very success of the computer produces less need for computer workers. Ⓐ People are becoming so familiar with computers, they will soon operate them as easily as they drive cars. ② Psychology is another young field where there are large changes. Research on the brain tells us that many mental illnesses are caused by chemical problems in our brains. Ⓐ If this is true, there won't be the need for the mental health care people we need now.

3. Although these jobs are disappearing, many others are being born. **1)** Your job is to develop the ability to cope with change. ① Ⓐ Find a sense of self that allows you to keep things in balance. Ⓐ Be strong enough to find or create other possibilities. Ⓑ Develop many different skills and interests. Ⓒ Have a good feeling of your own worth and you will be ready for an uncertain future.

중심소재: 컴퓨터 발달로 인한 사회 변화

1. 첫 번째 문단

1) 도입부 = 현상

Jurimetirics로 인해 법 또한 다른 직업과 마찬가지로 안전지대가 아니다.

①원인

모든 법적 기록을 컴퓨터에 저장하기 시작하면서 변호사의 필요성↓

Ⓐ부연

2. 두 번째 문단

1) 현상

①과학계

사회 변화의 영향력은 컴퓨터 과학에도 동일한 현상으로 발생

Ⓐ원인

컴퓨터의 발달로 오히려 전문 컴퓨터 작업자의 필요성이 낮아졌다.

②심리학 분야

심리학 분야도 상대적으로 오래되진 않았지만, 큰 변화를 겪고 있다.

Ⓐ심리학의 발달로 정신병은 뇌의 화학적 문제이기에 현재의 정신건강과 관련된 직업은 없어지게 된다.

3. 세 번째 문단

1) 현상

지금까지 언급한 변화로 인해 직업이 사라지는 반면, 새로 생기는 직업도 있다.

①대안

변화에 대처하는 능력배양

Ⓐ모든 일에 밸런스를 유지하는 모습

Ⓑ기회 창조

Ⓒ다양한 기술과 취미

④자신의 가치에 대한 긍정적 사고와 불확실한 미래에 대한 대처

정답 **1** (A) **2** (C) **3** (B)

지문분석

본문은 현상에서 대안으로 이어지는 단순한 구조를 취하는데, 글의 요지는 바로 글쓴이의 대안에 해당된다.

해설

1 대조의 Although를 활용한다.

these jobs are disappearing ↔ [?]

2 Surely, it(computer science field) is one job area a college student can safely bet will exist after graduation. Wrong.에서 알 수 있듯이 컴퓨터과학 분야 또한 졸업 후 보장이 되지 않음을 알 수 있다.

3 본문은 「현상 → 대안」의 단순한 구조를 취하는 글로, 젊은 세대들에게 변화하시는 사장의 요구에 맞게 대처해

야 함을 주장하는 글이다. 선택지 (B)의 목적을 가진 글로 볼 수 있다.

지문해석

변화는 항시 직업들에 영향을 미쳐왔다. 새롭고도 무서운 사실은 너무나 많은 직업들이 변화에 영향을 받고 있다는 점이다. 법조계도 더 이상 안전한 영역이 아닌데, 수많은 변호사들에 대한 수요를 없앨 수 있는 계량 법학이라는 신규 영역이 있기 때문이다. 컴퓨터가 법률 정보를 보관하고 처리한다면 변호사가 필요 없게 될 것이다. 대신에 오늘날 돈을 찾으러 "은행"에 가는 것처럼 사람들은 "법률 은행"에 갈 것이다. 사람들은 "법률 은행"에서 그들의 소송 사건에 관한 정보들을 입력할 것이다. 컴퓨터는 그와 유사한 모든 소송 사건들을 분석한 후 판결을 내릴 것이다. 컴퓨터는 변호사보다 더욱 저렴하고 더욱 손쉽게 정보를 수집할 수 있다. 심지어 판사보다 더욱 공정하게 판결을 내릴는지도 모른다.

컴퓨터 과학 분야의 변화는 어떠한가? 분명히 이 분야는 대학생들이 졸업한 후에도 존재할 것이라고 틀림없이 확신하는 직업 영역이다. 하지만 이는 틀렸다. 바로 그 컴퓨터의 성공이 컴퓨터 분야 노동자들에 대한 수요를 감소시킨다. 사람들은 컴퓨터에 익숙해지면서 머지않아 마치 운전을 하는 것처럼 손쉽게 컴퓨터를 작동시키게 될 것이다. 심리학은 커다란 변화가 일어나고 있는 또 하나의 새로운 영역이다. 뇌 연구에 따르면 많은 정신질환이 우리의 두뇌 속 화학적 문제들로 인해 발생된다. 만일 이것이 사실이라면 우리가 지금 필요로 하고 있는 정신 건강 의료진들에 대한 수요가 없어질 것이다.

비록 이러한 직업들은 사라지고 있지만 다른 많은 일자리들은 생겨나고 있다. 당신이 해야 할 일은 변화에 대처할 능력을 개발하는 것이다. 당신이 상황을 잘 통제할 수 있도록 하는 자아의식을 발견하라. 다른 가능성들을 찾거나 만들 수 있을 정도로 강해지라. 다양한 기술과 관심을 개발하라. 스스로의 가치에 대해 호감을 가지면 불확실한 미래에 대한 만반의 준비가 될 것이다.

Passage 7

1. To those familiar with its principle navigation tools (browsers, e-mail programs etc.), the Internet is not exactly an undiscovered country, but it is certainly a shifting landscape. It is being constantly changed by those who engage it, and by transactions, input, programming languages and devices that further diversify its modes of communication, its routes, and the means through which it is seen and navigated. 1) The impetus for this comes from a spectrum of sources that include both the profit and non-profit sectors of its "community." But undoubtedly its extension is fueled most of all by the corporate sector. 2. Navigation of this terrain requires guidance that not only supplies directional information, but also encourages a critical understanding of informational structures and the systems of micro-power with which they are interwoven. ① The digital landscape is being shaped not just by the convergence of various new media and information technologies, but also, by a convergence of industry interests from all sectors, especially entertainment and electronics. Ⓐ The "Information Revolution", therefore,

중심소재: 인터넷 변화

1. 도입부 = 현상(주제)
인터넷에 관여하는 사람과 인터넷 상에 영향을 미치는 다양한 요소로 인해 인터넷이 변화하고 있다.

1) 변화의 동인(뒷받침 진술)
인터넷을 중심으로 형성된 비영리 단체와 영리단체 중 특히나 인터넷 확장의 주된 원동력은 영리단체인 기업

2. 요지문
인터넷 사용 시 정보구조와 거대한 힘의 구조에 대한 비판적 이해가 필요하다.

① 뒷받침 진술
디지털 영역은 다양한 영역의 이해 관계로 집결된 곳

is changing the nature of our participation in all spheres of society, and both the way, and the means, by which we perceive these activities. The integration of digital technologies in daily life has especially reconfigured the relationship between the areas of work and leisure, which may share the same tools of information access, only adjusted for the different context.

Ⓐ 정보혁명의 영향
사회참여 방법·직장과 여가활동의 관계에 영향

정답 1 (D) 2 (A) 3 (C) 4 (B) 5 (D)

지문분석

본문에서 「현상 → 현상에 영향을 미치는 요소 → 주의사항」이란 큰 틀을 확인할 수 있다.

해설

1 본문은 인터넷 변화에 영향을 미치는 요소에 관한 글을 다루고 있다.

2 Navigation of this terrain requires guidance that not only supplies directional information, but also encourages a critical understanding of informational structures and the systems of micro-power with which they are interwoven. 부분을 통해 인터넷 사용자는 인터넷상에 제공되는 정보 구조와 시스템에 대해 비판적 이해의 필요성을 파악할 수 있다.

3 인터넷 확장의 주된 요인은 "민간기업"이라고 명시되어 있다.

4 마지막 문장을 보면, "일과 여가는 서로 다른 활동이지만, 도구는 동일하다"는 것을 의미한다.

5 a spectrum of는 "다양한"의 의미이다.

지문해석

인터넷의 주요 검색 수단들(웹 브라우저, 이메일 등)에 익숙한 사람들에게 그것은 미지의 나라라기보다는 분명 계속해서 바뀌는 풍경이다. 인터넷은 거기에 종사하고 있는 사람들에 의해, 또한 거래, 입력, 프로그램 언어, 통신 모드와 경로 · 인터넷을 보고 검색하는 수단들을 훨씬 더 다양하게 하는 여러 장치들에 의해 끊임없이 변하고 있다. 이를 위한 추진력은 인터넷 "공동체"의 영리, 비영리 분야를 포함하는 다양한 출처들로부터 생겨난다. 그러나 의심할 여지없게도 인터넷의 확장은 그 무엇보다 기업 부문에 의해 촉진된다. 이 영역의 항해에는 방향 정보뿐만 아니라 서로 얽혀 있는 정보 구조와 마이크로 파워 체제에 대한 비판적 이해를 장려하는 안내가 필요하다. 디지털 풍경은 가지각색의 신매체와 정보 기술의 융합뿐만 아니라 모든 분야, 특히 연예와 전자공학 분야의 산업적 이익의 융합에 의해 구체화되고 있다. 따라서 "정보 혁명"은 사회 전 영역에 걸쳐 우리가 참여하는 본질과 이런 활동들을 이해하는 방식 및 수단을 변화시키고 있다. 일상에서의 디지털 기술의 통합은 특히나 일과 여가 영역 간의 관계를 재정립해 왔는데, 이 두 가지는 서로 다른 상황에 대해 감안하는 경우에 한해 동일한 정보 접근 수단을 공유할 수도 있다.

Passage 8

1. Logic is the study of the methods and principles used to distinguish 'correct' from 'incorrect' reasoning. 1) This definition must not be taken to imply that only the student of logic can reason well or correctly. To say so would be as mistaken as to say that to run well requires studying the physics and physiology involved in that activity. ① Some excellent athletes are quite ignorant of the complex processes that go on inside their bodies when they perform. And, needless to say, the somewhat elderly professors who know most about such things would perform very poorly were they to risk their dignity on the athletic field. Even given the same basic muscular and nervous apparatus, the person who has such knowledge might not surpass the 'natural athlete.'

중심소재: 논리

1. 도입부 = 중심소재 도출

논리란 옳고 그른 논증을 구별하는 방법과 원칙에 대해 연구하는 분야

1) 주제문

논리를 공부해야 올바르게 추론할 수 있다는 의미는 아니다.

① 뒷받침 진술

이는 달리기를 잘하기 위해 이와 관련된 물리학이나 생리학을 잘 해야 한다고 주장하는 것이나 다름없다.

정답 **1** (E) **2** (C)

해설

1 앞서 언급한 내용과 같은 맥락의 뒷받침 내용을 연결하는 표현은 E밖에 없다.

2 Some excellent athletes are quite ignorant of the complex processed에서 선택지 (C)는 옳은 진술임을 파악할 수 있다.

지문해석

논리학은 옳은 것과 옳지 않은 추론을 구별해내는 데 사용하는 방법과 원리를 연구하는 것이다. 이런 정의가 논리학을 배운 학생만이 잘 혹은 바르게 추론할 수 있다는 것을 의미한다고 생각해서는 안 된다. 그렇게 말하는 것은 잘 달리기 위해서는 달리기와 관련된 물리학과 생리학을 공부해야 한다고 말하는 것만큼이나 바르지 못한 것이다. 몇몇 우수한 운동선수들은 자신들이 운동할 때 신체 안에서 일어나는 상세한 과정에 대해서는 잘 알지 못한다. 그리고 그런 과목에 대해 해박한 지식을 가진 노년의 교수가 경기장에서 자신의 명예를 걸고 뛰어야 하는 경우라 하더라도, 당연한 말이지만, 좋은 성적을 낼 수는 없을 것이다. 그런 지식을 가진 사람이 타고난 운동선수(natural athlete)를 능가하지는 못할 것이다.

TEST 17

Passage 1

구체적 진술의 시그널을 확인하고, 1인칭 시점의 이야기체 글로 주인공과 주변 인물 사이에 발생한 사건을 중심으로 내용을 파악한다.

1. When I worked as a part-time bank teller in college, a good-looking young man began making almost daily trips to my window to withdraw or deposit money. I wasn't sure it was because of me until he presented this note with his bank book: "Dear J: I've been SAVING this question in the hope that I might gain some INTEREST. If free Friday, would you care to DEPOSIT yourself beside me at a movie? I've taken into ACCOUNT that you may be previously engaged; if so, I'll WITHDRAW my offer and hope for Saturday. At any RATE, your company would be much enjoyed, and I hope you'll not ASSESS this as too forward. CHECK you later. Sincerely, B." I couldn't resist such a charming and original approach.

중심소재: 주인공과 은행 직원간의 서신

1. 은행 창구 직원에게 연애 신청을 하는 한 남자의 재치 넘치는 쪽지의 내용을 중심으로 글이 전개된다. 본문의 대문자에서 알 수 있듯이, 은행 용어를 사용하여 연애신청서를 작성했다는 점에서 여직원에게 큰 점수를 따냈다.

정답 1 (D)

해설

은행 용어를 연애와 비유하면서 재치 있게 연예편지를 쪽지에 작성한 재치 넘치는 글이다. 본문에 언급된 쪽지에 적힌 saving(간직하다, 저축하다), interest(이자, 관심), deposit(놓다, 저금하다) 등의 다의어를 재치 있게 사용했기 때문에 필자가 청년의 데이트 신청을 받아들였다고 볼 수 있다. 마지막의 Check you later는 헤어질 때의 인사말로 "나중에 또 봐"라는 뜻인데, check는 은행용어로 "수표"라는 뜻도 있다.

지문해석

내가 대학에서 파트타임 금전 출납원으로 일했을 때, 한 잘생긴 젊은 남자가 돈을 인출하고 예금하러 거의 매일 내 창구에 왔다. 나는 그가 통장에 이런 쪽지를 남길 때까지 그것이 나 때문이라는 것을 확신하지 못했다. "친애하는 제이 씨에게: 나는 조금이라도 관심을 얻길 소망하며 이 질문을 저축해 왔습니다. 만일 금요일에 시간이 있으시다면, 영화관에서 내 옆에 당신을 맡기시겠어요? 나는 당신이 선약이 있을 수도 있다는 것도 고려해왔습니다. 만일 그렇다면, 저는 제안을 철회하고 토요일을 희망하겠습니다. 어쨌든, 당신과 함께 있으면 대단히 즐거울 것입니다. 그리고 너무 주제넘은 제안이라고 생각하지 않기를 바랍니다. 나중에 (만나) 확인합시다. 친애하는, B." 나는 그렇게 매력적이고 독창적인 교제 신청을 물리칠 수 없었다.

Passage 2

1. Although speech is the most advanced form of communication, there are many ways of communicating without using speech. 1) Signals, signs, symbols, and gestures may be found in every known culture. 2) ① The basic function of a signal is to impinge upon the environment in such a way that it attracts attention, as, for example, the dots and dashes of a telegraph circuit. Coded to refer to speech, the potential for communication is very great. Less adaptable to the codification of words, ② signs also contain meaning in and of themselves. A stop sign or a barber pole conveys meaning quickly and conveniently. ③ Symbols are more difficult to describe than either signals or signs because of their intricate relationship with the receiver's cultural perceptions. Ⓐ In some cultures, applauding in a theater provides performers with an auditory symbol of approval. ④ Gestures such as waving and handshaking also communicate certain cultural messages.

2. Although signals, signs, symbols, and gestures are very useful, they do have a major disadvantage. 1) They usually do not allow ideas to be shared without the sender being directly adjacent to the receiver. 2) As a result, means of communication intended to be used for long distances and extended periods are based upon speech. Radio, television, and the telephone are only a few.

중심소재: 비언어적 소통

1. 첫 번째 문단

1) 도입부 = 문단 주제문

언어를 사용하지 않고도 다양한 의사소통 방법이 있다: Signals, signs, symbols, and gestures

2) 뒷받침 진술

① 예시와 함께 시그널의 기능을 설명하고 있다.

② 기호의 효율적 의사소통 측면 기술

③ 세 번째 예로 상징을 들고 있다. 속성으로 앞에서 언급된 시그널과 기호보단 해독이 어렵다는 점과 그 이유를 밝히고 있다(because)

Ⓐ 예시부연

④ 몸짓

2. 두 번째 문단

1) 문단 주제문

시그널, 기호, 상징 그리고 몸짓의 단점

2) 뒷받침 진술

공간적 제약

글 전체는 두 문단으로 구성되어 있다. 각 문단의 주제를 설정하고 이를 종합해 전체 주제를 설정하도록 한다.

TEST 17

정답 1 (A) 2 (D) 3 (C) 4 (D) 5 (C) 6 (B) 7 (A)

해설

1 신호, 기호, 몸짓 등 의사소통의 여러 가지 형태에 관해 이야기하고 있으므로, 각 요소를 포괄하는 선택지 (A)의 "의사소통"이 가장 적절하다.

2 첫 번째 문장인 speech is the most advanced form of communication을 통해서 "의사소통의 가장 발전된 형태"임을 파악할 수 있다.

3 The basic function of a signal is to impinge upon the environment in such a way that it attracts attention, as, for example, the dots and dashes of a telegraph circuit.를 통해서 신호는 사람의 주의를 끈다는 점에서 주변 환경을 "침범"하는 즉, 방해하는 형태의 의사소통임을 파악할 수 있다.

4 potential = possibility

5 In some cultures, applauding in a theater provides performers with an auditory symbol of approval.에서 "박수치기"는 상징의 한 예임을 파악할 수 있다.

6 마지막 문단에서 신호, 기호, 상징과 몸짓의 공간적 한계를 언급하면서 효율적 장거리 의사소통으로 라디오, TV, 전화가 언급되고 있으므로 "장거리에서도 의사소통을 하고 싶어 했기 때문"이라는 선택지 (B)가 정답이다.

7 신호, 기호, 상징과 몸짓은 의사소통의 여러 형태들을 살피고 있으므로 결론으로 가장 적절한 것은 (A)이다.

지문해석

비록 언어가 의사소통의 가장 발달된 형태이지만, 언어를 사용하지 않고도 의사소통하는 방법은 많다. 신호, 기호, 상징, 몸짓은 우리가 알고 있는 모든 문화에서 사용된다. 신호의 기본적 기능은 전보 회로의 점과 대시(–)같이 주의를 끄는 식으로 주위 정황에 영향을 주는 것이다. 언어를 지시하기 위해 암호화된 의사소통의 잠재력은 매우 대단하다. 단어들의 성문화(成文化)에 덜 융통성 있는 기호 또한 그 내면과 그 자체에 의미를 내포하고 있다. 멈춤 신호나 이발소 간판대는 '급히, 편리하게'를 의미한다. 상징은 수신자의 문화적 지각과의 복잡한 관계 때문에 신호나 기호보다 말로 설명하기가 어렵다. 어떤 문화에서는, 극장에서 박수갈채하는 것은 연주가들에게 청각적인 지지를 제공하는 것이다. 손을 흔들거나 악수하는 등의 몸짓도 특정한 문화적 메시지를 전달한다.

비록 신호, 기호, 상징과 몸짓이 매우 유용하다고 해도, 그것들은 커다란 단점을 갖고 있다. 그것들은 송신자가 수신자와 아주 가까이 있지 않으면 생각을 전하기가 힘들어진다. 결과적으로, 의사소통의 수단들은 장거리에 쓰이게 될 것이며 그 확장 범위는 언어에 근거한다. 라디오, 텔레비전과 전화기가 조금 사용되고 있다.

Passage 3

1. Simply put, positive psychology is the scientific study of human happiness. 1) ①Positive psychology focuses on what makes people feel good rather than what causes them to feel bad. Ⓐ Until recently, the prevailing focus in the field of psychology has been on mental illness rather than mental wellness. Psychologists asked questions such as why people get depressed, irritable, or anxious. Now some psychologists are examining what makes people happy rather than what makes them sad. ② Martin Seligman, the illustrious psychologist and professor at the University of Pennsylvania, is the father of positive psychology. Seligman first introduced the world to positive psychology in 1998. The overall goal of positive psychology is to enhance people's experience of love, work, and play. ③ One way to achieve this goal is to teach people how to incorporate personal qualities such as humor, originality, and generosity into their interactions with others to achieve happiness. Ⓐ So what does make us happy? Research suggests that once our basic needs are met, factors such as money, education, high intelligence, sunny weather, or even youth have only a modest effect on happiness. What researchers are discovering is that things such as friends and strong family connections directly affect how happy you are with your life. Ⓑ According to Seligman and other positive psychologists, there are certain personal qualities, or strengths, that directly affect happiness. ⓐ For example, qualities such

시간의 대조는 내용의 대조임을 파악한다: Until recently ↔ Now

실험을 통해 발견한 사실은 요지 또는 요지를 뒷받침하는 내용임을 기억한다.

중심소재: 긍정의 심리학

1. 도입부 = 중심소재 도출
인간의 행복을 연구하는 긍정의 심리학

1) 구체적 진술
① 목적
사람을 행복하게 만드는 것에 대한 연구
Ⓐ 부연
정신질병에 초점을 두었던 과거의 심리학과 달리 긍정의 심리학은 "행복"에 초점을 맞춤
② 기원

③ 방법
긍정적인 개인의 자질을 다른 사람과의 상호작용에 적용하는 방법습득
Ⓐ 실험부연
친구, 가족 유대 등이 행복에 직접적인 영향을 미친다.
Ⓑ 행복에 영향을 미치는 중요한 요소와 이미 가지고 있는 장점 활용
ⓐ 예시

as curiosity, optimism, courage, humor, kindness, and generosity are very important in leading a happy life. 2. Seligman encourages people to build on the qualities they already possess. For example, if you are already a generous person by nature, then you should try to practice being generous with friends, coworkers, and even strangers on a daily basis. The more generous you are to others, the more meaning you will have in your life and the happier you will be. Seligman firmly believes that everyone has the ability to be happy. You just have to put some work into it. Seligman should know, because he is actually a self-proclaimed pessimist and has been very open about his own depressive tendencies. He believes optimism is a quality that can be developed. Seligman argues that it does not matter how naturally optimistic or pessimistic you are. People can learn to expand upon their own ability to feel good and develop qualities that lead to happiness. In other words, anyone can lead a happy, if not happier, life.

2. 결론(요지)
행복해지려는 노력의 중요성을 언급하면서, "행복을 느끼려는 능력을 확장하고, 행복에 이르는 특징을 개발할 수 있다"는 내용을 전달하고 있다.

정답 1 (B) 2 (A) 3 (D)

해설

1 본문은 긍정의 심리학의 정의와 함께 사람을 행복하게 만드는 요소에 대한 내용을 실험을 통해 구체적으로 밝히고 있으며, 본문 말미에 이러한 요소를 잘 활용하는 방법의 중요성을 강조하고 있다. 선택지 (B)가 정답이다.

2 바로 뒤에 이어지는 연구의 내용에서 행복의 중요한 요소로 친구와 가족의 유대를 꼽고 있다. 그러므로 선택지 (A)를 넣어야 앞뒤 내용이 자연스런 문맥을 형성한다.

3 주어진 문장은 인간이 긍정적인 특성 중 관대함에 대해서 설명하고 있다. 두 번째 단락의 마지막 문장에서 인간의 관대함에 대해서 설명하고 있으므로 주어진 문장은 (D)에 들어가는 것이 적절하다.

지문해석

간단히 말해서, 긍정심리학은 인간의 행복에 대한 과학적 연구이다. 긍정심리학은 사람이 기분을 안 좋게 만드는 것보다는 좋게 만드는 것에 주목한다. 최근까지, 심리학 분야는 정신적 건강보다는 정신병에 그 초점을 두었다. 심리학자는 왜 사람들이 우울하거나 흥분하거나 불안해지는가와 같은 질문들을 했던 것이다. 그러나 이제 심리학자들은 사람들을 슬프게 만드는 것보다 행복하게 만드는 것을 검토하고 있다. 펜실베이니아 대학(University of Pennsylvania)의 저명한 심리학자이자 교수인 마틴 셀릭만(Martin Seligman)은 긍정 심리학의 아버지(창시자)이다. 셀릭만은 1998년에 긍정심리학을 처음으로 세상에 소개했다. 긍정심리학의 전반적 목표는 사람들이 사랑, 직업, 놀이에 대한 경험을 더 많이 하도록 해주는 것이다. 이 목표를 달성하기 위한 한 방식은 사람들에게 행복해지기 위한 유머, 독창성, 관대함과 같은 개인적 특성들을 다른 사람들과의 상호 작용에 발현시키는 법을 가르쳐 주는 것이다. 그렇다면, 우리를 행복하게 만드는 것은 무엇인가? 연구에 따르면, 일단 우리의 기본적인 욕구가 충족되고 나면 돈이나 교육, 높은 지능, 좋은 날씨나 심지어 젊음 같은 요소들은 행복에 큰 영향을 미치지 않는다. 연구자들이 알아내고 있는 것은 친구와 강한 가족의 유대관계와 같은 것들이 당신이 삶을 얼마나 행복하게 살아가느냐에 직접적으로 영향을 준다는 것이다. 셀릭만과 다른 긍정 심리학자에 따르면, 행복에 직접적으로 영향을 주는 특정한 개인적 특성이나 장점들이 존재한다. 예를 들면, 호기심, 낙천주의, 용기, 유머, 친절, 그리고 관대함 같은 특성은 행복한 삶을 이끌어 나가는 데 매우 중요하다. 셀릭만은 사람들에게 자신이 이미 가지고 있는 특성들을 더 발전시키라고 권장한다. 예를 들어, 당신이 선천적으로 친절한 성격이라면 매일친구와 동료, 심지어 낯선 사람들에게 친절해 지는 것을 연습할 필요가 있다는 것이다. 당신이 다른 사람들에게 친절하면 친절할수록 당신의 삶은 더욱 의미가 있고 당신은 더욱 행복해질 것이다. 셀릭만은 누구나 행복해질 수 있는 능력을 가지고 있다고 확실하게 믿는다. 당신은 그저 그것에 대하여 몇 가지 노력을 하면 된다. 셀릭만은 잘 알 것이다. 그는 실제로 자칭 비관주의자이고 자신의 우울한 경향에 대해서 매우 솔직하게 말해왔기 때문이다. 그는 낙천주의가 발전될 수 있는 특성이라고 믿는다. 셀릭만은 당신이 본질적으로 낙천적이냐 아니면 비관적이냐 하는 것은 중요하지 않다고 주장한다. 사람들은 저마다 기분 좋게 느낄 수 있는 능력을 키우고 행복을 초래하는 특성을 개발하는 것을 배울 수 있다. 다른 말로 하면, 더 행복한 삶은 아니라 하더라도, 누구나 행복한 삶을 이끌어 갈 수는 있는 것이다.

Passage 4

통념의 시그널과 전반적으로 대조의 글 전개가 활용됨을 확인한다.

통념을 드러내는 시그널의 종류

1) People say(believe/consider/think) that S V = It is said(believed/considered/though) that S V
2) We say That S V
3) Contrary to the popular thought(belief) = Contrary to what people say

1. When it comes to leisure activities, Americans aren't quite the funseekers they've been cracked up to be. 1) ① For one out of five, weekends and vacations are consumed by such drudgeries as housecleaning, yard work, and cooking; ② only one third of American workers enjoy the luxury of lolling in the sun, going camping, playing sports, or simply relaxing. Ⓐ One thousand employed Americans were recently asked how they occupy themselves on days they are not at work. According to the poll, older people, ⓐ the affluent, and the well-educated are most apt to spend their spare time doing the things they 'want to do' rather than those they 'have to do'.
Overall, high-salaried respondents were more active than those with lower incomes—they reported watching less television and were more likely to engage in social and cultural activities.
ⓑ People who are divorced, widowed, or separated, the survey concluded, are the least likely of any group to take a vacation—and the least likely to attach any importance to it.

중심소재: 여가활용

1. 도입부 = 통념비판
미국인들은 그다지 활발히 여가활동을 즐기지 않는다.

1) 뒷받침 근거
① 실제로 5일 중 4일은 청소, 정원, 요리 등의 집안일
② 직장인의 3분의 1만이 여가활용
Ⓐ 뒷받침 부연(설문조사)
ⓐ affluent, well-educated, high-salaried → active participants in social and cultural activities
ⓑ divorced, widowed, or separated → rarely take a vacation

정답 1 (C) 2 (E)

지문분석
설문을 통해 객관성을 확보하면서, 미국인들의 여가활동에 관한 내용을 다루고 있다.

해설
1 미국인들의 여가활동에 관한 글로 조사 등이 나오는 것으로 보아 신문기사체가 가장 적절하다.
2 high-salaried respondents were more active than those with lower incomes—they reported watching less television and were more likely to engage in social and cultural activities.의 밑줄 친 표현에서 선택지 (E)의 내용은 본문과 일치하지 않는다.

지문해석
여가활동에 관해서라면, 미국인들은 평판만큼 그렇게 놀이를 즐기는 사람들이 아니다. 미국인들은 다섯 명 중 한 명꼴로 집안 청소, 마당 일, 요리 등과 같은 허드렛일을 하면서 주말과 휴가를 보낸다. 미국 근로자들

중 단지 3분의 1만이 햇볕을 쬐며 빈둥거리거나, 캠핑을 가거나, 스포츠를 하거나, 그냥 푹 쉬는 호사를 즐긴다. 최근 1,000명의 미국 직장인들에게 일이 없는 날 무엇을 하는지 설문조사를 하였다. 그 조사에 따르면, 나이 든 사람들, 부유한 사람들, 고등교육을 받은 계층들은 그들이 해야 하는 일보다 하고 싶은 일들을 하면서 여가 시간을 보내는 경향이 가장 많았다. 전체적으로, 고소득 응답자들은 저소득 계층보다 더 활동적이었다. 즉 그들은 텔레비전을 덜 보고 사회와 문화 활동에 참여하는 경향이 더 많다고 답변했다. 이혼자들, 배우자를 사별한 사람들, 별거한 사람들은 휴가를 떠날 가능성이 가장 적으며, 휴가를 중요하다고 생각하는 경향이 가장 적다고 설문조사는 결론지었다.

Passage 5

1. 1) The philosophers tell us that art consists essentially, not in performing a moral act, but in making a thing, a work, in making an object with a view not to the human good of the agent, but to the exigencies and the proper good of the object to be made, and by employing ways of realization predetermined by the nature of the object in question. ① Art thus appears as something foreign in itself to the sphere of the human good, almost as something inhuman, and whose exigencies nevertheless are absolute: for, needless to say, there are not two ways of making an object well, of realizing well the work one has conceived—there is but one way, and it must not be missed.

2. 1) The philosophers go on to say that this making activity is principally and above all an intellectual activity. Art is a virtue of the intellect, of the practical intellect, and may be termed the virtue proper to working reason. ② But then, you will say, if art is nothing other than an intellectual virtue of making, whence comes its dignity and its ascendancy among us? Why does this branch of our activity draw to it so much human sap? Why has one always and in all peoples admired the poet as much as the sage? **2.** It may be answered first that to create, to produce something intellectually, to make an object rationally constructed, is something very great in the world; for man this alone is already a way of imitating God. And I am speaking here of art in general, such as the ancients understood it—in short, of art as the virtue of the artisan.

중심소재: 예술

1. 첫 번째 문단

예술에 대한 철학자의 견해

1) 견해 1 = 주제문

예술이란 도덕적 행위가 아니라 물체가 가진 내적 속성에 의해 이미 규정된 것을 실현할 수 있는 방법을 찾아 만드는 것

① 뒷받침 진술

예술이란 인간적 선의 영역과는 별개이며 그 내적 요건은 절대적이고, 이를 예술적 행위로 옮기는 방법은 하나뿐임

즉, 물건을 만드는 예술 행위는 단지 그 물건의 내적 요건과 타당한 가치의 목적에 맞게 만드는 것 하나밖에 없다는 뜻임.

2. 두 번째 문단

1) 견해 2

예술은 지적행위이다.

② 의문점 제기(문단 주제)

예술이 만드는 행위의 지적 미덕이라면 그것의 우월성은 어디에서 오는 것인가?

2. 답변(요지)

창조자이신 하나님을 흉내 내는 것이기에 예술은 장인의 가치

정답 1(C) 2(B) 3(A)

해설

1 첫 번째 문단에서 예술은 특정 대상의 내적 가치에 의해서 규정된 특징을 실현하는 것이라 했으므로 선택지 (C)가 정답이다.

2 (A)은 첫 번째 문단 마지막에 나온다. 본문분석에서 나눈 두 번째 문단 중 if art is nothing other than an

intellectual virtue of making, whence comes its dignity and its ascendancy among us?의 내용을 보면, "예술은 지적행위이며, 예술의 위엄과 우월성은 어디에서 발생하는가"라고 물은 후 이에 대한 답이 따르므로 선택지 (B)는 잘못된 진술이다. 같은 맥락에서 선택지 (C)은 본문과 일치함을 파악할 수 있다. Art is a virtue of the intellect.부분에서 선택지 (D)도 옳다.

3 Why has one always and in all peoples admired the poet as much as the sage? 문장에 대한 답변을 보면, 현인만큼 시인을 찬미했던 이유는 신과 같은 위대한 창조적 행위를 실천하는 사람이기 때문임을 파악할 수 있다.

지문해석

철학자들은 우리들에게 예술이란 본질적으로, 도덕적 행위를 수행하는 것이 아니라 물건을 하나의 작품으로 만들어내는 것이며, 행위자의 인간적 선을 목적으로 해서가 아니라 만들어지는 물체가 갖고 있는 요건과 그 물체에 타당한 선을 목적으로 해서, 그리고 해당 물체의 본성에 의해 미리 정해져 있는 실현 방법을 써서 물건을 만드는 것이라고 말한다. 따라서 예술은 인간적 선의 영역에 비추어볼 때는 그 자체로서는 이질적이고, 거의 비인간적인 어떤 것으로 보인다. 그럼에도 불구하고 그것의 본질적인 요건은 절대적인 것이다. 왜냐하면, 말할 필요도 없이, 물건을 잘 만드는 방법, 사람이 상상한 작품을 제대로 실현시키는 방법에는 두 가지가 있는 것이 아니기 때문이다. 그것은 단 한 가지 방법밖에 없으며, 그것을 놓치지 말아야 하는 것이다.
철학자들은 더 나아가 이러한 제작행위는 주로 그리고 무엇보다도 지적인 행위라고 말한다. 예술은 지성의 미덕이며, 실제적 지성의 미덕이며, 그리고 실용적 이성에 적합한 미덕이라 부를 수도 있다. 그러나 그러면 당신은 이렇게 말할 것이다. 만약 예술이 무엇인가를 만들어내는 지적 미덕이기만 하다면, 예술에 대해 우리가 느끼는 위엄과 우월성은 어디로부터 나오는 것인가? 왜 인간의 행위 중 유독 예술 분야가 그렇게도 많은 인간의 생기를 끌어당기는가? 왜 사람들은 항상 그리고 모든 민족 속에서 시인을 현자만큼 많이 찬미해왔던가? 우선 이렇게 대답해야 할 것이다. 창조한다는 것, 무언가를 지적으로 생산해낸다는 것, 이성적으로 구성된 물체를 만든다는 것은 이 세상에서 매우 위대한 것이라고 말이다. 인간에게 있어서는 이 행위만이 이미 신을 모방하는 방법으로 되어 있는 것이다. 그리고 나는 여기에서, 고대인들이 이해하고 있던 바와 같은 그런 일반적인 예술에 대해 말하고 있는 것이다. 한마디로 말해서, 장인들의 미덕으로서의 예술에 관해서 말하고 있는 것이다.

Passage 6

1. Lucas and Speilberg both achieved fame as the brightest young talents in Hollywood in the late 1970s and early 1980s, Lucas's *Star Wars* and Speilberg's *Close Encounters of the Third Kind*, appeared in the same year, 1977, placing both in the race for an Academy Award. 1) The two science fiction films used special effects that had never been seen before. ① Special computerized cameras were invented and miniature models of spaceships were designed. The effects on screen kept audiences breathless. When Lucas and Speilberg worked together on *Raiders of the Lost Ark*, they once again captured the imagination of the audience and made them feel as if they were a part of the action. 2. This is what made their films so successful.

중심소재: 루카스와 스필버그의 성공요소

1. 도입부
루카스와 스필버그는 어린 나이에 명성을 얻고, 아카데미상을 위한 경쟁을 함

1) 이유(요지)
특수효과

① 구체적 진술
특수효과를 통해 관객의 상상력을 사로잡고 마치 실제와 같은 경험을 하게 함으로 관중의 마음을 사로잡음

2. 요지 재진술
특수효과를 통해 성공하게 됨

지문분석

주제를 드러내는 중심소재 설정은 독해의 시작이자 끝이라 할 수 있을 만큼 중요하므로 이에 대한 끊임없는 연습이 요구된다.

정답 1 (B) 2 (D)

해설

1 special effects that had never been seen before를 보면 "전에는 전혀 볼 수 없었던 특수효과"라고 언급되어 있으므로 "너무 멋져서 숨을 쉴 수 없다"는 해석이 가장 적합하다.

2 두 사람이 공동 제작한 것은 Raiders of the Lost Ark이다.

지문해석

루카스와 스필버그는 둘 다 1970년대 후반과 1980년대 초에 할리우드에서 가장 총명한 젊은 인재로 명성을 얻었다. 루카스의 '스타워즈'와 스필버그의 '미지와의 조우'가 같은 해인 1977년에 나와 두 사람이 아카데미상을 놓고 경쟁하게 되었다. 그 두 공상과학 영화는 전에는 전혀 볼 수 없었던 특수효과를 사용하였다. 특수 컴퓨터 카메라가 발명되었고 우주선 미니어처가 만들어졌다. 화면상의 특수효과는 관객들을 숨죽이게 만들었다. 루카스와 스필버그가 '레이더스'에서 공동 작업을 했을 때 그들은 다시 한 번 관객들의 상상력을 사로잡았으며 관객들이 마치 그 액션의 일부가 된 것처럼 느끼게 만들었다. 이것이 그들의 영화를 성공하게 만든 요소이다.

Passage 7

1. Bangladesh's worst ever ferry accident has recently added pressure upon the authorities to improve safety in the shipping sector. 1) ① According to the official statistics, there have been about 250 ferry accidents in Bangladesh since 1977. These have resulted in more than 2,000 deaths. The latest sinking is typical of many accidents, taking place during the holiday rush at the end of the year. The accident happened in what is believed to be one of the riskiest river channels in the country, an area where accidents occur regularly.

② However, the channel remains one of the most important communication links between southern Bangladesh and the capital city, Dhaka. Ⓐ ⓐ Most of the boats that use this route are constructed in local shipyards, and are often built below international maritime standards. ⓑ Experts say that the high casualty figures on such vessels are due to a combination of poor manufacturing techniques and the failure of the boat owners to implement adequate safety precautions. The experts point out that although the provision of life jackets or emergency rings is mandatory, the rule has rarely been enforced. ⓒ Experts also say that many crews and captains lack proper navigation training. They say that the employment of an unskilled workforce

현상의 시그널을 확인한다.

중심소재: 여객선 사고

1. 도입부 = 현상

방글라데시에서 일어난 사건

1) 구체적 진술

① 1977년 이래 2,000명 이상의 사망자를 낸 끊임없는 여객선 사고 발생. 주로 휴가 때 발생하며 가장 위험한 해협에서 일어남

② 한편 이 해협은 상업적 요충지로서의 역할을 함

Ⓐ 원인

ⓐ 배를 만드는 제조 기술의 낙후

ⓑ 적절한 안전수칙 실천 미약 (주의할 것은 안전수칙에 대한 개념이 없는 것이 아니라 배의 주인이 실천하지 않는다는 점)

ⓒ 항해 훈련 부족

2. 대안(요지)

현 규제강화의 필요성보다 실천이 더욱 중요함을 강조

in the industry is widespread. 2. Officials at the Shipping Ministry say that they have devised tougher regulations for improving safety standards, but that the problem is one of enforcement rather than of legislation.

정답 1(D) 2(C) 3(D) 4(B) 5.(C)

해설

1 페리선 침몰로 인한 사망률이 높은 원인으로서 (D)는 본문에 언급되어 있지 않다.

2 although the provision of life jackets or emergency rings is mandatory, the rule has rarely been enforced를 보면, 법으로 구명조끼를 요구하고 있지만, 지켜지지 않음을 파악할 수 있다. 세부내용 파악 문제의 경우 지문(원문)보다 문제의 핵심내용을 먼저 파악하고, 지문을 읽을 때 이를 기억해 푸는 것이 효율적이다. 본 문제의 경우 life jackets이 제시되는 본문을 집중해서 읽도록 한다.

3 2번 문제와 마찬가지로 문제에서 요구하는 사항을 본문에 정확히 파악하여 답하도록 한다. The latest sinking is typical of many accidents, taking place during the holiday rush at the end of the year.

4 they have devised tougher regulations for improving safety standards, but that the problem is one of enforcement rather than of legislation에서 밑줄 친 표현에서 알 수 있듯이 법의 제정보다는 "법 실행 여부"가 관건임을 파악할 수 있다.

5 페리선 침몰 사고의 복합적인 원인들을 분석하는 글로 다음과 같은 전형적인 패턴을 따르는 글이다.

지문해석

방글라데시 최악의 여객선 사고로 인해 당국이 해운 부문의 안전 대책을 개선해야 한다는 압력이 최근 들어 거세지고 있다. 공식적인 통계에 따르면 1977년 이래로 250건의 여객선 사고가 방글라데시에서 발생했다. 이 사고로 지금까지 2,000명 이상의 사망자가 발생했다. 가장 최근의 침몰사고는 그 동안 일어난 많은 사고들의 전형적인 유형으로 분주한 연말 휴가 기간에 발생했다. 사고는 이 나라에서 가장 위험한 운하 중 한 곳으로 알려진 곳에서 발생했는데, 이곳은 사고가 빈번하게 일어나는 장소이다.

그러나 그 운하는 남부 방글라데시와 수도인 다카(Dhaka) 사이를 이어주는 가장 중요한 교통의 요지 중 하나이기도 하다. 이 수로를 이용하는 대부분의 배들은 지방의 여러 조선소에서 건조되는데, 종종 국제 해상 표준에 못 미치는 수준으로 제작된다. 전문가들은 그러한 선박에서 발생한 높은 사상자 수는 형편없는 제조 기술과 적절한 안전 예방책을 실시하지 않은 선박 소유주들 때문이라고 말한다. 전문가들은 구명조끼나 비상용 튜브 비치가 의무 조항임에도 불구하고 이 규정이 좀처럼 지켜지지 않는 점을 지적한다. 또한 전문가들은 많은 선원과 선장들이 적절한 항해 훈련을 받지 못한 점을 지적한다. 그들에 따르면 그 업계에서는 미숙련 노동자를 고용하는 일이 빈번히 발생한다. 해운 부처의 공무원들은 안전기준 개선을 위해 보다 엄격한 규정을 마련했지만 문제는 규정 제정이기보다는 오히려 시행이라고 말한다.

Passage 8

1. During the evolution of the factory system in the 19th-century, the merchant class became more and more significant in English national life. 1) Cities multiplied in population, labor and life were cheap, and the industrialists developed a philosophy of individualism that would justify their enterprise without involving obligations to society. 2) ① The Romantic writers were enemies of the idea of social injustice, but they knew little about actual social conditions; they themselves did not come from the ranks of wage earners. ② But the romantic writers were powerfully affected by the theories developed in France establishing the principles of Liberty, Fraternity and Equality. Before social abuses could be cured, these principles had to be established. The Romantic writers did much to promote them.

중심소재: 19세기 산업사회 현상

1. 도입부 = 현상

19세기 공장의 진화로 상인계급은 중요한 계층으로 성장함

1) 문제점 지적

사회적 책임감이 결핍된 개인주의의 발달

2) 낭만주의 작가들의 대안

① 한계점

낭만주의 작가는 임금노동자의 출신이 아니다 보니 현실적 대안을 제시하지 못함

② 의의(요지)

하지만 자유, 박애 그리고 평등을 주장한 프랑스 이론에 영향을 받아 사회의 부조리 척결을 위한 원칙을 바로 세우는 데 이바지 했음

앞서 제시된 내용의 논리적 반전을 이끄는 역접의 But 이후는 글의 요지가 되므로 집중에서 읽도록 한다.

TEST 17

정답 1 (B)

지문분석

본문은 19세기에 발생한 문제점을 언급하면서 프랑스에서 전개된 '자유, 박애, 평등'의 원칙을 대안으로 내세운 로맨틱 작가들의 내용을 다루고 있다. 마지막 문장에서 알 수 있듯이 "19세기 현상과 로맨틱 작가들의 업적"을 다루는 내용이다.

해설

본문의 중간에 "자본가들은 사회에 대한 의무를 포함하지 않으면서 자신들의 기업경영을 정당화시킬 수 있는 개인주의의 철학을 발달시켰다."의 언급된 내용으로 보아 선택지 (B)는 본문과 일치하지 않는다.

지문해석

19세기에 공장체제가 발달하는 동안 상인 계급이 영국의 국가적 삶에서 더욱더 중요하게 되었다. 도시들은 인구가 증가했고, 노동과 생명은 싸구려였으며, 자본가들은 사회에 대한 의무는 포함되지 않으면서 자신들의 기업경영을 정당화시킬 수 있는 개인주의의 철학을 발달시켰다. 낭만주의 작가들은 사회적 부정이라는 생각에 대해 적이었지만 그들은 실제 사회의 상황에 대해 거의 알지 못했다. 그들 자신이 임금 노동자 계급 출신이 아니었기 때문이었다. 그러나 낭만주의 작가들은 자유 형제애(박애), 그리고 평등의 원칙을 확립한 프랑스에서 전개된 이론들에 강력한 영향을 받았다. 사회 악습들이 치유되기 전에, 이러한 원칙들이 확립되어야만 했다. 낭만주의 작가들은 그 원칙들을 발전시키기 위해 많은 일을 했다.

TEST 18

Passage 1

나열의 시그널을 확인한다.

1. Nearly everyone is shy in some ways. If shyness is making you uncomfortable, it may be time for a few lessons in self-confidence. You can build your confidence by following some suggestions from doctors and psychologists. 1) ① First, make a decision not to hold back in conversations. What you have to say is just as important as what other people say. ② Second, prepare yourself for being with others in groups. Make a list of the good qualities you have. Then make a list of ideas, experiences, and skills you would like to share with other people. Think about what you would like to say in advance. Then say it. ③ Finally, if you start feeling self-conscious in a group, take a deep breath and focus your attention on other people.

중심소재: 수줍음

1. 도입부 = 주제문

수줍음을 문제점으로 파악하고 이에 대한 대처법 소개

1) 뒷받침 진술

① First - 하고 싶은 말을 주저 없이 하라.

② Second - 다른 사람과 생각, 경험, 기술을 함께 나눌 수 있도록 이야기 할 내용을 리스트로 작성하여 모임에 대한 준비를 하라.

③ Finally : 혼자가 아님을 기억하고 다른 사람에 집중하라.

정답 1 (B)

해설

저자는 수줍음에 대처하는 방법을 추천해주기 위해서 이 글을 썼다.

지문해석

어떤 면에서 거의 모든 사람들은 수줍어한다. 만일 수줍음이 당신을 불편하게 하고 있다면, 지금이 자신감에 대한 몇 가지 교훈을 받아들일 때일지 모른다. 의사와 심리학자들이 말하는 몇몇 제안들을 따름으로써, 당신은 자신감을 증진시킬 수 있다. 먼저, 대화중에 해야 할 말을 망설이지 않기로 결심을 해라. 당신이 이야기해야 하는 것은 다른 사람들이 이야기하는 것만큼이나 중요하다. 둘째로, 집단 내에서 다른 사람들과 함께 있도록 스스로 준비하라. 당신이 가지고 있는 장점의 목록을 적어보아라. 그러고 나서 당신이 다른 사람들과 나누고 싶은 생각들, 경험들과 기술들의 목록을 적어 보아라. 당신이 말하고 싶은 것을 미리 생각해 두어라. 그리고 그것을 말해라. 마지막으로, 만일 당신이 집단 내에서 수줍은 느낌이 들기 시작하면, 크게 숨을 한 번 쉬고 다른 사람들에게 당신의 주의를 돌려라. 기억해라, 당신은 혼자가 아니다. 아무도 수줍음을 완전히 극복할 수는 없다. 그러나 대부분의 사람들은 수줍음과 더불어 사는 법을 배운다. 수줍음을 억제하려고 노력하는 것만으로도 많은 대가를 얻을 수 있다. 그러나 아마도 수줍음을 없애려는 가장 큰 이유는 당신에 대해 더 많은 것을 알 기회를 다른 사람에게 주기 위한 것이다.

Passage 2

1. Language is not a medium, but a system. This system is not determined by what happens outside of it, in some pre-linguistic space. (But) It is built around an internal arrangement of difference. 1) In a famous analogy, language is compared to pieces in ① a game of chess. You can use anything as chess-pieces (medieval figurines, dolls based on your favorite sit-com, button found in the street), as long as it is clear to the players what defines the system of differences between the various pieces that allows them to move in specific ways. It is not important what you use as king, queen, rook and pawn, as long as everyone knows which is which. In the case of signifiers, it does not matter which particular marks and sounds are used to denote a certain object. What makes language work is the difference between one signifier and all others. Language efficiency depends not on the perfect way the marks 'cat' define a certain quadruped, but on the complex web of differences which allows us to recognize the minute but crucial distinction between 'cat', 'bat' and so on. Indeed, although this distinction is minute, we are so sensitized to language as a system of differences that we consider those who cannot recognize the distinction to be either non-users of our language or suffering from a learning disorder.

글의 구성은 아주 간단하다.

일반진술(주제문)
구체적 진술 : 비유를 통해 주제문에서 밝힌 내용을 자세히 설명하고 있다.

중심소재: 언어

1. 도입부 = 주제문
언어란 도구가 아니라 내적차별에 의한 체제다.

1) 뒷받침 진술
① 비유(chess)를 통해서 언어가 체제이며, 이것이 차별에 의해서 체제가 형성된 것임을 부연하고 있다.

* 본문이 다소 까다롭게도 느껴질 수 있지만, 비유를 통한 부연을 비롯해 글 전체에서 a system of difference라는 표현이 반복되고 있다.

정답 **1** (A) **2** (C) **3** (C) **4** (D)

해설

1 빈칸 뒤에 이어지는 내용(language is compared to pieces in a game of chess)을 보면, 언어를 체스경기와 비유하고 있다. 선택지 (A)가 정답이다

2 언어를 체스와 비유하는 글이다. You can use anything as chess-pieces부분에 해당하는 내용은 선택지 (C)이다.

3 첫 번째 빈칸은 각 단어를 대입하여 문맥에 가장 적절한 표현을 이끌어 내야 한다. 이럴 경우 빈칸의 답은 주변의 문맥을 통해 쉽게 파악할 수 있는 두 번째 빈칸부터 접근하는 것이 효율적이다. 두 번째 빈칸의 경우 바로 앞에 'but'으로 연결된 접속사를 보아 바로 앞의 minute와 상반된 의미를 지니는 미묘하지만 "아주 중요한"의 의미를 전달하는 crucial이 가장 적절하다. 세 번째 빈칸의 경우 바로 앞의 양보의 although가 이끄는 대조 및 「so ~ that」의 인과를 활용하여, "비록 이러한 구별이 아주 미묘하지만" 우리는 자신의 언어에 아주 "민감(sensitized)하기 때문에"로 이어지는 것이 문맥에 가장 적절하다.

4 언어란 체스의 서로 다른 독특한 말이 말을 두는 사람에게 뚜렷한 차별성을 지니는 것과 같이 특정 대상을 지칭하는 특정 표시(signifier)가 다른 표시와 구별되기 때문에 가능하다고 말하고 있다. 그러므로 언어는 각 표시의 독특한 특성의 차별성을 바탕으로 한 체계임을 알 수 있다. 선택지 (D)가 본문의 요지를 가장 잘 전달하고 있다.

지문해석

언어는 도구가 아니라 체계다. 이 체계는 언어 밖의 세계, 즉 어떤 언어 이전의 영역에서 발생하는 것에 의해서 결정되는 것이 아니다. 이것(체계)은 내재적 차이의 배열을 중심으로 세워진다. 유명한 비유로 보자면, 언

어는 체스의 말에 비유된다. 당신은 어떤 것이든(중세 시대의 작은 조각상이든, 좋아하는 시트콤을 따서 만든 인형이든, 거리에서 발견할 수 있는 단추든) 체스의 말로 사용할 수 있다. 체스를 하는 사람들이 체스 말들이 특정한 방식으로 움직이도록 하는, 다양한 체스 말들 사이의 시스템적 차이를 구별할 수 있다면 말이다. 모든 사람들이 당신이 사용하는 말을 구별해낼 수만 있다면 당신이 왕으로, 여왕으로, 장이나 졸로 어떤 것을 사용하는지는 중요하지 않다. 기표(signifier)의 경우 어떤 특정 표시와 소리가 일정한 물체를 지시하도록 사용되는지는 전혀 중요하지 않다. 언어가 운영되도록 만드는 것은 바로 한 기표와 다른 모든 기표들 사이의 차이점이다. 언어의 효율성은 '고양이'라는 표시가 특정 네발짐승을 정의하는 완벽한 방법에 의존하는 것이 아니라 '고양이', '박쥐' 등 여러 개 사이의 미묘하지만 아주 중대한 구별을 인식하도록 허용해주는 차이점들의 복잡한 망에 의존한다. 비록 이러한 구별이 아주 미묘하지만, 우리는 차이의 체계로서 언어에 아주 민감하기 때문에 이러한 구별을 하지 못하는 사람은 우리 언어를 사용하지 않는 사람이거나 학습 장애를 경험하고 있는 것으로 간주한다.

Passage 3

통념의 시그널을 확인한다.

1. A very large number of people cease when quite young to add anything to a limited stock of judgments. After a certain age, say 25, they consider that their education is finished. Ⓐ It is perhaps natural that having passed through that painful and boring process, called expressly education, they should suppose it over, and that they are equipped for life to label every event as it occurs and drop it into its given pigeonhole. **1)** But one who has a label ready for everything does not bother to observe any more, even such ordinary happenings as he had observed for himself, with attention, before he went to school. He merely acts and reacts.

2. For people who have stopped noticing, the only possible new or renewed experience, and, therefore, new knowledge, is from a work of art. **1)** Because that is the only kind of experience which they are prepared to receive on its own terms, they will come out from their shells and expose themselves to music, to a play, to a book, because it is the accepted method of enjoying such things. **2.** True, even to plays and books they may bring artistic prejudices which prevent them from seeing that play or comprehending that book. Their artistic sensibilities may be as crusted over as their minds.
But it is part of an artist's job to break crusts, or let us say rather that artists who work for the public and not merely for themselves are interested in breaking crusts because they want to communicate their intuitions.

중심소재: 교육

1. 도입부 = 통념
특정 시기가 지나면 교육이 끝났다고 생각함
Ⓐ 이유 부연

1) 문제점 지적
새로운 시각으로 사물을 바라보지 못하고, 단지 수동적으로 삶을 살아감

2. 대안
새로운 경험과 새로운 지식은 예술 작품을 통해서만 가능하다.

1) 뒷받침 근거
예술 작품을 통해서만 이들이 새로운 지식과 경험을 받아들일 준비가 되어 있기 때문이다.

2. 요지문
예술적 편견으로 인해 이들이 연극이나 책을 제대로 이해하지 못할 우려도 있으며, 이미 이들의 예술적 감수성이 굳어져 있을지 모르지만 예술가는 앞에서 지적한 문제점을 인식하고 대중의 예술적 감수성을 깨워야 한다.

정답 1 (D) 2 (B) 3 (A)

지문분석

통념비판으로 시작하여 "예술을 통한 평생교육"을 다루는 글이다.

해설

1 평생교육의 차원에서 예술을 통한 새로운 경험과 지식을 배양해야 한다는 내용이므로 제목으로 가장 적절한 것은 "교육과 예술의 역할"이 적절하다.

2 "음악, 연극, 책" 같은 예술형식을 가리킨다.

3 crust over는 "~가 …위를 껍질로 덮다"의 뜻이다.

지문해석

아주 많은 사람들은 상당히 젊은 나이에 제한된 용량의 견식에 뭔가를 더하기를 멈춘다. 특정한 나이 대, 25살 정도가 지나면 그들은 자기들의 교육이 끝났다고 여긴다. 이것은 아마도 고통스럽고 지루한 과정이 명백한 교육을 겪어온 그들에게는 그게 끝났다고 여기고 평생 일어날 모든 사건들에 라벨을 붙여 칸막이함에 넣기에 충분히 준비가 되었다고 여기는 것이 자연스러울 것이다. 하지만 모든 일에 라벨을 붙일 준비가 된 사람은 더 이상 관찰하지 않는다. 학교에 들어가기 전에는 정말 평범한 일에도 주의 깊게 관찰하던 사람이라도. 그는 단지 행동하고 반응한다.

발견하기를 멈춘 사람들에게 오직 새롭거나 새삼스러워서 결국 새로운 지식이 되는 경험은 예술 작품이다. 그들이 이러한 식으로 받아들일 준비가 되어있는 유일한 경험이기 때문에 그들이 그들의 껍질에서 나와 자신을 음악과 연극과 책에 노출할 것이다. 왜냐하면 이것이 이런 것들을 받아들이는 방법이기 때문이다. 연극이나 책에도 그들이 예술적인 편견을 가져와서 연극을 보거나 책을 이해하는 것을 막을 수 있는 것도 사실이다. 그들의 예술적 감수성은 그들의 마음만큼 껍질로 덮여있을 수 있다.

하지만 이런 껍질을 부수는 것이 예술가의 일이다. 차라리 자신만을 위해서가 아니라 대중을 위해 일하는 예술가는 직관적으로 소통하기 원하기 때문에 그 껍질을 부수는 데 관심이 있다고 말하자.

Passage 4

1. Lend money to a friend, and you're liable to lose both. But when someone close hits you up for a loan, it can be tough to say no. 1) ① The first consideration, say financial experts, is whether you can afford it. If you can't afford to give the money away, you can't afford to lend it. ② Next, get it in writing. For big amounts, a repayment schedule helps to legitimize the loan. "It protects the lender, and can make the recipient more comfortable, so they don't see the loan as charity," says Howard Levine, a chartered accountant. ③ Should you charge interest? It's not mandatory, and may have tax implications. But if your money would be earning 5% on a term deposit, charge the same 5%. Or structure it as a loan but forgo the interest on repayment. ④ And if a pal defaults? For lenders, it's not just the amount that can cause a rift, but the feeling that you're being taken advantage of. Levlne advises borrowers not to avoid the topic: "Pay back what you can, even if it's just a bit. If you can't pay back, be up-front. Don't just ignore it."

중심소재: Lending Money

1. 도입부 = 주제문

친구에게 돈을 빌려줘야 하는 상황에서 주의해야 할 사항

1) 뒷받침 진술

①첫 번째 고려사항

②두 번째 고려사항

③세 번째 고려사항

④네 번째 고려사항

나열의 글 전개를 나타내는 시그널을 확인한다.

TEST 18

정답 1 (A) 2 (A)

해설

1 If you can't afford to give the money away, you can't afford to lend it.를 보면, "돈을 주어도 형편이 되지 못하면, 빌려주지 말라"는 의미인데, give away는 받을 것을 기대하고 빌려준다는 의미의 단어가 아니라 "그냥 주다"의 의미이다. 그러므로 "돈을 주어도 되는 여유가 있는 상황에서만 돈을 빌려주어라"라는 의미로 해석해야 한다.

2 부연진술의 기능을 하는 콜론을 활용한다. Pay back what you can, even if it's just a bit. If you can't pay back, be up-front. Don't just ignore it.에 해당하는 주체는 돈을 갚아야 하는 채무자(borrower)이다.

지문해석

친구에게 돈을 빌려주면, 친구와 돈을 모두 다 잃을 수 있다. 그러나 가까운 친구가 당신에게 돈을 빌려 달라고 재촉할 때, 거절하기란 참으로 힘들다. 금융가들이 말하는 첫 번째 고려사항은 당신이 돈을 빌려줄 여유가 있는가 하는 점이다. 돈을 줄 수 있는 여유가 없다면 빌려주어서는 안 된다. 그 다음 고려할 점은 빌려 준 것을 기록해 두어야 한다는 것이다. 큰 액수일 때, 상환 계획은 돈 빌려주는 것을 보다 정당한 느낌이 들도록 해준다. "그것이 빌려준 사람을 보호하고, 빌려 간 사람을 보다 편안하게 할 수 있고, 그래서 양쪽 모두 대출을 자선으로 보게 되지 않는다."라고 공인회계사인 하워드 레빈(Howard Levine)은 말한다. 이자를 혹시 부과해야 할 것인가? 이자는 의무적인 것은 아니며, 이자를 받으면 세금을 내야 할 수도 있다. 그러나 당신의 돈을 정기예금으로 맡겼을 때 5% 소득을 얻을 수 있는 것이었다면, 빌려준 돈에 대해 똑같이 5%의 이자를 부과하라. 아니면 그것을 대출로 설정한 후, 상환 시에는 이자를 포기하라. 그런데 만약 친구가 돈을 안갚는다면? 빌려준 사람에게 있어서, 친구와의 사이를 갈라지게 할 수 있는 것은 단지 돈의 액수가 아니라, 이용당했다는 감정이다. 레빈은 채무자들에게 다음과 같은 말을 기억하라고 조언한다. "갚을 수 있는 것은 그것이 작은 액수라도 갚아라. 갚을 수 없다면 갚을 수 없다고 솔직히 말하고 그것을 떼먹으려고 하지 말라."

Passage 5

1. The economic world is extremely complicated. There are millions of people and firms, thousands of prices and industries. One possible way of figuring out economic laws in such a setting is by controlled experiments. 1) ① A controlled experiment takes place when everything else but the item under investigation is held constant. Thus a scientist trying to determine whether saccharine causes cancer in rats will hold "other things equal" and only vary the amount of saccharine. Ⓐ Same air, same light, same type of rat.

② (But) Economists have no such luxury when testing economic laws. They cannot perform the controlled experiments of chemists or biologists because they cannot easily control other important factors. Like astronomers or meteorologists, they generally must be content to observe.

Ⓐ If you are vitally interested in the effects of the 1982 gasoline tax on fuel consumption, you will be vexed by the fact that in the same year when the tax was imposed, the size of cars became smaller. Nevertheless, you must try

대조의 글 전개를 확인한다.

구체적 진술을 이끄는 시그널을 확인한다.

중심소재: 경제법칙

1. 도입부 = 주제문
복잡한 경제 환경에서 법칙을 찾아내는 방법은 통제 실험이다.

1) 뒷받침 진술
① 자연과학자들의 접근방식
통제변인설정
Ⓐ 예시부연

② 경제학자들의 실험
중요한 변수를 통제하기 힘들기 때문에 관찰에 의존하는 천문학자나 기상학자에 가까움

Ⓐ 예시부연
특정 경제 현상을 예를 들면서 경제학자들은 어떻게 일반적 법칙을 만들어 내는지 설명하고 있다.

to isolate the effects of the tax by attempting to figure out what would happen, if "other things were equal." You can perform calculations that correct for the changing car size. Unless you make such corrections, you cannot accurately understand the effects of gasoline taxes.

정답 1 (A) 2 (B)

해설

1 문맥 상 "~을 제외하고"라는 표현이 들어가야 한다.

2 글의 도입부에서 주제문이 제시되는 두괄식 유형의 전형이다. 주제문 = One possible way of figuring out economic laws in such a setting is by controlled experiments.

지문해석

경제계는 극도로 복잡하다, 수백만의 사람들과 회사가 존재하고, 수천 가지의 가격과 산업이 있다. 이런 상황에서 경제 법칙을 이해할 수 있는 한 가지 방법은 대조 실험을 통해서이다. 대조 실험은 조사 중인 항목 외에 모든 조건을 일정하게 유지하는 상황에서 실시된다. 그러므로 사카린이 쥐에게 암을 유발하는지 여부를 판단하려는 과학자는 "다른 조건들은 일정하게" 유지하고 사카린의 양만을 달리 할 것이다. 즉, 동일한 산소, 동일한 빛, 같은 종류의 쥐여야 한다.

경제학자들은 경제 법칙을 검증할 때 이와 같은 사치를 누리지 못한다. 그들은 화학자들이나 생물학자들이 하는 대조 실험을 수행할 수 없는데, 다른 중요한 요소들을 쉽게 통제할 수 없기 때문이다. 천문학자나 기상학자들처럼 경제학자들은 관찰하는 것으로 만족해야 한다.

만약 당신이 1982년 연료 소비에 대한 석유세의 효과에 대단히 관심이 있다면 세금이 부과된 해에 자동차의 크기가 더 작아졌다는 사실에 짜증이 날 것이다. 그럼에도 불구하고 만약 "다른 것들이 동일하다"면 무슨 일이 일어날지 알아내려고 시도하면서 세금의 효과를 분리시키려 노력해야만 한다. 당신은 자동차의 크기 변화를 감안하는 계산법을 실행할 수 있다. 만약 그런 조정을 하지 않는다면 석유세의 효과를 정확히 파악할 수 없다.

Passage 6

1\. 1) Mainstream scientific organizations worldwide concur with the assessment that most of the observed warming over the last 50 years is likely to have been due to the human-caused increase in greenhouse gas concentrations. 2) However, some critics of the consensus view on global warming have argued that the appearance of overlapping groups of skeptical scientists, commentators and think tanks in seemingly unrelated controversies results from an organized attempt to replace scientific analysis with political ideology. 1) Some claim that the promotion of doubt regarding issues that are politically, but not scientifically, controversial became increasingly prevalent under the Bush Administration and constituted a 'Republican war on science.'

중심소재: 온난화

1\. 도입부 = 중심소재 도출

온난화 원인에 대한 논의

1) 구체적 진술 = 주류 과학계의 견해: 지난 50년간의 온난화는 인간에 의한 온실가스로 발생한 것일 가능성이 높다.

2\. 요지문

some critics 상반된 견해: 온난화의 원인에 대한 공통된 견해는 사실 과학적 견해를 정치적 이데올로기로 대체하려는 시도에서 기인한 것이다.

1) 뒷받침 사례

정답 1 (D) 2 (B)

해설

1 주류 과학계의 관점은 인간의 인위적 활동으로 인해 온난화가 일어난다는 내용이고, however 이후 "온난화의 원인에 대한 공통된 견해는 사실 과학적 견해를 정치적 이데올로기로 대체하려는 시도에서 기인한 것이다"라고 밝히고 있다. 그러므로 "온난화에 관한 정치적 성향"이라는 선택지 (D)가 제목으로 가장 적절하다.

2 주류 과학계는 온난화에 대한 과학적 접근은 바로 인간의 인위적 활동으로 인한 온실가스의 증가로 일어나는 것이라는 입장이다.

지문해석

전 세계 주류 과학단체들은 지난 50년간 관찰된 지구 온난화의 대부분이 인간이 유발한 온실가스 농도의 증가에 기인한 것이라는 평가에 동의한다. 그러나 지구온난화에 대해 합의된 견해에 대한 일부 비평가들은 겉으로는 관련 없어 보이는 논쟁에서 회의적인 과학자들과 논평가들 그리고 두뇌집단들(think thanks)이 중복되어 단체별로 출현하는 것이 과학적 분석을 정치적 이데올로기로 대체시키려는 조직화된 시도에서 비롯된 것이라고 주장해 왔다. 어떤 이들은 과학적으로가 아니라 정치적으로 논쟁적인 사안들에 대해 의혹을 조장하는 행위가 부시 행정부 하에서 점차 일반화되었고 '과학에 대한 공화당의 전쟁'을 야기했다고 주장한다.

Passage 7

1. External relationships are just as important as internal ones in predicting team success. 1) ① A lot of the time that a team spends building trust and a collegial spirit would be better spent scouting for outside sources of new ideas, generating enthusiasm for what the team is doing among upper managers and communicating with everyone the group's work touches, from customers to tech support. ② Conventional wisdom about what makes a team work, such as clearly delineated roles and team spirit, tends to correspond to team-member satisfaction, but those variables often don't line up with financial metrics like sales revenue. Companies that thrive in the knowledge-driven global economy are Ⓐ spread out, with loose hierarchies, not rigid centralized structures. Ⓑ They depend on complex, constantly changing streams of information that can't be contained by any one source. Ⓒ And the tasks of groups within these firms link them to people within the company and without. The distributed-yet-interconnected character of contemporary work dictates reaching outward, but years of morale-building retreats and consultants persuade us to keep looking in.

중심소재: 조직성공의 조건

1. 도입부 = 주제문

조직이 성공하기 위해선 내부관계뿐 아니라 외부관계도 중요하다.

1) 뒷받침 진술

① 외부자원을 찾는 데 시간을 투자하는 것이 현명하다.

② but 이후 성공한 기업의 특징 기술

Ⓐ 느슨한 관료제로 엄격한 중앙집중 구조가 아니라 외부로 확장하려는 성향

Ⓑ 한 특정 소스에 의해서 얻을 수 있는 것이 아닌 복잡하고 항상 변화하는 정보의 흐름에 의존

Ⓒ 내외적 인맥 확장

정답 1 (A) 2 (C)

해설

1 such as를 활용하여 빈칸에 들어갈 답의 범위를 좁힐 수 있다.

A such as B
A ⊃ B이므로 결국 B와 같은 맥락의 표현을 고르는 문제다.

B의 내용이 clearly delineated roles and team spirit이므로 "이미 정확히 기술된"에 해당하는 표현은 바로 conventional에 해당함을 알 수 있다. 문맥적 의미를 통해서 답을 구할 수도 있지만, 기능어를 통해 문장 내 표현 간의 관계를 통해서도 답을 구할 수 있다는 점을 기억한다.

2 팀 성공이 "회사의 판매 수익에 영향을 받는다"는 내용은 본문에 언급되어 있지 않으므로 선택지 (C)는 옳지 않다.

지문해석

기업 내 조직의 성공을 예측하기 위해서는 내부 관계만큼이나 외부 관계가 중요하다. 조직이 신뢰와 사기를 쌓는데 소비한 수많은 시간은 새로운 아이디어의 외부 원천을 찾고, 조직이 하고 있는 일에 대한 열의를 고위 경영자들에게서 이끌어 내며, 소비자에서 기술지원에 이르기까지 조직의 업무에 관련된 모든 이들과 소통하는 일에 쓰이는 것이 더 나을 것이다. 분명하게 기술된 역할 및 공동체 정신과 같이 조직을 일하게 만드는 것에 대한 일반적인 통념은 조직 구성원들의 만족에는 부합하지만, 그런 변수들은 종종 매출 수익과 같은 재무지표에 부응하지 않는다. 지식 중심의 세계 경제 속에서 번영하는 기업들은 엄격한 중앙 집권 구조가 아닌 느슨한 계층 구조를 가지고 뻗어 나간다. 그들 기업은 어느 하나의 출처로는 담을 수 없을 만큼 복잡하고 지속적으로 변하는 정보의 흐름에 의존하고 있다. 그리고 이러한 기업 내 조직의 업무는 그들을 기업 내외부의 사람들과 연결시켜 준다. 분산되었으나 서로 연관된 동시대의 업무 성격은 외부 확장을 강요하지만, 수년간의 사기 진작을 위한 단합 대회와 상담역들은 계속해서 내부를 살피라고 우리를 설득하고 있다.

Passage 8

1. A margin account sounds mysterious to the uninformed. Actually, it is nothing more than a loan the stockbroker makes to you using your securities as collateral to support the loan. 1) Here's how it works: ① Say you open a margin account by depositing $3,000. (All brokers require a minimum deposit for a margin account, and the Board of Governors of the Federal Reserve System requires an initial margin requirement of 50 percent of the value of securities purchased.) Then, you buy 100 shares of ABC stock at $ 50 a share. Thus, you bought $5,000 worth of stock, ignoring commissions, with only a $3,000 deposit; obviously the other $2,000 came from your bsroker. Now, what happens if the stock goes up or down in value? No problem, if it goes up. You can sell whenever you like and repay the $2,000 loan plus interest and pocket the difference. If it goes down, keep one simple fact in mind—the loss is all yours. You don't share it with the broker. So if ABC goes down to $30 a share and you then sell, the broker still gets $2,000, plus interest, and you still pocket the difference—$1,000 in this case. You lose $2,000, which is $20 a share times the 100 shares.

중심소재: 마진계좌

1. 도입부 = 중심소재 파악

마진계좌의 정의

1) 주제

마진계좌의 운영 원리

① 예시

'Here's how it works'에서 알 수 있듯이 마진에 대해서 잘 모르는 일반인(uninformed)에게 마진계좌가 어떻게 운영되는지를 구체적 예와 함께 설명하는 글이다.

구체적 진술을 이끄는 시그널을 확인한다.

정답 **1 (A) 2 (B)**

해설

it is nothing more than a loan the stockbroker makes to you using your securities as collateral to support the loan을 보면, "주식 중개인이 융자를 지원하기 위한 담보물건으로 당신의 유가증권을 사용해 당신에게 내주는 융자에 불과하다"고 했으므로 중개인이 빌려주는 돈임을 알 수 있다.
①은 5,000달러어치의 주식을 샀는데 100주이므로 한 주 가격은 50달러가 맞고 ②는 2,000달러 손실인데 한 주 가격이 20달러이므로 100주에 해당한다.

지문해석

증거금 계정은 이에 대해 알지 못하는 이들에게는 불가사의하게 들린다. 실제로 그것은 주식 중개인이 융자를 지원하기 위한 담보물건으로 당신의 유가증권을 사용해 당신에게 내주는 융자에 불과하다. 운용되는 방식은 이렇다. 당신이 3천 달러를 예치해 증거금 계정을 개설한다고 하자.(모든 중개인들은 증거금 계정을 위해 최소한의 예치금을 요구하고 미국연방준비제도이사회는 매입 유가증권 가치의 50%를 초기 증거금으로 요구한다.) 그러고 나서 당신은 주당 50달러에 ABC 주식 100주를 산다. 그렇게 되면 당신은 수수료를 무시할 때 단지 3천 달러의 예치금과 당신의 중개인에게서 나온 2천 달러로 5천 달러어치의 주식을 산 것이다. 이제 주식 가격이 오르거나 내리면 어떤 일이 발생하는가? 오를 때에는 아무 문제가 없다. 당신이 원하면 언제든지 팔아서 2천 달러에 이자를 더해 상환하고 그 차액을 가지면 된다. 만약 하락하면 간단한 사실 하나를 명심하라. 즉 그 손실 전부가 당신의 것이지 중개인과 나누지 않는다는 것이다. 그래서 만일 ABC가 주당 30달러로 하락하고 당신이 그때 판다면 중개인은 2천 달러와 이자를 여전히 받고 당신은 차액을 챙기면 되는데 이 경우에 차액은 1천 달러이다. 당신은 2천 달러를 잃게 되는데 이는 주당 20달러에 100주를 곱한 것이다.

TEST 19

Passage 1

1. Communication scholar Kames McCroskey, who has studied communication apprehension for more than twenty year, defines it as "an individual's level of fear or anxiety associated with either real or anticipated communication with another person or persons." 1) As this definition suggests, communication apprehension is not limited to public speaking situations. We may feel worried about almost any kind of communication encounter. ① If, for example, you are preparing to have a conversation with a romantic partner who, you think, is about to suggest ending the relationship, if your professor has called you into her office to discuss your poor attendance record, or if a police officer has motioned you to pull off the road for a "conversation," you know what communication apprehension is all about.

중심소재: 의사소통 불안

1. 도입부 = 중심소재 도출

의사소통 불안을 개인적 수준에서 정의

1) 주제문

의사소통 불안은 공적인 장소에서 말하는 것에만 한정되는 것이 아니라 개인적 수준의 다양한 상황에 적용된다.

① 뒷받침 예시

글의 도입부에서 정의되는 대상은 일반적으로 중심소재에 해당한다.

구체적 진술을 이끄는 시그널을 확인한다.

TEST 19

정답 1 (D)

해설

본문분석에서 볼 수 있다시피, communication apprehension is not limited to public speaking situations. We may feel worried about almost any kind of communication encounter가 주제문이다. 즉 의사소통 불안이란 공적인 장소에서만 발생하는 것이 아니라 다양한 개인적인 상황에서도 발생하는 것이다. 선택지 (D)가 이를 가장 잘 반영하고 있다.

지문해석

의사소통 학자인 케임스 맥크로스키(Kames McCroskey)는 20년 넘게 의사소통 불안에 관해 연구해 왔는데, 의사소통 불안을 "다른 사람 또는 사람들과의 실제 혹은 예상했던 의사소통과 관련된 공포 또는 불안의 개인별 수준"이라고 정의한다. 이 정의가 시사하듯이 의사소통 불안이 공석에서 말하는 상황들에만 국한된 것은 아니다. 우리는 거의 모든 종류의 의사소통과 맞닥뜨릴 때에 마음을 졸일 수 있다. 예를 들어 당신이 스스로 생각하기에 관계를 정리하자고 할 것만 같은 애인과의 대화를 준비해야 하는 경우, 교수가 당신의 저조한 출석률에 대해 이야기를 하자고 교수실로 부르는 경우, 경찰관이 당신에게 차를 세우고 "대화"를 나누자고 몸짓하는 경우에 당신은 의사소통 불안이 어떤 것인지 알게 된다.

Passage 2

1. Thus the critic need not humbly efface himself before the work and submit to its demands; on the contrary, he actively constructs its meaning: he makes the work exist; 1) "there is no Racine en Soi ... Racine exists in the readings of Racine, and apart from the readings there is no Racine." None of these readings is wrong, they all add to the work.
2. So, a work of literature ultimately consists of everything that has been said about it. As a result, no work ever dies; "A work is eternal not because it imposes a single meaning on different men, but because it suggests different meanings to a single man, speaking the same symbolic language in all ages: the work proposes, man disposes."
1) Barthes's masterpiece, S/Z, remains the exhilarating monument to this total rejection of the critic's passive role. To this one should add Barthes's concomitant insistence on a new emphasis on literature as it really is: a signifying system which characteristically and autonomously employs the specific activities of reading and writing, and which is not simply concerned to deliver a pre-ordained content to the reader.

요지를 드러내는 시그널을 파악한다.

중심소재: 문학작품

1. 도입부
비평가의 역할: 작품 속에서 새로운 의미를 만들어 내는 것이다.

1) 부연

2. 요지문
결과적으로 문학작품은 의미가 고정되어 있지 않아 영속하다(항상 새로운 의미가 부여된다는 의미).

1) 뒷받침 진술
권위 인물을 통해 요지를 뒷받침하고 있다.

* 요지를 담는 강조구문 확인 : not A but B, B not simply A (B강조)

정답 1(A) 2(B) 3(A)

해설

1 요약정리의 Thus를 활용한다. 문학작품을 대하는 비평가의 역할에 대한 내용이 언급되는 것으로 보아 앞선 단락에선 비평가의 역할과 위상에 대해서 다뤄졌을 것을 추론할 수 있다.

2 문학작품이 절대 죽지 않는 이유는 비평가에 의해 새로운 의미가 지속적으로 부여되기 때문이라고 했으므로 선택지 (B)가 옳다.

3 앞선 단락의 요지를 특정 작가의 작품에 적용하는 단락이므로 "작품에 지속적인 의미를 부연한다"는 맥락에서 내용을 파악한다. 빈칸에 들어갈 표현은 앞 뒤 문맥상 비평가의 수동적 역할(the critic's passive role)을 나타내는 표현이 들어가야 하므로 선택지 (A)가 가장 적절하다.

지문해석

그러므로 비평가는 작품 앞에서 자신을 겸손하게 낮추거나 작품의 요구에 따를 필요가 없다. 오히려 그는 작품의 의미를 활발하게 그려낸다. 그는 작품이 존재하게 만든다. "Racine en Soi는 존재하지 않는다. Racine은 Racined의 글에 해석에 존재하고, 그 해석을 떠나 Racine은 존재하지 않는다." 어떠한 이런 해석도 틀리지 않으며 이들은 모두 작품에 추가적인 요소를 제공한다.

그래서 문학작품을 궁극적으로 이것에 대해 언급한 모든 것에 구성된다. 결과적으로 어느 작품도 결코 죽지 않는다. "작품이 영원한 이유는 이것이 다양한 사람에 단일의 의미를 부여하기 때문이 아니라 이것이 모든 시대에 동일한 상징적 언어를 말하면서 단일의 사람에 다양한 의미를 드러내기 때문이다. 작품은 제시하고, 인간은 그것을 처리한다(의미를 부여한다)."

Barthes의 걸작 S/Z는 비평가들의 수동적 역할을 전적으로 거부하는 유쾌한 기념비적인 작품이다. 문학의 중요성에 대한 Barthes의 동시적 주장을 추가해야 한다. 읽기와 쓰기의 구체적인 활동을 극적이고 자발적으로 채택하고 독자에게 이미 정해진 내용을 단순히 전달하는 데에만 관심을 보이지 않는 의미를 부여하는 체제를 추가해야 한다.

Passage 3

1. In everyday life we surround ourselves with an invisible "bubble" that constitutes what we consider our personal space, an area around our body that we reserve for ourselves, intimate acquaintances, and close friends. 1) These personal spaces vary greatly from one culture to another and within cultures when people of different age, race, sex, and social class categories interact. ① Middle Easterners, for example, have much smaller distance requirements for casual interaction and men often embrace or kiss on the cheek when introduced for the first time—something that makes American men very uncomfortable. Despite living in a very densely-populated country, the Japanese often maintain a larger social space when interacting with strangers. When two Japanese men are introduced, they bow toward one another, an act that requires a distance of about 180cm to prevent bumping heads. In the United States, women are generally far more comfortable touching, hugging, or kissing one another than are men, and women generally will allow other women within their intimate distance, something a man rarely allows from another man, even if they are blood related.

중심소재: 개인공간(bubble)

1. 도입부 = 중심소재도출
개인적 영역이면서, 친밀한 관계를 유지하는 'bubble'이란 공간에 관한 글이다.

1) 주제문
이러한 영역은 문화와 문화 내 존재하는 나이, 인종, 성 그리고 사회 계층에 따라 다양하다

① 뒷받침 예시
각 나라별로 개인적인 공간인 'bubble'을 어떤 식으로 유지하는지 기술하고 있다.

뒷받침 예시의 시그널 확인

예시의 두 종류

① 뒷받침 예시

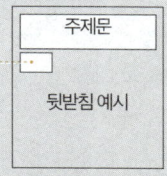

주제문

뒷받침 예시

For example

② 부연 예시

주제문

뒷받침 1. ________

뒷받침 2. ________

부연 예시

뒷받침 3. ________

* 예시가 나왔다고 해서 바로 앞 내용이 주제문이라 생각해선 안 된다.

정답 1 (B) 2 (A) 3 (B)

해설

1 빈칸 뒤에 이어지는 구조는 〈주어+동사〉의 절의 구조가 아니라 동명사구가 따르는 전치사구에 해당한다. 동명사를 바로 취하면서 부사구를 형성할 수 있는 것은 전치사 Despite 뿐이다. 문맥적으로 보면, "일본은 좁은 땅덩어리에 밀집하여 살고 있다"와 "낯선 사람과 상호작용을 할 때 거리감을 두면서 사회적 공간을 유지한다"는 서로 대조되는 개념이다. 그러므로 빈칸에 들어갈 단어는 Despite가 가장 적절하다.

2 Middle Easterners, for example, have much smaller distance requirements for casual interaction and men often embrace or kiss on the cheek when introduced for the first time—something that makes American men very uncomfortable.을 통해서 미국 남자들은 다른 사람이 자신의 bubble(영역)에 들어오는 것을 불편해함을 파악할 수 있으므로 선택지 (A)는 본문과 일치한다.

3 비교급을 강조하는 표현이 아닌 것은 (B)이다.

지문해석

일상생활에서 우리는 개인적 공간이라 간주하는 것으로 구성되는 눈에 보이지 않는 "bubble (버블지구)"로 둘러싸여 있다. 즉 개인적 공간이란 우리가 우리 자신과, 잘 알고 있는 사람들, 그리고 가까운 친구들을 위해 보존하고 있는 주변 지역을 의미한다. 이런 개인적 공간들은 문화마다 다르며, 각 문화 안에서도 서로 상호작용하는 사람들의 나이, 인종, 성, 그리고 사회적 계층이 다름에 따라 달라진다. 예를 들어 중동 사람들은 격식을 차리지 않은 상호작용을 할 때 훨씬 더 가까운 상호 간의 거리를 요구하며, 처음으로 소개를 받은 남자들이 종종 포옹을 하거나 뺨에 키스를 하는데, 이것은 미국 남자들을 매우 불편하게 만든다. 매우 인구가 밀집된 좁은 나라에 살고 있음에도 불구하고, 일본인들은 낯선 사람과 상호작용을 할 때 더 큰 사회적 공간을 유지한다. 일본인 두 사람이 서로 소개될 때 그들은 서로에게 절을 한다. 이것은 머리가 부딪치는 것을 막

기 위해 약 180센터미터 떨어진 거리를 요구하는 행동이다. 미국에서는 여성들이 일반적으로 남자들이 그런 것보다 훨씬 더 편안하게 접촉하고, 포옹하며, 서로에게 키스를 한다. 그리고 여성들은 일반적으로 친밀한 거리 내에 다른 여성들을 허용하는데, 이는 남자는 비록 혈연 관계일지라고 다른 남자에게 좀체 허용하지 않는 행동이다.

Passage 4

현상의 시그널을 확인한다.

1. ① During the past two decades the rise in the real income of manual laborers has been not only great in absolute terms, but also greater in comparison with that of non-manual workers. ② The effect of this has been to blur the old division between the working and middle classes, many manual workers' families now acquiring habits, tastes, and, to some extent, attitudes which were formerly regarded as "middle class." 1) Due to considerable upward mobility of the working class, social distinctions based on occupation have become less clear-cut. Whether they exist and what they consist of depend on what part of the country one is looking at, but people today should not assume that a doctor is regarded as several steps on the ladder above a garage keeper, or that the headmaster of the local state school is regarded as a higher being than the skilled worker who now earns not one quarter of his salary, but just as much as he does, if not more.

중심소재: 노동자 수입증가

1. 도입부 = 주제문(현상)

① 노동자의 실질 수입이 절대적·상대적 관점에서 증가

② 노동자와 중산층 계층의 경계가 불투명해짐

1) 뒷받침 진술

본문 끝까지 노동자 계층의 경제력 상승으로 인해 발생한 결과(직업을 바탕으로 한 사회 계층 간 경계가 불투명해짐)와 주의사항이 기술되고 있다.

정답 1 (B) 2 (C)

해설

1 육체노동자 계급과 사무직 노동자 계급 간의 오랜 구분이 점점 흐려짐 = 임금을 바탕으로 한 경제적 계급은 불분명해짐(less clear-cut)

2 내용일치/불일치 문제 중 내용일치를 묻는 경우 글의 요지가 답이 될 가능성이 높다. 선택지 (C)의 내용은 본문에서 전달하고자 하는 요지이며, 나머지는 모두 본문과 일치하지 않는다.

지문해석

지난 20년 동안 육체노동자들의 실제수입 상승은 절대적인 면에서 클 뿐만 아니라 사무직 노동자들의 수입 인상에 비해서도 더 컸다. 이러한 수입 상승의 결과 노동자 계급과 중류 계급들 사이의 오래된 구분이 흐려져서, 이제는 많은 육체노동자 가족들이 예전에 중류 계급의 것으로 여겨졌던 습관과 기호, 그리고 어느 정도 태도를 습득하고 있다. 노동자 계급의 상당한 신분상승 때문에 직업에 근거한 사회적 구별은 덜 분명해졌다. 그러한 사회적 구별이 존재하는가 그리고 그러한 사회적 구별은 무엇으로 이루어지는가는 사람이 그 나라의 어떤 부분을 바라보는가에 의존한다. 그러나 오늘날 사람들은 의사가 차고 관리인보다 몇 단계 위에 있다고 여겨진다거나 지역주립학교의 교장이 숙련 노동자보다 더 높은 사람으로 여겨진다고 생각해서는 안 되는데, 숙련 노동자가 이제는 교장 급여의 4분의 1을 버는 것이 아니고, 교장보다 더 많이는 아니라 하더라도 교장만큼은 버는 것이다.

Passage 5

1. 1) **A thousand years ago**, when the earth was reassuringly flat and the universe revolved around it, the ordinary person had no last name, let alone any claim to individualism. The self was subordinated to church and king. 2) **Then** came the Renaissance explosion of scientific discovery and humanist insight and, as both cause and effect, the rise of individual self-consciousness. All at once, it seemed, humanity had replaced God at the center of earthly life. And perhaps more than any great war or invention or feat of navigation, this upheaval marked the beginning of our modern era. 3) There are **now** 20 times as many people in the world as there were in the year 1000. Most have last names, and many of us have a personal identity or reasonable expectation of acquiring one. 2. This special issue examines the transformation of identity through different lenses and concludes with reflections on how hard it is, in a time of gathering global conformity, to find one's own way.

중심소재: 개인의 정체성 발달

1. 도입부

1) 중세

지구가 평평하다는 점과 천동설을 언급하는 것으로 보아 교회중심의 중세의 배경을 파악할 수 있고, 개인의 정체성은 존재하지 않음

2) 근대

과학혁명과 인간중심 사상이 태동함으로 개인이 세상의 중심이 됨

3) 현대

과거보다 20배나 많은 인구가 모두 이름을 가짐 = 개인주의에 따른 개인의 정체성 확보

2. 글의 종류와 의도

"This special issue"에서 알 수 있듯이 출판물의 잡지임을 알 수 있고, 특정 글의 서문에 해당하는 글이다.

본문은 시간의 흐름에 따른 글 전개방법을 취하고 있다. 특정 대상의 역사, 발달과정, 기원 등과 관련된 내용을 다룰 가능성이 높으므로 이에 주의하며 접근하도록 한다.

TEST 19

정답 1 (D) 2 (A) 3 (D) 4 (B) 5. (E)

해설

1 본문분석을 참고한다.

2 let alone는 "~는 말할 것도 없고"라는 뜻으로 보통 부정문에 사용된다. 같은 의미로 사용되는 not to mention은 긍정과 부정문에 모두 활용된다.

3 르네상스 이전에는 개인은 교회와 왕에 속했다는 문장을 파악할 수 있다(The self was subordinated to church and king).

4 issue는 출판문의 "호"에 해당한다.

5 it은 to 이하를 받는 가주어로 사용되었다.

지문해석

지구는 분명 평평하고 우주가 지구의 주위를 돌고 있다고 믿던 1천 년 전, 평범한 사람들은 개인의 독자성을 요구할 권리는 말할 것도 없고, 성(姓)조차 가지고 있지 않았다. 자아(自我)는 교회와 왕에 종속되어 있었다. 그 후 르네상스 시대에 과학적 발견과 인본주의적 통찰력이 대대적으로 생겨났고, 또한 그것의 원인과 결과로서 개인의 자의식(自意識)도 등장했다. 갑자기, 인간이 지상의 삶의 중심에서 신을 대신하는 듯 보였다. 그리고 아마 그 어떤 커다란 전쟁이나 발명 또는 항해의 위업보다도 이 격변이 근대의 시작이 되었을 것이다. 지금 세계는 서기 1000년보다 스무 배나 많은 인구가 있다. 대부분의 사람들이 성(姓)을 가지고 있으며, 대부분이 개인의 정체성이 있거나 정체성이 있는 것이 당연하다고 생각한다. 이번 특별 호에서는 다양한 렌즈를 통해 (개인의) 주체성이 변천하는 모습을 살펴보고, 전 세계적인 합의가 가능한 시대에, 자신만의 길을 찾는 것이 얼마나 힘든지를 깊이 생각해보는 것으로 결론을 맺는다.

Passage 6

1. Surgery that can improve the way a person looks is becoming more and more popular. 1) This kind of surgery is called cosmetic surgery, and both men and women are turning to this treatment ① as a way of keeping their appearance young as well as keeping competitive in their jobs. Men especially are beginning to turn to face-lifts, liposuction, and implants to help them look younger. As companies downsize and move younger employees into higher position, older employees in their late forties and early fifties feel the need to look and act younger in order to stay competitive. Ⓐ A younger look through cosmetic surgery may give an older employee a few more years on the job. These operations are not without dangers, however.

중심소재: 성형수술

1. 도입부 = 주제문(현상)
성형수술이 점점 인기를 얻고 있다.

1) 구체적 진술
① 배경
과거와 달리 특히 남성이 경쟁력을 위해 수술을 하는 인원이 늘어난다는 내용과 구체적 연령대까지 언급하고 있다.

Ⓐ 부연
부작용

정답 1 (D)

해설
"현상 → 원인"으로 전개되는 글이다. 글의 요지에 원인에 해당하는 내용을 반영해야 한다. 성형수술을 통해 더 젊어지면 나이든 직원도 그 직장을 몇 년 더 다닐 수 있으므로, (D)의 어떤 사람들은 직장을 계속 다니기 위해 성형수술을 한다는 것이 답으로 가장 적절하다.

지문해석
한 사람이 보이는 방식을 개선할 수 있는 수술이 더욱더 인기를 끌고 있다. 이런 종류의 수술은 성형수술이라고 불리고 남성과 여성 모두 직업 측면에서 경쟁력을 유지할 뿐 아니라 젊어 보이게 하는 방법으로써 이 치료법에 눈을 돌리고 있다. 남성들은 특히 더욱 젊게 보이기 위해 주름 제거 수술과 지방 흡입술, 이식 수술에 의지하기 시작하고 있다. 기업들이 인원을 축소하고 젊은 직원들을 고위직으로 승진시킴에 따라 40대 후반에서 50대 초반의 나이든 직원들은 경쟁력을 유지하기 위한 방편으로 더욱 젊어 보이고 더욱 젊게 행동해야 할 필요를 느낀다. 성형수술을 통해 더 젊어진 생김새는 나이든 직원을 그 직장에 몇 년 더 있게 해 줄 수도 있다. 그러나 이러한 수술들에 위험이 없지는 않다.

Passage 7

1. 1) I was in high school when I finally accepted the fact that I was homeless. Until that point I was in complete denial. ① During those miserable times, my brother and I learned how to become expert liars. Ⓐ We never let our friends in school know where we were living. Ⓑ In some cases we were lucky enough not to be going to the local school, so no one ever walked home with us. If the shelter was near our school or one of our friends caught us coming out of the "bums" building, as the kids in the neighborhood used to call it, then we would tell them our mother worked there and we had to meet her there after school. It is difficult

during those miserable times의 표현에서 현실을 받아들이기 전 상황에 대한 내용이 기술될 것을 예상할 수 있다.

1. 첫 번째 문단

1) 도입부 = 개인의 경험담
노숙자의 신분을 끝까지 부인하다 마침내 현실을 받아들였다는 내용

① 이전 상태
현실을 받아들이지 못하고 거짓말쟁이가 되었다는 내용

Ⓐ 친구들에게 집이 어디에 있는지 말하지 않음

Ⓑ 아이들이 "bums"가 사는 건물에서 나오는 것을 목격 → 주인공과 형은 어머니가 거기에서 일한다고 거짓말함

enough to fit in when you are a kid, and worse yet you can never invite anyone home to visit because you don't have a home.

2. 1) Being in those shelters, though, helped me to see that the biggest cause of homeless is not lack of money to pay rent. There were a lot of broken families in these shelters, broken by drugs, alcohol abuse, divorce, AIDS, early pregnancy, lack of education and, most important, lack of information about how to get out of these troubles. ① Many of the kids I knew at the shelter really wanted to change their circumstances but few of them did—few of them knew how. There weren't many social workers around, and even when they were around and noticed a problem, they rarely followed up. 2) The children in these situations need a listening ear, someone to turn to consistently.

2. 두 번째 문단

1) 현상(문제점)의 원인

단순히 돈이 없어서가 아니라 무엇보다 자신의 어려움에서 빠져나가는 방법에 대한 정보의 부재

① 부연

2) 대안(요지)

자신의 상황을 들어주고, 이러한 상황에 도움을 줄 수 있는 의지할 사람이 필요하다.

개인적 경험담 사회적 문제점으로 일반화하고 있음을 파악한다.

TEST 19

정답 **1** (C) **2** (A)

해설

1 We never let our friends in school know where we were living.부분에서 선택지 (C)가 정답임을 알 수 있다.

2 Being in those shelters, though, helped me to see that the biggest cause of homeless is not lack of money to pay rent.부분을 통해서 선택지 (A)의 내용을 이끌어 낼 수 있다. 선택지 (C)의 경우 아이들이 자신의 문제점을 인식하지 못하는 것이 아니라 현 상황을 벗어나기 위한 방법에 대한 부재(lack of information about how to get out of these troubles)임을 본문에서 파악할 수 있다.

지문해석

내가 노숙인이라는 사실을 마침내 받아들였을 때 나는 고등학생이었다. 그때까지 나는 이를 완전히 부정하고 있었다. 그런 비참한 시절에 나와 내 남동생은 전문적인 거짓말쟁이가 되는 법을 배웠다. 우리는 우리가 어디에 사는지 학교 친구들이 절대로 알지 못하게 했다. 어떤 경우에 우리는 운이 좋아서 동네 학교에 다니지 않아도 되었고, 따라서 아무도 우리와 함께 집까지 걸어가지 않았다. 만약 노숙자 보호시설이 학교 근처에 있거나 친구 중 하나가 이웃에 있는 아이들이 "부랑자들이 사는" 건물이라고 부르곤 했던 곳에서 우리가 나오는 것을 목격했을 경우 우리는 그 친구들에게 어머니가 그 곳에서 일하셔서 방과 후에 만나야 했다고 말했다. 어렸을 때는 적응하는 것만으로도 쉽지 않은데 더욱 나쁜 것은 집이 없어서 어느 누구도 집으로 초대할 수 없는 것이었다. 그러나 그런 보호시설에서 지내는 것은 노숙의 가장 큰 원인이 집세를 낼 돈이 없는 게 아니라는 점을 깨닫게 해주었다. 보호시설에는 결손 가족들이 많았는데 이들 가정은 약물, 알코올 남용, 이혼, 에이즈, 조기 임신, 교육의 부족, 그리고 가장 중요한 이런 고난에서 어떻게 벗어날 수 있을지에 대한 정보 부족에 의해 파괴되었다. 보호시설에서 알고 지냈던 많은 아이들이 그들의 주변 환경을 너무나 변화시키고 싶어 했지만 실제 그렇게 하는 아이는 거의 없었고 어떻게 해야 할지 아는 아이도 거의 없었다. 주변에 사회복지사들이 많지 않았고, 사회복지사들이 주변에 있고 문제를 인식했더라도 그들이 계속해서 관심을 갖고 돕는 경우는 드물었다. 이런 상황에 처한 아이들에게 필요한 것은 계속 이야기를 들어주고 지속적으로 의지할 수 있는 사람이다.

본문은 글쓴이의 견해가 지속적으로 드러난다. 부정적 현상과 대안의 패턴을 파악한다.

Passage 8

1. The school wall is repainted for the fourth time to get rid of graffiti. 1) Creativity is admirable **but** people **should** find ways to express themselves that do not inflict extra costs upon society. Why do you spoil the reputation of young people by painting graffiti where it's forbidden? ① Ⓐ Professional artists do not hang their paintings in the street. Instead they seek funding and gain fame through legal exhibitions.

Ⓑ Buildings, fences and park benches are works of art in themselves. It's really pathetic to spoil this architecture with graffiti. I can't understand why these criminal artists bother as their “artistic works” are just removed from sight over and over again.

중심소재: graffiti

1. 도입부 = 현상(문제점 파악)
학교 벽 낙서를 지우기 위해 4번이나 페인트칠을 다시 했다.

1) 주제문
불필요한 사회적 비용을 늘리는 않도록 자신을 표현할 수 있는 방법을 찾아야 한다.

① 뒷받침 근거
Ⓐ 진정한 예술가는 거리에 자신의 예술작품을 걸지 않음
Ⓑ 공공시설 자체도 예술

정답 1(C)

해설
낙서(graffiti)에 대한 부정적인 견해를 근거와 함께 피력하고 있다.

지문해석
학교 벽은 낙서를 제거하기 위해 4번이나 다시 칠해졌다. 창의성은 훌륭하지만 사람들은 사회가 추가비용을 물게 하지 않으면서 스스로를 표현할 수 있는 방법을 찾아야 한다. 왜 여러분은 금지된 곳에 낙서를 해서 젊은이들에 대한 평판을 훼손하는가? 전문적인 예술가들은 자신들의 그림을 길거리에 내걸지 않는다. 대신에 그들은 지원금을 얻어서 합법적인 전시회를 통하여 명성을 구축한다. 건물, 담장 그리고 공원 벤치들은 그 자체로 예술 작품이다. 이러한 건축물들을 낙서로 훼손하는 것은 정말 안타까운 일이다. 나는 그들의 ‘예술적인 작품들’ 이 단지 계속해서 지워진다고 해서 이러한 어리석은 예술가들이 왜 기분 나빠 하는지 이해할 수 없다.

TEST 20

Passage 1

1. Have you ever wondered why the supermarkets you have ever been into are all the same? It is not because the companies that operate them lack imagination. 1) It is because they are all versed in the science of persuading people to buy things. ① For example, the first thing people come to in most supermarkets is the fresh fruit and vegetables section. For shoppers, this makes no sense. Fruit and vegetables can be easily damaged, so they should be bought at the end, not the beginning, of a shopping trip. But psychology is at work here: selecting good wholesome fresh food is an uplifting way to start shopping, and it makes people feel less guilty about reaching for the stodgy stuff later on. For another example, everyday items like milk are invariably placed towards the back of a store to provide more opportunity to tempt customers. The idea is to boost "dwell time": the length of time people spend in a store.

중심소재: 슈퍼마켓의 구조

1. 도입부 = 주제

슈퍼마켓은 왜 항상 똑같은 구조로 되어 있는가?

1) 답변(요지)

소비자의 심리(②)를 이용하여 물건을 사게 유도하도록 과학적으로 배치된 것이다.

① 뒷받침 진술

뒷받침 예시의 시그널을 파악한다.

정답 1(D) 2(D)

해설

1 가게가 효율적으로 배치되어 있다는 점은 소비자의 측면이 아니라 판매자 즉, 경영자의 효율성을 고려한 것이기에 선택지 (D)는 틀린 표현이다. 옳지 않은 것을 고르는 문제의 경우 문제를 먼저 읽고, 이를 바탕으로 본문의 내용이 대략 어떤 내용으로 전개될지 예측하는 연습을 반복적으로 한다.

2 세부내용 파악은 문제에서 물어보는 내용을 본문에서 찾아 답해야 한다. 그러므로 문제를 먼저 읽은 후 내용을 기억한 후 본문을 읽는 것이 시간의 측면에서 효율적이다. selecting good wholesome fresh food is an uplifting way to start shopping, and it makes people feel less guilty about reaching for the stodgy stuff later on.부분을 통해 "건강한 음식의 선택은 느끼한 음식을 선택해 발생하는 죄책감을 덜 느끼게 만든다"고 했으므로 이러한 맥락에서 선택지 (D)가 정답이다.

지문해석

왜 당신이 들렀던 슈퍼마켓들이 모두 똑같은지에 대해 의문을 가져본 적이 있는가? 그것은 슈퍼마켓을 운영하는 회사들이 상상력이 부족하기 때문이 아니다. 그것은 사람들이 물건을 사도록 설득하는 과학에 회사들 모두 정통해 있기 때문이다. 예를 들어 대부분의 슈퍼마켓에서 사람들이 들어와 가장 먼저 마주치는 것은 신선 과일과 야채 구역이다. 구매자들로서 이것은 이해가 되지 않는 일이다. 과일과 야채는 쉽게 손상될 수 있기 때문에 그것들은 쇼핑의 처음이 아니라 가장 나중에 사야 한다. 하지만 심리학이 여기서 작동하는데, 맛있고 건강에 좋은 신선 식품을 고르는 것은 쇼핑을 시작해 사기를 높이는 방법으로 나중에 느끼한 식품을 사는 것에 대한 죄책감을 덜어준다. 다른 예로 우유 같은 일용품은 항상 가게 뒤편에 놓이는데 이는 손님들을 유인하는 기회를 더 많이 제공하기 때문이다. 이 발상은 사람들이 가게에서 보내는 시간의 길이인 "머무는 시간"을 증가시키려는 것이다.

전체는 네 문단으로 나뉘져 있다. 문단별 소주제와 함께 각 문단의 관계 및 전체 주제를 설명할 수 있어야 한다.

Passage 2

1\. 1) Frankenstein has achieved a distinction earned by very few other novels: based on myth, it has itself becomes a myth. The story is of Frankenstein, a scientist who has acquired the ability to light the spark of life in matter. Seeking for perfection and beauty in the creature he makes, and for it to adore him, he creates instead a monster, sewn together from bits of various humans.

2\. Frankenstein's monster is monstrous only in physical appearance. In agony from the wounds that hold it together, the 'monster' inspires loathing in all who see it. Eventually Frankenstein's creation destroys him, his brother, his friend and his bride. Frankenstein pursues it to the Arctic, determined to kill it, but is himself killed as the monster appears to decide that Frankenstein will be his last victim, and he/it will kill himself.

3\. The bare outlines do not do justice to the weight of the story. 1) Frankenstein is an emblem for modern science, the lust for knowledge which creates a power for destruction which it cannot control, and which will eventually destroy the creator and itself. 2) The monster is a symbol of the outsider, subject to fear, loathing and to being an outcast simply through its being different and through society's knee-jerk reaction to destroy anything that appears alien.

4\. 3) It is also a version of the myth of the Noble Savage, where something essentially good is corrupted by so-called civilization. 4) There are also hints of the Faust myth, as there are in so many Gothic novels. Frankenstein is seeking to transcend the limitations of humanity, seeking to do what only God is empowered to do, namely give the gift of life. For this he must be destroyed, and in true tragic form that destruction will not be limited to him but also affect many innocent people and society in general. To that extent Frankenstein is also a tragedy, in the classical and neo-classical sense of the word.

중심소재: 소설 속 프랭크슈타인 → 상징적 의미

1. 첫 번째와 두 번째 문단

1) 도입부

프랭크슈타인 소설의 줄거리 소개

3. 세 번째 문단

소설 속 프랭크슈타인의 두 가지 상징적 의미

1) 상징 1

파괴의 힘을 창조하는 현대 과학

2) 상징 2

나와 다른 외부인에 대한 두려움과 혐오를 드러내는 외부인의 상징

4. 네 번째 문단

문단은 나눠지지만 여전히 프랭크슈타인의 상징적 의미를 기술

3) 상징 3

문명의 타락성

4) 상징 4

파우스트 신화: 신에 대한 인간의 월권행위 및 그로 인한 비극

정답 **1** (B) **2** (A) **3** (C) **4** (D) **5** (E)

해설

1 Seeking for perfection and beauty in the creature he makes, and for it to adore him, he creates ⓐ ______ a monster, sewn together from bits of various humans.에서 빈칸 앞뒤의 내용을 보면 완벽하고 아름다운 창조물을 만들려고 했으나 괴물을 만들었다고 했으므로 대조의 instead가 빈칸에 가장 적절한 부사이다.

2 do justice to는 "바르게 나타내다, 평가하다"의 뜻이다. The bare outlines do not do ⓑ ______ to the weight of the story.에서 bare outlines는 있는 그대로의 이야기를 말하는 것이데, 작품 내면의 상징적 내용을 파악하지 않으면 글의 장중함을 잘 전달하지 못할 것이라는 내용이다. bare outlines ↔ weight of the story임을 파악한다.

3 knee-jerk는 "무릎 반사"로 "자동적으로(예상대로) 반응하는"이란 뜻이다. 문맥으로 파악하자면 나의 기준에 비추어 다른 모습을 하는 대상에 대해 적대감을 보인다는 내용이다.

4 give the gift of life하려는 프랑켄슈타인의 시도를 지칭한다.

5 Frankenstein has achieved a distinction earned by very few other novels: based on myth에서 선택지 (A)는 옳다는 것을 알 수 있다. Frankenstein pursues it to the Arctic, determined to kill it, but is himself killed as the monster appears to decide that Frankenstein will be his last victim, and he/it will kill himself.에서 선택지 (B)도 본문과 일치함을 파악할 수 있다. 선택지 (C)의 내용은 Frankenstein is an emblem for modern science, the lust for knowledge에서 파악할 수 있으며 선택지 (D)의 경우 Seeking for perfection and beauty in the creature he makes에서 알 수 있다. Frankenstein's monster is monstrous only in physical appearance.에서 선택지 (E)는 본문과 일치하지 않음을 알 수 있다.

지문해석

1 프랑켄슈타인은 독특함을 이뤄냈다. 이는 다른 소설이 거의 얻지 못한 업적이다. 바로 신화에 근거를 두면서, 그 자체가 신화가 되어버린 것을 말한다. 그 이야기는 물질에서 삶의 기운을 불러일으킬 수 있는 영감의 능력을 가지게 된 프랑켄슈타인이라는 한 과학자의 이야기이다. 그는 자신의 창조물에서 완벽과 미를 추구하며, 그것이 자신을 숭배하기 원했지만, 오히려(instead) 그는 다양한 사람들로부터 조금씩 짜깁기를 한 괴물을 만들어내고 만다.

2 프랑켄슈타인의 괴물은 외관만 괴물의 모습을 띄고 있다. 그를 지탱하고 있는 상처들에서 오는 고통 때문에, 이 '괴물'은 그것을 보는 모든 이로 하여금 혐오감을 불러일으킨다. 결국 프랑켄슈타인의 피조물은 자신과 자신의 형, 친구, 그리고 아내를 망가뜨린다. 프랑켄슈타인 박사는 북극까지 쫓아가 이 괴물을 죽이기로 마음먹지만, 그 괴물이 프랑켄슈타인 박사를 마지막으로 죽이고 자신도 죽겠다고 결심하면서, 결국 박사 그 자신이 죽음을 당하게 된다.

3 겉으로 드러난 이러한 이야기의 개요는 작품의 중요성을 제대로 보여주지 못한다. 프랑켄슈타인은 현대 과학의 상징이며, 자신이 통제하지 못하는 파괴력을 만들어내, 결국 창조자와 그 자신 모두를 망가뜨리게 되는 지식에의 욕망이다. 이야기 속 괴물은 단순히 남과 다르다는 점과 외부인으로 보이는 것은 무엇이든지 파괴하려는 우리 사회의 자동반사적 행동으로 인해 두려움과 혐오, 그리고 추방의 대상이 되는 외부인의 상징이다.

4 이는 또한 '고귀한 야만인' 이라는 신화의 한 가지 형태이기도 하다. 이 고귀한 야만인은 근본적으로 선한 것이 소위 문명이라는 것으로 인해 타락하는 것을 일컫는다. 이 이야기 속에는 아주 많은 고딕 소설에서처럼, 파우스트 신화를 암시할 수 있는 다양한 실마리들이 존재한다. 프랑켄슈타인은 인간의 한계를 뛰어넘으려 하고, 오직 신만이 할 수 있는 것, 즉 생명의 선물을 선사하는 일을 하려고 애쓴다. 이로 인하여 그는 파괴되어야만 하며, 이러한 파괴가 그에게만 한정되는 것이 아니라 많은 무고한 사람들과 사회 전반에게까지 영향을 미치는 진정한 비극의 형태가 온다. 이러한 점에서 프랑켄슈타인은 고전주의와 신고전주의적 관점에서 비극이기도 하다.

첫 번째 문장에서 알 수 있듯이 시간의 흐름에 따라 특정 인물의 이야기를 다루는 글이다. 서사체의 글의 경우 주제문이 따로 존재하지 않고, 등장인물들의 행동과 이들을 중심으로 발생하는 사건 등을 잘 파악하는 것이 중요하다. 시간의 흐름을 나타내는 시그널을 잘 파악하고 각 시기에 구체적으로 어떤 사건이 발생했는지 표시를 해 두어야 한다.

Passage 3

1. 1) William Kidd's story begins in 1696 when he sailed to England from his home in the New York colony. Kidd wanted to captain a Royal Navy warship in the king's army. Unfortunately, the British Board of Trade had other plans for him. Kidd happened to arrive in England during the time that the Board of Trade was coming up with a plan to combat the rampant outbreak of piracy that was just then causing damage to Britain's commercial shipping routes. ① A "privateer" to do aggressive battle against the pirates on the high sea was wanted by the board. They also wanted their privateer to engage in a little of its own piracy by preying upon French merchantmen. ② The board more or less roped their reluctant Kidd into doing their dirty work for them by "suggesting" that he might have trouble getting past customs when he returned home to New York. By the time Kidd set sail in his thirty four-gun ship, the Adventure Galley, in February 1696, he had already been pressed into paying the board twenty thousand English pounds bond. In addition, he had contracted that a 10 percent share of any valuables captured be given to the king. Furthermore, Kidd and his crew were to receive their payment out of the loot they confiscated from the pirates and the French.

중심소재: William Kidd's story

1. 도입부 = 구체적 진술

1) unfortunately를 기점으로 주인공이 원했던 것과 실제 발생한 일이 무엇인지 파악하도록 한다.

① 영국 상무원이 Kidd에게 구체적으로 어떤 임무를 맡기를 원하는지 기술되고 있다.

② 자신의 의도와는 달리 강압적으로 체결한 계약의 구체적 내용이 기술되고 있다.

정답 1(C) 2(B)

해설

1 영국 상무원이 Kidd에게 하기를 원했던 것은 창궐하던 행적행위였고 Kidd가 원래 원했던 것은 왕실군함을 지휘하는 것이었지만, 영국 상무원은 그가 창궐하는 해적행위를 저지하고, 심지어를 프랑스 상선에 해적행위를 해줄 것을 꼬였다고 했으므로 선택지 (C)가 정답이다.

2 1번 문제와 맥락에서 영국 상무원이 원하는 것은 기존의 해적소탕과 함께 프랑스 상선에 대한 해적행위다. A "privateer" to do aggressive battle against the pirates on the high sea was wanted by the board.의 내용을 보면, 상무원은 "privateer"를 통해서 이러한 일을 수행하기를 원했다는 점으로 보아 선택지 (B)가 정답임을 파악할 수 있다.

지문해석

William Kidd의 이야기는 그가 뉴욕 식민지에 있는 그의 집으로부터 영국으로 항해한 1696년으로부터 시작된다. Kidd는 왕의 군대인 영국 해군 군함의 선장이 되고 싶었다. 불운하게도, 영국 상무원은 그를 대상으로 다른 계획을 품고 있었다. 마침 Kidd가 영국에 도착한 때는 상무원은 걷잡을 수 없게 발생하여 바로 그 당시 영국의 상업해상운송 루트에 피해를 유발하던 해적행위에 맞서기 위한 계획을 내놓은 시기였다. 공해상에서 해적에 대항해 공격적으로 싸울 "사나포선"이 상무원에 의해 요구되었다. 상무원은 또한 자신 휘하의 사나포선이 프랑스 상선을 약탈하는 식으로 자체적으로 어느 정도는 해적행위를 하기를 원했다. 상무원은 Kidd가 다시 뉴욕에 돌아갈 때에 세관을 통과하는 데 어려움을 겪을 것이라고 "제안"하는 식으로, 다소 꺼려하던 Kidd가 자신들의 궂은일을 해 주도록 다소는 꼬드겼다. Kidd가 Adventure Galley란 이름의 43문의 포가 달린 선박을 타고 항해에 나선 1969년 2월경에는, 그는 이미 상무국에 영국돈 2만 파운드를 보석금으로 지불하라는 압력을 받았었다. 또한 그는 포획한 귀중품 중 10% 몫을 왕에게 바치기로 계약을 맺었다. 게다가 Kidd와 그의 선원들은 해적들이나 프랑스인들로부터 압수한 노획물로부터 보수를 받게 되어 있었다.

Passage 4

1 The writing of poetry, which has been generally regarded in the West as the most imaginative and loftiest of all literary forms, was in China a common, everyday undertaking of the intellectuals. 1) ① Chinese poets, unlike some of their Western counterparts who happily built their castles in the air, were on the whole earthbound and mundane. They were disturbed neither by poetic agonies and aesthetic aspirations, nor by the thrills of romantic excursions into the mind and the universe.

② Instead, they were content with weaving songs out of the materials of daily life and occupation. ③ Almost every educated Chinese was a poet who turned out verses as fast as there was an occasion for them. Ⓐ And in China there were official occasions for poetry: court celebrations and religious festivities; weddings and funerals; garden parties, where the beauties of the peonies and chrysanthemums were felicitated; convivial feasts during which, after a generous flow of wine, companies were promoted, merged and dissolved; trips to scenic spots, where even the latent poetic talent would burst into bloom—these and a thousand and one other occasions, on which, no matter how trivial they seemed, poetry was the language that spoke understandingly and pleasurably to the heart.

중심소재: 동양의 시

1. 도입부 = 주제설정
동양의 시는 지식인들 사이의 일상적 창작활동

1) 구체적 진술

①특징 1
세속적이고, 일상적인 내용

②특징 2
일상적 삶과 자신이 하는 일을 소재로 시를 지었다.

③특징 3
많은 기회와 함께 많은 시를 지었다.

Ⓐ 부연
다양한 행사 부연과 함께 아무리 사소한 행사라도 시가 존재했으며, 일반인도 즐김

대조를 활용하여 특정 대상의 특징, 속성을 밝히는 글이다.

TEST 20

정답 1 (A) 2 (D) 3 (B)

해설

1 They were disturbed neither by poetic agonies and aesthetic aspirations, nor by the thrills of romantic excursions into the mind and the universe.를 보면 중국 시인들의 마음이 흔들리지 않았다는 점을 언급한 후 빈칸 이후에는 그들이 만족했다고 했으므로, "그 대신"의 뜻인 instead가 적절하다.

2 (G)의 경우 말 그대로 "맛있는 포도주"의 뜻이므로 trivial(사소한)이라는 의미와는 관련성이 없다.

3 빈칸 이하에서 행사의 예를 많이 들었으므로 (B) numerous(수많은)가 적절하다. (C) funerals까지는 공식적이라 할 수 있어도 garden parties는 공식적이라기보다 오히려 사적 성격의 행사이다.

지문해석

서구 세계에서는 일반적으로 시의 창작 행위를 창의력이 제일 풍부하고 고상한 형태의 문학 표현이라고 생각한다. 그러나 중국의 지식인들 사이에서 시의 창작은 흔하고 일상적인 일이었다. 중국 시인들은, 행복하게 공중누각을 세웠던 서구의 시인들과는 달리, 굉장히 현실적이며 일상의 일을 이야기했다. 그들은 시적 고뇌나 미적인 열망, 혹은 정신과 우주로의 낭만적 여행에도 흔들리지 않았다. 대신, 그들은 매일 같은 삶과 일에 따른 소재로 노래를 만드는 데에 만족했다. 거의 모든 중국의 지식인들은 기회가 주어지면 재빠르게 시를 지

어내는 시인이었다. 그리고 중국에는 시를 지을 수 있는 기회가 매우 많았다: 궁중 기념행사와 종교 축제, 결혼식과 장례식, 모란과 국화의 아름다움을 찬양하는 가든파티, 포도주를 잔뜩 마신 뒤, 서로 모이고 흩어지며 사교를 증진시키는 즐거운 축제, 숨은 시적 재능마저 만개시켜줄 경치 좋은 곳으로 잠시 떠나는 여행 등이 있었던 것이다. 이런 기회들과 더불어, 이 외 수많은 다른 행사에서, 그 행사가 아무리 사소해 보일지라도, 시는 즐겁게 그리고 우리가 이해할 수 있도록 우리의 마음에 호소하는 목소리였다.

Passage 5

글쓴이의 경험을 통해 궁극적으로 전달하는 사항을 파악하는데, 과거와 현재의 대조를 주목하도록 한다.

현상의 시그널을 확인하도록 한다: over the years, have + p.p

1. Over the years we have hired many MBAs to work for us. In fact, in my more impressionable days I guess this was one of my own conditioned reflexes: If you have a problem, hire an MBA. As we grew and got to areas in which we had less confidence or expertise, 1) I reasoned that by virtue of their education the MBAs were the best people to run these areas for us.
① What I discovered was that a master's in business can sometimes block an ability to master experience. Ⓐ Many of the early MBAs we hired were either naive or victims of their business training. The result was a kind of real-life learning disability—a failure to read people properly or to size up situations.
2. In fairness to some of our employees, we do have a number of MBAs working for us who have made the adjustment to the real world quite nicely. But to assume, as I once did, that advanced degrees or high IQ scores automatically equal "business smarts" has often proved an expensive error in judgment.

중심소재: 고학력과 실적

1. 도입부 = 현상
과거에는 MBA 출신을 많이 고용

1) 이유
교육을 많이 받은 사람 = 실무 능력이 뛰어난 사람

① 요지문
학위가 오히려 경험을 배우는 데 방해가 된다.
Ⓐ 뒷받침 진술

2. 요지 재진술
But 이후 학력과 실적이 비례하지 않음을 다시 언급하고 있다.

정답 1 (A) 2 (B)

해설

1 고등 학위나, 높은 IQ 점수가 실제 업무 능력을 보장하는 것은 아니다.

2 to assume, as I once did, that advanced degrees or high IQ scores automatically equal "business smarts" has often proved an expensive error in judgment.에서 똑똑하다는 것이 사업을 잘 하는 것과 동일하지 않다는 내용이 직접적으로 언급되어 있다. 선택지 (B)본문의 요지와 정 반대의 내용이다.

지문해석

수년간 우리는 많은 MBA(경영학 석사) 출신들을 우리를 위해 일할 직원으로 고용해왔다. 사실 내가 보다 외부의 영향을 많이 받던 시절에는 이것이 조건 반사 중 하나였다. 즉, "어떤 문제가 있다면 MBA 출신을 고용하라"는 것이다. 회사가 성장하고 확신이나 전문지식이 부족했던 분야에 진출하면서, 나는 MBA 출신들이 그들이 받은 교육 덕분에 회사의 이런 부문들을 경영해 나갈 최적의 사람들이라고 생각했다.
그러면서 내가 알게 된 것은 경영학 석사학위가 때로는 경험을 터득하는 데 장애가 될 수 있다는 점이다. 우리가 고용했던 초기 MBA 출신 직원들 대다수가 미숙했거나 경영학 수업의 희생자였다. 결과는 일종의 실전 학습 장애였는데, 즉 사람들의 마음을 제대로 읽거나 상황을 판단하는 데에 실패한 것이다.
우리 직원들 중 일부를 공정하게 평가해 보면 현실 세계에 꽤나 잘 적응해 일했던 MBA 출신 직원들도 상당

수 있다. 하지만 내가 이미 그랬듯이 고등 학위나 높은 지능지수가 자동적으로 "사업적 분별력"과 동일하다고 판단하는 것은 종종 판단에 있어서 비싼 대가를 치러왔다.

Passage 6

1. Drug makers are well aware of the power of public relations, and they spend millions of dollars winning and dining the physicians who can make or break their products. Drug makers routinely take physicians to dinner, send them on vacations, or get them tickets to the Super Bowl. 1) Although the physicians who accept these gifts claim that they are not influenced by them, this claim seems hard to believe. 2) In fact, according to Dr. John C. Nelson, an obstetrician who is also a spokesperson for the American Medical Association, studies have shown that a doctor is more likely to prescribe a particular drug if its makers have recently taken the doctor to lunch or dinner. ① Alarmed by the romance between many doctors and the drug makers, Dr. Robert Goodman, an internist, has set up a website called www.nofreelunch.com. Intended for health care providers, the site makes disturbing reading for patients. For example, in a study run by Harvard Medical School, eighty-five doctors were asked questions about two popularly prescribed drugs. The doctors said that their answers were based on academic research. But the study found that 70 percent of the physicians were repeating information found only in the ads created by the drug makers.

중심소재: 제약회사의 관행

1. 도입부 = 제약회사의 관행
의사의 마음을 얻기 위해 사적 대접 - 부연

1) 의사들의 주장
사적인 대접에 영향을 받지 않는다고 주장

2) 주제문(문제점 지적)
의사들은 사적인 대접을 해준 회사의 약을 처방하는 경향이 있다.

① 뒷받침 진술
Robert Goodman가 운영하는 웹사이트를 통해 뒷받침 사례(for example)가 제시

논리적 반전을 이끄는 역접의 기능을 확인하도록 한다.

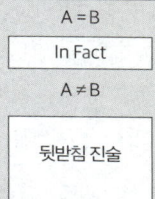

A = B
In Fact
A ≠ B
뒷받침 진술

정답 1 (D) 2 (A)

해설

1 they(drug makers) spend millions of dollars winning and dining the physicians who can make or break their products.를 보면, 제약 회사의 경우 의사들의 마음을 빼앗기 위해 엄청난 돈을 쓰고 있다. 이유는 자사 상품의 승패가 이들에게 달렸기 때문이다. 그러므로 선택지 (D)는 본문과 일치한다는 것을 알 수 있다.

2 이어지는 구체적 사례(for example)를 통해서 답의 근거를 찾을 수 있다. 85명의 의사를 대상으로 가장 많이 처방되는 두 종류의 약에 관해 물었더니 의사들은 "based on academic research" 처방했다고 대답했지만, 실제 70%는 repeating information found only in the ads created by the drug makers라는 결과가 나왔기 때문에 이러한 발견을 disturbing이라 표현한 것을 파악한다.

지문해석

제약회사들은 홍보활동의 힘을 잘 알고 자신들의 상품의 성패를 결정짓는 의사들을 푸짐하게 대접하기 위해 수백만 달러를 쓴다. 제약회사들은 정기적으로 의사들에게 저녁 식사를 대접하거나 휴가를 보내주거나 슈퍼볼 경기 입장권을 쥐어준다. 비록 이 같은 선물을 받는 의사들은 자신들이 제약회사로부터 영향을 받지 않는다고 주장하지만 이들의 주장은 믿기 어려워 보인다. 실제로 산부인과 전문의이자 미국의학협회(American

Medical Association)의 대변인인 존 C. 넬슨(John C. Nelson)에 따르면 의사는 제약회사가 최근 그에게 점심이나 저녁을 대접했다면 그 회사의 특정 약을 처방할 확률이 높아진다는 것을 연구 결과가 보여준다고 한다. 많은 의사들과 제약회사 간의 밀월 관계에 놀란 내과 전문의인 로버트 굿맨(Robert Goodman)은 www.nofreelunch.com이란 이름의 웹사이트를 개설했다. 의료인들을 대상으로 만들어진 이 사이트는 환자들에게 충격적인 읽을거리를 제공한다. 예를 들어 하버드 의대가 실시한 한 연구에서는 85명의 의사에게 흔히 처방하는 약 두 가지에 대해 물었다. 의사들은 자신들의 대답이 학술 연구에 기반을 둔 것이라고 대답했다. 하지만 연구에 따르면 응답한 의사 중 70%가 제약회사에서 만든 광고에만 나오는 정보를 되풀이해 말할 뿐이었다.

Passage 7

1. It's a warm evening in Baghdad and, not for the first time today, filming of "Love Under Occupation"—Iraq's first soap opera since the second Gulf War—has ground to a halt. **1)** Once again the culprit is postwar life. ① Ⓐ The U.S. Army shut down a radical Islamic newspaper a few hours ago and Ⓑ now thousands of angry Shiite Muslims are demonstrating outside. Ⓒ The crew packs its equipment into a battered car.

2. Kassem al Malak, the rubber-faced actor who is touted as Iraq's answer to comedian Jim Carrey, looks unfazed. Since filming began in February, gun battles and bomb blasts haven't been confined to the script. When al Malak describes acting as a life-and-death job, he doesn't sound like a drama queen.

3. Before the toppling of Saddam, the mere notion of making an Iraqi soap opera was impossible. Any drama touching on ordinary lives would have had to mention state-sanctioned torture and secret police—subjects that would earn a writer first-hand experience of both.
The few "real-life" dramas produced had very little action. Now it's the opposite. In the first series alone, al Malak's character, Fawzi Nabil, is arrested on suspicion of being a resistance fighter, gets embroiled in a kidnapping, and loses his devoted mother Zakir in a car-bomb attack.

중심소재: 이라크 드라마 중단

1. 첫 번째 문단

1) 도입부 = 현상(중심소재 파악)

이라크의 첫 번째 드라마가 중단되었다.

①원인

미국과 과격 이슬람 간의 전쟁

Ⓐ 과격 이슬람 신문사를 닫는 미군

Ⓑ 수천의 시아파 무슬림의 반대

Ⓒ 장비를 챙기는 드라마 직원

2. 두 번째 문단

이라크의 유명한 연기자가 언급되고, 현 상황에 전혀 당황하지 않는 모습(현실을 그래도 반영하는 소재 활용)

3. 세 번째 문단

사담집권 전후의 상황을 대조하면서 과거에 불가능했던 소재를 중심으로 한 드라마가 만들어지고 있음을 언급하고 있다(요지).

시간의 대조는 내용의 대조

과거	⊕
↕	
현재	⊖

정답 1 (E) 2 (B) 3 (D)

지문분석

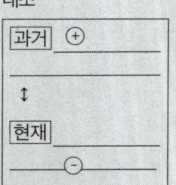

사담이 축출된 후 이라크 내 일상의 삶을 있는 그대로 그려내는 드라마가 출현하고 있다는 내용을 다루고 있다.

해설

1 culprit는 원래 "범죄자"라는 뜻으로 어떤 사건을 유발한 주체라는 뜻이다. 본문에서는 "범죄 드라마 제작이 중단된 "주요 원인"을 뜻하므로 Love Under Occupation의 촬영이 중단된 원인을 나타낸다.

2 Kassem al Malak, the rubber-faced actor who is touted as Iraq's answer to comedian Jim Carrey,

looks unfazed.에서 밑줄 친 표현은 "코미디언 짐캐리에 필적할 만한"이라는 뜻이다. 즉, answer는 "필적한 사람"으로 쓰였기 때문에 선택지 (B)는 옳지 않다.

3 Any drama touching on ordinary lives would have had to mention state-sanctioned torture and secret police—subjects that would earn a writer first-hand experience of both.를 보면, 일상의 주제를 다루는 드라마는 고문과 비밀경찰을 언급해야 했기에 아예 드라마를 만들지 못했다. 그렇게 했다가 작가가 이러한 고문과 비밀경찰을 경험할 수 있었기 때문이라고 하고 있으므로 선택지 (D)와 같이 과거에 비밀경찰이 드라마의 인기 있는 주제였다는 내용은 옳지 못하다.

지문해석

바그다드의 따뜻한 저녁이다. 그리고 오늘이 처음은 아니지만 제 2차 걸프전 이후 첫 이라크 TV 연속극인 "점령된 사랑(Love Under Occupation)"의 촬영이 중단되었다. 이번에도 그 범인은 전쟁 후의 삶이었다. 미군은 몇 시간 전에 한 급진적인 이슬람 신문사를 폐쇄했고 지금 분노한 시아파 성도 수천 명이 밖에서 시위를 벌이고 있다. 제작진은 장비를 낡은 차에 챙겨 넣고 있다. 코미디언 짐 캐리(Jim Carrey)에 필적할 만한 배우로 이라크에서 홍보되는, 천의 얼굴을 가진 남자배우 카셈 알 말락(Kassem al Malak)은 당황하지 않은 것처럼 보인다. 2월에 촬영이 시작된 이후로 총싸움과 폭탄 폭발은 대본에 제한되어 있지 않았다. 알 말락이 연기를 생사가 걸린 일이라고 설명할 때 그는 드라마 여왕마냥 말한 것이 아니다.
사담 후세인이 실각되기 전에는 이라크에서 TV 연속극을 만든다는 단순한 생각이 불가능한 일이었다. 평범한 삶을 다루는 그 어떤 드라마도 국가가 승인한 고문과 비밀경찰을 언급했어야 했으며, (실제 못했는데, 그렇게 했다면) 작가가 직접 경험했을 두 가지 주제이기도 했다(즉, 정작 연속극을 만들었다면 국가가 승인한 고문을 당했을 것이라는 의미). 이미 제작된 몇 편의 "실생활" 드라마는 거의 액션 장면이 없었다. 지금은 상황이 정반대이다. 첫 번째 시리즈에서만 알 말락이 맡은 극중 인물인 파지 나빌(Fawzi Nabil)은 독립투사 혐의로 체포되고, 유괴에 휘말리며, 자동차 폭탄 공격으로 그의 헌신적인 어머니 자키르(Zakir)를 잃는다.

TEST 20

Passage 8

1. The Romance languages of today came originally from Latin, which was the official language of the Roman Empire. 1) As the Empire spread gradually across a great part of Europe, Latin was introduced everywhere as the official language of government and administration. Spoken Latin was consistent from one area to another in the early days of the Empire. But later, when the Empire began to fall apart, the Roman administrators began to disappear. Gradually, the Latin of each region began to develop in its own way. Separated from each other by great distances and naturally influenced by the speech of the local people, each area slowly developed its own distinctive characteristics to the point where separate languages were formed. The modern Romance languages include the national languages: Italian, French, Spanish, Portuguese and Rumanian.

중심소재: 로망스어

1. 도입부 = 주제문
로망스어는 라틴어에서 유래했다.

1) 뒷받침 진술
주제문의 내용을 뒷받침하는 내용이 본문 끝가지 기술되고 있다.

기원에 관한 글임을 come from, originally, introduce, develop, form에서 쉽게 파악할 수 있다. 현재에서 과거, 과거에서 현재로 전개되는 시간의 흐름을 파악한다.

정답 1 B)

해설

로망스어의 기원에 관한 내용이므로 선택지 (B)가 제목으로 적합하다.

지문해석

오늘날의 로망스어는 원래 라틴어에서 유래했다. 라틴어는 로마제국의 공식 언어였다. 로마 제국이 유럽 대륙 전역으로 점차 확대되면서 라틴어가 도처에서 정치 · 행정의 공식언어로 채택되었다. 로마제국 초창기에 구어(口語) 라틴어는 지역마다 같았다. 그러나 이후에 로마제국이 붕괴되기 시작하자 로마 행정관들이 사라지기 시작했고, 각 지역의 라틴어는 점차 저마다의 방식으로 발전하기 시작했다. 각 지역은 서로 멀리 떨어져 있었기 때문에 자연히 토착인들의 언어에 영향을 받아 점차 지역 나름대로의 독특한 특징이 발달하게 되었고, 결국 독자적인 언어가 형성되었다. 현대 로망스어에 속하는 언어에는 이탈리아어, 프랑스어, 스페인어, 포르투갈어, 루마니아어 등이 있다.

TEST 21

Passage 1

1. In the past few years, there has been an explosion in a type of television programming called "reality TV." 1) As its name suggests, reality TV is about real people in real situations. ① Unlike traditional television shows, reality TV shows are completely Ⓐ unscripted. They allow viewers to watch how real people react in certain situations. ② Today, about 69 percent of the world's television watching is devoted to reality TV. Ⓐ In fact, some TV situations are completely dedicated to reality TV shows. Whether you are a fan of reality TV or not, it is definitely good business.

중심소재: 리얼리티 TV

1. 도입부 = 현상
리얼리티 TV의 폭발적 증가
1) 구체적 진술
① 정의 및 특징(대조)
Ⓐ unscripted
Ⓐ 부연
② 리얼리티 TV의 대중성
Ⓐ 부연강조(in fact)

현상의 시그널을 확인한다: in the past few years, has been

정답 1 (D) 2 (A) 3 (C)

해설

1 오늘날 69퍼센트의 TV 프로가 리얼리티 TV라고 했으므로 폭발적 증가라는 표현을 넣어야 한다.

2 unscripted는 "미리 써놓고 않은"의 뜻이므로 선택지 (A)와 그 뜻이 가장 유사하다.

3 현상의 글의 주제 또는 제목은 현상 자체가 되며, 이는 곧 글을 통해 전달하고자 하는 내용이 된다. 같은 맥락에서 내용일치문제를 낸 것이므로 "리얼리티 TV의 폭발적 인기"를 가장 잘 전달하는 것은 선택지 (C)이다.

지문해석

지난 몇 년 동안 '리얼리티 TV'라고 불리는 텔레비전 프로그램 유형이 폭발적으로 증가했다. 그 이름이 말하듯 리얼리티 TV는 실제 상황 속의 실제 사람들에 대한 것이다. 기존의 TV 쇼와는 달리 리얼리티 TV쇼는 대본이 전혀 없다. 리얼리티 TV는 시청자들이 실제 사람들이 특정 상황에서 어떻게 반응하는지 지켜볼 수 있게 해준다. 오늘날 세계적으로 약 69%의 TV 시청이 리얼리티 TV에 할애되고 있다. 사실 어떤 TV 방송은 완전히 리얼리티 TV쇼로만 되어 있다. 당신이 리얼리티 TV의 팬이든 아니든 리얼리티 TV는 확실히 좋은 사업이 된다.

However를 기준으로 특정 대상에 대해 상반된 견해로 전개되는 대조이며, However 이후 글쓴이가 드러내는 궁극적 내용이 전개되는 글로 구조는 간단하나 내용파악이 쉽지 않은 글이다.

Passage 2

1. 1) From the ancient Greek historian Thucydides to historical scholars of the Enlightenment and the Romantic periods, historians have maintained in different ways a fundamental distinction between objective knowledge about the past and poetic re-inventions of it. 2) In the last quarter of the 20th century, however, this distinction was challenged by a number of writers and thinkers. Taking their cue from French linguistic theories, ① these writers have argued that since the human mind understood everything through

중심소재: Text로서의 역사

1. 도입부
역사에 대한 입장
1) 과거 역사가들
객관적 역사와 재창조의 구별에 대한 다양한 견해 제시
2) 역사에 대한 20세기 역사가의 입장
① 모든 것은 텍스트 자체로 간주되어야 한다.

시간의 대조는 내용의 대조이므로 이러한 시그널을 놓치지 말고, however를 기준으로 근대에 해당하는 내용을 강조한다(글의 무게중심 이동).

순접부연의 접속부사를 파악한다.

the medium of language, everything could be regarded, in some sense, as a text. Nothing, indeed, could be shown to exist outside texts. ② Moreover, the language of which texts were composed bore no demonstrable, direct relation to the concepts of the things to which it referred; it took its meaning from the linguistic context around it. Ⓐ Thus for example chien no more suggested in itself a meat-eating, social, four-legged, barking animal than did dog or Hund — the word in question was only understood to have such a reference because it formed part of a larger system of words, a language.

② 텍스트의 언어는 그것이 지칭하는 대상과 직접적인 연관성이 없다: 언어의 임의성

Ⓐ 부연예시

정답 1 (B) 2 (E) 3 (B) 4 (A)

해설

1 However를 중심으로 기술되는 대조되는 견해를 파악한다. 과거에 대한 객관적 지식(역사적으로 발생한 사실)과 이러한 지식의 재창조(문학적 재창조) 사이에는 근본적 차이가 있다는 주장과 달리 20세기 이후 세상 모든 것은 언어를 통한 텍스트로 간주할 수 있다고 주장하고 있다. "문학 텍스트로서의 역사"가 본문의 제목으로 가장 적절하다.

2 this가 지칭하는 내용은 objective knowledge about the past and poetic re-inventions of it이다. 과거에 대한 객관적 지식은 실제 발생한 사건인 fact에 해당하고, 이를 시적(문학적)으로 재창조한 것은 fiction으로 볼 수 있다.

3 프랑스 언어학자의 이론에서 단서 또는 힌트를 얻었다는 이야기는 "이들의 이론을 사상적 기반으로 따랐다"는 의미이다.

4 언어는 그것이 지칭하는 대상과 직접적인 관련성을 지니지 않는다는 말은 특정 대상의 내재적 속성에 따라 이름을 칭하는 것이 아니라 인간이 임의적으로 그 대상에게 이름을 지어준다는 의미이다. arbitrary가 반영된 선택지 (A)가 정답이다.

지문해석

고대 그리스 역사학자 투키디데스(Thucydides)에서 계몽주의와 낭만주의 시대의 역사학자에 이르기까지, 역사가들은 과거에 대한 객관적 지식과 그것의 시적 재창조 사이, 여러 면에 있어서 근본적인 구별이 있음을 주장해왔다. 그러나 20세기 후반에 이러한 구분은 수많은 작가와 사상가들에 의해 도전을 받았다. 프랑스 언어학의 이론에서 근거를 들면서, 이 작가들은 인간의 마음은 언어라는 매개체를 통해서 모든 것을 이해할 수 있기 때문에 모든 것은 어떤 면에서 텍스트로 간주될 수 있다고 주장했다. 어떤 것도 텍스트 밖에서 보여질 수 없다(존재할 수 없다)는 것이다. 게다가 텍스트를 구성하는 언어는 언어가 지칭하는 사물의 개념을 증명할 수 있는 직접적인 관계를 띠지 않았다. 이러한 관계는 이것의 외부 언어적 문맥에서 그 의미를 취했다. 따라서 예를 들어 Chien(불어로 '개'를 가리킨다)은 dog, 또는 Hund(독일종의 개)와 마찬가지로, 그 말 자체로서는 고기를 먹고, 사회성을 지니며, 네 개의 다리를 가지고 짖는 동물을 가리키지는 않는다. 이 단어가 이러한 것을 지칭하도록 이해되는 것은 이것이 언어라는 더 큰 체제의 일부분을 형성하기 때문이다.

Passage 3

1. 1) ① North Americans do not maintain eye contact during a conversation; however, South Americans do. Ⓐ A person from North America usually meets the other person's eyes for a few seconds, looks away, and then back again, but a South American looks directly into the other person's eyes and considers it impolite not to do so. ② The South American uses many gestures. The North American, however, uses them only occasionally. ③ The North and South American have more in common regarding the distance each maintains from the person he or she is talking with. Ⓐ Unless a close friendship exists, both the North and the South American stand(s) about two to three feet from one another. ④ Another difference is the contrast in using hand movements while speaking. 2. By studying the differences in body language of a group of North and South Americans, we could probably figure out where each person comes from.

중심소재: 남미와 북미의 대화방법

1. 도입부 = 중심소재 도출

1) 구체적 진술

①차이점 1

Ⓐ부연진술

②차이점 2

③공통점

Ⓐ부연진술

④차이점 3

2. 결론(요지)

두 대상의 차이점을 드러내는 대조의 글로 however, but, difference와 같은 표현을 확인할 수 있다.

TEST 21

정답 1 (A) 2 (B)

해설

1 북미와 남미의 공통된 점(more in common)을 다루고 있으므로 선택지 (A)의 내용이 들어가야 자연스런 문맥을 형성한다.

2 문장삽입의 문제를 풀 때는 주로 ① 접속사 ② 대명사 ③ 부정관사 a와 정관사 the ④ 순차적 행위를 나타내는 동사 ⑤ 글 전개방식과 유형 등을 활용한다. "또 다른 차이점은 대화중 손동작"이라 했으므로 이후 북미와 남미의 서로 다른 손동작에 대한 구체적 내용이 나와야 한다. 제시된 문장은 [II]에 가장 적절하다.

지문해석

북미 사람들은 대화 중 눈을 계속 마주치지 않는 반면, 남미 사람들은 계속 마주친다. 북미 출신 사람은 대개 상대편의 눈을 수 초간 마주친 후, 눈길을 피했다가 다시 쳐다본다. 그러나 남미 출신 사람은 상대의 눈을 똑바로 쳐다보며, 그렇게 하지 않으면 무례하다고 여긴다. 또 다른 차이점은 대화를 하는 중 손동작에서 나타난다. 남미 사람들은 많은 동작을 쓴다. 그러나 북미 사람들은 가끔씩 동작을 한다. 북 · 남미 사람들이 이야기를 나눌 때 상대방과 유지하는 거리를 살펴보면 공통점을 발견할 수 있다. 만일 친한 사이가 아니라면 북미 사람들과 남미 사람들 모두 서로 2내지 3피트 떨어져서 있다. 북 · 남미 사람들의 몸동작에서의 차이점을 연구함으로써, 우리는 각각의 사람들이 어디 출신인지 알 수 있게 된다.

Passage 4

1. 1) Washington, D.C. has traditionally been an unbalanced city when it comes to the life of the mind. ① It has great national landmarks, from the Smithsonian museums, to the Washington Monument, to the Library of Congress. But day-to-day cultural life can be thin.

Ⓐ Washington has a good claim to be America's intellectual capital. [I] It regularly sucks in a giant share of the country's best brains, It is second only to San Francisco for the proportion of residents twenty-five years and older with a bachelor's degree or higher. [II] But far too much of the city's intellectual life is devoted to the minutiae of the political process. [III]

3. 1) This is changing. On October 1st, 2007 the Shakespeare Theater Company opened a 775-seat theater in the heart of downtown. [IV] This not only provides a new stage for a theatre company that has hitherto had to make do with the 450-seat Lansburgh Theatre around the comer, but it will also provide a platform for a large number of smaller arts companies. [V]

① The danger for Washington is that this intellectual and cultural renaissance will leave some citizens untouched. The capital remains a city deeply divided between well-educated white itinerants and under-educated black locals.

중심소재: 워싱턴 D.C

1. 첫 번째 문단

1) 도입부
워싱턴 D.C는 정신적(문화적) 삶의 측면에서 불균형한 도시였다.

① 뒷받침 근거
정치 분야와 달리 문화생활은 아주 취약하다는 내용을 전달하고 있다.

Ⓐ 두 번째 문단
워싱턴 D.C의 지나친 정치적 성향부연

과거와 대조되는 새로운 현상은 곧 글을 통해 궁극적으로 전달하려는 요지가 된다.

3. 세 번째 문단(요지)

1) 현상(요지)
새로운 극단회사가 도시 중심에 극장을 열면서 워싱턴 D.C 내 이전에 부족했던 새로운 문화생활의 활기를 예감하고 있다.

① 부연
특정 시민에게 이러한 문화생활이 적용되지 못할 것 같다는 우려를 통해 이에 대한 대응이 필요함을 간접적으로 전달하고 있다.

정답 **1** (A) **2** (C) **3** (C)

지문분석

글 전체로 "과거와 현재의 대조"를 파악하고, 영문단락은 언제나 과거를 대조로 현재를 강조하는 내용으로 전개됨을 기억한다.

해설

1 It is second only to San Francisco for the proportion of residents twenty-five years and older with a bachelor's degree or higher.를 통해 워싱턴 주민의 교육 수준은 샌프란시스코 다음으로 제일임을 알 수 있다. second to none은 "누구에게도 뒤지지 않는"의 뜻으로 "최고"라는 의미이다.

2 시민들의 식사대화가 대선으로 쉽게 옮겨진다는 것은 그만큼 시민들이 정치에 관심이 많다는 이야기이다. 선택지 (C)가 정답이다.

3 "이것이 변하고 있다"는 "새로운 극장의 개관으로 시민들이 일상에서 정치 외의 문화적 활동을 더욱 즐기게 되었다"라는 뜻이다.

지문해석

Washington D.C.는 예로부터, 정신적 삶에 관하여 균형이 맞지 않는 도시였다. 워싱턴에는 스미소니언 박물관(Smithsonian)에서 워싱턴 기념탑(Washington Monument), 그리고 국회 도서관(Library of Congress)에 이르는 대단한 역사적 건조물들이 있다. 그러나 일상적인 문화생활은 빈약하다.
워싱턴은 미국의 지적인 수도라고 주장할 만한 이유가 충분하다. 워싱턴은 미국의 최고 두뇌들의 상당수를 끌어모으고 있다. 워싱턴은 학사학위 이상을 소지한 25세 이상의 주민 비율이 샌프란시스코(San Francisco) 다음으로 제일 높은 곳이다. 그러나 이 도시의 지적인 삶의 너무나 많은 부분이 정치적 절차의 세세한 부분으로 기울어져 있다. 예를 들면, 요즘은 저녁 테이블의 대화가 아주 쉽게 대통령 선거에 관한 이야기로 바뀔 수 있다.

이것이 변하고 있다. 2007년 10월 1일에 셰익스피어 극단(Shakespeare Theater Company)은 시내 중심부 한가운데에 775석 규모의 극장을 개관했다. 이것은 지금까지 변두리에 있는 450석 규모의 랜즈버그 극장(Lanburgh Theartre)으로 그런대로 해나가야 했던 극단에게 새로운 무대를 제공해줄 뿐만 아니라, 수많은 소규모 예술 단체들에게도 활동무대를 마련해줄 것이다.

워싱턴의 위기는 이러한 지적이고 문화적인 부흥이 일부 시민들에게는 영향을 미치지 못할 것이라는 점이다. 수도인 워싱턴은 고등교육을 받은 백인 이주자들과 교육을 많이 받지 못한 흑인 지역주민들 사이의 괴리가 심각한 도시로 남아있다.

Passage 5

1. Have you ever flipped a coin to decide whether or not to do something? 1) People have been flipping coins for more than two thousand years.
① Julius Caesar began the practice when he was the dictator in ancient Rome. A picture of Caesar's head was printed on one side of every Roman coin. When Caesar flipped a coin and saw his head, that meant the Roman gods gave a "yes" response to a question. If he didn't see his head, the answer was "no."
② Romans began flipping coins to help make important decisions. Coin flips helped people know whom to marry, what house to buy, or who was guilty of a crime. Seeing Caesar's head meant the dictator and the Roman gods agreed with a person's decision.

중심소재: 동전던지기

1. 도입부 = 중심소재 도출
독자의 경험을 통해 주의를 환기시키며, 중심소재인 동전던지기를 언급하고 있다.

1) 구체적 진술
동전던지기는 2000년의 역사를 가진다.
① 동전던지기를 처음 시작한 배경
② 시저로 시작된 동전던지기가 일상생활의 일반적 관행으로 확대

기원을 밝히는 글이다. 도입부에 주제를 드러내는 중심소재와 함께 다음과 같은 글 전개방식을 취한다.
① 과거 → 현재(현상)
② 현재(현상) → 과거

정답 1 (B) 2 (C)

해설

1 When Caesar flipped a coin and saw his head, that meant the Roman gods gave a "yes" response to a question.의 밑줄 친 내용을 보면, "시저의 얼굴을 보면 긍정의 응답"이라는 의미이므로 시저의 얼굴은 "동의"가 된다.

2 글의 도입부인 첫 번째 문단에서 중심소재인 "동전던지기"를 개인의 경험담과 통해서 소개하고, 이후 동전던지기의 기원에 관한 중심내용을 다루고 있다. 일반적으로 기원의 글은 「 현재 → 과거 → 현재 」의 패턴의 응용으로 본문은 일반적으로 과거의 내용이므로 과거시제가 활용됨을 기억한다.

지문해석

당신은 뭔가를 할지 안할지 결정하기 위해 동전을 던져 본 일이 있는가? 사람들은 2천여 년 넘게 동전을 던져 결정해 왔다. 율리우스 시저(Julius Caesar)는 고대 로마의 독재자일 때 그 관행을 시작했다. 시저의 머리 그림이 모든 로마동전의 한 면에 새겨졌다. 시저가 동전을 던져서 머리를 보게 되면 그것은 로마의 신들이 질문에 "좋다"라고 한 것이었다. 만약 그가 그의 머리를 보지 못하면 응답은 "안 된다"였다. 로마인들은 중요한 결정을 하는 데 도움을 얻기 위해 동전을 던지기 시작했다. 동전 던지기가 사람들이 누구와 결혼할지 어

떤 집을 살지 혹은 누가 범인인지를 알게 도와주었다. 시저의 머리를 확인하는 것은 그 독재자와 로마의 신들이 한사람의 결정에 동의한다는 것을 의미했다.

중심내용을 파악한다.

나열의 글 전개 확인

Passage 6

1. Virtuality tends to skew our experience of the real in several ways. 1) ① First, it makes denatured and artificial experiences seem real — let's call it the Disneyland effect. Ⓐ After a brunch on Disneyland's Royal Street, a cappuccino at a restaurant chain called Bonjour Caféat an Anaheim shopping mall may seem real by comparison. After playing a video game in which your opponent is a computer program, the social worlds of Multiple User Dungeon (MUDs) may seem real as well. At least real people play most of the parts and the play space is relatively open. One player compares the roles he was able to play on video games and on MUDs. "Nintendo has a good game where you can play four characters. But even though they are very cool," he says, "they are written up for you." They seem artificial. In contrast, on the MUDs, he says, "There is nothing written up." He says he feels free. MUDs are "for real" because you make them up yourself.

② Another effect of simulation might be thought of as the artificial crocodile effect. Ⓐ In The Future Does Not Compute: Warnings from the Internet, Stephen L. Talbott quotes educators who say that ⓐ years of exciting nature programming have compromised wildlife experiences for children. The animals in the woods are unlikely to perform as dramatically as those captured on the camera. ⓑ I have a clear memory of a Brownie Scout field trip to the Brooklyn Botanical Gardens where I asked an attendant if she could make the flowers open fast. For a long while, no one understood what I was talking about. Then they figured it out: I was hoping that the attendant could make the flowers behave as they did in the time-lapse photography I had seen in Disney films.

중심소재: 가상현실

1. 도입부 = 주제문

가상현실은 현실을 왜곡한다.

1) 뒷받침 문장

① 첫 번째 왜곡

가상현실은 인위적인 경험을 실제화한다(= Disneyland Effect)

Ⓐ 뒷받침 부연

② 두 번째 왜곡

가상현실에 드러나는 과장된 현실로 인해 아이들의 실제적 경험을 약화시킴(= Artificial crocodile effect)

Ⓑ 뒷받침 부연

ⓐ 예시 1

카메라에 잡힌 동물과 진짜 숲속의 동물과는 너무나 딴 판이기에 혼돈을 일으킬 수 있다는 점

ⓑ 예시 2(경험담)

exciting nature programming에 노출된 주인공은 꽃을 보고, 디즈니 영화에 잡힌 꽃이 피는 현상을 그대로 현실에서 기대하고 있다(과장된 영화 내 현상과 현실을 구별하지 못함을 드러냄).

정답 1 (B) 2 (A) 3 (B) 4 (B) 5. (D)

해설

1 가상현실은 인공적인 경험들을 실제처럼 보이도록 한다고 언급되어 있으며, 아래 A and B는 A = B라는 관계를 활용하여 artificial과 가장 근접한 표현이 보기 (B)임을 알 수 있다. 선택지 (A), (C), (D)는 모두 같은 맥락의 유사어에 해당한다.

it makes (A) and artificial experiences seem real A = artificial

2 뒤에 이어지는 구체적 사례를 통해서 답을 이끌어 낼 수 있다. The animals in the woods are unlikely to perform as dramatically as those captured on the camera.부분에서 보는 것과 같이 사진에 담긴 동물의 모습이 실제 동물보다 더 dramatical하다는 것을 알 수 있다.

3 대조되는 Nintendo 게임은 they are written up for you라고 했으므로 MUDs는 선택지 (2)의 you make them up yourself로 표현하는 것이 가장 적절하다.

4 우선 compromise에 "(신용 · 명성 · 평판 등을) 위태롭게 하다, 손상하다, 더럽히다; (능력을) 약화시키다"의 뜻이 있음을 알고 있어야 한다. 앞뒤 문맥을 통해 왜 compromise가 답이 되는지 생각해보도록 한다.

5 전체적으로 가상현실로 인해 현실이 위협받고 있다는 의미이므로 선택지 (D)가 답으로 가장 적절하다. 첫 번째 문장을 통해 주제를 설정해 보도록 한다.

지문해석

가상현실은 몇 가지 방식으로 우리의 현실 경험을 왜곡시키는 경향이 있다. 첫째로 그것은 본성을 바꾸고 인위적인 경험들이 실제인 것처럼 보이도록 만든다. 그것을 디즈니랜드(Disneyland) 효과라고 일컫자. 디즈니랜드의 로얄 스트리트(Royal Street)에서 아침 겸 점심을 먹고 난 후 애너하임(Anaheim) 쇼핑몰의 봉쥬르 카페(Bonjour Caféat)라는 식당 체인점에서 마시는 카푸치노 한 잔이 상대적으로 더욱 실제처럼 보일 수 있다. 컴퓨터 프로그램이 적군인 비디오 게임을 하고 나면 다자간 지하감옥 게임(일명 머드 게임) 속 사교계 역시 실제처럼 보일 수 있다. 하다못해 실제 인물들이 그 역할들의 대부분을 수행하고 있고, 놀이 공간은 상대적으로 공개되어 있다. 한 게이머는 그가 비디오 게임과 머드 게임에서 맡을 수 있는 역할을 비교하며 "닌텐도는 당신이 네 가지 배역을 맡을 수 있는 괜찮은 게임이다. 그러나 그것들이 매우 멋질지라도 당신에게 맞춰 만들어진 것일 뿐이다"라고 말한다. 인위적으로 보인다는 것이다. 반면에 머드 게임에는 "미리 만들어진 것이 하나도 없다"고 그는 말한다. 그는 자유를 느낀다고 말한다. 머드 게임은 "실제인데" 당신이 게임을 직접 만들어가기 때문이다.

시뮬레이션의 또 다른 효과는 인공 악어 효과라고 생각해 볼 수도 있다. 스테판 탈보트(Stephan L. Talbott)는 그의 저서 《미래는 계산하지 않는다: 인터넷의 경고》에서 대자연에 대한 흥미로운 다큐멘터리 영화를 수년 간 시청하는 것이 아이들의 야생 경험을 손상시켰다고 말한 한 교육자의 말을 인용하고 있다. 숲 속의 동물들은 좀처럼 카메라에 잡힐 때처럼 과장되게 행동하지 않는다. 나는 브라우니 스카우트(Brownie Scout) 견학 여행으로 브루클린(Brooklyn) 식물원에 갔던 기억이 선명한데, 당시 한 안내원에게 꽃을 빨리 피게 할 수 있는지 물었다. 한동안 어느 누구도 내가 무슨 말을 하고 있는지 이해하지 못했다. 이후 그들은 이해했다. 나는 안내원이 내가 본 디즈니 영화의 저속도 촬영에서처럼 꽃을 서서히 움직이게 할 수 있는지를 기대했던 것이다.

Passage 7

1. Most households now own two cars, and quite a few own three or four. 1) Sometimes that is necessary—if there are two wage-earners, for example, and both have to commute by car because no other options are available. But if you want the extra car only because it will be a little more convenient, stop and consider two things. ① Ⓐ First, the mere purchase of a car harms the environment because it encourages the manufacturing of more automobiles. When you picture that new car in your driveway, imagine instead the four tons of carbon and nearly 700 pounds of ordinary pollutants pumped into the atmosphere as a result of its manufacture. Ⓑ Second, not having an extra car will discourage you from making unnecessary car trips and force you to make more effective use of the car you have. ⓐ This suggestion is a bit like advising a smoker who is trying to quit to keep cigarettes out of the house, or a dieter to buy no sweets. Without that care always at hand, you just might find yourself doubling up with your spouse on trips to the store, hitching rides with friends, perhaps even bicycling or walking.

중심소재: 차량구매

1. 도입부 = 현상
한 가정에 차가 두 대 또는 서 네 대 보유

1) 주제문
추가적인 차량을 구매할 때 고려해야 할 두 가지 사항

① 뒷받침 진술
Ⓐ 첫 번째 이유
환경적 측면
Ⓑ 두 번째 이유
불필요한 여행을 줄이고, 현재 가지고 있는 차를 더 잘 관리하는 효과가 있다.
ⓐ 부연
현재 소유하고 있는(at hand) 자동차를 잘 관리해야 하는 이유 부연

정답 1 (C) 2 (D)

해설

1 if there are two wage-earners, for example, and both have to commute by car because no other options are available의 밑줄 친 표현으로 보아 선택지 (C)가 정답이다.

2 the mere purchase of a car harms the environment because it encourages the manufacturing of more automobiles.에서 "더 많은 자동차의 생산은 환경에 부정적인 영향을 미친다"는 것을 파악할 수 있다.

지문해석

오늘날 대부분의 가정은 두 대의 자동차를 보유하고 있고, 상당수의 가정이 세 대 또는 네 대를 보유하기도 한다. 때로는 그럴 필요가 있기도 한데, 예를 들어 맞벌이를 하고 다른 선택 안들이 없어서 부부가 자동차로 통근해야 하는 경우가 그렇다. 하지만 만약 여러분이 단지 좀 더 편하기 때문에 여분의 자동차를 원한다면 멈춰 서서 두 가지 사항에 대해 생각해 보라. 첫째, 단지 자동차를 사는 것만으로도 환경에 해를 끼치는데 그것은 더 많은 자동차 생산을 조장하기 때문이다. 여러분이 (집 앞) 사유 차도 위에 세운 새 차를 마음속에 그려볼 때 그 대신에 그 새 차를 생산한 결과 대기에 배출된 4톤의 탄소와 약 700파운드의 일상 오염물질을 상상해 보라. 둘째, 여분의 차를 갖지 않는 것은 당신이 불필요한 자동차 여행을 하지 않도록 하고 현재 가지고 있는 차를 더욱 효율적으로 사용하게끔 할 것이다. 이 같은 제안은 금연하려고 노력하는 흡연자에게 담배를 집 안으로 가지고 들어오지 못하게 하고, 다이어트 중인 사람에게 단 것을 사지 못하게 하는 것과 같다. 항상 곁에 있던 그 보살핌(자동차)이 없다면 당신은 배우자와 둘이서 가게에 가거나, 친구들의 차에 끼어 타거나, 어쩌면 자전거를 타거나 걷고 있는 스스로의 모습까지 발견할지 모른다.

Passage 8

1. Gift cards are America's most popular present. 1) Retailers like them because they are profitable. But like most goods in the recession, they have become harder to sell, prompting some radical redesigns. ① Gift cards are profitable Ⓐ because retailers receive money for them up front, and around 10% of them are never redeemed. Ⓑ When people do use them, they often spend more than the amount given, and Ⓒ on products with high margins. ② But sales of gift cards were down by around 6% last year in America, to about $25 billion, partly Ⓐ because discounts in stores were so steep that customers saw more value in buying merchandise directly. Ⓑ Bankruptcies among retailers also scared people away from gift cards, for fear that stores would not be around to honour them. Ⓒ Some financial-services companies that offer gift cards which can be used in various stores came under fire for charging monthly maintenance fees on unspent balances.

중심소재: 상품교환권

1. 도입부 = 현상
최근 상품권 구매가 줄어듦.

1) 뒷받침 근거(이유)
① 도매상의 입장
Ⓐ 선수금 및 10%는 돈으로 상환이 안 됨
Ⓑ 정해진 금액 이상 소비
Ⓒ 마진이 큰 품목 구매로 이어짐

2) 소비자 입장
Ⓐ 일반 상품 세일이 높아 돈으로 직접 구입
Ⓑ 도매점의 부도위험
Ⓒ 상품 유지 수수료

최근에 발생한 현상과 그 이유·원인을 밝히는 글이다.

TEST 21

정답 1 (A)

해설
sales of gift cards were down by around 6% last year in America, to about $25 billion, partly because discounts in stores were so steep that customers saw more value in buying merchandise directly.를 보면 "상점의 할인 폭이 커 기프트 카드보단 직접 돈을 주고 사는 것이 가치 있다(싸다)"고 언급하고 있으므로 선택지 (A)의 내용은 본문과 일치한다.

지문해석
기프트카드는 미국에서 가장 인기 있는 선물이다. 소매업자들도 기프트카드를 좋아하는데 수익성이 좋기 때문이다. 하지만 불경기에 판매되는 대부분의 상품이 그렇듯이 기프트카드 역시 판매하기 어려워졌고, 이는 몇 가지 근본적인 개편을 촉구하고 있다. 기프트카드는 수익성이 좋은데, 소매업자들이 기프트카드에 대해 선불로 돈을 받고 기프트카드의 약 10% 정도는 교환되지 않기 때문이다. 사람들은 기프트카드를 사용할 때 종종 카드에 주어진 금액보다 많이 쓰고 수익성이 높은 상품에 카드를 사용하기도 한다. 그러나 기프트카드 매출은 작년에 미국에서 6% 정도 감소하여 약 250억불을 기록했는데, 부분적으로는 상점의 할인 폭이 너무 커서 고객들이 직접 상품을 구입하는 것을 더 가치 있다고 생각했기 때문이다. 또한 소매업자들의 부도는 사람들로 하여금 기프트카드를 멀리하게 하는데, 상점들이 기프트카드를 사용할 때까지 남아있지 않을 수 있다는 두려움 때문이다. 다양한 상점에서 사용될 수 있는 기프트카드를 내놓은 일부 금융회사들은 쓰지 않은 잔액에 대해 월 유지비를 책정해 비난을 사고 있다.

TEST 22

Passage 1

1. 1) Research studies have shown that ① high-achieving people are able to envision a detailed, three-dimensional picture of their future in which their goals and aspirations are clearly inscribed. ② In addition, they are able to construct a mental plan that includes the sequence of steps they will have to take, the amount of time each step will involve, and strategies for overcoming the obstacles they are likely to encounter. Ⓐ ⓐ Such realistic and compelling concepts of the future enable these people to make sacrifices in the present to achieve their long-term goals. ⓑ Of course, they may modify these goals as circumstances change and they acquire more information, but they retain a well-defined flexible plan that charts their life course.

1. 도입부
실험의 결과(show)가 바로 드러난다.

1) 구체적 진술

① 높은 성취력을 보이는 사람일수록 자신의 목표를 구체적으로 설정한다.

② 목적을 달성하기 위한 구체적 단계 설정 + 중간에 직면하게 될 걸림돌에 대한 대처법(전략)

Ⓐ 세부부연

ⓐ 앞에 언급한 현실적이고 강력한 미래에 대한 계획으로 장기적 미래를 위해 현재를 '희생'할 수 있게 됨

ⓑ 상황이 변한다고 해도 그 상황에 맞는 유연한 계획을 가지고 있다.

정답 **1** (B)

지문분석

실험을 통해 밝히려는 사항이 무엇인가? 본문은 실험을 통해 '성취도가 높은 사람들의 특징'을 파악하는 글이다.

해설

역접의 접속사를 활용하는데, of course A but B는 "물론 A이지만 B이다"의 의미이다. A와 B는 서로 대조되는 관계가 되므로, 상황에 따라 목표를 바꾼다는 내용이 나온 후 but이 나오므로 빈칸에 들어갈 표현은 글 전체의 문맥을 감안할 때 "상황에 따라 목표를 바꾸지만, 명확한 계획을 가지고 장기적인 관점에서 진행한다"는 선택지 (B)가 가장 적절하다.

지문해석

성취도가 높은 사람들은 그들의 목표와 열망이 분명하게 그려져 있는, 자신의 미래에 대해서 상세하고 입체적인 그림을 상상할 수 있다는 것이 연구를 통해 보여지고 있다. 게다가 이러한 사람들은 밟아야 할 일련의 단계들과 각 단계에 소요되는 시간, 그리고 발생할 수 있는 장애를 극복하기 위한 전략 등을 마음속으로 계획할 수 있다. 이렇듯 미래에 대한 현실적이고 설득력 있는 개념은 이 사람들이 장기적인 목표를 달성하기 위해 현재에서 희생을 할 수 있게 해준다. 물론, 그들은 주변상황이 바뀌고 정보를 더 얻으며 목표를 수정할지도 모르지만, 인생의 진로를 나타내는 명확하고 유연한 계획은 그대로 유지한다.

Passage 2

1. 1) A writing system is a type of symbolic system used to represent elements or statements expressible in language. ① Writing systems are distinguished from other possible symbolic communication systems in that Ⓐ ⓐ one must usually understand something of the associated language to comprehend the text. By contrast, other possible symbolic systems such as information signs, painting, maps, and mathematics often do not require prior knowledge of a spoken language. ⓑ Every human community possesses language, a feature regarded by many as an innate and defining condition of humankind. However, the development and adoption of writing systems have occurred only sporadically. (a) Once established, writing systems on the whole change more slowly than their spoken counterparts, and often preserve features and expressions which are no longer current in the spoken language. ⓒ The great benefit of writing systems is their ability to maintain a persistent record of information expressed in a language, which can be retrieved independently of the initial act of formulation. 2. 1) All writing systems require the following things. ① Ⓐ First, a set of defined base elements or symbols, individually termed characters or graphemes, and collectively called a script. Ⓑ Second, a set of rules and conventions understood and shared by a community, which arbitrarily assign meaning to be base elements, their ordering, and relations to one another. Ⓒ Next, a language (generally a spoken language) whose constructions are represented and able to be recalled by the interpretation of these elements and rules. Ⓓ Last, some physical means of distinctly representing the symbols by application to a permanent or semi-permanent medium, so they may be interpreted.

중심소재: 문자 체계

1. 첫 번째 문단

1) 도입부 = 중심소재 도출

상징 체계로서 문자를 언급하고 있다.

① 주제문

문자 체계는 다른 상징적 언어 체계와는 다르다.

Ⓐ 뒷받침 진술

ⓐ 문자의 특징 1

the associated language 이해의 필요성

ⓑ 문자의 특징 2

문자의 발달과 채택은 간헐적으로 발생

(a) 부연진술

ⓒ 문자의 특징 3

장기적 보존

2. 두 번째 문단

1) 주제문

문자의 조건

① 뒷받침 진술

Ⓐ 조건 1

characters와 script인 기본요소 또는 상징의 집합체

Ⓑ 조건 2

규칙과 약속: 의미의 임의성

Ⓒ 조건 3

언어의 구조는 문자의 요소와 규칙에 의해 표현되고, 다시 회상될 수 있어야 함

Ⓓ 조건 4

영구 또는 반영구적 수단에 의해 상징을 표현할 수 있는 수단 필요

두 문단으로 나눌 수 있다. 각 문단의 중심 내용을 파악하고, 전체 주제를 설정하도록 한다. 두 문단 모두 나열의 글 전개를 활용하고 있다.

대조를 통해서 다른 상징체계와 달린 문자만의 특징을 언급하고 있다.

나열의 시그널을 확인한다.

정답 1 (B) 2 (A) 3 (D)

해설

1 문자의 정의를 다루는 글이다. 일반적으로 정의로 시작하는 글은 두 가지 유형이 있는데, 하나는 글의 중심소재가 되는 특정 대상에 대한 간략한 소개 이후 주제의 폭을 좁혀 특정 사항만을 집중적으로 다루는 유형이 있는 반면, 본문과 같이 특정 대상에 대해 다양한 정보를 제공하는 백과사전식 글이 있다. 객관적 입장에서 특정 대상을 기술한다는 점도 기억하도록 한다. 선택지 (B)가 가장 적절하다.

2 By contrast, other possible symbolic systems such as information signs, painting, maps, and mathematics often do not require prior knowledge of a spoken language.를 보면 다른 상징체제(문자와 달리)의 경우 prior knowledge of a spoken counterpart는 필요하지 않다고 했으므로 문자의 경우 prior

knowledge of a spoken counterpart가 필요함을 유추할 수 있다. 선택지 (A)는 본문과 일치한다. However, the development and adoption of writing systems have occurred only sporadically.에서 보기 (B)는 본문과 일치하지 않음을 파악할 수 있다. 선택지 (C)와 같이 only, never, always와 같이 극단적 표현은 본문에 명시되어 있지 않는 이상 오답일 가능성이 높다.

3 characters는 문자 하나하나의 개별적 요소이고, script는 개별적 문자가 집합적으로 모여 형성된 것이다.

지문해석

문자(writing system)는 일종의 상징 체계로 언어로 표현할 수 있는 문장 요소 또는 문장을 표현하는 데 사용된다. 문자는 텍스트를 이해하기 위해 누구든 조합된 언어의 무언가를 이해해야 한다는 점에서 가능한 다른 상징적 의사소통 체계와는 구별된다. 대조적으로 정보 기호, 그림, 지도 그리고 수학과 같은 다른 가능한 상징 체계의 경우 구어를 이해하기 위한 사전 지식을 필요로 하지 않는 경우가 많다. 모든 인간 공동체는 언어를 소유하고 있는데, 많은 사람들은 언어를 인간의 내재적 특징이며, 인간을 규정하는 조건으로 간주하고 있다. 그러나 문자의 발달과 채택은 산발적으로 발생했다. 일단 문자가 만들어지면, 문자 체계는 말 체계보다 더 천천히 변화하며, 종종 말 체계에서는 더 이상 사용되지 않는 특징과 표현을 가지고 있다. 문자의 가장 큰 장점은 한 언어에서 표현된 정보를 일관성 있게 지속적으로 기록하는 능력이며, 이는 초기 표현의 형성과는 상관없이 다시 이끌어 낼 수 있다. 모든 문자는 다음의 요소가 필요하다. 먼저 일련의 기본 요소, 혹은 상징이 필요하다. 이는 개별적으로는 부호, 혹은 문자소라 불리며, 전체로는 스크립트라 불린다. 다음으로 특정 공동체에서 이해되고 공유되는 규칙과 관습이 필요하다. 이러한 공동체는 기본적 요소와 그 순서, 그리고 요소들 간의 관계에 임의적인 의미를 부여한다. 마지막으로 이러한 요소들과 규칙의 해석에 의해 표현되며 기억될 수 있는 언어(일반적으로 말)가 필요하다. 마지막으로 영구 또는 반영구적인 도구에 적용되어 상징을 뚜렷하게 제시하여 해석될 수 있는 특정한 외적 수단이 필요하다.

Passage 3

실험의 결과(show)는 글의 요지다.

1. Experiments have shown that relaxing before a learning session positively affects the results. 1) When you take a few minutes to relax deeply, Ⓐ your brain waves slow down. When we experience alpha, or slower, waves, our mind is better able to focus because it's less distracted by muscle tension or irrelevant thoughts. Ⓑ Relaxation also appears to allow the two sides of our brain—the logical, linear left brain and the creative, holistic right brain—to work together. 2. All in all, alpha waves seem to tune up our brains for increased mental performance.

중심소재: 휴식과 학습효과의 관계

1. 도입부 = 주제문

실험의 결과(show) : 수업시간 이전 취하는 휴식(중심소재)이 학습효과에 긍정적 영향을 미친다.

1) 뒷받침 진술

휴식을 취하면 왜 학습효과가 높아지는지를 설명하고 있다. 휴식을 취하면, 알파파 증가로

Ⓐ 집중력 강화

Ⓑ 좌뇌와 우뇌의 협력 증진

2. 요지 재진술

알파파는 정신활동을 증가시킨다 (휴식은 알파파를 증가시키고 이것이 학습을 위한 정신활동을 증가시킨다는 내용).

정답 1 (D)

해설

휴식이 학습효과에 미치는 영향을 다루는 글이다.

지문해석

실험에 따르면 수업시간에 들어가기 전에 긴장을 푸는 것이 결과에 긍정적 영향을 미친다고 한다. 몇 분 동안 깊이 긴장을 풀면, 당신의 뇌파는 늦춰진다. 우리가 알파파 즉, 느린 뇌파를 경험하면, 우리의 정신은 더

욱 집중하기가 쉬워지는데, 이는 근육의 긴장이나 불필요한 생각으로 정신이 산만해지는 경우가 적기 때문이다. 또한 긴장을 풀면 논리적이고 직선적인 좌뇌와 창조적이고 통합적인 우뇌가 둘 다 같이 협력할 수 있는 것으로 보인다. 전체적으로 알파파는 정신적인 성과를 증대시킬 수 있도록 우리의 뇌를 조율하는 것으로 생각된다.

Passage 4

1. Textbooks for primary school students have been accused of containing illustrations that could create a gender bias. 1) ① Male characters appear about 30 percent more often than girls in textbook illustrations and are portrayed as main characters according to a paper coauthored by Prof Kwon Chi-soon of Seoul National University of Education and Kim Kyung-hee, a teacher at Euncheon Elementary School in Seoul.

Ⓐ "Male characters play important roles in many cases while female characters often play passive roles," the research team said in the paper. "Children are vulnerable to the biased role models and textbook writers have to remove those sexual stereotypes."

ⓐ The paper said men are depicted as a president, polticitian, judge, doctor, and university professor, while women appear as a teacher, nurse, and bank teller. Male characters play the main roles about 60 percent more often than their counterparts in textbooks, it said.

중심소재: 초등학교 교과서 내용

1. 도입부 = 주제문
초등학교 교과서는 성 편견이 반영된 삽화를 담고 있다

1) 뒷받침 진술
① 남성이 30% 이상 중요한 역할을 담당하는 것으로 묘사

Ⓐ 근거부연

ⓐ 부연사례

TEST 22

정답 1 (A) 2 (C)

해설

1 남자가 중요한 역할을 하고 여자는 수동적인 역할을 하는 것으로 보아 남성우위의 성(gender) 편견의 내용이다. more often than이 적절하다.

2 vulnerable은 "~에 취약한, 상처입기 쉬운"이란 뜻으로 (C)와 그 뜻이 가장 유사하다.

지문해석

초등학교 학생들이 보는 교과서는 성역할에 대한 편견을 조장할 수 있는 삽화를 사용한다는 비판을 받아왔다. 교과서 삽화에서 남자들은 여자들보다 약 30%정도 더 자주 나오며, 중요한 인물로 묘사된다고 서울 교육대학 권치순 교수와 서울 은천 초등학교 김경희 교사가 공저한 논문에서 밝혔다. 남자들은 주로 중요한 역할을 하는 데 비해서 여자들은 보통 수동적인 역할을 한다고 연구팀은 논문에서 말했다. 어린이들은 치우진 역할 모델에 영향을 받기 쉬우니 교과서 집필자들은 저러한 성적인 고정관념을 배제해야 한다. 그 논문에 따르면 남자들은 대통령, 정치인, 판사, 의사나 대학교수로 묘사되는데 여자들은 선생님이나 간호사나 은행 금전출납원으로 나타난다. 남자들은 교과서에서 여성보다 약 60% 정도 더 주요한 역할을 한다고 그 논문은 말한다.

Passage 5

1. Henri Matisse and Marc Chagall were both famous artists. The two men painted in France in the early twentieth century. Their paintings influenced many other artists of their time.
1) ① Henri Matisse was born in a small town in France in 1869. He grew up in a wealthy family and showed no early interest in art. Then, while recovering from a surgery in 1890, he began to pass the time by painting. From then on, he considered himself a painter.
Ⓐ In his paintings, Matisse used color in a way that no artist had before. His bold and unusual use of color let the viewer see the world in a new way. When he grew ill and could no longer paint, Matisse did not give up being an artist. He cut out large and colorful paper shapes and arranged them on a canvas. In this way, he was able to create beautiful art until the end of his life.
② Ⓐ Marc Chagall was born in a small Russian town in 1887. His family was poor, but young Chagall begged his parents to let him study art. After working for some time as an artist, Chagall decided to go to Paris. He studied and worked there for four years before returning to Russia, where he met and married his wife. Eventually, he moved his family to Paris, where he stayed for most of his remaining years.
Ⓑ His later work included murals and stained-glass windows. Chagall's paintings reminds people of scenes they might see in a dream. Animals and people float in the air. Wonderfully unusual colors add to the dream-like quality. Chagall used ideas from Russian fairy tales and Jewish folk tales in many of his works.
2. Matisse and Chagall each used art and color to show ideas in new and unusual ways. Today their paintings hang in fine museums all over the world. Along with artists like Monet and Picasso, they are considered pioneers of modern art.

중심소재: 앙리 마티스와 마르크 샤갈의 그림

1. 도입부 = 주제문
동시대의 사람인 앙리 마티스와 마르크 샤갈은 프랑스 예술로 당대의 많은 예술가들에게 영향을 미침

1) 구체적 진술
① 앙리 마티스
간략한 성장배경과 그림을 그리게 된 동기

Ⓐ 예술적 특징과 예술에 대한 열정

② 마르크 샤갈
Ⓐ 간략한 성장배경

Ⓑ 예술적 특징

2. 정리(역사적 의의)
시대를 앞서간 마티스와 샤갈은 예술과 색상을 사용해 독특한 방법으로 자신의 사상을 전달한 현대 예술의 선구자

정답 1 (D) 2 (B) 3 (B) 4 (A) 5. (C)

해설

1 첫 단락 두 번째 문장에 20세기 초반에 파리에서 작품 활동을 했다고 언급되어 있다. 따라서 정답은 (D)이다.

2 샤갈과 마티스 회화의 공통점은 독특한 색채라고 했으므로 정답은 (B)이다.

3 마티스와 샤갈은 작은 마을에서 자랐다고 했으므로 선택지 (B)가 정답이다.

4 말년의 두 화가의 차이를 묻는 문제이다. 마티스는 그림을 그릴 수 없어 종이를 오렸다고 했고 샤갈은 벽화를 그렸다고 했으므로 정답은 (A)이다.

5 마지막 문장을 보면 마티스, 샤갈, 모네, 피카소의 공통점은 현대미술의 개척자라는 언급하고 있으므로 정답은 (C)이다.

지문해석

앙리 마티스와 마르크 샤갈은 모두 유명한 화가였다. 이들은 모두 20세기 초반 프랑스에서 회화작업을 했다. 그들의 회화는 당대의 많은 화가들에게 영향을 미쳤다.

앙리 마티스는 1869년 프랑스의 작은 마을에서 태어났다. 그는 부유한 가문에서 성장했고 어린 시절에는 그림에 관심을 보이지 않았다. 그러다 1890년 수술에서 회복하는 도중에 그는 그림을 그리면서 시간을 보내기 시작했다. 그때부터 마티스는 자신을 화가라고 여겼다.

자신의 그림에서 마티스는 이전의 다른 어떤 화가들도 쓰지 않았던 방식으로 색채를 사용했다. 그의 대담하고 독특한 색채의 사용으로 인하여 관람자들은 새로운 방식으로 세상을 보게 되었다. 병이 들어 더 이상 그림을 그릴 수 없었지만 마티스는 화가이기를 포기하지 않았다. 그는 크고 화려한 종이를 잘라 캔버스에 배열했다. 이런 방식으로 마티스는 생을 마감할 때까지 아름다운 예술을 창조할 수 있었다.

마르크 샤갈은 1887년 러시아의 작은 마을에서 태어났다. 그의 가족은 가난했지만 어린 샤갈은 부모에게 미술을 공부하게 해 달라고 졸랐다. 화가로 얼마간 일을 한 후에 샤갈은 파리로 가기로 결심했다. 그는 파리에서 4년간 공부하고 작업한 후 러시아로 돌아와서는 아내를 만나 결혼했다. 결국 그는 가족과 파리로 갔고 그곳에서 여생의 대부분을 보냈다. 그의 후기 작품에는 벽화와 창문의 스테인드글라스가 있다.

샤갈의 회화는 사람들에게 꿈에서 볼 수 있을 법한 장면을 환기시킨다. 동물과 사람들이 공중에 떠다닌다. 경이로울 정도로 독특한 색채는 그의 그림에 꿈같은 성격을 더해준다. 샤갈은 러시아의 동화와 유태인의 구전에서 온 아이디어를 자신의 많은 작품에 이용했다.

마티스와 샤갈은 각각 새롭고 독특한 방식으로 자신의 사상을 보여주기 위해 회화와 색채를 이용했다. 오늘날 그들의 회화는 전 세계의 훌륭한 미술관에 걸려 있다. 모네와 피카소 같은 화가들과 더불어 이들은 현대미술의 선구자로 간주된다.

Passage 6

1. 1) As boys, we are taught that masculinity and a concern for style are incompatible. ① Ⓐ Fashion is the domain of the woman, and too early an immersion in it might put us on the path to becoming sissies. Ⓑ This idea is hammered into us by our fathers and friends throughout childhood and adolescence, typically until we reach our early twenties. Ⓒ Then, an abrupt and complete reversal in philosophy is thrust upon us. Suddenly, "image is everything," "shoes make the man," and "women love a well-dressed man."

2. 1) We set out on a scrambled shopping trips to get ourselves up to date, but, with no acquired style savvy to steer us, we mistakenly let ourselves be guided only by price tags and our favorite colors. The unhappy result? A generation of men that spends too much money on clothes that don't look good on them. Clearly, this is not a sustainable state of affairs. We need to remedy it. Now we're

1. 첫 번째 문단

1) 도입부

시간의 글 전개방식에 따라 남성의 패션 변화를 기술하고 있다.

① 구체적 진술

Ⓐ 소년이었을 때
남자다움과 패션을 양립할 수 없는 관계

Ⓑ 청소년기
지나치게 패션에 신경을 쓰면 여성화가 되기에 아버지와 친구의 견제를 받는다.

Ⓒ 20대 초
갑작스럽게 외모에 신경을 쓰게 됨

2. 두 번째 문단

1) 문제점 지적

옷을 고르는 올바른 지혜가 부족하기 때문에 가격과 유행하는 색상에 따라 옷을 고르고 지나치게 많은 돈을 낭비하게 된다

not about to suggest that men set about raising their sons differently, because we think we're generally doing a good job at that. 2) What we will do, however, is provide males with the information that they need to make it through that troubling transition from not knowing how to dress to knowing how to dress.

2) 요지(대안)
남성에게 옷을 입는 올바른 방법에 대한 정보를 제공해야 한다.

정답 1 (A) 2 (B)

해설

1 글을 쓴 궁극적인 목적인 요지가 마지막 부분에 드러난다. What we will do, however, is provide males with the information that they need to make it through that troubling transition from not knowing how to dress to knowing how to dress.를 통해서 "남성에게 옷을 입는 올바른 방법에 대한 정보를 제공하는 글"임을 파악할 수 있다.

2 사고의 반전(reversal of philosophy)이란 이전에는 패션이 여성의 전유물이었지만, 시대가 변하면서 남성 또한 옷을 잘 입는 데 관심을 보여야 한다는 의미로 파악할 수 있다.

지문해석

소년일 때 우리는 남성다움과 멋에 대한 관심이 양립할 수 없다고 배운다. 패션은 여성의 영역이고 너무 일찍 거기에 몰입하는 것은 우리를 여자같이 되도록 할지도 모른다. 이런 생각은 어린 시절과 청소년기를 거쳐 보통 20대 초반까지 아버지와 친구들에 의해 주입된다. 그런데 이제 우리는 갑작스럽고 완전한 사고의 반전을 강요받고 있다. 갑자기 "이미지가 전부다", "신발이 남성을 만든다", "여성은 옷 잘 입는 남자를 좋아한다"고 한다. 우리는 스스로 최신식의 사람이 되기 위해 뒤죽박죽인 쇼핑여행을 계획하지만, 길잡이가 될 만한 스타일에 대한 상식을 습득하지 않은 채 가격표와 좋아하는 색상만을 따라가는 실수를 범한다. 이로 인한 불행한 결과는 무엇인가? 어울리지 않는 옷에 남성들이 너무 많은 돈을 쓰는 것이다. 분명하게도 이것은 지속 가능한 상황이 아니다. 우리는 이를 해결할 필요가 있다. 우리는 지금 남성들이 그들의 아들들을 다르게 키워야 한다고 제안하려는 것이 아니다. 왜냐하면 대체로 우리는 그 일을 잘 해내고 있다고 생각하기 때문이다. 하지만 우리가 할 일은 옷 입는 방법을 모르는 남자에서 옷 입는 방법을 아는 남자로의 그 성가신 변화를 완수해야 할 필요가 있다는 것을 남성들에게 알려주는 것이다.

Passage 7

사형제도의 역사적 추세를 살피는 글이므로 시간의 글 전개가 활용될 것을 예상할 수 있다.

1. The new reluctance to punish by killing is part of a historical trend. 1) ① There was a time when death and torture were spectator sports, when crowds flocked to see prisoners drawn and quartered or beheaded. In some parts of the world, flogging and stoning are still public spectacles. ② But in the 19th century, supposedly "enlightened" states began looking for more humane ways to serve final justice to kill people without causing too much suffering to either the victims or their executioners. Ⓐ The authorities tried hanging, firing squads, electrocutions, gas chambers, and, more recently, lethal injection. Ⓐ Each method was

중심소재: 사형제도

1. 도입부 = 주제문
사형을 꺼리는 새로운 행위는 역사적 추세이다.

1) 뒷받침 진술
①과거
사형과 고문은 공공장소에 이뤄진 흔한 장면
②19세기
계몽국가의 출현으로 좀 더 인간적으로 사형을 취하려는 시도가 이뤄짐

supposed to be an improvement over the last. But the results could be ghastly. Too much depended on the uneven skills of the executioners.
③ Jurors and prosecutors are steering away from the death penalty because they are both more and less afraid: Ⓐ more apprehensive about killing the innocent and less fearful of crime. As crime rates fell in the 1990s and the first few years of the new century, jurors became more lenient in capital cases. Ⓑ At the same time, prosecutors began to be wary of seeking the death penalty. With legal costs soaring in death cases, states are finding it cheaper to pay for lifetime prison sentences. Ⓒ There may be no such thing as a foolproof system for killing people fairly and painlessly. The smallest glitch can make too much of a difference.

Ⓐ 예시 및 부연
예시와 함께 과거의 사형과 비교했을 땐 좀 더 인간적으로 향상되었지만, 여전히 문제점 존재
③ 현대
배심원과 검사가 사형을 꺼리는 이유
Ⓐ 무고한 사람을 죽일 수 있다는 것에 대한 우려와 범죄에 대한 우려가 줄어들었다(결과적으로 사형제도에 더욱 관대해 짐)
Ⓑ 비용절감
Ⓒ 궁극적으로 무고한 사람에 대한 잘못된 판단으로 인한 살인을 면하려는 의도

정답 1 (B) 2 (D)

해설

1 시대적으로 후기에 나오는 처형방법은 이전의 것보다 인간적이고 개선된 것으로 간주되고 있으므로 독극물 주입이 가스실 이용보다 더 인간적인 처형방법이다.

2 선택지 (A), (B), (C) 모두 사형집행 시 발생할 수 있는 상황에 대해 언급하고 있지만 (D)의 의사들이 기꺼이 사형에 참여한다는 언급은 ①의 예외가 될 수 없다.

지문해석

최근 들어 사형에 처하는 것을 꺼리는 것은 역사적인 추세의 일부이다. 사형과 고문이 많은 관객을 동원하는 스포츠이던 때가 있었는데, 당시에는 죄수들이 끌려나와 능지처참되거나 참수당하는 것을 보려고 군중들이 몰려들었다. 전 세계의 일부 지역에서는 여전히 태형과 투석형이 대중의 구경거리이다. 그러나 19세기에 추정컨대 '개화된' 국가들이 사형수나 사형 집행인들에게 지나친 고통을 야기하지 않고 사람을 죽이기 위해 마지막 정의를 구현하는 보다 인간적인 방법을 찾기 시작했다. 관계당국은 교수형, 총살, 전기의자, 가스실, 그리고 보다 최근에는 치사 주사를 시도했다. 이 각각의 방법은 이전의 것보다 개선된 것으로 여겨졌다. 그러나 그 결과는 끔찍할 수도 있었다. 너무나 많은 것이 사형 집행인들의 들쭉날쭉한 기술에 좌우되었다.
배심원들과 검사들은 사형을 회피하고 있는데 그들이 한편으로는 더 많은 두려움을, 다른 한 편으로는 더 적은 두려움을 갖고 있기 때문이다. 즉 무고한 사람들을 죽이는 것은 더 염려하고, 범죄에 대해서는 덜 두려워한다. 1990년대와 금세기 초 몇 년 동안 범죄율이 하락함에 따라 배심원들은 사형에 해당하는 사건에 보다 관대해졌다. 동시에 검사들은 사형 구형을 조심하기 시작했다. 사형 사건에 드는 법적 비용이 치솟음에 따라 국가들은 종신형 선고에 따른 비용을 지불하는 것이 돈이 덜 든다는 것을 깨닫고 있다. 사람을 공정하고 고통 없이 죽이기 위한 아주 간단한 제도 같은 것은 없을지도 모른다. 가장 작은 결함도 큰 차이를 만들 수 있다.

개인의 경험담을 바탕으로 한 구체적 진술에 일반진술로 전개되는 패턴을 파악하도록 한다.

* 실험의 목적/의도
= 주제, 제목
* 실험의 결과
= 요지(주제, 제목 도출)

개인의 경험담을 일반화하고 있다. I(woman) → women. 요지는 일반진술에서 파악한다는 점에서 개별사례가 일반화되는 시점을 파악하는 능력은 주제, 요지, 제목을 설정하는 데 아주 중요하다.

Passage 8

1. Last week I went to dinner with an eligible doctor. As we were finishing the main course, I struck up conversation with the owner (Marco) in Italian—I speak five languages. My date nearly choked on his linguini and spent the rest of the date mute. I had committed the worst dating faux pas: I had outshone my suitor. Yet it would seem I am not the only woman who is wondering whether it is time to hang up her brain. 2. In America, research shows that successful women are hiding their accomplishments for fear that their academic achievements and financial kudos will scare off potential suitors.

1. 도입부 = 구체적 진술
글쓴이 I의 경험담

2. 일반진술
실험의 결과를 통해 글의 요지인 현상을 제시하고 있다.

정답 1 (D) 2 (C)

해설

1 5개 국어를 자유자재로 구사하는 여인을 보고, 상대방이 취한 태도는 My date nearly choked on his linguini and spent the rest of the date mute. I had committed the worst dating faux pas: I had outshone my suitor.의 밑줄 친 표현으로 보아 상대는 "똑똑한" 여성에 대해 그리 관심이 없음을 추론할 수 있다.

2 I had committed the worst dating faux pas: I had outshone my suitor.부분에서 여성이 최악의 실수를 범했다고 했는데, 이는 바로 앞에 전개되는 이탈리아어로 말한 내용을 지칭한 것이다.

지문해석

나는 지난주에 결혼상대로 훌륭한 어느 의사와 저녁 식사를 했다. 우리가 주 요리를 거의 다 먹었을 때 나는 식당 주인인 마르코(Marco)와 이탈리아어로 잡담을 나눴는데, 나는 5개 국어를 구사한다. 나의 데이트 상대방은 링귀네 요리에 목이 막힌 듯하더니 이후 데이트 내내 아무 말 없이 있었다. 나는 최악의 데이트 실수를 저질렀던 것이다. 즉, 나는 내게 구애하는 남자보다 돋보였던 것이다. 그러나 언제 자신의 두뇌를 잠깐 쉬게 해야 하는지를 잘 모르는 여성이 단지 나 혼자만은 아닌 것 같다. 한 연구에 따르면 미국 내 성공한 여성들이 그들의 학업 성취와 재정적 성공이 잠재적인 구혼자들을 겁을 주어 쫓아낼 것을 우려해 자신들의 성취를 숨기고 있다고 한다.

TEST 23

Passage 1

1. Many mathematicians play chess, but few excel at it. 1) While creating mathematics and playing chess may require the same kind of thinking, the pace is different. ① In his work a mathematician can correct his errors upon reflection; in a game he must commit himself quickly and irrevocably, and mathematicians are not exceptionally good at snap decisions. Ⓐ A few mathematicians have exceptional spatial visualization and computational skills. Some have an intuitive feeling for the relationship, for example, between a five-dimensional object and a seven-dimensional space that surround it. And some even have the ability to solve long and complicated problems in their head. As a rule, however, mathematicians cannot do arithmetic as rapidly as accountants.

중심소재: 수학자와 체스

1. 도입부
수학자들은 체스에 뛰어나지 않다.

1) 뒷받침 근거
수학 또한 체스와 비슷한 사고과정을 거치지만 속도가 틀리다

① 이유부연
순간적인 결정에서 수학자와 체스를 두는 사람의 근본적 차이가 있음

Ⓐ 수학자 중 예외적인 경우를 언급하고 있지만, 결국 수학자는 빠른 계산에 취약함

대조와 인과의 글 전개를 파악한다.

정답 1 (D)

해설

in a game he must commit himself quickly and irrevocably, and mathematicians are not exceptionally good at snap decisions.에서 알 수 있듯이 체스는 빨리 해야 하는데 수학자는 빠른 결정(make a snap decision)에 능하지 못하다고 했으므로 (D) "빠른 결정을 함에 있어서의 취약성이 이유"로 적절하다.

지문해석

많은 수학자들이 체스를 둔다. 그러나 뛰어나게 잘 두는 수학자는 몇 안 된다. 수학을 하는 것과 체스를 두는 것은 같은 종류의 사고를 요하는 반면에 속도가 다르다. 수학연구에 있어 수학자는 재고하면서 에러를 수정해 갈 수 있지만 체스에서는 빠르게 그리고 되돌릴 필요 없을 정도로 (게임에) 전념해야 하는데, 수학자들은 특히나 빠른 결정을 잘하지 못한다. 몇몇 수학자들은 예외적으로 공간 시각화와 계산 능력을 갖고 있다. 예를 들어 몇몇의 수학자들은 5차원적 사물과 그 사물을 둘러싸고 있는 7차원 공간의 관계를 직관적 느낌으로 안다. 또한 일부 수학자들은 길고 복잡한 문제를 암산으로 푸는 능력도 갖고 있다. 그러나 일반적으로 수학자들은 회계사들만큼 빠르게 계산을 하지는 못한다.

Passage 2

통념비판(Myth-breaking)의 글로 실험을 통해서 비판의 근거를 확보하고 있다.

1. Ⓐ Among the most widespread myths shared by college students is that charm, the social graces, and campus activities will be more important to the first employer after college than any other single fact, such as grades. Ⓑ Another myth suggests that there is a significant connection between the courses we take in college and employment. 1) Facts explode both of these myths. ① The most concrete information we have relating to college achievement and job performance is the now famous Bell Telephone Study of 1962. 2. Bell examined the careers of 17,000 of its employees. Success with the company was checked against the employees' academic performance, extracurricular activities, as well as which college they attended. Academic excellence closely correlated to success with Bell Telephone. Those who had ranked high in their classes were found to be receiving the highest salaries at Bell. It was also found that two thirds of all college graduates are in afield completely different from that for which they thought they were preparing in college.

중심소재: 수업성취도와 사회적 성공

1. 도입부 = 통념

Ⓐ 통념 1: 성적보단 매력, 예의범절 그리고 교내 활동이 더 중요하다.

Ⓑ 통념 2: 대학에서 수강하는 과목과 업무성취도의 연관성이 높다.

1) 요지문

앞선 통념은 잘못된 것이다.

① 뒷받침 진술

실험을 통해 통념 비판

- 실험이 등장하는 글 -
실험은 주장을 뒷받침하는 도구 중 하나이다. 실험의 결과는 곧 글에서 드러내고자 하는 요지에 해당한다.
* 실험의 목적/의도: 주제, 제목
* 실험의 결과: 요지, 주장 ←주제, 제목 도출 가능

정답 1 (D) 2 (C)

해설

1 통념비판(myth-breaking)의 글이다. 대학생 고용과 관련된 통념과 연구를 통해 잘못된 통념을 깨고 있다.

2 "반에서 상위권에 있었던 학생들이 그 회사에서 가장 높은 봉급을 받고 있는 것으로 밝혀졌다."는 내용은 "성적 = 봉급"의 관계이므로 이를 반박하는 내용은 성적보다는 성격을 강조하는 선택지 (C)이다.

지문해석

대학생들 사이에서 공유되는 가장 널리 퍼져 있는 잘못된 통념 중의 하나는 바로 매력, 사회적 품위, 그리고 캠퍼스 활동이 졸업 후 첫 직장 고용주에게 성적과 같은 단일 요소보다 더 중요하리라는 생각이다. 또 다른 통념은 대학에서 수강하는 강좌와 고용 사이에는 중요한 연관성이 있다는 것이다. 진실은 이 두 가지 통념을 모두 타파한다. 대학 학업성취도와 직업 업무성취도에 관해 우리가 가지고 있는 가장 구체적인 정보는 이제는 유명해진 1962년의 벨 전화 회사 연구이다. 벨은 그 회사 사원 17,000명의 경력을 연구하였다. 회사에서의 성공을 그 사원들이 어느 학교를 다녔는지 뿐 아니라 학업 성적과 과외 활동 등과 견주어 점검해 보았다. 학업 우수성은 벨 전화 회사에서의 성공과 밀접한 관계가 있었다. 반에서 상위권에 있었던 학생들은 그 회사에서 가장 높은 봉급을 받고 있는 것으로 밝혀졌다. 또한 모든 대졸 사원의 2/3는 그들이 대학 시절 준비했던 분야와는 완전히 다른 분야에 있다는 사실도 밝혀졌다.

Passage 3

1. Historical criticism seeks to understand a literary work by investigating the social, cultural, and intellectual context that produced it—a context that necessarily includes the artist's biography and milieu. 1) ① Historical critics are less concerned with explaining a work's literary significance for today's readers than with helping us understand the work by re-creating, as nearly as possible, the exact meaning and impact it had on its original audience. Ⓐ A historical reading of a literary work begins by exploring the possible ways in which the meaning of the text has changed over time. ② Reading ancient literature, no one doubts the value of historical criticism. There have been so many social, cultural, and linguistic changes that some older texts are incomprehensible without scholarly assistance. But historical criticism can even help one better understand modern texts. Ⓑ To return to Weldon's Kee's "For My Daughter" for example, one learns a great deal by considering two rudimentary historical facts—the year in which the poem was first published (1940, when war had broken out in Europe, and America was recovering from the Depression) and the nationality of its author (American)—and then asking how this information has shaped the meaning of the poem. Even this simple historical analysis helps explain at least part of the pessimism of Kee's poem, though a psychological critic would rightly insist that Kee's personality also played a crucial role. 2 **Thus**, in writing a paper on a poem, you might explore how the time and place of its creation affect its meaning.

중심소재: 역사비평

1. 도입부 = 주제문

역사비평의 목적: 문학작품이 만들어진 다양한 배경을 연구함으로 특정 작품을 이해하려는 시도

1) 뒷받침 진술

① 역사 비평의 관심사

특정 작품이 의도한 원래 독자에게 미친 영향력과 의미

Ⓐ 역사 비평의 시작

텍스트의 의미가 시간이 흐르면서 (시대적 배경이 달라지면서) 변하는 다양한 방법에 대한 탐구

② 역사비평의 유용성

범위 : 단지 고대의 작품뿐 아니라 현대의 작품을 이해하는 데도 도움이 된다.

* but(even)의 역할 - 역접이 아니라 추가 강조임을 확인

Ⓑ 예시부연

2. 요지문

특정 작품에 대한 논문을 쓸 때는 그 작품이 만들어진 시대와 장소에 대한 이해가 앞서야 한다.

요지를 이끄는 시그널 확인한다.

TEST 23

정답 **1** (A) **2** (B) **3** (B)

지문분석

양괄식 구조를 파악한다.

해설

1 첫 번째 문장(Historical criticism seeks to understand a literary work by investigating the social, cultural, and intellectual context that produced it)에서도 밝혔다시피 특정 작품을 살펴 볼 때는 작품 외적의 요소에 대한 이해가 선행해야 한다는 선택지 (A)가 빈칸의 내용으로 가장 적절하다.

2 1번 문제와 같은 맥락에서 작가가 처한 환경에 대한 이해는 글의 요지와 일맥상통하기에 선택지 (B)가 정답이다.

3 1940, when war had broken out in Europe, and America was recovering from the Depression에 드러난 사회적 배경으로 볼 때 선택지 (B)가 정답임을 파악할 수 있다. 선택지 (D)의 경우 before the Depression에서 before가 아니라 after가 되어야 한다.

지문해석

역사 비평은 그 역사를 만들어낸 사회적, 문화적, 지적 배경을 조사하는 방식을 통하여 문학 작품을 이해하기 원하며, 이러한 배경은 반드시 작가의 일생이나 (그가 겪어온) 사회 환경에 대한 내용을 포함하고 있다. 역사 비평가들은 작품이 오늘날의 독자들에게 문학적으로 지니는 중요성을 말하는 데에는 그다지 신경 쓰지 않는다. 오히려 정확한 의미를 다시 만들어내어 그것을 우리가 이해하고 그것이 그 원래 관객에게 미쳤던 영향을 이해하도록 돕는다.

문학작품을 역사적 관점에서 읽는다는 것은 텍스트가 지니는 의미가 시간이 지나면서 계속 변화하는 방식들에 대한 탐구로부터 시작된다. 고대 문학작품을 읽으면서, 그것이 지니는 역사적 비평의 가치를 의심하는 사람은 아무도 없다. 사회적, 문화적, 언어적 변화가 굉장히 많기에, 어떤 고대 문헌들은 학자들의 도움 없이는 해석이 불가하다.

그러나 역사적 비평은 우리가 현대의 문헌들을 더 잘 이해할 수 있게 도와줄 수도 있다. 예를 들어 Weldon Kees의 "나의 딸을 위하여"로 다시 돌아가 보자. 우리가 두 가지 기본적인 역사적 사실, 즉 그 시가 처음 출간된 해인 1940년은 유럽에서 전쟁이 발발했고 미국은 대공황에서 회복하는 시기였다는 것과, 그 작가가 미국인이라는 사실을 알고 나면, 그리고 이 정보가 그 시의 의미를 어떻게 만들어냈는지를 보면 우리는 많은 것을 알 수 있다. 이렇게 간단한 역사적 분석조차 적어도 Kees의 시에 담긴 염세주의 사상의 일부를 설명해내는 데 도움이 된다. 심리 비평가들은 응당 Kees의 성격 또한 아주 중요한 역할을 했다고 주장하겠지만 말이다. 따라서 시에 대한 리포트를 쓸 때, 그 시가 쓰여진 시대와 장소가 시의 의미에 어떤 영향을 끼쳤는지를 살펴보아야 한다.

Passage 4

1. 1) Most people are astonished to learn that there are real, stable differences in personality between conservatives and liberals—not just different views or values, but underlying differences in temperament. ① Ⓐ NYU professor John Jost has demonstrated that conservatives and liberals boast markedly different home and office decor. Liberals are messier than conservatives, their rooms have more clutter and more color, and they tend to have more travel documents, maps of other countries, and flags from around the world. Conservatives are neater, and their rooms are cleaner, better organized, more brightly lit, and more conventional. Liberals have more books, and their books cover a greater variety of topics. Ⓑ And that's just a start. Multiple studies find that liberals are more optimistic. Conservatives are more likely to be religious. Ⓒ Liberals are more likely to like classical music and jazz, conservatives, country music. Liberals are more likely to enjoy abstract art. Conservative men are more likely than liberal men to prefer conventional forms of entertainment like TV and talk radio. Liberal men like romantic comedies more than conservative men. Liberal women are more likely than conservative women to enjoy books, poetry, writing in a diary, acting, and playing musical instruments.

중심소재: 자유주의와 보수주의적 성격의 차이

1. 첫 번째 문단

1) 도입부 = 단락주제문
보수주의자와 자유주의자의 성격차이

① 뒷받침 진술
Ⓐ 집과 사무실의 장식의 뚜렷한 차이점

Ⓑ 추가적 차이점
자유주의자들이 보수주의자들에 비해 좀 더 긍정적인 반면, 보수주의자들은 종교를 좀 더 중요시 여김
Ⓒ 예술적 경향의 차이점

2. 1) Personality differences between liberals and conservatives are evident in early childhood. ① In 1969, Berkeley professors Jack and Jeanne Block embarked on a study of childhood personality, asking nursery school teachers to rate children's temperaments. They weren't even thinking about political orientation. Twenty years later, they decided to compare the subjects' childhood personalities with their political preferences as adults. They found arresting patterns. As kids, liberals had developed close relationships with peers and were rated by their teachers as self-reliant, energetic, impulsive, and resilient. People who were conservative at age 23 had been described by their teachers as easily victimized, easily offended, indecisive, fearful, rigid, inhibited, and vulnerable at age 3.

2. 두 번째 문단

1) 단락주제문

자유주의자와 보수주의자간의 성격적 차이점은 어린 시절부터 드러난다.

① 뒷받침 실험

정답 **1**(C) **2**(A) **3**(B)

해설

1 특정 대상 또는 대상 간의 다양한 특징이 제시되는 지문의 경우 내용일치문제를 내기에 매력적이다. 따라서 본문의 내용을 파악할 때, 각 대상에 번호를 매기면서 특징을 체크해 놓으면 내용일치문제 풀이 시 시간을 절약할 수 있다. (C) "보수주의자들은 진보주의자들보다 더 염세적이면 몸차림이 단정하다"는 Conservatives are neater, and their rooms are cleaner, better organized, more brightly lit, and more conventional." 과 People who were conservative ... described ... victimized, easily offended, indecisive, fearful, rigid, inhibited, and vulnerable at age 3.부분에서 옳다는 것을 알 수 있다.

2 마지막 문단은 어린 시절의 성격에 어른이 되어서 가지는 정치적 성향과의 연계성을 밝히는 내용이다. 자유주의적 성향의 사람들은 어린 시절 동료들과 잘 지내고, 선생으로부터 self-reliant, energetic, impulsive, and resilient와 같은 긍정적인 평가를 받은 반면, 보수성향의 어른은 어린 시절 easily victimized, easily offended, indecisive, fearful, rigid, inhibited, and vulnerable와 같은 평가를 받았다. 그러므로 선택지 (C)와 같이 stable(conservative)한 성격의 아이들은 동료들과 잘 지낸다는 것은 옳지 않으며, 정당정치를 피하는 경향이 있다는 점도 본문과 일치하지 않는다.

3 본문의 내용으로 비추어 John Jost와 Block의 동료들은 심리학자라고 보는 것이 가장 적절하다.

지문해석

대부분의 사람들은 보수주의자들과 진보주의자들의 성격에 있어 실질적이며 변하지 않는 차이가 있다는 것을 알게 되면 놀라움을 감추지 못한다. 단지 시각이나 가치의 차이가 아니라, 근본적 기질에 있어서 차이가 있는 것이다. 뉴욕 대학의 교수인 존 요스트는 보수주의자들과 진보주의자들이 자신들의 집과 사무실을 장식하는 데 있어서 두드러진 차이를 나타낸다는 것을 보였다. 진보주의자들은 보수주의자들보다 더 지저분하며 실내의 방은 더 난잡하고 많은 색으로 장식이 되어 있다. 그리고 그들은 여행관련 문서와 다른 나라의 지도와 세계 여러 국가의 국기를 더 많이 가지고 있다. 이에 반해 보수주의자들은 더 깔끔하다. 실내의 방은 더 깨끗하며 정돈이 더 잘 되어 있고 좀 더 밝게 조명이 켜져 있으며 더 평범한 모습이다. 진보주의자들은 더 많은 책을 가지고 있고 그 책들은 상당히 다양한 주제를 다룬다. 이런 차이는 단지 시작에 불과하다. 다양한 연구에 의하면 진보주의자들이 더 낙천적인 반면, 보수주의자들은 종교적 성향이 더 짙다. 또한 진보주의자들은 클래식과 재즈를 더 좋아하는 것 같고 보수주의자들은 컨트리 음악을 더 좋아하는 듯하다. 진보주의자들은 추상예술을 더 즐기며, 보수주자들은 TV와 라디오 토크와 같은 일반적 형태의 오락을 더 좋아하는 것 같다. 진보주의 남자들은 보수주의 남자들보다 로맨틱 코미디를 더 좋아하며, 진보주의 여자들은 보수주의 여자들보다 일기를 쓰고 악기를 연주하면서 책과 시를 즐겨 읽기를 더 좋아하는 것 같다.

진보주의자들과 보수주의자들 간의 성격 차이는 아동기에서도 분명하게 나타난다. 1969년, 버클리 대학의 교수 잭과 쟝 블락은 아동기 성격에 관한 연구에 착수했다. 그들은 보육 학교 교사들에게 어린이들의 기질을 평가해줄 것을 요구했다. 그들은 심지어 정치적 성향에 대해서는 고려하지도 않고 있었다.

20년 후, 그들은 피 실험자의 아동기 때의 기질과 성인이 된 후의 정치적 선호도를 비교하기로 했다. 그들은 주목할 만한 패턴을 발견했다. 진보주의자들은 그들이 어린 아이였을 때, 동료들과 가까운 관계를 발전시켰으며, 그들의 교사는 그들은 자기 의존적이고 정력적이며, 추진력이 있고 활발한 아이로 평가하였다. 23세 때에 보수주의자로 성장한 사람들은 3살 때, 그들의 교사에 의해 쉽게 희생당하며 쉽게 화를 내고 우유부단하며, 엄격하고 억압되어 있으며 상처를 받기가 쉬운 아이로 평가되었다.

Passage 5

1. 1) Seeds of Peace takes up where governments leave off, ① attempting to fulfill the hope of peace treaties that are signed but that remain essentially pieces of paper. Ⓐ Seeds of Peace carries out a task that governments are neither equipped for nor very interested in: transforming the hopes for peace into a new reality on the ground among populations that have been taught for decades to distrust and hate one another. ② The program fosters education, discussion, and emotional growth through both competitive and cooperative activities and emphasizes the importance of developing non-violent mechanisms of resolving conflict. In the three years of its operation, over three hundred male and female teenagers have come from Israel, Palestine, Egypt, Jordan, Morocco, and, for the first time last summer, from Serbia and Bosnia-Herzegovina. ③ Campers are selected in a competitive process; Ⓐ the only prerequisite is that they must have a working knowledge of English. Ⓑ Initially each candidate is recommended by his or her school and then asked to write an essay on the following subject: "Why I want to Make Peace with the Enemy." The final step of the selection process is a personal interview. Candidates are awarded extra points if they demonstrate skill in speaking English. Points are also awarded to children from refugee camps or other underprivileged backgrounds.

중심소재: 평화의 씨앗(단체)

1. 도입부 = 중심소재 도출

평화의 씨앗이란 단체에 관한 글이다.

1) 구체적 진술

① 목적

실천되지 않은 상태로 남아 있는 평야조약의 희망 실천

Ⓐ 목적부연

서로 미워하고 불신하도록 배운 사람들 사이에 평화에 대한 희망을 새로운 현실로 이 땅에 실천하는 것

② 프로그램의 구체적 방법

경쟁과 협력의 활동을 통해 교육, 토론 그리고 정서적 성장을 양육하고 분쟁의 비폭력적 방법의 개발을 강조

③ 선발조건과 과정

Ⓐ 조건

가장 중요한 사항: 영어

Ⓑ 과정

후보는 특정 주제에 대한 에세이를 작성과 인터뷰 진행. 이때, 영어실력이 좋거나 난민 캠프나 다른 소외계층 출신 추가점수

정답 1 (B) 2 (A)

해설

1 populations that have been taught for decades to distrust and hate one another부분과 "십대들", "이스라엘과 팔레스타인", "세르비아와 보스니아-헤르체고비나" 등으로 보아 (B) "서로 갈등 관계에 있는 국가들에서 온 십대 청소년들에게 교육과 대화를 통해 평화의 씨앗을 심는 프로그램"임을 알 수 있다.

2 "평화의 씨앗" 프로그램에 참여하기 위한 자격요건은 Candidates are awarded extra points <u>if they demonstrate skill in speaking English.</u>에서 알 수 있듯이 영어 말하기 능력이다. demonstrate는 "(능력 따

위를) 증명하다, 보이다"의 뜻이다.

지문해석

"평화의 씨앗"은 정부가 그만 둔 일을 맡아 한다. 서명은 받았지만, 사실상 종잇조각으로 남아있는 평화조약의 희망을 성취하려는 시도를 하면서 말이다. '평화의 씨앗'은 각국 정부들이 준비하지 못한, 그리고 관심도 없는 임무를 수행한다. 그 일은 바로 수십 년간 서로를 불신하고 증오하도록 길들여진 사람들 사이에서 평화에 대한 희망을 현장의 새로운 현실로 바꾸어놓는 일이다. 이 프로그램은 경쟁과 협동을 통해서 교육, 토론 및 정서발달을 촉진하며, 갈등을 해결하는 비폭력적 체계를 개발하는 일이 중요함을 강조하고 있다. 3년간 운영되는 동안, 300명 이상의 십대 청소년들이 이스라엘, 팔레스타인, 이집트, 요르단, 모로코, 그리고 지난 여름 처음으로 세르비아와 보스니아 헤르체고비나에서 찾아와 이 프로그램에 참여했다. 캠프 참가자들은 경쟁과정을 통하여 선발되는데, 이들이 갖춰야 할 유일한 필수조건은 실제로 활용할 수 있는 영어지식 단 하나이다. 먼저 각 지원자는 자신의 학교에서 추천을 받은 후, 다음과 같은 주제에 대해 에세이를 쓰도록 요청받는다. "내가 적들과 평화롭게 지내기를 원하는 이유는 무엇인가." 선발과정의 마지막 단계는 개별 인터뷰이다. 지원자들은 영어 말하기 능력이 입증되면 추가 점수를 받는다. 난민 캠프나 다른 소외계층 출신의 어린이들에게도 추가점수가 주어진다.

Passage 6

1. 1) ① In the United States, there are more women in the work force at higher levels than in any other country in the world—and they still make less than their male counterparts. ② In Sweden, women's wages are high, but their role in the work force remains relatively traditional. ③ In Germany, maternal leave is generous, but many women drop out of the work force once they have children. ④ In Japan, the gap is not just in wages but also in the basic structure of the way men and women are employed.

2. 1) ① In good times and in bad, women's wages have become an increasingly important component of household income and consumer spending. ② The shift toward service-based economies in the industrialized world has favored women in the work force—one reason they have poured into the labor market over the past three decades.

3. But what they find once they get there differs considerably throughout the developed world. That has less to do with gender politics than it does with macroeconomics, 1) and it results in women still being paid less than men in most places and for most jobs. ① The reasons for this persistent inequity are complex, and they vary with geography.

1. 첫 번째 문단

1) 도입부 = 주제문(현상)
활발한 사회진출과는 달리 여성의 임금이 아주 낮다.

① 미국
다른 어느 나라보다 일터에 여성의 비율이 높지만 여전히 남자에 비해 임금이 적음

② 스웨덴
일터에서 여성의 역할이 상대적으로 전통적인 반면 임금은 높다.

③ 독일
임신 휴가가 후한 반면, 아이를 가지면 대부분 일을 관둔다.

④ 일본
단지 임금뿐 아니라 남자와 여성의 고용 구조 자체에서 차이를 보임

2. 두 번째 문단

1) 사회진출 배경(현상의 원인)
① 가정수입과 소비지출의 중요한 역할
② 서비스 산업으로 전환

3. 세 번째 문단

1) 주제문 재진술
여성의 중요한 사회적 위치와 달리 임금은 여전히 적은 현실

① 임금 불균형의 원인
복잡하고, 지역마다 다름

정답 1 (B) 2 (B) 3 (A)

해설

1 문맥상 빈칸에 들어갈 접속사로 적절한 것은 "일단 ~하면"이란 once가 적절하다.

2 내용일치 여부 문제로 (A)의 "임금에 있어서 남녀평등은 선진화된 사회에서도 아직 이루어지지 않았다"는 본문의 "남성들보다 훨씬 더 적은 임금을 받는"을 통해 일치하며, (C)의 "임금에 있어서 남녀 차이는 성 정치학의 문제라기보다는 경제학의 문제이다"는 본문의 "성정치학보다 거시경제학에 더 관련이 있으며"를 통해 일치한다. (D)의 "서비스에 기반을 둔 경제로의 변화는 여성들에게 유리하게 되었다"는 본문의 "산업화된 사회에서 서비스에 기반을 둔 경제로의 변천은 노동력에서 여성들을 유리하게 한다"를 통해 일치함을 파악할 수 있다. 그러나 "여성의 경제력은 아이를 가진 여성들에 대한 관대한 출산휴가가 주된 원인이다"는 선택지 (B)의 내용은 In Germany, maternal leave is generous, but many women drop out of the work force once they have children.의 내용과 일치하지 않으며, 이를 일반화할 수도 없다.

3 빈칸의 앞의 this로 보아, it results in women still being paid less than men in most places and for most jobs.에서 드러나는 "임금불균형"이 들어가야 함으로 선택지 (A)가 정답이다.

지문해석

미국에서는 전 세계 어떤 나라들보다 고위직에 종사하는 여성 인력이 많지만 그래도 그들은 여전히 남성 인력보다 수입이 적다. 스웨덴에서는 여성의 임금이 높긴 하지만 직장에서의 역할은 비교적 구식이다. 독일의 경우 출산 휴가에 관대하지만 많은 여성들이 아이를 가지면 직장을 그만둔다. 일본에서는 임금뿐만 아니라 남녀가 고용되는 방식의 기본적인 구조 측면에서부터 차이가 있다.

경기가 좋든 나쁘든 여성의 임금은 점점 더 가계 수입과 소비 지출에서 중요한 요소가 되고 있다. 산업화된 사회에서 서비스에 기반을 둔 경제로의 전환은 노동 인구 측면에서 여성들에게 유리하게 작용했다. 이는 지난 30년간 여성들이 노동 시장에 대거 유입된 하나의 이유이기도 하다.

그러나 일단 노동 시장에 진출하고 나서 여성들이 발견하는 것은 선진국들마다 상당히 다르다. 그것은 성정치학보다 거시경제학과 더욱 관련이 있고, 대부분의 지역과 일자리에서 여성은 남성보다 적은 임금을 받는 결과를 초래한다. 이런 지속적인 불평등의 원인은 복잡하고 지역에 따라 다르다.

Passage 7

1. In its battle against the financial crisis, the U.S. government has extended its full faith and credit to an ever-growing swath of the private sector: first homeowners, then banks, now car companies. Soon, Barack Obama will put the government credit card to work with a massive fiscal boost for the economy. Necessary as these steps are, they raise a worry of their own: 1) Can the United States pay the money back?

① The notion seems absurd: Banana republics default, not the world's biggest, richest economy, right? Ⓐ The United States has unparalleled wealth, a stable legal tradition, responsible macroeconomic policies and a top-notch, triple-A credit rating. U.S. Treasury bonds are routinely called "risk-free," and the United States has the unique privilege of borrowing in the currency that other countries

중심소재: 정부의 적극적 경기부양

1. 도입부 = 현상

경제위기 대처의 일환으로 민간부분에 대한 정부의 적극적 개입을 통한 경기부양 실시예정

1) 의문문(주제)

그럼 과연 미국정부는 이러한 빚을 모두 갚을 여력이 있는가?

① 일반적 견해

어리석은 질문

Ⓐ 근거

바나나공화국(아프리카를 상징)과 달리 세계 최대 경제대국인 미국은 무리 없다.

like to hold as foreign exchange reserves.

② Yes, default is unlikely. But it is no longer unthinkable. Thanks to the advent of credit derivatives—financial contracts that allow investors to speculate on or protect against default—we can now observe how likely global markets think it is that Uncle Sam will renege on America's mounting debts. Ⓐ Last week, markets pegged the probabilities of a U.S. default at 6 percent over the next 10 years, compared with just 1 percent a year ago. For technical reasons, this is not a precise reading of investors' views. Nonetheless, the trend is real, and it is grounded in some fundamental concerns.

② 답변(요지문)
미국이 자신의 엄청나게 늘어나는 부채를 갚지 못하는 상황
Ⓐ 뒷받침 근거

TEST 23

정답 **1** (D) **2** (B) **3** (A) **4** (D)

해설

1 Last week, markets pegged the probabilities of a U.S. default at 6 percent over the next 10 years, compared with just 1 percent a year ago.로 보아 미국의 부채 상환율이 악화됨을 알 수 있다. 그러므로 "상환율 증가세"라는 선택지 (D)는 틀린 진술이다.

2 But 이후에 글의 요지가 드러나고, 이에 대한 근거가 뒤따른다. 글쓴이는 일반적 견해와 달리 미국의 채무상환 능력을 문제 삼고 있다. unthinkable의 선택지 (B)를 넣어야 글의 논리적 흐름에 맞다.

3 renege는 사전적 의미로 "약속을 어기다"이다. 본문의 문맥으로 볼 때 "채무를 이행하지 못함"을 의미한다.

4 글의 요지는 미국이 부채를 갚지 못할 가능성이 높다는 내용이다. For technical reasons, this is not a precise reading of investors' views. ________, the trend is real, and it is grounded in some fundamental concerns.에서 this와 the trend는 모두 "미국이 부채를 상환하지 못할 가능성이 높다"는 내용을 가리킨다. 투자자들이 바라보는 관점은 글쓴이가 다르다는 것을 알 수 있는데, 빈칸 뒤에 이어지는 내용은 글의 통일성 관점에서 글쓴이의 견해와 일치해야 함으로 역접의 접속사가 필요하다.

지문해석

금융 위기와의 전쟁에서 미국 정부는 충분한 신뢰와 신용*을 계속해서 커져가는 민간 영역의 행렬에 연장시켜 왔는데 처음에는 주택 소유주들, 다음은 은행들, 이제는 자동차 회사들에까지 확대되었다. 조만간 버락 오바마(Barack Obama) 미국 대통령은 자국 경제를 위한 막대한 재정 부양을 위해 정부의 신용카드를 사용할 것이다. 이런 조치들이 필요하긴 하지만 그 나름대로 걱정거리를 일으키기도 한다. 미국이 그 돈을 갚을 수 있을 것인가?
그 생각은 터무니없어 보인다. 바나나공화국들이나 채무를 이행하지 않지 세계에서 가장 크고 부유한 나라가 그러진 않지 않은가? 미국은 비할 데 없는 부와 안정된 법률 전통, 책임감 있는 거시경제 정책, 최고의 AAA 신용등급을 가지고 있다. 미국 재무부 채권은 통상적으로 "무위험" 채권이라고 불리고, 미국은 다른 국가들이 외환보유고로 보유하고 싶은 통화로 돈을 빌릴 수 있는 특권을 유일하게 가지고 있다.
그렇다. 채무 불이행은 일어날 법하지 없다. 그러나 더 이상 생각할 수 없는 일도 아니다. 투자자들로 하여금 채무 불이행에 투기를 하거나 채무 불이행을 막도록 하는 금융 계약인 신용 파생상품의 출현 덕분에 우리는 이제 세계시장이 미국 정부가 미국의 늘어가는 부채를 갚지 못할 가능성에 대해 어떻게 생각하는지를 살펴볼 수 있다. 지난 주 시장은 미국의 채무 불이행 가능성을 향후 10년간 6%라고 평가했는데, 이는 고작 1%로 평가되었던 1년 전과는 비교되는 것이다. 기술상의 이유로 이것이 투자자의 시각을 정확하게 읽어낸 것은 아니다. 그럼에도 불구하도 이 추세는 사실이고 몇 가지 근본적인 우려에 근거를 둔 것이다.

*full faith and credit: (美 법률) 충분한 신뢰와 신용. 각 주(州)는 다른 주의 일반 법령 · 기록 · 재판 절차를 승인하고 따라야 한다는 미합중국 헌법이 규정하는 의무.

Passage 8

1. Yesterday, residents were urged to evacuate about 250 homes, and about 300 guests had to leave a resort hotel as the wind drove the fire downhill into Ventana Canyon. 1) ① Ventana Canyon is in the foothills of the Santa Catalina Mountains, where the fire has raged since June 18. It has blackened about 85,000 acres. ② The fire destroyed 415 homes last month in and around the mountaintop vacation hamlet on Mount Lemmon. It skirted fire lines last week and burned a handful of cabins in Willow Canyon. However, a change in weather calmed a wildfire burning about a half-mile from an exclusive desert neighborhood today, greatly reducing the danger to dozens of homes. Relatively high humidity of 30 to 50 percent extinguished flames in some areas above the homes in Ventana Canyon and cooled the fire in others. Still, fire officials said that flare-ups were possible.

중심소재: 산불

1. 도입부 = 현상

화재로 인해 주민들을 대피시킨 내용이 언급되고 있다.

1) 구체적 진술

① 불길이 발생한 장소에 대한 간략한 배경설명

② 사건의 구체적 내용전개

정답 **1** (C)

해설

선택지 (A)에서 cabin이 탄 곳은 Willow Canyon이다. 선택지 (B)에서 불길을 잡은 것은 비가 아니라 high humidity of 30 to 50 percent이며, 화재로 인해 사람들이 벤타나 협곡의 가옥과 리조트 호텔로부터 대피했다는 것은 이 협곡이 항상 공공의 출입을 금지하고 있지 않음을 의미하므로, 선택지 (D)는 옳지 않다.

지문해석

어제 불길이 바람을 타고 내리막을 따라 벤타나(Ventana) 협곡으로 번지자 거주자들은 250여 개 가옥들로부터 대피하도록 권고되었고, 300여 명의 여행객들은 관광호텔을 떠나야만 했다. 벤타나 협곡은 산타 카탈리나(Santa Catalina) 산의 작은 언덕에 있는데, 그곳은 6월 18일 이후 불길이 사납게 일고 있다. 이 화재는 8만5천 에이커를 불태웠다. 화재로 지난달에만 레먼(Lemmon) 산꼭대기에 있는 작은 휴양 마을과 그 주변의 415개 가옥이 파괴되었다. 지난주에는 방화선을 피해 화재가 번져 윌로우(Willow) 협곡에 있는 수 개의 오두막이 불탔다. 그러나 오늘 기상 변화로 인해 근처 외곽 사막에서부터 반마일 가량을 불태웠던 불길이 진화되었고, 수십 가옥들이 처한 위험을 낮췄다. 30에서 50퍼센트 가량의 비교적 높은 습도는 벤타나 협곡에 있는 가옥들 위쪽 지역의 불길을 진화했고 다른 지역에서의 불길을 진정시켰다. 그러나 소방 공무원들은 갑작스런 불길이 여전히 가능하다고 말했다.

TEST 24

Passage 1

1. 1) Anorexia nervosa literally means "loss of appetite for nervous reasons." It is characterized by weight loss. ① However, anorexia nervosa sufferers have not lost their appetite. Ⓐ ⓐ They have lost weight because they are suppressing their urge to eat. Most anorexia sufferers cannot easily suppress the feeling that they are fat or at risk of becoming fat if they fail to keep their eating in control. Such feelings are usually quite independent of their actual weight. This is referred to as having a distorted body image. ⓑ There is also a strong cultural component. Anorexia nervosa is more common in Western post-industrialized nations, and, in the United States, whites are more affected than African Americans or Hispanic Americans. While the culture of thinness in which we live is certainly an influential factor in the development of anorexia, it is by no means the sole cause.

2. 1) Anorexia is a response to a complex mix of cultural, social, familial, psychological and biological influences unique to each person. Some possibilities are discussed below. ① Ⓐ One plausible theory is that people develop anorexia because they seek control over themselves and their lives. ⓐ Food and weight can be controlled when other aspects of life cannot. Restricting food intake while in the presence of enticing foods evokes feelings of accomplishment. Ⓑ A high Percentage of people struggling with anorexia have a history of abuse, neglect, or other traumatic experiences, and develop anorexia as a coping mechanism. ⓑ Losing weight provides a concrete way to cope with difficult circumstances because it serves to distract the sufferer from the pain.

3. 1) The following two features seem to be characteristic of many sufferers. ① Ⓐ First, most have low self-esteem. Ⓑ The second feature is that they find it difficult to deal openly with problematic emotions. This may have something to do with their personality. ⓐ For instance, they may be obsessional and perfectionist. In general, eating disorders seem to arise in the midst of the difficult business of growing up and developing as a person.

중심소재: 신경성 식욕부진

1. 첫 번째 문단

1) 도입부 = 중심소재 도출

신경성 식욕부의 간략한 정의와 특징 기술

① 주제문(문제점 지적)

신경성 식욕부진을 겪는 사람이 실제 식욕부진을 겪지 않음

Ⓐ 뒷받침 진술

ⓐ 원인 1

실제 식욕부진이 아니라 먹고 싶은 욕망을 억제하는 것임(근본적 문제는 잘못된 신체상)

ⓑ 원인 2

날씬함을 강조하는 사회와 그렇지 않은 사회를 대조하면서 문화(사회)적 요인을 지적

2. 두 번째 문단

1) 단락 주제문

식욕부진의 원인

① 뒷받침 진술

Ⓐ 자기 통제

ⓐ 부연진술

Ⓑ 과거의 아픈 기억에 대처

ⓑ 부연진술

3. 세 번째 문단

1) 단락 주제문

두 가지 종류의 증상

① 뒷받침 진술

Ⓐ Low Self-esteem

Ⓑ 문제점으로 지적되는 감정을 열린 마음으로 다루지 못함(개인의 성격과 관련됨)

ⓐ 예시부연

정답 1 (C) 2 (D) 3 (A) 4 (C)

해설

1 신경성 식욕 부진증의 원인들과 증상을 다루고 있다.

2 이어지는 내용을 보면, 식욕 부진증의 원인을 왜곡된 신체상에서 찾는 것으로 보아 실제 몸무게와는 관련이 없음을 파악할 수 있다. 또한, 글의 도입부에 나오는 anorexia nervosa sufferers have not lost their appetite에서도 힌트를 얻을 수 있다.

3 "그럴듯한"이란 뜻과 가장 유사한 의미는 feasible이다.

4 Anorexia nervosa is more common in Western post-industrialized nations, and, in the United States, whites are more affected than African Americans or Hispanic Americans.의 밑줄 친 표현에서 알 수 있듯이 신경성 식욕 부진은 개발도상국보다는 선진국에서 좀 더 흔하게 나타나고, 미국 내에서도 같은 맥락에서 백인들에게 경제적 측면에서 열악한 환경에 사는 흑인 또는 히스패닉계 사람보다 더 흔하게 발생한다고 나타나 있다.

지문해석

Anorexia nervosa는 문자 그대로 "신경성의 이유 때문에 식욕을 잃는 것"을 의미한다. 그것은 체중 감소에 의해 특징된다. 그러나, 신경성 식욕 부진증[거식증] 환자들은 그들의 식욕을 잃지 않았다. 그들은 먹고 싶은 욕구를 억누르고 있기 때문에 체중이 빠졌다. 대부분의 anorexia 환자들은 그들이 뚱뚱하다는 느낌이나 그들의 먹는 것을 제어하지 못해서 살찔 수 있는 위험에 처한다는 느낌을 쉽게 억누를 수 없다. 그러한 감정들은 보통 그들의 실제 체중과 꽤 독립적이다. 이것은 왜곡된 신체 이미지를 가지는 것으로서 언급된다. 또한 강한 문화적 구성요소가 있다. 식욕 부진증은 서구의 산업화 이후의 나라들과 미국과 백인들이 아프리카인들이나 스페인계 미국인들보다 더 영향을 받는다. 우리가 살고 있는 얇음의 문화가 분명히 신경성 식욕부진의 영향력 있는 요인이지만 그것이 결코 유일한 원인은 아니다. 신경성 식욕부진은 각 사람에게 독특한 문화적, 사회적, 가족적, 심리적이고 생물학적인 영향들의 복잡한 혼합물의 반응이다. 몇 가지 가능성들이 아래에서 토의된다. 한 가지 그럴듯한 이론은 사람들이 그들 자신과 삶에 대한 통제력을 찾기 때문에 그들이 식욕부진을 발전시킨다는 것이다. 음식과 체중은 삶의 다른 면들이 통제될 수 없을 때 제어할 수 있다. 음식을 꼬드기는 면전에 있는 동안 음식 섭취를 제한하는 것은 성취감을 불러일으킨다. 식욕부진과 싸우고 있는 높은 퍼센트의 사람들이 남용, 태만, 혹은 다른 외상 경험을 갖고 있고 대처하는 기계장치로서 식욕 부진증을 발전시킨다. 체중을 줄이는 것은 어려운 환경에 대처하는 구체적인 방법을 제공해준다. 왜냐하면 그것이 고통으로부터 환자를 흩뜨리는 역할을 하기 때문이다.

다음의 두 특징들은 많은 환자들의 특징인 것처럼 보인다. 첫째, 대부분의 환자들은 낮은 자긍심을 갖고 있다. 두 번째 특징은 감정들을 공개적으로 처리하는 것이 어렵다는 것을 발견하는 것이다. 이것은 그들의 개성과 어떤 관련이 있을지도 모른다. 일반적으로, 먹는 장애들은 한 사람으로서 성장과 발전의 어려운 일의 한 가운데서 생겨나는 것처럼 보인다.

Passage 2

1. Few people over the age of 10 would list "Happy Birthday" among their favorite songs. But Harvey Alter, now 62, has a special fondness for it. 1) It helped teach him how to talk. One morning in June 2003, Alter, then a self-employed criminologist, was putting a leash on his dog, Sam, in preparation for a walk when suddenly he felt dizzy and disoriented. "My thoughts were intertwined, not making sense," he said in a recent interview. "I knew I was having a

중심소재: 생일파티 노래

1. 도입부

10세 이상이 되면 생일노래를 부르지 않는 반면 62세의 나이에도 이 노래를 매우 좋아한다.

1) 구체적 진술

이 노래를 좋아하게 된 배경을 상술하고 있다.

예외적 상황은 언제나 이유가 따른다는 점을 기억하도록 한다.

stroke." At St. Vincent's Hospital, doctors diagnosed an ischemic stroke, caused by a blockage in blood flow to part of the left half of his brain. As a result, the right side of his body was temporarily paralyzed, the right side of his face drooped and he had trouble coming up with the right words and stringing them into sentences—a condition called aphasia. Within hours of his stroke, Alter met with Loni Burke, a speech therapist. At first he was completely nonverbal; within a few days he could say small words. "Mostly, he said, 'No,'" Burke recalled, "because he was frustrated that he couldn't speak." After two years of painstaking therapy, Alter's paralysis had mostly disappeared and his smile was back to normal. But while he could communicate through small words and the help of a chalkboard, complex verbal communication remained elusive. Using standard speech therapy techniques like reviewing lists of numbers and the days of the week, Burke helped her patient piece together short phrases. But they came slowly and sounded robotic. ① Then one day, she asked him to sing. "How can I ever sing? I can't talk," Alter recalled thinking. But as soon as Burke began to sing "Happy Birthday," he chimed in. "It sounded good," he said. "Almost like I didn't have anything wrong." 2. The technique, called melodic intonation therapy, was developed in 1973 by Dr. Martin Albert and colleagues at the Boston Veterans Affairs Hospital. The aim was to help patients with damage to Broca's area—the speaking center of the brain, located in its left hemisphere. 1) These patients still had relatively healthy right hemispheres. And while the left hemisphere is largely responsible for speaking, the right hemisphere is used in understanding language, as well as processing melodies and rhythms.

① 노래를 통해 언어를 치료하는 내용

2. 일반진술

언어치료에 도움이 되는 melodic intonation therapy를 소개

1) 원리

언어의 이해와 음악을 처리하는 우뇌를 통해 좌뇌의 언어구사 능력을 돕는다.

앞서 기술된 구체적 진술의 내용을 일반화하고 있다.

구체적 진술의 시그널 one day는 글을 통해 전달하려는 중요내용을 담는다.

정답 1 (C) 2 (D)

해설

1 a blockage in blood flow to part of the left half of his brain. As a result, the right side of his body was temporarily paralyzed에서 왼쪽 뇌에 이상이 생겨 오른쪽 몸이 일시적으로 마비된 것으로 기술하고 있으므로 선택지 (C)는 본문과 일치하지 않는다.

2 while the left hemisphere is largely responsible for speaking, the right hemisphere is used in understanding language, as well as processing melodies and rhythms.에서 언어와 관련된 뇌의 기능은 전적으로 왼쪽에 치우쳐 있지 않다는 내용을 파악할 수 있으므로 선택지 (D)의 내용은 본문과 일치함을 알 수 있다.

지문해석

열 살이 넘은 사람들 중, 가장 좋아하는 노래 목록에 "Happy Birthday"를 올릴 사람은 거의 없을 것이다. 그러나 지금 62세인 하비 알터는 그 노래를 특별히 좋아한다. 그것이 그에게 말하는 법을 알려주는 데 도움이 되었기 때문이다. 2003년 6월 어느 날 아침, 당시 사설 범죄학자였던 알터는 자신의 개 샘을 가죽 끈으로 묶고 산책을 준비하고 있었는데, 그때 갑자기 현기증을 느끼고 방향 감각을 상실했다. 그는 최근 인터뷰에서 "내 생각들이 서로 엉키며 의미가 통하지 않았어요. 나는 뇌졸중이 오고 있다는 걸 알았지요."라고 말했다. 성 빈센트 병원에서 의사들은 이를 허혈성 뇌졸중으로 진단했는데, 이는 그의 좌뇌 중 일부로 들어가는 피의 흐름이 막혀서 유발된 것이었다. 결과적으로 그의 우반신이 일시적으로 마비되었으며, 안면 우측이 축 처지고, 적당한 단어들을 생각해서 그것들을 문장으로 배열하는 데 어려움을 가지게 되었다. 즉 실어증이라고 불리는 상태였다. 뇌졸중 진단 후 몇 시간 지나지 않아, 알터는 언어치료사 로니 버크를 만나게 되었다. 처음에는 그는 완전히 말을 하지 못했다. 며칠이 지난 뒤에는 짧은 단어들을 말할 수 있게 되었다. "그는 대부분 '아니오.' 라고 말했어요. 말을 할 수 없다는 것에 좌절했기 때문이었지요." 라고 버크는 회상했다. 2년간의 힘든 치료 후에 알터의 마비 증세는 대부분 사라졌고, 그의 미소는 정상으로 되돌아왔다. 그러나 짧은 단어들과 칠판을 통하여 의사소통은 할 수 있었지만, 복잡한 언어적 의사소통은 여전히 어려운 상태였다. 숫자와 요일의 목록들을 검토하는 것과 같은 표준 언어치료기법들을 사용하여 버크는 환자가 짧은 어구들을 이어 맞추는 것을 도와주었다. 그러나 그 짧은 어구들은 천천히 나왔고 로봇 같은 소리로 들렸다. 그런데 어느 날, 그녀는 환자에게 노래를 하라고 했다. 알터는 "어떻게 노래할 수 있단 말인가? 말을 할 수도 없는데"라고 생각했다고 나중에 말했다. 그러나 버크가 "Happy Birthday"를 노래하기 시작하자마자 그가 가락을 맞추었다. "노래는 좋게 들렸어요. 거의 틀리게 부른 부분이 없는 것처럼 말이죠" 라고 그는 말했다. 그 기법은 멜로디 억양 치료법이라고 불리는 것으로, 마틴 알버트 박사와 그의 동료에 의해 보스턴 보호병원에서 1973년에 개발되었다. 그 치료법의 목적은 뇌의 좌반구에 있는 언어중추인 브로카 영역에 손상을 입은 환자들을 돕는 것이었다. 이러한 환자들의 우뇌는 상대적으로 건강한 우뇌들을 여전히 가지고 있었다. 언어적 행위를 담당하는 부분은 좌뇌이긴 하지만, 우뇌도 가락과 리듬을 처리하는 것뿐만 아니라 언어를 이해하는 데 사용된다.

Passage 3

but을 중심으로 언어에 대한 한계점의 내용으로 글의 무게중심이 이동한다.

앞의 예시와 같은 맥락에서 추가적인 예가 제시되고 있다. 순접부연의 기능을 확인한다.

1. Language is our most flexible and most sophisticated medium of expression, but everyone has felt, at one time or another, that it has its limitations. **1)** It is accurate enough to convey only the most commonplace distinctions. ① We have a word, "green" for describing the color of a leaf, and we are able to distinguish between light green, dark green, and a certain number of other shades. But a green leaf that is in the shadow has a very different appearance from one that is in sunlight. Yet our language provides no easy and familiar way of communicating this distinction. Similarly, we have an extraordinary wealth of words for sounds, such as quaver, rattle, bump, squeak, and splash; but there is no one expression for the phenomenon of a single loud sound followed by gradually diminishing overtones that is heard when a gong or a piano-key is struck. **2.** These deficiencies do not reflect the inadequacy of language. They are simply consequences of a fact with which everyone is familiar,

중심소재: 언어

1. 도입부 = 주제문
언어는 나름의 한계점을 가진다.

1) 뒷받침 진술
명확한 구별만을 전달한다.

① 예시부연
예시를 통해서 언어의 한계점을 뒷받침하고 있다.

the fact that even the most ordinary experience is far more complicated than language can possibly be.

2. 한계점의 의의
경험은 언어보다 훨씬 복잡하기에 언어로 모든 것을 표현할 수는 없다.

정답 **1 (A) 2 (A) 3 (A)**

해설

1 접속사 문제는 문장 또는 문단 간의 결속성(응집성)을 파악하는 능력을 묻는다. (가) 이후의 내용은 바로 앞에서 전개된 글쓴이의 견해인 '언어의 한계성'을 뒷받침하는 추가적 내용을 제시하고 있으므로 선택지 (A)가 가장 적절하다.

2 첫 번째 문장이 주제문인 두괄식 구조의 글이다. Language is our most flexible and most sophisticated medium of expression, but everyone has felt, at one time or another, that it has its limitations.에서 선택지 (A)가 주제(=제목)를 이끌어 낼 수 있다.

3 the most ordinary experience is far more complicated than language can possibly be에서 선택지 (A)는 본문과 일치함을 알 수 있다.

지문해석

언어는 우리가 지닌 가장 융통성 있고, 가장 섬세한 표현의 도구지만, 때때로 언어에는 한계가 있다는 것을 우리 모두는 느낀다. 언어는 가장 흔한 차이점들만을 전달하기에 충분할 만큼 정확할 뿐이다. 우리는 나뭇잎의 색상을 묘사하는 '녹색'이란 단어를 가지고 있고, 옅은 녹색, 진한 녹색 그리고 특정한 수의 다른 (녹색)색조를 구별해낼 수 있다. 그러나 그늘 아래에 있는 녹색 잎은 햇볕 아래 놓인 잎과는 전혀 다른 모습을 가진다. 사실 우리의 언어는 이러한 구별을 쉽고 익숙하게 전달해내지 못한다. 마찬가지로, 우리는 떨리다, 방울뱀 소리를 내다, 찍찍 울다 그리고 튀기다와 같이, 소리를 표현할 수 있는 아주 풍부한 어휘를 가지고 있지만, 징이나 피아노 건반이 때려지고 난 후 들리는, 점차적으로 사라지는 소리를 포함하는 한 번의 큰 소리를 내는 현상을 표현할 말은 하나도 없다. 이렇게 알맞은 표현이 없다는 사실이 언어의 불충분함을 반영하는 것은 아니다. 이런 결핍은 단지 모든 이가 익히 알고 있는 사실의 결과인데, 그 사실이란 바로 가장 평범한 일조차 언어로 표현될 수 있는 것보다 훨씬 복잡하다는 것이다.

Passage 4

1. 1) Contrary to the image of rolling sand dunes and scorching heat, deserts are much more diverse than most people envision. ① In addition to the blazing hot temperatures of popular imagination, there are also vast, icy stretches of land known as cold deserts, and though hot deserts and cold deserts are different in some respects, they are similar in ways related to climactic patterns. The climactic differences between hot deserts and cold deserts are obvious from their names. Without cloud cover or water to moderate temperatures, hot deserts can reach up to 120°F during the day. The Sahara:, the largest hot desert in the world, holds the record for the hottest daytime temperature ever recorded at 135°F. Meanwhile, the highest

중심소재: 사막의 다양성과 특징

1. 첫 번째 문단

1) 단락 주제문
다양한 종류의 사막이 있다.

① 뒷받침 진술
cold desert와 hot desert라는 두 사막의 차이점을 예와 함께 상술

TEST 24

average temperature in the wannest month in the Antarctic Desert is 20°F.

2. 1) Although their temperatures are extreme opposites, all desert regions are defined by the same factor, which is their lack of precipitation. ① The lack of rain in deserts is caused by either of two phenomena: rain shadow or extreme distance from a source of moisture. Ⓐ A rain shadow is created when air masses lose all their moisture as they travel over mountains, leaving no precipitation for the areas on the other side of the mountain. Ⓑ The Antarctic Desert, the largest desert in the world, amazingly receives less than ten millimeters of precipitation per year. Combined with high altitude, precipitation is sparse in Antarctica because weather fronts do not reach inland.

2. 두 번째 문단

1) 단락 주제문(현상)

강수량의 부족

① 뒷받침 진술(원인)

Ⓐ 원인 1

Ⓑ 원인 2

정답 **1** (C) **2** (D) **3** (A)

해설

1 선택지 (A)는 본문 마지막에 언급된 "비 그늘" 현상을 말하는 것으로 "수분이 반대쪽에 가라앉는다"는 것은 산을 넘어오면서 수분을 잃어버린다는 의미이다. 그러므로 (C)와 같이 다습한 공기 덩어리가 사막지역에 "도착해서야" 뜨거운 열기로 인해 증발한다는 것은 본문과 일치하지 않는다. Combined with high altitude, precipitation is sparse in Antarctica because weather fronts do not reach inland.의 마지막 문장에서 (B)와 같이 "특정 기상전선은 내륙에 미치지 못한다"는 것을 파악할 수 있다. (D)는 rain shadow or extreme distance from a source of moisture에서 밑줄 친 강수량 부족의 두 번째 원인으로 언급된 것이다.

2 추운 사막인 남극 사막의 최고 평균 온도가 화씨 20도라고 밝힌 이유는 더운 사막인 사하라사막의 화씨 135도와 극명하게 대비시키기 위한 것이므로 선택지 (D)가 정답이다.

3 빈칸 앞뒤의 두 문장은 더운 사막인 사하라사막과 추운 사막인 남극 사막의 기온을 대조적으로 나타내고 있다. 따라서 두 문장을 대조할 수 있는 의미로 접속부사 meanwhile이 정답이다.

지문해석

움직이는 모래 언덕과 작열하는 열기(熱氣)의 모습과는 반대로, 사막은 대부분의 사람들이 상상하는 것 이상으로 다양하다. 일반 사람들이 생각하는 엄청나게 더운 고온 지역 이외에도 추운 사막이라고 알려진 광대한 얼음으로 펼쳐져 있는 지역도 있다. 더운 사막과 추운 사막은 몇 가지 면에서 다르지만, 기후 패턴과 관련된 여러 가지 점에서는 유사하다. 더운 사막과 추운 사막의 기후 차이는 그 이름만 봐도 명확하다. 온도를 조절해주는 구름층과 물이 없기 때문에, 사막은 낮 동안에는 온도가 화씨 120도까지 올라갈 수 있다. 세계에서 가장 큰 더운 사막인 사하라 사막은 낮 온도가 지금까지 기록된 최고온도인 화씨 135도까지 상승한 기록이 있다. 한편, 남극 사막에서는 가장 따뜻한 달의 최고 평균기온이 화씨 20도이다. 이 두 사막의 기온은 극과 극으로 정반대이지만, 모든 사막지역은 동일한 요인으로 정의되는데, 그것은 강수량이 적다는 것이다. 사막에 강수량이 적다는 것은 두 가지 현상 중의 하나에서 기인하는데, 그것은 산으로 막혀 강수량이 적어지는 비 그늘과 수원에서 멀리 떨어져 있다는 것이다. 비 그늘 현상은 공기 덩어리가 산을 넘어 이동하면서 가지고 있던 수분을 다 잃어버려서, 산 넘어 다른 지역에는 비가 오지 않게 될 때 발생한다. 세계에서 가장 큰 사막인 남극 사막은 연간 강수량이 놀랍게도 10밀리미터 미만이다. 고도가 높다는 것과 아울러 기상전선이 내륙에까지 미치지 못하기 때문에 남극의 강수량은 적다.

Passage 5

1. A style of singing in Tuva, known as "throat" singing, but, more precisely called overtone singing—the ability to single out and control overtones, phrasing them two or more at a time—finally became known outside of this remote region at the dawn of the 1990s. 1] ① While everyone has natural harmonics in his or her voice, the Tuvans were able to focus on one of these harmonics, or overtones, create a drone with one overtone and then, vocally, grab a higher pitch, which shapes a melody on top, allowing them to sing duets with themselves.
② Tuvans divide various overtone styles into three major types, all of which use nature to describe the sounds. Ⓐ ⓐ Sygyt, for example, is simply an imitation of singing birds or gentle breezes. ⓑ Xoomei tends to suggest stronger winds, while ⓒ Kargyraa portends storms. ③ No doubt, people this connected to nature realized that in the birds and rivers and rocks were the spirits. Overtone singing, then, was used shamanically. ④ There are mountains in the region that make sounds by holding winds before releasing them into the valleys below. Rivers also create sound patterns that vary according to the rocks they hit; supposedly, their sounds contain the origins of overtone singing.

중심소재: 투바 사람들의 배음창법

1. 도입부
간략한 정의와 함께 글의 중심소재인 투바 사람들의 배음창법을 소개하고 있다.

글의 도입부에서 정의되는 대상은 중심소재에 해당한다.

1) 구체적 진술
① 배음창법의 구현
일반인과 달리 투반사람들은 자연화법 중 하나의 화성에 초점을 두어 지속적인 저음을 깔고, 여기에 높은 음의 멜로디를 형성하여 홀로 이중창을 냄
② 자연의 소리를 활용하는 세 종류의 배음창
Ⓐ 예시부연
ⓐ Sygyt: 새소리 또는 산들바람
ⓑ Xoomei: 강한 바람 소리
ⓒ Kargyraa: 태풍
③ 자연소리를 활용한 이유
이들을 신령으로 인식
④ 배음의 기원 = 자연소리

정답 1 (A) 2 (D)

해설

1 바로 앞에 "자연물에 신령이 있다"는 내용으로 미루어 (A) shamanically가 적절하다.

2 hrasing them two or more at a time에서 선택지 (A)에서 옳음을 파악할 수 있고, (B)의 경우 Tuvans divide various overtone styles into three major types, all of which use nature to describe the sounds.에서 옳다는 것을 파악할 수 있다. "부드러운 산들바람(gentle breezes), 강풍(stronger winds), 폭풍(storms)"의 언급으로 보아 선택지 (C)도 옳은 진술이다. (D)의 "투바 사람들의 성대구조는 다른 민족과 다르다"는 내용은 본문 어디에서도 파악할 수 없다.

지문해석

'후음(throat)' 창법이라고 알려진 투바(Tuva)의 노래방식, 더 정확히 말하자면 배음(overtone)창법—배음을 뽑아내고 조절하여 한꺼번에 두 가지나 그 이상의 음정을 표현하는 능력—은 1990년대 초 이 외딴 지역의 외부로 알려지게 되었다. 사람들은 누구나 목소리에 배음(화음)을 타고나지만, 투바 사람들은 이러한 배음 중 하나에 집중하여 한 배음으로 지속적으로 저음을 내고 그러고 나서 높은 소리로 멜로디까지 부름으로써 혼자서 이중창을 부르는 효과를 낼 수 있었다. 투바 사람들은 여러 가지 배음 방식을 세 가지 유형으로 나누는데, 이 유형들 모두가 소리를 묘사하기 위해 자연을 이용한다. 예를 들어 시기트(Sygyt)는 단지 지저귀는 새나 부드러운 미풍을 모방한 것이다. 후미(Xoomei)는 강풍을 암시하는 듯하며, 카르기라(Kargyraa)는 폭풍을 상징한다. 이 정도로 자연과 연관된 사람들은 틀림없이 새와 강물과 바위에는 신령이 있다고 인식했을 것이다. 그러면 배음창법은 주술적으로 이용되었다. 이 지역에는 계곡 아래로 바람을 보내기 전에 바람을 끌어 모으면서 소리를 만드는 산들이 있다. 강물 또한 부딪치는 바위에 따라 서로 다른 소리의 형태를 만들어 낸

TEST 24

다. 아마 이들의 소리에 배음창법의 기원이 있는 듯하다.

Passage 6

1. The fact is that recent economic numbers have been terrifying, not just in the U.S., but around the world. Manufacturing, in particular, is plunging everywhere. Banks aren't lending; businesses and consumers aren't spending. Let's not mince words: This looks an awful lot like the beginning of a second Great Depression.

1) We weren't supposed to find ourselves in this situation. For many years most economists believed that preventing another Great Depression would be easy. In 2003, ① Robert Lucas of the University of Chicago, in his presidential address to the American Economic Association, declared that the "central problem of depression-prevention has been solved, for all practical purposes, and has in fact been solved for many decades."

② Milton Friedman, in particular, persuaded many economists that the Federal Reserve could have stopped the Depression in its tracks simply by providing banks with more liquidity, which would have prevented a sharp fall in the money supply. Ⓐ Ben Bernanke, the Federal Reserve chairman, famously apologized to Friedman on his institution's behalf: "You're right. We did it. We're very sorry. But thanks to you, we won't do it again."

③ It turns out, however, that preventing depressions isn't that easy after all. Under Mr. Bernanke's leadership, the Fed has been supplying liquidity like an engine crew trying to put out a five-alarm fire, and the money supply has been rising rapidly. Yet credit remains scarce, and the economy is still in free fall.

2. Friedman's claim that monetary policy could have prevented the Great Depression was an attempt to refute the analysis' of John Maynard Keynes, who argued that monetary policy is ineffective under depression conditions and that fiscal policy—large-scale deficit spending by the government—is needed to fight mass unemployment. The failure of monetary policy in the current crisis shows that Keynes had it right the first time.

앞선 내용의 논리적 흐름을 전환하는 역접의 however를 확인한다.

중심소재: 경제위기와 정책실패

1. 도입부 = 현상
미국뿐 아니라 세계경제의 위기를 언급하면서 대공황 재현의 심각성을 언급하고 있다.

1) 경제 정책 실패의 배경
① Robert Lucas의 주장
대공황 예방은 쉬우며, 핵심적인 문제는 이미 해결이 되었다.

② Milton Friedman의 주장
은행의 유동성↑ → 통화공급감소 예방
Ⓐ Friedman의 주장을 받아들이는 연방준비은행장

③ Milton의 말대로 연방준비은행은 유동성을 공급하면서 통화공급을 증가시켰지만 신용과 경기는 자유낙하의 상황

2. 결론
Friedman의 통화정책은 경기부진 때 통화정책은 효력이 없고, 정부지출을 늘려야 한다는 재정정책인 케언즈의 분석을 반박하려는 시도였는데, 이것은 오히려 케언즈의 분석이 옳았다고 말하고 있다.

정답 1 (B) 2 (A) 3 (B)

지문분석

본문은 "현상(문제점) → 잘못된 정책 지적"의 형태를 취하고 있다.

해설

1 세 번째 단락의 내용인 Milton Friedman ... the Federal Reserve could have stopped the Depression in its tracks simply by providing banks with more liquidity, which would have prevented a sharp fall in the money supply.에서 프리드만의 이론에 찬성하는 경제학자들은 경제침체를 극복하는 방안으로 통화정책을 선호했다는 것을 알 수 있다.

2 밑줄 친 부분을 좀 더 자세히 표현하자면 "당신의 말이 옳습니다. 당시 연방 준비이사회에서는 케인스의 말대로 했습니다. 그러나 이제는 당신의 주장이 옳음을 알고 있는 덕분에 다시는 케인스의 말대로 하지 않겠습니다"와 같다. 따라서 버냉키는 프리드만의 주장과 같은 현재의 통화 공급 정책을 옳다고 믿고 있고, 앞으로도 바꿀 생각이 없음을 파악할 수 있다.

3 현 경기침체에 대한 프리드만 경제정책은 실패했다. The failure of monetary policy in the current crisis shows that Keynes had it right the first time.에서 알 수 있듯이 케인스의 정책이 옳았음이 입증되었다. 케인스는 대규모 적자 지출이라는 정부의 적극적인 개입(active government intervention)을 통해 경제위기를 타파할 수 있다고 믿었다.

지문해석

최근의 경제 수치가 미국에서뿐만 아니라 전 세계적으로 위협적이라는 것은 사실이다. 특히 제조업은 도처에서 요동치고 있다. 은행은 대출해주지 않고 기업과 소비자들은 지출하지 않고 있다. 돌려서 말하지 않겠다. 이것은 끔찍하리만치 제 2차 경제 대공황의 시작처럼 보인다.

우리는 스스로가 이러한 상황에 처하리라고 예상치 못했다. 여러 해 동안 대부분의 경제학자들은 또 다른 대공황을 막는 것이 수월하리라고 믿었다. 2003년 시카고대학의 로버트 루카스(Robert Lucas)는 미국 경제협회를 대상으로 한 회장단 연설에서 "경기침체-예방에 있어서 핵심적인 문제는 사실상 해결되었고 실제로 해결된 지 수십 년이 되었다"고 선언했다.

특히, 밀턴 프리드만(Milton Friedman)은 연방준비제도이사회가 은행들에 더 많은 유동성을 공급했다면 통화 공급량의 급격한 감소를 막았을 것이고 그러면 대공황을 그 자리에서 간단히 막을 수 있었을 것이라고 많은 경제학자들을 설득시켰다. 연방준비제도이사회의 의장인 벤 버냉키(Ben Bernanke)는 그의 기관을 대신해 프리드만에게 다음과 같이 사과했던 것으로 유명하다. "당신이 옳습니다. 우리는 그렇게 했습니다. 매우 유감스럽지만 당신 덕분에 우리는 다시는 그렇게 하지 않을 겁니다."

그러나 경기 침체를 막는 것이 결코 그렇게 쉽지 않은 것으로 밝혀졌다. 버냉키의 지도하에 연방준비제도이사회는 초대형 화재를 진압하려는 소방대원처럼 유동성을 공급해왔고 통화 공급량은 급속히 증가해왔다. 그러나 신용은 부족하고 경제는 여전히 거침없이 추락하고 있다.

통화정책으로 대공황을 막을 수 있었다는 프리드만의 주장은 존 메이나드 케인스(John Maynard Keynes)의 분석을 반박하려는 시도였는데, 케인스는 통화정책이 경기침체 여건에서 효율적이지 못하고 대규모 실업과 싸우기 위해서는 재정정책, 즉 정부에 의한 대규모 적자 지출이 필요하다고 주장했었다. 현 위기에서 통화정책이 실패한 것은 케인스가 처음에 옳았다는 것을 보여준다.

Passage 7

1. 1) Back in my early twenties I tried a diet that was limited to just a few healthy foods. Three weeks into it, I had nearly reached my goal of losing eight pounds. ① But my progress wasn't as sweet as I had expected. One night I abandoned the diet and gorged on every food I'd been missing. Over the next two weeks, I ate more than ever. No surprise that I quickly regained eight pounds, and put on two more. It sounds like the old diet-binge cycle that we've all heard about so often. ② My brazen act of indulgence was the direct effect of a boring, restrictive diet. Ⓐ "If you tell someone they cannot have, say, a piece of cheesecake, then that is the first thing they want to have," says Dr. Hubbert. "And then when they eat that piece of cheesecake, they say, 'Oh, now I've blown it, so I might as well blow it every day.'"

2. At Tufts University in Boston, researchers studied 71 healthy men and women aged 20 to 80 years who provided detailed reports of everything they ate for six months. 1) People who routinely ate a variety of nutrient-dense foods such as vegetables, fruits, and whole grains tended to be lean. The researchers found that when people eat a variety of desirable foods, especially vegetables, they eat fewer nutrient-poor, calorie-dense foods such as cookies, candy, and chips. Overall, they consume fewer calories without consciously restricting their intake.

실험의 결과는 글의 요지에 해당한다.

중심소재: 다이어트

1. 구체적 진술

1) 선별적 음식 다이어트

개인의 경험담을 통해 건강하지만 몇 가지 음식에 제한된 다이어트 언급

① 문제점

폭식을 하게 되면서 단 시간에 다이어트 이전 상태보다 더 살이 찌게 됨

② 원인

지루하고, 음식이 제한적이라 오래 지속하기 힘듦

Ⓐ 심리적 원인 부연

특정 음식을 먹지 말라고 들으면 그 음식을 더욱 먹고 싶어짐

2. 실험

1) 결과(요지)

영양분이 가득한 다양한 음식과 야채를 많이 먹는 사람들이 날씬하며, 칼로리를 덜 섭취한다.

정답 1 (E) 2 (E) 3 (B)

지문분석

본문은 개인의 경험담을 통해 문제점을 제시하고, 실험을 통해 이에 대한 대안을 제시하는 글이다.

해설

1 본문은 개인의 경험담을 통해 엄격하게 제한된 몇 가지 음식을 바탕으로 한 다이어트의 문제점을 지적하고, 실험을 통해 영양가가 풍부하고 다양한 음식을 먹을 것을 추천하는 글이다. 선택지 (E)가 본문의 중심내용을 가장 잘 반영한 주제/제목이 된다.

2 나는 몇몇 건강에 좋은 음식만 먹는

3 본문분석을 참조한다.

지문해석

옛날에 20대 초반이었을 때, 나는 몇몇 건강에 좋은 음식만 먹는 다이어트를 시도했었다. 시작한 지 3주 정도 후에 나는 8파운드를 빼는 나의 목표에 거의 도달했다. 그러나 그 과정은 내가 예상했던 것만큼 즐겁지는 않았다. 어느 날 밤에 나는 다이어트를 포기하고 먹고 싶었던 모든 음식을 실컷 먹었다. 그 후 2주 동안 나는 그 어느 때보다 더 많이 먹었다. 당연히 나는 8파운드가 다시 쪘고 게다가 2파운드가 더 쪘다. 그것은 우리가 너무 자주 들어온 '다이어트-과식' 주기처럼 들린다. 나의 제멋대로의 뻔뻔한 행동은 지루하면서 제한적인

다이어트의 직접적인 결과였다. "만약 당신이 어떤 사람에게, 이를테면, 치즈 케이크를 먹지 말라고 말하면, 그러면 그것을 가장 먼저 먹고 싶어 한다. 그리고 그들은 치즈 케이크를 먹을 때 '아 이제 치즈 케이크를 먹었네. 그러니까 매일 먹는 게 더 낫겠다'라고 말한다"고 허버트 박사(Dr. Huhhert)는 말하고 있다. 보스턴의 터프츠 대학(Tufts University)에서 연구진들은 자신이 6개월간 먹은 모든 것에 대한 자세한 보고를 한 20세에서 80세에 이르는 71명의 건강한 남성과 여성을 연구했다. 일상적으로 야채, 과일, 전곡과 같은 다양한 영양가 높은 음식을 섭취했던 사람들이 마른 경향이 있었다. 연구진은 자신이 원하는 다양한 음식을, 특히 야채를 사람들이 먹을 때 그들은 쿠키, 사탕, 과자와 같은 영양가 낮고 칼로리가 높은 음식을 덜 먹는다는 것을 발견했다. 전반적으로 그들은 의식적으로 자신들의 섭취를 제한하지 않으면서 칼로리를 더 적게 섭취한다.

Passage 8

1. Almost every office is looking for additional space. 1) <u>One easy way to get it is to use moveable partitions instead of, or in conjunction with, the solid interior walls of your existing office space. These walls provide several important benefits.</u> ① Ⓐ First, they let you take maximum advantage of existing space. No more conflicts where one office is just a little too small and another is just a little too big—just move the partition over a foot to adjust the space for everyone. Ⓑ Second, you can change the positions of the partitions as your business needs change. If one project ends and another begins, you can easily change the office space to accomodate project needs. Ⓒ Finally, new materials make these walls both sound-absorbent and lightweight, so they provide the privacy of built-in walls with the advantages of flexible space.

중심소재: 사무실 공간 확보

1. 도입부 = 중심소재 도출
사무실 공간 확보

1) 주제문
이동식 칸막이 사용

① 뒷받침 근거
Ⓐ First - 첫 번째 이점
Ⓑ Second - 두 번째 이점
Ⓒ Finally - 세 번째 이점

정답 **1** (B) **2** (C) **3** (D)

해설

1 이동식 칸막이에 관한 글로 그 장점을 중심으로 기술하고 있다.

2 칸막이는 "칸막이가 필요한 곳이면 어디든지 칸막이를 옮겨 놓을 수 있기 때문에" 공간을 만들 수 있다.

3 If one project ends and another begins, you can easily change the office space to accomodate project needs.에서 선택지 (D)가 정답임을 알 수 있다.

지문해석

거의 모든 사무실이 부가적인 공간을 찾고 있다. 그것을 확보하는 가장 손쉬운 방법은 현재 사무실 공간을 차지하는 견고한 내벽 대신에 혹은 내벽과 함께 이동식 칸막이를 사용하는 것이다. 이런 이동식 벽들은 몇 가지 중요한 장점을 가지고 있다. 첫째, 이들은 현재의 공간을 최대한 이용할 수 있도록 해준다. 어떤 사무실은 약간 작고 다른 사무실은 약간 큰 경우 모든 이들을 위한 공간을 조절해 칸막이를 1피트만 옮겨 놓으면 더 이상의 갈등은 없다. 둘째, 당신의 업무가 변화를 필요로 할 때 칸막이의 위치를 바꿀 수 있다. 만약 하나의 프로젝트가 끝나고 다른 프로젝트가 시작되면 프로젝트의 요구사항을 반영해 사무실 공간을 손쉽게 바꿀 수 있다. 마지막으로 새로운 소재를 이용해 이런 벽들을 소음을 흡수하고 가볍게 만들어 융통성 있는 공간의 이점들과 함께 붙박이 벽의 사생활을 제공한다.

TEST 25

Passage 1

1. In Under New Appleby, the author paints a stark yet vivid canvas of a small scottish town, Appleby. **1)** ① Some of the homes in Appleby date back to the 17th century, but now the awesome-powers and tradition-upsetting realities of the 20th century arrive in the form of a nuclear power plant, a proposed fishery, and a Pakistani immigrant family. Ⓐ How the new Appleby, hence the title, deals with these events becomes the subject of a quiet but captivating drama that is sure to move every reader.

중심소재: Under New Appleby이란 책

1. 도입부 = 중심소재 도출

Under New Appleby라는 작품에 관한 글로 책의 구체적 내용이 무엇인지 파악하는 데 주목한다.

1) 구체적 진술

Appleby라는 작은 도시를 생생하게 묘사한 작품으로 ①에서 보는 바와 같이 but을 중심으로 과거와 대비되는 현재를 기술하고 있다.

Ⓐ 앞에서 언급된 이러한 요소는 독자들에게 감동을 주는 조용하지만 매력적인 이야기의 주제로 작용할 것으로 보고 있다.

정답 1 (B) 2 (B)

지문분석

본문은 새로 발간된 책에 대한 리뷰에 해당하는 글이다.

해설

1 스코틀랜드 어느 작은 마을의 빠른 변화에 관한 책이다.

2 마지막 문장에 "모든 독자를 감동시킨다(to move every reader)"고 했으므로 선택지 (B)의 As passionate가 적절하다.

지문해석

《Under New Appleby》라는 작품에서 작가는 스코틀랜드의 작은 마을 Appleby의 황량하지만 생생한 배경을 화폭에 담고 있다. Appleby의 몇몇 집들은 17세기로 거슬러 올라가 지어진 것이지만, 지금은 두려움을 느끼게 하는 힘과 전통을 뒤엎는 20세기의 실체들인 핵발전소, 기업형태의 양식장, 그리고 파키스탄에서 이민 온 한 가족 등등이 이 마을에 들어섰다. 그러므로 제목에 드러나듯이 이 새로운 Appleby가 이런 사건들을 어떻게 다룰 것인가는 잔잔하지만, 분명 모든 독자를 감동시키는 매혹적인 드라마의 주제가 될 것이다.

Passage 2

1. Writing plain English is hard work. No one ever learned literature from a textbook. I have never taken a course in writing. I learned to write naturally and on my own. I did not succeed by accident: I succeeded by patient hard work. 1) Verbal dexterity does not make a good book. Too many authors are more concerned with the style of their writing than with the characters they write about. There are too many writers whose styles are often marred by verbosity and self-importance. Few great authors have a brilliant command of language. ① The indispensable characteristic of a good writer is a style mark by lucidity.

② A good writer is wise in his choice of subjects, and exhaustive in his accumulation of materials. ③ A good writer must have an irrepressible confidence in himself and in his ideas. ④ Good writers know how to excavate significant facts from masses of information. ⑤ The toughest thing for a writer is maintain the vigor and fertility of his imagination. ⑥ Most writers fail simply because they lack the indispensable qualification of the genuine writer. They are intensely prejudiced. Their horizon, in spite of their education, is a narrow one.

중심소재: 명료한 글쓰기

1. 도입부 = 중심소재 파악

명료한 글쓰기는 인내의 노력으로 이뤄진다.

1) 구체적 진술

Good Writer의 요건(Implicit)

① 요건 1

명료한 스타일

② 요건 2

현명한 주제선택과 자료수집

③ 요건 3

스스로와 자신의 생각에 대한 자신감

④ 요건 4

정보의 홍수에서 중요한 사실을 추려내는 기술

⑤ 요건 5

풍부한 상상력

⑥ 요건 6

선입견이 없어야 하고, 시야가 넓다.

정답 1 (C) 2 (A) 3 (D)

해설

1 말이 많음을 의미하는 단어는 선택지 (C)이다.

2 I did not succeed by accident: I succeeded by patient hard work.를 통해 선택지 (A)는 본문과 일치함을 알 수 있다.

3 (다)의 경우 often marred by (나) verbosity와 같은 수동태의 형태를 취해야 하고, (라)의 경우 보어자리이므로 동명사 또는 부정사가 오는데 The toughest thing is to v의 부정사 형태를 가진다.

지문해석

쉬운 영어를 사용해 글을 쓰는 것은 어려운 작업이다. 이제껏 어느 누구도 교과서에서 문학을 배운 사람은 없다. 나는 한 번도 글쓰기 수업을 받아본 적이 없다. 나는 자연적으로 스스로 글쓰기를 배웠고 나는 어쩌다 보니 성공한 사례가 아니었다.

나는 끊임없는 노력으로 인해 성공을 거뒀다. 언어적 재능은 좋은 책을 만들지 않았다. 너무나 많은 작가들이 자신이 쓰고 있는 캐릭터들보다 본인의 글쓰기 스타일에 더 신경을 쓴다. 또한 스타일이 장황하고 거드름을 피우는 태도로 인해 스타일이 망가진 작가들로 아주 많다. 뛰어난 언어 코맨드를 가지고 있는 훌륭한 작가는 별로 없다. 좋은 작가가 가지는 필수적인 요소는 명료성으로 특징지어지는 스타일이다.

훌륭한 작가는 주제의 선정에 있어 현명한 태도를 보이며, 자료를 모으는 데 있어 철저하다. 훌륭한 작가는 자기 자신과 자신의 생각에 있어 억누를 수 없는 자신감을 가져야 한다. 훌륭한 작가는 수많은 정보 중에서 중요한 사실들을 가려낼 줄 안다. 작가에게 있어 가장 어려운 것은 자신의 상상력을 활력 있고 풍요롭게 유지하는 것이다. 대부분의 작가들은 단순히 천재 작가들은 반드시 가지고 있는 특징을 가지지 못하기에 실패한다. 이들은 심할 정도로 선입견을 지닌다. 그들은 교육을 받았음에도 불구하고 시야가 아주 좁다.

Passage 3

1. Every day more than 100 million people hear the sound of background music. They hear it while they are working in offices, shopping in stores, and eating in restaurants. They even hear it while they are sitting in the dentist's chair. 1) Why is background music layed in so many places? ① The answer is easy. Music is such a powerful force that it can affect people's behavior.

2. 1) Studies show that background music can affect the sales of business. ① Ronald Milliman, a marketing professor, measured the effects that fast music, slow music, and no music had on customers in a supermarket. Ⓐ He found that fast music did not affect sales very much when compared with no music. Ⓑ However, slow music made a big difference. Listening to music played slowly made shoppers move more slowly. When slow music was played, shoppers bought more and sales increased 38 percent. ② Milliman also found that restaurant owners can use music to their advantage. Ⓐ In the evening, playing slow music lengthens the amount of time customers spend in the restaurant. Ⓑ At lunch time, restaurants want people to eat more quickly so that they can serve more customers. Playing lively music at lunchtime encourages customers to eat quickly and leave.

의문문은 글의 주제에 해당하고, 답변은 요지임을 기억한다.

실험의 결과 또한 요지를 드러낸다.

중심소재: 배경음악과 행동의 관계

1. 도입부 = 현상
1억이 넘는 인구가 매일 일상의 생활 속에서 배경음악을 듣는다.

1) 주제도출
왜 이런 배경음악이 도처에서 들리는 걸까?
① 답변(요지)
음악은 사람들의 행위에 영향을 미치기 때문이다.

2. 뒷받침 진술

1) 실험을 통해서 "음악이 사람들의 행위에 영향을 미친다"에 뒷받침 진술을 제시하고 있다.
① 실험 1(쇼핑센터)
Ⓐ 빠른 음악: 빠른 음악 상품 구매에 별 영향력 없음
Ⓑ 늦은 음악: 소비자에게 더 많은 상품을 구매하도록 영향을 미침

② 실험 2(레스토랑)
Ⓐ 저녁: 늦은 음악
Ⓑ 점시: 빠른 템포의 음악

정답 1 (C) 2 (D) 3 (B) 4 (C)

해설

1 느린 음악이 식당에 손님이 머무르는 시간을 연장한다는 맥락이므로 lengthen이 적합하다. elongate는 물리적 길이를 연장한다는 뜻으로 주로 쓰인다.
2 로날드 밀리만은 음악이 마케팅에 미치는 효과를 연구한 사람임을 파악한다.
3 패스트푸드 식당은 손님이 빨리 와서 먹고 빨리 나가야 하므로 빠른 음악을 틀 것이므로 선택지 (B)가 정답이다.
4 실험이 등장하는 지문에서 요지는 실험의 결과임을 기억한다. 실험을 통해 밝힌 사항은 "음악은 사람의 행위(상품 구매)에 영향을 미친다"이다. 선택지 (C)가 요지로 가장 적절하다.

지문해석

날마다 1억이 넘는 사람들이 배경음악소리를 듣는다. 이들은 사무실에서 일을 하면서, 상점에서 쇼핑을 하면서, 식당에서 식사를 하면서도 배경음악을 듣고 있다. 심지어는 치과병원 의자에 앉아있는 동안에도 듣는다. 왜 배경음악이 이렇게 많은 장소에 깔리는 것일까? 답은 쉽다. 음악은 사람들의 행동에 영향을 미칠 만큼 강력한 요소이기 때문이다.
몇몇 연구들에 따르면, 배경음악은 영업 매출에 영향을 미칠 수 있다. 마케팅 학과 교수 로날드 밀리만(Ronald Milliman)은 빠른 음악과 느린 음악, 음악이 없는 상태가 슈퍼마켓의 고객들에게 미치는 영향을 측

정했다. 그는 빠른 음악이, 아주 음악이 없는 상태에 비해 판매에 그다지 큰 영향을 미치지는 않음을 알았다. 반면 느린 음악은 큰 차이를 낳았다. 느리게 연주되는 음악은 쇼핑객들을 느리게 움직이게 했다. 느린 음악이 연주될 때 쇼핑객들은 더 많이 샀고 판매는 38퍼센트 증가했다.

밀리만은 또한 식당주인도 음악을 이윤을 내는 데 이용할 수 있음을 알아냈다. 저녁 때 느린 음악을 연주하는 것은 고객이 식당에서 보내는 시간을 연장시킨다. 점심시간에 식당은 사람들이 식사를 빨리 하게 하여 더 많은 손님들을 받고 싶어 한다. 점심시간에 생기 있는 음악을 연주하면 손님들은 빨리 식사를 하고 빨리 식당을 떠나게 된다.

Passage 4

1. If our educational system were fashioned after its bookless past we would have the most democratic form of 'college' imaginable. 1) ① Among the people whom we like to call savages all knowledge inherited by tradition is shared by all. It is taught, to every member of the tribe so that in this respect everybody is equally equipped for life.
② Education in the wilderness is not a matter of monetary means. ③ All are entitled to an equal start. There is none of the hurry which, in our society, often hampers the full development of a growing personality. ④ There, a child grows up under the ever-present attention of his/her parents: Therefore the jungle and the savannah know of no 'juvenile delinquency.' Ⓐ No necessity of making a living away from home results in neglect of children, and no father is confronted with his inability to buy an education for his child.

중심소재: 바람직한 교육제도

1. 도입부 = 주제문

책이 없었던 과거의 교육제도는 가장 민주적형태의 교육의 장

1) 뒷받침 진술

① 전통적으로 전해지는 모든 지식을 모든 공동체 구성원이 공유하기에 모든 이가 동등하게 삶을 위한 준비를 갖출 수 있다.

② 전통적 교육이란 '돈을 위한 목적'의 수단이 아니다.

③ 모든 이가 동일한 시작의 권리를 부여받기에 온전한 인격적 성장에 방해가 되는 서두를 필요가 없다.

④ 부모의 지속적인 보호와 관찰이 있기에 청소년 비행이 없다.

Ⓐ 부연

정답 1 (C) 2 (D)

해설

1 No necessity of making a living away from home results in neglect of children. and no father is confronted with his inability to ______ an education for his child.문장에서 이중부정의 no를 먼저 파악하여야 올바른 해석이 가능하다. no는 주부와 서술부 모두를 부정하기 때문에, "집을 떠나 생계를 꾸릴 필요성이 없었기에 아이들을 소홀히 하지 않았다"로 해석하게 된다. 글의 문맥에 따라 해석을 하더라도 이중부정의 no를 몰랐다면 혼동이 될 수 있으므로 주의한다. 생계는 곧 경제적 능력과 직결됨으로 교육을 돈으로 사야(buy) 하는 무능력에 직면하지 않았음을 유추할 수 있다.

2 선택지 (D)는 there is none of the hurry라는 부분과 일치하지 않는다.

지문해석

만약 우리의 교육 체계가 책이 없던 과거를 따라 만들어진다면 우리는 상상할 수 있는 가장 민주적인 형태의 '대학'을 갖게 될 것이다. 우리가 야만인이라 부르고 싶어 하는 사람들은 전통으로 전수된 모든 지식을 공유하고 있다. 그 지식은 부족의 모든 구성원에게 전수되기 때문에 결과적으로 이러한 면에서 모든 사람이 삶에 대한 준비를 평등하게 갖추게 된다.

황무지에서의 교육은 금전적인 수단의 문제가 아니다. 모든 이에게 동등한 출발권이 주어진다. 우리 사회에서 자주 볼 수 있는, 인격의 전인적인 성장을 방해하는 그런 서두름은 전혀 없다. 그곳에서는 아이가 항상 부

모의 관심을 받고 자란다. 따라서 정글과 사바나는 '청소년 비행'이라는 것이 없다. 집에서 멀리 떠나 생계를 이어야 할 필요성이 없으므로 아이들을 소홀히 하는 일은 생기지 않으며, 아버지가 아이들에게 돈을 들여 교육을 시킬 수 없는 처지에 놓이게 되는 일도 없다.

Passage 5

1. It might be poisonous emissions wafting from a nearby manufacturing plant. Or it might be the odor surrounding a plant being pushed in Washington that would make it harder for neighbors and local officials in hundreds of communities to know what potentially deadly pollution risks they are being exposed to. 1) Twenty years ago, in response to demands from public safety officials and ordinary citizens across the country, Congress passed the Emergency Planning and Community Right-to-Know Act. ① It came in the wake of the worst industrial accident in history, a chemical spill at a U.S.-owned insecticide plant in India that killed more than 15,000 people, and a serious chemical accident at the same company's plant in West Virginia. ② The law mandated a publicly accessible annual report, known as the Toxics Release Inventory, on poisonous substances being pumped into the air, water and ground by refineries, chemical plants and others ranging from food processors to makers of kitchen counter tops. ③ By spotlighting where dangerous pollutants come from, it has helped reduce toxic chemical releases by almost 65% over the past two decades.

중심소재: 환경오염

1. 도입부 = 현상(문제점)

제조 공장 주변 유독가스 또는 악취

1) 대안

비상기획과 지역주민들의 알 권리 법안 통과

①배경

②내용

③효과

정답 1 (B) 2 (C) 3 (D)

해설

1 주민들(they)이 오염에 노출되어 있다는 점과 현재 상태가 계속 진행 중에 있으므로 수동태진행(being exposed to)을 사용한다.

2 mandate는 "의무화하다, 명령하다, 권한을 주다"의 표현이다.

3 선택지 (A)의 always와 같은 극단적 표현은 답이 될 가능성이 낮다. 다음 문장을 통해서 선택지 (D)는 본문과 일치함을 알 수 있다. By spotlighting where dangerous pollutants come from, it has helped reduce toxic chemical releases by almost 65% over the past two decades.

지문해석

그것은 근처에 있는 제조 공장에서 나와 떠돌아다니는 유독성 배출물일지도 모른다. 혹은 워싱턴에서 등 떠밀리고 있는 공장을 둘러싸고 있는 냄새일 수도 있는데, 이는 지역 사회 수백 곳의 주민들과 공무원들이 일종의 잠재적으로 위험한 오염 위험에 그들 자신이 노출되어 있는지 알기 어렵게 만드는 것이다. 20년 전 전국에 있는 공중안전 공무원들과 평범한 시민들의 요청에 응하여 의회는 비상사태 계획 및 지역 사회의 알권리 법안을 통과시킨 바 있다. 그 법안은 인도에 있는 미국계 살충제 공장에서 발생한 화학 물질 유출 사고로 15,000명 이상이 사망한 역사상 최악의 산업 사고와 동일 업체의 웨스트 버지니아(West Virginia) 소재 공장에서 발생한 중대한 화학 물질 유출 사고의 결과로서 탄생했다. 그 법은 공개적으로 접근 가능한 연례 보고서를 의무화했는데, 이 보고서는 독성 방출 목록이라고 알려진 것으로 정유공장, 화학공장, 식품 제조업자부터 부엌조리대 덮개 제조업자에 이르는 기타 공장들이 대기와 수면, 토양에 배출하는 유독성 물질에 관한 것이다. 위험한 오염물질의 출처를 집중 조명하는 방식으로 그 법은 지난 20년 동안 유독성 화학물질 배출량을 약 65% 줄이는 데 일조했다.

Passage 6

1. Increasing energy use, climate change, and carbon dioxide (CO2) emissions from fossil fuels make switching to low-carbon fuels a high priority. 1) Biofuels are a potential low-carbon energy source, but whether biofuels offer carbon savings depends on how they are produced. ① Ⓐ Converting rainforests, peatlands, savannas, or grasslands to produce food-based biofuels in Brazil, Southeast Asia, and the United States creates a 'biofuel carbon debt' by releasing 17 to 420 times more CO2 than the annual greenhouse gas (GHG) reductions these biofuels provide by displacing fossil fuels. Ⓑ In contrast, biofuels made from waste biomass or from biomass grown on abandoned agricultural lands planted with perennials incur little or no carbon debt and offer immediate and sustained GHG advantages.

중심소재: 바이오연료

1. 도입부

저탄소 에너지 전환의 시급

1) 주제문

바이오연료의 저탄소효율성은 어떻게 생산되는지에 달려 있다

① 뒷받침 진술

Ⓐ 방법 1

열대우림, 피트 지대, 사바나 등을 바이오연료로 전환 - 이 경우 이산화탄소 발생율이 더 높아져 바람직하지 않음

Ⓑ 방법 2

바이오매스 폐기물 또는 다년생 식물의 유기된 농노에서 재배된 바이오연료 - 탄소배출을 즉각적으로 줄이는 효과

중심소재의 폭이 low-carbon fuels에서 biofuel로 좁아짐을 파악하도록 한다.

TEST 25

정답 1 (A) 2 (D)

해설

1 바로 뒤에 이어지는 두 가지 바이오연료 생산방법을 보면 서로 생산방식에 따라 그 효율성에 큰 차이를 보임을 알 수 있다. 이로 보아, 선택지 (A)가 정답임을 알 수 있다.

2 비농경지의 바이오연료 재배용 농지로의 전환은 바이오연료가 억제하는 이산화탄소량보다 17~420배 많은 양을 배출한다. 즉, 이산화탄소를 줄이기 위한 바이오연료 재배가 오히려 더 많은 이산화탄소를 배출하는 모순을 지적하고 있다. 따라서 이산화탄소 억제에 있어서 비효율적인 방법임을 나타내는 (D)가 적절하다.

지문해석

에너지 사용량의 증가, 기후 변화, 화석연료로 인한 이산화탄소 배출 등의 문제로 인해 저탄소 연료로의 전환이 매우 중요한 사안이 되었다. 바이오연료는 잠재적인 저탄소 연료이지만 이 연료가 탄소배출을 줄일 수 있는 가능성은 재배 방식에 달려 있다.

브라질, 남부 아시아, 미국 등지에서 열대우림, 이탄(연대가 오래지 않아 완전히 탄화하지 못한 석탄)지대, 사바나(열대초원) 또는 초지(목축용, 농업용 토지)가 곡물 중심의 바비오 연료 생산지로 전환되면서 '바이오연료(로 인한) 탄소 부채'가 발생된다. 그 양은 화석연료 대신 바이오연료를 사용함으로서 줄일 수 있는 온실가스(GHC)량보다 적게는 17배, 많게는 420배에 이르는 양이다. 반면 바이오매스(에너지원으로서의 동식물자원) 폐기물이나, 다년생식물과 함께 재배된 바이오매스에서 생산된 바이오연료는 탄소 부채가 매우 적거나 전무하다. 따라서 즉각적이고도 지속적인 온실가스 감소 효과를 볼 수 있다.

Passage 7

1. 1) ① The animals that inhabit the Earth total about one and a quarter million species. Of these, some 80 percent are insects, animals classified in the phylum Arthropoda, the group of joint-legged creatures. ② Numbers alone indicate the success of the class Insecta, but they have also colonized the world more widely than any other group.

③ There are only a few marine insects; some are surface dwellers, others live between tide marks and one midge even lives on the sea bed. But wherever else other animals go, so do the insects—either as free-living forms adapted to an enormous variety of habitats or as parasites living in or on other animals. The insects are a dominant life form from the artic to the equator. Some exist beneath the snow and ice, others in deserts, still others in salt lakes and hot springs.

2. One of the chief factors in insect success is their ability to fly; 1) apart from the more primitive forms, most species have achieved the freedom of the air, enabling them to colonize new areas and habitats, to escape from predators, to find mates, and to prospect for food much more easily than their nonairborne invertebrate relatives.

① Although the insects have scored a great evolutionary success through their powers of flight, their weight/wing ratio is such that theoretically, flight should not be possible. Actually, however, their wing muscles build up energy and then release it rapidly, the speed of the wing-beat compensating for a theoretical lack of lift.

중심소재: 곤충

1. 도입부 = 중심소재 도출

1) 곤충의 엄청난 번식력

①곤충의 수
지구상의 동물 중 가장 많은 종

②곤충의 분포
전 세계에 널리 분포되어 있음

③곤충의 적응력·생명력
어떠한 환경에서도 살아남는 강인한 생명력으로 세계 도처에 분포되어 있음

2. 이유(요지)
곤충의 성공적 번식력의 요인은 비행능력

1) 뒷받침 진술

①부연
몸집에 비해 날개가 작지만, 움직이는 횟수↑

정답 1 (A) 2 (C) 3 (A) 4 (D) 5 (B)

해설

1 이 글은 곤충이 진화에 성공한 것을 수적 증가와 분포지역의 확대 그리고 그 성공요인인 비행능력을 중심으로 다루고 있다.

2 One of the chief factors in insect success is their ability to fly.에서 파악할 수 있듯이, 비행능력이 곤충이 생존할 수 있는 한 요인으로 파악할 수 있는 것이지 날 수 있는 곤충만이 생존한 것은 아니므로 선택지 (C)는 옳은 진술이다. 세 번째 문단에 나오는 apart from the more primitive forms, most species have achieved the freedom of the air... to find mates의 밑줄 친 표현에서 선택지 (A)와 (D)는 틀린 진술임을 파악할 수 있다.

3 제시된 문장에 Numbers와 colonized the world more widely(분포지역)가 나란히 언급되어 있으므로, 곤충의 수를 이야기하는 첫 번째 단락과 분포지역을 설명하므로 그 사이 두 번째 단락 사이에 제시된 문장을 넣는 것이 적절하다.

4 세미콜론 다음의 tide marks(조수점)와 sea bed(해저)로 보아 해양곤충임을 알 수 있다.

5 고산지대에 대한 언급은 없다.

지문해석

지구에 서식하는 동물은 약 125만 종에 이른다. 이들 중 대략 80%는 곤충인데 이 곤충들은 다리에 마디가 있는 동물 집단인 절지동물군에 분류되는 동물이다. 그 수효만으로도 곤충강의 성공은 분명하지만, 곤충들은 또한 다른 어느 집단보다 더 널리 세계를 식민지화했다.

해양 곤충은 단지 소수에 불과하다. 그중 어떤 종들은 해상표면에 서식하고 또 다른 종들은 조수점 사이에 (썰물 때만 뭍으로 드러나는 곳에)서식하며, 어떤 작은 곤충은 심지어 해저에서도 서식한다. 그렇지만, 다른 동물들이 그 밖의 어디에 있든 곤충들도 거기에 있다. 이를 테면 엄청나게 다양한 서식지에 적응하여 자유롭게 서식하는 형태의 곤충들도 있고 다른 동물의 몸속이나 표면에 기생하는 곤충들도 있다. 곤충은 북극지방에서 적도에 이르기까지 지배적인 생물형태이다. 일부 곤충은 눈과 얼음 밑에서 존재하고 다른 곤충은 염분이 있는 호수와 온천에서 생존한다.

곤충의 생존성공에 있어 주요한 요소들 중 하나는 날 수 있는 능력에 있다. 보다 원시적인 종을 제외하고 대부분의 종들은 공중을 자유로이 날 수 있게 되었는데 이로 인해 새로운 지역과 서식지를 차지하고 천적으로부터 피하고 짝을 찾고 곤충과 비슷하지만 날지 못하는 무척추비류보다 훨씬 더 쉽게 먹이를 찾는 것이 가능하게 되었다.

곤충이 비행능력을 통해 진화상의 큰 성공을 이루긴 했지만, 그들의 날개에 대한 몸무게의 비율이 너무나 커서 이론적으로는 비행이 불가능한 것이다. 그렇지만, 실제로는 그들의 날개 근육이 에너지를 증강시킨 후 그것을 빠르게 방출한다. 날갯짓 속도가 이론적으로 부족한 부양력을 메워주는 것이다.

Passage 8

1. Men and women make different career choices, and we cannot expect an equal distribution of the sexes within every profession. 1) ① At one extreme, it is foolish to expect equal outcomes for men and women in organizations like the armed forces. Not only are men stronger and more aggressive but the psychology of both sexes has evolved to trust men (and not trust women) in combat, precisely because of this aggression and strength. ② At the other end of the scale, it is probably an opposite mixture of evolved aptitudes and attitudes that causes the domination by females of professions such as nursing. This is not to say there can be no good female soldiers or male nurses. Patently, there can. 2. But it is not clear evidence of discrimination that they are rarer than their counterparts of the opposite sex. We cannot say where the equilibrium would lie in a world free from discrimination. But we can say with reasonable confidence that this equilibrium will often not be 50/50.

중심소재: 직업별 남녀성별 분포

1. 도입부 = 주제문

모든 직업에서 남녀 성별의 동등한 분포를 기대할 수 없다.

1) 뒷받침 진술

① 극단적 예시 1: 군대

② 극단적 예시 2 : 양육

2. 요지

한 쪽 성이 다른 성보다 특정 직업에서 많이 차지하고 있다고 해서 차별이 존재한다고 볼 수 없다. 오히려 남녀 균형은 5대 5가 아니라고 말하는 것이 더 합리적인 사고이다.

정답 **1** (C) **2** (C)

해설

1 첫 번째 문장인 Men and women make different career choices, and we cannot expect an equal distribution of the sexes within every profession.을 보면, 남녀가 서로 다른 직업을 선택하고, 동등한 성분

포를 기대할 수 없다고 했다. 글의 후반부를 통해 직업에 따라 성분포의 차이가 발생하는 것은 성 차별에 의한 결과가 아니라 특정 직업에서 50/50의 균형이 발생하지 않는 것이 이성적으로 옳다고 말하고 있고, 마지막 문장을 통해서도 직업선택의 차이점은 성차별에 의한 결과가 아니라는 파악할 수 있기에 선택지 (C)가 요지로 가장 적절하다.

2 빈칸이 들어간 문장과 앞문장이 서로 but으로 연결되어 있다는 점에서 "남성이 주류를 이루는 직업군인에 여성이 없는 것은 아니지만 여성이 남성보다 흔하지 않다"는 맥락으로 흘러야 글의 요지와 일맥상통한다.

지문해석

남자와 여자는 다른 직업을 선택하고, 우리는 모든 직업 내 동등한 남녀 성 분배를 할 수 없다. 극단적으로 군대와 같은 조직에서 남녀의 동일한 결과를 기대하는 것은 어리석다. 남자가 좀 더 힘이 세고 공격적인 뿐 아니라 남녀 모두의 심리는 전장에서 남성을 믿고 여성을 믿지 않는 것으로 진화했는데, 이는 엄밀히 말해 이런 공격성과 힘 때문일 뿐이다. 다른 극단으로는 간호와 같은 전문분야의 여성들에 의해 지배되도록 진화된 적성과 태도가 혼합된 상반된 상태이다. (그렇다고 해서) 이것이 훌륭한 여성 군인이나 남성 간호사가 없다는 것을 말하는 것은 아니다. (이들은) 명백하게(Patently) 존재한다. 그러나 이들이 상대방 성보다 흔하지 않다고 해서 차별의 명백한 증거가 아니다. 우리는 차별로부터 자유로운 세상에 균형이 어디에 존재하는지 말할 수는 없다. 그러나 우리는 이러한 균형이 종종 50/50이 아니라는 것은 합리적 자신감으로 말할 수 있다.

READING INNOVATOR

◆ **저처럼 독해에서 구조나 주제 찾기 힘드신 분들에게 굉장히 유용할 것 같네요!**

이 책은 해설 부분이 너무 잘 되어 있습니다. 지문을 그대로 해설지에 사용해서 구조를 보여주고, 중심내용이랑 주요한 부분들을 한눈에 들어오게 잘 정리가 되어있어요. 그리고 지문도 몇 개는 수능지문보다 쉽지만 몇 개는 퀄리티가 좋아요. 중심내용이나 글의 구조를 분석하는데 도움이 되었습니다. 저처럼 독해에서 구조나 주제 찾기 힘드신 분들에게 굉장히 유용할 것 같네요 추천합니다!

- 독자 서평 (t*******3 - 예스24)

◆ **이 책을 통해, 독해를 하는 스킬과 문제 푸는 스킬을 향상시킬 수 있었습니다!**

편입 준비를 하는 많은 사람들이 이 책을 추천하길래 구매를 해봤는데 사길 잘했다는 생각이 들었습니다. 내용과 구성 면에서 군더더기 없이 깔끔했고, 설명도 상세하게 잘 적혀 있었습니다. 유형별로 공부하기가 편했고 이 책을 통해, 독해를 하는 스킬과 문제 푸는 스킬을 향상시킬 수 있었습니다. 독학으로 공부하기에 참 좋은 책이라고 생각합니다~ 정말로 강추합니다!

- 독자 서평 (m****4 - 예스24)

◆ **독해실력을 한 단계 더 업그레이드하고 싶다면 이 책을 적극적으로 추천드립니다!**

실전편도 기본편과 마찬가지로 지문들이 다양한 주제로 되어있어 지루함이 없습니다. 이 책은 공무원, 수능, 편입 시험 등을 앞두고 본인의 실력을 검증할 수 있는 책인 것 같습니다. 그동안 공부해 왔던 것들을 이 책을 통해 확인할 수 있는 책이었습니다. 지문 포인트도 장황하게 나열하지 않고 딱 포인트를 명시해서 오히려 더 좋은 것 같습니다. 독해실력을 한 단계 더 업그레이드하고 싶다면 이 책을 적극적으로 추천드립니다.

- 독자 서평 (as******* - 교보문고)

◆ **독해 문제풀이 접근방법을, 실전을 통해 배울 수 있도록 만들어진 책!**

'이제는 실전이다!'라는 문구 그대로 실전문제 25회 분량을 직접 풀어보고 해설을 확인할 수 있다. 문제+해설집 2권이며, 해설집에는 기본 해설 및 해석은 물론이고, 상세한 본문 분석이 빼곡히 채워져 있다. 독해 문제를 풀기 위해 어떠한 방식으로 접근해야 하는지를 실전을 통해 배울 수 있도록 만들어진 책!

- 독자 서평 (dh**** - 교보문고)

◆ **해설 설명도 잘 되어 있고, 구성도 좋고 여러모로 편하게 공부할 수 있도록 되어 있는 책!**

언어는 사용하지 않으면 퇴화한다는 말이 사실인가 보다. 영어를 사용하지 않는 환경이 되니까 예전에는 잘만 하던 말들도 안 나오고, 지문을 봐도 바로바로 독해가 안 되고, 미드를 보면서도 들리는 말이 별로 없어졌다. 그래서 영어 공부를 다시 시작해야겠다는 생각으로 추천받아서 구입한 교재인데, 아무래도 내 수준을 너무 높게 평가하고 추천한 모양이다. 살펴본 결과 해설 설명도 잘 되어 있고 구성도 좋고 여러모로 편하게 공부할 수 있도록 되어 있는 책이며 내가 딱 원했던 스타일의 문제집이지만, 지문의 수준이 내가 공부하기에는 조금 어렵다는 생각이 들었다. 그 이유는 첫 번째 챕터에서 정답을 맞힌 문제보다 틀린 문제가 더 많았기 때문이다. 심지어 정확하게 해석하지 못하는 문장들도 있어서 나도 모르게 좌절했다. 그래도 현존하는 영어 공부 책 중에 제일 좋다고 하니 아무래도 리딩이노베이터 기본편을 구입해서 그것부터 공부하고 실전편으로 넘어와야 할 것 같다.. 기본편에서 만나요.

- 독자 서평 (s*****3 - 예스24)